GEORGE
WASHINGTON'S
WAR

THE FORGING OF
A REVOLUTIONARY
LEADER AND THE
AMERICAN PRESIDENCY

BRUCE
CHADWICK, Ph.D.

SOURCEBOOKS, INC.®
NAPERVILLE, ILLINOIS

Published by Sourcebooks, Inc.
P.O. Box 4410, Naperville, Illinois 60567-4410
(630) 961-3900
FAX: (630) 961-2168
www.sourcebooks.com

Library of Congress Cataloging-in-Publication Data
Chadwick, Bruce.
George Washington's war: the forging of a Revolutionary leader and the
American presidency / by Bruce Chadwick.
p. cm.
Includes bibliographical references and index.
ISBN 1-4022-0222-9 (alk. paper)
1. Washington, George, 1732-1799—Military leadership. 2. Command of
troops—History—18th century. 3. United States. Continental Army—
History. 4. United States—History—Revolution, 1775-1783—Campaigns. 5.
Generals—United States—Biography. 6. Presidents—United States—
Biography. I. Title.

E312.25.C48 2004
973.3'3'092—dc22

2004003566

Printed and bound in the United States of America
BG 10 9 8 7 6 5 4 3 2 1

For Margie and Rory

TABLE OF CONTENTS

Chapter One: Christmas, 1776 1

Chapter Two: The Squire of Mount Vernon 37

Chapter Three: The Army Will Die 71

Chapter Four: The Patriot King 101

Chapter Five: Rebuilding the Army 137

Chapter Six: The Army's War Machine 171

Chapter Seven: Valley Forge 193

Chapter Eight: The Angel of Death 231

Chapter Nine: The Fall from Grace 253

Chapter Ten: A New American Army .279

Chapter Eleven: Starving to Death 305

Chapter Twelve: A War of Attrition and Ungrateful Hearts 335

Chapter Thirteen: A Hero Turned Traitor 367

Chapter Fourteen: The Great Slavery Debate 403

Chapter Fifteen: Coup d'Etat 433

Chapter Sixteen: Cincinnatus 447

Epilogue: "I Do Solemnly Swear..." 463

Acknowledgments 501

Bibliography 503

Notes 513

Index 563

About the Author 570

"*We are, during the winter, dreaming of Independence and Peace.*"
—George Washington, commander-in-chief of the
Continental Army in the American Revolution

"*The qualities we seek in a great man are vision, integrity, courage, understanding, power of articulation and...a profundity of character.*"
—Dwight D. Eisenhower, Supreme Allied Commander, World War II

Chapter One

CHRISTMAS, 1776

"Victory or Death."
—George Washington

During the early evening of December 19, 1776, a thick snow began to fall throughout central New Jersey and the greater Philadelphia area. It landed silently, coming down in straight lines, and within hours the countryside was covered with a blanket of white. The snow draped itself over the tops of large wooden barns and small homes. Slender columns of smoke from fireplaces inside cabins cut through the storm and drifted toward the sky. The snow made low rock outcroppings disappear as it piled high, filling up gullies and cascading in soft pillows over wooden wagons left outdoors. The snow rested on the branches of thousands of trees and lined the banks of creeks. It covered dirt roads and meadows near the Delaware River, which separated Trenton, New Jersey, from McKonkey's Ferry, in Pennsylvania, seven miles north.

The snow continued to fall through mid-morning of the following day. It was accompanied by light winds and a brisk twenty-four–degree temperature. Winter had finally hit Trenton and Philadelphia. The home of William Keith, near Newtown, Pennsylvania, now served as headquarters for George Washington, the commander-in-chief of the Continental Army. The Keith home, a two-story gray stone building, was covered with snow. Washington's officers, coming in and out of the Keith house, stamped their feet to loosen the powder from their boots and brushed the snow from their coats. On the first floor, two large fireplaces burned throughout the day and evening, providing the only heat for the officers and for George Washington, who was trapped by both the British Army and the vicissitudes of the icy weather.

The American Revolution had ignited in glory on a spring day, April 19, 1775, when colonists in Massachusetts battled British regulars at Lexington and Concord, forcing them to retreat back toward Boston after the firing of the famed "shot heard 'round the world." The colonists had chased the British, shooting at them from behind trees and stone walls, from the windows of houses and from atop the roofs of barns. Later, residents had cheered when the British vacated the city at the end of the winter of 1776, forced out by a threatened artillery bombardment led by George Washington. The British army, under the command of General William Howe, had retreated from Boston to spend the remainder of the winter in Nova Scotia, Canada.

Washington's leadership had made him a hero. From the Carolinas to New Hampshire, thousands of men joined the Continental Army, determined to free the thirteen colonies from the yoke of what they considered unacceptable British oppression. The army, funded by the new Continental Congress, had the emotional support of many of the colonists, despite pockets of Loyalist, or pro-British, sympathizers. Soon it grew in strength from a collection of militia totaling ten thousand men to an army numbering more than twenty thousand soldiers and carrying with it more than two hundred cannon. Public support for the cause ran high in many of the states. The American revolutionary spirit reached its zenith on July 4, 1776, when members of the Continental Congress issued the Declaration of Independence. By that date, some colonists, particularly New Englanders, naively assumed that the hated "redcoats" would soon leave American soil and sail back to England.

The British had no intention of losing their colonies. A week after the Declaration of Independence had been signed, British general Henry Clinton left the coast of South Carolina with his troops in order to join forces at Staten Island with General Howe, who had brought nine thousand of his own men down from Nova Scotia. By the middle of August, Howe's brother, Admiral Richard Howe, had joined him. Together, they had assembled thirty-two thousand men—a quarter of them Hessian auxiliaries—along with one hundred and thirty warships and transports, twenty frigates, and more than three hundred cannon, all gathered at considerable expense to defeat the American colonists. The numbers seemed overwhelming. By the end of the summer, there were, in fact, four thousand more British soldiers in New York than the entire population of Philadelphia, America's largest city.

Washington, who left Boston for New York earlier that year, spent the summer organizing his own defenses across Long Island, in forts along the Hudson River as well as earthworks on Brooklyn Heights. But despite his careful preparations, there was little he could do against the power of the British forces, especially since he seemed intent on battling them head-on, army against army, a misguided strategy that he would soon have to correct.

British troops at first overwhelmed the Americans at Brooklyn Heights, pushing them back toward the East River behind heavy cannon and musket fire. The vicious Hessians needlessly killed more than five hundred soldiers, bayoneting many of them in the back and shooting others as they tried to surrender. The British, under Howe, had the Americans boxed in on three sides, their backs to the river. Washington feared the annihilation of his entire army. He needed an escape route. It was then that he devised a method of retreat—one that he would use continuously throughout the war.

Washington had access to hundreds of small flatboats that he had been collecting from the New York area. On the night of August 29, the general ordered soldiers, former fishermen, from Marblehead, Massachusetts, under the command of Colonel John Glover to quietly organize the boats into a flotilla and to wait for the beginning of a massive evening evacuation by the entire army. When darkness descended, the fishermen watched as regiments of men, moving quietly and in perfect order, climbed down from the heights above them and scrambled into the boats. Glover and his men then poled them across to Manhattan and out of danger under the cloak of a fortuitous fog. Finally, after the hours of watching the slow, soundless evacuation, George Washington, the last man on the east side of the river, climbed into the final boat and made his escape. When the British attacked in the morning, they found the campfires still burning, but the Heights empty.

Washington's sleight-of-hand did little more than buy time. American forces were again routed at Harlem Heights, at White Plains, and finally at Fort Washington, where some soldiers managed to escape by scrambling into Glover's boats and crossing the Hudson into New Jersey, where the commander led his men on a long retreat toward Philadelphia. More than five thousand Americans had been killed or captured in the New York campaign, one of the worst defeats in American military history.

The British chased what was left of the Continental Army across the state. Fear of the British, with their long columns of professional soldiers and hundreds of cannon—and the tenacious Hessians—prompted thousands more soldiers to desert and go home as Washington and the army slowly made their way across the dirt highways of New Jersey. Entire companies of soldiers fled. Finally, on December 7, the Continental Army crossed the Delaware to escape the British, under General William Howe and Lord Charles Earl Cornwallis, who stopped on the New Jersey side of the river. The English were in no hurry. Neither general had any regard for the Americans or their leader. Howe's top aide, Ambrose Serle, reported that the generals considered Washington "a little paltry colonel of a militia of bandits."

By then, the American revolutionary forces led by the general, more than nineteen thousand a few weeks before, had dwindled to just five thousand men. The New York routes had been accompanied by news of the devastating defeat of American forces involved in an ill-planned invasion of Canada. One of the two other armies under Washington's command, led by General Horatio Gates, was still marching through northern New Jersey. Incredibly, General Charles Lee, who was in charge of the other army, had been unluckily captured by the British on Friday the 13 when he foolishly stopped at a tavern in Basking Ridge. His second in command, General John Sullivan, was, like Gates, still on the march. But he had only had about one thousand men, half the number that General Washington anticipated.

Half of them were sick and unfit for combat. The British had captured nearly all of the American cannon in New York. Now, as the snow fell, Washington could count only eighteen pieces of artillery. Many had wondered if the general would even make it across New Jersey. "I feel for Washington, that best of men," wrote worried Congressional delegate William Hooper to a friend at the end of November.

As Washington marched across the state he had become dismayed at the feeble reaction of the people to the revolution. Many New Jerseyans, like other Americans, were as despondent about the future as the men who had deserted the army. Men were now reluctant to join the army or support the cause and leave their families. The commander fumed about their lack of help in letters to friends and relatives: "I think our affairs are in a very bad situation...from the defection of New York, the Jerseys and Pennsylvania. In short, the conduct of the Jerseys has been most infamous. Instead of turning out to defend their country and affording aid to our army, they are making submission as fast as they can."

Washington's soldiers were in tatters. There was no new clothing to replace their dirty and ripped uniforms. Some, particularly those in the militia, substituted their own jackets, shirts, and breeches. Following the westward Delaware crossing, men had stumbled out of the boats nearly naked, covered with only a coat, shivering and ill. Many had no shoes and had cautiously wrapped their callused and bleeding feet in rags to protect them from the snow. Some men bled through their rags, lining the snow that lay on the ground with red. Of half-naked soldiers he met on the retreat, New Jerseyan George Ross said sadly that "they fall dead on the roads with their packs on their backs and are found perishing in haylofts."

Crude hospitals were set up in two small homes near Washington's headquarters on the western shore of the Delaware. There were no nurses, soap, or sanitary facilities. Sick men were placed on beds of straw covered with the blood of other sick men who had recently died. Washington's men sneered at locals who charged the army for the food and blankets they brought.

The soldiers in camp were getting sicker by the day from jaundice, dysentery, and other ailments. Primitive medical treatments of the era did little to help them. Just before Christmas, aides told Washington that nearly 1,200 of the 2,400 men in his camp were too ill to fight. The heads of the Pennsylvania militias who had promised Washington that their men would already be in Philadelphia to defend the city against an attack by Howe's army were nowhere to be found.

Worse still, the enlistment of most of the men in his army would be up at the end of the month. The soldiers, most of them young, some under eighteen, had stuck with him through the disastrous New York campaign and flight across New Jersey, while others had deserted. But now, trapped and with the war possibly about to end with one last British assault, most of them would simply go home to their families. And Washington knew that Congress had no more money to pay the soldiers who did re-enlist.

The New Jersey provincial government had disbanded at the news that the British were starting the invasion of their state. Members of the Continental Congress, certain of the imminent British takeover of Philadelphia, the capital and financial center of the colonies, had fled the city and moved to Baltimore. Dozens of leading businessmen and Philadelphia families left with them. On the run, the members of Congress would have great difficulty directing the country and raising money to pay the soldiers and purchase the supplies that Washington so desperately needed.

The people of Philadelphia were terrified, certain the British would seize the city. The Redcoats had "rushed like a torrent through the Jersies," according to Richard Henry Lee of Virginia, a delegate to Congress who watched them as he packed his own bags to flee. "The enemy move rapidly this way," wrote Congressional delegate William Hooper. "It was impossible for such a handful to make a stand against this superior force." Businessman Robert Morris, sitting alone in Philadelphia as the last Congressional delegate in the city, watching the evacuation out of his window, sadly lamented that events "leave no room for joy in the mind of a true friend to his country."

There were rumors, too, that the British planned to recruit an additional thirty thousand or more troops to join their force in America in the spring, bringing the total to more than sixty thousand—against some five thousand Americans. The leaders of the Congress were so fearful of the future that they sent Washington an extraordinary note on December 12: "...that until they should otherwise order, General Washington should be possessed of all power to order and direct all things relative to the department and the operation of the war." The note made him a military dictator, for Congress had now placed him in charge of not just the army, but, in effect, the entire country. It had also left him to fend for himself.

On December 20, as the snow continued to fall, the commander-in-chief feared that he would lose the army, and the country, as the British moved about on the other side of the Delaware. Howe had placed 1,200 Hessians in Trenton, on the eastern side of the river, easily seen through the trees made barren by winter. They were under the charge of Col. Johann Rall, the tough German commander who had overseen the deaths of the helpless Americans in Brooklyn.

Washington dreaded the winter as much as he feared the British. If the frigid temperatures caused local rivers, creeks, and ponds to freeze over, it would create a thick ice bridge for the British and the Hessians to cross the Delaware, just seventy-five yards wide at some points. There, they could easily attack his army. Even if the British did not advance, the cold, snow, and sickness would destroy the Colonial army within weeks. And if they did survive the weather, the end of enlistment on December 31 would probably bring about its collapse. "You may as well attempt to stop the winds from blowing or the sun in its diurnals as stop the regiments from going when their term is expired," the dismayed general told one colleague about the troop exodus he feared.

Washington worried about everything. He put his apprehensions bluntly before Congress in a letter written to John Hancock on December 20. "The enemy are daily gathering strength," he warned. "This strength is like a snowball rolling. It will increase the progress of the enemy's arms. Militia may possibly [stop them] for a little while, but in a little while, also, the militia of those states which have been frequently called upon will not turn out at all…Could anything but the Delaware River save Philadelphia?" He then wrote about Howe, "I do not see what is to hinder him as ten days more will put an end to the existence of our army."

Washington frantically sought help in a flurry of letters to politicians and generals, writing Connecticut Governor Jonathan Trumbull about the troop crisis that "I am almost led to despair" and informing Rhode Island Governor Nicholas Cooke that "the prospects are gloomy." He was just as grim in notes to army colleagues, complaining to Major General William Heath that "my situation, and that of the Cause, is critical and alarming."

That same week he talked to some of his officers about a private plan, later abandoned, to sell off his Virginia estate, Mount Vernon, and thus all of his assets and equipment, emptying his bank accounts to raise enough money to pay the soldiers to remain in the army.

In an earlier letter to his cousin Lund, Washington said that he could not make a stand in Pennsylvania against the British. "I tremble for Philadelphia," he wrote, and, after listing all of his troubles, from the unreliable militia to the capture of Lee to the lack of support from the people, he grimly concluded that soon "the game will be pretty well up."

He again implored Congress to raise troops and send him money to pay them. He was strident in his writing, but never desperate. The tone let his officers and politicians know that the situation was critical, but that somehow a solution could be found. It was a tone he would maintain throughout the war, constantly preparing his correspondents for the worst, but hoping for the best. A perfect example of this strategy was a letter he wrote to Congress on Christmas Eve. The general was privately furious about Congressional control of all military promotions. This system produced unqualified officers and unhappy troops. Instead of railing about it, he diplomatically wrote Hancock that Congress should "devise some other rule by which the officers, especially the field officers, should be appointed" and noted that his army was top-heavy with officers from the larger eastern states, which angered their men, who were from other states. "[This] means that several deserving men could not have been provided for, had the utmost pains been used for the purpose, and many others of great merit have been neglected in late appointments and those of little worth and less experience put in their places, or promoted over their heads."

Washington ordered the leaders of any militia company in Pennsylvania he could find to march to Philadelphia. He told his officers to demand that local farmers sell the army the grain it needed to make bread to prevent the men from starving. Everyone under his command was urged to use their personal powers of persuasion to convince local militia leaders that the men in their community, their friends and neighbors, were all essential to the cause and should enlist. Officers who were stationed near small communities, such as Morristown, New Jersey, were called upon to build strong ties between the civilian population, whether village leaders or area businessmen, and the army. The general's all-encompassing plans even embraced tribes of American Indians up and down the eastern coast of America; he begged them to refuse any British requests to fight alongside them against the Americans.

There seemed to be no respite from the cold as the temperature remained below freezing on most days in the week before Christmas. The snow stayed on the ground, making any troop movements extremely difficult. Washington rode along the riverbank, watching with dismay as the water along the western side began forming a thin, icy shield. In the middle, large chunks of flat ice flowed southward. In the distance, in and around Trenton, he saw the Hessians in their bright blue coats with their red collars, straw-colored vests and breeches, and signature brass headgear.

Shortly after Washington's December 20 letter to the Continental Congress, Lee's army, under General John Sullivan and Lord Stirling, arrived in camp along with men from the army of Horatio Gates. Washington's forces now totaled 2,400 men, with another three thousand camped farther south. On December 14, Howe, in charge of the main British army, had left Rall and his Hessians in Trenton to keep an eye on Washington and returned to New York to wait until spring, declaring the winter campaign over. Critics later said that he didn't chase the Americans, or move toward Philadelphia, because he wanted to return to a lover in New York, Mrs. Elizabeth Loring, the wife of a local physician. But certainly, Howe did not believe a delay of a few months would make any difference in the outcome of the war. The British, who never fought in winter, could crush the Americans, and do it quickly, whenever they chose. Why not wait until spring? He was so confident of victory that he even told Lord Cornwallis, in charge of his secondary force near New Brunswick, to pack his bags and go home to England.

Washington, completely at home in all kinds of weather, began to think about ways in which winter might possibly help him. Perhaps there was a way in which he could harness the snow, ice, sleet, and wind to work in his favor. Pacing in his headquarters at night, he began to formulate a plan. Finally, gathering his top officers, some of whom would become the founding fathers of the nation—such as Henry Knox, the first Secretary of War and Alexander Hamilton, first Secretary of the Treasury (James Monroe, the fifth president of the United States, was a captain with the troops that night)—he outlined his idea for an attack on Trenton, an assault that would become a stunning victory.

His officers were at first shocked by its boldness, but quickly agreed and began to work out the details. First, the date—Washington knew from nearby residents whom he employed as spies that the Hessians always held feasts on Christmas Day and that there would be much eating and drinking. He did not believe that the regiments of Howe's army in New Brunswick, fifteen miles away, were prepared to march on Trenton on short notice.

Washington decided to build his entire strategy on the information provided by a local farmer said to be one of his spies, John Honeyman. He was a Scotch-Irish immigrant who had lived with his family on a small farm outside of Trenton for several years. Honeyman had been a weaver in Scotland and still practiced his craft as a sideline after his farm chores were over. The jovial Honeyman, still affecting his brogue, had gained the trust of Rall and other Hessian officers on numerous visits to supply them with meat and other farm produce. Now, when details on Hessian daily routines were needed most, Honeyman provided Washington with precise information on the Hessians, the town, the land around it, the roads, and the best places to cross the river. The spy told him how many soldiers were in the town, in which homes, and how many sentries were sent out each evening and morning, and where they patrolled.

The most important information Washington sought from Honeyman, and obtained, was on Colonel Rall. He needed to know everything about the tough fifty-year-old colonel who had served in the German military since he was fifteen and was known as "The Lion." Honeyman described Rall as a disciplinarian but an officer who separated his professional and social life. Washington learned that Rall usually stayed up late and slept until about 9 A.M. each morning. He loved to take morning baths and often stayed in his tub until 10 A.M. or later.

He was also known as a lion at parties. One of his top aides, Lieutenant Andreas Wiederholt, commented that, "He was a very sociable man who knew how to give a party and make it a nice one." Some of his soldiers grumbled that Rall was prouder of the military band he liked to lead on parade than his troops. Washington learned, too, from Honeyman, that his soldiers worried about how Rall would act under pressure. Wiederholt, who shared in Rall's revels, wondered about his leadership capabilities and told others that the Colonel "lacked cool presence of mind."

The Americans might be able to launch a surprise attack on Trenton, using night and the weather as a cover, but only if they began to move on Christmas Day. Washington knew that it would be bitter cold and that the task of loading his cannons and horses on boats would be difficult. Their passage across the river would be even more arduous. He knew, too, that getting the men across would be equally troublesome because the ice chunks would constantly hit the boats. His greatest fear was that another snowstorm would strike, delaying the army's arrival at Trenton and forcing the men to fight in a snowfall.

At the same time, he understood that if the weather worsened, his chances were better. The sleepy Hessians would never expect an army, particularly the underclothed, underfed, depleted Americans, to cross a large river and launch a major attack in the middle of a snowstorm on Christmas Day. The gambler in him told him he could do it.

And so he made his fateful decision. His belief that the attack would either turn the course of the war or bring about the annihilation of his army was reflected in a note he wrote to himself. Balled up and found by a physician visiting him, it simply said: "Victory or death."

The general decided that his wing of the army would begin to cross the Delaware at twilight on the night of Christmas Day. They would march through New Jersey under the cover of darkness and attack Trenton from two directions at dawn. At the same time, about one thousand men under General James Ewing would cross the river just below Trenton and march on the town from that direction. A third force under General John Cadwalader, numbering about two thousand men, would attack farther south to capture any fleeing soldiers. Washington's three forces probably could not defeat the superbly trained and well-equipped Hessians in a face to face, open-field battle, but they might be able to beat them in a surprise strike. That was, if the weather did not turn into a storm.

It did. Meteorological reports indicate that early on Christmas Day, the worst storm in decades hit the southeastern colonies, dumping as much as two feet of snow on the ground in some sections of Virginia. The storm moved north and northeast; its northwest corner swept over Philadelphia, dumping several inches of snow. However, the weather was still clear when Washington's men arrived at McKonkey's Ferry slip, a long wooden dock that jutted out into the Delaware fifty yards from McKonkey's two-story gray-stone Inn and Tavern. The men began to board the boats just after 4:30 P.M. Washington anticipated snow as he looked up at the dark-hued sky. He knew that a snowfall would delay the crossing. He pressed the officers to load the men into the boats faster. His plan called for precision. The entire army had to start moving across the river as the sun went down to avoid detection by British spies. Everyone had to be across the river by 2 A.M. The army had to move the entire distance to Trenton, a seven and one half mile trek, in the darkness, unseen until they arrived at dawn. Then, as the sun came up, the army would begin its surprise attack.

Washington would be left to fight alone. The storm that hit south of Trenton was so severe and the ice so thick that only some of Cadwalader's and Ewing's troops could take any boats or equipment across the Delaware. Most were stranded on the Pennsylvania side of the river. Those who made it to the New Jersey side never reached Trenton. "Very stormy," a local woman who lived near the point where Ewing planned to land wrote in her diary. Washington, unaware of their inability to reach New Jersey, was on his own.

The commander was certain he could succeed. He had been assured by Colonel John Glover and his Marblehead, Massachusetts, fishermen that they could transport the army, horses, and artillery across the river using long poles to propel the flatbottom boats and that the boats, forty feet long and about eight feet wide, were large enough to make it across no matter how bad the ice floe in the middle of the river became. Glover and his men had rescued the army from Brooklyn in boats and they could do it again.

He also had the assurance of portly Henry Knox, the physical giant who had been the head of his artillery for eighteen months. Knox was a huge man; at six foot two, he was as tall as the commander-in-chief. But unlike the muscular Washington, Knox weighed 280 pounds, with little muscle. His body was distinguished by his huge belly, fat hands, and tree trunk–sized thighs. The stout Knox was an unforgettable figure with a round and cheerful face, sharp gray eyes, and a sunny disposition.

Knox, who possessed a booming voice that could be heard throughout the camp, had never fired a cannon in his life when he became head of artillery in 1775. He was a local bookseller in Boston who was fascinated by weapons. He had read just about every book published on ordnance and convinced Washington to put him in charge of his artillery, even though his wife Lucy Flucker's father was a local British official. Knox had moved fifty-five large cannons overland from Fort Ticonderoga, in New York, to Boston in the snow and cold of the 1775–76 winter, using sleds pulled by oxen, a feat which earned him the nickname Henry "The Ox" Knox. He had gained his reputation working in bad weather. He and Washington agreed that, with surprise on their side, there was a chance they could win.

Washington wanted to give the men some kind of inspirational speech before they boarded the boats, but knew that he was no orator. So, instead, he handed out copies of the latest patriotic essay by Tom Paine, *The American Crisis*. Paine had gained national notoriety just months before when he published *Common Sense*, said to have been read by nearly every adult in the colonies. *The American Crisis* spoke of the need to fight on against all odds. It was perfect for his soldiers. The officers were told to read it to their men just before they began the crossing of the river. They stood in groups, the weather getting colder, the sun receding, the snow on the ground hard against their feet. They moved their legs up and down, as if marching in place, to keep warm. As the night descended upon them, they listened to Paine's words:

> These are the times that try men's souls. The summer soldier and the sunshine patriot will, in this crisis, shrink from the service of their country; but he that stands it *now*, deserves the love and thanks of man and woman. Tyranny, like hell, is not easily conquered; yet we have this consolation with us, that the harder the conflict, the more glorious the triumph.

Then, as the sun went down, the crossing of the Delaware began. It soon became apparent to all that the movement of the troops across the river would take more time than Washington had planned. The wooden ferry landing grew slippery, making the soldiers move carefully into the boats, taking up precious time. The men kept patting their arms with their hands to keep warm. The narrow walkways on the side of the boats began to freeze. The boatmen had to move more slowly as they thrust their poles into the dark water. The ice chunks in the river—large, flat, and thick—were more numerous than on previous days. They slammed into the vessels repeatedly, banging them hard, pushing them downstream and requiring more work for the boatmen. Fortunately, the boats had bows that cut through the ice sheets that covered parts of the river, particularly near the shores. The water was higher than usual and the current moved south at a faster pace than normal.

Just after 11 P.M., the snow began to fall, landing softly on the clothes of the men. The snow further impeded the crossing. It caused havoc with the loading of the horses and cannons. Knox, aware that the crossing was running an hour late already, began to bellow at the men to move faster in loading his heavy and cumbersome artillery onto the ferry boats. The men could barely make out even a man as large as Knox in the storm, but they heard his unmistakably deep, resonant voice cutting through the night. His loud exhortations spurred them on and, slowly, the big guns were lashed to the boats and poled across.

"The army crossed the river…with almost infinite difficulty," Knox told his wife, Lucy. "The floating ice in the river made the labor almost insidious." The men traveling with him agreed. A tired Thomas Rodney, of Delaware, marveled as the boats, top-heavy with the big cannons, slowly made it to the other side. "It was as severe a night as I ever saw," Rodney said. "The frost was sharp, the current difficult to stem, the ice increasing and the wind high. It was only with the greatest care and labor that the horses and the artillery could be ferried over."

George Washington had crossed earlier with some of the soldiers. He sat on the New Jersey side, his great blue cloak wrapped about his large frame, a stoic look upon his face as he watched the landings. He looked up from time to time at the snow, which was falling quickly now, sticking to the snow already on the ground. It fell thickly at a rate guaranteed to reach several inches, which Washington knew would collect quickly and make the movement of the troops, already late, even more difficult. A fierce wind had started up from the northwest, cutting into the faces of the men. The temperature after midnight hovered at about twenty-nine degrees and never climbed above freezing. Finally, at 4 A.M., the last horses and cannons landed, a full two hours late. It was then that the storm became even more intense as sleet and hail mixed with the snow, making walking difficult and seeing almost impossible.

One soldier, Thomas McCarty, commented that it was "the worst day of sleet rain that could be" and another swore that the sleet "cuts like a knife." Washington spoke of "a violent storm of snow and hail."

There would be no going back, however. The commander was determined to attack Trenton, even if the army arrived two hours late. The storm and the clock had trapped him on the eastern shore of the Delaware. If he abandoned the assault and tried to ferry his men back across the river, the army would be seen by British spies on both shores at dawn. They would be trapped on the water, and the army would be destroyed. "There was no making a retreat without being discovered," Washington explained to member of Congress. "...I determined to push on at all events."

Washington knew that if he spurred his men hard on the march, they could reach Trenton before breakfast. It would still only be 8 A.M., a full hour before his spies told him Colonel Rall would awaken. The storm might have caused Rall to cancel his evening patrols. The sentries outside the town might have slept late because of their Christmas Day feast and the snow, now blanketing the region.

By now, Washington realized that winter was not his weakness, but his strength. The forty-four-year-old farmer-turned-general knew from years of experience in Virginia that storms like this, with freezing temperatures and heavy snow, could last for hours. The storm appeared as though it would continue, perhaps all morning or all day. The weather would be the army's cover as it marched toward Trenton. The wind was behind them, which meant it would blow the snow and sleet right into the faces of the Hessians, who would have to fight facing northward. The Americans would be charging at the enemy out of a fierce snowstorm. If Washington was right, the winter weather would be a more powerful force than all of his men and cannons together.

Washington and his officers encouraged the men to move quickly. Their forced march probably saved lives because the men did not have enough time to freeze (two soldiers who stopped to rest froze to death). The general exhorted them to move faster in a stern, but understanding, way. "Press on boys, press on," he shouted from his horse. The men realized how important the march was by his demeanor. "I have never seen Washington as determined as he is now," wrote Captain Rodney.

The men were as focused as their leader. That new feeling was expressed a few days earlier, when they sensed that something was going to happen. A Connecticut soldier wrote his wife: "As for what few troops we have, you would be amazed to see what fine spirits they are in; and the Continental troops are really well disciplined, and you may depend will fight bravely...we shall do honour to ourselves."

They kept up the fast pace through the night and early morning, their hopes renewed by the chance to attack the enemy instead of retreating from him. Alexander Hamilton, overseeing the artillery, was impressed. The men were "ready, every devil one of them...," he said, "to storm hell's battlements in the night."

Both armies arrived on the outskirts of Trenton a few minutes before 8 A.M.. During the night, Washington had split his troops in two, taking his men southward on Princeton Road while Sullivan led his soldiers down River Road, closer to the Delaware. Washington waited for the sound of gunfire from Sullivan's men as a sign that both armies were ready to assault the town.

Trenton was a small village with two main streets, King and Queen, which both terminated at Front Street. There were two small side streets. The town of one thousand residents contained approximately one hundred homes and buildings. The general's plan was to assault from Princeton and River roads and then enter the village. Knox would set up his eighteen cannon at the northern ends of King and Queen streets and begin firing as the Hessians emerged from their houses. The men would move in following the artillery barrage, which the general hoped would cause significant disorder among the enemy.

The town was quiet, as Washington had hoped. Rall slept late. His two-story wooden home seemed quiet. The other houses were also silent as the Hessians slept off their holiday celebration. Just as Washington had hoped, Rall had not sent out night patrols. Nor had the early-morning sentries that usually checked the two roads leading into Trenton ventured out into the storm. At 8 A.M., the weather was still brutal.

The American commander believed that no one had seen him, but someone had spotted the general. A local resident, a Loyalist, had watched the army moving through the storm late at night and sent his servant with a written warning to Colonel Rall. The German leader, probably still in the middle of eating or playing cards, ignored it. Washington had guessed, correctly, that none of the Hessians believed any army, much less the badly equipped Americans, could march through a snowstorm. In fact, on December 21, British General James Grant, in New Brunswick, relying on reports from local residents, told his Trenton commander that he had nothing to fear from Washington. "Grant writes me the enemy are naked, hungry and very weak and that it is not necessary to place troops [sentries]," Rall told his officers.

Trenton scouts reported stirrings in Washington's camp during the days before Christmas and said that Americans had been spotted in rowboats during the daytime. Rall, certain the Americans forces were depleted, did not worry. Residents said that the American soldiers they had seen were incapable of attacking anyone and would probably not survive another month. Rall was so confident that the Continentals would not strike that he had even ignored an earlier order from Cornwallis to build defensive earthworks outside the town. He feared no river crossings. "We were sure the rebels could not do so," wrote one of the German grenadiers, Johannes Reuber.

With the first shots of Sullivan's guns, Washington ordered the attack. His men moved to a position north of the town, on a slope overlooking the two streets. Knox set his cannons up in the snow and began the bombardment. His artillerists, amateurs but capable, hit the Hessians as they emerged in small groups from their houses. The initial bombardment caused confusion and disorder, as Washington had hoped. Men racing into the streets found themselves facing north. The wind was coming at them, and they could not see as the snow and sleet hit their faces. One of the first groups was cut down by an artillery battery commanded by Hamilton. After a few moments of heavy cannon fire, Washington ordered the men to attack. Some men had wrapped their musket locks in blankets and were able to use them, but the wet snow and sleet had caused many muskets to misfire or not to fire at all. Washington ordered those soldiers to attack with bayonets and drawn swords.

The Hessians, still sleepy and reeling from the surprise, rushed into the fields outside of town but found themselves cut off by some of Sullivan's men on the south and west and Washington's troops on the north and east. They were unable to form into groups or position their cannon properly because the screams from the civilians rushing into the streets drowned out commanders from their officers. Colonel Rall, finally awake, was unable to get his men together in any one section of town. He quickly mounted his horse and attempted to rally his men. "My brave soldiers, advance!" he yelled, but his command was ineffective. He was shot as he waved his sword, and he fell from his horse, mortally wounded.

Several Hessians scrambled through the snow and found their cannon. They tried to fire at the Americans, but Knox's artillery barrage was too much for them. One blast hit a German field piece and broke its axle, disabling it. Knox then ordered his soldiers to attack the men behind the piece, and those behind a second cannon. The Americans, led by Lt. James Monroe, charged, wielding swords, screaming as loud as they could. The Hessians fled, but not before one of them shot Monroe in the chest, nearly killing him.

The battle was over in just an hour. Some thirty Hessians had died and 920 were taken prisoners. The Americans captured six cannon (the best result they had ever seen), one thousand muskets, forty hogsheads of rum, and even the musical instruments for Rall's beloved band. Just two Americans had been killed. "This is a glorious day for our country," Washington told Private James Wilkinson as the enemy troops surrendered.

There was little time to celebrate. About two hundred Hessians did manage to escape toward Burlington and the British Army post there. It would only be a matter of time before Redcoats would begin to march toward Trenton. Washington was also certain that word would soon reach Lord Cornwallis, still packing in New Brunswick, twenty miles away, and that he would march his superbly equipped force toward Trenton as well. It was time for the Americans to disappear once again into the snowstorm.

Washington ordered the men and their prisoners, plus their supplies, north to the Delaware crossing site. The storm had not abated and the snow, wind, and sleet were as formidable as ever. Again, slowly and deliberately, the men crossed the river. So much ice had caked on the boats in just thirteen hours that the captured Hessians were ordered to help the Americans chip it off.

The Hessians were kept prisoners at McKonkey's Ferry that night and later sent to Philadelphia, where they were marched through the streets as prisoners of war, a sorry end for the men who were supposed to storm the city and subdue it without trouble.

Henry Knox could not believe how smoothly the daring raid had gone. "Providence seemed to have smiled upon every part of this enterprise," he wrote his wife, Lucy.

Washington was proud of his men: "Their behavior upon this occasion reflects the highest honor upon them," he told John Hancock with great pride. To Cadwalader, he recalled: "The officers and the men who were engaged in the enterprise behaved with great firmness, poise, advance and bravery and such as did them the highest honor."

Although flush with victory, Washington had little time to celebrate. He knew that the British would be furious and come after him. This time they would build or commandeer boats to cross the Delaware. They might take Philadelphia or crush the American army with their superior forces. The men in Washington's army were still dressed in rags and continued to be hungry, tired, and sick. And the enlistments were due to expire on December 31.

Across the Delaware Once More

Lightning does not often strike twice, but Washington decided that he might. The snow had stopped late in the evening of December 26, leaving between four and six inches of powder on the ground throughout the area. He had crossed the Delaware once in snow and he could do it again. If the British did not expect a river crossing the first time, they would certainly not expect the same maneuver again. There was even more snow on the ground, and it would be harder to transport men and cannon. Surprise would still be on his side. He was determined to re-cross the Delaware and strike once more. His top officers agreed with his latest daring plan.

Washington had other reasons to attack. He did not want to have simply come back across the Delaware and go into winter camp, avoiding a confrontation with the enemy. Nor did he want to give any appearance of retreat, only of victory. He also believed that a second engagement would substantially change the public view of the army and the revolution, especially in New Jersey, where he desired to set up a winter camp. The army needed the support of the people. The crushing losses of late 1776 had eroded it. A second victory would rally them. The commander-in-chief also felt that a second triumph would swell the size of the army, particularly the militia units throughout the colonies. He had written of the men in the militia with great disdain in his winter letters, but he believed they would stay in the service, and that their ranks and enthusiasm would grow, if the Americans could score a second victory over the haughty British. He already had reports of more militia units joining the fight right after Trenton, and on New Year's Eve Washington would issue a general call to all men in New Jersey to join the volunteer units. Another victory over the British would reinforce the idea that the Americans could win and help him gain critical support in Europe, where the great nations, particularly France, whose officials supported him in secret, gave his army little chance of defeating the mighty British crown.

The army moved across the Delaware again on December 29 and marched toward Trenton, where Washington believed he might find small units of the British Army. He was hopeful of defeating a minor force of redcoats in the region north of the village and avoiding a full-blown engagement with Cornwallis.

He wanted to engage the British quickly because the enlistments ended in two more days. That night, Washington decided to make a personal plea, asking his men to stay. He rode to a New England regiment that had been ordered to form up for inspection. Astride his handsome chestnut horse Nelson, the six-foot-three general sat ramrod straight, his broad blue hat and large cloak making him appear even larger as he looked over his men. Many of them were young, just sixteen or seventeen years old. Some were much older. Many were farmers, some merchants, others blacksmiths. Some had complete uniforms, but most did not. Many had no shoes. They were thin from a lack of food. The men were sick. They coughed as he approached them. Some leaned on their muskets to stand. It was cold and the breath of many soldiers froze in the air.

The commander spoke to them as he always did, with sincerity and determination, but without theatrics. On top of his seventeen-hands-high horse that night, he had the same confidence that the men had come to admire despite their losses. He explained how personally proud he was of each man and reminded them that their stunning conquest at Trenton had turned the course of the war. He could not lose them; the colonists could not lose the war. He described the desperate situation to the men and explained earnestly that he needed them to stay in the army. He had an unusual proposal: each man would receive a ten-dollar bonus, above his wages, if he agreed to stay for six more weeks. That time would give the army a chance to score one or more additional victories over the British and then head toward winter camp. An officer asked the men agreeing to the proposal to step forward as Washington rode to the side of the grounds near a creek to watch. No one moved.

Frustrated and solemn, the general nudged his horse and rode back in front of the men. He looked over the head of his horse and leaned forward and gazed down at the soldiers with his blue-gray eyes. The men seemed uncertain. They admired this man. They loved their country. They wanted independence. But they had done all required of them. They had fought hard. They had suffered greatly. Now it was time to go home. Washington knew how they felt, but he needed them.

The general decided to make one last plea, trying to find the right words. "You have done all I asked you to do, and more than could be reasonably expected," he said. "But your country is at stake, your wives, your houses, and all that you hold dear. You have worn yourselves out with fatigues and hardships, but we know now how to spare you. If you will consent to stay only one month longer, you will render that service to the cause of liberty, and to your country, which you probably never can do under any such circumstances."

Washington was a man of few words and tonight he was grasping for the right ones, again trying to clearly define what it was they were fighting for. He talked on about what they had accomplished and what needed to be done and the urgency of keeping the army together. Finally, he told them that what they faced in the next few days was "the crisis which is to decide our destiny."

He looked at the men and then down at the ground again and walked his horse to the side and waited for a response. For long moments, no one moved. The men looked at the snowy white ground in front of them. They shifted their weight from one leg to another, gazing left and right, to see what actions others would take. Still, no one moved. The minutes passed.

Finally, one veteran slowly stepped forward. He told the general that he could not go home when the army needed him. A few more stepped up; others followed. Within minutes, more than half of the men agreed to stay and fight on. Many of those who chose to go home were sick or too badly dressed to last much longer in the winter. The same appeal to the men was made by other generals and other officers, invoking Washington's name. The response was also positive. The army would hold together; it would fight on.

The troops did not know that Washington had misled them. There was no bounty money. They also did not know that he had absolutely no authorization from Congress to offer any bonuses.

Now, having given his word, the commander had to raise the money. He sent Robert Morris, the chief financier of the Continental Congress, and one of the colonies' leading businessmen, word of his plight. He begged Morris to find money, hard cash as well as script, and have it delivered to him immediately. "We have no money to pay the bounty and we have exhausted our credit by such frequent promises," he explained to Morris. Then he implored him to help. "Borrow money where it can be done," he said, and invoked patriotism as he told him the revolution was out of time. "Every man of interest and every lover of his country must strain his credit upon such an occasion. No time is to be lost."

Morris wrote back that he was overwhelmed with earlier requests from Washington and Congress and had little time to raise money for what amounted to an illegal offer. Everyone knew, though, that if anyone could find money in a bankrupt city, it was Morris. The elegantly dressed, slightly overweight, forty-two-year-old delegate to Congress was a partner in Willing and Morris, Philadelphia's leading mercantile business, which earned enormous profits in manufacturing, shipping, banking, and assorted other enterprises. Morris was a financial genius who had earned money for everyone who ever worked with him. He was also an ardent patriot and had led the revolt against the Stamp Act in the city in 1765 and was one of the authors of the local non-importation agreement, which barred purchases of most British goods by local merchants.

Morris found the money, borrowing it from other men in the city's financial community. He managed to stuff two bags full of script plus Spanish dollars, English crowns, shillings, and French francs and dispatched them to Washington. On the very last day of 1776, a courier arrived with new orders from Congress, now settled in Baltimore. Recognizing the fragile state of the fledgling country, and proud of the army and its victory at Trenton, Congress had changed its mind and authorized the general to do anything necessary, including bonuses, to keep the army together.

There was critical news from spies the next morning. The British, as Washington suspected, were embarrassed by the defeat at Trenton and the loss of 920 of their best troops. They had moved out of New Brunswick and marched through Princeton, pushing aside a small American force Washington had placed there earlier. The main force of seven thousand men was on its way toward Trenton and a smaller, but still large, British army remained at Princeton. Washington assumed the men headed toward him north of Trenton were under Howe, but unfortunately they were commanded by Lord Cornwallis, who had stopped packing at the news of the defeat at Trenton and called out his army for a counter-attack.

Although Washington knew the terrain, he found himself boxed in, and by a better general than Howe. Since the Redcoats were massing north of Trenton, all the Americans could do was back up toward the

Delaware and post soldiers east of tiny Assunpink Creek, which ran parallel to the river, as their sole line of defense. Washington had no boats to flee across the Delaware and, with the enemy arrayed in front of him, the last thing he wanted to do was attack the larger and much better trained and equipped British under the wily veteran Cornwallis.

The weather, too, was no longer in his favor, becoming warm after the storm. The temperature rose above freezing on the morning of December 30 and climbed to 36 degrees by the middle of the afternoon. It remained at 36 degrees on December 31 and then, on New Year's Day, shot up to 51 degrees. The snow melted, and the ground thawed. Then, late that afternoon, a low-pressure system moved into the region, creating a fierce rainstorm. The dirt roads and meadows, softened by the warm weather and pounded by the rain, quickly turned to mud that was, as artist and Pennsylvania Lieutenant Charles Wilson Peale wrote, "over our shoetops." The soggy ground made any troop or artillery movement by the Continentals nearly impossible as Cornwallis arrived on January 2. Washington had the British in front of him and the impassable river behind him and an army stuck in the mud.

Cornwallis attacked in late afternoon and drove the Continentals back from their defensive line in front of the creek, forcing them to retreat over the single bridge crossing it. They went past Washington, stern and steady on his white horse. He stood mounted there like a rock while bullets whizzed through the air. Washington remained near the bridge to give his men some confidence. Later, he moved back.

Dusk began to fall and Cornwallis decided against pursuing the Americans further. Why bother to chase Washington that afternoon, he told aides, in what was to become familiar British reasoning for wasting opportunities. "We've got the old fox safe now," Cornwallis told another general, "We'll go over and bag him in the morning."

The American soldiers knew that their chances against the British army the next day would be tenuous. "Even the most sanguine among us could not flatter ourselves into thinking with any hope of victory," wrote Massachusetts private Samuel Shaw, who said his comrades were certain that the army would be crushed in the morning.

As evening approached, British sentries watched as dozens of Americans walked about, dismantling wooden farm fences for firewood and carrying large stacks back toward their camp. The movement of men stopped a few hours later and numerous campfires were started so that the men could cook dinner and keep warm. Except for a few dozen easily observed sentries, the camp became quiet as the men appeared to sleep, attempting to rest before the British assault, which would surely come soon after the sun rose.

But the Americans were wide awake. The weather was changing. The rain had stopped falling in the morning and the temperature had held at 39 degrees all day. Washington had watched the treetops carefully and noticed that a steady northwest wind blew throughout the afternoon. As night fell, the wind continued and the temperature began to drop. From his years as a farmer, the general knew that these were all the signs of a sudden cold front that would cause a frost. If the weather held, and the wind remained constant, the ground would freeze later in the night. The weather that evening was similar to that on dozens of nights in his years at Mount Vernon, all carefully recorded in meticulous weather diaries he had kept since 1759.

He remembered periods such as the last week of March, in 1768, when the same weather patterns had plagued his farming. He had carefully written:

Mar. 22—Calm, clear and pleasant, snow melting fast.
Mar. 23—Calm and cloudy, with a little rain in the morning.
Mar. 24—Clear and cool—wind at No. West.
Mar. 25—Morning cool and wind at No. West. Ground froze.

He was certain that the muddy dirt roads would freeze, allowing the men to march on them, and that the narrow highways would be solid enough to bear the weight of heavy artillery. These conditions would not last. He had to watch for the cold to descend, move the army eighteen miles to Princeton, engage the enemy, and leave the town by late afternoon before another thaw arrived, once again turning the ground to mud and making additional travel difficult. Washington kept one eye on his large fires and another on the sky, waiting for a frost to provide an opportunity to evacuate.

Shortly after midnight, the ground began to freeze. Officers circulated throughout the camp with news of the general's plan. They would keep their fires burning and sentries posted to make the British think the army was soundly encamped for the night. Then, slowly and quietly, the entire army would move back toward the river and then on to the Quaker Bridge Road, a little-used narrow dirt road that would take them northeast through riverside farmlands, well away from any British sentries and north toward Princeton. The men were to gather up their equipment and muskets silently. Blankets were tied around the wheels of the cannon caissons to quiet them. Washington had silently evacuated his untenable position at Brooklyn Heights in the middle of the night during the previous summer, using boats instead of a road, in the same manner. He had been able to fool Howe then and he was hopeful of tricking Cornwallis now.

When the sun rose, the troops walking north on Quaker Bridge Road realized that the temperature had changed drastically. "The morning was bright, serene and extremely cold, with a hoar frost which bespangled every object," reported Lt. James Wilkinson. And the highway was easy to walk on. "The road which the day before had been mud, snow and water...had become hard as pavement," said Captain Stephen Olney of New York.

The British, watching his fires burn in the distance, never suspected anything. In the morning, Cornwallis rose early, prepared to attack, but found the fields and woods on the other side of the creek empty. Washington and the rebels had simply vanished.

Just before 9 A.M. outside Princeton, the Americans encountered two regiments of England's crack Fourth Brigade, led by Lt. Col. Charles Mawhood, who was riding, as always, with his two pet dogs near him. At first, Mawhood paid little notice to the large Continental Army, which seemed to clog up the road for quite a distance. He assumed, naturally, that it was Cornwallis' army, returning after crushing the rebels the day before near Lawrenceville. When he realized that it was Washington, he quickly sent his men across a bridge to engage them. General Hugh

Mercer, Washington's longtime Virginia friend, led an American attack through an orchard at the Clark farm.

The Americans found themselves in a fierce early-morning fight that was described well by Delaware's Thomas Rodney, who almost lost his life in the battle:

> About 150 of my men came to this post, but I could not keep them all there, for the enemies fire was dreadful and three balls, for they were very thick, had grazed me. One passed within my elbow, nicking my great coat and carried away the breech of Sergeant McKnatt's gun, he being close behind me. Another carried away the inside edge of one of my shoe soles. Another nicked my hat and indeed they seemed as thick as hail.

The British were too strong and the Americans were routed. Mercer was bayoneted to death. The British prepared to launch another bayonet charge at his troops, now moving back in disarray.

By this time, Washington, riding hard over the fields to see what was happening, appeared behind the men in Mercer's regiment. He leaned down and spurred his horse on through the trees, yelling out to the militia to follow him. The appearance of the commander-in-chief bolstered the confidence of the frightened men. They stopped running, turned, and followed the general as he continued through the woods, exhorting the troops to turn and face the enemy. They were joined by a newly arrived New England regiment of some 500 men (American regiments were supposed to number 790 men, but usually varied between 350 and 600). Washington then rode up to the front of the men and led a charge against the Redcoats. High on his horse, he took off his hat and waved it above him as he yelled for the men to follow him, an easy target for the British soldiers who recognized him. He took the Americans to within a few dozen yards of the British lines, where their infantry was aided by artillery. They fired.

"Halt!" he yelled and the men stopped, raised their muskets, and aimed. Some were alarmed that Washington was right in front of them, an easy target for the enemy.

"Fire!" yelled the commander-in-chief. Both sides fired at the same time. The morning was thick with smoke and the sound of musketry as hundreds of bullets cut through the air around Washington in what a man there called a "very heavy platoon fire." The general never moved as the barrage erupted around him. He sat implacably on his horse, his eyes glowering at the British. His men were amazed that he had not been killed by the fusillade; they were also impressed that a general would stand right in the line of fire with them.

The British troops were unnerved by the heavy American fire and the bravery of their commander. There was a fast second volley from the Americans; the British fled. They expected some militiamen to chase after them, yelling in victory, as was the custom, but were astonished to see Washington himself leading the chase on his horse.

"It's a fine fox chase, boys!" the general yelled back over his shoulder as the men raced after him, shouting, muskets in the air, joining him in the chase of the British. The general led it for a few moments and then stopped, letting the men follow the Redcoats, shouting happily as the British raced away over the meadows. It was one of the first truly jubilant moments in the war.

While Washington rallied the men around him, in a nearby field General Sullivan's men defeated the men of the British Fifty-fifth regiment, and Alexander Hamilton's artillery battery shelled Nassau Hall, the main building of the College of New Jersey (now Princeton University), where nearly two hundred Redcoats were stationed. One of the cannonballs shattered a window and ironically smashed into a painting of King George I hanging in a room of the building. The British, hovering inside, hung a white flag of surrender out one of the windows. After a few shots were heard in the distance, the fighting ended. The men lowered their muskets. "It is impossible for any troops to behave better than ours did," wrote a very pleased Shaw.

All of the British not captured were in full retreat toward Trenton and New Brunswick. The battle of Princeton had taken only forty-five minutes. The rebels had lost thirty enlisted men and fourteen officers, including Mercer. Many of the dead had been brutally bayoneted. In contrast, the British had suffered enormous losses. Washington estimated the total at about three hundred killed and three hundred captured. The victory seemed to those closest to Washington a sign from above. "I thank the God of the Universe for producing this turn in our affairs of America," Knox told his wife. "This sentiment I hope will prevail in the hearts of the people."

Just after the fighting, Dr. Benjamin Rush tended to the wounded soldiers and officers. Men from the Princeton militia loaded captured British supplies onto the wagons. Washington had heard from scouts that Lord Cornwallis was a one-hour march away, to the south, astonished that the entire American army had slipped away to Princeton under his nose. A major confrontation against Cornwallis, following the furious battle just completed, could not be risked that afternoon.

Now there was little time to think about pursuing British troops fleeing across the meadows or even burying the American dead in a nearby field. The British, moving as fast as possible from Trenton, even with their cumbersome supply wagons and artillery corps, would soon arrive in the area. If Washington's calculations about the weather were correct, the freeze would not last much past mid-afternoon (it ended at 1 P.M.). The general considered all of his varied options and determined that he should put distance between himself and Cornwallis before the roads once more turned to mud, making travel impossible. Shortly after 11 A.M., just two hours after the last shots of the battle had been fired, Washington directed his officers to hastily form their regiments into columns and align their wagons in a train so that the army could move out of Princeton and north toward the tiny village of Morristown, fifty miles away. The commander-in-chief later told Hancock that if he had commanded more troops, fresh ones that had not been used in the Princeton skirmish, he might have marched on New Brunswick, fifteen miles away, before Cornwallis could catch up to him, destroyed the British ammunition magazines there, captured the remnants of their army waiting in the town, confiscated $2 million in cash kept there, and ended the war.

Over the course of the next two hundred years, historians would write hundreds of books and articles about the victories at Trenton and

Princeton that week, but in all of their eloquence they never described the defeats of the British as well as the plain-spoken Dr. Jonathan Potts, a surgeon with the Continental Army, who said of the enemy: "They were drubbed and out-generaled in every respect."

In just seven days, Washington and the Americans had scored startling victories over the vaunted Hessians in Trenton, outfoxed England's best general, Cornwallis, captured Princeton, killed 330 men, taken 1,230 prisoners, and sent the British reeling back toward the safety of New York.

The rather remarkable success of the Continental Army in the two encounters did much to change the attitude of the officers and men concerning the Revolution. They believed for the first time that the war could be won. "The enterprises of Trenton and Princeton...[were] the dawnings of that bright day which afterwards broke forth with such resplendent luster," wrote Hamilton, who, like so many others, was proud of his own bravery during the fighting.

Members of the Continental Congress, waiting in temporary quarters in Baltimore until they could return to Philadelphia, were impressed and even thrilled by the twin triumphs over the British. "The news from General Washington has given new life and spirits to everybody here," wrote a buoyant delegate James Smith to his wife.

An English journalist traveling in the colonies at the time, Nicholas Cresswell, said of the Americans now: "A few days ago, they had given up the cause for lost. Their late successes have turned the scale and now they are all liberty-mad again."

The surprising military successes also changed the tenor of press coverage of the war by colonial newspapers. Prior to the crossing of the Delaware, only about one third of the forty-four newspapers in America favored the war. Some opposed it or, as was more likely the case, maintained an interested neutrality and waited to see what would transpire. Now, just about all of the editors of the newspapers decided to support the rebellion, convinced that the war could, indeed, be won, and independence achieved. It was the victories that had changed their minds, not any increased intellectual or political fervor. The editors had not merely observed the American army win two battles over an enemy force that had badly defeated it numerous times before in New York; they had seen the rebels thoroughly thrash the mighty British. Empowered by these victories, they used their columns to urge all Americans to be proud of their army.

"The late success of General Washington in the Jersies must afford the most heart-felt pleasure to every American," an editor at the *Pennsylvania Evening Post* told his readers. Of the soldiers, an editor of Philadelphia's *Freeman's Journal* bragged: "The men behaved with the utmost bravery." An editor at the *Connecticut Journal* saw a crack in the British armor and hinted that they were now "in utmost confusion."

The press saw the British army much like the huge, seemingly invincible boxing champion whose lightly regarded opponent has suddenly knocked him to the canvas, to the astonishment of the crowd. The champion will get up, groggy, shaking his head to regain his senses, and continue the fight, but now he will move about carefully, very defensively, to avoid another knockdown. And now, unlike before, he will fear his opponent.

Politically, the departure of the British from New Jersey (except for small garrisons in New Brunswick, Elizabeth, and Perth Amboy) meant that both that state's legislature and Congress could regroup, their sense of panic and doom gone. The state legislature in New Jersey, which had disbanded in fear just a month before, reconvened and began to go about its business. The Continental Congress had been, unkind as it may seem to say, hiding out in Baltimore, waiting to see whether or not the Redcoats would crush Washington on the shores of the Delaware and capture Philadelphia. Little of the nation's business was conducted in the Maryland seaport because delegates did not know if they would have a nation left. Now, with most of the British driven back to New York, with New Jersey in the hands of the Continentals, and with Philadelphia secure, Congressmen could breath a sigh of relief and begin to resume their legislative functions, raise money for the army, step up the recruitment of troops, and continue negotiations to cajole the French into entering the war on the side of the Americans. And the delegates could also begin to pack for the trip back to Philadelphia, which was once again safe to enter.

Militarily, George Washington, who had spent the early months of the war educating Congress about army matters, had received an education himself. He had learned that his much smaller army, unencumbered by numerous regiments of soldiers clogging up the roads and long lines of supply wagons such as those needed by the larger enemy force, could move much faster than its opponents. It could attack more rapidly than the British and it could retreat quicker, keeping the men alive to fight future battles. It could, in fact, fly from an attack on a moment's notice, as it did the night before the encounter at Princeton and, earlier, at Brooklyn Heights and Fort Washington. The army's ability to escape was just as important as its ability to attack. This was of critical importance to Washington. The British could lose their Hessian army of nine hundred men at Trenton and still have thirty-one thousand troops left. Washington could not lose his army; there was no other.

Guerrilla warfare would often be the hallmark of the army for several years. Washington's men could not defeat the British in classic head-to-head fighting, as had been proven in New York, but they could win battles if they fought unconventionally, with daybreak assaults, sneak attacks, and trickery. Trenton and Princeton had not only proven that these tactics could be used successfully by the Americans, but that the British did not know how to defend themselves against this creative form of warfare.

Washington had learned, too, that the British had great difficulty fighting in the winter. They had no experience fighting in snow, ice, and sleet, and even the strident urging of their generals and officers had not been enough for them to conquer the elements as well as the Americans. Howe had returned to New York in early December, even announcing that the campaign was over until the spring. Cornwallis had begun to pack his bags for a winter voyage back to London, where he had planned to stay for as long as possible to care for his sickly wife.

This reluctance of the British high command to engage any enemy with snow on the ground, or in chilly weather, might, Washington mused, give him the time he needed in the winter of 1777 to rebuild the Continental Army.

The American commander had learned that he could use the savage elements of winter—snow, sleet, frost and numbing weather—to his advantage. It might be possible, again and again, to utilize the harshness of winter as a cloak for himself and the army, enabling it to strike with surprise. The success of the army had not only given it new life, but the public appearance of an army that had not merely conquered the enemy, but done so with great panache. It had become something more than the military extension of the revolution; it had become an entity of its own. The Continental Army was now a viable physical force in the land. People need symbols to create nations. Revolutions need declarations of independence, slogans, and flags. Most of all, revolutions need an army and a leader.

Washington was a man of steely determination who had reacted to events and personalities, and the trying vicissitudes of winter, with speed, boldness, imagination, and success. In ten critical days, Washington had undergone a significant transformation. He had become not only the heralded leader of the army, but of the revolution and the struggling new nation as well.

When the news of the American forces' twin victories arrived in Europe a few weeks later, government leaders from nations small and large reacted with great surprise. The news did not spread throughout the capitals of Europe like a tiny ripple in a pool of calm water; it moved like a tidal wave. The news, and the way it was played in European newspapers and conveyed in backrooms of legislatures and in the hallways of royal palaces, had a dramatic effect throughout the continent.

The French government had been reluctant to actually declare war on England, its leaders opting instead to give American negotiators who had been in Paris for some months little more than verbal promises that they might formally take sides with the revolution at some future date. Now, though, news of Washington's smashing victories led them to a decision to send much-needed gunpowder, muskets, flints, and cannon to the Continental Army. They ordered four ships laden with artillery and gunpowder to sail for America as quickly as possible.

In Germany, the Prince of Hesse, home base to the Hessians captured at Trenton, was stunned by the defeat and the loss of an entire army. He said the capture of the town was "a painful shock" and ordered a full investigation of the whole Hessian enterprise in the American colonies. The prince's subordinates, as bewildered as their leader, wondered out loud if the Hessians' reputation as fighters had been shattered for good. Frederick the Great would say that the victories were "the most brilliant of any recorded in the annals of military achievement."

The newspapers of European countries, always eager to trumpet any failing of the British, gave considerable attention to the winter victories, presenting Washington as a new and significant military figure on the world stage and demeaning the British. There did not seem to be a major European city where the American triumphs were not much discussed news. A German wrote that "George Washington's coup...was the sensation of the world."

In England, members of Parliament, stung by Trenton and Princeton, became extremely critical of their army. The generals, they argued, had woefully misjudged the Continental Army. Their numerous delays in pursuing the Americans, from September until December, had been inexcusable lapses in judgment. They wondered, as many in Britain did, how an army of thirty-two thousand of the best soldiers in the world could be defeated by much smaller, generally untrained, and badly equipped forces, and how the most brilliant and seasoned generals in the Empire could be out-foxed by a wheat farmer. King George's most influential ministers weathered the criticism and defended the army, but they knew that their forces had received a significant blow. Or, as Lord George Germain, head of the Colonial Office and director of the war effort, said in a letter to Howe, "all of our hopes were blasted by that unhappy affair at Trenton."

Officers in the British army were even more savage than London newspaper editors, members of Parliament, or the public in their condemnation. Their criticism was hurled not at the foot soldiers, but directly at Howe and Cornwallis. Many were in accord with General Sir Henry Clinton, who accused Cornwallis of "the most consumate ignorance I ever heard of in any officer above a corporal."

Later, British historian George Trevelyan wrote about the battles: "It may be doubted whether so small a number of men ever employed so short a space of time with greater and more lasting effects upon the history of the world."

And as his men trudged through the middle of New Jersey toward Morristown, as the snows began to fall once more, George Washington would need all of those skills to deal with a series of wintertime catastrophes that would again threaten the existence of his army and with it the future of his new country.

Chapter Two

THE SQUIRE OF
MOUNT VERNON

*"I can truly say I had rather be at Mount Vernon
with a friend or two about me than to be attended
at the seat of government by the officers of state and
the representatives of every power in Europe."*
—George Washington

When the Second Continental Congress was called into session in
Philadelphia during the summer of 1775, it was not at all clear
that George Washington would be nominated as commander-in-chief of
the Continental Army. He was sent from Virginia, the House of
Burgesses said, "for the wisdom of his counsel."

Soon after Washington, forty-three, had arrived in the city, he began
to wear his new Virginia militia uniform to the daily sessions of Congress. He cut a commanding figure; he seemed ready for war. Washington always claimed that he wore his uniform because he wanted the
delegates to see some visible sign that Virginia was willing to fight, and
that he was willing to lead his colony's forces. In his mind, he had resisted war again and again. It had taken him years to stir up the old military passions that had faded away at the end of the French and Indian

War, where he had served as a very young man. He knew now, though, that events had gone too far and that there would be a war. America would need experienced soldiers.

The delegates were looking for men with military experience to place on a special committee in order to determine what kind of an army the colonies needed and to develop the procedures required to assemble it. Washington exercised great influence on the members of the committee. Striding through Carpenter's Hall in his uniform, he impressed everyone. In committee meetings, the retired colonel had shown that he knew far more than any of the delegates about military matters. Although he had never led an army or overseen any significant military strategy during his three years in the army in the 1750s, he had led men in combat. He had been shot four times. It may have been true that his administrative responsibilities as head of a regiment of Virginia militia on the frontier were limited to the operations of a single main fort at Winchester and a smaller fort at Cumberland, but he had convinced delegates that the running of the forts was akin to the command of an army, but on a much smaller scale. Washington had left the army in 1759, sixteen long years before, and all the delegates could remember about his days in uniform was that he had fought well and been considered a young hero. The creation of his own militia that spring and his dramatic vow to raise an army and march on Boston had already become legendary throughout the colonies. In Philadelphia, he was seen as a fierce patriot.

Washington's notion that he might only lead an army of Virginians in a wider war ended rather quickly as discussions about a national army and the need for a commander-in-chief progressed. The British would have no fear of a war against an armed militia just from Massachusetts. Soldiers had to be recruited from each of the colonies for a truly American force. The commander of that army would not only have to be a fine general, but a man who truly represented the national interests of the United States. He could not be an amateur, like the willing John Hancock, or a former British officer, such as Charles Lee, now commanding Americans in Boston.

Washington's name was mentioned often. The men who met him and worked with him in Philadelphia all quickly realized that his military training and political and business experience had made him unique. They all remarked that he had a presence about him, a man used to success who could instill confidence in those around him. Jedediah Morse, who knew him later, summed up the feelings of most men and women when they first met Washington: "His features strong, manly and commanding; his temper reserved and serious; his countenance grave, composed and sensible. There was in his whole appearance an unusual dignity and gracefulness which at once secured him profound respect, and cordial esteem. He seemed born to command his fellow men."

Delegates talked to him about the possibility of assuming a leadership position in the army. He never advanced himself for the job. He never politicked for it, hinted at it, or insinuated through sly conversation that he wanted it or would take it. He kept away from people talking of him as the commander. But he *did* wear his uniform every day.

Washington knew far better than any of the delegates that success in a war against England would be difficult. He agreed with their view that Americans would make good fighters because they would be protecting their homeland and opposing the outrageous policies of the Crown, that the patriot's enthusiasm was unbounded. He agreed that God and virtue would be on their side. But as a practical former colonel he knew that they would be the underdogs. "The resources of Britain were, in a manner, inexhaustible; that her fleets covered the ocean and that her troops had harvested laurels in every quarter of the globe. We had no preparation. Money...was wanting," he philosophized, analyzing the military situation with great precision, while concluding coldly that "the sword was to be forged on the anvil of necessity."

Delegates from North and South saw Washington as an acceptable choice. They were satisfied, too, with his demeanor. Over the weeks of their sessions, they had come to know him. He was modest, not a braggart, mature, and a man who could act as both general and leader of the cause. "He seems discreet and virtuous, no harem scarum ranting swearing fellow but sober, steady and calm," wrote delegate Eliphalet Dyer after

Washington's selection. Another delegate, Thomas Cushing, assessing his personality and status in life, concluded: "He is a complete gentleman. He is sensible, amiable and brave. His agreeable behavior and good conduct will give great satisfaction to our people of all denominations."

Many were impressed that their new military leader was also a wealthy patrician, a man who, with his stature, certainly did not have to join the army, much less lead it. Although they rarely discussed it, the delegates knew that the British would execute the leaders of the Revolution if the enterprise failed, just as they had executed the heads of a Scottish rebellion in 1747. The first on that list would be the commander of the army. Here, in front of them, in his pristine blue and red uniform, then, was a man who had absolutely nothing to gain and everything to lose. "There is something charming to me in the conduct of Washington, a gentleman of one of the first fortunes upon the continent, leaving his retirement, his family and friends, sacrificing his ease," wrote John Adams, who had come to know him well.

Back home in Virginia, the selection was hailed by all, and the *Virginia Gazette* called Washington "the generalissimo of American forces."

Newspaper editors and Congressmen seemed to understand, too, before he even mounted his horse, that the job of commander-in-chief of the American army could be special. He might soon become, as Adams wrote, "one of the most important characters in the world."

George Washington had not started his life as a patrician. Like many Americans, he had risen from humble origins. His great-grandfather John came to America as an indentured worker in 1658. He was representative of many other European men and women who had settled on the Atlantic Coast at that time, all seeking opportunities in the new world. John Washington was soon joined by his brothers and a sister as he worked off his indenture fees, gained independence, and prospered. He began to buy up land and slaves.

The Washingtons acquired more property and slaves over the next seven decades. John's grandson, Augustine, an unusually tall and muscular man, married Jane Butler. They had two sons, Lawrence and Augustine. Jane died in 1730 and Augustine Washington married Mary Ball, who gave him seven more children. The first was a son, George Washington, born on February 22, 1732, at their farm, Pope's Creek Plantation, in central Virginia.

A few years later, the Washingtons moved to Ferry Farm, on the northern bank of the Rappahannock River across from the small but bustling river port of Fredericksburg. They lived adjacent to a busy ferry stop, moving there to be closer to the iron mine that Augustine ran. Washington's father died there in 1743. George's older stepbrothers received the bulk of his father's wealth and land, which his mother, close to young George, resented. Lawrence was given a sizable plantation on the Potomac River, which he later named Mount Vernon. George, eleven at the time, was given Ferry Farm, which he ran with his mother and the farm's nineteen slaves. They grew tobacco, corn, and wheat.

The boy enjoyed reading, even if he did not do much of it at school. At home, he spent his time devouring classics such as *Don Quixote* and *Tristram Shandy*, but his favorite book was a popular pamphlet of the day called *The Rules of Conduct and Politeness*. The pamphlet, translated into several languages, offered tips on conversation, manners, love of God, temper management, honesty, and a respect for one's elders. For Washington, it was a blueprint for success in Virginia society. He memorized most of it, reading it numerous times and even copying sections of it in longhand. Adherence to the pamphlet's advice enabled him to grow into a respected teenager who could assimilate into the life of the Virginia gentry.

His older brother Lawrence, whose wealth had increased substantially when he married into the influential Fairfax family, suggested that George, who had met dozens of sailors at Fredericksburg, join the Royal Navy when he turned fourteen. Surely the family knew someone who could pull strings to have him assigned as a cabin boy aboard the ship of a famous sea captain. Family friends urged Mary Washington to keep her son away from long ocean voyages on ships where unsanitary conditions brought on extended and sometimes fatal illnesses. Mary was also in no hurry to have her son leave for one- and two-year voyages and then perhaps move to London. It appeared to be the wrong choice.

Her son seemed more enamored with the land. Washington had grown up amid the rolling hills and wide fields of eastern Virginia and loved them. He began to work as a land surveyor just after he turned seventeen in 1749. He quickly gained a reputation as a fast learner who pleased his clients. He offered careful and accurate surveys of land for dozens of large farmers in the area who appreciated the detail of his reports. Later, details would be the hallmark of his years in the army. Other farmers, hearing of his meticulous work, hired him. Many Virginia planters had little cash because they had their money invested in land and slaves. It was common practice to pay professionals like Washington in land. Soon, the surveyor owned more than 1,400 acres.

By the time he was eighteen, a restless Washington had moved in with Lawrence at Mount Vernon. Already, he appeared physically imposing. At six feet, three inches tall, he weighed 175 pounds and his shoulders sloped above a thick torso, thin hips, and very thick thighs. He had long, muscular arms and very large hands. His feet were large too; he wore size 13 shoes. He had a round face with a long and flat nose and blue-grey eyes that sat in oversized sockets. Those who greeted him contended his eyes were sometimes animated and at other times grave. His hair was reddish brown, tied in a cue, highlighted against a rather fair complexion. His pale skin tended to burn easily in the hot summer sun. Washington did not smile much, friends said, because he did not want people to see his badly angled and defective teeth.

But he was, as a friend, George Mason, later said of him, someone to be reckoned with: "In conversation, he looks you full in the face, is deliberate, deferential and engaging. His demeanor is at all times composed and dignified. His movements and gestures are graceful, his walk majestic." Mercer also observed, as so many others did during Washington's lifetime, that even at eighteen he possessed "a commanding countenance."

George Washington was a very athletic and strong young man, like his father. Once, on a dare, he joined a group of young men who were engaged in a contest to see who could toss a heavy bar of iron the farthest. They picked it up, held it away from their bodies, spun about two or three times and then heaved it, much like a discus thrower. Even though he had never tried the heave before, Washington joined in, and on his first and only toss threw the iron bar more than a dozen yards farther than any of the astonished young men. It was at this time, too, that the legend concerning Washington's tossing of a silver dollar across the wide Rappahannock began. In truth, it was a stone, not a silver dollar, that his cousin Fielding Lewis insisted he saw George heave across the river, some 130 yards wide in front of Ferry Farm.

By this time, he had also become an exceptional horseman. His abilities on his mounts made surveyor's work much easier as he galloped his favorite horses across the Virginia countryside. There were few areas as lush, with dozens of creeks, thick forests, wide tobacco fields, and meadows for riding. Those sections of the state that hugged the Potomac River, where his brother lived, were particularly beautiful. To ride through Virginia, his horse surging forward and the cool spring breeze blowing across his face, would become sheer joy for him. He was able to maneuver his horses through thick forests, getting them to leap over fallen trees, race through gullies, and gallop as fast as any farmer in the area had ever seen. "He is a very excellent and bold horseman, leaping the highest fences and going extremely quick without standing upon his stirrups, bearing on the bridle, or letting his horse run wild," said a man who rode with him.

He had grown into a popular and sought-after young man. He did not have much of a sense of humor, but ingratiated himself to others by laughing heartily at their jokes and stories. He was always eager to try a new ale. Card games became his vice and he played as often as possible, carefully marking down, in great detail, his winnings and losses. Women, the prettier the better, became another vice.

He was blossoming into a respected and successful man when he surprised friends by applying for and winning the job of military adjutant for one of Virginia's two militia companies. That job would be a stepping stone, he certainly hoped, to a prestigious commission in the British Army. It is uncertain where this yearning for the military life came, whether it was his envy of brother Lawrence's time in the army, a teenage romance with battle, or simply a way to move away from his overbearing mother, with whom he had a difficult relationship all of his life. But at twenty, Washington found himself in charge of the military for the British in the state's southern district. He became head of the militia at a time when France was flexing its muscle in North America. The French, eager for more trade in the Ohio Valley and Great Lakes, began building forts and signing trade agreements with the various Indian tribes that populated that section of the country.

This alarmed Governor Dinwiddie, who sent Washington on a mission through the Ohio Territory to take a message to the French at Lake Erie warning them to stop building forts and to withdraw from the area. Washington and a guide, Christopher Gist, left Williamsburg in November and reached a French fort near Lake Erie in mid-December. The commandant refused Dinwiddie's request and sent Washington home. He and Gist soon found themselves on a three-week, four hundred–mile journey in the midst of a severe winter. During the trip, their raft overturned on the Allegheny River; Washington nearly drowned. Walking with the aid of snowshoes and later using horses, the pair managed to struggle through snowfalls, rain storms, freezing temperatures, and attacking American Indians. The young militia leader had learned the dangers of the wildnerness firsthand.

In the spring of 1754, the French sailed down the Allegheny and easily seized a British fort located at the current site of Pittsburgh. They demolished it and constructed a larger one, Fort Duquesne. Washington, now a lieutenant colonel, was sent to attack it. On the way, on May 28, part of his militia, numbering several dozen, confronted the French. They killed ten men, including the French commander Jujmonville de Villiers, a well-known diplomat. They also captured twenty-one French soldiers in what was the first skirmish of the French and Indian War. Washington then supervised his men in the hasty construction of a garrison he aptly named Fort Necessity. It was a disaster. The French arrived six weeks later, forcing Washington to surrender. The Virginians, led by a now-humbled young colonel, were forced to march sixty miles to the safety of Will's Creek.

News of the loss of the fort, the death of the French diplomat, and questions about his command greeted Washington upon his arrival at Williamsburg, and a disgusted Washington resigned. He was back in the spring of 1755, though, when he learned that Edward Braddock, one of England's most distinguished generals, had arrived in Virginia with a force of four thousand well-trained British soldiers who were planning a march on Fort Duquesne.

Washington asked for a regular officer's commission in the British Army, but Braddock turned him down. The British General wanted to take the Virginian with him because he knew the territory around Pittsburgh, but because Washington was an American he could only go as a volunteer officer. Washington, angry at the snub from the English, but eager for the campaign and a chance to serve with the legendary British commander, agreed.

His ardor for war cooled considerably when he came down with malaria in late June 1755. Washington, sick and frustrated, had to ride all the way through the wilderness in a covered wagon, battling a fever. Tired of the ride, the twenty-three-year-old Washington finally climbed down from the wagon, strapped one of his pillows to the saddle on his horse, and mounted. He was weak, with pains shooting through his stomach, but he rode on. It was not long before his regiment caught up to Braddock, who had marched into a wilderness trap and had been surrounded by the French and hundreds of American Indians.

Washington, appalled that the British were lining up in their bright red coats for a frontal assault on a hill well-guarded by the French and their Indian allies, begged the general for permission to lead a group of men in an Indian-style assault on the hill from the woods. Braddock refused, and sixty-three of the eight-six officers in the formal attack were killed or wounded. Washington lost two horses in the battle and was shot four times, each musket ball ripping through his coat but miraculously missing his body. Braddock was shot through the chest. He would soon die.

The leaderless army was in a full rout. Washington, one of the few officers left, took charge. Despite bullets whizzing about him, he managed to reach the British leader's side where he had soldiers lift the general on to a stretcher and move him out of the area of fire. Washington then had the British regulars and the American militia regroup; he led them in an orderly retreat through the woods and saved the army.

Although the combined British and American forces suffered a devastating defeat, the twenty-four-year-old Washington was hailed as a hero back in the colony's capital. The governor awarded him a bonus, promoted him to full colonel, and gave him control of the colony's one thousand–man defensive force. Virginians saw in him a young man who was not only brave, but extremely cool and creative. He was, they believed, a man who in time of crisis would not panic and could show exemplary leadership skills.

The French and Indian War continued in the Americas until 1763, but there was little action on the Virginia frontier. Washington served as an administrator for two more years, building a few forts, representing the state with local public officials, defending farms, recruiting troops, and hunting Indian war parties (he found few). He wound up feuding with Dinwiddie over the appointment of officers under his command and in militia units throughout the state and seethed over public and private criticism by the governor over his work. Then, in 1758, Washington became quite ill. Fed up with the military, Washington retired that year, at the age of twenty-six. However, the events of the war remained deeply etched in his mind. He had learned that he and others could survive harsh conditions when required and that he himself was inventive. Washington had also learned much about how American Indians fought. They traveled light, never went head-to-head against a larger foe, retreated as adroitly as they attacked, and specialized in sneak attacks and subterfuge. Most important of all, he had learned that the British could be beaten.

Meeting Martha

His brother Lawrence, whom George loved deeply, had died from tuberculosis during the war and left his large plantation at Mount Vernon to his widow, who leased it to George and bequeathed it to him when she died a few years later. George began farming there, working with his brother's slaves, white indentured servants, and tenant farmers to produce large tobacco crops.

It was then that he met Martha Custis.

Martha was not his first love. His first love had been the unattainable

Sally Cary Fairfax, the wife of his close friend George Fairfax. He had visited the Fairfaxes often at their large nearby plantation, Belvoir, with its handsome manor house. He had become smitten with Sally, a beautiful, slender, witty, and well-educated woman, albeit flirtatious and teasing, who had befriended him. His love for her was apparently never consummated. All that remains of their relationship is a series of awkward letters in which both seemed to hint at, but never admit, their feelings for each other.

Martha Custis was different. She was not a textbook beauty like Sally. She stood just over five feet tall, seemed overweight, had a round face and small hands, and was, by most accounts, rather plain looking. The daughter of a rich planter, she had been raised to marry a planter and help run his farms. As a teenager, Martha had been trained as a cook and taught how to supervise a large kitchen and produce meals for the family and guests. Older women had given her lessons in the fine art of playing hostess at large parties for her wealthy neighbors. She had been taught how to work with and handle slaves.

She was a refined young woman who had her social coming out at the age of fifteen. At seventeen, she married Daniel Custis, one of the wealthiest men in Virginia, who was thirteen years her senior. She bore him four children. Two died before his own death of heart failure in 1757. Martha, twenty-five, became one of the richest widows in America. She owned several plantations and one of the largest mansions in Williamsburg, a looming red-brick home not much smaller than the Governor's Palace. She soon found herself pursued by many young men mildly in love with her and very much in love with her money.

Martha Custis and George Washington had met at several balls and parties, but did not engage in a long conversation until the afternoon she was visiting her next-door neighbor, William Chamberlayne. Washington was riding through the area on his way back to Mount Vernon and stopped to pay a courtesy call on Chamberlayne. Here, he met Martha. He told his servant, riding with him, to wait outside for a few hours while he visited. Soon, the afternoon turned into evening. George and Martha sat up late into the night as Chamberlayne discreetly vanished. The pair talked again for hours in the morning before Washington finally rode away.

Washington, a twenty-seven-year-old bachelor, was trying to forget Sally Fairfax, who was still writing to him. He was very much aware that most of his friends had already married and settled down. Martha, nine months older than George, was searching for a husband her own age and a man who could take care of her and help bring up her small children.

The couple, quite taken with each other after their initial meeting, soon developed a deep affection. She saw him as a handsome young man and a war hero. She was so entranced by his military exploits that—all of her life—she kept one of the white military gloves that he wore that day. He did not consider Martha beautiful like Sally or some of the vivacious actresses he had seen in Williamsburg. He saw in Martha a loving companion and a friend, a woman whom he could trust and a woman who always be there as a wife and counsel.

George and Martha married four months later. Martha arrived at Mount Vernon to a festive reception carefully orchestrated by her new husband. He told his servant John Alton to buy eggs and chickens for Martha's first meals and to "prepare in the best manner you can for our coming." The groom reminded him to make the beds, air out the rooms, clean up all of the chairs and tables in the main house, and, thinking of everything to impress his new bride, even told Alton that "the staircase ought also to be polished in order to make it look well."

Washington seemed to ease rather quickly into plantation life and the social life of the Potomac. He confided to a friend with obvious satisfaction: "I am now, I believe, fixed at this seat with an agreeable consort for life. And I hope to find more happiness in retirement than I ever experienced amidst the wide and bustling world."

And he did. Washington became fascinated with farming and became quite successful. He always sought new ways to use the thousands of acres of land at Mount Vernon. His brother, like just about every other planter in that area of Virginia, had raised tobacco and made substantial profits with it. Lawrence, like others, had also raised wheat and corn, but mainly to feed his family and the slaves who worked for him. George continued to plant tobacco for several years, selling as much as ninety-three thousand pounds annually. But soon, he cut back his production as the demand for American tobacco declined in England.

Washington followed European news carefully and realized, like other Virginians, that bad harvests on the continent since the early 1760s had created a demand for wheat. He greatly expanded his production of wheat, and corn for commercial sale. It worked. Within a few years his wheat, cut differently than most, was considered some of the best in the colonies. He began to have his harvest threshed indoors so that rains would not cut down the number of days the wheat could be produced. By 1769, Washington and other planters were producing and selling twice as much wheat to Europe. He raised sheep when no one else did and had servants use the wool from his stock of one thousand to produce most of the winter clothing for the vast plantation work force. He extended his livestock to large herds of cattle, each branded "GW." Washington even attempted the breeding of buffalo.

Washington frequently grew new crops in previously exhausted soil, constantly utilizing his existing land, a practice not normally followed because so much land was available. He bred mules to use along with horses, convinced they were sturdier animals for plantation chores. He grew grapes and produced wine. Fisheries were built in the Potomac and his workers caught thousands of pounds of fish for food and sale, using a ship he bought expressly for that purpose. New tools were invented and old ones improved upon by him.

His holdings were vast. Mount Vernon alone covered nine thousand acres, or thirteen square miles. Martha's farms included another seventeen thousand acres. George broke up each of the farms into smaller units and hired overseers to run each one. The overseers were not only in charge of several hundred slaves (160 at Mount Vernon alone) and white tenant farmers, but responsible for detailed daily and weekly reports on the productivity of their sections. He often took their advice in order to improve operations.

Washington did not delegate authority and managed every single aspect of his plantations, coordinating everything from slave sales to the purchase of nails and medical supplies, often complaining about rising prices. He was a workaholic. He rose before dawn each day and spent an hour or more keeping detailed account books and notes on the plantation business in the southeast study of his mansion, where he also shaved and dressed to avoid waking Martha in their bedroom directly above. He left the office and walked fifty yards south, down a slight incline, to his brick stables to mount one of his favorite horses and ride through his farms and to meet with overseers, still rubbing their eyes as they spotted their early-rising employer. He frequently worked with his tenant farmers or slaves in the field and did not finish the day's business until after nightfall, when he went back to the main house and tended to the problems of his family. Explaining why he spent so much time toiling at Mount Vernon with his workers, Washington told his close friend Bryan Fairfax, probably with a grin, that the plantation jobs "goes on better whilst I am present than in my absence from the workmen."

His busy days were chronicled in short notes in his diary. His brief entry for a stormy April 10, a day when Martha was sick, revealed much about his farming and personal life:

> Mrs. Washington was blooded by Doctor Laurie, who stayed all night.
>
> This morning my plows began to work in the clover field, but a hard shower of rain from the northeast (where the wind hung all day) about 11 o'clock stopped them for the remainder of the day. I therefore employed the hands in making two or three hauls of the river and found that the herrings were come.
>
> Val Crawford brought four Hhds. [wagonloads] of my mountain tobacco to the warehouses at Alexandria, two in my own wagons and with a plow such as they use mostly in Frederick. Came here in the night. He informed me of my worthy overseer Hardwick's lying since the 17th in Winchester of a broken leg.

Washington, a good judge of land, bought up neighboring farms for further development. Over the years, he expanded his operations at Mount Vernon. He owned other farms, some his and some formerly

Martha's, that covered another twenty-three thousand acres. They were productive and prosperous. He spent considerable time, alone and with others, exploring lands for possible purchase in the far western sections of Virginia, on the frontier borders, lands he had traversed in the 1750s as surveyor and colonel. His land development, experimentation, and business genius enabled him to become one of the wealthiest men in Virginia by the time he reached the age of forty (upon his death relatives assessed his wealth at about $75 million in today's money).

Washington was apparently sterile and could not father children, but he never acknowledged that, sometimes telling friends that Martha was probably not capable of bearing more children after having given birth to four. He became the devoted father to Martha's two children: Jack Custis and Patsy, and his heirs would be their children. He never neglected to go out of his way to spend time with the children or buy them things. His very first shipment of purchased goods from London after his marriage included a number of toys and children's books.

Martha was obsessively protective of her remaining offspring and always kept them near her side. It wasn't until Jackey was seven that she traveled without him. Away from Mount Vernon, she constantly worried about him, explaining to her sister Nancy Bassett about a trip that "I carried little Patsy with me and left Jackey at home for a trial to see how well I could stay without him. Though we were gone but a fortnight, I was impatient to get home. If I at any time heard the dogs bark or a noise out, I thought there was a person sent for me. I often fancied he was sick or some accident had happened to him so that I think it is impossible for me to leave him."

Martha and George spent enormous amounts of money on clothes, academic tutoring, and music and dancing lessons for Jack and Patsy. They made certain that friends and relatives visited Mount Vernon often and that they spent time with the children. But Martha's fear that danger would come to one or the other proved correct.

For no apparent reason, Patsy first collapsed and went into convulsions when she was eleven as George and Martha enjoyed tea. The fits, which were epileptic seizures, continued on a regular basis. Doctors bled her, gave her medicines, and put an iron ring on her finger to bite on when she was overcome by a seizure. Nothing helped.

George Washington did everything he could for the girl. At enormous cost, he hired a succession of doctors from Virginia to treat her. He then hired specialists trained in Europe who prescribed medicine for malaria and even ether. Unable to do much for her medically, Washington began to shower her with presents. Over the next few years he spent large sums of money to buy her games, combs, dresses, necklaces, earrings, books, and magazines. Her parents took her with them to as many receptions and parties as they could. Fearful of further seizures, they looked in on her as she slept and tried to keep an eye on her whenever they could during the day.

They were ebullient when she was healthy, as evidenced by a cheerful note Martha sent a friend in 1760, telling her that "my dear little girl is much better. She has lost her fits and fervors and seems to be getting well very fast."

After a string of seizures, at age thirteen Patsy did seem to get a little better. During the spring and summer of 1773, when she was sixteen, her health seemed to improve. She attended parties in nearby towns and frequently visited Washington's brother Jack, with whom she was very close. She continued her music lessons and developed friendships with several teenage girls in the Tidewater area.

Patsy was sitting with her parents, her uncle Jack, his family, her brother's fiancée, and her girlfriend at dinner on July 19, 1773, when she suddenly went into convulsions, slipped off her chair, and collapsed onto the floor. The women and girls shrieked. George Washington leaped out of his seat and ran to her. He held her in his arms and tried to quiet her shaking body. There was nothing he could do. "[She] expired in less than two minutes without uttering a word, a groan or scarce a sigh," he explained to Martha's sister. The ordinarily stoic Washington showed great emotion in the letter, telling her that "yesterday the sweet innocent girl entered into a more happy and peaceful abode than any she has met with in the afflicted path she hitherto has trod." He stumbled for words to describe his wife's grief and finally said that "this sudden, unexpected blow I scarce need add has almost reduced my poor wife to the lowest ebb of misery."

Jack was in good health, but presented Washington and Martha with an entirely different set of problems. Washington never knew what to do with him as the boy grew into a rowdy and undisciplined teenager. Martha's concern for Patsy carried over to Jack and she protected him mercilessly, permitting him to grow up as a pampered and hopelessly overindulged child.

Jack was sent off to a nearby academy with two horses and a servant. The tutors there did the best they could, but made little headway. Washington wrote his tutor, Jonathan Boucher, that his stepson's mind was more interested in "dogs, horses and guns" than in obtaining an education. Boucher agreed and told Washington "I must confess to you that I never in my life knew a youth so exceedingly indolent…one would suppose nature had intended him for some Asiatic Prince." At one point, the frustrated Washington even cut off Jack's charge accounts at local stores. The boy seemed hopeless to his stepfather. "He lacks that attention which is necessary to advance him in his studies," he told Boucher in the spring of 1771. Once, in anger, Washington snapped that his parenthood of Jack was "lost time."

As Jack aged, it was reported to Washington that it was difficult for his son to pay much attention to his lessons because he was paying too much attention to girls. At nineteen, Jack stunned his parents by announcing his engagement to Nellie Calvert from Annapolis, Maryland. Washington was as upset as Martha at this sudden prospective marriage and complained to friends that he doubted his son "has ever bestowed a serious thought of the consequences" of marriage. Under pressure from his stepfather to forestall marriage, Jack did agree to at least completing his education before he walked down the aisle with Nellie.

Washington then took Jack to New York to study at King's College, now Columbia University. His father encouraged Jack to finish school because he wanted him to have a fine education; he also was eager to put as much distance between his stepson and the vivacious Nellie as possible. Patsy's death ended that educational endeavor. A severely depressed

Martha, left with only Jack, having lost three of her children, insisted that Washington permit him to return home. Life at Mount Vernon without at least one of her children was simply unbearable for her. Jack came back and soon married Nellie.

Washington never regretted the marriage and forgave Jack all of his juvenile transgressions. He was happy if his son was happy. He did everything he could for the new bride and groom, and doted on the 1774 wedding plans with his wife. He invited Jack and his new wife to Mount Vernon as often as possible for dinners and parties, rode to see them whenever he could, and maintained a warm and loving relationship with Jack for the rest of his son's life.

The love he had for his son was returned. Jack adored his stepfather. He thanked Washington for his love of him and Nellie in a 1774 letter where he said that the only way he could respond was to say that he was "at a great loss for words" in expressing his love for his father. He said that he felt "affections and regard—both of which did not I possess in the highest degree for you. I...shall strenuously endeavor by my future conduct to merit a continuance of your regard and esteem." Later, during the war, Jack continually wrote to his mother begging for assurances that his father was safe.

Throughout those years at Mount Vernon, George Washington grew into a highly responsible man, a church and civic leader and a person of great integrity. He was known throughout Virginia for his humility. He never bragged about his wealth or his military exploits as a young man. When called upon for a speech, after a vote to give him official thanks for his French and Indian War military service at a session of the Burgesses, he could say nothing. "Your modesty is equal to your valor," the House speaker told him.

He became an elder in his Anglican Church at nearby Pohick, in charge of aiding the poor, and attended services with his family just about every Sunday. The owner of Mount Vernon was a regular parishioner at the Bruton Parish Church whenever he was in the capital on business. Washington was a member of the Fairfax County Court for many years, serving as one of the justices for criminal and civil hearings and working on committees to oversee the maintenance of public buildings and county roads. His civic responsibilities extended to nearby Alexandria, where he served as one of the town's trustees.

Washington's great vice, like that of so many rich Virginia men, was gambling. He was a fanatic for the lotteries that were very popular at that time and could not seem to spend two dollars on lottery tickets without spending thousands. He once bought $3,600 in lottery tickets (today's money) from Lord Stirling, a New Jersey friend. On another occasion he borrowed three thousand dollars from a friend to buy tickets for a local lottery he found out about late one night at a tavern. Washington even ran his own lotteries. He played cards for money constantly, sometimes just about every night for weeks on end, often against his own relatives, such as his sister Betty, who lived in Fredericksburg. His diaries showed that he usually put at risk some twelve to fifteen thousand dollars per year in today's money at card tables in the gaming room of local taverns such as Christiana Campbells' in the state capital, parlors jammed with card tables at society balls, and even at the Governor's mansion, where he played against Governor Dunmore for hours. He loved horseracing. Washington put up purses for horse races and then bet heavily on them at tracks in Williamsburg, Alexandria, and Annapolis. He also bet on dice games and billiards. Although his overall betting records are sketchy, he probably gambled some thirty to thirty-five thousand dollars per year, a substantial sum.

Washington loved to see plays with Martha and became a regular at the theater in Williamsburg, one of the best in the colonies. He sometimes went as often as four days in a row, viewing matinees when saddled with some other commitment in the evening. He had become an extremely fine dancer and was often invited to parties where music would be played. His friends loved to watch him dance the minuets, country reels, and jigs at parties well attended by the gentry that often lasted until dawn. Washington even arranged to have dance instructors brought to Mount Vernon to teach dancing to his children and their friends.

He was said to be among the most avid fox hunters in North America, and usually led or took part in several hunts each week during the spring and summer. Later, during the war, his love of fox hunting would earn him the British nickname "the fox." His competitive nature in the fox chases was extraordinary, as it was in just about everything he did. Washington recorded the exact time, down to the minute, it took him to catch a fox (and his anger at not finding any). The end of the hunt was always celebrated with wine that Washington and his workers had produced on the plantation. He kept 110 gallon kegs of it in storage for his consumption and parties. He joked to friends that Mount Vernon was one of the colony's best taverns.

The master of Mount Vernon was a very fashionable dresser and imported most of his clothes, and those of Martha and his children, from London clothiers. He also purchased clothes at the best stores in Virginia. One merchant's invoice notes that in October 1761, Washington ordered "a handsome suit of clothes, for winter wear, a handsome suit of thin, ditto, for the summer, a fashionable cloak for a man six feet high, and proportionable, and two best beaver hats, plain...." He understood that in Virginia society expensive clothes were necessary, but never forgot that they were merely for show. "Do not conceive that fine clothes make fine men, any more than fine feathers make fine birds," he reminded friends.

He and Martha bought silverware with great care and spent large amounts of money on elegant furniture. Many of those pieces were imported from England. Mount Vernon itself, a large, three-story high white house with a columned porch the length of the building, afforded a wonderful view of the broad Potomac River and was kept in museum condition by the fastidious Washington and the hard-working Martha. The couple always seemed to be involved in the renovation and expansion of the mansion, and in 1770 finished the two-story expansion of the south wing, which contained their spacious bedroom. In 1775, construction was started on the north wing. Unforeseen events would delay the latter's completion for ten long years.

Washington derived enormous pleasure from his life at Mount Vernon. "No estate in United America is more beautifully situated than this," he wrote one man in 1793 about Mount Vernon. "It lies in a high, dry and healthful country three hundred miles by water from the sea...and on one of the finest rivers in the world."

He also seemed to take pride in the village he had created around the main house. The buildings in this tiny community included a kitchen, smoke house, greenhouse, blacksmith's hut, carpenter's shed, a spinning house for production of clothes for his slaves, a laundry house, stables, and a series of warehouses for his farm products. A village of a dozen homes for domestic slaves sat within one hundred yards of the mansion.

Washington's six brothers and sisters, especially his brother Jack and sister Betty, visited him frequently at Mount Vernon, as did friends and neighbors. The Washingtons hosted numerous parties and asked anyone they knew to visit and stay overnight. Throughout the 1760s, they played host to far more than two hundred overnight guests per year (they had 677 overnight guests in 1798). They all found him a genial host who tried to make visitors feel comfortable. Nicholas Cresswell, a British traveler who attended a party at Mount Vernon before the revolution, was enamored with Washington's taste and style. "He keeps an excellent table and a stranger, let him be of what country or nation, he will always meet with a most hospitable reception at it," he wrote, and added, with apparent delight, that Washington "took great pleasure in seeing his friends entertained in the way most agreeable to themselves."

Martha's friend Elizabeth Powel expressed the same feeling when she wrote her of the "elegant hospitality exercised at Mount Vernon, where the good order of the master's mind, seconded by your excellent abilities, pervades everything around you and renders it a most delightful residence to your friends."

Washington enjoyed helping people with problems in any way he could, either with money or a favor. He paid for the entire college education of the son of a friend who once worked with him on surveys, asking for nothing in return. He often advanced money, with no expected repayment, to the sons of friends who were enlisting in the British army. He gave Robert Stewart, a friend from their French and Indian War days, sixty thousand dollars so that Stewart could buy himself a commission in the British Army. He paid the expenses of an old army friend, George Mercer, for five long years while Mercer lobbied to earn a veteran's land commission in the Ohio territory. Washington paid for the education of his twenty-two nieces and nephews. During the war, he ordered his plantations managers never to turn away anyone seeking food or shelter. All of this generosity was done in secret, and the beneficiaries were sworn to keep it so.

Virginians were impressed by the image he carefully maintained, in both his private and public life. He was tall and strong. The planter wore expensive clothes that fit him well. He held his head high and walked with assurance. He managed his affairs as a successful businessman, ran his plantations as an accomplished manager, and lived in a well-appointed home. Politically, he held his own in late-night discussions with the best minds in the region. Socially, he mixed just as easily with his frontier riflemen as the well-bred gentlemen at their elegant balls. In public, seated on any horse, well dressed and secure, George Washington always looked successful. Some thought that he was born to his role. "The general seems by nature calculated for the post he is in. He has a manner and behavior peculiar to himself and particularly adapted to his present station and rank in life," wrote one British visitor.

So it was that at the age of forty-two, Washington was seen by most Virginians as a distinguished, trustworthy, and honorable man. He had achieved more than most men in the colonies and deserved the gentle and pleasant life of semi-retirement that he had created for himself along the Potomac amid the sprawling lawns and thick forests at his beloved Mount Vernon. But events that would follow Jack and Nellie's wedding in 1774 would soon change everything and create a second life for the squire of Mount Vernon.

Political Beginnings

It was inevitable that Washington's wealth and status as a war hero would have led his neighbors to insist that he become involved in the political life of Virginia. Washington had first been elected to the House of Burgesses, the state's governing body, in 1759, to the "great satisfaction" of members, and was reelected faithfully to each of its sessions (his first bill was to ban hogs from running wild in the streets of Winchester). He offered few bills but served on numerous committees, wrote reports, and helped others in their legislative duties. Just as Patrick Henry had become a popular member for his flowery oratory, Washington had become a respected member because of his hard work, open-mindedness, and ability to listen to everybody before casting a vote.

His real skills were revealed behind the scenes in the political corridors of Williamsburg. He could not speak in public with any of the power of men like Patrick Henry. Like others, he marveled at Henry's oratory as he denounced the Stamp Act as a bill that would "destroy American freedom" and told the assembly that "if this be treason, make the most of it." (Jefferson, in the hall that day, called Henry's words "torrents of eloquence.") What Washington could do, and with great effect, was use his reputation and powers of persuasion, and his resolute personality, to win votes for the policies he favored at parties, dinners, and lunches with fellow Burgesses, the British governor, and Crown officials. His diary records dozens of dinners at the home of House speaker Peyton Randolph and hunting expeditions and dinners with Lord Dunmore in the 1770s. He spent endless hours playing cards at taverns with politicians and office holders, and in that time lobbied for his causes not with lilting speeches, but with sound logic and dogged determination. And, like any politician, he was not above flattery, complimenting legislators on their dress and telling the Royal Governor on one occasion that he was so happy to see him on his last scheduled visit to their parish that "Colonel Fairfax and myself looked every hour for eight or ten days, for your Lordship's yacht," and that his visits to their homes was always "very pleasing."

He was proud to be a member of the governing body and was pleased, like all Americans, that the colonies had achieved such success since their founding more than 150 years before. George Washington had come to believe, as had other influential Virginians, that America had, in reality, become a separate country from Great Britain. That belief was held not only by elitist planters and prominent businessmen but by the growing American middle class and its farmers, merchants, and shopkeepers. By 1775, when he rode to the Continental Congress, Americans had developed a wholly new life, free and independent from England.

With the emergence of that new middle class in the 1760s and 1770s, commerce boomed. Whether it was farming in Pennsylvania, ironworks in New Jersey, shipbuilding in Massachusetts, or tobacco production in Virginia, Americans had developed a prosperous way of life. They honored freedom of religion and, regardless of class, seemed to get along with each other. They had reached the point where they felt they really no longer needed to be a part of England and, in fact, resented her control over their lives.

During the 1760s, the colonists began to complain that the British government had become corrupt, that England had been weakened by greedy and unscrupulous politicians, unfeeling royals, and dishonest business moguls. They saw Parliament as a decaying governing body that unfairly ruled the British Empire, and America, with an iron fist, leaving no room for criticism by its subjects.

The Crown thought nothing of simply shutting down the colonists' assemblies when British leaders were unhappy with their actions. Massachusetts's royal governor had closed that colony's assembly in 1767 and again in 1774. Virginia's governor, Norborne Burkeley, shut down his state's assembly in 1769 when he was displeased with proposed legislation.

As for freedom of the press, the British seemed determined to undermine American newspapers when their writers became too radical. At times, the newspapers had been extremely critical of the Crown, and governors had shut down several newspapers and tried to drive others out of business by threatening to withdraw needed government advertising. Americans held the independent press sacred; ten of the thirteen colonies had press-freedom clauses in their constitutions.

The colonists also feared the disruption of their highly successful free-market economy. Merchants traded up and down the Atlantic coast and had expanded their shipping to the Caribbean and Europe. That was abruptly curbed by British laws that forced colonists to trade only with England (American trade represented one third of the British economy). Colonial prosperity was threatened by rising business taxes as well. Farmers in Pennsylvania complained that a full 22 percent of their gross sales were lost in the cost of doing business and high taxes. Increased taxes would make any business profits impossible for planters, merchants, and farmers. They were incensed that members of Parliament, and the British people, did not understand their unhappiness.

More taxes followed in the wake of the French and Indian War to pay British costs in the conflict and to maintain the British army in the colonies. The stamp tax of 1765 was the most notorious of these levies. The act required many businessmen, and all lawyers, to purchase stamps to place on paperwork; all newspapers required them. The bill was just one of several. It had been preceded by the Sugar Act, which included new taxes on molasses and rum; the Iron Act (no American sales of carriages, plows, or equipment in England); and the Currency Act, which outlawed colonial paper money. These measures were followed by the Townshend Acts of 1767, which authorized taxes on just about anything Americans sold to England, such as tea, glass, and paper.

Washington's business, like that of other Virginia planters and merchants, and those in other colonies, had suffered from Parliament's restrictive legislative acts and taxes. His own taxes on furniture and luxuries for Mount Vernon had risen, as had commissions he had to pay British middlemen in the tobacco industry. He had wanted to restart his father's old ironworks, but was forbidden by new British laws. Another recent law forbid colonists to settle lands west of the Appalachian Mountains, cheap lands he himself had long planned on developing.

The rich planter, just like the yeoman farmer, believed he was being taxed to death. There seemed to be a British tax on everything. Americans not only had to pay general taxes on goods they purchased, but on piece chairs they put in their homes; even doorknobs were taxed. Anyone who ordered spoons from London had to pay not one, but two different taxes. Americans began to see themselves as unwanted relatives, as second-class citizens. Washington, like others, felt an economic noose starting to tighten around his neck. He, like so many others, began to believe that independence was not only the best path to follow, but the only one available. In a letter to Joseph Reed written a few months before the signing of the Declaration of Independence, an angry Washington expressed the feelings of most colonists:

We had borne much; we had long and ardently sought for reconciliation upon honourable terms, that it had been denied us, that all our attempts after peace had proved abortive, and had been grossly misrepresented, that we had done everything which could be expected from the best of subjects, that the sprit of freedom beat too high in us to submit to slavery, and that if nothing else could satisfy a tyrant and his diabolical ministry, we are determined to shake off all connections with a state so unjust and unnatural.

Washington's anger was not just directed at Parliament, but at the businessmen he had dealt with in England as a farmer and a consumer. He complained that taxes on tools and plows sent to him in Virginia for farming were too high and that equipment was substandard. He boiled over with anger in 1768 when a very costly carriage he had purchased from a London company began to fall apart after just two months of use. He told friends that British businessmen held their American buyers in the same low esteem as the British government. He, like so many other Americans, believed that they would always be nothing more than second-class citizens in the British Empire.

Psychologically, the residents of the colonies also had come to believe that they were actually better British citizens than the British themselves and were working harder to uphold the freedoms of the British empire than the British. They felt compelled to keep intact all of the freedoms they had gained as Americans, freedoms they now saw threatened by Parliament and King George III. They were certain that they had also, over all those generations, established an ideological philosophy of government, based on deep beliefs about personal liberty, that they could not now relinquish. They had grown to embrace a distinctive American ideal, a vision of a nation and people that loved liberty and hated tyranny. It was an ideal that could not, after all those years, be discarded. It was an ideal, Thomas Jefferson said, that now had to be embraced at any cost.

Americans were convinced that they had grown into a people imbued with an extraordinary sense of honor, integrity, and moral nobility. Their assumption was that only a virtuous people could be given the responsibility of self-governance, and so it was fitting that the colonists complained about British moral shallowness. Americans firmly believed that the economic success of the colonial upper classes and the jealousy of that success in the middle class put them in danger of corruption and that they were drifting toward what they saw as the moral decay of Europe. They believed that a separation, and even a war, might be necessary to protect their virtuous nature. The purity of their character would bring them victory and permit them to develop a democracy that would be the envy of the world.

This view made it possible for them to condone any acts of civil disobedience aimed at the Crown and, if need be, for them to engage in an armed rebellion. The planters, farmers, and shopkeepers in all of the thirteen colonies had come to believe, by the mid-1770s, that they had already created a political, economic, and social revolution in America. A war would merely validate it.

Like most Americans, Virginians protested the various acts of Parliament that they considered oppressive. Virginian representatives met officially at the House of Burgesses and unofficially in private homes or local taverns. Virginians later set up a secret Committee of Correspondence, of which Washington was a member, to communicate with radicals in the other colonies.

The turning point in Washington's political life was certainly the passage of the Stamp Act, which infuriated lawyers and newspaper editors. The bill caused raging controversy throughout the colonies, starting in Massachusetts, where thousands vowed not to pay the new tax. In Virginia, where a county court declared it illegal, there was such protest that the stamp collector refused to enforce it. Virginia's governor dissolved the state assembly when that body passed Patrick Henry's resolution condemning it. Stamp collectors and Crown officials were beaten up in other colonies. Arguments against it filled the pages of colonial newspapers for weeks, especially in Virginia, where just about everyone read the *Virginia Gazette*, perhaps the colonies' best newspaper. The debates continued until the Stamp Act was repealed a year later. Washington said the colonists saw the stamp levy as a "dreadful attack upon their liberties" and felt the same way about the Townshend Acts, which, also generated much hatred toward the Crown until they were eventually repealed.

Washington advanced from philosophical opposition to outright and heated verbal criticism of England over those years. "No man should scruple to hesitate a moment to use arms in defense of so valuable a blessing on which the good and evil of life depends is clearly my opinion," he wrote neighbor and friend George Mason in 1769, adding that the British "would be satisfied with nothing else than the deprivation of American freedom."

Washington stood with others in the House of Burgesses on May 15, 1769, to applaud a resolution that said Britain's taxes "violated the rights of Americans." He stood with his colleagues again the next day when the chamber voted to send the resolution to the governor with their "hearts filled with anguish." Furious, Governor Francis Fauquier dissolved the assembly.

Washington and Mason then retaliated by authoring Virginia's nonimportation agreement, which called for state residents to join a group they called the Virginia Association to boycott British goods to force the Crown to drop its taxes and legislation. He was so irritated over the issue that he personally rode through the state and talked more than one thousand Virginians into joining the Association and signing a pledge to not purchase any more British products. He urged Virginians to withhold valuable Virginia exports, such as tobacco, from markets in England.

The one tax Parliament would not repeal was on tea, and that refusal on Britain's part angered Washington, as it incensed so many. Then, suddenly, in late December 1773, the members of the Sons of Liberty dressed as Mohawk Indians, boarded the *Dartmouth* in Boston Harbor, and dumped all of its cargo of tea into the water. In March, they did the same to tea on a second ship. Parliament reacted swiftly by announcing in early May what became known as the "intolerable acts," which included forcible quartering of British soldiers in American homes, the deportation of "political prisoners" to London for trial, and the closing of Boston Harbor, which crippled the economy of New England.

The Intolerable Acts caused an uproar in Virginia and in the other colonies. The debate was fierce in Virginia, where a livid Washington argued again that the British were wrong to impose taxes on the colonies. They exhibited, he said, "an unexampled testimony of the most despotic system of tyranny that was ever practiced in a free government."

It was after the closing of Boston Harbor that Washington told Virginia legislators that he was prepared to raise a regiment of one thousand men, pay for their clothing and muskets, and march them to Boston to prepare for war if it came. He told the state assembly: "Shall we, after this, whine and cry for relief, when we have already tried it in vain? Or shall we supinely sit and see one province after another fall a prey to despotism?"

On their own, Washington and Mason authored the highly publicized Fairfax Resolves, which urged Virginians, and all Americans, to again boycott British goods and to stand up for their rights against England. The sharply worded resolves began with the charge that the colonists, loyal British subjects for 150 years, now saw themselves as a "conquered country." Both men were also insulted that despite this endless succession of crippling legislative blows, George III still insisted that he was not trying to subjugate Americans.

Washington and other state legislators denounced the closing of Boston's port and called for a day of national fasting at sessions on May 24 and 25, 1774. They drew up a resolution that called the Boston Harbor closing a "dangerous attempt to destroy the constitutional liberty and rights of all North Americans" and "reduce the inhabitants of British America to slavery."

The resolution was published on the morning of May 26. That afternoon, Virginia's governor, Lord Dunmore, dissolved the legislature. Events moved rapidly. Several nights later Washington and most of the other seething Virginia legislators gathered at Raleigh Tavern in Williamsburg and, amid candlelit tables and tankards of beer, argued about what to do. They finally voted to issue their confrontational resolutions anyway via the press.

They also agreed with a Massachusetts suggestion for a Continental Congress to be held in Philadelphia so that representatives from all the colonies could meet to decide the future of America. "The crisis is arrived when we must assert our rights or submit to every imposition that can be heaped upon us till custom and use shall make us as tame and abject slaves as the blacks we rule over with such arbitrary sway," an increasingly incensed Washington wrote his friend and neighbor Bryan Fairfax just before he left as a delegate. After all, he told Fairfax, Americans had done everything possible already—with no result. "Have we not addressed the Lords, and remonstrated to the Commons? And to what end? Does it not appear, as clear as the sun in its meridian brightness, that there is a regular, systematic plan formed to fix the right and practice of taxation upon us? Does not the uniform conduct of Parliament for some years past confirm this? Do not all the debates…in the House of Commons on the side of the government expressly declare that America must be taxed? Is there any thing to be expected from petitioning after this?"

Washington had the full support of his wife in these dangerous political endeavors. That confidence in her husband, and her gracious personality, perhaps the key to her loving relationship with George, were summed up warmly in a letter written by Edmund Pendleton, a fellow delegate to Congress, who stayed at Mount Vernon and left for Philadelphia with Washington.

"I was much pleased with Mrs. Washington and her spirit," he wrote with apparent pleasure. "She seemed ready to make any sacrifice and was cheerful though I know she feels anxious. She talked like a Spartan mother to her son on going into battle [saying] 'I hope you will stand firm…I know George will.' When we set off in the morning she stood in the door and cheered us in the good words, 'God be with you gentlemen.'"

It went unnoticed by anyone that George Washington, Virginia's most distinguished military veteran, had formed, with others, several private, armed militia regiments. Washington took charge of his own militia, the Fairfax Independent company, paid for the uniforms and expenses of all of its members, and, ominously, donned a brand new, carefully cut red and blue uniform, which he designed himself, to lead his men in drills, his sword very visibly strapped to his waist.

The Continental Congress

In Philadelphia in the fall of 1775, Washington said little officially, and there is no record of any speech he gave in the public sessions. Privately, though, according to his diaries, as always, he engaged in long conversations with other delegates and joined them, and Philadelphia residents, for dinner parties where politics were discussed late into the night. He, like they, felt that the rights Americans had gained over more than a century and a half were being destroyed by the Crown. He impressed everyone he met as thoughtful, responsible, and hardworking. Later, Patrick Henry picked Edward Rutledge and Washington as the two most impressive men in the first Congress.

Washington agreed with those who voted more economic reprisals against the Crown, a colony-wide boycott of taxed goods, and a general call to meet force with force if Parliament did not back off on its campaign to break the economic back of America.

Events had cascaded throughout the winter and spring of 1775. Farmers in Massachusetts had engaged in two pitched battles with British regulars at the villages of Lexington and Concord in April; eight Americans were killed and ten injured at Lexington. Hundreds of men, American and British, had been killed at the battle of Bunker Hill in Boston. Ethan Allen and the Green Mountain Boys had attacked a British fort in New York, Ticonderoga, and captured it. Benedict Arnold and his men had captured St. John's, in Quebec Province, sunk five British vessels, and captured four others.

Boston's Sons of Liberty continued to incite insurrection. Armies of New Englanders had begun to assemble and surround Boston. The New England newspapers called out for action. People throughout the colonies feared that in revenge Britain would send its huge fleet to close every harbor in the colonies and impose even harsher taxes. They were worried that the fleet would also bring thousands more of the dreaded Redcoats and their flashing bayonets. An emergency Second Continental Congress was called in the summer of 1775. Delegates appointed by their states convened in Philadelphia to discuss their grievances against the king, the organization of militia in different states, the union of different state militias into one national army, and methods to raise taxes to pay for the army.

Delegates from New England, such as John Adams, reported on the British outrages and urged colleagues to prepare for war. Men from the southern states, who had not experienced any military trouble, complained that British policies had started to affect their farms and businesses. Others urged the passage of resolutions aimed at again placating England. They were convinced that sensible measures now would bring about agreeable British reaction. The British would realize that the delegates, and the Americans, were reasonable. They would back off from their occupations and taxes, the patriots would back off from their threats, and peace would be restored. Many members simply did not know what action to take.

John Adams thought Washington could lead the army of seventy-five thousand men Congress promised to raise. He had fought gallantly in the French and Indian War and showed genuine leadership qualities; there were very few men who had been entrusted with command in that war who could lead American forces now. On his plantation and in his responsibilities to his church, county, and Alexandria, he had gained extensive administrative experience. In his well-tailored uniform, Washington had the look of a military leader. As a longtime member of the House of Burgesses and both Continental Congresses, he was certainly a man who would understand the political ramifications of events and could work with Congress.

Most importantly, his southern roots were crucial because Congress was bogged down in regional squabbles. The Massachusetts men could not get any of their own voted commander by the delegates from the other states, and they knew it. They had to find someone from the southern colonies for political harmony. It would be helpful to have a commander from Virginia because it was the second-most radical colony in the Americas, behind Massachusetts. It was the most populated and prosperous colony and its political leaders were among the best-educated and wealthiest men on the Atlantic seaboard, men whose help would be essential if a full-scale war developed. And in Virginia's Washington, the members of Congress had a former soldier, wealthy planter, and staunch patriot.

Congress elected Washington as the general of a yet-to-be-formed army for a yet-to-be-formed nation. The ever-modest Washington stood up in the hall where the delegates met, his six-foot, three-inch frame a towering presence, and delivered a very brief acceptance speech. In it, he told the men that he would serve without pay, just expenses, for however long he was in charge of the army. The ever-humble colonel told them that he was not worthy of the job. "I this day declare with the utmost sincerity that I do not think myself equal to the command I am honored with," he said with sincerity, and sat down.

Privately, too, he was worried about his abilities to lead an army. "I have launched into a wide and extensive field, too boundless for my abilities, and far, very far, beyond my experience. [It is] an honor I did not aspire to; an honor I was solicitous to avoid," he wrote to the captains of several companies of his own Virginia militia.

He was even more worried in a discussion with his trusted brother-in-law, Burwell Bassett: "I am now embarked on a tempestuous ocean from whence, perhaps, no friendly harbor is to be found. It is an honor I wished to avoid, as well from an unwillingness to quit the peaceful enjoyment of my family as from a thorough conviction of my own incapacity and want of experience."

Washington was even more humble in a letter to Martha. He explained to her that it seemed "a trust too great for my capacity." Most of all, he did not want to leave her. "I should enjoy more happiness and felicity in one month with you, at home, than I have the most distant prospect of reaping abroad, if my stay were to be seven time seven years. But it has been a kind of destiny that has thrown me upon this service. I shall hope that my undertaking of it is designed to answer some good purpose," he wrote. Several days later he wrote, telling her, "I retain an unalterable affection for you which neither time or distance can change." He entrusted his fate to God. "I shall relay therefore, confidently, on That Providence which has been heretofore preserved, and been bountiful to me, not doubting that I shall return safe to you in the fall."

And then he made out his will.

The members of Congress did not know what would happen to its new Continental Army, which was really just a collection of regiments on paper. They were not certain how they would merge the different collections of ill-trained farmers with flintlocks around Boston into a force or how they would recruit men. They had no idea how these soldiers would be able to take the field against the greatest army in the world. For the moment, though, they knew that they needed a respected commander-in-chief. Now they had one. A resolution was hastily drawn up: "This Congress doth now declare that they will maintain and assist and adhere to him, the said George Washington, with their lives and fortunes."

They did not know it then in the chaotic spring of 1775, as events whirled about them with astonishing speed, but they had pledged to the new general far more than just their lives and fortunes. They had pledged to him the future of an entire country.

Chapter Three

───────── ❦ ─────────

THE ARMY WILL DIE

MORRISTOWN, 1777

"The distress of another winter and the force of another campaign will reduce all to subjugation."
—Ambrose Serle, aide to Lord Howe

"The people here are a set of sly, artful, hypocritical rascals, cruel and cowards. I must own I cannot but despise them completely."
—Hugh Earl Percy

T he Continental Army moved slowly up the highway from Princeton toward Morristown, New Jersey, on the afternoon of January 6, 1777. The soldiers walked hunched over, their muskets slung awkwardly on their shoulders. They wore thin, torn mittens. Ice formed on the hair of some. Most of their uniforms were dirty. "Many of our poor soldiers are quite barefoot," lamented Washington.

The military hats—for those who still owned them—were pushed back recklessly in a futile gesture to cover the soldiers' streaming and unkempt hair. Most men squinted to avoid the garish glare that greeted their eyes, raw from the rays of the midday sun, bouncing off the glistening smooth bed of thin snow, which covered the road and rolling meadows around them.

They did not march in perfectly straight lines, or shoulder to shoulder, or with their heads held high, or in carefully formed regiments, as the British always did. They struggled north that day in a broken, crooked line toward a strange town and an uncertain future.

There was an advance guard of several hundred men, spread out, checking for the British. Behind them came captured British officers, dressed in their splendid red uniforms. They were followed by the American light infantry, formed into columns, four men across. Washington rode with them, saying little. Next was a large group of British infantrymen, ordered to walk single file. To their rear was a small, slowly moving column of American artillery. Teams of horses, as tired as the men, pulled the cannons, which bumped along as they hit holes in the road. They could not be seen through the crust of snow. General Henry Knox rode with them. Sturdy wooden carts carried the wounded.

Trailing Knox and his cannons was the main vanguard of soldiers, marching in a single line with wide gaps of space between them. The commander had ordered men and prisoners to walk that way in order to trick any British spies into thinking his army was much larger than its actual size. Riding among them were Washington's other generals, including Nathaniel Greene, John Sullivan, and Lord Stirling.

Greene was a thirty-four-year-old Quaker from Rhode Island who was one of the better-educated men in the army. He learned to read Latin fluently while a teenager and used money he earned doing chores to buy books, which he read by candlelight. His nonviolent Quaker friends were shocked when he joined the army. Greene, who walked with a pronounced limp, was one of the first generals named by Congress—and the youngest—when the hostilities began. After more than two years of service, he had become a trusted confidant and close friend of the commander-in-chief.

Sullivan, thirty-six, a New Hampshire lawyer, was named a general in June 1775, based on his service as head of a local militia unit. He had conducted himself adequately in combat, but fellow officers and many of his men disliked him because of his argumentative personality and hot temper. And, they said, he was always complaining about something.

Lord Stirling had been William Alexander for so long that friends in the Morristown area had trouble calling him by his fancy, newly found "title," and those who disliked him—and there were many—practically choked on it. The high-living Alexander, who ran an ironworks in Morris County and resided in a stone mansion on the top of a gently sloping hill in Basking Ridge, had for years always seemed on the verge of bankruptcy following failures in a string of badly run businesses, including lotteries. He had learned that he might be remotely connected to British royalty, the late Earl of Stirling, and sailed to England to claim his title. Despite his constant lobbying, Parliament delayed bestowing the title on him for several years because his claims to the Earl's lineage were murky. Tired of waiting, Stirling simply told everyone he knew, in England and America, that he was the Earl of Stirling, with or without Parliament's blessing. The self-appointed "Lord" came back, mustered some financial backing for his ironworks, and managed to hold off his creditors. He became a patriot and joined the army as soon as the war began. He had become friendly with Washington prior to the war, and his many critics claimed that was why he was named a general. Morristown would serve as the army's winter camp, with men billeted there and in several nearby communities. There were several reasons for its selection: 1) the town had a large number of patriots and was home to several state leaders; 2) Charles Lee's army had stayed there in early December and found the people hospitable; 3) Morristown was the center of a vast ironworks industry that was already producing shot and shell and could produce cannons; 4) the area had its own seven hundred–man militia, one of the few in New Jersey, plus a light horse company; 5) Morristown and its nearby hamlets seemed to be very religious communities, which Washington believed important since most ministers supported the war.

Morristown was also about midway between the large cities of New York and Philadelphia and near the main highway that connected the two bustling ports. The army could move quickly toward either in an emergency to cut off any British advances. It was also centrally located for communications and movement of troops between Washington's other armies in New York, Rhode Island, Princeton, and Connecticut. The village sat in the middle of very hilly terrain, protected on the east by the formidable Watchung Mountains, and would be easy to defend in case of attack. Washington wanted to keep the British in New York, New Brunswick, and the Amboys and leave the vast American countryside to the rebels.

Washington's greatest worry on that cold January day was an attack. Howe had twenty-two thousand men in New York and another ten thousand in New Jersey. "A storm will burst soon, somewhere," Washington warned financier Robert Morris shortly after his arrival, "and the [British] aim will be at this army." He was nervous, and his apprehension showed in another letter, this one to his former aide, Joseph Reed: "We are now in one of the most critical periods which America ever saw."

The general was not just looking for a military base in a winter camp. He was seeking a politically stable community, a town within whose confines he could go about the difficult business of rebuilding his drained army. He needed a town where he would have the complete cooperation of local officials. He did not want to camp near a large city with its taverns, houses of prostitution, and gambling dens. He needed time and quiet so that the army could lick its wounds and spend the winter preparing for a spring campaign against what were said to be even larger forces (one frequent rumor was that the Russians were going to send twenty thousand soldiers to fight for England).

New Jersey, wedged between New York and Pennsylvania, had never developed an identity of its own. It had no major cities, and its large towns, such as Newark and Elizabeth, were close to New York and its residents felt more affinity for New York than their home state. New Jersey had a number of different religious denominations and ethnic groups. Its politicians represented many different locales—agricultural and manufacturing—and, some said, never seemed to agree on anything. There were a large number of Loyalists in the area. Residents of the state had been reluctant to enlist in militias when the rebellion began, and the general had fumed at the lack of help for his army as it fled across the region in the fall.

However, Washington felt comfortable with New Jersey's new revolutionary legislature, headed by hard-working Governor William Livingston. The Morristown area also seemed to be a safe political haven. The Rev. Jacob Green, a man of politics as well as a man of God, was the pastor of an area Presbyterian Church and also one of the authors of the recent state constitution. Green was famous for his statement that America was "the asylum for the sons of liberty and noble spirits of all parts of the world." Jacob Ford Jr., from one of the wealthiest families in Morris County, was already in the militia and was operating a gunpowder mill for the army.

The head of the regular militia there was the blustery Colonel William Winds, like Washington a veteran of the French and Indian War. Winds had become a figure of note during the Stamp Act crisis a decade earlier when, unwilling to buy paper with the Crown's official stamp, he stripped white birch bark from trees and used it as legal stationery. It was Winds's militia that arrested Governor William Franklin, the Loyalist son of Ben Franklin, when the Crown's government in the state fell. Phillip Dickerson, who owned a local tavern, had formed a small militia company and funded it himself. Silas Condict was a member of the state's provincial congress and his brother Ebeneezer enjoyed great influence locally. Morris, like most counties in America, was run by an eight-member Board of Magistrates; the Morris magistrates were among the best. The people of Morristown governed themselves efficiently, working together at town meetings to make decisions.

Morristown was a community of about seventy homes positioned around an eight-acre village green. It had been founded in the early part of the century by men who arrived to start the iron industry. The town had a population of about 350. Several thousand more people lived nearby in what are today the villages of Madison, Westfield, Chatham, Whippany, Boonton, Rockaway, Bound Brook, Parsippany, and Basking Ridge, where troops would be stationed. There were numerous churches in the area, mostly Presbyterian. The town was home to two silversmiths, Gary Dunn and John Dickerson; a chairmaker, Frederick King; and a saddlemaker, Dan Smith. Judge Samuel Tuthill and a lawyer, William Dehart, supervised the county jail and courthouse with its quaint white cupola, which sat on the edge of the village green. A small general store sat across the green near Jacob Arnold's three-story tavern. A local teacher, Dorothea Cooper, tutored the village children. Most of the men and women in the surrounding area worked on small farms that produced wheat, corn, rye, oats, vegetables, and a variety of fruits.

Mrs. Theodorick Bland, an officer's wife who lived there in the spring of 1777, was enchanted by the area and talked about it as if she were describing a painting. "You cannot travel three miles without passing through one of these villages," she wrote in a letter to a friend, "all of them having meeting houses and courthouses, decorated with steeples which gives them a pretty, airy look, and the farms between the mountains are the most rural sweet spots in nature, their meadows of a fine, luxuriant grass which looks like a bed of velvet interspersed with yellow, blue and white flowers."

No "luxuriant" small village such as Morristown was prepared to house even a small militia. Now, suddenly, the entire Continental Army, with its creaking cannon caissons and commissary wagons with their jangling pots and pans, had arrived on a bitterly cold afternoon. Where do you put an army?

Most of the the buildings in Morristown were clustered around the village green or on the roads leading out of town. There was little room for a camp in the community itself, so most of the army stayed in flat, open fields to the southeast in hastily pitched tents. Hundreds of men collapsed from exhaustion when they arrived just before sunset and had to be awakened by officers to prevent them from freezing. The considerable population of sick soldiers who barely made it to Morristown were placed in the town's Presbyterian and Baptist churches, which had been turned into hospitals by their pastors at Washington's request. They were cared for by local physicians and several ministers who served as part-time amateur doctors. Many of the men were wrapped in blankets and laid down on church pews; others were simply put on the floor and had rolled up jackets stuffed under their heads as pillows.

Just about all of the officers and men lived in area homes after a few days in their tents. Community leaders, contacted by messengers sent from Washington days earlier, went from house to house to ask residents if they could take in soldiers as boarders. They were asked just how many they could squeeze into their residences. At first, some homeowners balked at the suggestion, but eventually they agreed. Most took in two to four soldiers, but some welcomed a dozen. Rev. Green, at one time, housed fourteen men. He let them sleep in his attic under the eaves. Uzal Kitchell took in sixteen. Jacob Ford Jr. housed the officers and men of the Delaware light infantry in his spacious, two-story mansion, one of the grandest homes in the state, piling five and six of them into each of his numerous bedrooms. Others were housed in public buildings, barns, and stables. Most of the troops slept on the floor. Artist Charles Wilson Peale, a lieutenant in a Pennsylvania militia, wrote that many complained of their hardwood mattresses and that the "floorboards were rather cold."

Some officers ignored the crowded housing conditions and concentrated on more important things, such as the young women of the area. One of them was Lieutenant James McMichael, who noted with great satisfaction that the ladies of Morristown "are very fond of the soldiers."

Local homes were also used to shelter several prominent New York–area families that had fled the Redcoats, including businessman Elias Boudinot and banker John Morton, and stragglers, whether couples or individuals, who had been driven out of their homes by the enemy.

Upon their arrival, troops began to convert local buildings and barns into warehouses to store food, muskets, tents, wagons, paper, clothes, boots, medicine, and other supplies. Buildings were constructed for commissary offices and the camp tailors, blacksmiths, wheelwrights, cooks, and carpenters. A slaughterhouse was erected. The little village seemed ready to burst.

The officers and men quartered in residences needed shelter, warmth, and meals, of course, but Washington had another motive. He wanted spies to see that his army was so large that the traditional camp could not hold all of its men, that his army was too big for an entire town.

Washington continually thought of ruses to fool spies or over-curious Tories in the area. One of his most effective methods was the daily drill and carefully orchestrated parades. No matter what the weather conditions were, the troops went through these exercises on the village green. These were conducted for hours, with regiments coming and going down narrow dirt lanes, so that at the end of the day any observer had to believe that the army was much larger than it was.

The general accepted Arnold's offer to use his tavern as headquarters. It was on the western side of the green, across from the courthouse. The white, wooden-sided building had comparatively elegant furnishing for the day and large rooms that became useful for army business. Arnold had craftily constructed a bunker under a trap door on the first floor where he stored dozens of muskets and ammunition in case of a British attack. A wide ballroom on the third floor contained numerous tables and chairs that were pushed together for officers' conferences. The tavern was crowded, also serving as headquarters for the local chapter of Free Masons, the New Jersey Council of Safety, and even for Governor Livingston. Washington used one of the two second-floor rooms that overlooked the green as his office and the other as his bedroom. He would spend the winter running the army from the tavern.

Following him into Arnold's that first day, lugging their baggage up the stairs, were Billy Lee, a slave who had been a longtime servant at Mount Vernon; a woman housekeeper; and a steward, along with the General's three aides, Tench Tilghman, John Fitzgerald, and Robert Harrison, who would later be joined by others. Washington called his aides his "family." All were young, well educated, and from good homes. All venerated him ("He is the honestest man that I believe ever adorned the human race," Tilghman told his father). Some of the first, such as Tilghman and Harrison, were the sons of family friends. His aides helped him run the army. They wrote out his dictated orders, took care of all mail, oversaw daily appointments, procured newspapers and pamphlets, acted as go-betweens with other officers, and worked as liaisons with local public officials and townspeople.

Their real importance, though, was to serve as the commander-in-chief's confidants and sounding boards. They were sworn to keep secret everything that happened inside the tavern, even from family. ("I cannot discuss politics," Tilghman wrote in a letter to his father, whom he felt had become too inquisitive about army business.) They were never to relate any stories about the general, grudges he might have held, his criticism of Congress, or turbulent meetings he may have presided over. They had to help him preserve his strong, stoic image within the army and the country.

His aides were also among the few to see Washington lose his temper. He managed to keep it in control most of the time, contemporaries marveled, but he could explode. He ripped the militia during the disastrous New York campaign, fuming to his aides about their unreliability in battle as he dictated a scathing letter to Hancock and Congress. "Great number of them have gone off, in some instances almost by whole regiments," he charged, and said they exhibited "an entire disregard of that order and subordination necessary to the well doing of an army." Pleading for a professional army like the British, Washington agonized to his aides, hastily jotting down his remarks for a letter, that "our liberties must of necessity be greatly hazarded, if not entirely lost, if their defense is left to any but a permanent standing army."

He fired off an angry letter to Governor Nicholas Cooke of Rhode Island, assailing him for ordering militia to his own communities instead of Washington's headquarters. He blasted William Duer, a New York colonel, for intercepting clothes intended for the men in Morristown. "Your troops are in comfortable barracks, while ours are marching over frost and snow, many without a shoe, stocking or blanket," he snapped at him. His tart tongue was loose again in early April when he lashed out at gunpowder makers in New York after they maintained that they produced better powder than anyone else, a claim with which the general obviously disagreed. "There certainly must be roguery or gross ignorance in your powdermakers," he vented to General William Heath about his local workers, "because the powder made in the other states is esteemed better than that imported from Europe."

The generals could annoy him, too, and his quill was filled with as much acid as ink when he replied to General Sam Weedon, who told him in early March that he was going home and would return sometime in early summer. "Surely you meant this by way of a joke. Can you possibly conceive that any consent would be obtainable for such an absence as this? Could I stand justified do you think, in the opinion of the public, to suffer the officers of the states to be absent so long at the most important and active part perhaps, of the campaign? No, sir...," he told him. And then Washington, who had not been home for nearly two years, lashed out at Weedon for his claims of being homesick:

> No man wishes more to gratify officers than I do—nor can any man feel more for their private inconveniences, because no person suffers more by an absence from home than myself. But when I forgo all the advantages of private interest, and have more cause to regret my confinement and may suffer more by it from a peculiarity of circumstances than any other man in the service from a sense of duty to the public, it cannot be presumed that that sense which totally restrains my own wishes can give unbounded indulgencies to others.

Ordinarily, Washington held his anger whenever he spoke openly about Congress, but his patience was often tested by the delegates. On March 2, 1777, he blasted Congress in a lengthy letter to Robert Morris. He at first complained that the delegates passed legislation without regard to consequence, bills that "cannot be carried into execution without a train of evils that may be fatal in their consequences." Then he berated delegates for their armchair generaling—hundreds of miles away. "When they are at a distance, they think it is but to say 'Presto! Be gone' and everything is done," he snickered. He could complain about petty things, too, such as his inability to find good housekeepers and wine stewards in New Jersey. He told an aide in Philadelphia to hire someone there, but added sarcastically, that person preferably should not be known for stealing liquor. After the war, it was learned, too, that Washington's cursing included salty language that would have shocked sailors.

Security in Morristown was tight. There had already been one plot to assassinate the commander-in-chief in New York, for which Thomas Hickey, one of his own guards, was hanged. General Sullivan urged him not to ride toward New York, even surrounded by dozens of his men, because he feared Loyalists would kill him somewhere along the desolate highways that meandered through northern New Jersey. (Sullivan even had a morbid dream in which Washington was murdered.) Washington had also received an anonymous note warning him that unsavory-looking strangers had been loitering on the green in front of his headquarters. So, regardless of the weather, twenty-six soldiers guarded the tavern and the general twenty-four hours a day. His aides even devised an elaborate plan to protect him. At a given signal, men would surround Arnold's Tavern, some on the roadway in front of the main entrance and some at a perimeter, muskets ready. Inside, riflemen would wedge themselves together at each window in the building in order to both fire at attackers and shield the general, who was hustled into the middle of the building, away from view. Then, in an often-practiced drill, a dozen men with rifles or drawn swords would surround Washington (and Martha when she stayed with him).

The general did what he was advised, but was never apprehensive about kidnapping. An expert horseman, he believed he could outrace any assailants who accosted him while he was riding. He never believed that a small party of kidnappers could penetrate deep enough inside his camp to capture him at his office. The drills were held often and Washington expressed his unhappiness with their frequency with a sigh or frown. After a few years of these drills, Mrs. Washington, who also had no fear of capture, refused to participate and merely flung her bedcovers over her head for "protection" when the drill alarm sounded, eliciting a smile from her husband.

The general went to great lengths to maintain a careful personal image in the army, just as he had in private life. He had spent years at Mount Vernon developing the persona of the aristocratic planter and seasoned state representative. He did it in the way he dressed and acted in both public and private, whether socially with the other gentry or when overseeing the plantation and its slaves and indentured laborers. Nobody looked more like a successful planter or businessman than George Washington.

As John Adams said in nominating him to lead the American army, nobody looked more like a general than George Washington, either.

He was cognizant that perception would be as important as experience. The soldiers, from colonels on down to privates, needed to know that their commander was a better soldier than all of them, that he was not only capable but the best possible person to lead them into battle. And, in the civilian theater, members of Congress, the press, and public needed to know that the leader of their army was just as distinguished as the most respected European military figures. If the commander-in-chief was impressive, then the army under him would be seen as impressive, too.

Washington manipulated his image in several ways. He paid the best clothiers to make several copies of a blue and buff uniform that he personally designed, with a large colorful sash that went around his waist to indicate that he was the commander-in-chief. He wore the uniform every day; he never looked casual. He never simply rode his horse, but sat astride him with purpose, as though someone were about to paint him. Throughout his army years, he always had a housekeeper, a steward, and servants, as the British generals had. He insisted that all dressed as well as he did. A detailed note he sent to an aide in Philadelphia ordering uniforms for his servants is symbolic of the importance he attached to his own appearance and to that of those around him: "Two waistcoats, and two pair of breeches. The coats may be made of light colored cloth of any kind and lined with red shalloon—a bit of red for the capes, or collars, to them. Buttons and every kind of trimming must be sent, as nothing of the kind is to be had here."

Washington began the day at dawn, as he had for years at Mount Vernon, and worked through the late hours of the evening. His meetings with individuals or groups of officers were structured and professional. In them, he made certain that he acknowledged the significance of the men at the sessions so that they, in turn, could acknowledge his. He always let them know that he did not consider them underlings or subordinates, but important men whom he needed.

His aides ran his headquarters like that of a head of state, instilling deference for him in all who came to call. Everyone, whether important or not, was careful in their conversations with him; none dared offend him. He insisted that all correspondence to him from Americans in or out of the military be addressed General Washington. Letters from the British had to be addressed "His Excellency, George Washington, Commander-in-Chief of the Continental Army." He would not open any mail from British generals without the formal title. He walked with his head high and with a purposeful stride, exuding confidence and appearing even taller than six feet, three inches. He looked more like royalty than most royalty. "Not a King in Europe but would look like a valet by his side," said Abigail Adams.

The opinion held of the general by the soldiers who fought for him reflected that of the charming and influential Mrs. Adams. One soldier who saw him for the very first time on a hot July day in 1775 in Boston marveled at his appearance. "I have been much gratified this day with a view of General Washington," he wrote in his journal. "His Excellency was on horseback, in company with several military gentlemen. It was not difficult to distinguish him from all others. [He is] tall and well proportioned. His dress is blue coat with buff-colored dress and an elegant small sword; a black cockade is in his hat. His personal appearance is truly noble and majestic." A chaplain who was present at his arrival in Boston to take charge of the army wrote that "his look and bearing impressed everyone and I could not but feel that he was reserved for some great destiny." And a young schoolboy who saw him ride past on a New England roadway remembered, "Never shall I forget the impression his imposing presence made upon my young imagination, so superior did he seem to me to all that I had seen or imagined of the human form."

In his relationships with the men, he maintained the distance of the superior to underlings. He spent many afternoons riding through Morristown to see the soldiers at work, but rarely dismounted. He talked to soldiers, regardless of rank, but never on an intimate or overly friendly basis. He kept his distance, and while some considered his manner aloof and condescending, most realized that he had to conduct himself that way as the commander-in-chief. The general always maintained a serious public attitude; few could remember him laughing when on official business. He was always the colleague of anyone, but clearly above everyone.

He always conveyed the impression to his men, and to anyone who saw him with his men, that he was not the head of some disorganized band of badly equipped farmers involved in an impetuous rebellion. He was in fact, as anyone could see, the commander-in-chief of a great nation's army.

Washington was able to carry himself with such distinction and confidence because he did not try to fit himself into the role of a commander-in-chief. In his mind, he *was* the commander-in-chief. The job had never existed before. Generals throughout the world only had to be heads of the army reporting to a monarch or parliament. He had to be the head of the army and, in the middle of an ongoing revolution, a political and cultural figure as well. He had to create the job of commander-in-chief of the American army. He simply molded the job to all of his considerable personal skills and strengths. And because he saw the commander-in-chief as himself, it was much easier for him to be comfortable, confident, and successful. He did not have to fit prescribed contemporary or historical descriptions of the job, as so many others did. He simply had to be himself.

The final flourish was his personal guard. He needed a large contingent of troops for his protection, but he also needed them for his image. Everybody had to know, American or British, that they were dealing with the most important man in the army—and the country. The government of the United States was, in reality, wherever the army was. Events had forced Washington to become a national executive as well as a military general. He had formed a personal guard in the spring of 1776, but it was depleted by departures. With great care, he created a new one in the winter of 1777. The men were carefully selected to impress all who saw them. Each had to be members of well-connected families, of good character, "sober, young and active," Washington insisted, and stand five feet, nine inches or five feet, ten inches, which was very tall for an era in which the average male was approximately five feet, five inches tall. They also had to be native-born Americans, although the always politically careful general made that a secret condition so he would not offend officers and men from other countries. He ordered brand-new and exquisitely designed uniforms, with special hats, new muskets, and the best horses for his guard. The unit consisted of fifty-eight infantrymen, thirty-eight cavalry, and their own fife and drum corps. Over the next few years, as his need for protection grew, the guard would expand to nearly two hundred men. When they moved through the countryside with the commander-in-chief, music playing and flags flying in the afternoon breeze, they created a parade as splendid as people had ever seen.

The victories at Trenton and Princeton had caused a significant shift in popular opinion about the army, the war, and Washington. His stock was now at an all-time high, and the general knew it. He had sensed it in the cheers of townspeople whom he met as the army moved north and camped at Pluckemin for several days on the way to Morristown. He knew it from letters he received and from the tone of writers in the colonial newspapers he had delivered to him throughout the winter. The Philadelphia *Freeman's Press* urged Americans to join him in the ranks. "Show yourselves worthy of possessing that inestimable jewel, liberty, and reflect that you have nothing to dread while you are engaged in so glorious a cause and blessed with Washington for a leader." The *Pennsylvania Journal* editor gushed over his accomplishments and said that "had he lived in the days of idolatry, he had been worshipped as a God."

Many saw him as an eighteenth-century Moses, summoned by the Almighty to lead the Americans to their own promised land of independence. This also allowed all of the colonists, regardless of their wealth or social standing, to embrace Washington as an all-purpose biblical deliverer, and none held his wealth, influence, or position in society against him, as they did just about all the rich who served in the army or the government.

Knowing he had to maintain his stature and hold fast the growing public affection in order to achieve victory, Washington began an intricate public-relations campaign to obtain help for the rebellion not just from Congress, but from state governors and legislators, merchants, farmers, ministers, newspaper editors, foreign diplomats, and munitions makers. The army, in his mind, was the military extension of the political and social revolution that had already transformed America.

He was no longer the inexperienced commander who had not seen action since the French and Indian War twenty years before or the fledgling leader whose decision to engage larger British forces head on in traditional battle had proved so disastrous in the fatal string of encounters in New York. He had been transformed, in just a two-week period of time, into a great general in the eyes of the people.

The troops admired him for working so long without any pay as their own officers constantly bickered over salary and promotions, and privates and corporals refused to fight unless given bonuses. The men of the militia came and went on three-month call-ups, the veterans fought for a year and then went home, and hundreds deserted. But, day after day, the commander was always there. He had not taken a single day off in the nearly two years he had led the army and would not until the fall of 1781, four years later. They trusted him, too, because, unlike most generals, he fought with the men. The soldiers believed that he was responsible and could make decisions that would win the war and save their lives. He had crossed the Delaware and marched through the snowstorm to Trenton with them and stood in the line of fire alongside them at Princeton. His devotion to the cause of independence was unquestioned. All could agree with soldier Sam Shaw, who referred to Washington as "our brave general...fearless of any danger."

And he completely understood that the function of all good leaders was not to make the men under him, the Congress, or the public care about what happened to him, but what happened to them. His political genius was to understand that the successful leader in a democracy gains power and status not by assuring his own success, but the success of the people.

Washington's position in America had transcended that of a mere general. He had come to represent all that was good in both the army and, more importantly, the country. By the end of 1775, parents had started to name their newborn baby sons George and girls Martha. Soldiers, ministers, politicians, and newspaper editors began to refer to General Washington as "His Excellency." Communities, starting with Stoughantom, Massachusetts, began naming themselves after him. Many groups and individuals, urged on by newspapers, began to celebrate his

February birthday as a national holiday. "War and Washington," a rousing drinking song, was written about him. Painters in both America and England produced paintings of him, always in heroic poses, as early as the autumn of 1775. Dozens of poems celebrating his life began to appear in pamphlets and newspapers by January of 1777, and several suggested he be coronated as a king.

All of this resulted from his triumphs at Trenton and Princeton. It was almost as if, in the minds of Americans thirsty for victory, the losses in New York did not matter. All that counted now, in January 1777, was the subjugation of the British at Trenton and Princeton. Winning those two alone did not suddenly make him a revered leader, however. Washington was held in such high esteem because his victories there reminded people of why he had been chosen to lead the American forces in the first place. They concluded, like financier Morris, that "heaven, no doubt for the noblest purposes, has blessed you with a firmness of mind, steadiness of countenance and patience in sufferings, that give you infinite advantages over other men." People saw him as a man of high integrity and honor. Americans saw themselves and their nation as virtuous. The man who led the army then had to be virtuous too, and there was no one better to fit that order than the tall commander from Virginia.

The American ideal in 1777 was the man who believed in freedom, pledged his life and fortune to protect liberty, and was willing to give up everything for the cause. He was a man, in or out of the army, who fervently believed that America could and should be independent and, once freed from England, would prosper. George Washington met all of those criteria. He embodied all the best qualities of the citizen/soldier.

Washington was not a fiery commander, an inspiring speaker, or a man who could produce instant melodrama. He did not have the type of personality that would later be called charismatic. The general was a calm man of stern determination and steady nerves, a man who was inventive in combat and resourceful enough to change tactics quickly when the tide of the battle turned. He was a man of solid morals. Washington fit the description of what Carl Von Clausewitz would later term "military genius," despite his New York losses, because most importantly, as Von Clausewitz said of great leaders, Washington had "strength of character."

Since Americans from Congressional leaders to battlefield generals to merchants and farmers believed that he had all of these virtuous and exemplary qualities, and saw the nation's future in him, then, of course, in some sort of transference, they believed that these same qualities had to be deep down inside of them, too.

Many members of Congress had come to lionize him. They had selected him not just because he was one of the few men in the country with military experience, but because as a veteran state legislator and member of both Continental Congresses he understood how to work with an assembly of political figures. They knew now, after eighteen months as the head of the army, that Washington would always treat Congress with respect. He was just as careful to acknowledge their political power as they were to acknowledge his in the military. He understood that to be successful he had to work with Congress and not against it, despite all of their frequent failures to aid the army. There was never a time that they worried that he would use the army to take over the government of the struggling new nation.

The Congressmen, like the soldiers, appreciated the general's complete absence from the political stage and applauded his efforts to focus all of his energies on winning the war and not interfering with Congressional discussions of public policy. That, of course, was his greatest strength. He did not want money, title, or position. He sought nothing from anyone for his service to his country. There did not seem to be any need for power or glory in him. He did not seem to have any ambition at all, unlike just about everyone in Congress, the army, or in state governments. Whenever asked about ambition, he brushed off the suggestion. "To merit the approbation of good and virtuous men is the height of my ambition," he told Thomas Jefferson, and, when asked about it by fellow Virginian Benjamin Harrison, he said that "to stand well in the good opinion of my countrymen constitutes my chiefest happiness."

Washington was, of course, an intensely ambitious man. He had harbored a burning desire to succeed at whatever he tried all of his life, whether it was fox hunting, card playing, farming, or the revolution. He had been a good state legislator by working behind the scenes and never appearing to be a public politician. In bringing together merchants, munitions makers, newspaper editors, and ministers to join him in championing the rebellion, he had shown extraordinary political skills. Yet his real skill was to convince everyone that he had no political skills at all; he was just a general in the service of his country. Nothing more. He was a soldier above politics. His ability to make others see him in this manner—a man with no personal agenda—gave him the freedom to pursue all of his goals throughout the war, a freedom he never would have had if dragged down by the baggage many politicians carry.

And so, by the time he had arrived in Morristown, he had become a unique figure, idolized by the press, adored by the public, respected by Congress, feared by the British, and cheered by the people. Most felt like Alexander Hamilton's tutor, Dr. Hugh Knox, that "Washington was born for the deliverance of America."

These opinions would change when the army's fortunes declined, and the commander-in-chief knew that, but for a while, in the winter of 1777, he basked in the admiration of all.

The Smallpox Epidemic and Washington's Great Gamble

Washington's much-anticipated plans to rebuild the army were put on hold during the first week of January, when Mrs. Martha Ball came down with smallpox and began to die. Smallpox had claimed a Morristown man in 1770; two men, two women, and a child in 1771; and another man in 1774. Mrs. Ball would die on January 11. Within days of her passing, Morristown citizens began to fall prey to one of the worst smallpox epidemics in American history—brought by the army.

The soldiers and officers of the Continental Army had lived in unsanitary conditions for months. They had few doctors, little medicine, and, when in need, were treated in makeshift hospitals. The soldiers were badly clothed and unprotected from the weather. Most of the men lived in tents whose sides did little to shield them from frigid winds. The soldiers had become physically vulnerable to any diseases, especially smallpox, which attacks people living in overcrowded conditions.

Smallpox had been the scourge of Europe in the decades before the American Revolution. A series of epidemics that passed through London between 1718 and 1746 killed tens of thousands of people. Thousands died in epidemics that swept through Geneva and Berlin during that same period. The disease claimed the lives of forty thousand people in Belem, Brazil, in 1750. It had hit America, too. Nearly 15 percent of the population of New York, some 1,200 people, were wiped out in that city's 1731 smallpox scourge. The 1760 smallpox attack in Charleston, South Carolina, killed 10 percent of the population. Boston had been hit with smallpox several times, the 1721 epidemic taking the lives of 15 percent of the residents. Boston's latest battle with the disease was in 1776, when the Americans were camped there. Another epidemic had hit New York when Washington was engaged in battles there in 1776, and yet another claimed the lives of more than two hundred residents of Nova Scotia that year.

Smallpox struck quickly and usually took the lives of 10–15 percent of its victims, but sometimes claimed up to 40 percent. The infected developed severe fevers, fast pulse, throbbing headaches, aches in the loins and limbs, and painful vomiting. On the third or fourth day, pus-filled eruptions appeared on the skin. These blotches and pimples then spread over the rest of the body. The victims' heads swelled and their skin turned dark blue. For many, death came within a few days.

The disease might have been carried by soldiers in the regiments that passed through Morristown in mid-December or possibly was carried into the village by the army's advance scouts following the battle of Princeton. It was also brought by the men who arrived on January 6. They walked, weak, into Morristown and then fell desperately ill. Soldiers who became ill promptly infected the people in whose homes they were quartered. General Washington was alarmed. He had been a victim of smallpox as a teenager and still bore pockmarks on his cheeks to show for it. He had seen smallpox claim the lives of dozens of farmers in Virginia over the years, and as a state legislator argued for inoculations for the neighbors of those who became sick. An epidemic in Virginia in 1760 had claimed the lives of several of his slaves, despite considerable efforts by him to save them.

Washington's fear of smallpox was so great that he refused to allow any soldiers who had not previously built up an immunity to go into Boston when the British left the city. When he was summoned to Philadelphia by Congress in the spring of 1776, he told his wife that she had to be inoculated upon arrival because of smallpox rumors. The general was in charge of three thousand soldiers and officers in the Morristown area camps in January 1777, and was worried that smallpox would devastate his troops. "Instead of having an army we shall have a hospital," he told Horatio Gates.

There was additional trouble. He had learned from couriers that new outbreaks of smallpox had been reported in New York, Connecticut, Maryland, Virginia, and again in Pennsylvania, all places where his troops were quartered. "The smallpox is so thick in the country that there is no chance of escaping it," wrote John Adams from Baltimore, where the disease spread through neighborhoods and threatened the health of Congress, which had stopped dispatching couriers to Philadelphia because of the epidemic there.

The Congressional medical committee was alarmed at the spread of the disease in the Carolinas and Virginia, and its chairman, Dr. Benjamin Rush, told the general that the men in those states were near panic. "We beg leave to remind you that the southern troops are greatly alarmed at the smallpox and that it very often proves fatal to them," he said.

The biggest problem Washington faced as he sat in his office on the second floor of Arnold's tavern was that the disease was striking with too much speed. He had troops scattered throughout northern New Jersey. If the troops fell ill, they could infect tens of thousands of civilians in those areas. Infected troops in other camps, such as those near Philadelphia, Newport, Rhode Island, and Peekskill, New York, could do the same—they could trigger a national epidemic.

There was a relatively successful inoculation procedure to stop smallpox, but it was time-consuming. Doctors in Europe and in America put patients fearful of catching smallpox on a six-week preparatory diet and administered medicine, often a combination of milk and mercury. They were forced to vomit and also bled at regular intervals in order to purge their blood. Then they were inoculated. The inoculation itself was a simple procedure. Postules, tissue from a previous victim, would be injected into patients via a small incision under the skin. The patients' infected tissue would then fight off the smallpox when it attacked the body. Post-inoculation procedure included weeks of rest, diet, and medicine that was little more than a powdery flour. The method was, claimed Boston doctor Zabdiel Boylston in the 1750s, "the most beneficial and successful ever discovered."

Doctors studied ways to shorten the prep period because the disease killed its victims so quickly. In 1760, British doctor Daniel Sutton saved the lives of many potential victims of smallpox with a preparation period he cut to just ten days. Dr. Lewis Williams was reported to have prevented a handful of people in England from dying during a 1763 epidemic by inoculating them without any preparation at all. During the early 1760s, American doctors, who had minimal training in battling it, followed Sutton's example. They gave patients generous doses of medicine every few days and urged them to maintain a light diet. American doctors, like their European counterparts, waited ten days before inoculation. Washington did not have time; he had to stop the disease immediately. He cringed when he thought about the ravages of the disease, he told Patrick Henry, and said that, "I know it is more destructive to an army in the natural way than the enemy's sword and I shudder when I think of [it]."

The general had multiple sicknesses with which to deal. Dozens of men had dysentery, including one of his best generals, John Sullivan, who fell ill when he arrived in the area and was bedridden in Chatham, unable to move. Others suffered from venereal disease, pleurisy, and high fever.

Washington, running out of time, consulted Chief Army Doctor William Shippen and several others, and then made a gutsy decision: he would ignore long-standing medical practice and order immediate inoculations, with no preparations at all, for his camps and the civilian population.

He issued orders to Shippen to begin inoculations on January 6, the day he arrived in Morristown, fully cognizant of the risk he was taking. "Finding the smallpox to be spreading much and fearing that no precaution can prevent it from running through the whole of our army, I have determined that the troops shall be inoculated. This expedient may be attended with some inconveniences and some disadvantage but yet I trust in its consequences will have the most happy effects," he told him, adding that it seemed not only appropriate but necessary. "For should the disorder infect the army, and rage with its usual virulence, we should have more to dread from it than from the sword of the enemy."

All of the three thousand troops in the Morristown area were to be inoculated immediately and army inoculations would be done on a volunteer basis for civilians in the neighboring villages. All troops in the Peekskill, Princeton, Philadelphia, and Connecticut regiments were to be inoculated, and already-infected troops were to be quarantined in hospitals that the army would set up with civilian assistance. Soldiers were forbidden to go into Philadelphia, where the epidemic was growing. All new recruits arriving for duty were to be inoculated upon arrival. The inoculations were to be kept top secret.

It was a decision Washington made with no approval from the Congressional delegates in Baltimore. Congress did not decide to take a vote on whether or not to ask Washington to act on the smallpox crisis until February 13, five weeks after he made his decision to begin inoculations. The delegates did not object to his orders without their approval because he had all of the power they had given him to issue the orders and, just as importantly, their trust. It was a decision Washington made "for the public good," as he would often explain his unusual revolutionary dual role of national executive and military leader, a determination that had to be made immediately, without lengthy Congressional debate. It was, in essence, the very first use of "executive order," a snap decision by a national executive in a health emergency, the kind of decision that would be made so often in the future by presidents of the United States.

There was some dissent in his own inner circle of officers about the decision. Sullivan argued that all smallpox victims should be taken by wagons to some remote village and isolated. One colonel even refused to participate, fearful his men would die, and had to be ordered to comply. The general was adamant about the need for immediate action, and was confident, as he often was, that one man with power, certain from experience that he was right, had to act alone, sometimes without the counsel or approval of others, in order to succeed. He never doubted his decision, and confided to his aide Harrison, as he had to Dr. Shippen, that "I shudder at the consequences of this disorder if some vigorous steps are not taken to stop the spreading of it."

It was a ground-breaking medical, military, and political decision. An entire army of any nation had never undergone mass inoculations for any disease before. The problem, of course, was that the soldiers would be unable to fight for weeks as they lay in the hospital recovering. The army could easily be overwhelmed by an enemy, as both Washington and members of Congress feared. And, too, the entire army would become infected with smallpox and thousands of soldiers and civilians would die if the bold procedure backfired. It was a huge risk, one of many the commander would take in the coming winter months.

It was a risk that he wanted the civilians in the area to take with him. Many local residents were fearful that the experimental inoculations would fail, and that the postules introduced into the systems of the soldiers without traditional preparation would not only bring about their deaths, but would sweep through the country.

It was one of Washington's first opportunities to create a working coalition between the army and the public, which he knew was vital to the success of the revolution, and he eagerly sought to make it happen. The general summoned all of the clergymen in the county, most of whom also worked as part-time doctors. They arrived on horse-driven sleds over a new snowfall, brushed their coats off, and walked up to the third floor of the Arnold Tavern. They included men from every denomination: Dr. Timothy Johnnes of the Presbyterian church of Morristown, Rev. John Gano of the Baptist Church, Rev. Green of Hanover Presbyterian, Reverend John Lewis from Mendham, Rev. Azariah Horton from Madison, Samuel Kennedy from Basking Ridge, William Woodhull of

Chester, and John Derby, of Parsippany. Washington asked them all for advice and urged them to expand the hospitals in their churches, already full of sick soldiers battling other ailments, such as dysentery and tuberculosis, in order to care for the smallpox victims, civilian and military.

Then, Washington, probably showing his own pockmarks, explained his plan, which would be free to all of the civilians in the area. He also used the opportunity to work as a national executive and not merely a general, using the army as the government. The ministers knew that Congress had given him extraordinary powers to act in such a manner and they were pleased that the army, acting in the national interest, was going to help the people.

Fear of the dreaded smallpox was so great that a large public meeting was then held, chaired by Rev. Green, at the Hanover church. There, in a long talk to an overflowing crowd, General Washington again outlined the dangers of the epidemic already raging in the area and the steps he wanted to take to stop it. He told civilians that what he wanted to do was proper for the army and urged them to be inoculated, too. His fervent pleas did not persuade everyone to take advantage of his offer. The residents of the Morristown area were conservative and accustomed to traditional medical beliefs that favored weeks of careful diet and preparation prior to any inoculations. They were afraid that Washington's emergency measure would not work and that they would die. Some accepted the free inoculations, but many did not.

His lack of success at that meeting convinced him that he had to "order" civilians to be inoculated elsewhere and sent Dr. John Cochran, who had treated smallpox victims since 1771, to the Philadelphia area to stop the rapidly growing epidemic there. "Use every means possible in your power to prevent that disease from spreading in the army and among the inhabitants, which may otherwise prove fatal," he told him, and authorized him to establish hospitals for soldiers and civilians wherever he could and to force civilians to be inoculated.

The general sent word to his officers in different states to start inoculations of soldiers and civilians at once, regardless of public nervousness. "Vigorous methods must be adopted, however disagreeable and inconvenient to individuals," he said in a letter to aide Robert Harrison, then away from headquarters.

The army inoculations got underway immediately. Local doctors in Morristown assisted Dr. Nathaniel Bond, an army surgeon. Churches in the area were used as hospitals for recovering patients, but there were so many soldiers that the general had to ask residents to turn their homes into hospitals, putting themselves and their families at risk. Revs. Green and Johnnes were inoculated and then began to minister to the sick. The number of soldiers and civilians falling ill increased daily, and by early March Green was sadly writing in his diary, "many, many sick." The victims were "the most frightful and pitiable human beings I have ever seen." Green's small church was probably the busiest inoculation center with more than eight hundred soldiers and some civilians treated and housed there. There were so many patients being treated or recovering in the hall that Green's fourteen-year-old son Ashbel, who helped him tend the sick, said that the church was "wholly occupied with medicine."

Some of the Morristown women and children were afraid to undergo the procedure after doctors told them they might be scarred from the pock marks. One doctor told a mother that her daughter might be saved, but she would "be ugly for the rest of her life." As an elderly woman, Eunice Kitchell complained that the inoculation she had at age eight ruined her looks. Henry Knox's wife Lucy worried that the inoculation might wreck her beauty and turn away her husband. "You will want to know if I look as I did or whether there is danger of you not liking me as well as you did when you saw me last," she told him with great apprehension.

Other women who came down with smallpox, but survived it because they were inoculated soon enough, regretted what the disease did to their looks but were happy to be alive. Mrs. Martha Bland, wife of a colonel in Morristown, was one of the first civilians inoculated and one of the first women to look into a mirror to observe the ravages of the disease. She joked of her scarred face: "I had many pocks on my face, all of which are at present visible and I shall be pitied with them. [My husband] laughs at my poor forehead and [says] I threw honeyburs upon it, or, as the sailors say, threw black eyed peas upon it."

The experimental procedure was astonishingly successful. There were only a handful of fatalities among the three thousand troops who were inoculated in the Morristown area. The rest fought off the disease and were back on duty within weeks. The same success was reported throughout the states. More than one thousand troops from Virginia on their way to Philadelphia were inoculated and none died. Hundreds more were successfully inoculated in Baltimore, Philadelphia, Peekskill, Connecticut, and Rhode Island with no loss of life.

There was some humor in the recuperation of the troops. So many decided to remain "in recovery" well after they should have been healthy that Washington had to write special orders for loafers to be rounded up and put to work. The recuperating soldiers also managed, through laudable theatrics, to convince doctors that their return to good health would be considerably speeded up by jugs of rum, and the doctors, quite moved by their touching performances, convinced the quartermaster to procure the liquor. Recuperating privates with a sweet tooth also talked doctors in obtaining chocolate for them, and hastily written requisitions for ten- and twelve-pound boxes of it were common.

Unfortunately, many Morristown and Morris County area residents refused inoculation and perished. Records showed that in the Morristown area, sixty-seven residents died from smallpox that winter, or 20 percent of the population. Dozens of people who refused inoculation in the surrounding villages also died, including Ebeneezer Condict, brother of the influential Silas. So many residents had died from smallpox and other diseases that Washington ordered mass graves dug behind the Morristown Presbyterian church where the dead were wrapped in sheets and interred. The dozen who died in Chatham and Madison were buried in nearby apple orchards. That winter also saw a record nineteen deaths in the county from tuberculosis, which locals also claimed was brought to the area by the soldiers. Altogether, 207 area residents died from smallpox, tuberculosis, dysentery, and other diseases that winter, a record high.

There was local heroism and tragedy in the desperate battles against smallpox and other illnesses that assailed the winter camp. One of the state's most prominent physicians, Dr. Berne Budd, took time out from his busy office in Morristown to care for Washington's sick soldiers. He became so impressed with their valor and need for medical care that he gave up his practice and joined the army. The doctor, who could have remained safely in civilian life, died three months later of a fever he picked up in camp. A local minister, Rev. Azariah Horton, sixty-two, whose son had spent four months as a prisoner of war, was enjoying a safe and healthy retirement when some of his former parishioners contracted smallpox. Horton returned to the ministry and, like other pastors in the Morristown area, ignored danger and began to work in a local church hospital. He came down with smallpox and died on March 2. A merchant who knew something about medicine, Abiel Tompkins, volunteered as a nurse, contracted smallpox, and died a week later. Rev. John Lewis of the Mendham Presbyterian Church, who supervised the burying of his town's dead, also caught smallpox and died. He was interred by his own burial group.

One of Washington's prime concerns were members of his "family" of slaves and free laborers at Mount Vernon and his blood relatives. He had reports that more than three hundred workers at Mount Vernon had a touch of the smallpox through the winter, but that their early non-prep inoculations, ordered by Washington, had saved them. He had his brother Samuel's nephew in the army with him inoculated early. He made certain that all of his brothers and sister and their families were inoculated. His efforts saved the lives of all except Sam's wife, who was claimed by smallpox after what Washington later suggested was a botched inoculation.

His orders for the treatment of his workers and family members actually violated a 1769 Virginia law, which regulated smallpox inoculations and required months of pre-inoculation preparation. Washington did so without qualms and said the law should be overturned and a new law written that not only required inoculations for all adults and children, but even mandated them for babies.

Men in the army wrote home to urge family members and friends to take the emergency inoculation at once. Almost all of the civilians in towns near each of Washington's camps were saved by the inoculation, and they told friends and relatives in other communities to do it. Those people then told their own friends and neighbors in an effective word-of-mouth campaign. All of the soldiers and many civilians were inoculated at army camps by military and civilian doctors. Some civilians were inoculated by private physicians whom they asked to follow Washington's non-preparatory method.

Washington's decision to inoculate without preparations, saving the lives of tens of thousands of soldiers and civilians, was very satisfying to him. In assessing the success of the inoculations throughout the country, he told Connecticut Governor Joseph Trumbull, with great pride, that "Inoculation at Philadelphia and in this neighborhood has been attended with amazing success," and assured him that no one would die of smallpox in his state, either.

The British apparently did not learn of the mass inoculation of the army and citizenry until much later in that spring. There was a report about smallpox in the *Royal Gazette and Weekly Mercury*, a Tory newspaper in New York, on March 31, but the story merely reported some infections; the writer had no knowledge of the potential catastrophe and the story did not indicate that the British knew anyone was very sick. Washington's orders to keep the movement of troops into and out of the hospitals—usually at night—almost kept the secret of the mass inoculations that immobilized the entire army. The stealthiness with which it was done, along with ruses to fool the British, such as parading soldiers who were healthy and sending out troops on harmless raids to create diversions from the epidemic, proved successful. The British never attacked the weakened army. A medical historian later wrote that Washington's efforts to save the army and populace from smallpox was as important a factor in winning the war as victory in any battle.

Chapter Four

—————— ✑ ——————

THE PATRIOT KING

MORRISTOWN, 1777

*"Providence has fitted him for the charge
and called him to the service."*
—Rev. John Witherspoon

O nce the smallpox epidemic was under control, Washington could
return to his campaign to win support for the war from the public. The purpose of that crusade was never simply to recruit more troops;
the general's goal was more than a mere military victory. He believed that
a revolution was fought not just by colonels and corporals, but by everyone, whether housewife or blacksmith.

In Europe, there had never been much of a connection between the
common man and the ruler's army. Paid, professional, highly trained forces
fought for their countries, usually their kings; troops enlisted for years. Soldiering in Europe was profession, and many spent their adult lives in uniform. The European people went about their business as the king's army
went to war, usually against another emperor, prince, or king. For hundreds
of years, soldiering had been either a mercenary or an aristocratic profession.

Washington wanted to change that view. He knew that the people who wanted a revolution and independence had to fight for it. They could not simply hire others to do the job for them. Patriotic soldiers would make the best troops, far better than men who fought simply for money or an Old World sense of entitlement. He had to use the army to unite the people, not just to defeat the enemy. In the fall, he had expended all of his resources, fleeing from the British. Now, in winter, he had time to regroup and plan his strategy.

As the leader of the army with extraordinary powers from Congress to win the war, the commander-in-chief wanted to forge ties between the army and the local, state, and national governments. They had to halt their infighting. He could not win the war with different state and county legislatures squabbling about regional differences and local goals and ignoring the revolution.

An important part of that broad-based campaign for political consensus was his association with the states and their war governors. All of the states had provincial governments, legislatures, councils of safety, and elected executives who ran their affairs. Washington believed that good relations with the different governors and other state officials were necessary to obtain needed troops and supplies when Congress was ineffective at doing so, which was often. He also felt that friendships with the governors and legislatures would show the people that the army was working with public officials and was part of the local authority. "When the civil and military powers co-operate, and afford mutual aid to each other, there can be little doubt of things going well," he had written members of the New York Committee of Safety in that regard in 1776.

He knew many of the governors by the time he had crossed the Delaware. He had served in Congress with Governors George Clinton of New York, Caesar Rodney of Delaware, Richard Caswell of North Carolina, John Rutledge of South Carolina, Thomas Johnson of Maryland, and William Livingston of New Jersey. Joseph Reed, the president, or governor, of Pennsylvania, had worked as his personal aide for ten months. Patrick Henry and Thomas Jefferson, two of Virginia's governors during the war, were personal friends from the House of Burgesses. Clinton and

Rodney also served under him as generals during the first year of the war and understood his problems more than most.

He attempted to include the governors in any decisions he made concerning the protection of their states. He had met with the governors of the New England states in 1775. In 1776, on his way to New York for what would turn out to be a series of military disasters, he stopped to hold a conference with the governors of Rhode Island and Connecticut. He urged all of the governors to visit him in camp, particularly the winter camps. Clinton, Reed, and Johnson were frequent guests. Toward the end of the war, Virginia governor Thomas Nelson would live in the Continental Army camp during the siege of Yorktown. Washington told the governors that he wanted them to advise him and, through their personal visits, inspire the troops from their states. Camp visits by the governors were important because these meetings were held on Washington's ground, not theirs. They had to be impressed with Washington at his headquarters in Morristown— the soldiers standing at attention, the deference to the general by officers and civilians alike, the flags, swords, drills, and parades. He was able to use all of the trappings of his military office to create an aura of power and influence. This sense of Washington's position made the governors far more likely to help him when emergencies arose.

During their visits or in letters, the general made certain that each governor had the latest information on the progress of the war. An aide wrote letters concerning the army to the New York legislature twice a week. Washington assured them that he would work tirelessly to have prisoners from their state exchanged, particularly their personal friends or sons of friends. He promised to investigate any complaint brought by a state official concerning the army. State leaders were repeatedly told how courageously the men from their state had performed in battle; as an example, Washington wrote the Massachusetts legislature of the bay area men that "they have given the highest proof of their bravery" at Trenton and Princeton.

The general changed his own plans to give the governors troops they believed necessary to protect their states from invasion. He sometimes replaced commanding officers, even generals, that governors did not like.

Washington admitted to the officers he transferred that sometimes the military reasons might have been wrong, but the political reasons were right. He told General Israel Putnam, whom he relieved at the request of New York's Governor Clinton, that "my reasons for making this change is due to the prejudices of the people [Clinton], which whether well or ill-grounded must be indulged."

The care of the governors was never forgotten. Washington told any general or colonel anywhere near a state capitol to pay a courtesy call. He constantly wrote the governors. When Caesar Rodney left the service to become the governor of Delaware, Washington wrote him a flattering letter and told him that his military works "reflect the highest honor on your character and place your attachment to the cause in a most distinguished point of view."

It was in these relationships, too, that Washington first practiced what political scientist Fred Greenstein would later call "hidden hand" politics. The general, wanting some Congressional action but unwilling to petition for it directly for fear of being seen as a meddler, would ask a governor to make the request for him, through a Congressman from his state. The commander might be unable to get farmers to agree to prices on produce, so he would go to local magistrates and ask them to implore the farmers to do so without knowing he had met with them. Washington's "hidden hand" usually worked so well that few knew that he was behind many of the wartime appeals. He would rely very heavily on the "hidden hand" after independence was achieved.

He kept a watchful eye on politics through his reading of numerous newspapers and had aides keep him updated on the results of elections so that he could immediately send congratulatory letters to the winners. Knowing that those who lost might be back again, in that office or some other, he sent them letters too, thanking them for their service to their country.

He always told the governors that they were his close colleagues and that, in person or by letter, they could speak as friends. He went out of his way to defer to the politicians. Washington wrote Trumbull about some task, "which I can see you performed to the utmost of your abilities." He told Jonathan Bryan, the vice president (Lt. Governor) of Georgia: "I flatter myself that your state will cheerfully concur" with Washington's decision. He was always "pleased to see" or "honored" that some governor or legislator did what he suggested or visited winter camp.

He also told them that he considered them part of his inner circle, his military "family," and often sent them copies of stolen British plans, letters concerning spy discoveries, and copies of documents about news that pertained to their troops. As a master stroke in flattering the politicians, most of their letters from him in Morristown were in his own handwriting, not his aides' (he always reminded them of this).

He practically gushed in his thanks to them for any favor they did (which was usually what he expected of them anyway), telling Clinton at one point that the whole country was grateful to him for his hard work for the army. He told Cooke of Rhode Island in a letter full of extravagant praise that his "cheerful concurrence with me in public measures and zeal for the service calls for my best thanks."

His letters to governors and state assemblies were overly cordial and always aimed at obtaining their cooperation. In one he sent to the Massachusetts Assembly, he softly chastised them for not raising enough troops and exhorting them to find more:

I took the liberty in a letter of the 13th of February to inform your honorable board of the augmentation Congress has resolved to make to the Army they voted to be raised in September and to solicit your attention and your good offices in prompting the raising of your proportion of these latter levies. I trusted...the quota to be raised by your state to be just and your interest would have been exerted to fill them up in the same manner that it was to fill up the 15 battalions first voted. Finding this not to have been the case, and being assured from a variety of combining circumstances, and intelligence not to be questioned, that Britain this campaign will strain every nerve at home and abroad to effect her purposes, I beg leave again to repeat my solicitations upon this subject and to entreat that you will take the matter under your most early and serious consideration and give every aid you shall deem necessary and conducive to completing two of these corps with all possible expedition.

Washington wanted these men to feel like they were part of the revolution so that they could turn around and convince their state legislatures to be a part of it, too. They did. To a man, the governors encouraged patriotism—and recruiting—in their state chambers. Livingston, after one talk with the general, delivered a soaring speech to the New Jersey legislature, typical of the enthusiasm exhibited by the governors in their public rhetoric. "Let us do our part to open the next campaign, with redoubled vigor and until the United States have humbled the pride of Britain, and obtained an honorable peace," Livingston exhorted his legislators. He then promoted the army as he told them that New Jerseyans should "cheerfully furnish our proportion [of soldiers] for continuing the war—a war, on our side, founded on the immutable obligation of self defense and in support of freedom, of virtue, and everything tending to enoble our nature and render a people happy."

The winter of 1777 gave Washington his first full opportunity to work with state leaders. Throughout the winter, and over the next several winters, he would come to believe that a country of separate state governments could not work and that a much stronger national government was needed. That government, the work he had finished with governors had already shown him, needed a strong national executive.

Washington's relationships with state executives, even his friends Henry and Jefferson, paled with the deep personal friendship he developed with Livingston. In the radical Livingston he found a kindred spirit. The men met in Philadelphia during the second Continental Congress. They had much in common. Livingston, like Washington, was wealthy; he was the scion of one of the richest families in New York and a successful lawyer. Both were men who enjoyed writing; Livingston had published dozens of political essays in newspapers and magazines and was the master of literary satire. Both were devoted family men; Livingston had five daughters, three sons, and a wife whom he doted over (five other children had died). Both were excellent horsemen. Both enjoyed good wine and spirits. And both were physical giants. Livingston, at six feet, three inches, the same height as Washington, also towered over most of the men surrounding him. They were both good politicians and staunch patriots who shared common views. Alexander Hamilton later said that he had never met two men who thought so much alike as the governor and the general. (In 1788, Hamilton would call Livingston one of the five most important men in the war.)

Livingston feared kidnapping from his Elizabeth mansion, Liberty Hall, just across the harbor from British troops in New York, just as Washington's top aides feared the general's capture. For this reason, he frequently lived in different towns in New Jersey, running the state from a large trunk. Apprehensive about his welfare, Washington assigned three soldiers to act as his bodyguards throughout the war. The general finally told him to stop running and move to Morristown where he could work and be protected by the army. So, in the middle of the winter of 1777, the governor moved his family into the mansion of Lord Stirling in nearby Basking Ridge. He then began to see the commander-in-chief regularly. He visited him at headquarters and dined with him in Morristown or at Stirling's home.

Livingston developed a deep and lasting friendship with Washington, which was expressed with fervor in a letter he wrote the general a year later. "As for the personal friendship of your humble servant, if it is worth having at all," he told him in a heartfelt way, "you have it upon the solid principles of a full conviction of your disinterested patriotism; and will continue to have it, while that conviction continues to exist, all the Devils in hell, and all the envious intrigues upon earth, notwithstanding." From the winter of 1777 until 1783, the governor and general would share one of the closest relationships of any two men in the war.

In his relations with Livingston and the other governors, Washington was able to succeed thanks to his considerable powers of persuasion. The general, like any political leader, could never assume that other leaders would go along with his plans just because he told them he was right. He, like any leader, had to persuade the governors that they should help him not only because he was right, but because he could make them agree that he was. He also had to persuade them to do what he wanted because the results would be just as beneficial for them as for him. He had to use his power to convince people, a skill learned through years of backroom politics in Williamsburg as a legislator. He had to make them believe that in order to have them understand that in subjugating themselves to him they were not losing any of their power, but gaining some of his. He had enough fame by the winter of 1777, thanks to Trenton and Princeton, that any national, state, or local politician, editor, or businessman would want to do what he asked in order to gain power merely through their association with him.

Ties to the governors were just part of Washington's multifaceted public-relations campaign, a campaign which could only be conducted in winter, when he had time. The commander-in-chief also considered religion as vitally important to win the support of both the army and the people. Americans were very religious; many had moved to the colonies to flee religious persecution in England. The Great Awakening evangelical movement of the mid-eighteenth century had transformed the religious views of a large portion of the population. The movement, whose converts believed that they could find God within themselves and not through established churches, was begun by radical protestant ministers in New England in the early 1730s and then spread throughout the middle-Atlantic states during the next twenty-five years. Nowhere was the force of the crusade felt more than in Washington's native Virginia, where the reformation took root in the 1760s and continued to grow. There, England's official Anglican Church, of which the general, also a Free Mason, was a member, had been weakened. The New Light, revivalist Baptist churches had won over many of its parishioners, and revival Presbyterian churches had taken more. By 1771, New Light Baptist churches in the state were drawing surprisingly large crowds, sometimes more than five thousand people, to outdoor Sunday services.

The Great Awakening gave each man and woman a sense that they had a personal relationship with God that transcended the one they had with the established church. It also promoted the natural rights of the individual, given by God, not the church or the state, and upheld the idea that tyranny of any kind had to be overthrown, whether the religious tyranny of the established church or the governmental oppression of England.

The Awakening also changed the personal philosophy of many Americans. It made them believe that while they could not be of the same rank as others in wealth, land, education, or influence, they could be the moral equivalent of their neighbor, or anyone in the colonies. It helped to construct a model for the new American, built on integrity and character. The ministers of the Awakening preached that finding God within one's self not only gave a person religious piety, but enabled them to undergo a social transformation and to find true happiness. The movement stressed that men and women were not condemned to hell, but could attain heaven through a holy life. However, a large difference between the new evangelicals and traditional protestant sects was that heaven could also be obtained through social consciousness and good works. Noble works were not just in the service of the church, but in the service of the nation. The new movement had a dramatic effect throughout the country.

One of the men who best understood how the religious movement had changed people was George Washington, who had earlier left the army for private life just as the Awakening was sweeping through Virginia. How much the Awakening may have influenced Washington's private religious beliefs is difficult to determine, but in some cases his attitude clearly coincided with the ideas of the new religious movement. He told his mother-in-law in 1765, when a cutback on luxuries was deemed patriotic during the Stamp Act furor, that material possessions were not important, that "the necessaries of life are mostly to be had within ourselves." He wrote George Mason in 1769, discussing their boycott of goods, that it would cause the wealthy planters to live simpler and more moral lives and that it would help the poor to feel some equality with those above them on the social rungs because wealth would no longer be a yardstick for success; only virtue would.

The Great Awakening energized many religious sects and created new ones. Emotionally, it enabled people to exchange their religious fervor for political zealotry. Now, they could see that the Revolution was a war for natural rights and a battle to destroy British tyranny. The revolution was an end to one era and the beginning of another one, revivalists suggested. It created a new nation in a new land for a people with new religious insight. The revolution, preachers foretold, would bring about the first country in the world created on a new political framework at the same time that this new religion was changing the masses. Democracy and evangelism would grow together. Ministers, particularly Presbyterians and Baptists, preached to their flocks, too, that British corruption equaled the corruption of the soul and told soldiers that they could seek personal moral regeneration through victory in the war against England. One minister told his parishioners that "eternal happiness" in Heaven was the American victory in the war.

The ministers often quoted verses from the Old Testament, connecting the battles of the Hebrews to the revolution. One of the most fiery defenders of the rebellion was Massachusetts minister William Stearns. He bellowed from his pulpit that "When God, in his providence, calls to take the sword, if any refused to obey, Heaven's dread artillery is levelled against him…cursed be he that keepeth back his sword from blood; cursed is the sneaking coward who neglects the sinking state when called to its defense—O then, flee this dire curse—let America's valorous sons put on the harness, nor take it off till peace shall be to Israel." Stearn's dramatic bold call to arms was repeated often by other ministers in other churches throughout the states.

Many Americans echoed the sentiments of a Rutgers University student, Simeon Vanartsdalen, who, like so many, believed that independence had been ordained by the Almighty: "We may for a considerable time feel the effects of war, yet I rest assured that God will do justice and am also convinced that our cause is just and have great reason from various instances to suppose that He has and will interpose on our behalf."

Washington had always believed that freedom of religion was an important component of the revolution. "The liberty enjoyed by the people of these states of worshipping almighty God agreeable to their consciences is not only among the choicest of their blessings, but also of their rights," he said often and with great passion. He always linked religion to virtue, telling a group of ministers that "religion and morality are the essential pillars of civil society."

A few British officers understood that. Howe's aide, Serle, warned the Colonial office in London of religious passion in the states. He reminded them that hundreds of ministers in New York, delivering sermons on street corners and in parks as well as churches, spoke out against the Crown and that "the preachers look upon the war very much as a religious one." A British visitor to America that year wrote in his diary that "the Presbyterians are the chief instigators and supporters" of the rebellion.

The commander used that love of God to help the revolution in numerous ways. He had attended church regularly all of his life and continued at the Presbyterian Church in Morristown every Sunday (services were held outdoors in bitter weather because the church had been converted into an army hospital). He became friendly with the Presbyterian pastor, Rev. Timothy Johnnes, and the other ministers in the area, particularly the Rev. Jacob Green. He ordered all of the soldiers not on sick call to attend weekly church services. He hired as many chaplains as possible and paid them $40 per month. He understood the special relationship between the soldier and chaplain.

He also made sure he only hired chaplains who loved the rebellion as much as they loved God (half the chaplains in Washington's army were Presbyterians, as was Rev. George Duffield, the chaplain to the Continental Congress). He counted on them to inspire the men politically as well as spiritually and convinced church leaders throughout the states, such as his friend the Rev. John Witherspoon, president of Princeton University and a delegate at the Second Continental Congress, to have ministers give rousing recruiting speeches at the end of their Sunday sermons. The ministers never failed to connect the commander-in-chief to the Almighty. ("Providence has fitted him for the charge and called him to the service," said Witherspoon of the general.)

They did not let him down. Several chaplains in winter camp not only led prayers but tended the sick and convinced many weary, homesick men to stay in the army. Some even participated in battles.

Washington also referred to "Providence" liberally. He constantly told correspondents that he was certain of the "smiles of a kind Providence" on the American cause and that the revolution was "under the protection of a Divine Providence" and that "a bountiful Providence has never failed us in our hour of distress."

Reverend Green had several New Light preachers as guest speakers at his church over the years and as a young man had known some of the leading evangelists, such as George Tennant, George Whitefield, and Jonathan Edwards, and listened to them, he later said, "with wonder and affection." Johnnes's Morristown Presbyterian Church was a vibrant New Light church and had undergone two major revivals, in 1764 and in 1774, which added 144 more parishioners, all evangelicals. Johnnes and the other Presbyterians, and their guest speakers, preached just what Washington wanted his men to hear—that God encouraged people to not only embrace new religious views, but the Revolution as well. They offered material as well as spiritual aide. Rev. Johnnes not only supported the army from the pulpit, but gave Washington a dozen acres of church-owned land where army warehouses were built.

Washington was equally pleased with the reception the army received from a former minister at the local Baptist church, the Reverend Gano, a leader in the evangelical movement in the 1760s and 1770s. Gano and his fellow Baptists had passed a resolution at a New Jersey religious convention condemning the Crown and supporting the rebellion. Gano enlisted in the army as a chaplain; church elders turned their church over to the army as a hospital for the winter of 1777.

Presbyterian ministers and church leaders throughout New Jersey were solidly behind the revolution from the beginning, but their opposition to the Crown was especially strong in New Jersey in the winter of 1777. In the fall of 1776, while chasing Washington to Pennsylvania, British troops had burned down several Presbyterian churches. Like others in the revolutionary era, Washington would always insist on the separation of church and state, but as a national executive in the war, and in later life, he would always acknowledge the critically important role religion played in American life. He, and those who followed him in national leadership, understood that Americans firmly believed that they were good, decent, and righteous people because God was within them.

The help of the press was another part of Washington's winter strategy. The general read as many newspapers as he could: American, Tory, and whatever London journals friends could smuggle to him. He had friends in every major city in the states send him their newspapers and asked anyone scheduled to visit him to bring along the latest editions. He read them to find out how the press and public felt about the army—and him—but also to determine what the British were doing.

He realized sooner than anyone in Congress how valuable a zealous patriotic press could be to the Revolution. Its editors needed copy and were very pleased to run propaganda stories about the army and its great victories (its losses sometimes became victories in their columns). He also persuaded dozens of editors of newspapers throughout the colonies to publish his own campaign dispatches, slightly rewritten, as news stories, as well as his proclamations.

The press particularly enjoyed publishing any stories or letters involving alleged British atrocities against citizens. Washington urged anyone he met who had any kind of story that even hinted at British abuse against Americans to describe it in letter form and mail it to a newspaper. The atrocity stories—real or exaggerated (or sometimes fabricated)—helped to galvanize the public against the British. The papers could be used as a propaganda division of both Congress and the army to build public support for the war.

Washington and others implored Americans living in Europe to write favorable letters about the American cause to newspapers and magazines in the foreign cities where they resided, and was always pleased when his friends wrote articles in the language of the country (Livingston wrote in Dutch).

The general thought that positive newspaper coverage of the war was essential for reasons beyond mere support. There would be times when he would need substantial and/or emergency help from Congress, the states, and the people. He had to convince people, no matter their station or influence, to see him and the army in a favorable light so that they would help when called upon. If newspaper editors wrote praising stories about the commander-in-chief and the army, then that praise must be well founded. The knowledge that the press was convincing the people to support him gave Washington substantial political clout with local, state, and national public figures. They read the papers, too.

He was so upset that there were no newspapers to push the cause of the rebellion in New Jersey that on several occasions he asked Congress to appropriate money for a newspaper that would be published in camp and distributed to the troops and thousands of residents of New Jersey. He was turned down by Congress, but, at his persistent urging, and with Governor Livingston's influence, the New Jersey legislature did find funds for the founding of the highly partisan *New Jersey Gazette*, published in Burlington, in South Jersey, starting in late 1777. Washington never gave up on the idea of a completely controlled, army-backed newspaper for the troops and citizens.

Washington's officer councils, voluminous correspondence, dinners with aides, meetings with ministers, talks with his troops, and endless monitoring of British and national opinion through newspapers enabled him to always know the feelings of the people, a tenet of Machiavelli's "good prince." He personified, too, both in America and across the ocean, the idea of the "patriot king," first expressed by the English writer Henry St. John, the Viscount Bolingbroke. Bolingbroke was one of many who believed that people yearned for a monarch who was of royal heritage but always acted for the good of the common folk and not the rich or titled. Ironically, it was in the American Washington, and not the very royal George III, that English speaking peoples found him.

Analyzing the Enemy

Washington's great fear continued to be a British attack. The commander, who spent considerable time analyzing his English counterparts, knew that they did not like to fight in winter, even with their large army. If the British knew his real size, they would swat the Continental Army down like a defenseless gnat. "I believe the enemy have fixed their object and the execution will surely be attempted as soon as the roads are passable.

The unprepared state in which we are favors all their designs," he anxiously wrote Hancock in March.

He had to make the British unwilling to risk a confrontation with a sizable and well-armed American force, even if it didn't exist. First, he posted sentries as far as nine miles away from his camps. He had soldiers build beacon fire pits on hilltops that, if lit, could warn of British movement. The fires could easily be seen in Morristown and other villages where troops were quartered. Alarm horns were erected. He ordered General William Heath to take several thousand men and fake an attack on Kingsbridge, near New York, to make the British think he was prepared for battle at any moment. He ordered soldiers in the New Jersey camps to forage for food wherever they could and to fire on any British soldiers they found who were on forage missions of their own (in one skirmish, the Americans claimed to have killed several dozen British out on their own foraging expedition). These encounters were important, as Hamilton told Congress, because "they serve to harass and distress the enemy."

The soldiers involved in the foraging war saw firsthand how effective they could be. "Scarce a day passed without an attempt to forage and plunder, but the vigilance and bravery of our troops obliges the enemy to return commonly without plunder and often with a very great loss of their men. The enemy too well know the fate that must attend their passing the woods and mountains which leads to Morris County to hazard such an expedition," one soldier explained in a letter to a newspaper. The success of the foragers rattled British soldiers, who found themselves trying to find and fight an enemy in the forests and glens, where their training did them little good.

Washington wanted as many skirmishes as possible to impress the British. The foragers seemed to be everywhere, British scouts reported to Lord Howe. The heavy number of foragers meant, Howe believed, that they were needed to commandeer supplies for a very large army. It was an army, too, Howe was convinced from the false alarm at Kingsbridge and his disastrous encounters in Princeton and Trenton, that was ready to fight in any weather.

Washington told townspeople to keep an eye out for the British whenever they traveled and to report any soldiers they saw in uniform or odd-looking strangers. Later, he would employ spies to augment the work of this complex ring of protection.

Washington worked as closely as he could with local residents to build support for the army in the community. The people had to admire and respect the army before they could help it. To do that, the people had to admire and respect the leader of the army. He began the promotional campaign right after the fall of Trenton. He had soldiers distribute all of the belongings of the Hessians captured in that encounter to those citizens throughout central New Jersey whose homes were ransacked by the British. He also issued strict orders that forbid similar plundering by American troops and convinced state officials to do the same.

The commander went out of his way to hold meetings with civic and religious leaders in the communities where the army stayed for any period of time. He always sought out advice from locals and made them feel that they were important. He continually told them that the army could not survive without the help of the public. That public-relations campaign, which lasted throughout the war, created alliances with ordinary people that gave the army needed support. Carefully planned by the general, that effort slowly created a marriage between the army and the civilians. They soon came to believe that, whether in or out of uniform, they were all comrades in the rebellion.

These protective measures would give Washington the time he needed to hold the army together and slowly rebuild it through a spirited recruitment drive he intended to launch as soon as the men settled in at Morristown.

By the winter of 1777, Washington was getting better at strategic planning, an early weakness. He tried to think like the British in order to outwit them. He was satisfied, in January, that the British goal was to divide America by maintaining a large force in New York, the geographic center of the colonies, their most important port and its second-largest city. From there, Washington surmised, Howe would sail up the Hudson River, ordering Burgoyne's army down from Canada to join him; split

New England from the Middle Atlantic States; and then, in a series of strikes, move east and west to smash American forces; take Providence and Newport; and recapture Boston.

If they adopted that strategy, Washington would try to thwart them with his own small armies. Now, in Morristown, he had positioned his army to monitor any British movement across New Jersey toward Philadelphia or up the Hudson. He had Heath's army at Peekskill, on the Hudson, and Benedict Arnold's army nearby in Rhode Island ready to move at sudden notice to intercept the Redcoats. This was, in fact, Howe's exact plan. He had asked Lord George Germain, head of the colonial office, for thirty-five thousand more troops to accomplish it. Germain, although skeptical of the need for so many troops, agreed to it in principle and also ordered General John "Gentleman Johnny" Burgoyne to attack Albany from Canada. The British would not be able to move without tenacious harassment from the Americans, though. They would have to leave a large force behind to hold the large cities. They would always be forced to fight an offensive war.

The Americans, Washington believed from the time the first shots were fired at Lexington and Concord, could win by fighting differently. "The war should be defensive," he had told Congress. "We should on all occasions avoid a general action, or put anything at risk, unless compelled by necessity." He would fight a war of attrition. Unable to defeat the Americans, tired of losing men and equipment, and weary of the great cost of the American war and the criticism a long conflict would surely bring, Washington was certain, England would simply quit.

Although he complained endlessly about the local militias, he had learned how to use the militia along with his artillery, Continental Army regulars, and frontier riflemen to create an effective fighting force. He now knew where to deploy his forces if Howe or Burgoyne did make a move. And, finally, he had used the army to create an image of unified purpose to win sympathy from the people. He hoped the people would help the army wherever it went. As he worked hard to win the war, he continued to deplore it. "It is really a strange thing that there should not be room enough in the world for men to live without cutting one another's throats," he told the Marquis de Lafayette years later.

But to capitalize on his initial success, George Washington needed time. Any national leader needs as much time as events will permit to study available options before making a critical decision. Days and weeks not only give a leader time to think and sort out ways in which his policies can be pursued, but time to evaluate prior policy decisions and to determine the effect on any one action on others. Wise leaders make careful decisions, based on study and consultation with others; bad leaders make quick, impulsive decisions based upon personal instinct and with little consideration of alternative plans. Aware of this critical need, some leaders, such as Franklin Roosevelt, arranged their days and weeks to build in time for reflection and have frequently delayed decisions in order to have as much information as possible before deciding on a plan.

Following the hectic events of December and January, George Washington needed as much time as he could obtain in order to reorganize the army and decide upon future military policy. He needed time to discuss his plans with other officers and to solicit their opinion at his frequent officers' councils. The general had to assess the strength and morale of the American army before he could determine how to deal with the British in the spring. That estimation would require reports involving troop strength in Rhode Island, New York, and in Morristown, plus the health of the men. He would need the state of the supply warehouses and some estimations from Congress concerning future food and clothing shipments. Now, with winter upon both sides, he had to estimate the size of the English forces and determine what course of action Lords Howe and Cornwallis might take in the winter and spring. Washington always tried to think like the British would; how they would react to something the Americans did. He needed time in order to work with Congress and representatives in France to develop more persuasive methods to convince the government of King Louis to support the Americans.

It was critical, in a state where there were still so many British sympathizers, that Washington utilize all of his personal skills to rally the public to the cause of the rebellion. Victories at Trenton and Princeton had to be followed up with a public-relations campaign to ensure that America's new-found liberty frenzy lasted. He bought himself valuable time in the winter of 1777 and in all the winters of the war.

Washington's Most Pressing Problem: The Loyalists

Washington's recruitment drive to expand the size of the army and the public-relations campaign to win over the hearts of the people never properly developed as planned because during that first winter in Morristown, Washington was confronted with troubles that never seemed to end.

The most pressing was that of the Loyalists. He had chosen Morristown because it was home to a number of patriots, but the tiny community and the surrounding area was populated by thousands of British sympathizers. It was estimated that nineteen thousand Loyalists lived in New Jersey. Most of these men and women remained true to England because they did not believe the colonies should separate from the motherland. Others had ambivalent feelings toward the Revolution, and little love for England, but were certain that the rebels would fail and that they would profit by remaining loyal to Great Britain. Others were convinced that the continued war would mean the destruction of America's cities. They agreed with Joseph Galloway, a Loyalist publisher and former speaker of the Pennsylvania Assembly, who pleaded for a new plan in which the Americans would have some representation in Parliament. Several thousand Loyalists, fearful of reprisals, had abandoned their stores and farms and sailed to England. Many more huddled in Tory enclaves, such as New York, until they could leave, too.

Some joined the British army and fought against their neighbors. A Loyalist group in South Jersey ransacked the homes of patriots there in the winter and spring of 1777, causing one resident to write that "the inhabitants are afraid of every person they see." He was not alone. There were small Loyalist armies in several colonies, even in Washington's native Virginia, whose troops had been promised sums of money and/or land in return for their military service.

The Tories were despised by the rebels. One sharp-tongued New Jersey man called them "undesirables of the lowest order...corrupted vampires, unprincipled wretches, the dregs and offscourings of human nature." (Apparently on a personal front, Tom Paine complained bitterly that all of the prostitutes in America were Tories.) Some were driven out of towns and had their property confiscated. Others were beaten. Some were tarred and feathered and others threatened with hanging. Many lost their businesses when patriots boycotted their stores and refused to buy produce from their farms.

Loyalists were a very big problem and an immediate threat to the army in Morristown. Washington was sure they would refuse to aid his soldiers, who would need provisions and supplies, and, worse still, become spies for the British. The commander wanted to cleanse Morristown and the rest of the colonies of the British sympathizers. To do that, Congress might take months, which was too long.

Again, acting on the extraordinary authority granted to him by Congress, Washington assumed the powers of a national executive. On January 25, he had issued a proclamation that ordered any and all colonists who had sworn allegiance to the Crown to report to American army posts by the beginning of March in order to take a loyalty oath. "They have been lost to the interest and welfare of their country," the general said. Those Tories who did not report, Washington directed, had to move their families within British lines and would be declared "common enemies" of the American states. The proclamation was issued, according to the general, because "it had become necessary to distinguish between the friends of America and those of Great Britain."

There was another reason. Washington knew that thousands of Loyalists in New Jersey had been repulsed by British behavior when Howe chased the American army through the state in the fall of 1776. British troops had plundered farmhouses, crossroad villages, and even entire towns, such as Princeton. The British persecution had turned many of the Loyalists away from the Crown and toward the Americans. Now, in the winter of 1777, Washington hoped to crush the sympathies of the remaining Loyalists once and for all.

Washington never wavered in his drive to rid the colonies of Tories. The United States, he believed, had to be just that—united. "The more united the inhabitants appear, the greater difficulty Howe will find in reconciling them to regal government and consequently the less hope of conquering them," he wrote Congress and added that the oath would lead to "the destruction of the opposition."

Washington, thinking as a politician and not just a general, knew that he would be supported by Governor Livingston, who hated Loyalists and saw them all as traitors, as he told the New Jersey Assembly in a heated speech: "They have warred upon decrepit age and upon defenseless youth. They have committed hostilities against the possessors of literature and the ministers of religion....They have butchered the wounded, asking for quarter; mangled the dying, weltering in their blood."

Washington remembered that Livingston had been a Brigadier General in charge of all of the state militia companies and during the previous summer had rounded up dozens of Loyalists and sent them off, under guard, to state officials. As soon as he became governor in 1776, he formed a Committee on Safety, and appointed himself chairman, to punish Loyalists wherever they could be found. In his friend, Washington not only had a governor who would not oppose him on the loyalty issue, but an ally who would help him.

The loyalty oath created some opposition in state legislatures and Congress. It seemed dictatorial to some, particularly New Jersey legislator Abraham Clark, who said he was "alarmed" and told John Hart, speaker of the New Jersey Assembly, that "He [Washington] hath assumed the legislative and executive powers of government in all the states" and violated the civil rights of all Americans. Despite their protests, Congress later approved Washington's actions.

Following Washington's proclamation, all of the colonies passed various acts to punish those who refused to take the oath or were deemed Tories. It was what Washington had hoped for. It spurred civilian authorities to do what he wanted them to do, but under legislative and not military mandate.

It was a step down a dangerous path. The patriots often had difficulty winning over neutrals to their side because they frequently denied the liberty to others that they demanded for themselves. Patriotic gangs had physically beaten Tories. The property of British officials and English sympathizers had been destroyed or confiscated. Unpopular newspaper editors had been forcefully restrained while their offices were ransacked and their presses damaged or destroyed. And now General Washington had decided that there was only room for one set of political opinions—his.

The commander's insistence on the pledge of allegiance and the persecution of those who refused to take it was the first in a long series of loyalty oaths that would tarnish the reputations of several national leaders who followed him. In similar policy decisions, during the Civil War Abraham Lincoln suspended the writ of habeas corpus, had political foes arrested, and ordered the closure of newspapers that opposed his views. Woodrow Wilson would shut down more than a dozen newspapers that opposed American involvement in World War I. Senator Joe McCarthy conducted a witch-hunt for what he termed unloyal Americans in the 1950s. They all fell into the same controversial trap as General Washington, which was to violate freedom of some in order to protect freedom of many.

Washington wanted harsh measure taken, but did not want to appear vindictive, so he had Hamilton send out letters, under Hamilton's name, ordering other generals, and the civilian authorities, to be severe. The brassy Hamilton, acting on Washington's orders, even suggested hangings. "An execution or two, by way of example, would strike terror, and powerfully discourage the wicked practices going on," he wrote to the New York Committee of Correspondence. Hamilton told Livingston that the commander-in-chief wanted action: "It is the ardent wish of His Excellency that no delay might be used in making examples of some of the most atrocious offenders."

The general himself let subordinates know that he was not very concerned about the legality of any arrests and wanted a fast response. He sent a courier to General Samuel Parsons with a copy of the proclamation and told Parsons to begin arresting people without waiting for any official documents. "No form of an oath of allegiance is yet drawn up," he told him, "but you can easily strike off one that will answer the end designed." And Washington was in no hurry to undo any harms caused by the rush to round up Tories by the army or local boards, telling General Thomas Mifflin that he would not use his considerable influence to release a man Mifflin said had been unfairly arrested. "It is not in my power to release any man from confinement imposed upon him by the civil power," he told Mifflin.

The anti-Loyalist campaign grew to a feverish pitch and Tories were vehemently denounced. Congressional delegate William Whipple called them "pests to society," and delegate Roger Sherman said they were "most dangerous [people]." Delegate William Whipple said each state should simply "banish all the wretches." And New Yorker Nathaniel Whitaker called them "cowardly, selfish, cringing, lukewarm, half-way, two-faced people." Some states and counties created committees for the sole purpose of prosecuting the Loyalists. New York created the Committee and Commission for Detecting and Defeating Conspiracies. In the spring of 1777, following Washington's edict, the New York Committee promptly authorized the hanging of fourteen Loyalists.

The New Jersey Committee of Safety, which often met in Morristown, convened once a week in what soon would become a full-scale witch-hunt for real or imaginary Loyalists. The Council heard several hundred cases that winter and spring. Its members authorized Washington to make arrests and send the suspects to the Council and local judges to take the oath when military personnel were not available. On Washington's orders, officers arrested hundreds of Loyalists. At one point, the general even sent twenty-five soldiers from Morristown to South Jersey to help guard a large group of newly arrested Tories at the request of Governor Livingston. One group of suspected Loyalists was arrested in Maryland, incarcerated in Philadelphia, and then put on trial in New Jersey.

Washington was a key figure in the process and often met with the Council, which convened at the home of Silas Condict, a member, one block from his headquarters. If the Council did not have enough evidence against someone—usually given by neighbors—the man was simply jailed until it could be found. Men languished in prison for weeks. John Duyckman was held in a Philadelphia jail for two months, without charges ever being brought against him, before he was released. Many were kept under house arrest. John Johnson, his sister, and her son, of New York, spent several weeks in jail waiting until evidence could be found to incriminate them. They were finally released when it was determined that "nothing specially having appeared against them."

One of the most zealous boards held hearings in Dutchess County, New York. It had the local militia round up hundreds of Loyalists and held so many hearings that by the beginning of the summer of 1778 it had already used up its annual budget. That commission imprisoned large populations of men and women (children were considered, but then ignored). The commission often exceeded its authority to utilize the militia, once even ordering it to break up a local robbery ring. The Dutchess County board incarcerated so many local men and women on no or little evidence that it had to turn away captured British soldiers because the county jail was full of Tories.

Loyalists were incarcerated in unusual prisons. The Ulster County, New York, jail was quickly filled to capacity and judges began to imprison Tories in a flotilla of vessels anchored in the Hudson River. Some Tories arrested in Simsbury, Connecticut, were housed at the bottom of a local copper mine; their food was provided by buckets lowered by a winch.

Wholesale Loyalist raids were ordered. In the summer of 1777, General William Winds was sent to arrest seventy-three Bergen County Tories and other raids that summer resulted in more than one hundred arrests. September manhunts produced more. Fifty men were held in the small and badly ventilated Morristown jail to await trial. They did not have sufficient water and the summer heat was stifling. Many became sick; their families feared they would die.

A separate group of men were put on trial in the fall. As critics of the loyalty oath and its subsequent campaign predicted, more than half of those arrested were released because there was no evidence of criminality. Promised amnesty for enlistment, thirty men found guilty and given jail terms joined the Continental Army. Thirty-five were sentenced to death but were pardoned upon enlistment. The chilling finale of the trial involved the cases of Loyalists James Jeliff and John Mee. Both were sentenced to die with the others but then given a chance to confess to their particular crimes (recruiting for the British and fighting against the local militia) and join the army. The men refused. The county sheriff warned them repeatedly that they would be hanged if they did not confess. The two men, either staunchly loyal to the King or believing that General Washington would urge Governor Livingston to pardon them at the last minute, remained firm in their convictions. They were hanged. Washington, informed of the executions, said nothing (he also ignored property confiscations repeatedly brought to his attention).

The attacks on the Loyalists extended to households. Livingston and his Council kept lengthy lists of women in Newark who were married to departed Loyalists and asked local residents to keep an eye on them, always suspicious that they, too, were Tories. Other women and their children in that city were deported out of the state. The crusade even reached into churches when a minister from Newark was brought before the Council in Morristown on charges of disloyalty and jailed, even though his real crime seemed to be the high fees he charged his parishioners in his sideline business as a doctor.

During the campaign, undertaken with Washington's approval, a number of prominent residents had their lives ruined. John Hutchinson was a successful farmer in Parsippany when the Continental Army arrived. Although there was no evidence against him, Hutchinson had unfortunately sent three of his sons into the British Army to fight against Americans (two were killed in action). His punishment for parenthood was a fine plus a term in the Morristown jail. Then, in 1780, his third son, William, was captured in Elizabeth and hanged as a spy. Hutchinson, his wife and daughters, fearful of hanging or imprisonment themselves, fled, abandoning their large farm. Leaving his family in New York, Hutchinson tried to reach England, but perished when his ship sank.

Perhaps the most tawdry story was that of Mrs. Catherine Van Cortlandt, the wife of Loyalist Philip Van Cortlandt, who left Morris when he learned soldiers were on their way to arrest him. Men burst into his home later that night, swords brandished, and demanded to know where he was. Catherine, holding her children next to her, refused to tell them.

A detachment of soldiers remained at the home, hoping that Van Cortlandt would return. He did not; Van Cortlandt fled to New York, where he joined a Loyalist detachment of the British Army. The soldiers moved in and behaved, Catherine wrote her husband, "in a manner that would disgrace the most savage barbarians." She and her children became pariahs. The children were so harassed by other children at the local school that their mother pulled them out. Reverend Green soon began to denounce Van Cortlandt as a traitor from the pulpit of his church. Neighbors shunned her. Local farmers would not sell her food, and she and her children began to starve.

Finally, unable to endure her treatment any longer, Catherine went to see General Washington, who snubbed her and ordered her to turn her home into a hospital for smallpox victims; she could stay or leave. She went back to Washington. He would not see her, but gave her a safe-conduct pass so she could leave town.

Mrs. Van Cortlandt's flight to find her husband was perilous. She piled her children and some belongings into two wagons. She rode up front with one of her slaves. A second wagon with the remainder of her slaves and belongings followed. They drove to Hackensack in a snow-storm. At Hackensack Ferry, local militiamen fired a volley of shots over their heads. Other soldiers stopped the wagons and broke open chests, trunks, and boxes and looted them

Near New York, she asked a farmer if she could buy some milk for her children. The man prepared to give her children milk, but then asked who she was. She told him.

"I will not give a drop of milk to any Tory bitch," the man said.

Scared but determined to spirit her children out of New Jersey, Catherine Van Cortlandt ignored the insult and traveled on to New York, where she was reunited with her husband. Their family left with the British army when the war ended. They lived for a time in Canada, then Spain, and then England. The Van Cortlandts never returned to the United States and lost all of their property and belongings.

The New Jersey Council on Safety was led by the most ardent Tory hunter in America, Livingston. It was the governor who told the Council on Safety to imprison whomever they wanted without bail. He also gave the Council independent powers and even permitted them to demand special sessions of the assembly to address their needs. The New Jersey Council had the right to arrest people in one county and jail them in another. Any offer of aid or comfort of any kind to the British was considered a treasonous act. The governor, particularly overheated at one point, even decried that he would hang anyone in New Jersey who did not have a loyalty oath on their person when stopped by the militia.

The vendetta became extreme, particularly in Morristown, where local judges, in an effort to gain the good graces of General Washington, began to move beyond the oath and issued indictments against residents for merely disagreeing with the Revolution under a "seditious words" statute, and the number of people indicted for their opinions became substantial. Everybody seemed to be pointing a finger at someone in what was becoming a vicious witch hunt in the name of independence.

The Continental Congress became increasingly unhappy. The loyalty oath had divided friends and family, and in many places was judged to have done more harm than good. "Brother has been fighting against brother, a father against son and there is too much reason to fear that worse is to follow," wrote Congressman Henry Laurens to his son in the winter of 1777.

By late April, Washington, too, began to fear that the crusade was out of control. Through Hamilton, he urged local, county, and state committees to take their time in passing judgment on men and women brought before them because evidence might not be available to support charges, and many were probably turned in by neighbors who did not like them. The general asked local officials to simply dismiss all minor charges, prosecuting only those accused of major crimes, such as spying.

"Private pique and resentment had had their influence in causing some innocent persons to be apprehended; and that, in many instances, there was so slight a foundation of guilt as made it highly impolitic to meddle with them. It is always injurious to apprehend those whose cases are such as afterwards oblige us to acquit or discharge them," Hamilton wrote one governor on the commander's behalf. Washington now also insisted on combing through the records of those arrested and reading many of the charges himself. He then asked local committees to exonerate most of those arrested.

He also tried to make amends and rebuild communities fractured by the loyalty campaign. "It has been represented to me by Captain Kinney that there are many people in the county who are really innocent of any crime or evil design against their country, but having been seen in company with some notoriously disaffected who have been tampering with them, they fear they will be considered of their party and have therefore fled," he told the governing board of Sussex County, New Jersey. "Captain Kinney says he is informed that if they were certain of being well received, they would return to their homes, give any kind of security for their future good behavior and become peaceable inhabitants of the county and state. I therefore think you had better make the offer of pardon to such as you think deserve it and invite them to return."

Washington knew that by issuing the loyalty oath, he would set off a military and civilian firestorm. He knew that, in the end, he could control the army's response to the Loyalists but he could not control any of the actions of the states, sheriffs, and courts. He unleashed the persecutions, some just and some unjust, probably certain that hundreds of people would be injured in some way and that many would be ruined and some even executed. He did it, though, because he believed it was the only way in which he could rid Morristown, and the United States, of the Loyalists who might destroy the army. His goal as the commander was to keep the army alive and win the war. Harsh measures sometimes had to be taken to achieve that goal. So be it.

Just when the smallpox outbreak appeared to seem under control, more troubles arose. Washington was soon faced with creeping inflation that threatened to choke the army and the local economy. The American people, used to reliable currency such as the British pound or Spanish dollar, were reluctant to use the new Continental Congress script. The government had flooded the thirteen colonies with the paper money, but because the people clung to the "hard dollars," paper script was starting to become worthless. New Continental "loan certificates," which were issued in mid-December, just meant more useless paper to most people.

Shaken by the rising cost of nearly everything, Congress ordered states to force merchants to hold down prices. The New England states met at a financial summit in Providence, Rhode Island, in January 1777, and representatives agreed to a year of strict price controls. Massachusetts was the toughest of the states in enforcing the controls. To further uphold the value of script, Congress also ordered that all taxes and army bills had to be paid with it. The people paid little attention to the new state edicts or Congressional pleas. Efforts at national price controls failed following a raucous debate in Congress in mid-February. Some delegates favored it, such as the flustered Samuel Chase, who told Congress that "the [gold] mines of Peru would not support a war at the present high price of the necessaries of life." But others, such as Benjamin Rush, argued that price controls previously used by English and other European countries had not worked. Many agreed with delegates such as John Adams, John Witherspoon, and James Wilson, who said a democratic government could not fix prices. Adding a colorful historical touch, Wilson reminded the delegates that "the whole power of the Roman emperors could not add a single letter to the alphabet." The campaign to regulate prices died quickly.

Script was also devalued by a vast counterfeiting scheme, run by the British, designed to wreck the colonial economy. The rather simply designed script was easy to duplicate on special presses. The English also managed to reproduce nearly perfect duplicates of paper bills used by the different states. Howe's counterfeit unit produced millions of dollars in script. The British even advertised bundles of the money for sale, cheap, in Tory newspapers. Washington called the British counterfeiters "villains." Josiah Bartlett, when told of the counterfeit bills in New Hampshire, said it was "a diabolical scheme" to ruin America.

Prices soared. In the Morristown area, salt jumped from two to twenty-five schillings. The cost of a pair of shoes leaped from seven schillings to fifteen. A pound of butter increased from 2 to 2.6 schillings.

The price of a cord of firewood doubled; linen tripled. Inflation was everywhere. In New England, sugar costs were up 10 percent, tea 25 percent, and meat 66 percent. Prices of drinks increased and so did meals, hotel rooms, carriages, and horses. Merchants quickly realized they could buy price-controlled goods in Massachusetts and sell them at huge profits in their own state. Soon prices were rising throughout the whole Atlantic seaboard. "Everything here bears a high price," Oliver Wolcott of Philadelphia groaned to his wife. "The avaricious, the timid and the disaffected have all conspired to produce that evil."

The spiraling inflation impeded the army in Morristown, which relied on farmers and shopkeepers for food and necessities. Many farmers would set two prices, one for hard currency and a second, usually 15 percent higher, for script. Very few farmers would sell any food to the army on credit alone. Civilians argued over the price of everything with officers in charge of foraging and wrote damning letters about them to headquarters. If asked to lease wagons or other equipment for a day, they insisted on year-long contracts. An officer who hinted to one farmer that the army might simply requisition his goods without payment was threatened. "I will blow out your brains," wailed the farmer.

By the end of the winter in Morristown, troops and their wagons were traveling more than thirty miles to buy food for the army. Some farmers would not even accept script for purchases. (The refusal even extended to the soldiers recuperating from smallpox in local hospitals. One man recovering from the disease begged Henry Knox to loan him hard money because merchants would not sell him anything.)

Everybody began to raise prices on items the army needed. Congressional delegate William Whipple wrote Connecticut's Governor Trumbull a savage letter denouncing the high prices of cannons in his state. "It will be an example for all others to demand the like prices….and spread jealousy and discord among the United States, to say that the state of Connecticut had in this instance taken advantage of the [nation]."

An exasperated Hancock, on behalf of Congress, wrote an emergency circular to all the states concerning spiraling costs "to remedy the evils occasioned by the exorbitant prices of manufacture and articles of trade."

In Morristown, the General's quartermasters complained that they could not obtain any food. "The cry of want of provisions comes to me from all quarters—General Maxwell writes word that his men are starving. General Johnson, of Maryland, yesterday informed me that his people could draw none [food]," Washington wrote the head of the commissary and fumed later that "No army was ever worse supplied than ours."

No army was unable to pay its bills like the American, either. His aides continually reminded Washington that rising prices meant they could not buy food or get men to sign up for service with bounties that meant little. "The treasury has been for some time empty and the army has labored under the greatest inconveniences for want of money. I have complaints…of the want of money to carry on recruiting. If we are not supplied with that all matters must be at stand," Washington warned Congress.

At the same time, the general found himself in a lengthy correspondence with British generals and Congress in an effort to have the captured General Charles Lee returned to him, with no luck. The Americans had not captured anyone of Lee's stature and could not arrange an exchange of prisoners. Washington cared little for Lee, but he needed experienced field commanders.

All of this made Washington extremely agitated. In late February, he complained in a letter to his brother about "parasite" Loyalists, the "evil" deserters, fretted about what Howe would do next, and seemed despondent. He had lost Hugh Mercer, Jacob Ford and his son, and General Daniel Hitchock, all dead within the last month. The general had been so depressed in a mid-February letter to Robert Morris that the financier, concerned, wrote him back that he was too morbid and that things would be better for everyone if "the bright side of our affairs was to be sometimes painted by your pen." Washington sighed to a dinner guest that he and his aides worked morning until night on army business and "I give into no kind of amusement myself." Tilghman, who saw Washington each day, watched as the commander slipped further and further into despondency. His aide knew how drained he was. "The weight of the whole war…may be said to lay upon his shoulders," he said.

The endless work and increased worries had begun to take their toll on the general. As the winter months passed in Morristown, he became frustrated by Congress. The supervision of the smallpox inoculations required enormous personal effort. His campaign to woo the governors of the various states had worn him down, as had the increasingly complex efforts to rebuild the army. Friends in and out of the army often asked him to intercede in their family squabbles, and he was soon embroiled in a feud between Lord Stirling and his mother-in-law. And if all of those worries were not enough to demoralize him, in February, news discreetly arrived in Morristown that back in Virginia, Washington's mother Mary, never a champion of the rebellion, was again behaving in public very much like a British sympathizer.

He also found himself saddled with more and more army work because, at the same time, his "family" of aides had been dramatically reduced. He only had two experienced aides, Tench Tilghman and John Fitzgerald, to help him. In late February, he had dispatched Caleb Gibbs, head of his guard and an aide who handled administrative work, to Philadelphia and was making plans to send General Greene there as well. Another aide, Robert Harrison, had become so ill in mid-February that he had been unable to work or get out of bed. Yet another, George Baylor, rode to Baltimore to present the Hessian colors captured at Trenton to Congress and was then reassigned. Both Sam Webb and William Grayson had been given regimental commands during the first week of January and were gone. George Johnston, hired as an aide in mid-January, was still learning the job and not yet very effective. Washington had made Alexander Hamilton an aide, but he was not due to report until early March. Washington could not replace his missing aides with other top officers because he had sent most of them back home to their states in order to recruit men. The commander, overwhelmed with office work and with few to help him, wound up doing much of the work himself, in addition to his other duties. He soon became physically and mentally exhausted.

Then, on February 24, the worst snowfall in thirty-five years, "an extraordinary storm" according to an amateur meteorologist, hit the

Middle Atlantic states. Snow fell for twenty-four hours. There was so much snow in New York City that streets were impassable. The snow was particularly troublesome in Morristown. There, more than fifteen inches fell on top of a deep previous snowfall. Winds created drifts several feet high.

An ardent micro-manager, Washington surely led the storm cleanup. He emerged from his headquarters the next day and, on horse and on foot, traveled throughout the Morristown area to supervise the removal of snow. He spent the next several days supervising the cleanup, and during this time developed a bad cold and sore throat. He had fallen victim to sore throats all of his life. Now, in extremely severe weather, he became very ill with quinsy, a bad throat infection, and was bedridden.

The stricken general did not get better. He became much worse and was unable to sit up or get out of bed. Dr. Cochran rushed to his side. He used the standard, primitive medical practices of the day, including bleeding Washington to draw out bad blood and applying a glass cup to his head to suck out tainted sweat. These measures had little effect. His condition worsened and he developed an abnormally high fever. Phlegm filled his throat and he could hardly breathe. The general knew that he was very ill and told Cochran that he was afraid he was going to die; the men in his family had a history of dying young (his father had passed away at age forty-nine). The doctor did not want him to go this way. The physician wanted the great man to slip off peacefully. He would not. The general was angry about dying, and grew angrier each day. He was mad that he was dying young, mad that his wife was not there at the end, indignant that he would no longer be able to lead the army, and fearful that an army without him would disintegrate.

Washington communicated the best he could with his aides. He summoned Nathaniel Greene to his bedside and reportedly told him, in front of Hamilton and others, that if he did not survive he wanted him to serve as the interim commander-in-chief until Congress appointed a new one. Greene assured Washington that he would outlive everyone in the army. But a concerned Greene delayed a planned trip to Philadelphia just in case Washington did not show some improvement.

He did not.

Hamilton had arrived in Morristown by March 1. He, Tilghman, Harrison, and Johnston all believed the general might die and urged Greene to prepare himself to lead the army. The young aides even discussed the problems of holding Washington's funeral in the snow.

It is unknown how many men were aware that Washington was very close to death. His aides sent dispatches to only a few key military and political figures with ominously worded messages about his grave condition. Governor Livingston, Washington's friend, and who would be needed for political stability in New Jersey if the general died, was one of these men. In an abrupt note written on March 8, Greene told him that "His Excellency General Washington is very unwell." The top generals in the army had to be informed. On March 10, Hamilton sent an urgent message to General McDougall in Peekskill, New York. "He has been very much indisposed for three or four days past, insomuch that his attention to business is pronounced by the doctor to be very improper," he wrote of the general, and added that his young aides and Greene were handling nearly all of the army's business while he was sick. "The only answer he would give may be given by myself," Hamilton told McDougall, explaining that the commander was incapacitated.

His aides, and those who knew of his illness, were careful to keep the secret. No one in Congress was told until later. The soldiers had not seen the general riding through camp on his horse, or galloping across the countryside, but reasoned that the snowstorm had kept him inside. The colonial newspapers did not learn of his illness until March 27, when the *Continental Journal* reported that he had been sick for several days but is now "perfectly recovered." His hometown paper, the *Virginia Gazette*, fed news by his friends, did not know of his brush with death until April 4. Most importantly, the British did not know that he was seriously ill, either. Washington's aides kept his condition quiet by concocting an elaborate coverup. They elicited decisions whispered by the general and maintained a steady flow of orders and letters from headquarters, all written by them in Washington's name. They knew Washington so well that they wrote many notes without even consulting him, as Hamilton suggested. The general's personal bodyguards were casually told that he was under the weather, nothing more.

Martha Washington had left Mount Vernon in late February for her annual winter camp visit, unaware of his perilous condition. She stopped off in Philadelphia to rest for a few days before proceeding to Morristown. On the night she arrived in Philadelphia, she was greeted by soldiers who told her in hushed tones that the general was failing badly. Martha was alarmed because she knew how vulnerable he had always been to throat infections. She left with them as quietly as possible early the next morning, without telling anyone the ominous news, and rushed to his side, her carriage traveling as quickly as her horses could pull it over roads covered with snow and ice.

Her arrival on March 15 seemed to boost his spirits and she nursed him, using a special formula of molasses and onions that had cured his throat inflammations in the past. Her homemade Mount Vernon remedy, plus Cochran's continued care, saved the general. He was up and about a few days after her arrival. Everyone breathed a sigh of relief when "the old man" started complaining about the army; that proved he was feeling better. His recovery was a relief to all and summed up best by Congressman Gouverneur Morris, who later said it caused "universal joy."

Chapter Five

REBUILDING
THE ARMY

MORRISTOWN, 1777

*"I do not think that any officer since
creation ever had such a variety of difficulties
and perplexities to encounter as I have."*
—George Washington

B edridden, Washington had plenty of time to think following his brush with death. It had reminded him, once again, that he could not run the army alone. No general, or national executive, could operate alone. He needed help.

The third week of March saw considerable activity in Washington's rooms on the second floor of Arnold's tavern. Sentries outside could see the figures of Hamilton, Harrison, Tilghman, Martha Washington, and Dr. Cochran moving about, day and night, as they cared for the slowly recovering commander-in-chief, who dutifully gulped down his wife's concoction of onions and molasses. Slowly, Washington slipped back into his daily routine. He put his cleaned blue and buff uniform back on, tied his wide sash tightly about his waist, and met with officers and local officials. He resumed dictating orders to his staff. Messages were taken by couriers on horseback through frigid weather to his generals in different locations. Hamilton and the others had managed to keep the army running smoothly and the general simply picked up where they had left off.

Always able to recognize his weaknesses as well as his strengths, Washington knew that he needed more aides to help him with his work. He added John Walker and Richard Meade to his staff. Young Hamilton had been easily assimilated into the general's "family" and soon became Washington's ambitious chief-of-staff, although he was never actually given that title. It is uncertain how the two men became acquainted, but sometime between the losses in New York and the victory at Trenton the handsome, outspoken young lieutenant from the West Indies had captured Washington's attention. The general needed a chief-of-staff, and in Hamilton he saw a man with all of the qualities the post required: determination, organization, communication skills, and loyalty. Hamilton was also extremely political and understood how the various governors, state officials, and Congressional delegates viewed the war. He had even published a political pamphlet when he was nineteen. In addition to his other skills, Hamilton, highly recommended by Knox and Greene, also spoke perfect French (the general did not). Hamilton's fluency would be valuable when the French entered the war on the American side, an alliance that would prove crucial for victory.

Later, Washington would say of Hamilton, "There are few men to be found of his age who have a more general knowledge than he possesses, and none whose soul is more firmly engaged to the cause, or who exceeds him in probity and sterling virtue."

His encounter with death had forced Washington to reassess his opinion of his once mercurial abilities to manage large operations and control his military chain of command. He might have been able to oversee a few forts in the French and Indian conflict, or several hundred laborers at Mount Vernon, but a national army was different. Here, in a very complex organization, he had learned that he needed capable aides at his side and that he had to delegate more work. He now saw his aides as European commanders did, as a circle of confidants within his wider circle of generals. He relied on their counsel. He also relied on the advice of his top officers, with whom he met regularly for policy discussions at the tavern.

The staff worked through the day with the general as he dictated letters and orders and kept notes on his own activities, pacing back and forth on the wide, creaking boards of the hardwood floor of the ballroom or his office. They supervised his appointments, arranged his meetings, and interceded for him with other officers. They were also his eyes and ears around camp, reporting problems and offering suggestions, saving him time and headaches.

But it was the frail, thin, wiry Hamilton, a full eight inches shorter than the general, often reading classic literature when not in the office, who became the driving force of the staff. His remarkable intelligence was recognized by everyone. He had become friendly with Governor Livingston and his family while a student at a private school in Elizabeth before the war. He was an intellectual, but, unlike many men of great learning, he was also a well-organized, hard-working administrator who streamlined the chain of command and served as the buffer between the commander-in-chief and the entire army. In Hamilton, Washington had a brilliant thinker, and also someone who got things done.

Hamilton took much of Washington's dictation, but was soon writing out the general's letters and orders himself, his own thinking a perfect reflection of his commander's. Washington rapidly expanded Hamilton's duties, putting him in charge of all headquarters operations in order to give himself more time for other work. He gave Hamilton surprising powers, permitting him to interview deserters, meet spies, communicate with generals, chair meetings of officers, and talk to local ministers and merchants on his behalf. He also allowed him to write public proclamations and newspaper columns signed with Washington's name. The general had no objections to the frequent political and economic advice that the talkative Hamilton offered to congressmen, governors, state legislators, and anyone else who would listen. He saw a younger version of himself in Hamilton, but a more brilliant self. And, at twenty, Hamilton had not yet developed the serious character flaws that much later would bring about his downfall.

The two were constantly together, whether in the office, at dinner, or riding with exuberance with longtime servant Billy Lee through the countryside in the late afternoon as the sun started to set over the thick forests. One courier, on a winter visit to Morristown, recalled that when he entered a room at Arnold's tavern late one evening, he found General Washington, his blue cloak pulled tightly about him, slumped in a chair in front of a fireplace full of dying embers. Opposite him on a bench, wrapped in a thin blanket, was Hamilton, chattering away about politics.

Washington's judgment in aides was superb. Later, from among the thirty-two young men who worked on his staff during the war, the United States acquired six cabinet officers, diplomatic representatives to Spain and Portugal, an associate justice of the Supreme Court, four governors, three U.S. senators, a president of the Continental Congress, a delegate to the Constitutional Convention, and a Speaker of the House of Representatives.

The general's return to good heath enabled him to mount his favorite horse, Nelson, and once again visit his officers and troops. The commander often rode slowly through the dirt lanes of the tent cities, which served as the army's camp in Morristown or the nearby villages. Soldiers there later told friends that while the commander generally made it a point to keep his distance from the enlisted men, he sometimes stopped to talk with them. He would usually halt in front of a group sitting around a fire or doing some camp work and, bending over his saddle, and holding his horse's reins gently, engage in conversation. Sometimes he wanted to know what their needs were, especially when he knew supplies were low. At other times he just wanted to hold casual conversations that had no military importance at all. The soldiers saw these friendly visits, albeit brief, as evidence that he cared for them.

Washington had developed a strong bond with his troops since he took command of the army in the summer of 1775. He had shown personal bravery and strategic skill, but what mattered to the soldiers was that the commander-in-chief was trustworthy. They always knew where they stood with him and firmly believed that he had their interests at heart, that they were important to him. This unshakable trust permitted them, and all who knew him, to forgive his earlier military mistakes and to rely on his leadership to bring eventual victory.

Now that Martha had arrived, the general's gloom slowly disappeared. She had lived with him during the winter in Boston and would be with him for at least two months of every winter camp throughout the war. He enjoyed everything about his wife, and was also able to talk to her, with much animation, about his frustrations concerning Congress, the army, and the war. He could not let his guard down with his aides or generals, but he could unleash all of his pent-up venom to Martha, who would listen and nod knowingly, merely happy to be his audience. The pair had a very close relationship and corresponded regularly while he was away, but what was written disappeared in 1802, after Washington's death, when Martha burned their hundreds of wartime letters, correspondence which, if preserved, might have given scholars and public figures a remarkable insight into the life of America's first couple.

Mrs. Washington's arrival eased tension everywhere in camp. Her presence permitted evenings in Morristown to be far more social. In late March, Washington, surely at Martha's urging, allowed a number of officers to invite their wives to travel to Morristown and move in with them at their crowded homes. It was then that he encouraged Governor Livingston to do the same. The Governor moved into Lord Stirling's Basking Ridge mansion with his wife and family. At the end of the workday, Washington would often host dinner parties at Arnold's tavern or attend dinners at Stirling's home or at the home of John Jacob Faesch or other ironworks owners (dinner was usually served at 3 or 4 P.M. in the colonial era). When it was safe, he would ride with his aides over twenty miles of highways to Livingston's mansion in Elizabeth for dinners, sometimes protected by only a dozen men. He would be joined by the officers and their wives and any visiting governors, Congressmen, or foreign dignitaries who might be visiting Morristown with their wives.

The commander never sat at the head of the table at these dinners, which could last as long as three hours, always preferring a side seat so that he could lean back in his chair and enjoy the company. He looked forward to these dinners because he could slip out of his stoic military commander's persona and simply be himself. As they began lengthy dinners with the commander-in-chief, those who had never met him before at first were impressed with his august appearance. "Washington is brave without temerity, laborious without ambition, generous without prodigality, noble without pride, virtuous without severity," enthused a wealthy French philosopher and general, Chevalier de Chastellux, who dined with him often. An American army surgeon who was a dinner guest summed up the views of many when he wrote that "the serenity of his countenance, and majestic gracefulness of his deportment, impart a strong impression of that dignity and granduer which are his peculiar characteristics."

Yet, as the often three-hour dinner parties progressed, guests saw a different Washington than the stern military leader. First, he did not look at all like the hundreds of paintings of him that hung in public buildings and homes throughout America, or had been reproduced in books and magazines. "His face is much more agreeable than represented in his portrait," claimed Prince de Broglie, a dinner guest who felt like others, such as Jean Pierre Brissot De Warville, that "the General's goodness appears in his looks…in conversation they become animated." John Bell remarked that "there was a remarkable air of dignity about him, with a striking degree of gracefulness." One French officer at a dinner said of his face that it was "never stern, and, on the contrary, becomes softened by the most gracious and amiable smile. He is affable and converses with his officers familiarly and gaily." Another man added that "in conversation, His Excellency's countenance is peculiarly interesting and pleasing." After the war, aide David Humphreys often described the general's facial appearance in private as "animated."

Some of the best descriptions of the general at ease, though, were offered by women. Mrs. Martha Bland, an officer's wife who dined with him frequently in Morristown, was one. "He commands both sexes, one by his excellent skill in military matters, the other by his ability, politeness and attention. From dinner 'til night he is free for all his company," she said, like so many women who only saw his social side and were not witness to his military gruffness. Abigail Adams, writing years later when Washington was president, said that "he is polite with dignity, grave without austerity, modest, wise and good. These are traits in his character which peculiarly fit him for the exalted station he holds and God grant that he may hold it with the same applause and universal satisfaction for many, many years."

But one thing that those who met him privately constantly remarked upon, as did those who only saw him in public, was that George Washington not only dressed and acted like the leader of an army and the head of a nation, but did it with panache. Visitors' reactions were perhaps summed up best by French officer Count Axel de Fersen, who met him near the end of the war and wrote simply in his journal of Washington that "he looks the hero."

Everyone was impressed by his humility, and one visitor was stunned that "he speaks of the war as if he had not directed it; and of his victories with an indifference which strangers even would not affect." And all were transfixed by his blue-gray eyes, remarking to others years after the war how "lively" they were in private conversations.

Those invited to these dinner parties were also impressed by the general's aides, whose jokes, stories, debates, and discussions made the war disappear for awhile. One guest found Tilghman "modest and worthy," Fitzgerald "an agreeable, broad-shouldered Irishman," and said that Gibbs "kept the dinner table in constant laughter."

It was Hamilton, though, spouting his political views, telling stories, lampooning British politicians, and diving into every subject from literary criticism and haughty Philadelphia merchants to the softness of the sand on the beaches of the Caribbean, who was the charismatic figure at these parties, always encouraged by Washington. He, like the others, took great enjoyment in the stories and humor of Hamilton. So did Martha, who was concerned that all of the general's top aides were still bachelors. Determined to marry them all off, she talked Washington into loosening many of the social restrictions on the young men. They were soon sharing tea and stronger libation at the homes of Morristown's lovelier young women late at night.

Although usually social in nature, the dinners could be charged with politics. Washington and Livingston spent long hours discussing the ways in which the governor managed to expertly control the often cantanker-ous members of his state legislature. Washington was also impressed with the way in which Livingston worked with the courts and local leaders throughout the area. They were both intent on consensus rule, Livingston in his statehouse and Washington in the army.

Livingston's most critical contribution to the growth and education of his military friend, however, was his concept of visible moral authority. Livingston told Washington that a political leader, whether the head of a state or a national army, must also be the moral leader of his people. He explained to the general that the leader was responsible for more than merely running a political or military organization. He had to not only represent the people, but be the symbol of the people he governed. He had to represent all of their hopes and dreams. An appointed or elected administrator not only should aspire to being a political, social, cultural, and moral leader, but in fact *had* to do so. It was his responsibility. He had to use all available tools to do that, whether speeches, letters, newspaper columns, dinners, receptions, proclamations, broadsides, and routine activities such as handshaking and visits to hospitals to see the wounded. It was an expansive view of leadership in democratic government that Washington had never envisioned in his days in the House of Burgesses or in the army. Livingston's opinions, and his work as that kind of a moral leader as governor, substantially changed the general's thinking.

They all learned from the overly serious, brilliant John Jay, who had married Livingston's daughter Sally in 1774. Jay, thirty-one in the winter of 1777, was one of New York's top lawyers; he would become the chief justice of the state's courts in May. He was one of the authors of the state's new constitution. He had known Hamilton before the conflict. Jay and Washington met when both were delegates to the Second Continental Congress, and the Virginian was impressed. Jay argued forcefully with Washington and Livingston for the need of laws supporting whatever Washington did with his extraordinary military and civilian powers and in the actions of Congress and the states. Later, in 1787, Hamilton and Jay would be two of the authors of The Federalist Papers which, published in just about every newspaper in the country, helped to win ratification for the Constitution. Washington would later name Jay the first chief justice of the United States.

Mrs. Washington invited the wives of the officers and women in the Morristown area to visit her at the tavern whenever they desired. She encouraged them to join her in a sewing circle to produce much-needed socks for the troops. "Lady Washington" was certainly not the royalty they expected. "Her graceful and cheerful manners delighted us all," said one of the local women who joined the group, "but we felt rebuked by the plainness of her apparel and her example of persistent industry, while we were extravagantly dressed idlers in these perilous times. She seems very wise in experience, kind-hearted, and winning in all her ways. She talked much of the sufferings of the poor soldiers, especially of the sick ones. Her heart seemed to be full of compassion for them."

The Spymaster

The middle of January saw several small snowfalls and weeks of cloudy weather. Washington's mood was as dark as the gray skies above him. He had brought a victorious, but exhausted and sick, army of three thousand men to Morristown, but only about half of them were ready for active duty. Following the smallpox panic, the size of the army began to melt away. Again, the commander was faced with the possibility of the army, and the revolution, collapsing. He had to somehow hold the Continental Army together as winter continued. That became increasingly difficult for several reasons: desertions, three-month enlistments, an unreliable militia, lack of supplies, officer feuds, and sickness. His forces had shrunk as the army lost men every day to desertion and the refusal of troops to re-enlist. He begged Congress for help. "As militia must be our dependence, till we can get the new army raised and properly arranged, I must entreat you to continue your endeavors with the states of Pennsylvania, Maryland and Virginia to turn out every man that they possibly can, and for some longer time than they generally have stipulated for," he wrote Hancock on January 19, or, he warned, he would have "scarce...any army at all."

On the federal level, Washington continued his frantic pleas to Congress for more clothes, supplies, and, most urgently, men. He begged the states for help at the same time, a doubling of effort he would pursue throughout the course of the war. "We have a full army one day and scarce any the next and I am much afraid that the enemy one day or other, taking advantage of one of these temporary weaknesses, will make themselves masters of our magazines, stores, arms and artillery," he wrote to state heads in one circular, once again expressing his fears of a sudden enemy stroke against him.

He told Rhode Island Governor Nicholas Cooke that he had to implore him "in the most pressing terms" to recruit troops. "It is to the last importance to the interests of America that the new regiments be speedily levied," he wrote anxiously, explaining that he had to rely on the states as much as he did Congress and again to unite the states and Congress for the common cause of independence.

He was more blunt, and a little sarcastic, on the federal level. In a note to Hancock, he said: "Reinforcements come up so extremely slow that I am afraid I shall be left without any men before they arrive."

Until he had more troops, he had to convince the British that his army was far larger than it appeared. The general did that through a number of ingenious schemes. The soldiers in civilian homes and their numerous drills and parades on the village green helped to accomplish that goal. But what he relied upon most heavily was a carefully orchestrated disinformation campaign and the work of a trusted brigade of spies.

Washington first dabbled in disinformation in Boston in the spring of 1775. The army had far less gunpowder than expected, but he was able to convince both the residents and the British that he had four times as much as necessary by planting false information with an array of local gossips.

That success led him to a six-year-long disinformation crusade that he began in earnest when he arrived in Morristown. He enlisted Elias Boudinot, the New York businessman who had moved his family to Morristown for protection. Boudinot was his emissary to Howe during negotiations to free American soldiers being held prisoner in New York jails and on prison ships. His real mission, though, was to use the talks as a cover to meet men and women in New York whom he could recruit as paid spies. He also went to tell the British high command that Washington had forty thousand healthy troops at Morristown and that the commander-in-chief was invincible.

At the same time, Hamilton had befriended a local Morris County Loyalist whom Washington knew to be a British spy. Washington had Hamilton carefully lay a trap. The commander spent a long time writing, in his own hand, complete troop-strength lists, regiment by regiment, in a lengthy and very official report that he stretched out for twelve pages. In the report, Washington inflated the size of his army in Morristown from its actual strength of three thousand to twelve thousand troops. The "official" report was then casually left on the Hamilton's desk on the day that the spy was scheduled to visit Arnold's tavern. Hamilton, feigning overwork, left the room at one point to find papers, knowing that the spy would spot and read the fake report.

Boudinot's forty thousand figure was never believed by Howe because he knew Washington's force was much smaller than that. He believed the twelve thousand figure reported by the spy, though, because the agent was reliable, the figure was believable, and the report was in Washington's own handwriting. By creating two sets of higher false figures, Washington hid his true strength of just three thousand. The ruse was so convincing that when a British colonel later released from a Morris County jail rode to Howe and told him that in reality Washington led a small, ill-nourished, and very badly equipped army, the British Lord accused him of being a colonial collaborator and threatened to hang him.

Washington's crafty use of disinformation became legendary. His false information was so believable that he and others often had to remind officers and diplomats that much of what they read or heard was invented. Washington had to tell an overconfident General Samuel Parsons on March 6 that his troop strength was far below the rumors Parsons had heard. "Nothing but ignorance of our numbers and situation can protect us," he told him. In Europe, Washington's disinformation had spread rapidly and America's diplomats in France seemed as convinced as General Howe that he had quite a large army. They felt so secure that Congressional delegate Robert Morris had to secretly write them at the end of March to explain that they, too, had been fooled. "You might suppose him 10 or 15 or 20 thousand strong by the [false] commissaries and quartermaster returns, but never 5000," he told them.

Spies intrigued George Washington, who learned their value from the British twenty years earlier in the French and Indian War. He once told Anthony Wayne that "single men in the night will be more likely to ascertain facts than the best glasses in the day." He continually urged his officers to look for local residents, uncertain Loyalists, and even unhappy former British soldiers who might make reliable agents. Casual spying was not very difficult in New York in the winter of 1777. Americans not directly involved in the fighting carried on their business in New Jersey and New York and met dozens of British Loyalists. Taverns and coffee houses were full of British soldiers who talked too much.

Good spies, men and women who could procure reliable information without being compromised, were often hard to find. These were the people Washington wanted to recruit for a spy ring that practically became a division of the army, personally run by the commander-in-chief. He did not know how honest their love of the rebellion was and feared that they would be turned by British money. For this reason, he paid all of his spies, usually fifty dollars a month, along with a five hundred dollar advance.

Winter gave the general time to work on his espionage network. He had started on January 5 when he wrote General Israel Putnam, "You will keep as many spies out as you will see proper." He continued that on January 24 when he interviewed Nathaniel Sackett, from Dutchess County, New York, who promised to organize a ring of agents and deliver reliable information on British movements in his area. Sackett was said to be "a man of intrigue and mystery."

Sackett recruited others, and within a week he had placed men in New York, New Brunswick, and Perth Amboy. They all had good cover. One man, who passed himself off as an ardent Tory, had a father in the British Army who introduced him to several officers. Another man was deftly included in a group of eight unknowing deserters who snuck out of Washington's camp and joined the British army in New York. Another was a sailor who landed a job on a British warship and sent coded messages on the movement of the fleet. The spies were so secretive that just two weeks later, on February 6, General William Heath angrily demanded that Washington tell him who they were since they were working right under his nose and he did not know their identities.

The chain of command for espionage was streamlined. At the top was Washington. Second in command in headquarters was Boudinot. Second in the field was Captain Benjamin Tallmadge, who as an officer in Connecticut could ride throughout the metropolitan area collecting information from spies without attracting untoward attention. Under Tallmadge were the local spy-network directors, each of whom employed a half-dozen or so operatives. Information would go to Tallmadge, who would send it via courier to Washington. Information usually reached Morristown in a single day.

The local rings were quite effective. Robert Townsend, part owner of a coffee shop in New York frequented by British troops, where liquor was served under the counter, ran one of the best rings. He and his workers picked up frequent tips from intoxicated soldiers. He was never suspected because he wrote virulent anti-American columns in the New York *Royal Gazette*, a Tory newspaper. Sackett ran a ring in Dutchess County that included farmers, merchants, and laborers. Other rings flourished in Philadelphia, New Brunswick, and Rhode Island.

Some operatives were women. Washington thought highly of female agents because they could go about their womanly business, carrying bread or laundry, without much notice. A number of wives living in Philadelphia during the 1778 British occupation were informers. Lydia Darragh was a midwife and undertaker whose house was requisitioned by British officers when they occupied the city. She managed to overhear many plans by putting her ear to the floor of her room, directly above one used by the officers for meetings. Her husband wrote down the information in tiny shorthand notes that were folded and stuck into her palm-sized sewing needlebook. Her fourteen-year-old son then passed on the information to his brother, a lieutenant in the Continental Army.

Darragh also passed information to American officials in town, casually slipping them needlebooks in conversations about clothing repair.

One very attractive woman in New York, known only as agent 355, agreed to spy because she was in love with Townsend. In order to obtain information, she spent time at his coffee house. Apparently with his approval, she flirted with a number of British officers who considered themselves Romeos. What she learned over bottles of wine in the dark corners of taverns eventually reached Washington. Agent 355's intimate relationship with Townsend and her life as an agent came to a bitter end when, pregnant with Townshend's child, she was arrested and confined on the notorious British prison ship, the *Jersey*, awaiting execution. She died giving birth aboard the vessel. (Townsend, distraught, shut down his spy ring for six months, angering Washington.)

Entire families worked as spies. Joshua Mercereau, who regularly obtained information on Staten Island and relayed it to Washington, was head of a family of intelligence agents who operated for three long years. The head of the operation was not Joshua, but his young son John who, with a withered arm, easily passed as a harmless cripple. The Mercereaus were so trusted by the commander-in-chief that he even permitted them to work behind the scenes to arrange exchanges of prisoners.

Washington's frequent pleas for informers or men to control them produced unexpected results, as revealed in a recently uncovered collection of letters between the commander and a quartermaster stationed near New Brunswick. They offer a fascinating insight into how Washington ran his espionage network, his voracious appetite for information, and the success even unseasoned officers could have in running spy rings.

The episode began near the end of winter 1777 when, at the finish of a routine letter about a skirmish, John Neilson mentioned to Washington that he had met a New Jersey militia officer who had been held prisoner by the British for several months. The officer told him that General Henry Clinton's army at White Plains now had about eight thousand men and that the British fleet in New York was preparing to sail for Virginia. Neilson added that he knew people who lived in New York who did business with the British who might serve as spies to gather more information.

Washington, sensing the opportunity to establish another spy cell, wrote Neilson back that same day. In a letter filled with a sense of urgency, the commander-in-chief told Neilson to establish an espionage network and that "at this moment it is of great importance to learn their [British] motions and whatever may lead us to a judgment of their intentions." The general then added a half-dozen detailed requests for specific information on the number of British boats, their cargo, and infantry capacity.

Neilson moved quickly and contacted his men. The next day, he sent Washington the requested information. He added that he had, as ordered, put together a small ring of agents. "I expect information tomorrow morning from a person who is going over for the that purpose [to spy]," he told the general. Neilson was especially eager to do all he could to injure the British since Lord Howe had commandeered Neilson's New Brunswick home and turned it into his personal living quarters in December.

Neilson wrote Washington two days later with additional facts. The general wrote back that he was pleased, but peppered him for more information. He even begged for tiny details, such as the size of defensive earthworks near the boats and the number of soldiers assigned to each. He told the young quartermaster that every morsel of information he could obtain was useful and that he needed replies right away. "The moment you derive your intelligence you will be pleased to forward it by an express," he implored him.

Finally, Washington warned him to be careful and beware of double agents. "I wish you to use diligence, dispatch and secrecy, and to employ only such persons as you have reason to believe fit for the purpose," he wrote, careful, as always, to keep his espionage networks intact and his cell operators safe.

The Washington-Neilson letters were written out. Most spy notes were written in ciphers, in which individual words or letters, by previous arrangement, were plucked from a long letter to spell out a secret message. Many of the espionage letters were written in invisible ink, invented by Sir James Jay, the brother of John Jay, the young New York lawyer and leader of the revolutionary movement there. Spies would leave space at the top or bottom of ordinary business letters for their secret notes. The invisible ink was never detected by the enemy.

Washington employed double agents, too. Three of them were captured in Elizabethtown with papers they planned to deliver to the British concerning falsified American troop movements. The civilian court was ready to hang the men, who refused to talk. When alerted, Washington sought out Governor Livingston and explained their situation. Livingston, who always enjoyed being made a partner in the general's schemes, then ordered jailers to let the men escape. Their cover remained intact.

Washington always told his agents that they risked their lives. All knew the story of Nathan Hale, a young spy and friend of Tallmadge who was caught in September 1776 and promptly hanged after boldly telling the hangman that "I only regret that I have but one life to give for my country."

In retaliation, Washington did not hesitate to hang British spies. One of the first to be hung was the well-connected James Molesworth, a clerk to the mayor of Philadelphia, who was discovered hiring ship captains in a British plot to destroy American forts near the city. A huge crowd gathered in a Philadelphia square to witness the hanging. His death did little to deter British spies in Philadelphia, and just two weeks later a large ring of spies was uncovered. They were promptly denounced as "infernal foes of American Freedom" by John Hancock. As further protection against British spies, Washington ordered subordinates to open all of the mail the soldiers sent home, something he learned from the British, who had been doing that for years.

Washington's spies would remain under his personal control with no civilian intermediaries. That unusual one-on-one relationship would bring great future success. Washington's cleverness at disinformation and his fruitful spy rings helped to keep the British in New York so that he had the winter to rebuild the army, a job that gave him nothing but headaches.

The Desperate Need for Soldiers

Washington began his term as commander with his hands tied by Congress. It was Congress, not Washington, that appointed the generals in the army. Congress, not Washington, approved all promotions. Many were based on friendships, not military skills. It was an ineffective way to run an army, and Washington resented it.

He also strenuously objected to Congress's fanciful notion of a part-time army of citizen/soldiers. Congress had rejected Washington's plea for a permanent army with three-year enlistments, explaining carefully that the revolution was a people's war and he would have all the soldiers he would need from state militias. The militias turned out to be unruly and unreliable, which Washington predicted. He had boasted that if he had only had enough troops, he could have already ended the war. He told his cousin Lund, "The unfortunate policy of short enlistments is daily, and hourly, exemplified. If the troops which were enlisted last year had been engaged for the war, or even three years, I could, with them...have drove the British Army out of the Jersies."

Recruitment efforts to enroll men for even one year had failed, and those who stuck out the year were now ready to go home. Winter recruitment had not only been slow, but the recruiters had become corrupt, often pocketing the money Washington gave them as bonuses to be paid to the troops. A bounty program, which permitted men to pay others to serve in their place, produced only dissatisfaction.

In 1775, Congress had bragged that it would create an army of seventy-five thousand men. Now, looking out over the snow-covered grounds outside his Morristown headquarters in the winter of 1777, Washington could count less than three thousand soldiers, half of them sick and unfit for duty and dozens sneaking away daily. He had begged Congress for more troops in December. He told Hancock then that "all that is dear and valuable" would depend upon the enlistment of an entirely new army for 1777. "Let us have a respectable army...[T]he critical situation of our affairs and the dissolution of our present force require that every nerve and exertion be employed for recruiting the new battalions."

He pleaded with him once more on March 14, stating his troop totals: "The enclosed return…comprehends the whole force I have in Jersey. It is but a handful, and bears no proportion on the scale of numbers to that of the enemy…I confess sir, I feel the most painful anxiety when I reflect on our situation and that of the enemy. Unless the [troops] arrive soon we must, before it be long, experience some…melancholy event."

The general reminded Congress, and anyone who would listen, that the original idea of three-month enlistments for the various state and county militia had been unsuccessful. Personnel was constantly changing. Men would go back to their farms just when they had become accomplished soldiers, only to be replaced with recruits who had to be trained anew. Three-month enlistments did not give men the sense of being soldiers; they saw themselves as temporary volunteers.

Washington had little use for the militia: "To place any dependence upon militia is, assuredly, resting upon a broken staff. Men just dragged from the tender scenes of domestic life, unaccustomed to the din of arms, totally unacquainted with every kind of military skill, when opposed by troops regularly trained, disciplined and appointed, makes them timid," he said, but acknowledged that it was difficult to train men in a country that had never had an army and who were "men accustomed to unbounded freedom."

He was harder on their leaders. "Their officers are generally of the lowest class of people and, instead of setting a good example to their men are leading them into every kind of mischief," he said with great disdain, again raging about officers whom he believed were prouder of their promotions than their victories.

However, by the end of the winter, Washington was forced to seek men to join the local militias because he needed anybody who could carry a musket or put one foot in front of the other. He told them in a rather blunt general circular that if they did not join the army they would contribute to "the total loss of our liberties" and that "we shall lose all of the advantages we have providentially gained this winter."

The general was furious with state legislatures that had the power to recall his troops to defend their states in what *they* considered an emergency. Right in the middle of the winter of 1777, Pennsylvania did just that—bringing home an entire artillery battery. To Washington, this activity, approved by Congress, was yet another example that national Congressional power had to supercede state authority and that the head of the national government also had to be in control of the national army.

He was just as angry with the hundreds of bonus soldiers in his lines. Each soldier who signed up for a bonus, usually twenty dollars, also received a new suit of clothes every year and, at the end of the war, one hundred acres of land. Bonus soldiers also received a half-pay pension for the rest of their lives if they were wounded and unable to work. The bonus system had problems, however. Some soldiers signed up in several regiments at the same time to earn more money (this deceitful behavior decreased in popularity when Washington began to execute men who did so).

The commander-in-chief's biggest obstacle occurred when he had to compete for bonus soldiers with state militias. He might be offering twenty dollars to a new recruit but lose him to a state militia, which might offer more (Massachusetts gave $53). He was repulsed by news from Henry Knox that many men in New England were demanding an $86 bonus when offered $20 because, they argued with considerable economic clarity, they would need it to cover the inflation of a three-year enlistment. Washington never minded paying the bonuses, but always worried about the dedication of the men who pocketed them, just as he worried about those who substituted for them. He said these men had "a dearth of public spirit and want of virtue" and complained that "such a dirty, mercenary spirit pervades the whole that I should not be at all surprised at any disaster that may happen."

He would take men in good or bad health, even asking General Parsons to send him the men under his command who were still recovering from smallpox. Parsons did not have to send them into regiments, either. Anybody would do. "If...[sending] only one hundred men immediately they would, altogether, amount to a respectable number," Washington wrote.

The commander-in-chief even agreed to allow entire regiments of men stationed far away to return to their native counties for assignment if they would agree to re-enlist, and even struck one homecoming deal with a colonel just 24 hours before his men threatened to leave.

The general was unhappy about his situation in letters to governors and officers but despondent in letters to family and friends. In a January letter to his stepson Jack, he was highly critical of his troops; mocked the militias, referring to them as "a motley crew, here today gone tomorrow"; and complained that no one in military history was forced to work with these kind of soldiers. "I do not think that any officer since the creation ever had such a variety of difficulties and perplexities to encounter as I have. How we shall be able to rub along till the new army is raised I know not. Providence has heretofore saved us in remarkable manner and on this we must principally rely."

Despite a series of impassioned pleas to the Continental Congress, Washington could not get money for supplies or clothing either. The army had to leave just about all of their supplies behind at Fort Washington, New York, when they evacuated the post during the previous fall. Men were continually barefoot or wrapped rawhide around their feet to keep them warm in the snow. They wore no coats or those that were torn. Blankets were scarce. Congress never seemed to have money for clothes, and the general had to beg governors and local officials for them. He even turned to the mothers of soldiers, asking them to donate clothes for their sons and send them along in specially authorized wagons from Philadelphia.

Washington had also run out of funds to offer bonuses for enlistment. "The treasury has been for some time empty and the army has labored under the greatest inconvenience for want of money," he lectured Hancock in January and added that he was out of weapons, too. He said that new soldiers would need arms but "I do not at present see how they are to be supplied."

And no matter what he wanted, the residents selling those products continually raised their prices. "I have to deal with a set of the most discontented, disaffected wretches that ever existed," a supply officer fumed in exasperation to Washington when he had to report that agreed-upon prices for goods had been increased by local farmers yet again.

The general's biggest problem was resignation and desertion. Many of the men who agreed to fight on for six more weeks when begged to do so by Washington just before the battle of Princeton, then promptly left when their time was up. Three-month militiamen left, too. Others departed because they were afraid of catching smallpox. Some were just tired of being hungry. Dozens went home sick. Still more exited when asked to do so in pleading letters from their wives, who insisted that their families needed them more than the rebellion did. Some who said they fought for a virtuous nation quit after they learned of corrupt recruiters. Others objected to being housed next to men from other states. Some just could not find it in themselves to like the Frenchmen they found shouldering muskets in the same drills. Some had battled the cold for months and just wanted to go home to their farmhouses and sit in front of a fireplace.

Some left individually, some with friends, and some in large groups. A sizable contingent of militia troops under Lieutenant Isaac Preston left the army in early January. In one troubling incident, four hundred troops under Lord Stirling left after a dispute with him and returned home. On the way, they stopped many recently recruited men and talked them into going home, too. (Washington told Stirling that his argument with his men "gives me much pain"). Six weeks later, an entire Massachusetts militia regiment, consisting of several hundred soldiers, their enlistments over, marched back to Boston as a group, carrying their muskets with them, despite a personal plea from Washington himself to stay.

A number of officers quit after Congress refused to promote them. Others resigned when they saw new men from their home counties arriving with ranks much higher than theirs. "Any man that has friends here [state assembly] can get any commission he wants and the old veterans that have suffered a hard campaign must now be commanded by men that never knew service," complained John Eccleston, one of fifteen officers from a Maryland regiment who left the army when overlooked for promotion.

Many were just simply fed up and worn out, such as John Taylor, a Virginian. In a morose letter explaining the waves of desertions, he told fellow Virginian Edmund Pendleton, who was both a Congressional delegate and close friend of General Washington:

> Explicit and frequent promises have been made of good and speedy clothing. But we ourselves, although we were amongst the foremost of the troops, were detained week after week and at last sent off with one sixth of our men naked, and one third without blankets; and what is most monstrous of all is that although the resolution of Congress ran in the same disjunctive, promising the men a suit of clothes or twenty dollars, yet they begin now to talk of making the men pay any additional price that they may cost *over* the twenty dollars, which will in my opinion cause a mutiny if it should take place.

Washington was enraged by the wave of desertions. "This practice in the militia so generally prevails that unless some effectual check can be speedily applied, I apprehend the most fatal consequences," he wrote Congress, frustrated in his appeals to make the delegates see how pressing his problems were.

He was personally offended that the men from his native Virginia and other southern states were deserting as quickly as the New Englanders. "They often walk off for their homes a few days after they join the army," he complained of them. One of Washington's aides, in a letter to a friend, wrote that the number of deserters was "almost incredible." A dour Washington told Congress in mid-March that he only had eight hundred regulars and about six hundred militia left to fight Britain's thirty-two thousand professional soldiers.

The general took several steps to curb desertions. He ordered his officers to establish more efficient procedures to maintain discipline and convince unhappy soldiers to stay. He personally begged entire units about to depart to reconsider. He ended all officer furloughs so that they could keep an eye on their men. Officers were ordered to keep a daily roster of their companies and, to underline the importance of the count, to report anyone missing directly "to His Excellency." He even turned to the governors of the different states and pleaded with them to get townspeople to turn in deserters, telling them that without immediate action "our army...will waste away." He persuaded newspaper editors to print the names and physical descriptions of deserters so their readers could identify them. He pressured Congress into ordering deserters turned over to local courts for trial and to offer a five dollar reward for any apprehended. He asked Livingston to do that directly. The loss of men was getting so bad, he told John Hancock sarcastically, that he feared "we shall be obliged to detach one half of the army to bring back the other."

In Philadelphia, Congress saw the logic of his demands, as it understood most of his plaintive pleas, even if Washington did not believe that they did, and agreed to his requests. It authorized states to arrest deserters and bring them before magistrates before sending them back to the army. The vote caused a firestorm among the delegates not because deserters needed to be apprehended, but because the general's request forced them to decide whether or not the new national government could make individual states do their bidding. In the end, most agreed with John Adams, who said that Congress had authorized an army and had to maintain it.

The soldiers frustrated Washington because their narrow view of national service was so different from his own. Many believed that by fighting for three months they had served their country faithfully. They could go home now, they honestly thought, because their agreed-upon time was up. If the general needed more men to replace them it was none of their concern. Others shrugged their shoulders and told friends and relatives that they had fought hard and had done their job. They were, in fact, heralded by the press for their bravery and were, as everybody acknowledged, the heroes of Trenton and Princeton. Now it was time for them to go home; others could replace them and do *their* job.

Several members of Congress, such as Richard Henry Lee, fed up with low enrollments, suggested in steamy speeches national conscription for three-year terms. "I really believe that numbers of our lazy, worthless young men will not be induced to come forth into the service of their country unless the states adopt the mode recommended by Congress of ordering drafts from the militia."

Decisions to depart were not a matter of undue concern to soldiers who elected to go home. Lieutenant Peale reported in his diary that there was no controversy in his company about leaving in January when enlistment was up, only unanimity. "They are determined to go home," he wrote. There *was* stern talk about not going home in Lieutenant Thomas Rodney's Delaware company, but only by Rodney. "I tried all in my power to prevail upon them to stay," he wrote, but they did not. Late on the morning of January 14, after they attended Colonel Ford's funeral, Rodney's men left quietly.

Peale, Rodney, and other officers knew there was nothing they could do, but they did not like it. "Slept poorly on account of the un-Godly behavior of the men," wrote General Thomas Mifflin of the rapidly departing soldiers.

Washington had always relied on harsh punishment to keep deserters in line. He had raised numerous eyebrows in Virginia in the 1750s when he ordered one-hundred-lash floggings of captured soldiers who had fled camp. In an effort to boost morale, he adopted a lenient policy when he became commander-in-chief of the Continental Army, authorizing only thirty-nine lashes for deserters. Later, as he became angrier, floggings became more severe. From time to time, he ordered deserters shot.

Washington knew that he had to have men executed for serious crimes. The death penalty was required as just punishment and to maintain discipline. The general never flinched from sentencing men to the gallows or the firing squad. He never really wanted to shoot his soldiers, though, and often looked for a way out. His steely resolve, but merciful nature, was evident in a letter to General Israel Putnam concerning the execution of one man in a group of convicted soldiers. "With respect to the prisoner's sentence to die, you are the best judge of the circumstances of this crime and of the character of the man and if either of those should appear to you, in other respects, as well as in this instance, worthy of severity, I think it would be well, for example's sake, to inflict the punishment on him and pardon the others, especially as the regiment to which they belong has been particularly addicted to desertion," he told

Putnam of the need for punishment and example. Then, in the very next line, his harsh sentiments faded. "But if there are any palliative considerations, or if the general conduct of the man has been pretty good," he suggested, "I should wish you to incline on the side of lenity."

By the time he arrived in Morristown, the commander-in-chief had become less zealous in the way he treated men who left the army so that he could keep them. There were at least three men flogged each day, but each received only thirty-nine lashes. Washington would often order a certain amount of lashes to be inflicted upon a man and then cut the number in half. Sometimes he would forego the whip and instead force deserters to "run the gauntlet," weaving their way between hundreds of soldiers ordered to whip or club them. Sometimes he would have eight men court-martialed and drop charges against seven, only prosecuting the remaining soldier.

Not every soldier sentenced to death wound up in a coffin, either. The commander reprieved many, but in a cruel way. A favorite maneuver was to order ten men shot and pardon nine, having the man with the most severe case executed. Or he would order a man executed and then pardon him at the last moment. This was always done with great drama.

A soldier wrote of one Connecticut man's execution before a firing squad:

> When the day arrived, an embankment was thrown up to prevent the shots fired at him from doing other damage and all things requisite on such occasions were in readiness. The Connecticut troops were then drawn out and formed into a square and the prisoner brought forth. After being blindfolded and pinioned, he knelt upon the ground. The corporal with his six executioners were then brought up before him, ready at the fatal word of command to send a brave soldier into the eternal world....

Then, suddenly, a courier rode up at full gallop, holding up a piece of paper from the commander-in-chief and shouting at the top of his lungs, "Reprieve! Reprieve!"

An even more harrowing portrait of an execution and last-moment pardon was painted by Dr. James Thacher, present at the mass hanging of eight men convicted of participating in a forgery ring that sold more than one hundred counterfeit discharge papers to soldiers:

> The wretched criminals were brought in carts to the place of execution. Mr. Rogers, the chaplain, attended them to the gallows, addressed them in a very pathetic manner, impressing on their minds the heinousness of their crimes, the justice of their sentence, and the high importance of a preparation for death. The criminals were placed side by side on the scaffold, with halters round their necks, their coffins before their eyes, their graves open to their view, and thousands of spectators bemoaning their awful doom. The moment approaches when every eye is fixed in expectation of beholding the agonies of death—the eyes of the victims are already closed from the light of the world. At this awful moment, while their fervent prayers are ascending to heaven, an officer comes forward and reads a reprieve for seven of them from the Commander-in-Chief.
>
> The trembling criminals are now divested of the [ropes] and their bleeding hearts leap for joy…No pen could describe the emotions which must have agitated their souls. They were scarcely able to remove from the scaffold without assistance.…

The eighth man was then hanged.

Washington ordered reprieves carried out in this manner, an aide said, "to strike terror into their fellow soldiers." It did.

Washington was so angry about the depletions in the army that he even lashed out at men who left camp and went back to their homes to recover from their smallpox treatment. Several dozen men went home from the regiment of Colonel Samuel Webb, and his report on their departure irritated the commander-in-chief. Washington snapped to his aides that if recuperating soldiers dawdled in their homes all spring there would be no army left to fight the British.

An additional problem was that the departing soldiers took their uniforms, bedrolls, muskets, and ammunition with them. Washington told Hancock about rifles that "no human prudence could secure but a small part of those...from being embezzled and carried off when their time of service expired."

The soldiers who did not depart became problems, too. Stuck in tiny villages in the middle of New Jersey with no battles to fight, they suffered excruciating boredom. They constantly argued over pay and promotion. Alcoholism was prevalent and sentries often left their posts, drunk. The commander had to prohibit the commissary from dispensing liquor. Many did nothing but play cards or roll dice all day. One group of officers living in a local residence became so obsessed with card games that they did not notice that one of their group had died of a fever. His corpse laid in bed for nearly a day before a homeowner found him and complained to the general. Soldiers subscribed to private lotteries and even wagered pool bets on how many days it would be before the war ended.

Women went to headquarters and told the general's aides that the men living in their overcrowded homes were the most foulmouthed creatures they had ever met. They did not want the soldiers' profane language to blister the ears of their children any more. They had to stop swearing or move out. The complaints about language came to the second floor of Arnold's tavern so often that Washington finally had to issue one of the most unusual orders of that or any other war: no more cursing. He had to follow that general order up with another that forbid any kind of gambling, including cards, dice, and lotteries. He said that there were "few vices with more pernicious consequences" than gambling. His edict must have particularly endangered the men since Congress, in order to raise money, had just introduced a resolution to hold national lotteries. It must have annoyed the gambling general, too.

Local farmers complained bitterly to the general's aides that soldiers routinely stole fence posts from their fields to make fires and, late at night, snuck into their unlocked stables or barnyards and took livestock, as well as equipment ranging from axes to kettles (the farmers had some feeling of justice in the spring, however, when soldiers intent on stealing bee hives filled with honey often wound up attacked by the inhabitants of the hives).

Faced with unhappy men who could no longer play cards, buy lottery tickets, or curse each other (or, under their breath, him), and without an enemy to fight just yet, Washington needed something for the men to do. And so he began the long construction of what the men called "Fort Nonsense," a large military earthworks on a hill in Morristown. They gave it the nickname because they were convinced it was simply make-work. Washington angrily disputed that claim and told the men that the fort was constructed to defend the town in case of British attack. During the remaining years of the war, the fort was used by guards to defend military warehouses. It kept the men busy.

Washington also had many men he did not want. Congress's diplomats in France, eager to help the army add trained officers, and to induce the French government to ally itself with the Americans, made arrangements for hundreds of French officers to join Washington's forces. They could not speak English, knew little about the causes of the Revolution, could not get along with American troops, and even tried to replace American generals. Hamilton, speaking for Washington, told anyone who would listen that the Americans were "greatly embarrassed" by the French and that they were of "no use" to the army. The commander-in-chief disdainfully called them "adventurers," "a weight upon the army," and complained that in one ten-day period he gave up half his time "to hear their pretensions." And, he said, there were too many of them. "This evil," as he referred to them, "is a growing one, for from what I learn they are coming in swarms from old France and the Islands." He bristled when several generals, led by Knox, threatened to resign unless the Parisian dandies were sent back to the Left Bank of the Seine. Washington demanded that Congress get rid of them.

The commander-in-chief was also discouraged that many of the men had left the army in order to sail with captains of privateers, American merchant ships outfitted for combat that preyed on British shipping. The Continental Congress not only authorized privateers, but encouraged them. So did Washington. The ships sunk a number of British warships bound for America with supplies for Howe's troops. They subdued others and confiscated their rich cargoes. Their goods were sold and the sailors on the ships split the profits, with the owners, captains, and mates, earning the largest shares. All of these men not only helped the war effort, but made substantial amounts of money, far more than a man could earn as a soldier in the army.

Hundreds of tough fighters had chosen service in the privateers over the army. Still others, including valued soldiers, such as John Glover and his Massachusetts fishermen, who had been instrumental in the success at Trenton and the evacuation at New York, had refused to re-enlist in the army in order to sail with the privateers. Although Washington appreciated their service at sea, he fervently wished they were in his army instead. The privateers did not seem to understand that they would have no enemy ships to plunder if the army collapsed and the war ended.

By April, the general had become increasingly frustrated at his inability to stop desertions. Despite Congress's decision to order states to find and detain deserters, soldiers who had fled were still missing. Friends and neighbors were not turning them in, and community leaders were not hunting them down. Finally, unable to either capture deserters or lure them back into the ranks, and needing all the men he could muster to begin the spring offensive against the British, the general simply gave up punishment entirely and offered an amnesty to any soldier who had deserted. It was another example of how he had grown in office, adjusting rules when they did not work because the greater good called for change.

Still, he did not have much of an army left. His spirits rose a bit when officers in Connecticut guaranteed more than four hundred new men in arms, but fell a week later when they had to tell him that they would be lucky to sign up half that many. Washington wrote Congress in a letter that, "I cannot get a man to come near me."

The commander wrote bitterly to one governor on April 3 that he was forlorn; his army had crumbled throughout the winter and there did not seem to be any reason to believe that it could be rebuilt in time to take the field against the British. He told him, "I think I am excusable in drawing every man in the Continental Service to (Morristown); to give opposition to the grand army of the enemy who, except they are checked, will in turn overrun every state in the Union."

He had lobbied the governors, Congress, and state legislatures for troops, with little success. In one of the lengthiest letters he wrote during the war, he complained to Patrick Henry that the states—their own Virginia included—had let him down. He told him that the army did not need just untrained militiamen who only served for a few months or substitutes who were paid by others to serve in their place. He feared that a draft would be unpopular and might, in fact, bring about "convulsions in the people." Without long-term enlistees, which he hoped would come from the working class, he could not win the war, and securing those men did not seem possible. He spilled out his frustrations to his old comrade from the House of Burgesses, telling him that his hopes of a victory "has been unfortunately blasted."

Then, with what must have involved a deep sigh, he pleaded with Henry to raise all the troops he could, and by any means possible. "What then remains for us to do," he told him, "is nothing less than furnishing our full quota of Continental troops by any means that will insure success, our situation perhaps more critical now than ever. Policy directs that caution should be used in the choice. But whether it should be by an indiscriminate draft, or by making it the interest of the timid, the rich and the Tory to furnish soldiers, at his own expense, in place of themselves…is a subject well worthy of the most dispassionate and mature deliberation of your assembly."

Local officials commiserated with the general. Disgruntled Maryland leader Samuel Chase chastised his own Council of Safety for its failure to raise men.

John Adams understood Washington's plight. "Where is our army?" he questioned in an April 28 letter to his wife. "We have not a thousand men. We have been continually flattered, with assurances, that many men have enlisted and are marching to Ticonderoga and Morristown. But none of them or next to none arrive."

The commander-in-chief was angry with deserters, fed up with recruiters, frustrated by Congress, puzzled by price-gouging farmers, and depressed that he could not rebuild his forces as the end of winter camp approached far too quickly. Then, on April 26, word came from Connecticut that the British had captured Danbury and burned down all of the American supply and ammunition warehouses in the town. Washington, drained from all of the setbacks, succinctly expressed his feelings about the entire winter in a letter acknowledging the Danbury debacle to General McDougall, calling it, and certainly everything else in his life, "truly distressing."

Through it all—the diseases, Loyalists, desertions, enlistment fall-offs, military defeats, financial woes, and bad weather—the governors, congressmen, newspaper editors, merchants, and farmers throughout the states never lost their unshakable faith in Washington and his ability to hold the army together against all odds. "While Washington survives, the great American cause cannot die," wrote Delaware's Governor Rodney in an admiration shared by all.

This was not mere oratory. Governor Rodney and others had worked tirelessly to raise troops from the moment that the Continental Army arrived in Morristown and Washington began his series of plaintive letters. Perhaps they did not work as quickly as Washington desired, or perhaps he was not aware of their efforts as he dealt with his series of crises, but they did all they could.

It had been a long spring punctuated by warm spells and snowfalls. A private from Massachusetts, Jeremiah Greenman, reported that snow flurries had been seen in Morristown as late as May 3. But by the middle of that month, the weather improved and it became evident that George Washington's hard work had finally paid off. The amnesty for deserters had worked. Hundreds of men returned. The general's persistent lobbying for more troops with Congress was successful. The delegates had authorized both New York and Pennsylvania to call up thousands more militiamen and to send them to Washington. Hancock, president of the Continental Congress, sent him an encouraging note and assured him that Congress would always help: "It is the earnest desire of Congress that the army under your command may be made not only strong enough to confine the enemy within their present quarters and prevent them from getting supplies from the country, but totally subdue them," he said in one strident letter which pleased Washington.

Regiments of Continental regulars, signed on for from one to three years, and companies of local militia, spurred on by urgent pleas from local governors and Congressmen, as Washington had hoped, began to arrive on a regular basis amid the late snow flurries of spring. They were cheered by the men—and the commander-in-chief. Daniel Morgan and five hundred of his famed frontier riflemen from the backwoods of Virginia trudged to Morristown at the end of April after Patrick Henry told Morgan that an emergency existed and that "the safety of our country much depends upon the exertions of its army at this trying period." Fifteen hundred troops from New Hampshire marched toward Fort Ticonderoga after a frantic Congressman Josiah Bartlett told them: "The enemy armies are moving on all quarters. For heaven's sakes! For your country's sake! For your own sake! Exert yourself in getting your men and sending them forward without a moment's loss of time."

In late April came the "fighting Reverend," Peter Muhlenberg, and the 8th Virginia, made up of several hundred German Americans from the Shenandoah Valley. A week later came "Dandy" Anthony Wayne, the flamboyant Pennsylvanian who raised and trained his own regiment. Brigadier General John Armstrong brought four companies of men to Morristown from Carlisle, Pennsylvania. The state of Maryland had raised one thousand men and sent them to Morristown at the end of March. Delaware Governor Rodney let Washington know that he was raising 1,500 troops and that they would be ready for the first battle of spring. Another 1,500 troops left North Carolina at the end of winter to march toward New Jersey.

Several hundred men in newly created militia companies arrived from South Jersey. New regiments raised in Connecticut, New York, and Rhode Island arrived shortly afterward. To the astonishment of the commander, his greedy, pathetic, and unscrupulous recruiting officers, charged with bringing in new men just about any way that they could, had somehow managed to sign up several hundred new soldiers for one- to three-year enlistments in the regular army. Among them were men like

Lemuel Roberts, enlisting for the third time, who turned down the bonus and signed on for nothing in order to fight for his country.

By the time Washington's wing of the Continental Army marched out of the Morristown area in May of 1777, its numbers had swelled to more than nine thousand men, or three times the number of starving and freezing soldiers that had stumbled into the sleepy village in early January. His other armies had grown in size, too, and total American forces now numbered just over fifteen thousand—to the astonishment of the British, who never thought Washington and his men would survive the winter. The American army was now large enough to do battle with anybody.

Chapter Six

THE ARMY'S WAR MACHINE

MORRISTOWN, 1777

"I frequently hear that cannon of every kind are much wanted."
—Hibernia ironworks manager Joe Hoff

One of the major reasons George Washington marched the army to Morristown in January of 1777 was to camp near the flourishing iron industry that had recently become the heart of America's military arsenal. The dozens of ironworks in the area, which had spent decades manufacturing kettles, pots, utensils, plows, rakes, and carriages—items so much a part of American life—now belched with soot and smoke as their workers concentrated on weapons and ammunition.

Washington probably learned about this vast network of manufacturing foundries in Morris County as early as May 1773, when he was first introduced to Lord Stirling, who owned one of the biggest ironworks in the county. They met at the elite Jockey Club in Philadelphia, where Washington had stopped while accompanying his stepson Jack from Virginia to New York. There, the boy would enroll in King's College. The two men had struck up a friendship and traveled together through New Jersey to Basking Ridge, where Washington and his son spent two days as the guests of Stirling at his hilltop stone mansion. It is not known whether or not Stirling gave Washington a tour of his ironworks, or the iron country, but he surely must have discussed his business with Washington, who had a great interest in the industry. Washington's father had once operated a small mine and ironworks in the 1730s and in the late 1760s George had thought about reopening it. He had even discussed a partnership to build another ironworks with Virginian William Crawford in 1760.

Lord Stirling wasn't Washington's only contact. He also had kept up a steady correspondence with other foundry owners. In the fall of 1776, the commander-in-chief had authorized Jacob Ford to construct a secret gunpowder mill on his estate on the northeast perimeter of Morristown. Later that season, he told Jacob Faesch to begin manufacturing cannonballs at his Mount Hope works in Rockaway, while authorizing the production of thirty-five tons of shot at the Hibernia ironworks—owned by Stirling—as early as October 1776. (Stirling's critics charged that the land-rich, cash-poor lord was counting on war business and his friendship with the commander-in-chief to prevent bankruptcy).

Washington's relationships with the iron producers of the region were yet other examples of his strong strategic abilities. The commander had set out to create a war machine by deliberately cultivating close personal alliances with foundry owners to insure that they would continue to turn their interests from the manufacture of spoons and shovel to shot and shell—all for the public good. He worked with these local businessmen to help the military win the war, again creating the idea of a unified commitment to independence.

He had to lobby governors and Congress to write new laws, or make new ones himself, to help the factory owners maintain their labor force. He had to negotiate with Congress to fund the war production of cannons, muskets, and gunpowder. He had to use the army to build trains of wagons so that the munitions could be transported to camps throughout the area. Washington had to take unprecedented legal and political steps to obtain questionable laborers for war production. Jurisdiction of a huge private industry had to be given to a national executive, also in charge of the military, so that the country could protect itself. Washington understood that the transformation of the local and national ironworks into a military preserve for the United States was yet another example of leadership. He realized that the best way to mobilize a private industry for war production was through a persuasive single national executive who represented both the best civilian and military interests of the country. In short, as in so many other instances, Washington had to function as a national leader and operate outside of the army just as often as he worked within its boundaries to win the war and create a national coalition of citizens who knew that they did not have to carry swords to be a part of the war effort.

The first iron forge in Morris County was built in 1710 in Whippany, on the banks of the Whippany River. This forge was built by John Ford, who received his iron from mines on Mahlon Dickerson's land in nearby Succasunna. It was the second forge in the state. The first was built in Tinton Falls, in Monmouth County, in 1674 for Lewis Morris, one of the state's major landowners, who ran it with seventy slaves, a dozen indentured workers, and some local craftsmen.

Their success spurred others to develop forges in Morris County, cognizant of the growing market for iron in America and in England. The larger ones required investment capital and were often run by a principal owner who sometimes had to rely on others for financial backing. The smaller ones, with little financing, often went out of business. The Rockaway River, which wound its way through Morris County, was a major source of waterpower for the forges and blast furnaces. Ironworks soon sprung up along that river in what is now Rockaway, Randolph, and Denville, many owned by prominent local men.

By 1775, Morris County had three large iron mines, a dozen small mines, thirty-four small forges, and eight large ones. There were a dozen more large furnaces, and more mines, located in nearby Sussex, Warren, and Bergen counties, including the deep and prosperous Ringwood mines. The mining industry in New Jersey employed nearly three thousand men, or more miners than the populations of many small American cities at that time.

These ironworks of the eighteenth century were self-contained mining communities. An example was Mount Hope. There, as in all ironworks complexes, the iron-smelting buildings—one for the large blast furnace and another for the transformation of pig iron into cannons and shot—anchored the community. The furnaces were enclosed inside huge wood and stone structures, except for the open top of the blast furnace. Workers would push heavy wooden carts loaded with recently excavated iron ore, limestone, and charcoal over trestle bridges to the top of these furnaces, often twenty feet high and ten feet in diameter, enclosed by thick stone walls. There they would dump in the ore. It would be melted into pig iron by hot fires fanned by large bellows run by the force of paddlewheels whose power was generated from a nearby pond, river, or waterfall. The pure iron that was poured out of the furnace was taken to the ironworks building for casting into cannonballs and artillery.

The mining town contained a general store, stables, several storage buildings, and a church whose minister was often paid a full-time salary by the foundry. There were more than one hundred small cabins built for the workers and their families, some scattered and some on carefully designed streets. Another two dozen log cabins were located at random on the hills that surrounded the complex. Men who cut wood for charcoal lived in them. The areas around the ironworks were usually barren after thousands of trees had been felled for fuel.

The cabins were small and shabby. They were hot in summer and cold in winter. They often had dirt floors and were small for a family or even an individual. The workers were paid ten to twelve British pounds per month (about fifteen dollars a week) in wages. Since the ironworks were isolated, the workers bought all their food, clothes, and provisions from an on-site company store. They could pay cash or have the purchases deducted from their monthly wages. Owners reserved the right to make 10 percent on all store sales, in addition to whatever profit they built into the sale prices after purchasing goods wholesale in New York or Elizabeth.

The owners of the ironworks built large homes for themselves. The mansion of Faesch was on a small hill overlooking the manufacturing complex. It was a two and one half stories high, four thousand–square foot manse with twelve oversized rooms, nine-and-one-half-foot ceilings, and six fireplaces. Although not lavishly decorated, it was certainly one of the finest houses in the area. George Washington's life would be saved there three years later.

In the 1770s, slave labor made up a small percentage of the foundry workforce. Paid labor was costly. Most owners knew a little bit about the iron business, but had to hire a full-time manager. They needed between fifty and two hundred workers to man the ironworks, and had to pay them weekly salaries (sometimes they paid them in goods). These costs meant that throughout the 1740s, 50s, and 60s, profits were slim, sometimes nonexistent. A group of forge owners petitioned the New Jersey Assembly in 1751 for tax relief. They were turned down at first, but their businesses slumped so badly that in 1769 the state granted several tax exemptions for periods up to seven years.

A few foundries were marginally prosperous. The blast furnaces of Faesch and Stirling in Rockaway employed more than seventy workers each and manufactured an array of utensils aimed at a consumer market, as well as producing bars of iron. On May 20, 1775, Charles Hoff, the manager of the Hibernia Works, wrote the owner, Lord Stirling, that "the furnace is making 20 tons weekly."

The financial troubles of the ironworks in the 1750s and early '60s were symptomatic of the problems that would catapult the colonies toward revolution. Most historians credit the Stamp Act of 1765 as the catalyst for rebellion, but it was probably an earlier British parliamentary insult—the Iron Act of 1750—aimed at the ironworks managers in Morris County, New England, and Pennsylvania, that engendered heated dissent in the colonies against the Crown for the first time. That act permitted ironmakers to continue to transport and sell iron bars to England, but forbid the continuation or construction of new slitting or rolling mills—the mills used to turn iron into shovels, carriages, kettles, and other consumer products—at American ironworks. This meant that the real profits in the iron business would be reaped by Europeans who turned the iron bars into consumer goods. They sold some in England, some throughout the Continent, and shipped the rest back to America for sale. The profits for the Americans, now turned into mere wholesalers, became minimal. The ironworkers felt shortchanged, but because the colonies had no representation in Parliament, they could do nothing.

Another iron act passed in 1764 limiting export of iron outside the colonies to England alone, cutting off a substantial European market. John Dickinson, famed for his columns "Letters from a Pennsylvania Farmer," which ran in dozens of American newspapers, argued that this act crippled the American iron economy and was a perfect symbol of the low esteem in which Parliament and the Crown held the colonists.

Americans also began to believe that if England was allowed to treat the iron merchants in this manner, the Crown might soon be treating all American businesses in the same discriminatory fashion. The men who ran the ironworks were naturally bitter that an outside agency, Parliament, could manipulate their business, restrict trade, and eliminate their chance for profits. Unable to directly influence Parliament three thousand miles away, the iron manufacturers, like so many Americans tired of British control of business, turned to politics at home. The leaders of the iron industry had land, workforces, and money. They knew all the other rich and powerful people in their areas. Their drift into local, state and national politics—driven by their desire to make their businesses profitable—was a logical step. In a sense, the iron manufacturers were the first Sons of Liberty. By 1775, the ironworks owners had become economically and politically powerful.

The Urgent Need for Gunpowder and Cannon

On March 15, 1775, a month before Lexington and Concord, the British began curbing sales of gunpowder after the colonists started destroying cargo at different seaports, including Elizabeth. The powder was needed to cause explosions that dislodged chunks of iron ore from inside the mines that ran through the area. Without powder, the workers could not extract any ore from the hills and production had to be halted. That meant no work for anyone and potential ruin for both the mines and the ironworks. Politics had, at long last, crept into the iron business. Foundry managers feared that any American violence against British camps or ships might bring on more restructions. On the same day that the British first started to curb their sales, Joe Hoff, the twenty-one-year-old manager of Lord Stirling's ironworks, heard, as did many others, that the rebels had struck another blow at the British at a nearby seaport: "I was much alarmed this day by a rumor prevailing here [Elizabeth] that the cargo of the ship 'Beulah' was burnt by the [American] Committee of Correspondence on their orders at Staten Island." (It turned out to be a rumor, but it sent shudders through everyone in the iron industry.)

A week later, Hoff, after talks with businessmen in Elizabeth and New York, realized he was going to have trouble getting powder. Any large British cutback on powder meant that he had to curb all commercial work at Hibernia. A complete British cutback would force him to consider closing the ironworks. This would undercut his efforts to retain his already shaky workforce. On May 17, a month after Lexington and Concord, a frantic Hoff told Robert Erskine, the manager of the Ringwood Ironworks, that he couldn't get powder and feared an extended war. "All the powder in that place [New York] had been secured for the safety of the Province," he said. "I found the Committee of Safety of that place and all the powder we had there and they would not suffer it to be moved in this emergency. Were it to come to such desperate lengths that they must have come to blows with the parent state?"

Stirling did not think the war would be short, either. "Lord Stirling told me it was his candid opinion that every kind of intercourse between New York and Jersey would be immediately cut off by the port of the former being shut and that he thought it most prudent and highly necessary that you should be furnished with a list of such goods as must come from New York for the supply of the present Blast...." Hoff wrote to a merchant on June 30 in an effort to buy up everything he could to protect himself and his miners from the onrush of world events.

Finally, on September 4, 1775, the foundry manager wrote Stirling that he had so little powder that he might have to shut down the ironworks:

"Will you carry on works next year? I need to tell miners if they're employed...."

Men, apprehensive that the political situation would mean the elimination of their jobs, had already started to leave the Morris ironworks to look for work elsewhere. "I am afraid the miners will leave me as they have been doing for some days," Hoff wrote.

The Continental Army had lost thousands of men as prisoners when Fort Washington fell in the fall of 1776, but it also lost all but eighteen of its two hundred cannon. Now, in the winter of 1777, Washington needed more cannon, more shot, and more powder...and right away. He was going to get them in Morristown.

There was no doubt in Washington's mind that cannon were crucial to the success of the Revolution. That had been proved decisively in Boston in February 1776 when a row of cannons on Dorchester Heights forced the British to evacuate the city. His cannon had also played an important role at Trenton.

As soon as Washington took command of the army, he realized his need for cannon. It was then that he met Henry Knox, who volunteered to bring fifty-five cannons back to Boston from far-away Fort Ticonderoga in New York. Full of bravado, Knox rode off toward Ticonderoga right in front of the British artillery officers in Boston, who fired away, without hitting him, missing broadly. He sneered to friends: "And [the cannon fire] did what? Why, scraped a man's face with the splinters of a rail fence....nor am I afraid they will hit me..." At Fort Ticonderoga, Knox and a regiment of men put the cannon on large sleds that Knox had built inside the fort and transported them through snow all the way to Boston, an impressive feat.

Knox, though, was despondent in January 1777 when the Continental Army arrived in Morristown. He had written Colonel Richard Gridley fifteen months earlier that an army the size of what the Continental Army should be would require at least one hundred cannon immediately, perhaps more, just to keep the army on the field. Even one hundred more would have given him less than he had a year before. He needed money to have them cast and he knew that they could be, since a Morristown man had bragged to him that his forge alone could probably produce thirty-eight cannons each year.

Knox, fed up with his supplies, wrote the Continental Congress again on September 1, 1776, with Washington's approval, for money to begin a comprehensive program for the production of cannon, shot, and shell for the army for the duration of the war. It was a plea for the creation of what later would become the War Department and the U.S. Military Academy. He asked for an academy with instructors where gunnery and military tactics could be taught and funds to build dormitories for students who would follow an extended curriculum. For now, he wanted 3,660 cannon, 100 wagons, 300 horses, and money to pay foundries to cast cannons.

One reason Knox wanted to utilize the ironworks near Morristown to manufacture cannon was to obtain uniform artillery (this was never completely accomplished). Throughout most of the war, Knox used cannon taken from somewhere else, such as the British guns at Ticonderoga or cannon delivered or sold by foreign manufacturers, such as the French or the Swedes. His men had to employ cannons that used different ammunition and were operated in different ways. The British artillerists used uniform guns. They were easier to use, and their operators were easier to train.

Washington pressed Knox to obtain more cannon and ammunition and to lobby Congress for funds. Finally, Congress appointed a five-man committee to fulfill the army's munitions needs. The committee authorized the production of 290 cannon and accepted bids from several foundries. Months of haggling over contracts followed, with little success. Finally, Congress reached an agreement with the Hughes Ironworks of Philadelphia, but the contract was never completely filled.

The army's need for gunpowder, shot, and cannons was constant. It was crippled without them. In the summer of 1776, the army repeatedly ran out of gunpowder and was forced to cancel one bombardment of Boston because there was no powder left. The artillery pieces from

Ticonderoga helped, but Knox needed many more. He was in trouble. He wanted to fight but had nothing to fight with. Artillery shortages prevented many American commanders from even engaging the British because they had no cannon. An example came on March 25, 1777, when Col. Alexander McDougall learned that the British planned to send several frigates and a landing party to raid Peekskill, a community on the Hudson River. Several cannons would be enough to defeat the raiding party and, at the same time, to sink frigates, which would have been a coup for the Continentals. However, he could not engage them without artillery. The British raided Peekskill and all McDougall could do was burn a small percentage of the stores there and retreat.

Upon his arrival in Morristown, Washington met frequently with the owners of the local iron mines and forges to begin emergency production of cannon, shot, and shells, as well as gunpowder. The general's relationships with the iron owners was social as well as military right from the start. He held dinners for the ironworks owners and managers at his headquarters at Arnold's tavern. He often rode out to their ironworks to watch production and dined with them at their homes, constantly using his personal powers of persuasion to get them to help the army, to make them see that what was good for the country was good for them. He became friendly with many, even appointing some, such as Stephen Jackson, as members of his personal guard. These friendships lasted a lifetime. Aaron Kitchel, an ironworks owner and one of the local politicians, remained a close friend to Washington all of his life. At these dinners and visits, and through their developing friendships, Washington learned that the local patriots had been busy.

Gabriel Ogden ran a large forge in Pompton Plains, where he began to produce cannonballs and shells. Like Ford, Ogden at first started producing munitions in secret, relying on discrete patriotic workers. After a few months, in the winter of 1777, nothing was secret. Ogden's production picked up quickly and his men began to stockpile the shells he manufactured. He wrote Knox: "Have weapons...Hurrying...As many 13 inch shells as they [wagons] can carry. Fast as possible. Will arrive tomorrow." Hoff wrote: "Willing to cast all the cannon we can."

All of the ironmakers had turned from business to the war and began to produce grapeshot, bayonets, shovels, picks, buckets, kettles, and some cannon for the Continental Army. The production was incredible for its time. Hoff, who had so much trouble getting powder in 1775, had plenty of it in 1777 thanks to Ford's mill, plus gunpowder brought into the country by the French Navy. He was able to keep his blast furnaces going day and night, and was producing fifteen tons of iron each month, most "for use by the Continentals." The Ogdens, Faesch, and John Cox, owners of the large ironworks, started to produce a few cannons using different-sized molds. Tiny three pounders came first, but within two months the ironworks were producing—and shipping to the front—nine- and twelve-pound field cannons. Production had become so great that the Continental Congress, which once had to beg for a single wagon of ammunition, was routinely taking orders for shells.

Production became so abundant that by March 12, 1777, Washington would write to General Philip Schuyler: "I have given Directions to Managers of the Iron-Works [in Morristown] to have the Shot...conveyed to some convenient Landing place, 'till the River [then frozen] opens, and then to be forwarded to You with all Dispatch."

During his very first week in Morristown, Washington received a crash course in the construction and operation of an ironworks from the local iron managers. He knew so much about the management of an ironworks and production of shot, shell, and cannon that by January 16 he could send an extremely complicated operations order to Col. Benjamin Flower in Philadelphia concerning the construction of a munitions works in Carlisle. He asked for sixty cannons, noted the different sizes he needed, authorized the hiring of more than one hundred workers, and assigned sixty soldiers to guard the factory, along with their own fife-and-drum unit. He showed his expertise in asking for "...an air furnace to be constructed there, to hold 3,000 weight of fluxed metal...."

The order, clearly written with an ironworks manager or using his notes, was an example of Washington's interest in the manufacture of ammunition, and it also showed that he was able to grasp complicated concepts rather easily. It was an example, too, of how he was able to apply the experiences of his life to the war and then, listening carefully to others, enhance his knowledge and grow as a leader.

The production urged by Washington began quickly. The ironworks owners now had access to gunpowder, had their furnaces in full blast, and were glowing from the way in which the commander-in-chief himself had taken such pains to associate with them and take them into his confidence. Washington's decision to befriend the ironworks owners, and not work with them via couriers or underlings, was a political masterstroke, gaining their admiration and loyalty not only for the duration of the war, but for a lifetime. Work increased and production boomed throughout the winter of 1777. (Benoni Hathaway, head of security for the Ford Powder mill, did not rely merely on hard work by his men; he nailed a lucky horseshoe over the front door of the building.)

War production consumed the ironworks. The owners and managers did not take on standard business and practically eliminated production of wheels and carriages, a staple of their trade and source of profit, to produce ammunition. The ironworks and the mines that fed them had quickly become America's first war machine. "The furnace is now altogether for the public use," wrote Hoff with great pride.

The output was prodigious and the foundries outdid each other in order to impress Washington. In the summer of 1776, just after the signing of the Declaration of Independence, Henry Knox met with Hoff and, worried about low supplies of shot and shell, asked the foundry administrator if it was possible, pushing his men as hard as he could, to manufacture fifteen tons of ammunition in the next year.

"We'll give you 50 tons," said the twenty-one-year-old Hoff proudly, and proceeded, remarkably, to give Knox 120 tons in that year.

The ironworks of Morristown were not alone. At the time of the Revolution, Virginia had eight large ironworks with furnaces and a dozen small forges. Maryland had eight ironworks and nine forges. Rhode Island had one large ironworks, owned by Samuel Waldo, in the village of Scituate, which began producing cannon and shot. A bigger ironworks was located at Springfield. Both Knox and Washington believed that the Springfield plant could become the major munitions producer in the

United States. It was already an efficient and productive factory and employed patriots. It was located at the intersection of major highways and was on the banks of the Connecticut River, which made it easy for the workers there to transport shot, shell, and cannon up and down the river with relative ease. Located in western Massachusetts, it was far enough away from Boston and major cities in Connecticut and New York to be safe from British raids.

Wooing the Iron Men

The men who owned and ran the ironworks in and around Morristown were a complex and ethnically diverse mix. The families of some had been in America for one hundred years; others had just arrived. Faesch, the gifted iron baron who ran the Mount Hope complex, came from Switzerland on a seven-year work contract and stayed. Peter Hasenclever, who ran the Ringwood works, came from Germany. Robert Erskine, manager at Ringwood, was from Scotland and in 1775 had raised and paid the expenses of his own militia company in Morris. The owners who toiled day and night to produce those tons of cannonballs were not the red, white, and blue musicians depicted so gloriously in many later paintings. They were disenfranchised men, the new Americans who saw, like so many others, new hope in the Revolution. Washington's ability to convince these divergent individuals from foreign lands to mobilize their ironworks to produce weapons and ammunition for the American rebellion was yet another sign of his mercurial personal ability to persuade people to help him.

Many of the ironworks in New Jersey used slave labor. Sometimes there were gangs of slaves that numbered anywhere from thirty to seventy men. Other ironworks only used two or three slaves. Hughes's works, which was typical, employed six. Bondage was common in New Jersey at the time of the Revolution, and in 1776 there were more than ten thousand slaves in the state. Some slaves worked in stores, some worked on farms, and some made cannon and shot for the army at the various ironworks. Many who worked as house servants for wealthy families came to know Washington when he visited. They hoped that a victory over England and independence might mean a new attitude about slavery and freedom, but they were wrong.

Inside the bulky, gray, overheated, smoky ironworks, the slaves toiled alongside hundreds of indentured servants who came to America from a number of European countries. Those people agreed to work without pay, or very cheaply, in return for passage, housing, and freedom at the end of five to seven years on a contract. They had the freedom to move about in the state, but had to be at their ironworks whenever required for seven long years. They, too, sweated day and night for a Revolution they hoped would change their lives.

In the 1770s, New Jersey still contained several hundred American Indians, who resided in the southern half of the state, and many of them worked in the iron mines and forges. Charles Read's Atsion Ironworks grew rapidly in the 1760s and included a saw and grist mill as well as a large ironworks. Lacking sufficient local labor, he hired American Indians who lived nearby. To induce more Indian laborers, Read let all the Indians buy goods at the company store, including liquor. The Indians he employed worked long hours to produce equipment and ammunition for the Continental Army, the same Continental Army that would burn down the villages of other Indians in New York.

In 1777, new additions to the fully engaged ironworks, and by far the strangest, were Hessian prisoners of war. Washington captured hundreds of Hessians at Trenton and in other battles. He did not want to imprison all of them and certainly did not want to march them from battle to battle with his army. Letters and memos from ironworks managers show that an agreement was quickly reached with several ironworks to induce dozens Hessian POWs to work there from 1777 until the end of the war to help produce weapons and ammunition to be used against their own army, in violation of accepted European rules of war.

Charles Hoff, who had replaced his brother as ironmaster at Hibernia and worked with Hessian POWs in the winter of 1777, wrote to the Continental Congress on July 4, 1778, offering to employ more Hessians. "I am informed that a good many deserters both of the British troops and Hessians [have] come in and sent to Philadelphia. I have sent the bearer…to engage as many men as he thinks proper with such to be used to cut wood in the winter and [who] can assist in the coaling."

Congress and the commander-in-chief not only authorized Hessian workers for the ironworks, but let the iron managers pick and choose whom they wanted from a laundry list of Hessians, who before the war worked as carpenters, artisans, blacksmiths, wheelwrights, and wagoners. By the spring of 1778, twenty-five to thirty Hessians were working at each of the Mount Hope, Hibernia, Picatinny Forge and other Morris County ironworks and another fifty to ninety were working at mines in Ringwood.

Washington approved of three classifications for Hessian prisoner-of-war workers. The first and largest group were German soldiers who agreed to desert from the British army and were promptly employed by ironworks and local farms as paid laborers. The general had this goal in mind when Trenton was captured. The Hessian prisoners were sent to German-American communities for incarceration so that German residents there could induce them to desert and become Americans; many of these "recruiters" were young women (including Washington's sister Betty and her girlfriends, who visited Hessian POWs in Fredericksburg). Some were prisoners of war who were "loaned" to ironworks and farms as unpaid laborers. Others were prisoners who were ordered to work in the weapons industry as prisoners, without salary, and were kept in servitude after the end of the war, in violation of the 1782 peace treaty, until the British paid ironworks owners to release them. The army labeled the men in the latter two categories "indentured servants" to get around the rules of war concerning prisoners. Communications were not difficult because the owners of several ironworks spoke German and others employed dozens of German-American workers.

Washington could impress the Hessians into weapons and farm work, in violation of accepted rules concernings POWs, because Americans despised the Hessians. They saw them as butchers who had bayoneted hundreds of soldiers to death in the New York battles. They were mercenaries, cold-blooded killers for hire. And they were foreigners. The British POWs, conversely, were seen as professional soldiers doing their job—and they were English, too.

One of the reasons the Hessians were required was because many American iron workers were unhappy with life in the mining camps. They worked long twelve- to fourteen-hour days at hard labor, earned little money, and, as soon as the war started, rarely had sufficient food and clothing because of British embargos. Some left the camps to join the Continental Army. Others, in no hurry to join the military, moved west to the Ohio territory to farm.

The ironworks managers had a difficult time finding miners during the early days of the war. They turned to the women and children of other miners and put them to work. They had more trouble obtaining supplies to sell the miners because the British had cut off the sale of most goods. This was a major problem because the mine managers, doing most of their work for the army and minimal for commercial clients, had so little cash on hand that they began to pay workers half their wages in money and half in goods from the company store. Now there were no supplies coming in.

Conditions at the mines worsened. Hibernia's manager had written to his supplier as early as May 27, 1776: "People here begin to think we have no coarse linen coming and they are almost naked. Many will certainly leave us if it is not here next week. Immediately send. We could sell goods to our people now of almost any kind."

Two weeks later, he wrote his chief supplier in New York: "We have lost some fine fellows this week because they were naked and could work no longer. It will be impossible to keep [the furnace] going."

To quell the starving and badly clothed miners, ironworks owners bought up all the rum they could find to sell to their men. They sometimes gave away rum each day to keep the men working. Often, this enticement was not enough. Men, without food and clothing, departed. Others joined the army, depleting the workforce considerably, even with the addition of the Hessians. To keep their men, and to lure new workers, the iron owners began a steady campaign with Washington, the Continental Congress. and New Jersey's legislature to exempt ironworkers from required service in the local militia. Charles Hoff asked for the exemptions, as did other iron producers, directly from Washington as well as Governor Livingston, citing the workers' war production and patriotism. They had won a temporary, local exemption in 1776 from the governor, but had to ask for another in 1777.

The draft-exemption crisis underscored the close relationship the iron owners and managers had with Washington. They not only had easy access to him, but were among the few people permitted to argue with the commander. Ringwood manager Robert Erskine went to see him in Morristown in late February, just before Washington fell ill, and apparently had a heated debate over the need for exemptions to prevent the wholesale departure of workers and the shutdown of the ammunition factories. Erskine was turned down. Unhappy, he then turned to New York Governor George Clinton, who lobbied on his behalf with the general.

Some iron producers were more diplomatic, such as Hibernia's Hoff, who wrote a careful letter outlining the need for an exemption to the general. "Every preparation should be made for putting the furnace in blast which has been done with a considerable expense and should the workmen be required to leave the business in its present situation, great damage must result from it." Hoff added that he was "happy in the service of my country."

Washington had similar requests from governors and Congressmen in other states on behalf of their ironworks. He had problems with the requests at first, and told Richard Henry Lee that exemptions meant discrimination. "Why should the ironmasters' men be exempt and farmers not?" he said, fearful that exemption for them would cripple his already-sputtering recruitment drives.

Reluctantly, and under intense pressure from public officials and Knox, Washington agreed to the exemption of thousands of ironworkers, but only if their foundries were manufacturing cannon, shot, and shell "for the public good." Workers not involved in the war effort would get no exemptions. Washington also took the step to prevent ironworkers and their companies from simply withholding services on the grounds that they did not have enough men.

At Washington's insistence, Congress granted the exemption to the ironworkers in New Jersey, and other states, and did so each year through the end of the war, acknowledging the emergency: "It is highly expedient that the army and navy should be furnished as speedily as possible with cannon, cannon shot, refined bar iron, shovels, axes, and other implements of iron, which the furnaces at Mount Hope, and Hibernia, with the forges at Brookland, Mount Pleasant, Longwood and Middle Forge...are well adapted to supply" read a Congressional resolution on the matter. State legislatures then granted the exemptions from militia duty.

Fifty men were exempted at Mount Hope and twenty-four at Hibernia. Between twenty and fifty were exempted at several other ironworks and four at Ford's powder mill. The ironworks, of course, used their exempt status to lure workers, as evidence in their newspaper advertising. An ad for Batsto ironworks on June 26, 1777 read: "Wanted at Batsto and Mount Holly—a number of laborers, colliers, nailers and two or three experienced forgemen to whom constant employment and best wages will be given....The workmen at these works are by law of this state exempt from military duty."

Even the exemptions were not enough of a lure to hold workers at some ironworks. In early April 1777, Gabriel Ogden, who owned a foundry at Pompton Lakes, convinced Washington to take an unusual step and assign forty soldiers to labor as ironworkers in order to meet cannon and ammunition orders.

From time to time, the general had to stop making war against the Redcoats in order to keep the peace among the iron managers. They feuded with each other constantly in the early days of the conflict. They all hated Stirling. He owed most of them money from pre-Revolutionary days and was seen by them as an opportunist (and a bad general). Their antagonism reached its high point just after the war began when Stirling, in a dispute with workers during a visit to another foundry, pulled out his whip and began hitting several workers with it. And he was not a solitary figure of controversy. Other foundry managers engaged in lengthy disputes with each other over everything from pricing to workers to favoritism within the ranks of the army quartermaster corps. Washington was constantly called upon to make peace between them.

His statesmanship at the foundries was successful and by late winter 1777, the iron owners began to coexist peacefully (one reason was that Washington suggested that the ailing Stirling spend most of the winter at his home in Basking Ridge, eleven long miles from the foundries in Rockaway). By the end of the war, their cooperation with each other had improved so much that even Lord Stirling routinely bought shot and cannons from his competitors and made a point to note how highly he thought of them. On October 15, 1781, he wrote the militia chief at Springfield: "I have desired Mr. John Jacob Faesch of Mount Hope to send on to this place for my account three tons of refined bar iron....I now also enclose an order for Mr. Faesch for one ton of his iron casting in such articles as you will direct. You will settle the price of both the bar iron and castings with Mr. Faesch on whose *honor* [author italics] you may depend in all dealings."

The ironworks owners helped in other ways. Bird, who ran the Hopewell Furnace, later helped to save the starving army during the brutal winter of 1777–78 at Valley Forge. At the outbreak of the war, Bird personally paid for the uniforms, firearms and food supplies for his entire three-hundred–man company. He was unable to move goods by land because of deep snow and the British Army. He took advantage of rising waters on the Schuykill River to send one thousand barrels of needed flour to Washington's army via boats he commandeered. Historians credit the flour, even though it only meant food for a week, as a major reason the army survived. Other ironworks, such as the foundry in Ringwood, New Jersey, permitted editors fearful of being arrested by the British to use their facilities to secretly produce newspapers.

Washington listened to any ideas forthcoming from his friends in the ironworks. Many were practical, such as the portable iron ovens cast at Ringwood and later used for cooking at Valley Forge. The idea that most intrigued Washington was the construction and placing of an iron chain across the Hudson River to stop all British shipping. Engineers designed a series of wooden pontoons connected by a long, thick iron chain that would stretch across the river near Poughkeepsie, anchored by iron cables to the floor of the waterway. The first chain was finished in the winter of

1777, but was captured and destroyed by British land forces the following fall. The chain was manufactured at Erskine's Ringwood Ironworks and transported ninety miles to the Hudson by caravans of wagons. A second chain was produced a year later and put in place in the summer of 1778, with chain and links from Ringwood, Lord Stirling's Hibernia plant and companies in Sterling, New York, and Pennsylvania. That chain, guarded by detachments of men at forts on both sides of the waterway, remained in place throughout the war and prevented any British transportation up the river.

Not all of the iron manufacturers were patriots. Several remained loyal to the British Crown. Charles Read Jr., the son of the man who built several ironworks in the Pine Barrens and worked in them, at first joined the Continental Army. He changed his mind just a month later, quit, and joined the British Army. He was captured and sent to Philadelphia as a prisoner of war. Other Loyalist iron owners were forced to flee during the war.

Toward the end of the winter, Washington and Knox lobbied Congress to reform its administrative structure to permit several subclassifications for army supplies. This allowed the manufacture and procurement of cannon, muskets, gunpowder, and other armaments as separate categories, with more men for each. The general was hopeful that this would create a stronger department.

The commander-in-chief also had word in early spring that production of cannon and ammunition was progressing at the smoke-belching ironworks in Morris County and elsewhere in New Jersey. The Mount Holly Furnace in South Jersey, one of the nation's largest, began to make cannon and had hired dozens of ironworkers and woodcutters to begin production of ammunition. A large munitions factory had finally been completed north of Philadelphia, and the one in Carlisle, to which Washington had sent personal designs, was just about ready to begin producing cannonballs. The ironworks in Morris County had become so productive—they had manufactured dozens of cannons and thousands of cannonballs during the winter—that Washington decided to leave a company of soldiers in the area to protect them and guard their storehouses. The foundry in Springfield, Massachusetts, was now operational.

However, the production of cannon and the large manufacture of ammunition in Morristown and the surrounding area was never quite sufficient. Despite the best efforts by the foundries, cannons often did not function properly. Some cracked during their first use. Repairs were sometimes impossible. In one test at the Hopewell factory, all 155 cannons, which took months to manufacture, misfired and were deemed useless. The brand-new ammunition industry had human tolls, too. Numerous workers were injured in the intensified efforts to manufacture ammunition. Nigah Peacock, the manager of a small gunpowder plant in South Jersey, was killed when his mill blew up during production.

Greene and Knox complained throughout the war that they never had enough artillery and ammunition, regardless of how many requests they sent Congress and how much urgent pleading they did. They were right. A two-year plan to lay siege to New York, and end the war, had to be called off twice because there was not enough cannon and shot.

Despite Washington's unhappiness that the winter failed to produce the hundreds of cannon that he dreamed about, the Morris foundries, and those in other states, did, however, manufacture enough cannon, and far more than enough shot, to permit the Continental Army to fight on when the snows of 1777 melted. And, in mid-April, dozens of cannons, 12,500 muskets, and thousands of stands of ammunition arrived in Philadelphia, delivered from the first of several French warships to bring needed military help to America.

"I have as many as tolerable," Washington told Schuyler of his cannons with satisfaction. The army had enough artillery and ammunition to hold its own in most battles against the British. This fact was leaked to Tory spies. The artillery allowed General Washington to keep his army on the field, which was his main goal throughout winter camp in Morristown.

The commander had used his considerable personal skills, powers of persuasion, and reputation to forge friendships with the foundry owners in Morristown and the neighboring villages. As a general, he had persuaded them to give up personal goals and profits for the good of the army. As a general, he had pulled strings and cut corners to land them contracts and have their workers exempted from military service. As a national executive, he had learned valuable lessons in how to serve as an administrator of a large war machine and the importance of munitions factories to both win the war and, later, perhaps, keep the peace. He had learned, again, that his role as commander-in-chief had grown to substantially more than just that of a military officer. He was functioning as both the civilian and military head of the nation, a job of great responsibility and danger, roles that would benefit him later.

Lord Howe and the British, who were planning an attack on Philadelphia, were taken aback. Just one year before, British Earl Hugh Percy had haughtily written Lord Germain from New York that the Americans could not survive very long and that "this business is pretty much over." Now, circumstances had changed dramatically and Howe had to send a secret note to Germain to inform him that the war could no longer be won as quickly as planned. "The rebels will not be able to raise their [projected] army...yet they will have numerous militia, with a tolerable train of artillery," he wrote, and regrettably predicted at least another year of fighting.

The American soldiers were happy to leave camp and enthusiastic about the coming campaign. "We shall be able, with the blessings of heaven, to make a good summer's work of it," predicted an optimistic Lieutenant Sam Shaw.

Washington's Morristown force had become so strong by the end of winter that the cocky Hamilton boldly wrote to a Congressional delegate that the mighty British were now afraid of the Americans and that "it would be madness in them...to risk all in any capital attempt [in a battle with us] and I am confident they will not do it."

Chapter Seven

VALLEY FORGE

VALLEY FORGE, 1777–78

"Here comes a soldier; his bare feet are seen through his worn-out shoes, his legs nearly naked from the tattered remains of an only pair of stockings, his breeches not sufficient to cover his nakedness, his shirt hanging in strings, his hair disheveled, his face meager, his whole appearance pictures a person forsaken and discouraged. He comes, and cries with an air of wretchedness and despair, 'I am sick, my feet lame, my legs are sore, my body covered with this tormenting itch…and all the reward I shall get will be—'poor Will is dead'."
—Dr. Abilgence Waldo, a surgeon with the Continental Army

"I am now convinced, beyond a doubt, that unless some great and capital change suddenly takes place, this army must inevitably be reduced to one or other of these three things: starve, dissolve or disperse."
—George Washington

"We have not so merry a Christmas."
—Henry Dearborn, a private at Valley Forge

The fateful decision to establish the 1777–78 winter camp of the Continental Army at Valley Forge, twenty miles northwest of Philadelphia in Chester County, was made by George Washington following careful consideration and under enormous political pressure. In the major action of the summer/fall campaign, the British army, after sailing from New York, had defeated Washington's American forces of eleven thousand men at Brandywine Creek, south of Philadelphia, on September 11 and then seized the city on September 26. The Redcoats entered Philadelphia in a parade, rows upon rows of smartly dressed soldiers marching with precision steps followed by the army's fife-and-drum bands playing heroic music that wafted through the city's neighborhoods. The British were cheered mightily by that town's Tories, who lined the streets to welcome them.

Determined to recapture Philadelphia, Washington attacked the British at Germantown, just outside the city limits, a week later. Despite hard fighting by the Americans and daring maneuvers by Washington, the Continental Army was beaten back. Philadelphia was secured for the Crown. Continental Army efforts to defend two American forts on the Delaware River near Philadelphia in the following weeks were unsuccessful; the British captured them and secured a firm route of supply for their forces.

On October 7, an American army led by Horatio Gates and Benedict Arnold achieved a stunning victory at Saratoga, New York, capturing the army of General John Burgoyne, buoying American spirits. But the fall of Philadelphia and the defeat of Washington's army in successive battles and in several small skirmishes between the middle of October and late December were major military reversals. Philadelphia was the largest city in America and one of the world's busiest seaports. The community was also the nation's capital, home to the Continental Congress for two years and the site of the signing of the Declaration of Independence. It was in Philadelphia that Washington had been given command of the army and in Philadelphia where Thomas Paine's *The American Crisis* was first published. Its fall to the Redcoats, assisted by Hessians, a joint force of seventeen thousand men, and the hasty evacuation of the city by Congress, was not only a reminder of England's overwhelming numbers and resources, more than thirty-four thousand men to Washington's eleven thousand, but a severe public-relations setback.

The surrender of the river forts signaled the end of the 1777 campaign, and Washington began to consider sites for a winter camp. The commander-in-chief wanted to keep his army within striking distance of Howe's forces if they moved out of Philadelphia, just as he had at Morristown, thirty miles from the British in New York, the previous winter. Now, though, he had additional pressures to camp near the city. The Continental Congress had fled to cramped headquarters in York, Pennsylvania, one hundred miles west, and wanted protection from a British assault on them there. The Pennsylvania Supreme Executive Council, evacuated to Lancaster from Philadelphia, demanded that Washington camp nearby to guard the towns and farms in the nearby area, using the military force for a political goal. The head of the council, Thomas Wharton Jr., snarled at Washington that if he camped anywhere besides the general Philadelphia area, he would be leaving the residents there "open to the ravages and insults of the enemy."

Members of the council were also afraid that without the Continental Army nearby, hundreds of the state's residents in the farms and villages around Philadelphia who were still neutral about the rebellion would flock to the British banner. They also demanded a major attack on Philadelphia by Washington to liberate it, a military operation he refused to undertake because of his weakened forces.

Washington's real winter needs for the army were shelter, clothing, and food. During the previous winter, Washington had billeted his much-smaller army in several communities in northern New Jersey near Morristown, and his force of some three thousand troops had ample shelter and food in village homes. But now he had a much larger army. He commanded more than thirteen thousand men in the winter of 1777–78 and had decided to house almost all of them, except two brigades sent to Wilmington, Delaware, in a single camp, which would, because of its size, immediately become the fourth-largest city in America. Washington could not house an army of thirteen thousand men in local homes, as he did the previous winter; Congress had passed a law forbidding it following complaints from Morristown residents. To feed, clothe, and provide for that many men, and offer medical services for those wounded in autumn battles and suffering from illness, would require enormous resources and administrative skill. And he had little money to pay for anything because, as he told Congress, "the military chest is bare."

Valley Forge was named after a local iron forge that had been destroyed by the British in the fall, but the camp was not in a valley. The area was a high plateau set on top of slightly rolling farmland at the intersection of Valley Creek and the Schuykill River. The plain there contained large meadows surrounded by thickets of trees. The plateau, with small creeks slicing through it, presented a luscious appearance at the height of summer and seemed to be an artist's palette of different bright hues in fall, when the leaves turned color. But its trees were barren and its meadows stark when winter set in.

The general was naturally worried about spending the winter in Valley Forge. He had been assured that the local sawmills could produce enough wood for thousands of soldiers' cabins and that the locals, from one of America's largest population centers and fertile farmlands, could provide ample food and clothing (even the British referred to Philadelphia as the "wheat capital of the world"). Valley Forge was buttressed by a wide river on one side, looked down over miles of terrain on the other three sides, and would be easy to defend in case Howe attacked. Washington needed a strong local militia to augment the size of the army and assist its leaders with their knowledge of local geography when skirmishes occurred. The commander was promised a huge militia, perhaps the largest in America. Politically, Washington enjoyed the continued vigorous support of both Congress and the Pennsylvania Supreme Executive Council. Still, it was a huge undertaking and Washington knew that both armies had devoured much of the available food in the area during the previous three months.

Valley Forge was advocated by two of Washington's most trusted generals, Lord Stirling and Peter Muhlenberg; the latter had lived in the area years before. They were familiar with Chester County and assured Washington that the site would meet his needs. Despite their personal guarantees, though, twelve other generals voted against Valley Forge and suggested other Pennsylvania towns, such as Lancaster and Reading; Wilmington, Delaware; and sites in New Jersey. Congressional delegate Abraham Clark vociferously pushed for any New Jersey site, fearful that the Redcoats would overrun the state.

Many disagreed and strongly urged him to reconsider with arguments that, later, seemed prescient. General William Weedon warned against a camp in open farm country; the army would not be near any medical services or town where clothing could be manufactured. Several others told Washington that while he could not house soldiers in homes, there were numerous barns, halls, and public buildings that could be used in towns such as Wilmington. Brigadier General Jedediah Huntington of Connecticut said that a nearby community was necessary. The soldiers, he insisted, were exhausted and needed as much comfort as they could find. Upon arrival at Valley Forge, and a quick first inspection, Huntington wrote that "our men, our horses and carriages are almost worn out with the constant marches and fatigues of the campaign and there is scarcely a single convenience about us but wood and water."

The most vigorous opponent of the decision was Major General Baron Johann DeKalb. A longtime critic of Washington, DeKalb worried that both American and British forces had already consumed much of the farm supplies in the area during the winter of 1776–77 and that the Continentals had been subsisting off of what was left for the last three months. How could the area still supply an entire army? "Good advice was not taken," DeKalb wrote of the Valley Forge choice. "The idea of wintering in this desert can only have been put into the head of the commanding general by an interested speculator or a disaffected man.…[I]t is a pity that he is so weak and has the worst advisors in the men who enjoy his confidence." The general noted, too, that in the weeks prior to the army's arrival at Valley Forge, food supplies had been dangerously low and wondered "what will be done when the roads grow worse and the season more severe?"

Still, Washington chose Valley Forge. In seeking "the best winter quarters," in the end Washington picked the plateau near the Schuykill for one main reason—the Pennsylvania politicians' insistence that he protect the local population from the British. The general would simply make the best out of a disputed choice for political necessity; it was a skill he acquired now that would serve him well later, when he became president and again had to help regional politicians serve their constituents while he served his.

"We should [not] leave a vast extent of fertile country to be despoiled and ravaged by the enemy, from which they would draw vast supplies and where many of our firm friends would be exposed to all the miseries of the most insulting and wanton depredation. A train of evil might be enumerated," he said. "These considerations make it indispensably necessary for the army to take such a position."

Long before the arrival at Valley Forge, Washington knew that he had mushrooming problems and that Congress had done little to solve them. His worries led him to write a long series of plaintive letters outlining his dilemma. Washington relayed his fears of insufficient provisions for the winter to Governor Livingston of New Jersey on October 1, complaining to him that the clothing department finds it "impossible to comply with the full demands of the whole army." On October 13, he complained to Congress that he was already short on food and uniforms. On November 6, he wrote Thomas Jefferson that he did not have enough clothes to get through the winter. Two days later, he informed Congress that he was out of money and that most of his troops had not been paid in two months. On November 10, he warned officers of a clothing crisis, referring to "our ragged men and half naked soldiers." The absence of shoes had become such a problem that the commander had to authorize a contest, with a ten-dollar reward, to the soldier who could design the best shoe substitutes using the plentiful rawhide in the warehouses.

A few days later, Washington sent a gloomy letter to Patrick Henry: "The stock of goods that were on hand are so nearly consumed that I look with the greatest concern upon the sufferings of the soldiers for the remainder of this year...."

Three weeks later, General John Sullivan wrote Washington that clothing had become such a problem that the army might not be saved no matter where winter camp was built. Upon arrival at Valley Forge, a Massachusetts officer reported that three-quarters of his men could not turn out for parade because they had no stockings or shoes. A Pennsylvania officer counted twenty-six men in his regiment without shirts and seventy-four without breeches and blankets. Anthony Wayne told a friend that he was surrounded by barely clothed and ill men. "My people...naked as to clothing. They are in that respect in a worse condition than Falstaff's recruits for they have not one whole shirt to a brigade."

A British spy who watched the American march toward Valley Forge confirmed their condition in a report. "They are destitute of shoes, stockings and shirts—the men tear the leather off their cartridge boxes to wrap around their feet," he said.

General Washington had monitored the clothing crisis since the battle of Germantown and, fearful of the army becoming victim to the elements as winter approached, as early as November 12 had peppered the Clothiers Department with demands for jackets and breeches. That same day, the general threatened to court martial any men who sold their jackets or breeches to buy food, a practice which had become common, and urged officers to keep daily records of the clothing of each man in the army. Exasperated, he asked one officer to simply attempt to "provide each man with a good blanket and shoes."

There was no one that the army could turn to for the instant production of clothing that was so hastily needed as they prepared to leave Whitemarsh, their camp for the last two months, for the Schuykill. The British Army could always depend upon its mills back home to produce uniforms, which could be transported to the states by its Navy. America had no clothing industry prior to the war and imported almost all of its woolens from England, nearly one million pounds per year. There were a few weavers located in distant villages, but no textile mills or any other means for the mass production of clothing, especially for a large national army.

In late November, the commander-in-chief ordered patrols to scour the countryside to demand for the army—with payment—any extra clothing the inhabitants might possess. After he watched a large number of men parade nearly barefoot, he posted a notice asking for anyone with information on where hundreds of pairs of shoes could be obtained locally to report to his office. Despite the burgeoning woes that were befalling his men, Washington tried to cheer them up as they began their day-long march to Valley Forge. Sitting in his field tent, its canopy shut down to keep out the chilly breezes, in his orders of the day Washington penned an inspirational message: "The officers and soldiers, with one heart, and one mind, will resolve to surmount every difficulty, with a fortitude and patience, becoming their profession, and the sacred cause in which they are engaged...."

Food shortages were just as vexing. On November 23, Deputy Commissary General of Issues Thomas Jones had complained to Washington and others that they were nearly out of food and warned of "the approaching calamity which I expect here every moment. [We have] not a single barrel of flour...."

The army arrived on the plains of Valley Forge on a chilly December 19 for a winter that would live forever in United States history. Historians, journalists, painters, poets, and movie directors have convinced generations of Americans that it was the harsh winter that nearly dissolved the army and that it was the ability of Washington and his men to overcome snowstorms and freezing temperatures that won the war. Who has not seen, sometime in their life, paintings of Washington on his knees, praying in the bloodstained snow at Valley Forge, or soldiers there barefoot and shivering in the cold, or read that nearly half the soldiers in the army died there? Somehow the Americans' ability to survive Valley Forge came to symbolize their gritty ability to overcome adversity of any kind over the next 225 years.

There were six snowstorms from December to March, with bad ones on Christmas Day and on January 11, but their snowfall only averaged four inches and they caused minimal inconvenience. Although there were several days of bone-chilling weather, the temperatures recorded during those months was not unusually low, and many soldiers used phrases like "pleasant for the season" to note the mildness. Sgt. Ebenezer Wild kept a diary that showed mild temperatures ("very fare and pleasant") on eleven of the first fourteen days of January. The Valley Forge winter, despite the folklore that surrounded it, was actually quite moderate.

What caused all of the deaths, the starvation, and an army in rags was not the weather, but the collapse of the army's commissary, quartermaster, and clothier divisions; feuds between Pennsylvania state authorities and Congress; badly run hospitals; and the general difficulty of any large army to live off the land all winter. Congress was of scant help in remedying these woes, which all surfaced at the same time that the army arrived at Valley Forge.

The administration of supplies had become a four-headed dragon designed by Congress. The Commissary Department was created to procure and supply food at the start of the war, but in June 1777, Congress inexplicably separated it into two divisions, Commissary General of Purchases and the Commissary General of Issues, the former to buy supplies and the latter to oversee their delivery. The Quartermaster's Office was created to hire wagons and drivers and to organize the transport of provisions. Under new Congressional rules, though, the Commissary Department could also hire wagons and transport supplies. An extensive set of recently adopted regulations, which required hundreds of hours of additional paperwork, was introduced. Neither department's top administrators lived in camp and worked with the army; they were civilians working for Congress in Philadelphia, then York. The military stores administration was also bogged down in misadministration. Chaos was inevitable.

The administrators of these divisions were often chosen for political purposes. The Commissary head was Joseph Trumbull, the son of Connecticut Governor Jonathan Trumbull. Roundly criticized for his inability to provide the necessary supplies and tired of the exhausting work, Trumbull resigned in August. He was replaced by William Buchanan, a Philadelphia merchant recommended by members of the Pennsylvania delegation in Congress. Buchanan was an incompetent who slowly led the Commissary Department into disarray, a condition that peaked just as the army moved to Valley Forge.

In October 1777, General Thomas Mifflin, the army's quartermaster, quit in anger. Mifflin, a Philadelphia politician before the Revolution, had been one of Washington's first aides and a major general. The commander-in-chief admired his administrative and recruiting abilities, but would not give him a combat command because he had no military experience. Mifflin, stationed in Philadelphia, was also highly critical of Washington for not defending the city sooner. Mifflin fled the city along with members of Congress and several thousand others as the British entered it. He did not move to York with Congress, but went home to Reading and promptly resigned, leaving the all-important quartermaster's job vacant at a time when someone was needed most. Incredibly, Congress did not replace Mifflin until March of 1778.

Food was so scarce because the men in charge of the Commissary Department had badly misjudged and sometimes misrepresented the amount of food available. As an example, Trumbull told Congress that the department had enough flour in various warehouses, 7.6 million pounds of it, to last the army throughout the entire winter. Yet a final check of flour in storage, undertaken as the army went into winter camp, showed that in reality there was only half that amount. It was further reported that the commissary had enough cattle, or access to enough cattle, to keep the entire army at Valley Forge supplied for seven months. A final check in mid-December, though, showed that the actual supply of beef would only last eight days.

Washington, who monitored his supplies on a daily basis, sometimes checking on them every few hours, complained bitterly about the inefficient operations of the two departments. He had managed to keep his temper in check with success during most of the Morristown winter, but now, in this vast geographic setting of forests and meadows, he erupted at the inefficiencies that threatened the lives of his men. Washington was the single most powerful man in the country, civilian or military, and yet he exercised no authority over supplies. This need for departmental control at the very top of the government would later be one of his very first priorities as president. He excoriated the clothing department, telling Congress that their sad work was "further proof of the inability of an army under the circumstances to perform the common duties of soldiers," and said that hundreds of his men were "barefoot and naked" and had to sit around the campfire all night because they had no blankets to cover them. He called the inability of the department to supply his men "a great and crying evil."

Not only was there just a week's worth of meat in the storehouses as the army prepared to move to Valley Forge, but the prospects of finding and slaughtering more cattle to feed the men were not promising. The Commissary, Congress, Pennsylvania Council, and just about everyone connected to the provisions chain had made an enormous blunder in determining whether or not Chester and Philadelphia counties could support the army's beef needs. During its best years before the war, from 1770 to 1773, farmers living in the metropolitan Philadelphia region had exported an average of just 1.4 million pounds of beef per year, the amount available after they met their own needs. The Continental Army, as everyone should have known by then, consumed nearly a million pound of beef *per month*. And, too, beginning in 1774, when political troubles surfaced, farmers had reduced their wheat harvest to avoid being saddled with surpluses they might not be able to export. There was little wheat or flour to make bread for an army that was consuming nearly thirty-four thousand pounds of bread each day.

What provisions local farms did have were plundered by the British when they moved through the county that fall. As an example, one farmer said that when the British raided his farm, one of the largest, on September 19 they stole two horses, 120 pounds of cheese, 105 pounds of butter, 108 pounds of bacon, 9 sheep, 4 coats, 4 pairs of breeches, 12 pair of stockings, 20 shirts, and 20 yards of linen.

The locals did not have anywhere near the food necessary to feed a large national army for an entire winter. Many of those who rode past those farms following the defeat at Germantown on October 4, and through the Whitemarsh area later, observed that. Jedediah Huntington put it best in a letter to a friend when he referred to Chester County as "this starved country."

The resignations of Trumbull in August and Mifflin in October created a paperwork nightmare for the Commissary chief's successors, now literally running two departments instead of one, and for Henry

Lutterloh, asked to take over Mifflin's duties without being appointed quartermaster general. Orders were misinterpreted, delayed, or lost. Bills were misplaced. Lists of friendly farmers who would sell food to the army could not be found. Agreements with farmers to lease wagons and arrangements to hire civilians as drivers were forgotten. Records detailing the type and quantity of food in warehouses were mislaid.

One deputy quartermaster wrote sarcastically of the Commissary administrators that "the whole race [of them] look like cats in a strange garret at one another, and not one of them knows what he is about. Such are the happy effects of shifting hands in the midst of a campaign." Another, Peter Colt, in Connecticut, said that "no person knows how to act or what to do. Every kind of commissary business is here entirely stopped."

The problems with Trumbull's successor in Commissary, Buchanan, were much worse. He did little to end the well-known corruption in the department, which was brought to Washington's attention in numerous letters from officers who dealt with Buchanan's employees.

Unwilling to accuse anyone of malfeasance without proof, Washington on several occasions sent aides to investigate complaints of corruption and inflated payrolls in these departments. Their reports were shocking. "There is not a Cross Road, or a Village of three houses but a deputy Commissary and Quarter Master is fixed there, to do nothing…" charged one investigator.

The Commissary was run so badly that Buchanan admitted to his associate, Charles Stewart, that he was afraid that Congress would investigate the entire department. Buchanan blamed all of his troubles on depreciated currency, underlings who did not work hard, and farmers reluctant to sell to the army; at one point he even blamed Washington, telling the Board of War that the general had let his army grow too large.

The commissary rather quickly earned the hatred of the soldiers. "We have lived upon lean beef 'til we are tired of the sight of it [and] live hand to mouth for flour. We blame our providers," said General Jedediah Huntington in a biting letter to his brother. His language may have been curt, but he was nowhere near as furious as Colonel Charles Parker, who blamed the Commissary for inedible food and short supplies and beat one of its agents with a whip and then threatened to hang him.

The new president of Congress, Henry Laurens, already tired of complaints concerning the bunglers in the Commissary, commiserated with them. "I was almost a stranger in Congress when the appointment of a commissary general was on the tapis and candidly confess I was much misled by specious representations," he said in January, adding that he "prognosticated evils which we are now laboring under." In a private letter to his son John, Laurens said he was shocked when Congressmen he was talking to at a recent party broke into laughter when he brought up Washington's plea for a quartermaster.

Hundreds of sick and wounded had arrived at Valley Forge with the army, bundled up in the few thin blankets that were available, and kept together in wagons so crowded that the men, many burning up with fever, were sandwiched against each other. Others stricken by illness had already been sent on to hospitals in Reading and Bethlehem. The sick in Valley Forge had nowhere to go for protective shelter because there were no buildings in which to house them; for weeks, the winter camp was nothing more than a large field of tents. More than anyone, the ill soldiers needed food but had none. Without sustenance, they became sicker and began to die. The end of December brought no relief in the clothing crisis, either, and many men remained dressed in rags. They, too, became sick from exposure to the snow, rain, and cold. The men who were already bedridden in tents began to transmit their diseases to others, creating the first large wave of infections and death that would plague the camp all winter.

The convergence of these health, food, and clothing problems could not be solved by Washington because they were all the responsibility of Congress. Its president had no power to order anyone to do anything. The delegates could not overcome them because, they said, they had to rely on the states for supplies. The states insisted supplies were the responsibility of Congress. There was no federal administrative branch to which anyone could turn or a powerful president with Constitutional authority to get things done, something Washington would plead for when he became president, for he would vividly remember this debacle.

Engaged in feuds all autumn, no one at the federal or state level had paid even minimal attention to the burgeoning supply and medical problems. These had deepened and now threatened to cripple the army. Everything that could go wrong had—and at the same time.

Learning to Be an Administrator

By the end of 1777, George Washington had developed into one of the hardest-working and most efficient administrators in the United States. In his winter camps at Boston, Morristown, and Valley Forge, he not only supervised all of the army's varied military operations but oversaw the running of the cumbersome camps themselves. He supervised the production, collection, and distribution of all the food, clothing, and medical supplies for his hut city and coordinated transportation, building construction, crime and punishment, recreation, and sanitation. In essence, during the winters he simultaneously served as commander-in-chief of the army and the mayor of a large American city. The detailed administrative work he tended to at that time was of considerable help in preparing him for similar work as the nation's chief executive later.

First, he had to build his winter city with residential neighborhoods, warehouses, privies, squares, offices, slaughterhouses, cattle pens, granaries, parade grounds, large stables, wagon barns, blacksmiths sheds, and even athletic fields. He was fastidious in planning the winter camp. His three hundred slaves at Mount Vernon lived in fourteen-foot by sixteen-foot cabins, with fireplaces, sleeping in bunkbeds to conserve space. Up to twelve people could sleep in each cabin, more if they doubled up in beds. The sturdy cabins had served his slaves well at Mount Vernon and they would house his men at Valley Forge. He ordered the construction of more than two thousand of them, with explicit instructions for their completion, in perfectly arranged streets. The twelve thousand men would live in tents until the huts were built.

Valley Forge was isolated in the eastern sector of Chester County, adjacent to Philadelphia county, and there were few farmhouses in either.

None were near enough to serve as headquarters, so Washington had to rent a small, six-room, two-story, gray-stone home from merchant Isaac Potts on the banks of the Schuykill River. Pott's home soon became the most overcrowded office in North America. Four aides worked at desks practically side by side in a fifteen-foot by fifteen-foot first floor office that overlooked the front yard and the river. The general's office was another fifteen-foot square wood-paneled room heated by a fireplace; light poured in through two high, narrow windows on the east wall. The room contained a small, dark brown secretariat for Washington, a tiny wooden table, and a desk with a straight-back chair for an aide. The second floor of the small house contained a fifteen-foot by fifteen-foot bedroom for the commander-in-chief and his wife, when she arrived. The aides slept in two tiny rooms at the front of the building. They used folding beds so that the rooms could be employed as daytime offices for the staff. There was no room large enough for meetings, as there had been in Morristown, so in early February Washington ordered the construction of a spacious wooden hut as a meeting room–dining hall behind the Potts home.

As always, Washington rose just after dawn, washed and dressed, and then plunged into writing letters to his wife and friends in Virginia at the secretariat. Then he walked downstairs, careful to avoid banging his head on the low ceiling over the narrow staircase, and began the day's work with his aides. Later in the morning during those first weeks, the commander strode out of the Potts house to a stable fifty yards away, mounted a horse, and rode to the vast fields where the city of huts was slowly rising out of the ground. Work proceeded briskly there and Thomas Paine wrote that the soldiers looked "like a family of beavers." Washington, proud of his army of carpenters, even offered a monetary reward for the best-built hut.

The city of huts was fraught with problems. The sawmills in the area, sporadically shuttered by frozen streams that could no longer provide waterpower, were not able to supply the tens of thousands of needed cut logs, as hoped. Soldiers in organized teams had to chop down trees and split them into uneven logs. The officers who supervised the construction of the camp were not very diligent and approved shoddy work. The officers, who like the men were in a hurry for immediate shelter, cut corners and ignored some of Washington's instructions. The huts were built on a flat field, with dirt floors and without much drainage. Most walls and roofs were haphazardly built, and saplings, twigs, and sod were used to fill in the cracks between logs, allowing rain and melting snow to seep through, creating puddles of stagnant water. There were no windows for ventilation; the fireplaces often did not work.

Construction lagged and some cabins were not occupied until the middle of January. Hundreds of men living in tents and working in a rather rainy winter came down with pneumonia and other ailments in the meantime and wound up in the hospital. "To see our poor, brave fellows living in tents, bare-footed, bare-legged, bare-breeched, in snow, in rain, on marches, in camp and on duty without being able to supply their wants is really distressing," Sergeant John Brooks of Pennsylvania told a friend.

Men drank dirty water from nearby streams. Not enough latrines were built and those that were did not operate properly. Soldiers urinated on the ground near huts and warehouses. Bad meat was left to rot. Garbage pickup was haphazard and the piled-up debris attracted vermin carrying disease. The rotting carcasses of more than 1,500 horses that had starved to death throughout the winter were left lying on the ground and created more disease. The horses that remained were so thin the men were afraid to use them. These hardships sent hundreds and then thousands of men into the hospitals with a variety of infections, including dysentery and typhus, as well as pneumonia. Hundreds more suffered from the "itch," a skin infection that brought on scabs that covered the body for weeks and rendered soldiers afflicted with it unfit for duty.

Washington's ability to deal with this multitude of problems was curbed by the absence of two of his most trusted men, Hamilton and Knox. Whenever a crisis had occurred in the past, particularly in the winter of 1777, the general could always rely on the diligent Hamilton, with his extraordinary political acumen, to help him. Washington had sent him to procure troops from General Gates in New York at the end of November, and while there Hamilton had fallen so ill that doctors feared he might die. He was bedridden for months and would not return to the army until January 20.

Washington also missed Henry Knox, his artillery chief and long-time confidant, whom he had sent to New England to oversee the military stores department and, wherever he could, hunt for cannon, food, and clothing. Knox was away most of the winter. The general had dispatched Knox and Hamilton on these missions because he did not need them; he had, after all, been assured by the Pennsylvanians that he would not encounter any problems at Valley Forge.

The commander-in-chief did have his core staff of experienced aides to assist him as his problems were exacerbated, and had added John Laurens, the brilliant, personable, French-educated son of the president of the Continental Congress. But, still, under all this unplanned pressure, he missed Hamilton and Knox.

His reduced staff assumed more and more work until they, too, were overloaded with the varied tasks of confronting the burgeoning supply crisis. During the first few days at Valley Forge, officers made repeated efforts to obtain more flour or meat, but failed. On December 22, 1777, the commander-in-chief was told that the last cow in the pens had been slaughtered and no more cattle could be found to provide beef. Nearly all of the flour was gone. There was no wheat. Officers complained that the work on the huts moved too slowly and that their tents afforded little protection as the temperatures dropped. Hungry soldiers snuck out of camp at night and stole whatever provisions they could find at local barns and farm houses, a practice denounced by the commander-in-chief. That same morning, he was told that the men he had ordered out to engage a British foraging patrol could not report for duty because they were starving and too weak to move. And, he told Congress, he could not even defend the camp: "had a body of the enemy crossed the Schuykill this morning, as I had reason to expect from the intelligence I received at four o'clock last night, the divisions which I ordered to be in readiness to march and meet them could not have moved."

Washington exploded. He paced back and forth in his office and dictated a lengthy and angry letter to Henry Laurens about the food and clothing crises. In virulent language, he demanded Congressional intervention and predicted that the army would "starve, dissolve or disperse" and that the war would be over.

Anger growing, Washington described the numerous problems that would lead, he assured Congress, to the collapse of his forces within just a few days. His men, he said, were so fatigued that the night before a regiment hinted at mutiny if supplies did not arrive. There was no beef and a total of just twenty-five barrels of flour left to be shared by nearly thirteen thousand men; he called the heads of the Commissary and Quartermaster's Departments inept and insinuated that they were purposefully sabotaging the army. He told the Congressional head that his officers were turned down in their request to buy clothing from county residents (paying on credit) and assured that Congress would send them ample clothing within ten days but that "not one article of which has come to hand."

Washington wrote Laurens that his men could no longer perform the common duties of soldiers. "We have by a field return this day, made no less than 2,898 men now in camp unfit for duty because they are bare foot and otherwise naked and by the same return it appears that our whole strength in Continental Troops...is 8,000 fit for duty," he said and added that another two thousand men had no blankets and were too sick to move.

"No man, in my opinion, ever had his measures more impeded than I have, by every department in the army," he wrote in one blistering line. He added that he was deeply wounded by what he saw as the abandonment of the government and feared the reaction of the people when they learned the truth and falsely blamed him. "Much more is expected of me than is possible to be performed and that upon the ground of safety and policy I am obliged to conceal the true state of the army from public view and therefore expose myself to detraction and calumny."

A few days later, he sent an equally scalding letter concerning the complete disorganization of the Quartermaster's Department to Lutterloh, sarcastically advising him that "you ought to know where your resources of Waggons & Drivers are to be had, & no longer depend upon soldiers for this business."

While some in Congress ignored Washington's savage letter, Laurens was deeply moved by it. The president of Congress was a sentimental and emotional man, always linking the army and the future of the country and always exhorting people to help the troops. He wrote passionate letters about the soldiers, such as a circular to the states pleading for food and clothing for the men at Valley Forge. In it, he appealed to those "in whose bosoms the sparks of public virtue are not yet extinguished" and told them he knew "that all classes of men will unite with their former spirit and virtue against an enemy whose progress is marked with every vestige of barbarity and whose determined object is to establish a tyranny of the most dangerous and debasing nature over the inhabitants of a vast continent."

Laurens, a short, heavyset man, one of the overlooked figures of the war, was one of the most radical men in the colonies when the Revolution began. A wealthy South Carolina merchant, he served in the South Carolina Assembly from 1756 to 1765 and on the state's Council of Safety. He was elected head of the state in 1775 when the royal governor fled. The state assembly sent him to Philadelphia as a member of the Continental Congress in the summer of 1777, and he was elected its president in November. His brilliant son John, an aide with Washington in the winter of 1777–78, was seen as a future leader. The head of Congress was an extremely hard-working man whom the delegates respected, although he could be contentious at times. Like all presidents of Congress, he had no executive power and was limited to a term of one year. Unlike many, though, he, like the commander-in-chief, realized that his true strength was the power to persuade. He used that skill frequently to extract what power he could from his office to help the army. He admirably performed all those tasks that winter while spending most of his time in York extremely ill with the gout. He was forced to lie down for hours at a time with his feet elevated.

Laurens had met with Washington several times since his arrival at Congress and was impressed by the general. The South Carolinian saw the general as the representative of Congress wherever he was with the army, an extension of the civilian government and, in a way, the country's most visible public official. He trusted Washington and believed him whenever he outlined the problems of the army. He understood from his son John's frequent letters and their meetings that the general's description of the army's dire circumstances was not exaggerated. Laurens also knew that Congress had been drowning in inertia for months, torn with factionalism and unable to accomplish much. He recognized, as many in the army reminded him, that Congress in the winter of 1777 was made up of members who, while well intentioned, simply did not have the patriotic fervor of the original Continental Congress. Following the capture of Philadelphia, some had even lost their faith in Washington and the army. All of this had slowed Congressional activity to a crawl.

"My heart is full and my eyes overflow when I reflect upon a camp of a fourth and more of invalids for want of necessary covering, an army on the verge of bankruptcy. For want of food, that we are starving in the midst of plenty, perishing by cold and surrounded by clothing sufficient for two armies, but uncollected," the president of Congress lamented in a letter he penned to William Livingston after he read Washington's note. "Within a few days...you will be informed that our whole system is tottering, and God only knows whether we shall be able to prop it up."

Laurens worked at an enormous disadvantage in York. He presided over a Congress with an absenteeism rate that sometimes approached 50 percent. The new executive was just learning of the disorganization and deficiencies of the Commissary and Quartermaster's offices. His ailments were so debilitating that he often considered resigning the presidency, and his seat in Congress, and returning to South Carolina to recuperate. Even though ill, without support, and woefully understaffed, the Congressional chief took action at once. He reorganized the Board of War, giving it more power and assembling a five-man committee (a committee whose formation was urged by Washington), which was to ride to Valley Forge and remain there as long as necessary to ascertain the needs of the army and the mood of the public in the region. The president of the Continental Congress told delegates that they should begin an investigation into the commissary, quartermaster's, and hospital departments to discover why supplies were not moving to Valley Forge fast enough and to reorganize them. He told Governor Trumbull that now "not only the Commissarial, but other departments on which the salvation of the army equally depends are somewhat more than deranged; they are shattered and distracted." And, distraught, he told him and others that "I pray God to aid us in this moment of danger." But could these frantic measures bring help in time?

Overcoming the Lack of Support for the Army

The ability of the Americans to survive the Valley Forge winter was also undermined by the growing animosity between the army and the civilian population, friction that had been expanding since the start of the Revolution and now came to a head. Farmers and merchants had argued since the beginning of the war that Continental paper currency was always declining in value; they did not want to sell anything to the army unless payment was in hard money, preferably gold. That reluctance to sell goods to the army, despite its perilous situation, enraged officers and men.

The soldiers were unhappy that they froze and starved while many of the people living around them were warm and comfortable in their homes. The men were envious of the residents who walked about in heavy winter coats while they remained in tattered jackets. They were jealous of the families whose men did not go off to war and were prosperous while their own families, without the man of the house, struggled. They resented the rich young men who paid poor young men money to serve in their place in local militias. Most of all, many of the soldiers were enraged that the public ignored their needs while they were fighting for their freedom.

This view of the soldier's contempt for the civilian population was expressed graphically by a Connecticut soldier, Ichabod Ward:

I am sorry to hear of the uneasiness that seems to be at home concerning the soldiers. It seems by what I can understand that some are very uneasy because we have not killed all the enemy. They wonder what we are about [earning] forty shillings a month and nothing to do. I wish that some men were to undergo half so much as one of us have this winter in long marches and lying on our arms in the open field undergoing cold and hard lodgings.

And everyone seemed to know someone who said they had ridden past a local farm teeming with fat cattle and thousands of sheaves of wheat or, worse, citizens with locked barns full of produce. "The people of the country, even those who pretend to be our best friends, hide their stock from us," wailed Lord Stirling to the commander-in-chief.

Some charged all of the southeastern Pennsylvania residents with being British sympathizers, intent on starving the American army. Congressman Francis Lightfoot called them "the most infamous, vile, execrable, extortionate villains...in the whole world." General James Varnum seethed in his denunciation of them:

My fear is that of dying in a heathenish land, deprived of a Christian burial. Should that befall me, how can my body be found by those who are conversant only in holy places and with good beings? You are well acquainted that a man must die when his time comes; and should mine approach while confined in Pennsylvania, how can my soul find its way through this Tory labyrinth to a pure ether congenial to its own nature?

There was also universal despising of the large population of Quakers in southeastern Pennsylvania, who would not fight for religious reasons and yet, although avowing moral allegiance to the Revolution, would not sell their flour, grain, and cattle to the army on credit. "The cursed Quakers" was a phrase many of the soldiers used in reference to the Friends.

The locals were just as angry with the men in the army as the soldiers were with them. Because of the food shortages, particularly at Valley Forge, soldiers snuck out of camp and plundered farms. The locals expected the thievery they experienced from the British, but not from their own forces. They resented the growing number of men who boasted that they had made large sums of money by collecting bonuses for enlisting and knew that many, despite the threat of execution, managed to enlist several times and collect even more. Many steadfastly believed that they were honor-bound to take orders from state officials, but not from Congress. They objected to selling food or clothes to the army for Continental scrip, which had dramatically depreciated in value.

The war between the army and the Redcoats was quite easy to understand, Washington believed, but neither he or any of his officers, or delegates in Congress, could understand the complicated war between the army and some of its own people.

There are complex reasons why many residents of southeastern Pennsylvania—and in other regions in the remaining years of the war—were reluctant to assist the army. Clearly, anyone living in the area had an opportunity to see the daily deprivations of the soldiers. Many friends and neighbors visited the Pennsylvania soldiers and saw the partially naked men huddled around fires or inside huts. They were told of the starvation in letters. It was no secret. Washington's frequent pleas for help to residents of Pennsylvania, and later New Jersey, Connecticut, and the New England states, similar to his pleas for men and supplies in the winter of 1777 in Morristown, surely alerted everyone in public life to the trouble. The people certainly did have their own problems—many were just subsistence farmers and had little food beyond what they needed for their family—yet they would not turn over any excess clothing or food to the army without payment. If the army existed to defeat the British and win independence for the people, how could those same people abandon the army?

The answer is complicated and connected to the cultural and economic life of colonial America. The people genuinely did not believe that the army needed help. Some saw it as a wholly independent force, organized and funded by Congress and not by their states, counties, or towns. Congress and the states had collected extra taxes to support it and surely had enough money to pay for its operation. Others saw it as a traditional European army, standing on its own and separate from the public. Besides, thanks to Gates victory at Saratoga, the army seemed to be winning the war, despite the two losses at Philadelphia. It was only a matter of time, probably just months, perhaps sooner, until the war ended and the British sailed back to England. Had the American forces not defeated the best British troops at Trenton and Princeton? The people had been assured by their newspapers and pamphleteers that the war would be won. Simply put, many were convinced that the American army did not need the American people. And so the citizens were reluctant to help an army whose civilian administration had nearly ruined it.

In the Chaos of War, Washington Sees the Future

Washington's frustration with the Commissary and Quartermaster's Departments grew in the months following his letter of December 23. As a businessman who had run one of the largest collection of farms in America, he could not understand how national departments could be run without direct supervision from above. Sitting alone in his bedroom or conversing with aides and generals at their two- to three-hour mid-afternoon dinners, he continued to challenge the idea that the national legislative body not only should run departments, but *could*. He began to suspect that Congress, an adequate body to debate policy, pass laws, and request troops, was simply incapable of administering large national offices. The agencies seemed to have lives of their own and operated wholly apart from Congress. They were ostensibly responsible to Congressional committees, but the delegates knew little about supplies.

Now, in the Valley Forge winter, many men on those committees were not even in Congress; they had gone home. The president of Congress was really a nominal figure and he could not seem to make the lumbering administrative agencies function at all. There was no other branch of government to which the general could turn. There was just Congress and the army.

What was needed, he came to believe, was a separate, civilian administrative branch of government to operate all federal agencies, separate from Congress but with Congressional overseers. Those agencies had to be responsible to people in a chain of command leading up to division heads and a national executive of some kind (the U.S. president), just as departments in the army were run by the commander-in-chief. The Valley Forge experience was probably the first time that

Washington considered the future government of the United States, with separate branches and a single president with substantial powers.

Stalemated by Congress, Washington then turned politician and appealed to the states of Virginia, Pennsylvania, and New Jersey and their officials, imploring them to raise as much food and clothing as possible, and to find herds of cattle for slaughter and horses for transportation. He confided to his friend Patrick Henry, now the governor of Virginia, concerning clothes, that "knowing how exceedingly the service has been injured, how great the sufferings and loss of men through this want, I cannot but hope every measure will be pursued...to keep them supplied. I assure you, sir, it is not easy to give you a just and accurate idea of the suffering of the troops. Were they to be minutely detailed the relation so unexpected, so contrary to the common opinion of people distant from the army, would scarcely be thought credible."

A considerable drawback in this winter camp was the inability of the general to simply get on his horse and ride five minutes to the home of an influential local politician to seek help, or request that a local leader visit him at his headquarters. Washington had worked with local public officials in the Morristown area on a small scale during the previous winter and enjoyed considerable cooperation and camaraderie. He was encouraged in that policy of working with local officials by his friend Livingston. And, in Livingston, he had a personal friend as well as a political ally. He had used his success as a general to operate politically like a president to bring divergent groups together for the common good.

Here in Pennsylvania, though, the situation was very different. Federal and state officials did not get along—at all. There had been friction between Congress and the Pennsylvania Assembly, both sitting annoyingly close to each other in Philadelphia, ever since Congress threatened to override the Assembly and take over Pennsylvania when the Assembly seemed too hopelessly mired in its debates to draft a new state constitution in the summer of 1776. Now it exploded over Congressional demands that the Council force state residents to assist the army. The Council charged that it was the job of Congress, but the delegates and Washington insisted that the state had to take over supply functions.

Unlike Morris County, Chester and Philadelphia counties had no strong countywide governing body. Ever since the 1720s, Pennsylvania's counties had been nominally run by three-man boards of commissioners who collected taxes, heard complaints, repaired the roads, and supervised elections. They had little real power over the people, however, and were usually superseded by state authorities. The state's new constitution of 1776, which created an appointed judiciary, a strong Assembly to pass bills, and a Council of Safety, and a "president," or governor, to carry them out, continued the weak three-man commissions for the counties, overseeing their actions. Chester was a sprawling farm area, with villages that contained only a few dozen people, and the inhabitants had never felt the need for a large board to oversee county business. The farmers were requested to make their own highway and bridge repairs and were reimbursed by county-wide assessments. The residents paid taxes to the commissioners that were then sent to the state government. The state handled any emergencies, such as Indian raids.

County public officials were held in low esteem by the new State Assembly. In fact, in 1776 the leaders of the State Constitutional Convention kicked out any county delegates who had refused to support Congress's Declaration of Independence. The state officials who did so were, in turn, held in even lower esteem by the Continental Congress. Delegates there not only showed no appreciation for this patriotic nod from the Pennsylvania Assembly, but just four months later threatened to shut down the Assembly and govern Pennsylvania themselves unless some political disputes within the chamber were resolved. This threat to govern Pennsylvania resulted in the friction between federal and state officials that lasted throughout the war.

The absence of a strong local governing board would prevent Washington from working with public officials who knew the farmers near winter camp and could get things done, although a larger governing body still might not have been able to do much to persuade the large population of Quakers to aid the army. In New Jersey, he had state cooperation, but always knew he could turn to his neighbors if state officials resisted him. Here, he was forced to work with constantly feuding state officials.

Cooperation between the national and state governments and the army was further impeded by the creation of yet another governing body, the reorganized Board of War. The new board not only cavalierly sent orders to Pennsylvania's state council, but overrode the Commissary Department and established its own set of agents to purchase supplies, who competed with Congress and the Commissary. To make matters worse, at the Board of War's insistence, Congress then passed a bill that permitted it to countermand any legislation passed by the Pennsylvania Assembly, which increased the ill will that had developed in the state toward Congress. Confusion reigned.

The inability of the State Council or Congress to accomplish much certainly did not surprise Washington or his generals after nearly three years of legislative logjams. Perhaps General Nathanael Greene explained the slow workings of Congress best in late December when he wrote of an army request for militia:

> This measure must go recommended to Congress. From Congress after a week or ten days' consultation a resolve will take place, recommending it to the different states. The assemblies of each are to be called together, their deliberations and judgment to be had upon the property of the measure and then an order after ten or twelve days issued to assemble the militia. If the officers are slow and tardy, as usual, to collect and march them to camp will be the business of a month.

The commander-in-chief, who debated the foibles of national and state governments daily with his aides, shared Greene's view. "The disaffection of the people is past all belief," he complained in a fit of exasperation. In December, in one of his rare bursts of public anger, he chided both the residents and Congress for complacency:

> I can assure those gentlemen that it is a much easier and less distressing thing to draw remonstrances in a comfortable room by a good fire side than to occupy a cold bleak hill and sleep under frost

and snow without clothes or blankets....Although they seem to have little feeling for the naked and distressed soldier, I feel super-abundantly for them and from my soul pity those miseries.

His rather dim view of the slow workings of Congress was not disputed by Laurens, who agreed with him. In a rather charming phrase, Laurens frequently told Washington of bills in the halls of Congress that "the work has indeed been a long time on the anvil."

At the same time, Washington's pleas for the state council to provide him with wagons to transport food from farms some distance from Valley Forge wound up tabled for weeks as the council engaged in another bitter dispute with Congress over how much money should be paid for the wagons and their drivers. The state council caused more problems when it refused to go along with Congressional price controls to hold down the cost of supplies, which were increasing as the Continental dollar slipped in value. The issue was never resolved. Neither was the varying prices of just about everything, such as flour, which sold for twenty-six shillings per hundred weight in Mackensy, Pennsylvania, but just twenty at Easton.

In addition, there were supply miscues everywhere. Although the winter was not severe, infrequent ice sometimes caused problems. One officer with a shipment of provisions was forced to remain on the northern bank of the Schuykill River for nine days until ice on the river thawed and his barge could take the food across. A shipment of clothes from Virginia was lost when commissary agents tried to haul it across a river of thin ice on sleds and the ice broke beneath them, ruining the clothes. Shipments of food upstream from Reading had to stop when the river level dropped; the quartermaster corps never anticipated that and had no other means of transportation for the food, which never arrived.

An investigation by John Ladd Howell, of the Commissary Department, showed that there were thirty-five thousand barrels of vegetables, beef, fish, wheat, pork, bread, and salt in storage deports in Delaware and Maryland, but no one had bothered to pick them up. Fifteen tons of much-needed hay located on a New Jersey farm could not be retrieved because wagons could not be procured. Fearful that British foragers might seize it, Greene had it burned. Twenty miles away, Tench Tilghman discovered several thousand barrels of provisions that a patriotic farmer wanted to sell to the army, but no one in the vicinity had wagons to transport it. One farmer had gathered a substantial amount of supplies for the army and agreed to sell it for just an IOU to be paid later, but a paperwork mix-up ensued and the needed food was never acquired.

Officers at Wilmington intercepted wagons of supplies headed for Valley Forge and refused to let them continue, unloading them and seizing the clothes for themselves, arguing with their superiors that "dogs were never more naked." Reports came in from Boston that residents there had raised enough clothes to fill a large wagon train, but neither the quartermaster or commissary offices were capable of moving it to Valley Forge. Washington had lost so many shipments of promised provisions and clothing that at one point he told officers he sent to look for them to keep it a secret from the men, to avoid further anger.

The Ultimate Enemy: Starvation

The mild winter was often as much harm as help because unusually high temperatures would sometimes follow cold snaps or rainy nights, softening the ground and retarding any movements of the heavy wagons. On January 30, a Hessian officer in Philadelphia noted that "today was the most beautiful summer day but no one could move from one house to another because the mud was so deep." As early as Christmas, Washington was warning the Commissary Department that "bad weather and broken roads will render the transporting provisions from any distance...subject to considerable delay." He was right; impassable roads were a constant problem and food delays were commonplace. "The badness of roads have deprived a single wagon from coming to camp this several days," an army officer wrote in February. As late as April, officers were still reporting that the roads were "intolerably bad." The rainfall that winter was heavier than usual, too, creating more mud. Day after day, supply wagons became stuck in it.

General Nathanael Greene succinctly summed up the deprivations the army endured in a January 5 letter when he said that "the troops are worn out with fatigue, badly fed and almost naked. There are and have been some thousands in the army without shoes for months past. It is difficult to get sufficient supplies to clothe the army at large."

It was especially difficult because of James Mease, a man remarkably unsuited for administrative work who, with modestly endowed subordinates, was the civilian in charge of the army's clothing department. At varying times during the winter, he was criticized for refusing to purchase clothing because he thought the price too high, for failing to pick up available clothes, refusing to buy clothes outside of Pennsylvania, and bungling orders to transport anything. Washington never believed that Mease, a merchant before the war, truly understood that men were freezing at Valley Forge. The general repeatedly asked Mease to visit camp, just several hours away on horseback, for an inspection, once practically ordering him. But Mease never did, perhaps earning the distinction of being the only man in the war to refuse a request by the commander-in-chief.

Complaints against Mease began to pile up in Congress and became a torrent by January. Some Americans may have been dying of the measles, Anthony Wayne wryly remarked, but soldiers in the Continental Army were "dying of the 'Meases.'"

None of these accusations moved Mease, who, in fact, following Wayne's sarcastic remark, told friends that he was being treated unfairly and that the numerous charges against him only showed that soldiers in winter camp had nothing to do except gripe. "Complaining is the fashion at present," he said.

Congress, though, did nothing to force Mease to reorganize his department or work more efficiently, and the entire winter passed without any improvement in the Congressional supply of clothing.

Mease's counterpart, Colonel Benjamin Flower, Commissary General of Military Stores, was not much better equipped for his work. Flower, thirty, was a hat manufacturer before the war. He had joined the artillery corps and was named head of Military Stores in 1777. His job was to build and administer a weapons factory in the Philadelphia area and make certain that the army was always supplied with cannon, muskets, and ammunition. Flower's problem, though, was that he was often sick and unable to work. Right when the army needed its department administrators the most, in mid-February, Flower was again bedridden (he would die in 1781).

Needing someone, the Board of War named Cornelius Sweers, Flower's bookkeeper, and placed him in charge whenever Flower was ill or traveling in other states. Under Sweers, production and delivery slowed, to Washington's dismay. Sweers claimed that he did not have enough men to help him administer the department, that he was drowning in paperwork and had run out of cash to make purchases. Later that year, following an investigation, it was discovered that Sweers had embezzled a significant amount of money from the army and he was imprisoned.

Always the pragmatist, Washington came to believe that his traditional supply chains were not going to improve. He had never permitted the men to plunder the inhabitants of the county, referring to those who did so as "villains" and their work as "cruel outrage and robbery and injurious to the cause in which we are engaged." Unable to procure enough food or clothing, and unwilling to permit its theft, Washington realized that he had to devise alternative methods. All of them showed the skills that he acquired in the war that made him a successful public official as well as a commander, skills that later would be used collectively to make him the nation's capable first president.

He had earlier ordered Sullivan's men to build a bridge over the Schuykill River as a safe retreat for the army if it was attacked and to make it easier for militia in the area to move in and out of camp. Now, he authorized local farmers to set up food markets near the bridge on different days of the week to sell the men whatever excess food they could find at regulated but fair prices that he set himself. He dispatched Anthony Wayne into South Jersey to forage for as much food as he could to replenish the dwindling supplies in Chester County. Lord Stirling took other men and scoured the New Jersey countryside northeast of Philadelphia, where he was able to find and procure far more food than anticipated. Wayne not only succeeded in finding food, but discovered several huge herds of cattle, which he commandeered on credit and delivered to Valley Forge.

In another expedition to find food, Washington asked General John Armstrong of the Pennsylvania militia to take a company of men and beg local farmers to sell him any cows they did not absolutely need for themselves. Traveling farm to farm, making his pleas in the name of the commander-in-chief, Armstrong managed to bring two hundred cows back to camp. Washington ordered American patrols to hide near highways to intercept local farmers traveling to Philadelphia to sell their food to the British and seize it—on credit. Learning that a large British force was about to leave Philadelphia to forage for food in the communities on the west bank of the Delaware River, Washington sent Greene ahead of them to seize whatever food, cattle, and horses he could find, paying on credit but making it clear that no one could refuse.

The general also refused to pay exorbitant prices on goods and put the army to work to help itself. As an example, the cost of barrels for the storage of food became so high that Washington stopped purchasing them and ordered soldiers to manufacture them. The general gained authorization from Congress to plead with the governors of each state to appoint men in their largest communities to go door to door and beg for clothes from residents. His 219 tailors were then put to work making clothing repairs, and men who were shoemakers before the war turned tanned leather into footwear.

He contacted newspaper editors, whom he had courted since the beginning of the war, and persuaded them into running notices asking readers to send clothes to Valley Forge. In a rather simple move that achieved surprising results, Washington then asked soldiers to just write home to ask their families to send them clothes.

Unable to procure enough supplies from Congress and the neighborhoods around him, Washington resumed his fruitful relationships with the nation's governors in an effort to induce them to provide food and clothing from their states. He invited several, such as Reed and Livingston, to camp. They were treated as visiting heads of state and everyone in camp deferred to them. The politicians were given tours of camp, encouraged to hold meetings with soldiers from their states, and feted at dinners. Washington sometimes sent his aides on long journeys on horseback to meet with the governors and heads of the state legislatures to offer reports on the army and plead for assistance. It was not unusual for someone like Richard Meade or Tench Tilghman to ride to Lancaster, York, Albany, or Princeton and spend several days lobbying on the general's behalf.

Washington kept in touch with governors too distant to visit Valley Forge with a succession of long and personal letters, always underscoring the army's reliance on them, such as a letter he sent to Virginia chief executive Patrick Henry in the middle of February. The general told his friend that he did not believe the army could take the field in the spring and begged him to use his considerable influence to obtain provisions: "I address myself to you, convinced that our alarming distresses will engage your most serious considerations and that the full force of that zeal and vigor you have manifested upon every other occasion will now operate for our relief."

The food supply of the Continental Army was sporadic through January and February of 1778 as Henry Laurens tried to reorganize the Commissary Department, with little success. The men began to starve again in early February, and by the middle of the month the lack of food had reached crisis proportions. Soldiers wrote home that they went without sustenance for up to four days at a time. Washington would often ride or walk through the city of huts, and when he did the men would cry out, "No meat, no meat...." Many soldiers would sit by the roadside and angrily yell out at passersby on horseback or in carriages, people they suspected of living well, "No meat! No soldier!"

Many felt like Private Joseph Plumb Martin, who wrote in his journal that "the poor soldiers had hardships enough to endure without having to starve; the least that could be done was to give them something to eat."

The high command was just as exasperated about supplies as the infantrymen. John Laurens complained bitterly that the commissary agents were "useless" and that "the present managers have brought us to the brink of ruin."

The commander was just as frustrated as his aide and everyone else who spewed forth their anger. Washington told General Israel Putnam on

February 6 that "the army under my command is...literally reduced to a starving condition," and that same day told Connecticut Governor Trumbull that without food "we cannot but disband." He complained to Livingston that "we are supplied from hand to mouth, and frequently not at all. This is the second time in the course of the present year that we have been on the point of dissolution and I know not whether the melancholy event may not take place."

Washington had held his tongue about the continued food shortage in his letters to the Commissary and Congress, but in mid-February he wrote Buchanan, blaming him, charging that his ineptitude might cause "total want and dissolution of the army." And he pleaded with others to send whatever they could and as soon as they could, or "we shall have not a horse left."

It was in the middle of all this consternation that Washington had to grapple with the demon that would shadow him throughout the rest of the war—the declaration of martial law. Military rule had often accompanied revolutions and now, in February of 1778, amid so many concurrent crises, it seemed inevitable.

The first step toward martial law appeared to be the seizure of food from farmers who refused to sell to the army. Washington and Congress had done everything possible to assure the southeastern Pennsylvania farmers and merchants that Continental paper currency would always be valuable, but with little success. The farmers simply refused to sell for American scrip sustenance needed to keep the army alive.

The crisis moved the Pennsylvania Assembly to reluctantly give the commander-in-chief authority to impress food, wagons, and horses and anything else necessary when farmers or merchants refused to sell these goods to the army. Washington's officers would not have to pay for supplies, but would have to issue certificates of credit, to be redeemed at some future date.

The impressment of goods by the army was foreseen by state legislatures and governors only as a last resort. Americans had complained bitterly that the British impressed not only supplies, but men, to fight for the Crown in the French and Indian War in the late 1750s and had continued the practice during the post-war occupation of the colonies. Now it appeared that Americans would do the same.

Impressment laws were enacted in several states and by Congress. They gave the commander-in-chief the power to take what it needed on credit. However, army agents had to obtain an impressment writ from a local judge, sometimes with a county magistrate alongside them, and could only impress a certain amount of food, take a certain number of cattle, or use wagons for a specified number of days, usually less than seven. Under no circumstances could the army seize anything without credit payment and, Washington insisted, officers had to keep careful records of purchases. Some states, such as Pennsylvania, required approval from the State Council as well as a county or local official. The states and counties wanted to help the army win the war, but it was equally important to them to protect their citizens from martial law.

Whatever qualms these legislative bodies had about forcible confiscation without payment faded as the war droned on. Soon Pennsylvania and New Jersey would give their governors the power to impress without credit in an emergency and Congress considered that measure, too. Delegate William Ellery, like many in Congress agreeable to martial law, expressed the view that it was simply necessary: "Some recommendations [Congress] may give to the States may be thought inconsistent with the rights of individuals, but necessity and the accomplishments of the most noble intentions, will, I hope, in their opinion warrant what at another time and upon a less occasion might be thought unjustifiable."

Many members of Congress were angry that Washington had not declared martial law already. One said that the commander-in-chief's noble view was laudable, but that his refusal jeopardized the Revolution, that it "may, on critical exigencies, prove destructive to the army and prejudicial to the general liberties of America." Even his own men pressured him to dispense with his ideals and simply seize what he needed. "Nothing can be expected from them except what may be done of coercive exactions," George Gibson, an aide, told him.

Washington disagreed vehemently; he was against the severe practice for several reasons. The army, he believed, was merely an instrument of the government and at all times had to be subordinate to civilian authority. The general looked at impressment from a political point of view, too. Washington was seen by the public as a national leader as well as a military commander, and he used that dual responsibility to act as a political figure throughout the war. The supplying of the army through seizure was not a simple military issue and he understood that; it was political. The Revolution could only succeed with the support of the people, and that support might have to be maintained for several more years. The commander-in-chief could not do anything that might threaten it. The forcible appropriation of food and clothes did so and, despite governmental urging, he was reluctant to do it because it was the first step toward military rule.

He was further appalled when the Pennsylvania Assembly suspended the writ of habeas corpus, at the strident request of the Board of War, in order to permit the army to seize clothing without any payment from known and suspected Loyalists. Washington refused to do so. Afraid of civilian reaction following such a step, he wrote the Board of War that "such a procedure, I fear, would not relieve our wants and at the same time would greatly distress the people and embitter their minds" and told Congress that martial law was "an evil much to be apprehended even by the best and most sensible among us. I have been cautious and wished to avoid as much as possible any act that might [cause] it."

And Washington reminded Congress that in a democracy people had to obey the civilian authority, not the military. He was a military commander now, but for much of his adult life he had served as a member of the Virginia state legislature and was a firm believer in government by elected representatives. "The people at large are governed much by custom. To acts of legislation of civil authority they have been ever taught to yield a willing obedience without reasoning about their propriety. On those of military power, whether immediate or derived originally from another source, they have ever looked with a jealous and suspicious eye." That opinion led him to ask Governor Livingston to confiscate several tons of hay found along the New Jersey shore, explaining that he did not want the army to do it. "I am not without power and directions from Congress to act myself in such instances, but I would wish the business to be done by civil authority, as their acts will create less jealousy and disgust and be viewed in a much more unexceptionable light."

And, too, he remembered very clearly how his strident campaign against the Loyalists had nearly backfired the previous winter when, with his blessing, Loyalists were jailed and penalized on very fragile and often questionable evidence. He knew in April that his tough treatment of the Loyalists, applauded by state and federal officials, had been wrong. A man who always learned from his mistakes, he would not launch any more dictatorial campaigns against anyone, even the obstinate Quakers, whose stern opposition to violence he never understood.

He made his stand against martial law clear in letters he sent to state governors, too, including those who had been given that power themselves. "Nothing in nature can be more repugnant to my inclination than to be obliged to have recourse to military coercion for subsistence," he later told New Jersey's Livingston. He feared authorization to seize goods might induce starving soldiers themselves to harass farmers and turn the locals against the army. He already had reports of fierce arguments between officers and farmers over goods impressed for credit since December. Commissary agents told him they feared soldiers would physically attack farmers. He told Congress that too much power "never failed even in the most veteran troops, under the most rigid and exact discipline, to raise in the soldiery a disposition to licentiousness, plunder and robbery...ruinous to the inhabitants [and] to armies themselves."

The commander-in chief was even against confiscation on credit, but did so—reluctantly—on just a few occasions. Even then, he apologized for his actions, telling Maryland Governor Thomas Johnson in an impressment letter earlier, as an example, that "these requisitions are not the result of choice, but of painful necessity, and viewing them in this light I am well assured, you will not only excuse them, but will readily afford every relief in your power to give." He told his agents in other states to impress for credit goods and wagons only when their efforts to pay in Continental scrip failed and to only confiscate on credit "as the inhabitants can spare without greatly distressing their families."

But Washington refused all requests to simply seize whatever he wanted, without payment, at gunpoint. He understood the feelings of the people far better than any of the panicking civilian officials and knew that the seizure of supplies would be construed by the public as a first step toward brutish military dictatorship. The people were fighting a revolution to gain independence from tyranny abroad; they did not do so only to wind up with tyranny at home.

Despite continued complaints by his men that the locals were hoarding food and clothes, Washington knew by the middle of February that, in fact, the residents who lived in southeastern Pennsylvania just did not have anywhere near the amount of flour, wheat, and cattle necessary to supply the army any longer. Their resources had been stretched to the limit and he knew it. That feeling was reinforced in a letter from the magistrates of Trenton. "We are well disposed to further the operations of the army by every effort that can be reasonably expected from good citizens," they explained, but added that they were exhausted. "The inhabitants in and near this town…have already felt the calamities of war in a degree unknown to most other parts of America."

His commissary officers told him that there were no supplies left and so did his generals, such as Varnum, who concluded on February 12 that "the country in the vicinity of the camp is exhausted." Washington then turned to Nathanael Greene, his most trusted general, who told him the same thing, that "the country has been so gleaned that there is but little left in it." A week later, the state of Pennsylvania simply gave up and told Washington that its food was gone and that "this council must acknowledge that they are not equal to the task imposed on them."

Supplies were not only running out in southeastern Pennsylvania, his commissary agents informed him, but elsewhere. "All the magazines provided in the states of New Jersey, Pennsylvania, Delaware and Maryland, and all the immediate additional supplies they seem capable of affording, will not be sufficient to support the army more than a month," Washington confessed to New York Governor George Clinton on February 16.

The cupboard was bare.

Chapter Eight

THE ANGEL
OF DEATH

VALLEY FORGE, 1777–78

"No man, perhaps, ever had a greater combination of vexacious evils and uncontrollable obstacles to encounter than this incomparable patriot and warrior; and no one surely ever possessed in a more eminent degree the peculiar talents and qualities requisite for the discharge of the important duties assigned him. He has acquired the full confidence of every faithful officer and soldier under his command and his wisdom and judgment are considered adequate to the most trying exigencies. He rises in the midst of distress and gains strength by misfortune."
—Dr. James Thacher, an army surgeon, on George Washington

"The hospitals robbed the United States of more citizens than the sword…they are an apology for murder."
—Dr. Benjamin Rush, the Continental Army's chief surgeon
for Pennsylvania in 1777–78

In September 1777, hundreds of sick men accompanied the army to Valley Forge. Some of them were able to walk, hobbling along with the assistance of rough-hewn wooden crutches, thin linen bandages wrapped tightly around their legs and chests. Others leaned on fellow soldiers, trying to hold their ripped blue jackets tight over their bare stomachs. Most moved eastward on Gulph Mill Road crowded into heavy wooden horse-drawn farm wagons and were badly jostled as the vehicles bounced over the deep ruts in the roadway.

They all required immediate medical attention. Some shivered from dysentery and others burned up with fever, their shirts soaked with sweat. Most of those sick men in the overcrowded wagons had fallen victim to various diseases from their weakened physical state, brought on by fatigue, malnutrition, and a lack of clothing to protect them from the elements. They were joined by hundreds more who became ill during the first weeks at Valley Forge.

Although the winter was comparatively mild, there were times when the weather shifted dramatically, bringing on conditions which made all of the soldiers susceptible to illness. General Varnum said that "the weather frequently changes five times in twenty four hours." One British soldier in Philadelphia wrote that the weather "has been perpetually changing," noting that in January temperatures fluctuated between 40 and 51 degrees, but that a week of fair weather would be interrupted by a snowstorm or heavy rainfall, such as the twelve-hour downpour of January 17. The next day the sun appeared and a warm front moved in. A thaw on January 5, following several days of severe cold, brought on mud and flooding on the Schuykill. One American colonel traveling that afternoon reported "this day was the worst riding I ever saw on account of its being so muddy." Soldiers sometimes went to sleep with several inches of snow on the ground and woke up to a fifty-two–degree morning. Snowfalls of March 9 and 10 were followed by nine consecutive days of balmy weather. This wildly uneven weather caused common colds and then pneumonia and fevers for many.

The medical catastrophe at Valley Forge had begun months before. The wounded from the Philadelphia battles, and subsequent skirmishes, had been carted off to makeshift hospitals in Reading and Bethlehem, filling them to near capacity. Those men were now joined by these soldiers slumped down in the backs of the slowly rumbling wagons, their faces gaunt and their bodies haggard, or struggling to limp alongside wagons, blood seeping through their bandages.

Washington acted swiftly as soon as the army began to settle in at Valley Forge. There were far too many men to house in hospital tents, especially in winter, and so he authorized officers to request or simply commandeer the public buildings, barns, and, especially, the churches of Chester County and nearby counties and convert them into hospitals. He acted not just as the commander, but in his always expanding role as an unelected public official who had take steps to protect the army in what he saw as a clear health-care emergency.

One year before, in Morristown, the general had enjoyed the near-complete cooperation of ministers in Morris County and throughout New Jersey. Most of them were Presbyterians and fervent supporters of the Revolution. Now, though, he had to deal with religious leaders who were not so cooperative. Southeastern Pennsylvania was home to the large communities of Quakers and Moravians, plus smaller eclectic religious groups, such as a community of German mystics. These religious groups were all pacifists and opposed to all wars.

Washington let all of the local churchmen and villagers know that turning over their churches and Meeting Houses was mandatory, but told them what to do in cordial notes written to significantly lessen the impact of a wrenching experience for the villagers. He reminded one minister who objected that "I need not explain to you how necessary establishments of this kind are to the welfare of the army, and you must be sensible that they can be placed nowhere without occasioning inconvenience to some set of people or other. At the same time, it is ever my wish and aim to effect the public good with as little sacrifice as possible of individual interests."

Some local officials and ministers whose buildings he needed were amenable and some were not. Since there were few large towns with usable public buildings within seventy miles of camp, Washington needed every rural church he could find. He told his agents to make arrangements with traditional Christian houses of worship, such as the Lutherans, but to also gain access to the churches of the Moravians, Quakers, and mystics.

Despite the objection of their bishop, the local community of Moravians at Bethlehem turned out to be among the most helpful. Their Brethren's Single House, a large men's residence hall, had been turned over to the army earlier in the year by local brothers. The army kept sending more patients as winter continued, and the Moravians then offered the additional use of their large Fulling Mill, where linens were manufactured, and all of their barns. Moravians who ran another Brethren's House in the small town of Lititz also welcomed the army. The number of patients housed there soon topped 250, surpassing the total population of the community.

Acting on Washington's wishes to renovate large buildings into hospitals, doctors and officers rode to the community of German mystics in the small village of Ephrata. Here again, the sect's bishop had rejected the commander's request, but the local leaders acquiesced when the plight of the army was explained. The mystics at Ephrata gladly served as aides and nurses for the more than five hundred soldiers Washington sent there over the next few days.

The Trinity Lutheran Church, First Reformed Church, Friends' Meeting House, Court House, Brick House, and Potter's Shop at Reading were voluntarily turned into hospitals, as were public buildings and churches in the nearby communities of Lancaster, Buckingham, Rheimstown, Warrick, and Schaefertown (several had been functioning as army hospitals prior to December). Three large barns at Yellow Springs, the site of a collection of mineral springs that Pennsylvanians had visited for years, were converted into medical facilities, as were several local taverns. Hundreds of sick soldiers were housed in each town.

When those buildings filled up, the army turned to local residents. Although the soldiers routinely castigated all of the farmers in the area— accusing them of withholding needed food and clothes—there were dozens who took in sick and dying soldiers, such as John Rowland, who turned his farmhouse and barn into hospitals and cared for the sick along with his wife and children, who were "remarkably kind," according to one soldier who spent several weeks recovering there.

The only hospital built expressly for the army, at Yellow Springs, was already half-filled with those wounded at Brandywine and Germantown. The three-story-high facility, called "Washington Hall" by the physicians, was 106 by 36 feet, with nine-foot-wide porches on three sides, and large enough to house thirteen hundred patients at the same time.

Doctors and officers persuaded some Quakers to turn over their meeting houses to the army. Those who refused had to stand by as the army took possession by force. One Quaker Friend refused to give an army doctor the key to his Meeting House, and so the physician, with soldiers, broke down the door and seized the building, along with the sizable horse stable behind it. The church and parsonage of German Reformed Church at French Creek were similarly seized when the pastor refused to cooperate.

In immediately utilizing public buildings and churches, stables and barns, plus a tavern or two, the medical department was able to transport the men who needed hospitalization into protective shelter within a short period of time. Doctors set up offices, wards, and operating rooms in these converted hospitals as rapidly as possible. Wagon transportation systems to move men from camp to distant hospitals were in place within a week. Medicines began to arrive from Pennsylvania and New Jersey towns daily. In just three weeks, George Washington had overseen the creation of more hospitals in the areas surrounding his winter camp than existed in most large states.

All of these medical centers were hopelessly overcrowded. The Reading Hospital, which could hold 360 patients, was home to more than nine hundred. Brethren's House in Bethlehem had room for three hundred, but by early January it housed more than four hundred sick soldiers, many in beds set up in the kitchen and narrow hallways. Dozens more were put into large white canvas tents erected in the grassy yards next to the building.

The need for more hospitals grew and doctors soon urged Washington to order the construction of what he called "flying hospitals," named after his quick-moving "flying camps" of the 1776–77 winter campaign. These were short-term care hospitals for patients before they had to be transported to larger facilities. They were sixteen-foot by twenty-five-foot log cabin structures that were hastily built and soon overcrowded. By the middle of winter, as sickness spread throughout the camp, eleven of these had been constructed.

On the advice of the doctors, Washington also built additional huts to temporarily house all the men who were covered with sores and scabs from the "itch" or scabies so that doctors could treat them together. Scabies had been common in armies for hundreds of years. It was an infection caused by life in an unsanitary and overcrowded environment. The condition began as vesicles of clear fluid between the fingers. The vesicles then broke and scabs developed. The infection then spread from the fingers to other parts of the body and caused constant itching. Some men's bodies were covered with scabs from the neck down.

There was no truly effective cure for scabies. Some doctors treated it as a skin disease and bathed scabs with a sulfur ointment; others considered it an internal disease and had soldiers drink a mixture of fennel water, corn poppy blossoms, and diluted sulfuric acid. British doctors prescribed the consumption of large quantities of saline solution. Some soldiers from frontier areas told doctors that the cure in their villages was to whirl a black cat with a white spot around the patient's head three times and then administer a solution of nine drops of blood from the cat's tail and nine charred barley corns with the side of a woman's wedding ring while circling the patient three times (doctors at Valley Forge declined this eclectic method). Regardless of treatment, recovery from the scabies usually took six weeks. At any one time at Valley Forge, several hundred soldiers were confined to the huts because of scabies.

There was a constant shortage of doctors. Washington had sixty surgeons and thirty-three mates, or medical assistants. As he assayed his medical troubles at Valley Forge, he realized that a dozen or more physicians had been granted furloughs without his approval. Several surgeons, in daily contact with infected soldiers, became sick themselves and became patients in their own wards. A few doctors and mates, frightened or disgusted by the growing medical calamity, left camp and went home, reducing the care available to the soldiers. Washington ordered them right back, and if they did not return, as in the case of surgeon's mate James Sackett, had them arrested and court-martialed.

Whenever he heard complaints about the hospitals, Washington ordered immediate investigations to improve conditions as much as possible. The last was in early April 1778, when he instructed Brigadier General Lachlan McIntosh to conduct yet another survey of the hospitals, threatening, as always, to court-martial anyone mistreating his soldiers. MacIntosh was to do a thorough job. "You are authorized to examine, if necessary, the books of the directors, surgeons, commissaries, etc. You are to make a minute enquiry into the management of the sick, the care and attendance given them, their wants, and report the same to me with your opinion of the number and proper place or places to fix the hospitals as for the purposes of accommodating the sick, the more convenient superintending of them and reducing the expense by lessening the number of physicians, surgeons, etc. which are now employed and may be necessary in the present divided state of the hospitals," the commander told him.

All of the hospitals were general medical facilities, and soldiers with different diseases were placed near each other on whatever type of bedding could be found. There were no isolation wards or separate rooms for those suffering from a particular disease. Those in bed with one disease would soon be infected with that carried by the men next to them. Infections spread quickly because there was no medication available to halt them. There were few sheets or hospital clothing, and men had to lie in bed, suffering, in their uniforms. There was insufficient food and water. Men were cold because the hospitals were created in buildings with far too few fireplaces to provide the necessary heat for hundreds of men. Few guards were posted in the hospitals, and some patients stole clothes and money from others. Soldiers complained bitterly about their medical treatment in letters to family and state officials, underscoring the fatality rate. Elijah Fisher wrote of his release from a hospital that "I gits better but a number died. There were between fifty and sixty that died [in the hospital] in about a month."

Dozens of men would die in just a few days if an epidemic reached the doors of the hospital. An example was a horrific outbreak of typhus that swept through the wards of Brethren House in Bethlehem. A patient there said that "the misery…cannot be described; neither can it, without being seen, be imagined." A doctor who visited that hospital told Washington "that so violent was the putrid that 9 out of 11 surgeons were seized with it, one of whom died, and that out of three stewards, two died with it and the third narrowly escaped with his life. Many inhabitants of the village caught it and died."

Hundreds of men without shoes for weeks wound up in the hospital with gangrene and had to have toes or a foot amputated, then, recovering, they came down with typhus and died. Soldiers recovering from bayonet or musket ball wounds inflicted months earlier died of a fever caught there.

Some medical centers were so far away from camp that wounded men died en route or became worse as the wagons carrying them lurched violently over bad roads. One man arrived at one makeshift hospital only to find that there was no room. He was then transported by wagon ten miles to a second hospital, which was also full. Another wagon took him to the home of a local woman, where he was given a bed in her overcrowded house and remained there for weeks. Men who lived within seventy miles were sent home in wagons to alleviate overcrowding at the hospitals.

Shipments of medicine were lost by the army's disastrous transportation system. Apothecaries that were supposed to have medical supplies often did not, and no one knew where they were. "There are medicines in different places, of which I have no list," wrote an exasperated Dr. Jonathan Potts to the Commissary office, whose workers did not know where the medical supplies were, either.

None of the facilities were as well equipped as the hospitals in cities such as Philadelphia, Boston, and New York, but even there primitive medicines did little to curb fever epidemics or pneumonia. Patients witnessed ghastly scenes. Men gripped by the fever would sweat and shake to death in front of the others in their ward and then, dead, be coldly carted off by orderlies. Medical science in the 1770s offered no easy remedy to prevent severe arm and leg wounds from resulting in gangrene. The only way to prevent that, and save lives, was to amputate limbs. Doctors had little more than saws and low-level anesthetics, or just liquor, for amputations. Toward the middle of winter liquor had run out, too, and men were operated on with their arms and legs strapped to wooden tables as they clenched sticks in their mouth. Successive operations resulted in operating rooms covered with puddles of blood. The smell of operations, and the stench of death, seemed to be everywhere.

The death rates in these medical facilities were staggering. Doctors had no medicines to stop common killers such as typhus. Over one third of the patients housed at the Bethlehem Hospital during successive periods of the winter, more than five hundred, died there, including thirty-seven of the forty men from the 9th Virginia regiment. Half of the 250 soldiers at Lititz died, along with a local doctor, Moravian pastor, and five aides. Several hundred soldiers under care at Ephrata died, as did the doctor attending them. Later in the winter, hundreds died at Yellow Springs, along with their doctor. Hundreds more died in the other communities where public buildings and homes had been converted into hospitals. As an example, 214 of the 1,072 North Carolina troops who arrived at Valley Forge died there or in nearby hospitals, more than died from that state during the entire eight-year war. Death was so prevalent that in each successive week of February the death rate jumped by 33 percent, prompting one visiting Congressman to report "sickness and mortality have spread…to an astonishing degree."

Doctors in camp had never experienced the waves of diseases—and were despondent about the mounting fatalities. Dr. Benjamin Rush, the army's chief surgeon for the region, was one of them. "Young men under 20 years of age were subject to the greatest number of camp diseases. The southern troops were more sickly than the northern or eastern," he said, and, like others, blamed most deaths on typhus, contracted as often in the hospital as in camp. "Men who came into the hospitals with pleurisies and rheumatisms soon lost the type of their original diseases and suffered, or died [contracting typhus]. Many causes combined to produce and increase this fever: such as the want of cleanliness, excessive fatigue, ignorance or negligence." On New Year's Day, 1778, Rush told Washington that he considered all of the army's hospitals defective and that "Who, sir, can bear to see so many brave men, who have narrowly escaped a more glorious fall in the field, thus ignobly deprived life under pretense of being saved from death, without the tenderest emotions." Later that winter, Rush said that the hospitals "stink of human life," and joked that, "There cannot be a greater calamity for a sick man than to come into our hospitals." In another acidic remark, Rush told friends that the best way to end the war would be to march the British army through Valley Forge so that its soldiers would all die from diseases they caught there.

Generals, too, were vicious in their condemnation of both hospitals and doctors. In a stinging letter, General Varnum told Washington that patients "are treated with a degree of inhumanity that would add horrors to the glooms of Siberia! A senior surgeon of the hospital receives pay, if I am not mistaken, superior to a Brigadier of the army. Good God! For what?" and described surgeons skills as "quackery substituted for experience." General Jedediah Huntington told Washington of the army surgeons that all they did was bloodlet their patients and suggested hiring barbers because they were cheaper.

George Washington was under considerable stress in the early days of the Valley Forge encampment. His medical emergency would last for months. The general had to work with expediency in order to procure new hospitals for his hundreds of sick and dying men at the same time he was required to oversee the construction of the sprawling hut city. These two gigantic projects had to be completed at the same time; there was absolutely no time to delay either. The gifted administrator had his hands full with both, but just as he arrived at Valley Forge he was shaken by news that a yet another epidemic of smallpox had been detected in Virginia.

Washington had hoped he had seen the last of the deadly smallpox during the previous winter, when his unprecedented inoculation of the entire army had saved his men and thousands of civilians. Now a new wave of smallpox was sweeping through the Atlantic seaboard. It soon became evident, too, that thousands of Americans had *not* taken advantage of the army's free inoculation program the previous year; victims began to appear in several states. Washington's fear now was not only that the new epidemic would strike his camp at Valley Forge, but that his new recruits had already been infected. That apprehension was realized shortly when a camp doctor discovered that several men in a recently arrived regiment from Massachusetts were suffering from the disease and had to be hospitalized

The general at first ordered all recruits to be inoculated upon enlistment in their hometowns before they departed for Valley Forge, delaying their arrival at camp for several weeks. What appeared to be a cautious plan unraveled when it was learned that two recruits who had been treated for smallpox in Virginia had died because the inoculations were botched. Washington, not willing to risk any more lives with inoculations administered by untrained country doctors, then ordered all of the recruits from around the country to report to Valley Forge immediately, where they would be inoculated by doctors with smallpox experience.

Washington then ordered a canvass of Valley Forge to determine who among his veteran troops had not been inoculated and, to his chagrin, discovered that more than one-third of his troops had not been and were extremely vulnerable; the New Hampshire regiments alone had five hundred non-inoculated soldiers. Washington then knew that he had a double disaster on his hands. He now needed one string of hospitals for men ill with various diseases and another set of medical facilities for smallpox inoculation and recovery.

He told doctors they had to begin treatment right away, but there was no large hospital for the men to spend the recovery period of several weeks. He had nowhere to put these thousands of men because every available public building was already jammed with sick men and he did not want those recovering from the inoculations to be infected by them and die.

Some smallpox victims and those scheduled for inoculation were sent to the Yellow Springs hospital. Most of the men were simply inoculated and kept in their huts (or in the flying hospitals in camp) until they recovered. (In areas where isolated hospitals could not be built, such as Delaware, Washington ordered officers to commandeer local residences and turn them into isolation wards for inoculation and recovery.) Doctors ran the inoculation program so efficiently that by the middle of January they had already inoculated more than two thousand soldiers. More than four thousand troops would be treated before the last group of inoculated and recovered soldiers left their sickbeds and huts in the middle of April.

So many soldiers throughout the country had fallen victim to smallpox, and recovered, that their facial pock marks became a way to identify them if they went AWOL, as evidenced by this newspaper ad for a young deserter:

TWENTY SHILLINGS REWARD, EXCLUSIVE OF WHAT'S ALLOWED FOR TAKING DESERTERS

Deserted from Major General John Clark's quarters at Newtown Square on the 27th. Martin Nicholls, a soldier, about 5 feet 2 inches high, 18 years of age, a barber by trade, wears his hair tied, is of yellowish complexion and much pitted with the smallpox. Had on and took with him an old felt hat cocked, a blue cloth coat with metal buttons, almost new, a whiteish colored and round waistcoat buckskin breeches, white yarn stockings –a pair of half worn shoes with yellow buckles, a good blanket coat without buttons, two good white linen shirts, an old knapsack with some old shirts. He some time ago waited on General Mercer and last winter on Colonel Biddle, 'tis probable he may endeavor to go to Philadelphia, as his father lives there. All officers and soldiers are requested to apprehend him and give notice to John Clark, Aid de camp to Major General Greene.

This second mass-inoculation program prevented a much feared outbreak of smallpox in the army, and only ten soldiers died. The halt of any smallpox in the army meant, too, that no one in Chester County was infected by the soldiers and that, again, Washington's actions had saved thousands of lives.

Still, while he had to be pleased with the success of the smallpox program, Washington was unhappy that so many men were dying of other diseases and that there just did not seem to be a way that the medical services could save them. Dr. James Tilton was one of the many physicians repulsed by Valley Forge and its medical services. "It would be shocking to humanity to relate the history of the general hospitals in the years 1777 and 1778," he said. "[Hospitals] swallowed up at least half our army, owing to a fatal tendency in the system to throw all the sick of the army [together]."

Illness at Valley Forge became so rampant that Anthony Wayne told a friend, "I am not fond of danger, but I would most cheerfully agree to enter into action once every week in place of visiting each hut of my encampment where objects strike my eye and ear whose wretched condition beggars all description. The whole army is sick and crawling with vermin."

No one was angrier at conditions in the hospitals, and the men dying in them, than Washington. He received a letter from Dr. Rush the day after Christmas in which the physician had revealed the worst possible conditions for men confined to hospitals, and cringed that at Valley Forge each of those conditions had been met in abundance. The health of the army had deteriorated so badly that on New Year's Eve, instead of celebrating, the commander wrote a heartbreaking letter to his friend, New Jersey's Livingston:

I sincerely feel for the unhappy conditions of our poor fellows in the hospitals and wish my powers to relieve them were equal to my inclination. It is but too melancholy a truth that our hospital stores are exceedingly scanty and deficient in every instance and I fear there is no prospect of their being better shortly. Our difficulties and distresses are certainly great and such as wound the feelings of humanity. Our sick naked, our well naked, our unfortunate men in captivity naked!

The travails of the sick were never farther away than daily reports and letters Washington received at the Potts House from hospital patients, including an apologetic note from a young Virginia man, Joseph Holt, who respectfully requested permission to return home to die. "My disorder increases, a fact which alarms me very much. I am truly sorry to quit the army as it was my intention to continue in the service while men were wanting, but as I am by direction of Providence rendered incapable of serving my country any longer in the field. I think it my duty to myself and the public to retire from the army in hopes to find some remedy for my fatal disease that is fast growing on me," young Holt wrote. Washington put the letter down, picked up a quill, and approved Holt's resignation.

The doctors who stayed in the army complained bitterly that the men who came down with diseases in the hospital presented a more pathetic sight than men nearly killed in battle. Dr. James Thacher of Massachusetts, who would be an army surgeon for several years, described that feeling in an entry in his journal, written while he tended the sick at the army camp in Albany that winter: "If I turn from beholding mutilated bodies, mangled limbs, and bleeding, incurable wounds, a spectacle no less revolting is present, of miserable objects, languishing under afflicting diseases of every description—there are those harbingers of approaching dissolution—there are those with emaciated bodies and ghastly visages, who...just lift their feeble heads from the pillow of sorrow."

Stress and fatigue caused doctors to quarrel with each other over medical practices and lack of support from the army, Congress, and the state of Pennsylvania. Many threatened to resign over rank or the inability of the army to supply them with food or clothing. This infighting became so great that in early January, just when he was needed most, Rush resigned after he accused Dr. William Shippen, the military's chief surgeon, of misusing funds. Shippen was at first stripped of his procurement authority and later court-martialed (his eventual punishment resulted in just a mild censure). The Shippen-Rush altercation and recriminations between doctors friendly to each sent shockwaves throughout the medical establishment of the army, which did not help matters at Valley Forge.

The Shippen-Rush feud may have been the most publicized imbroglio in the medical corps that winter, but the two squabbling physicians were not alone. Doctors assigned to General Smallwood's camp at Wilmington, Delaware, threatened to resign en masse when they were denied new clothes captured from a British ship and distributed to regimental officers. Washington had to intervene to arrange for them to receive clothing and keep them in the service. Some doctors threatened to resign when they were not promoted. The doctors at the flying hospitals fought with the doctors at the main hospitals over procedures. The doctors at the main hospitals fought with Shippen and Rush. Shippen and Rush fought with each other. All brought their complaints to Washington.

On his own, Washington requested more medicine from Congress, making health care for the soldiers a political as well as military issue. He told the delegates that "the accommodation of the sick and the preservation of men's lives are the first and great objects to be consulted; the regimental surgeons ought not to be destitute of a reasonable quantity of medicines and other conveniences of which the sick stand in need....[T]hey [now] must remain without proper assistance 'til their diseases confirm themselves and with regard to many, get beyond the power of a cure."

He told officers to keep their men clean, "as nothing adds more to the look of a soldier, and nothing can contribute more to his health than cleanliness of person and wholesome diet, you are to be particularly attentive to both of these." Washington had ashes and tallow collected daily so that they could be made into soap and asked men to keep their hair clean and cut short to prevent lice. The general ordered doctors in the Northern Department, in New York, to send whatever medicine they had to Valley Forge and directed Shippen to search for medicine chests (wooden boxes containing a standard assortment of medicines) and forward them to Potts. Military stores workers were ordered to locate sulfur and oil and send them to the Valley Forge hospitals at once. Anyone who found blankets was to send them to the hospitals, where their shortage was "peculiarly distressing," as Washington put it, and in early January he ordered that four hundred blankets that arrived in a long-awaited shipment of goods should not go to the men in huts, but had to be sent to the hospitals. No matter how low food supplies became, the commissary was ordered to make certain that each patient in the hospitals had a daily supply of rice or Indian corn for sustenance.

In mid-January, Washington ordered an officer from each regiment to visit each day the hospital where his men were housed to offer some cheer. One week later, upon the advice of physicians, he ordered hospital administrators to let regimental leaders know where to send their sick and to keep track of hospital beds to prevent overcrowding. The commander ordered wagons kept in reserve to transport the sick after he was told many men died simply waiting for transportation to the hospital. At the end of the month, unhappy with his gradual steps, he issued a lengthy memorandum to all officers charged with visiting the hospitals with ten very specific instructions and authorized them to conduct investigations and report irregularities.

He asked Rush, before his resignation, to conduct an informal survey to determine what could be done to improve the organization of the hospitals, and pleaded with Congress to undertake an investigation of the entire medical department. "It is to be regretted that a department for which such ample provision has been made, and on which so much depends, should yet be inadequate," he told him. This would be one of several Congressional investigations Washington would request, and welcome, during the winter, viewing the inquiry as Congress's right and a check on the powers of the army. As president, he would set precedent by welcoming Congressional investigations of his own controversial actions in wars against Indian tribes.

The general was particularly unhappy about sanitation in camp, a major source of illness. He ordered horses buried as soon as they died and the daily collection of horse excrement. The commander-in-chief was alarmed when that was not done, complaining angrily that "the carcasses of dead horses lay in or near the camp, and that offal near many of the commissary stalls still lay unburied, that much filth and nastiness is spread among the huts which will soon be reduced to a state of putrefaction and cause a sickly camp." Washington ordered officers to have men constantly fill latrines with dirt to cover the day's excrement and dig new ones to reduce the smell and diseases they festered; new latrines were built quite a distance away to reduce stench.

He ordered cleanliness in huts and conducted surprise personal inspections, often to be disappointed. After one mid-January survey, he told the men that "the smell of some places is intolerable....[I] for the last time request that all kinds of dirt & filth to be raked together & burnt or buried." On the advice of Baron Von Steuben, from Prussia, who joined the army in February, he ordered a hospital patients' straw burned and bedding washed upon his death or discharge. The commander-in-chief had doctors turn in regular reports concerning the care of each man in each hospital, along with their medical or comfort wants.

The Commissary Department was ordered to make special shipments of flour, wheat, and beef directly to the hospitals so that patients would have decent food while they recovered. Washington went out of his way to write personal notes of thanks to agents who did, telling one that, "I am obliged to you for the trouble you have taken in removing the stores and more so for the rice, oil and fish...which will be particularly useful at this time at the hospital."

Later in the winter, as the weather improved, Washington ordered the men to tear out the sapling branches and mud between the logs of their huts, and to cut out windows, to provide much-needed ventilation and to air out their bedding each day. They had to regularly wash out their uniforms and bathe themselves in nearby streams. Garbage pits were dug and bad meat, bones, dirty straw, and filthy rags were burned.

One thing that infuriated the general were the venereal diseases many men caught from prostitutes who followed the army. He decided to ban them (they always drifted back) and fined each man who came down with the disease (ten dollars for officers and four dollars for enlisted men). These soldiers doubly angered him because he had repeatedly warned against consorting with prostitutes for that reason. He fumed that men did not pay attention to his orders. He was so annoyed that men urinated wherever they wanted, ignoring the latrines, that he ordered any man caught doing so flogged. Later, when the stench and sickness became worse, at Congress's suggestion, he ordered anyone caught urinating on the ground shot by sentries.

Yet, ironically, Washington, who personally did so much to prevent deaths at Valley Forge would, as president, do little to halt a yellow fever epidemic that would sweep through Philadelphia in 1793, leaving the medical decisions to the same Dr. Benjamin Rush who had been so ineffective at Valley Forge.

And then there were the more than one thousand American prisoners captured at Germantown and Brandywine living in grossly unsanitary conditions in old Philadelphia jails, crude warehouses, and drafty public buildings turned into prisoner-of-war facilities. American soldiers incarcerated in these dimly lit, badly ventilated, insufficiently heated, and overcrowded buildings received little clothing, minimal medical attention, and practically no food, which the British asked the Americans to provide under the rules of war. The Americans had none.

Conditions in the makeshift Philadelphia jails were dreadful. The Rev. James Morris of Connecticut, a minister confined in one for three months after the battle of Germantown, reported that each small room held between sixteen and thirty-two men who had to sleep against each other on the floor because there was little space. Consuming small rations or no rations at all, they were hungry all winter. Shortly after their confinement in the jail, an epidemic of typhus swept through the building, killing four hundred of the seven hundred prisoners-of-war. Their bodies were carried outside and buried in a long trench. "Such a scene of mortality I never witnessed before," said the minister. "Death was so frequent that it ceased to terrify; it ceased to warn; it ceased to alarm survivors."

Another former prisoner said that captured Americans ate grass, bark, and lime they scratched from walls, and sucked water out of stones to survive in the prisons. One man bit off his fingers and ate them. "Our brethren who are unfortunately prisoners in Philadelphia meet with the most savage and inhumane treatments that barbarians are capable of inflicting," said a doctor who knew the former prisoner.

Complaints of starvation, brutality, and exposure poured in to Congress. "Our soldiers in the hands of the enemy at Philadelphia…are treated in a most barbarous manner and a number of them have perished with famine. Some have died on the state house yard with grass in their mouths [for food]," complained Congressional delegate William Ellery. Another delegate, Daniel Roberdeau, charged the British in Philadelphia with "cruelty unheard of among nations [said to be] civilized."

The treatment of prisoners-of-war was one of the most contentious issues of the Revolution for Washington, who expected the British to treat American prisoners with the same dignity that he treated the English and Hessians his army captured. That was not the case. The British tossed the several thousand American soldiers they captured following the New York battles of 1776 into the holds of filthy prison ships anchored in New York, where a great number died.

Howe made no attempt to clean up the prison ships and now, once again, he was making no effort to sanitize his jails in Philadelphia. Washington wrote several letters of protest to the British general, complaining that American prisoners suffered from "cruel and unjustifiable treatment."

At first, Howe ignored him, denying all accusations of misconduct and assigning any charges of brutality to rumor. "I can only assure you that it has been entirely differently related to me by the latter [jailers], whose veracity I have no reason to suspect. I do not think it necessary to trouble you with farther assurances on these subjects. Nor will you expect I should seriously controvert the absurdities that have been officially reported as facts, relative to the insulting, starving, stripping and forcing prisoners to enlist. The complaints of the ill treatment of the officers and prisoners in Philadelphia are equally without foundation," he told Washington. Pressed relentlessly for better conditions by Washington, Howe told him to send an officer to inspect his prisons, but the man was turned away when he arrived.

Washington warned Howe that retaliation against British POWs might follow, hinting that he might not be able to protect them. Washington never followed through on his threat. Washington also charged that the British had violated the rules of war by imprisoning civilians on an assortment of what he claimed were unfounded charges; these men were now sick and dying.

Howe replied with a stinging rebuke for Washington's own severe treatment of Loyalists and Quakers the winter before in Morristown, a charge the American commander knew was true. Howe began with the residents he had imprisoned, telling Washington that "all these persons were notorious abettors of the rebellion, members of committees, collectors of arbitrary fines, and oppressors of the peaceable inhabitants." Then he scolded him for his Loyalist campaign. "The line of treatment which might be observed respecting them has been strongly marked by the sufferings of many of His Majesty's faithful subjects in the revolted colonies. You are not ignorant that numbers, even of the most respectable gentlemen in America, of that description, have been torn from their families, confined in jails and their property confiscated; that many of those in this city, whose religious tenets secured them from suspicion of entertaining designs of hostility, have been ignominiously imprisoned and without even the color of a judicial proceeding, banished from their tenderest connections into the remotest part of another province," he told Washington, who knew, too, that many were at that moment in faraway jails in his native Virginia, where some had even been visited by his own sister.

"Nor can it be unknown to you that many have suffered death from tortures inflicted by the unrelenting populace under the eye of usurped yet passive authority," he went on, with Washington the "authority." "That some have been dragged to trial for their loyalty and in cruel mockery of law condemned and executed; that others are now perishing in loathsome dungeons; and that penal edicts are daily issuing against all who hesitate to disavow by a solemn oath the allegiance they owe and wish to pay to their sovereign."

The records concerning prisoners-of-war held in Philadelphia that winter, by both British and Americans, were disorganized, but an estimated five hundred of the nine hundred prisoners perished.

No exact death toll was recorded at Valley Forge, but several estimates indicate that approximately two thousand soldiers died, plus half of the prisoners-of-war held in Philadelphia. Altogether, more than 2,500, or nearly one quarter, of the American army perished during the winter campaign, one of the highest death rates of any army in military history. It was Dr. Waldo who probably summed up the troubles of Valley Forge best: "Poor food—hard lodging—cold weather—fatigue—no clothes—nasty cookery—vomit half the time—smoked out of my senses—the Devil's in it—I can't endure it—why are we sent here to starve and freeze? What sweet felicities have I left at home....Here all confusion—smoke and cold—hunger and filthiness—pox on my bad luck! Here comes a bowl of beef soup, full of burnt leaves an dirt, sickness enough to make Hector spew...."

Conditions continued to deteriorate and then, on the last day of February, in what must have been one of his worst moments in his life, in or out of the military, a grim George Washington told hospital workers to strip the clothing from the emaciated patients who had died so that they could be distributed to men still alive in order to keep them warm.

Chapter Nine

THE FALL
FROM GRACE

VALLEY FORGE, 1777–78

*"I have been distressed to see some members of this house
disposed to idolize an image which their own hands have
molten. I speak here of the superfluous veneration that is
sometimes paid to General Washington."*

—John Adams

*"The people of America have been guilty of idolatry,
by making a man their God…No good may be
expected from the standing army, until Baal and
his worshippers are banished from the camp."*

—"Thoughts of a Freeman," anonymous letter found on a
staircase at the office of the Continental Congress

Adams and the anonymous critic did not have to worry about the
public veneration of Washington for very long. That adulation
began when Washington's army forced the British to evacuate Boston in
the spring of 1776, eroded with his humiliating defeats in New York, and

bloomed again with the Continental Army's stunning victories at Trenton at Christmas 1776, and at Princeton the following week. Public
esteem grew with the salvation and growth of the army during the winter at Morristown, all the accomplishments of George Washington.

The American public was fickle, though, and the enchantment of
some people with the commander-in-chief faded after he failed to defeat
the British Army at Brandywine in September and then again at Germantown on October 4. What had happened to his mercurial powers? The
defeats did not simply give the enemy some geographic advantage on a
map; these losses permitted the British to capture Philadelphia.

Many of the ministers who had supported the general had turned
silent. The Reverend Jacob Duche, a Loyalist, publicly asked Washington
to acknowledge the loss of the war and sue for peace. Some farmers and
merchants who had praised Washington's bravery just six months before
now muttered that he did not have the courage to launch another attack
on Philadelphia. They contended, as Nathanael Greene warned the general, that "success sanctifies everything."

Members of Congress grumbled about Washington's ineffectiveness,
too. The loss of Philadelphia had forced them to flee in confusion to
rather cramped new headquarters in York and to set up a national government all over again. The criticism of some delegates was pungent.
Jonathan Sergeant, who also served as the attorney general of Pennsylvania, called Washington's losses "such blunders as might have disgraced a
soldier of three months' standing," and said that America "would sink
with him." James Lovell, a Massachusetts delegate, said that Washington
was a "demi-God" who needed "a rap...on the knuckles."

Publicly, delegates were cautious in their language, but on December
10, 1777, they passed a critical set of resolutions in which Washington,
although of course never named, was blamed for spending too much
money to haul supplies from distant towns, for not using provisions in
nearby counties, and for not exercising the powers Congress gave him.
Important leaders of his own army complained about him, such as
Frenchman Baron DeKalb, who blithely wrote friends back in France
that any success Washington enjoyed was due to nothing but good luck.

Besides, the public had a new hero, General Horatio Gates, who had not only defeated the English at Saratoga with a force of seven thousand men, but captured Burgoyne and his entire army of six thousand men. Following that victory, shortly after the British occupation of Philadelphia and Washington's loss at Germantown, Gates began to receive dozens of laudatory letters from public officials and delegates in Congress. The colonial press fawned over him and, when news reached the Continent, he became the darling of Europe. He had become so popular, and so quickly, that when Hamilton met with him at Albany in November 1777 to deliver Washington's request for one third of his troops, the aide had to be cautious in relaying the orders, gingerly telling Washington, "I found myself infinitely embarrassed and was at a loss how to act. I felt the importance of strengthening you as much as possible, but on the other hand I found insuperable inconveniences in acting diametrically opposite to the opinion of a gentleman whose successes have raised him into the highest importance."

The triumph of Gates at Saratoga instantly became the public measure of the war. If Gates could defeat Burgoyne, why couldn't Washington defeat Howe? The religious questioned how Washington could lose when all Americans knew that God wanted them to win. If the Americans deserved victory because they were virtuous, why had Philadelphia fallen? What was Washington doing wrong?

Everything, insisted a small group of politicians, including delegates Samuel Adams, Lovell, Sergeant, Abraham Clark, and former Congressman Dr. Benjamin Rush, now serving as a surgeon in the army. They found Washington weak in discipline and unwilling to engage the British every time the Redcoats were seen, regardless of his own strength. They said that Washington relied too much on the militia, or that he did not rely on the militia enough. He spent too much time listening to advice from senile older generals, or he received too much advice from impudent younger men (Hamilton was their favorite culprit). They asserted that he did not listen to enough people; then they argued that he should never listen to anyone and use his best judgement. He waited too long to make decisions; he made decisions too quickly. And he was heavily criticized by his enemies in Congress and in the Pennsylvania Council when he decided to remain in Valley Forge for the winter and not attempt an assault on Philadelphia. Even John Adams, who nominated him as commander-in-chief, had turned critical.

Washington, of course, realized the necessity of protecting Philadelphia and wrote to Charles Lee a year before, "You know the importance of Philadelphia and the fatal consequences that must attend the loss of it." But what could he do?

Gates's star seemed to rise everywhere just as Washington's began to fall, as evidenced in remarks by John Adams when Congress declared a special day of Thanksgiving in 1777 to honor the army. Adams now ruefully wrote his wife that "one cause of [the Thanksgiving] ought to be that the glory of turning the tide of arms is not immediately due to the Commander-in-Chief." Lovell was harsher, even suggesting that Washington was a coward when he chortled in a note to Samuel Adams that "the army was not inclined to fight Howe when he gave them four days opportunity."

Washington himself was partially to blame for the change in public opinion. He had been too successful at fooling everyone into thinking that his army was several times as large as its actual size. His press releases to newspapers had created an image of himself and his troops that no one could possibly achieve. How could such a huge army with such a brilliant commander and so many gallant soldiers lose a single battle, much less the largest city in America?

Washington had no champions in the Philadelphia press at a time when he needed the backing of the media most. The editors of the Philadelphia papers, such as William Bradford of the *Pennsylvania Journal and Weekly Advertiser*, Benjamin Franklin of the *Pennsylvania Gazette*, and John Dunlap of the *Pennsylvania Packet*, had been his greatest supporters throughout 1776 and 1777, filling their columns with stories and letters praising the commander-in-chief. But the British occupation of Philadelphia in the fall had driven them all out of town. Bradford shut down the *Journal* for an entire year. Franklin was in Paris as a diplomat. His *Gazette* staff fled to York, carrying their large printing press, containers of ink, boxes of type, and other equipment in a wagon, where they published sporadically. The *Packet* relocated to Lancaster, publishing when it could. The only newspapers the residents of Philadelphia and Chester Counties could read were the Tory journals, the *Ledger, Royal Gazette,* and *Evening Post,* which excoriated Washington.

The people themselves must be assigned some of the blame for the sharp criticism of Washington that winter. They embraced unrealistic assumptions about the conflict. They wanted a quick end to the war, even though the Americans were constantly outnumbered and had no organized navy to battle England's, which was the most powerful in the world. The British possessed substantial supplies delivered from England, and funds to purchase whatever they might need in America from farmers and merchants willing to sell them goods. The British had vast treasuries full of gold and silver to back up their steady currency; the Americans were constantly bankrupt and issued depreciating paper money. Yet the people wanted the war to end within the week and naturally blamed the leader of the army when that goal could not be realized.

Anyone who wanted Washington removed as commander-in-chief had no real alternative general to succeed him, though, until the October 17 surrender of the British at Saratoga. Washington's critics now flocked to the banner of Gates. All of this attention delighted the cunning Gates, who had been stripped of command of the northern army the year before and had to watch Congress elevate Philip Schuyler, Washington's friend, to that post over him. At the insistence of John Adams, his longtime champion, Gates was reinstated by Congress in August 1777 after Schuyler lost Fort Ticonderoga. Saratoga followed, but in reality victory there was due just as much to the battlefield heroism of Benedict Arnold as any strategy by Gates.

In late November, as Washington mulled over his decision about where to spend the winter, a group of Congressmen, led by Lovell, Sergeant, and the "retired" Thomas Mifflin, toyed with the idea of replacing Washington with Gates. General Gates also began to receive letters from Continental Army general Thomas Conway. The Irish-born Conway had spent most of his adult life in the French Army and became a brigadier general when he arrived in the United States to fight on the American side. Conway was a man who hated to take orders, even when he agreed with them. He disliked Washington and allied himself with Gates. The commander had tried to block his proposed promotion to major general, which he thought was unfair, but he was especially angry that Washington had denounced him in letters to Congress, calling him a man "without conspicuous merit" and going so far as to say that his promotion—over those who deserved it more—would "give a fatal blow to the existence of the army."

To the commander-in-chief, the Conway elevation was the perfect example of the problems of a system in which Congress, and not the commander, determined promotions. In fact, Washington was so irate at the suggested promotion that he told Richard Henry Lee on October 17 that he might resign over Conway: "I have been a slave to the service; I have undergone more than most men are aware of to harmonize the many discordant parts; but it will be impossible for me to be of any further service if such insuperable difficulties are thrown in my way."

According to innkeeper John Jones, on October 28, James Wilkinson, a twenty-year-old aide to Gates, following a night of heavy drinking with other officers at a Reading, Pennsylvania, tavern where Lord Stirling had made his headquarters, told soldiers there that Washington "was not the man people imagined" and that it was "unpardonable" for him not to engage the enemy more often. Then Wilkinson informed his drinking companions of Conway's letter, a savage note with the admonition to Gates that "Heaven has been determined to save your country or a weak general and bad councilors would have ruined it."

A suspicious Stirling immediately informed Washington, who was crestfallen at the apparent appearance of a cabal to depose him. A rumor spread that Congress had already made the choice and narrowed down the list of men to succeed Washington to Gates (the favorite), Charles Lee, Mifflin, and Conway. His generals and aides were shocked. Lord Stirling called it "wicked duplicity of conduct." Hamilton said it was an extensive and deeply rooted scheme to depose Washington and called

Conway "vermin" and "a monster." The commander's other generals rallied around him to denounce Conway and Gates. Daniel Morgan, who had arrived at Valley Forge from Saratoga with his frontier riflemen, told everyone that Arnold, and not Gates, was the hero of Saratoga. Hearing of the Conway incident, Morgan snapped to John Laurens that he would never serve under Gates or any other general if Washington was fired, that Washington was "the sole defender of his country's cause."

Washington did not act immediately on Conway's letter because throughout November he was bogged down in battles to obtain more food and clothes, and in mid-December he led the army to Valley Forge. The commander finally turned to the Conway affair in late December and January. Washington sent Gates a curt note to let him know he had read the treacherous part of the letter, called Conway a "dangerous incendiary," and slyly told Gates that he did not know that he and Conway were such close friends. Washington then forwarded a copy of the white-hot section he had been given of Conway's letter to President Laurens in the middle of the month. Laurens had obtained a copy of the complete letter elsewhere. Shortly after, Laurens, his admiration for Washington growing, secretly mailed him a caustic three-page letter titled "The Thoughts of a Freeman," surely written by someone in Congress, which an aide found lying on a staircase. The letter brutally denounced Washington's conduct of the war.

Washington thanked Laurens for the correspondence, alerting him to enemies in York in a brilliantly crafted letter carried by courier on horseback on January 31. In it, Washington, as always, portrayed himself as an unambitious man who lived only to serve his country, reminding him that he was "doing all in my power to answer the important purposes of the trust reposed in me" and that he had no other goal except to "promote the public good." With great emotion, he told Laurens that "my heart tells me it has been my unremitted aim to do the best circumstances would permit." He had now been pounced upon by what he termed "a malignant faction," that, he charged, "take an ungenerous advantage of me." He blithely welcomed any and all investigations into his conduct, knowing that they would not be started by Laurens.

A mad scramble followed. Conway let Mifflin know that he was about to be exposed for disloyalty and Mifflin alerted the other Congressional conspirators, as well as Gates. Conway offered to resign.

What happened next was symptomatic of the inability of Congress to understand the workings of the army and the insistence of Washington's political enemies to harm him in some way. Instead of accepting Conway's resignation, Congress refused it and let him remain in the army. His friends in Congress then managed to gain approval to promote Conway to a major general, despite the uproar over the conspiracy, moving him ahead of twenty-three other generals. He was also named inspector general and ordered to investigate Washington's supply and medical problems.

At the same time, Congress reorganized the Board of War, which oversaw the operations of the army, in another effort to solve the provisions debacle. In another step to undercut the commander-in-chief, enough of his enemies banded together to force the whole body to name Gates the president of the board and added Mifflin as a non-military member to the five-man board. To add insult to injury for Washington, the Congressional caucus then approved Gates's alcoholic aide Wilkinson, whom Gates often referred to as "a military genius," as the board secretary.

Washington now had a considerable problem on his hands. The maneuvers of congressmen had placed his two apparent enemies, Gates and Mifflin, on the Board of War and the deceitful Conway in camp as the inspector general. Washington felt Congress was moving close to either replacing him with Gates, or at least forcing him to resign. No one knows what Washington actually said to his aides, but publicly he took pains to ignore the complicity of politicians in the contretemps, writing later that "whether any members of Congress were privy to this scheme, and inclined to aid and abet it, I shall not take upon me to say; but am well informed that no whisper of the kind was ever heard in Congress."

However, he told the Rev. William Gordon on January 23 that "I am told a scheme of that kind is now on foot by some." He informed fellow Virginian Patrick Henry in a personal letter in March that he was certain there were people trying to depose him, that he was the target of "intrigues of a faction which I know was formed against me. I cannot precisely mark the extent of their views, but it appeared in general that General Gates was to be exalted on the ruin of my reputation and influence." He added that Gates was a willing participant, along with Mifflin. Conway, Washington told Henry, "was a very active and malignant partisan." Washington seethed about Gates in a note to Lafayette, saying of Gates that he was driven by ego and a desire to harm Washington. And years later, as an old man, reflecting on the move to have him fired, he told Archibald Blair that there was definitely a coup afoot, but that the culprits were not in the army, but in politics. "The attempt was made by a party in Congress to supplant me in that command," he insisted.

Outwardly, Washington played the deeply offended, noble general who, since he was a soldier and not a politician, simply did not have the ability to fight back. He told his closest aides and generals to remain calm, even though he saw Conway as "my inveterate enemy." It would be best leave everything to fate, as he had told one officer on New Year's Eve.

That clever front, denying ambition and desire for "lucrative" gain, was designed to attract support from his generals and aides, which, as he expected, was instantly forthcoming in exactly the manner he anticipated. Lafayette put it best: "You shall see very plainly that if you were lost for America, there is nobody who could keep the army and the Revolution for six months. There are open dissentions in Congress, parties who hate one another as much as the common enemy, stupid men who without knowing a single word about war undertake to judge you, to make ridiculous comparisons; they were infatuated with Gates without thinking of the different circumstances, and believe that attacking is the only thing necessary to conquer. Those ideas are entertained in their minds by some jealous men and perhaps secret friends to the British Government."

His generals and aides, saddened and shocked at what had happened to their chief, and personally infuriated that Conway had been promoted over them, decided to act on Washington's behalf. A group of brigadier generals who usually did nothing but feud with each other mobilized to complain of Conway and Gates to Congress as a unit, authorizing General John Sullivan to lodge a formal complaint about Conway on January

2. In the letter, the group said the promotion of Conway "reflects disgrace and dishonor upon us." A sharp letter came from Laurens's son, John, who told his father that there was "universal disgust" concerning Conway's promotion and the whole affair.

A heated personal letter was sent to Henry Laurens from Lafayette. Much attention had to be paid to any letter from Lafayette. The handsome French general, just nineteen when he arrived in the United States, was the descendent of a wealthy European family and became even richer through recent inheritances and marriage. Like many other Frenchmen, the elegantly dressed and headstrong Marquis had embraced the rebel cause and sailed to America to join the Continental Army. He had little military experience in the French Army, but was attracted to the American cause by both a sense of romantic adventure and an intense dislike of the British.

The young marquis and his friends put considerable pressure on the U.S. envoy to France, Silas Deane, to have him named a major general upon his arrival in the United States. Several delegates in Congress were opposed to the idea of making the teenaged boy from Europe a general ahead of battle-worn American veterans, but Lafayette's offer to serve without pay and at Washington's behest won them over. They were also mindful of the need for French political support. Lafayette first met Washington in August 1777, and, despite language difficulties, the two men were attracted to each other and began a deep, personal friendship, a relationship so strong that Washington later said that he always thought of Lafayette as a son. There was some grumbling among American officers and enlisted men about Lafayette, whose English was severely limited, but that was dispelled after he fought bravely at the battle of Brandywine, where he was wounded in the leg. Then, after spending two months in a Pennsylvania hospital, he emerged to lead an attack on the British in Gloucester, New Jersey, that gained him even more popularity among the Americans.

Lafayette, like the others, insisted that he only wrote Laurens because the deeply hurt general was too distraught to reply himself. Lafayette warned that everyone at Valley Forge was behind the general and that to remove him from command would be "very dangerous." Besides, who would replace him? "If you should lose that same man [Washington], what would become of the American liberty? Who could take his place? Certainly somebody [you] should raise from the earth…for now I do not see anybody, neither in the south, neither in the north, neither Gates, neither Mifflin, neither Greene, who could keep an American army for six months. General Washington is my friend, my tenderest friend it is true; but I assure you that I have not the least partiality in what I wrote to you," he said.

The marquis then added that he had nothing but the highest regard for Gates, whom he said deserved all of the praise heaped upon him following Saratoga. However, having done that, Lafayette then skewered them all when he said "…but [they] do not bear any comparison with our general."

Washington maneuvered brilliantly. He waited until the day after John Laurens wrote his father to send Henry Laurens a curt note to let him know his feelings about Conway, simply calling him "my enemy." (Washington scratched out a much harsher sentence in which he feared the Board of War would ignore him in favor of Conway in the dispute and said his "feelings and opinion of [Conway] will never permit me without the grossest dissimulation, which I abhor and despise, to countenance the man as my friend.")

Through a series of letters, Washington then managed to force an unmasked and very nervous Gates to admit that his behavior in the apparent conspiracy was suspect. Gates extended his complicity by demanding an investigation to find out who leaked the letter Conway had sent him skewering Washington. Then, in a blundering letter, Gates indirectly accused Hamilton of stealing letters that implicated Conway, carrying himself squarely into the conspiracy. Washington wrote back immediately to accuse the now-scrambling Gates of lying about Hamilton and told Gates that the leak was from his own trusted aide, the tankard-hoisting Wilkinson. He then denounced Conway in perhaps the strongest language he used in any written letter during the war, charging that Conway "is capable of all the malignity of detraction, and all the means of intrigue, to gratify the absurd resentment of disappointed vanity or to answer the purposes of personal aggrandizement and promote the interests of faction." Gates responded with another confused note to Washington in which he denied the accusations and pleaded that "I solemnly declare that I am of no faction" and blamed everything on Conway.

Shortly afterward, his own role made public, Wilkinson tried to blame the accusations against Hamilton on another of Gates's aides, Robert Troup. Gates, knowing he was in trouble and looking for a scapegoat, then accused Wilkinson of lying about Gates's relationship with Conway. The young Wilkinson, probably after a few more nights at the tavern, then challenged Gates to a duel, which was fortunately called off. Gates then closeted himself at his office in York and refused to see anyone. Washington was upset that both Gates and Mifflin had been placed on the Board of War, but he did not expect either to have the nerve to travel to Valley Forge with the board to meet him face to face. They never did.

Conway was next. When exposed by Washington, he denied everything, telling Washington that as a general he should know that subordinates are often critical and write letters they may regret. Conway wrote a very strident and defensive letter about his qualifications as an inspector general to one of Washington's confidants, claiming that he did not want to do anything "to give the least cause of uneasiness to the Commander-in-Chief," which was scorned by all who were shown it.

Conway then wrote Washington a letter in which he sarcastically compared him to Frederick the Great, an insulting letter that prompted aide Tilghman to sneer "Conway wrote the General a letter for which he deserved to be kicked...." and that Washington "treated it with the contempt it deserved." Conway's letter did not win him any gratitude from Washington, who received his new inspector general at Valley Forge with a chill that could be felt throughout Chester County. Washington's aides and other generals snubbed Conway, walking out of any room he entered. "He is a great incendiary," said Nathanael Greene. Aide Tench Tilghman put it savagely, writing that people like Conway were "like moles who work in the dark."

Conway, unable to contain his anger, sent a sharp letter to Washington, accusing him of refusing to assist him in his newfound duties. This gave Washington the chance to write President Laurens a letter in which, offering eyewitnesses, he insisted that he had done everything possible to help Conway to do his job. Conway had lied. Besides, he wrote Laurens, why would he befriend Conway? "My feelings will not permit me to make professions of friendship to the man I deem my enemy and whose system of conduct forbids it." The next step Conway would take, Washington suspected, was to again offer his resignation. The commander-in-chief was also cognizant that Conway's protectors in Congress seemed to have disappeared following the storm. He knew, too, that Laurens, the president of Congress, hated Conway and had called him "guilty of the blackest hypocrisy" and charged that his actions had been "unpardonable."

While all of this politicking was going on, Congress had named Lafayette to lead an ill-planned expedition to Canada. Gates told Lafayette that Conway would be one of the generals assisting him. Lafayette then took a daring step to show his support for Washington. Mounting one of his horses at the stable adjacent to the Potts House, he rode to York as fast as he could and bluntly told Congress that he would not follow the orders as long as Conway would be with him, a move that could have ruined his career. Taken aback by this bold action of the popular Lafayette, and surely moved by his support of Washington, Congress overruled Gates and kept Conway home. (Somehow Conway wound up in Albany anyway: Lafayette snubbed him there and refused to continue with the expedition, which was then cancelled by Congress.) Lafayette was not the only general angry at Conway for trying to depose Washington. A few months later, General John Cadwalader challenged Conway to a duel and shot him in the face, nearly killing him.

The purported effort to oust Washington was not only the talk of camp, but of the country. Everyone seemed to *somehow* have been told about it. Washington's brother told him the plot was the talk of Williamsburg. Washington knew his Valley Forge generals would support him, but he needed alliances from outside the army and outside Congress. That support came quickly. State legislators and governors added their support to the commander through a series of letters to each other. One of the first was Joseph Reed, a Pennsylvania congressman who had been the generals' aide early in the war but quit following an argument.

"The attachments of this army to its Commander are extremely strong and natural," he wrote Jonathan Smith, a delegate from Pennsylvania:

> A long connection, winning manners, unspotted morals cast a luster 'round him which a want of success cannot obscure....In supporting him, [troops] support their own opinion. Those who are bold enough to think of a change would do well to reflect upon these circumstances....We are bound by every principle of honor, interest and gratitude to discourage every attempt to lessen his character and weaken or counteract his measures. If there should be any such system formed, as I have hinted, and any farther marks of it appear, let me entreat you...to oppose it.

The general's aides and friends were worried about the outcome of the activity of Gates, Conway, and the delegates all winter, but not Henry Laurens, who, a veteran of legislative wars in South Carolina, saw Washington as both an inventive military commander and clever politician. When the strife was at its peak, Laurens had calmly assured the effusive Lafayette, "Be not alarmed. I think it is not in the power of any junto to lessen our friend without his own consent. I trust his good sense and his knowledge of the world will guard against so fatal an error."

Indeed, no one should have worried about Washington's ability to defuse the plot against him through the shrewd use of a number of people to represent his interests and his own masterful ability to scheme. This is shown by a little-known note to aide John Fitzgerald written on February 28, four days after the episode ended with Washington's half-hearted forgiveness of Gates:

> I thank you sincerely for the part you acted at York respecting Conway's letter and believe with you that matters have and will turn out very different to what that party expected. Gates has involved himself

in his letters to me in the most absurd contradictions. Mifflin has brought himself into a scrape he does not know how to get out of with a gentleman of this state and Conway, as you know, is sent upon an expedition which all the world knew, and the event has proved, was not practicable. In a word, I have a good deal of reason to believe that the machinations of this junto will recoil upon their own heads....

Until the Valley Forge winter, George Washington had never been involved in a career-threatening political conspiracy; certainly no such dilemma ever presented itself in the staid House of Burgesses. In the Conway incident, though, he had shown deep understanding of his own people, in and out of the army, and had used considerable skills in pitting the conspirators against each other, flushing out Gates, and rallying support from his own friends. These were not the military skills of a seasoned general, but the political skills of a national leader, expertise he would need later when he stepped on to a larger stage as the first American president.

His indignation at the move to oust him showed, too, that he was both hurt and angry at any attack on his character or insinuation that he was not fit for command. He had similarly exhibited his wrath to criticism of his leadership in the French and Indian War. It was a thunderous reminder to everyone in the army that all must support the commander; there could be no exceptions for any reason. And it was a lesson, too, that a capable leader should not be removed from office on mere personal pique. Later, Washington and his political contemporaries, writing the U.S. Constitution, would insist that the president could be impeached only for "treason, bribery or other high crimes and misdemeanors."

Martha Comes to Valley Forge

Martha Washington arrived at Valley Forge in early February, just as the second food crisis of the winter was beginning. Her husband had never needed her more. He had been frustrated by Congress in attempting to solve the army's supply and medical problems at the same time that he was defusing the Conway conspiracy. The commander-in-chief was under considerable stress, so much that he must have smiled after he read a note from a general who told him that what he needed to relieve the pressure was "sending for Mrs. Washington, a generous glass of wine or riding on horseback almost every dry day."

But Mrs. Washington was far more depressed than her husband on that crisp February morning as a team of horses pulled her large wooden sled through a light snowfall in front of the Potts house. A snowstorm had made it impossible for her to travel beyond an inn at Brandywine Creek, thirty-five miles south, and her husband had sent an aide, Captain Caleb Gibbs, to meet her there and bring her to Valley Forge in the sleigh. Martha's sister Fanny Basset, who was very close to her, had just died; Martha believed that her death had ended a large part of her life. Martha had now lost her sister, father, first husband, and three of her four children. "If to meet our departed friends and know them was certain, we could have very little reason to desire to stay in this world," she said in a maudlin letter to her husband following the funeral. She added that "nothing in the world so I wish for more sincerely than to be with you," but was too grief-stricken to travel.

The general, who wanted her with him and knew that he and he alone could console her, asked her to come to Valley Forge. He knew, too, that she was the only person in the world who could comfort him. Martha could never say no to her husband. She had told a friend that if he asked her to come to camp, despite her depression, "I must go."

Her despondency must have deepened when she arrived in the wilderness of Valley Forge, with its barren trees and frozen creeks, to witness the deprivations and sickness there. The Potts House, which her husband had admitted was "a dreary kind of place," was cramped and full of men all day. The entire two-story building could have fit into one of the wings at Mount Vernon and still left enough space for a well-appointed ballrooom. Martha summed up her thoughts diplomatically in a note to a friend, Mercy Otis Warren: "The General's apartment is very small." The general had taken the largest bedroom in the home for himself, but it was only fifteen feet wide and fifteen feet long, and its canopy bed, tables, and chairs left little room to do much more than turn around. The Potts residence had a kitchen that was built for a family, not an army headquarters. Washington immediately had it expanded so that Martha could use it for cooking and as a workroom.

Martha lived the same Spartan life as everyone else at Valley Forge. The clothing shortage prevented decent clothes for the local women who worked as her servants (she complained that one girl working for her was "indecently and most shamefully naked").

Martha's arrival, as always, brought joy to her husband. He would complain to her about the conditions of the army, discuss his frustrations with Congress and the people, denounce Conway and others, and she would listen attentively. Martha Washington brought great calm to her husband and at Valley Forge; with men dying by day and cabals by his own generals plotted against him by night, he needed her. The Washingtons had little time for each other as the crises of the winter escalated, and the general was forced to spend most of the day meeting with aides to cope with them. To give themselves time, the general decided to have a one-hour breakfast with his wife each morning at precisely 7 A.M. The husband and wife had their morning meal in their bedroom on a small table in front of the south-side window; the general issued orders that he was not to be disturbed—by anyone—during that hour each morning.

She quickly resumed her role as the General's affable wife that had earned so much respect for the Washingtons at Morristown the previous winter. She again organized a sewing circle and invited the wives of officers in camp, and local women, to tea, which was served in the Washingtons' bedroom above the din of noise below. She talked with them about cooking and fashion, children and grandchildren; exchanged stories about the battles between husbands and wives; and decried the fall of Philadelphia—and its shops. Martha organized the small social life of the officers' wives at Valley Forge, women such as Kitty Greene and Lord Stirling's wife, whom she knew from Morristown. The women, and their husbands, enjoyed teas and coffees at evening receptions, which included singing (which was *not* among the commander-in-chief's many skills). Martha also organized a party on February 22 to celebrate her husband's forty-fifth birthday, highlighted by an outdoor concert performed by the Second Continental Artillery Company's band, whose members received a tip of fifteen shillings from a pleased Mrs. Washington.

She also worked with Charles Wilson Peale, the young Philadelphia artist who had joined the Pennsylvania militia in 1776 and painted various portraits, large and small, of General Washington and others. Martha wanted Peale to paint yet another portrait of her husband because she did not like his previous efforts and neither did the general. He despised posing for artists all of his life and made it a point to avoid much of a conversation with the different men who drew him, except for Peale, whom he liked because he was a soldier and sometimes dined with him in camp. Martha complained that Peale, and all the other artists, made the general's nose too long, deadened his eyes, and, in a common complaint of any wife, made him look old.

Martha took on unpleasant responsibilities, too, such as listening with a sympathetic ear to the stories of women who visited camp to see her husband about their problems, knowing that the general would not intercede on their behalf. At 1:30 P.M. on April 6, Elizabeth Drinker, a Quaker woman, came to present her woes. The Pennsylvania state government had imprisoned her husband, a Quaker merchant, for selling goods to the British. Mrs. Drinker wanted Washington to give her a pass to permit her to travel past American sentries to Lancaster to plead her case with the state government. She also wanted the general to use his political connections to have her husband freed. The woman met first with Martha, who listened attentively, and then the general, who only gave her a few minutes. Mrs. Drinker and her companion, Isabel Morris, were then invited to a 3 P.M. afternoon dinner with fifteen officers and the Washingtons. When dinner was over, Mrs. Washington asked Mrs. Drinker to join her in her upstairs bedroom. There, quietly, Martha told Mrs. Drinker that General Washington had decided against her request and that her husband would remain in confinement.

Martha's afternoon with Elizabeth Drinker was not unusual. She was often urged to soften a blow for women who arrived at camp to plead for their husbands or families concerning any number of issues.

Those who met the short, plump Martha for the first time in Pennsylvania formed different impressions of her. Some men who were introduced to her told friends that, physically, she was rather ordinary looking, but engaging. Other men were surprised that the most famous man in America was married to such an unattractive woman. "She is small and fat; her appearance is respectable. She was dressed very plainly and her manners were simple in all respects," said Chevalier Chastellux, a French diplomat who met her later. But all of the women who met her found her charming and one called her "a social, pretty kind of woman."

Martha had always been a nervous woman, and in the winter of 1778 she was again filled with trepidation. She never enjoyed leaving Mount Vernon, even for a few days' visit to a relative. She still disliked travel and again, as in the previous winter, had to endure a week-long carriage ride over bad roads in winter, avoiding British patrols, to reach her husband's camp. She worried about her son Jack and his family back home. She was apprehensive that her farm manager would not be able to run Mount Vernon without her and fretted, as always, over the health of her husband, who was very susceptible to throat infections in winter weather and had nearly died from one in Morristown. Yet she was sturdy, and no one seems to remember her complaining about Valley Forge. In fact, she spoke glowingly of the officers and men there and proudly told one woman that her favorite music was the sound of military fife and drums.

Rumors of Hope

General Washington had to constantly quell rumors at Valley Forge, as he did at Morristown. An early rumor that swept through camp in late December was that Gates had launched a surprise attack on New York City, seized it, and captured seven hundred British soldiers before all the rest fled. A second was that thousands of citizens of Canada had revolted and overthrown the British government there. In December, a rumor flew through the States that the Continental Army had swelled to more than fifty thousand men. As soon as this rumor was put to rest, a new rumor, that the army had sixty thousand men, supplanted it. And then, on March 27, a wild story circulated that fifty ships of the French Navy were about to land thousands of French soldiers in the Carolinas to join the American army. No, another rumormonger asserted, the French had already landed, but in Rhode Island, not the Carolinas, and it was a single ship, not a fleet. The ship, however, carried 67 cannons, 1,110 carbines, 3,000 muskets and a hold full of shot, shells, powder, and sulphur (this rumor was so strong that it was printed as a news story in the *Pennsylvania Gazette*).

Just before Christmas, a rumor reached camp from Boston that the British had formulated another plan to either capture or assassinate Washington. It was during the Valley Forge winter that Washington worked feverishly to have General Charles Lee freed through a prisoner exchange and a rumor now surfaced that Congress had been planning to name Lee commander-in-chief just before he was captured and might still do so. Another that floated through Pennsylvania was that Conway was going to be appointed commander-in-chief of the Georgia militia; a second had him being named U.S. Ambassador to France.

Throughout December and early January, Washington had lobbied with Congress to send an investigative committee to live at Valley Forge for several weeks so that delegates could witness camp deprivations with their own eyes. He also wanted to give Congress an opportunity to change the terrible image it had among the soldiers, who blamed it for all of their misery. "The cry against Congress still continued as high as ever," wrote one soldier in January, "men of no less rank than colonels spoke of them with the greatest contempt and detestation."

Washington, of course, had to be very careful about his comments concerning Congress. Privately, he was appalled that many Congressional delegates were at home during the worst crisis of the war. He was upset, too, that the most talented men in the country were not members of Congress, as they were when the war began, and that they had been replaced by men of moderate skills. The best men, Washington knew from his relations with governors and others, worked in the states. In a revealing letter to his brother Jack that winter, he lamented that men of quality were not available to help the army or to participate in a peace conference recently proposed by the British:

[Peace talks] will require all the skill, the wisdom, the policy of the first abilities of these states, to manage the helm, and steer with judgment to the haven of our wishes through so many shelves and rocks as will be thrown in our way. This, more than ever, is the time for Congress to be replete with the first characters in every state, instead of having a thin assembly and many states totally unrepresented as is the case at present. I have often regretted the pernicious and what appears to me fatal policy of having our [best] engaged in the formation of the more local governments and filling offices in their respective states leaving the great national concern, on which the superstructure of all and every one of them does absolutely depend, and without which none can exist, to be managed by men of more contracted abilities.

Throughout the winter, Washington devoted considerable attention to national and state politics and the ways in which individuals contributed to the federal and local governments. He kept track of the movement of public figures in each of the states and in Congress, corresponded and held long talks with them in camp, as he had done in Morristown. He saw that the states were becoming stronger with good men and that Congress was growing weaker with inexperienced legislators. It was slowly creating a balance of power that he did not see as fruitful for a country that had to be united in the war—and afterward.

The rumor of the prospective French alliance with the United States that reached London in early March led Lord North to change his objectives. Parliament would soon be faced with a war against France, and perhaps Spain and Holland, which could spill over into the Caribbean and drain its resources. It might be wiser to offer the colonists a settlement so that the empire could concentrate on this upcoming "world war." North offered the Americans a rather ill-defined peace treaty in the draft of a bill sent to Parliament. Under its terms, Americans would have a say in any taxes imposed by Parliament, the major pre-war complaint, and be considered an autonomous country within the British Empire, but not achieve actual independence. American leaders were not impressed with the offer. Washington said it contained "injustice, delusion and fraud" and hoped that it "will be attacked in every shape in every part of the continent."

The treaty was never actually tendered to the Americans. Howe was then ordered to send five thousand men with a fleet to battle the French in the West Indies, to evacuate Philadelphia, and return to New York and hold it. He was told by the Admiralty in London that "the object of the war being now changed, and the contest in America being a secondary consideration, our principal object must be distressing France and defending…His Majesty's possessions."

By the middle of winter, George Washington knew that he had made a grievous mistake in choosing Valley Forge as his winter camp. He could not admit that publicly, but in one forlorn moment in the middle of January acknowledged as much to Congress in a letter he dictated to an aide. "Unhappily, we begin to feel too sensibly some of the disadvantages apprehended from taking the present position of the army instead of retiring into more commodious, though more remote, winter quarters. The present position of this army, adopted in compliance with the prevailing current of sentiment among the people, the pressing remonstrances of the Assembly of this state and the apparent wish and inclination of Congress is not without its inconveniences," he said, and told the delegates he feared the worst. "We shall be likely to suffer still more at a more critical time." He stopped talking, paused, and then told the aide to strike the paragraph from the letter, attempting to eliminating it from history.

The four-man investigative committee Washington had requested from Congress to assess living conditions at Valley Forge—John Harvie, Francis Dana, Joseph Reed, and Nathaniel Folsom—arrived in late January and remained in camp through the end of March. The delegates were shocked when they visited the sick and the dying as well as by the badly built huts and lack of food and clothing. They were given tours of the empty, drafty food warehouses and taken to regiments where half the men could not go outdoors because they had insufficient clothing and laid on wet straw bunkbeds, their hands blue from exposure. They interviewed angry surgeons and were shown farmyards and meadows littered with unused tools that could be used by the army but could not be purchased. The delegates had a chance to interview local merchants and to examine financial records. They were given long explanations of the army's difficulties by Washington, who reiterated the need for able men as heads of the supply networks. They were shaken.

In letters sent from camp, and later in their formal report, the men bluntly told Congress that the army's supply system had to be completely overhauled. They made drastic suggestions. The Committee, at Washington's urging, recommended that the Quartermaster's post be filled immediately, but not by another civilian. They urged the selection of General Nathanael Greene and the creation of new posts for two assistant quartermasters to be chosen by him. Greene would run the department from within the camp itself, a more efficient system since Greene knew the needs of the army. They told Congress to hire a new head of commissary, Jeremiah Wadsworth, a Connecticut merchant and former seaman who had proved himself a capable deputy in the New England office.

The Committee did not offer any suggestions for the reorganization of the medical department, but forwarded recommendations from doctors at Valley Forge, who insisted on a decentralized system in order to permit doctors in camp to make immediate decisions and not have to wait while the director general considered their requests. They urged the director general should also be stripped of complete financial authority, a practice, they hinted, that engendered corruption (the source of Rush's resignation). Congress approved of the decentralization and also made the entire hospital department more accountable for its budget.

The language of the Committee members was blunt. They directly blamed the starvation of the army on the commissary and quartermaster divisions and accused their civilian leaders of gross malfeasance and negligence. They saw no hope unless drastic changes were undertaken. "A great proportion of the soldiers are in a very suffering condition for want of necessary clothing and totally unfit for duty, but even this evil would have been patiently endured had not another, irresistible in its nature, taken place, the want of provisions. We do not see from whence the supplies of meat are to come. The want of it will infallibly bring on a mutiny in the army...'tis probable this army will disperse if the commissary is so damnably managed," wrote Francis Dana to Congress.

Then, referring to Congress's determined invasion of Canada, Dana snapped, "Good God! How absurd to attempt an expedition into Canada when you cannot feed this reduced army!" Washington's wishes had been ignored concerning the Canadian venture. A number of Congressmen wanted Lafayette to take Canada for France to solidify the American–French Alliance. Washington was adamantly opposed; he did not want to give France, or any foreign power, a foothold in North America.

The members of the committee did not limit their vitriolic letters to Congress. They wrote a series of letters to influential governors to make certain that the states brought pressure on Congress to resolve the Valley Forge problems and did what they could to forward supplies. The committee also targeted corruption, charging that "the number of little piddling, pilfering plunderers in the character of deputies and deputies assistants is sufficient almost to form an army."

The acerbic letters to Congress and the pleas to the governors had an impact. At Henry Laurens's prodding, Congress moved to reorganize the departments with, for that ambling body, remarkable speed. The committee findings reached York by courier during the third week of February and a formal report was turned in a week later. By March 2, the recommendations had been adopted and Greene was appointed. Wadsworth was named on April 9. They took over the reins of their departments within days. It was recognition, at long last, that Congress could not do an effective job of overseeing the army. It was time, finally, to let the army attempt to run itself.

Washington was pleased. He was confident that his situation required drastic emergency help from Congress and that delegates had to make a personal visit to camp to see the deprivations firsthand. He had also been certain that he would be able to convince the delegates to recommend exactly what he wanted them to say, that his determined demeanor and powers of persuasion would prevail. He was right. Just as the people had come to see the Revolution through him, he had induced the congressmen to see all the problems through his eyes. The congressional investigative committee was a powerful vehicle in which the legislative branch could oversee any malfeasance in the army or other offices of the government. Washington would welcome these committees again as president, even when it his office they were probing, and the congressional investigative committee would become an important vehicle throughout history.

The committee recommendations at Valley Forge came just when all progress seemed halted and a malaise had permeated the camp, put best by assistant quartermaster Jones: "In short, everything seems to go against us and without the Almighty hand of Providence helping us somewhat better we shall all disband...."

Chapter Ten

꩜

A NEW
AMERICAN ARMY

*"The General is well, but much worse with fatigue and
anxiety. I never knew him to be so anxious as now."*
—Martha Washington

The deaths of a considerable number of men from sicknesses, deserters, and the hospitalization of another several thousand plus those recovering from smallpox inoculations, had substantially reduced the size of the American armed forces at Valley Forge as winter dragged on. By early February, there were fewer than six thousand soldiers left from the nearly twelve thousand that had arrived in December. Illness and the lack of food and clothing had weakened the rest. George Washington had to once again frantically lobby states for Continental regulars and militia and halt the growing tide of resignations and desertions.

The early results were disappointing. No state annoyed him like Pennsylvania. The state's council had promised sixty-two thousand able-bodied men for militia duty as an inducement to establish a camp in Valley Forge, but by early winter fewer than twenty-five hundred had arrived—and they were only there for sixty days and then went home. Militia called up to replace them took weeks to report.

The Pennsylvania Assembly told the general it had another war to fight, against American Indians raiding villages in the northern and western parts of the state, which abutted the Northwest Territories. They sent a militia company promised to Washington off into the wilderness to fight American Indians instead. The general did not balk because he, too, feared the growing problem of Indian aggression. In the summer of 1779, he would order General Sullivan to undertake a campaign against Indians in those areas, which resulted in the destruction of dozens of Indian villages and hundreds of Indian casualties.

Thomas Wharton Jr., the head of Pennsylvania's supreme executive council, told the commander-in-chief, too, that the state's residents did not get along with the general's soldiers and refused to serve. He added that there was "a great and growing disgust that is lately become general throughout the counties to serve in conjunction with the regular troops" and that Pennsylvanians believed them to be "defective and cowardly." Washington constantly pressed Pennsylvania for troops. Sometimes a company or two was mustered together and sent on, but on other occasions the state council blithely told him that they could not find anybody to enlist or to draft.

Despite frequent pleas by Delaware Governor Caesar Rodney, a friend of Washington's, enlistment there was unsuccessful and General William Smallwood, in camp in Wilmington, finally told the commander that "I have no expectation of any aid from the militia." There were one thousand continentals from New Jersey and five hundred from Virginia, but that was only on paper. Washington was unhappy about the men from his home state, too, and fumed at repeated complaints about rank and pay that had been sent to him by Virginians since the summer. To keep them in the army, he finally relented and permitted them a two-month furlough plus a Christmas vacation.

Slow enlistments angered his generals as much as they irritated Washington. General Alexander McDougall was one. "It is very surprising that this country cannot be taught experience, neither from the practice of ages nor their own sufferings," he told Washington. "All the civilized nations in Europe exert every nerve to recruit their army early in winter when they are at war to discipline their soldiers for the campaign. But America sends her recruits to her army by fifties, when the enemy is at our beards, and wonder the invader is not defeated, without considering that she has not furnished us with the means to do it, for men are not soldiers."

Washington needed more troops and so he turned to the state legislatures. This plea worked for him because his position enabled him to approach state officials as a political leader, not merely a general. This practice was so accepted that he would use it on several occasions as president during the Whiskey Rebellion and Indian Wars. "We may be assured," he told the state officials, "that Britain will strain every nerve to send from home and abroad, as early as possible, all the troops it shall be in her power to raise or procure. Her views and schemes for subjugating these states and bringing them under her despotic rule will be unceasing and unremitted."

This direct plea, plus numerous personal letters to governors and local politicians, a promise to pay eight dollars per new soldier to local recruiters, and even purchasing liquor as an inducement finally resulted in additional Continental troops, and some Indian recruits. But they were slow to arrive at Valley Forge and many were not in camp until April.

Although resignations and desertions were not as high as at Morristown, when so many enlistments ran out and the men went home, the general had lost hundreds of men by January. He was forced to plead with some and threaten others, in a very personal campaign, to keep the army in existence. He feared the exodus of thousands, even generals. General Samuel Holden Parsons, then in New York, was one. He wanted to resign in mid-January. The commander told him that his departure might have a grim result. "I am sorry to find you have thoughts of leaving the army," he wrote him. "I hope you will consider the matter well and the consequences which such a procedure may involve. Besides the loss of your own services, the example might have a disagreeable influence on other officers." The plaintive appeal worked and Parsons remained.

Washington was so fearful of resignations that he often refused to permit generals or officers to go home on furloughs, such as John Sullivan, who claimed his business was going bankrupt, and General James Varnum, who told the commander he only wanted to see his wife, whom he missed terribly. The commander urged any of his generals or colonels in the hospital, such as McDougall, to return as soon as possible. He ordered those officers already home, such as Brigadier Generals Peter Muhlenberg, and John Glover, to come back immediately, telling them, as he wrote Glover, that "the situation of the army is such that it can ill bear the loss of good officers." Even though he was pleased at the success of Henry Knox's expedition to locate cannon and clothing in New England, he ordered him back, too, telling him to return "as expeditiously as circumstances will admit."

Sometimes he used stiff, wooden language in his pleas, and in others he was heated. In early January, he received yet another request for a furlough from Colonel William Malcolm. The general exploded, telling Malcolm, who only recently joined the service, that if he wanted to go home he should stay home. "Resign…you will meet with no difficulty with me," he snapped at him. Washington admonished Charles Lewis of his native Virginia that his desire to go home indicated that apparently others "possess more virtue more attachment to the great and common cause" than Lewis and, referring to his own long service, told him that "there are none among us who do not experience great inconvenience from the service, but are we to quit it?"

He told his aides, as he told James Bowdoin, "I am astonished, considering the sufferings the men have undergone, that more of them have not left us" and that resignations were "an epidemical disease."

Many who wanted to stay in the service were under enormous pressure from their spouses to come home to salvage their collapsing farms. One man wrote, "our wives, our children, all that is dear to us at home are suffering. And these monopolizers extorting on our families, how can we stay here contented when our families are in such a suffering conditions?" Soldiers' friends in camp commiserated with them, "When an officer…finds a letter directed to him from his wife, filled with the most heart aching

The first official portrait of George Washington was this 1772 painting by Charles Wilson Peale. Washington posed in the uniform he wore as a colonial officer in the British Army during the French and Indian War. (Courtesy of Morristown National Historical Park.)

George Washington spent all of his adult life, except for the war years, living at Mount Vernon, a collection of large plantations on the banks of the Potomac River in Virginia. The last time Washington saw his plantation, on the day he died, it was covered in snow, as it is in this photo. (Courtesy of the Mount Vernon Ladies Association.)

There are few existing portraits of the Washington family together. This stipple engraving by David Edwin and Edward Savage shows George, Martha, and her children, Jack and Patsy Custis.

THE ORIGINAL ARNOLD TAVERN.
FROM PEN AND INK SKETCH BY MISS S. HOWELL.

Washington used the tavern of Jacob Arnold as his headquarters during the first winter at Morristown in 1777. (Courtesy of the Morristown-Morris Township Library.)

Painted by
MISS EMMA H. VAN PELT.

From Pen and Ink Sketch by
MISS S. HOWELL.

ORIGINAL FIRST PRESBYTERIAN CHURCH, 1738.

The Morristown Presbyterian Church was turned into a hospital for soldiers and townspeople afflicted with smallpox during the winter of 1777. (Courtesy of the Morristown-Morris Township Library.)

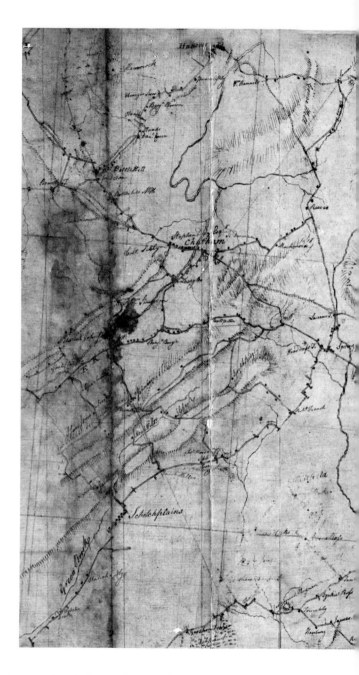

Washington asked his mapmaker, Robert Erskine, to draw this map of the New Jersey
region between his camp in Morristown, upper far left, and the Hudson River, to the
far right. The map shows Elizabethtown, the major port on the New Jersey side of
the river, and the three highways that merged at the village of Springfield into the
lone road leading to Morristown. The map shows the Newark Mountains, actually

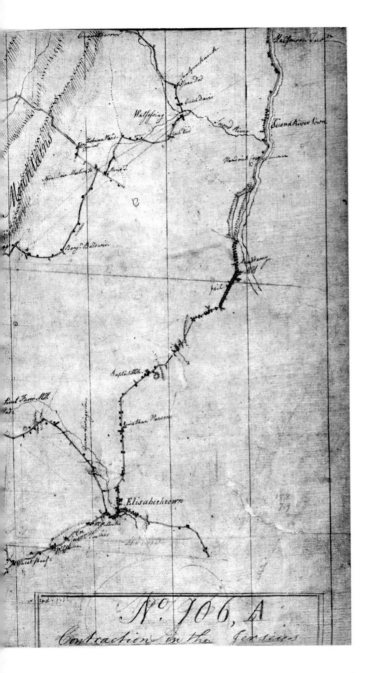

the Watchung, and the gap between them, at Short Hills and Springfield, that the British would have had to march through to reach Washington's army in any surprise attack. He used the map to set up a string of defenses that worked perfectly when he was finally attacked by the Redcoats in the spring of 1780. The Americans defeated the British at Springfield. (Courtesy of the Morristown-Morris Township Library.)

The commander-in-chief, in the forefront, holds his cape tightly while reviewing a small parade at Valley Forge. (Courtesy of Valley Forge National Historical Park.)

This small stone farmhouse served as Washington's headquarters during the terrible winter at Valley Forge. (Courtesy of Valley Forge National Historical Park.)

Washington frequently inspected cabins, slaughterhouses, hospitals, and other buildings at Valley Forge, although never alone, as shown in this sketch. (Frank Leslie's Weekly sketch courtesy of Valley Forge National Historical Park.)

Soldiers were sent on forays into the countryside to find and purchase whatever food, supplies, and firewood they could find.

Artistic license was often carried away when illustrators attempted to depict the hardships at Valley Forge. One widely published sketch showed these men living in a fragile lean-to, although no one did. They all lived in huts, although the huts were badly constructed havens for disease.

By the time the winter of 1777-78 ended, Washington's hard work resulted in the recruitment of thousands of new soldiers. They were trained by Baron Frederich Von Steuben. (*Harper's Weekly* sketches courtesy of Valley Forge National Historical Park.)

Mrs. Jacob Ford, whose husband and son had died in the Revolution, offered Washington the use of her home when he returned to Morristown for winter camp in 1779. Washington's office was on the first floor, at the rear. The home, open to the public, has undergone several renovations over the years. (Courtesy of the Morristown-Morris Township Library.)

When the army returned to Morristown in the winter of 1779, Washington ordered that the huts for his men be built with tighter walls and roofs to keep the rain out and additional windows for better ventilation. The army was camped at Jockey Hollow, today part of the Morristown National Historical Park, open to the public (these are recreated cabins). (Courtesy of the Morristown-Morris Township Library.)

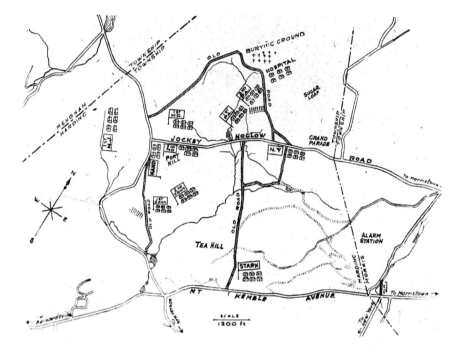

One of the few existing maps of the winter camp at Jockey Hollow shows some of the neighborhoods of huts, or cabins, in what was actually a well-designed military city that housed thirteen thousand men. The men survived one of the most brutal winters in American history. The hospital buildings are shown at the top of the map. One of Washington's alarm stations is on the right, on top of a high hill. Large cannons stationed here were fired by lookouts if the British Army was spotted. (Courtesy of the Morristown-Morris Township Library.)

Alexander Hamilton pleaded for a battlefield command for years and was finally rewarded when the general put him in charge of the Yorktown attack in 1781. This 1870 engraving, based on a portrait by Alonzo Chappel, shows Hamilton in the trenches before the victorious assault that brought an end to the Revolution. (Courtesy of Morristown National Historical Park.)

Washington's most reliable commander, General Nathanael Greene (shown here in a J.B. Forrest engraving), stayed with Washington during most of his winter camps. It was Greene's army that kept Lord Cornwallis in the Yorktown area of Virginia in the autumn of 1781 until Washington's army and the French fleet arrived to lay siege to the British army and end the war in triumph. (Courtesy of Morristown National Historical Park.)

The Marquis de Lafayette, a young and adventurous French nobleman, became a favorite with Washington after their meeting at Valley Forge. (Courtesy of Independence National Historical Park.)

Henry Knox was in charge of all American artillery and succeeded Washington as commander of the army when the general resigned in 1783. This engraving is based on a Charles Wilson Peale portrait. (Courtesy of Morristown National Historical Park.)

William Alexander called himself Lord Stirling, although his nobility was always in question. The American general, depicted here in a G.R. Hall engraving, was with Washington through most of his winter campaigns. (Courtesy of Morristown National Historical Park.)

#1839 Dickerson's Tavern, "Under The Hill".

Benedict Arnold, shown here in an H.B. Hall engraving, was court-martialed on corruption charges at the Dickerson Tavern, known locally as the Norris Tavern, in Morristown in the winter of 1779–80. Despite a spirited defense from an angry Arnold, the court-martial board found him guilty of some of the charges. Washington, who admired Arnold greatly, merely reprimanded him. Arnold was appalled by the reprimand and made up his mind to betray his country by selling the plans of West Point to the British. (Courtesy of Morristown National Historical Association. Dickerson Tavern sketch courtesy of the Morristown-Morris Township Library.)

Washington's closest political ally during the war was New Jersey governor William Livingston, who provided troops and supplies at critical junctures and served as a political confidant. (Courtesy of Morristown National Historical Park)

General Horatio Gates did not stop a conspiracy to have him replace Washington as commander-in-chief during the Valley Forge winter, when the army's prospects for victory were dim. (Courtesy of Independence National Historical Park.)

Philadelphia banker Robert Morris was dubbed the "financier of the revolution" for his uncanny ability to raise money for the army from numerous sources. (Courtesy of Independence National Historical Park.)

Samuel Huntington, John Hancock, John Jay, and Henry Laurens (clockwise from top left) were four of the presidents of the Continental Congress during the Revolution. Each man helped Washington in different ways during the winters, when it seemed the army would collapse. (Huntington photo courtesy of Morristown National Historical Park. Laurens, Jay, and Hancock photos courtesy of Independence National Historical Park.)

George Washington left Philadelphia on his soon-to-be-familiar white horse to take command of the American army outside of Boston in the spring of 1775. (Courtesy of Morristown National Historical Park.)

Paintings of Washington in the foreground, with his men behind him, were popular because they linked the commander of the army with the common soldier. (Courtesy of Independence National Historical Park.)

No painting conveys the heroic image of Washington held in the hearts of the American people so much as this 1824 portrait by Rembrandt Peale of the general on his white horse. (Courtesy of Independence National Historical Park.)

render of complaints a woman capable of writing [about the lack of food, clothing and money]...who would not be disheartened from persevering in the best of causes," wrote a doctor about men in his brigade.

Washington understood that: "If they were confined to bad officers, or to those of little or no character, they would be of no consequence....But it is painful to see men...who have rendered great services...and who are still...most materially wanted, leaving the army, on account of the distresses of their family."

The biggest reason, though, was the need for a pension system for officers, preferably the half-pay for life system used in some European armies. "Nothing else will preserve any degree of reputation in the army," Doctor Sam Tenney, one of several physicians threatening to go home, said of a pension.

Washington argued that the only way he could keep officers and men in the service, and recruit more, was through such a system, often discussed in lengthy debates in Congress. The general argued that his men had given up their jobs to join the army and might not get them back when the war ended. He told Congress, too, that their absence placed impossible pressure on their wives and sons to run their farms or businesses without financial help.

Those delegates in favor saw it as a just reward for service; those opposed saw it creating indolence among thousands of returning veterans. Washington never wavered in his support of the system. He warned Congress that resignations might soon become a tidal wave and he would not be able to "hold the army together much longer."

Several thousand soldiers were in the hospitals, sick and dying, and more would die in their huts. Only about half of the twelve thousand men who had marched into camp with him were available for duty by February. He knew that the final death toll would mean that he would have to add several thousand more men to restore the army to eleven thousand strong and that number was just half of the troops he had during the fall of 1777. He was given the usual promises of large militias from different states and more from recruiters who said that, with sufficient bonuses, they could sign up thousands of troops.

Washington acknowledged them, but pressured the states to send him more men. He also outlined to the congressmen visiting camp a broad plan to enlarge the army. In a lengthy memo, he insisted that the Continental Army needed more than forty thousand men to defeat the British the following summer, a figure they all knew was not possible, and that perhaps a draft was finally necessary. Washington also asked for more help in developing his artillery department under Henry Knox, who constantly asked for more men and cannon. If Congress did not act, he warned, the future was dim. He complained to New Jersey Governor Livingston that "…the fatal policy of host enlistments like an evil genius is now prosecuting us and marring all our operations."

And he oversaw a plentiful number of operations. Washington had resisted strenuous pressure from Congress and the Pennsylvania Council to attack Philadelphia in the winter, but he did approve of numerous small actions. In an imaginative attack, his men floated dozens of kegs loaded with explosives down the Schuykill River in an attempt to blow up British ships and barges in Philadelphia. And they engaged in dozens of skirmishes with British patrols in Chester, Philadelphia, and Bucks counties. These constant brief encounters, Washington assured Congress, would prevent the British from plundering supplies and preserving them for the Americans.

No one disagreed with Washington's need for more soldiers. The governors and Congress did all they could to recruit troops. Henry Laurens was the General's greatest supporter, complaining to friends that if the army was not able to fight in the spring, all would be lost. "If the states do not exert themselves, and speedily, too," he said of enlistments, "if delayed the whole fabric will tumble."

Rank among officers continued to be a problem for Washington. It had surfaced in the Morristown winter but died down during the spring and summer. The officers' complaints about rank seemed to grow in direct proportion with idle time; winter gave them much of it. They complained that the army, not Congress, should decide rank and make promotions, that men from certain states were favored over those from others, that Washington and the generals had favorites whom they advocated for promotion, and that foreign officers were given preference for advancement over Americans.

Rank was a source of great honor for the men in the army. Officers who had led comfortable lives before the war craved acknowledgment of their superior station in life by high rank. Those who led marginal existences before the conflict saw rank as not only a reward for service, but an elevation to a higher, and much deserved, station in life. The men saw the army as a metaphor for democracy; all should have equal opportunities to advance in the ranks. Squabbles among officers about rank and pensions became so great that two officers in the artillery were said to be "near daggers points."

Many soldiers felt like the overlooked James Eldredge, who told Washington in a typical letter, "my reasons for leaving the service are principally…I have seen with much impatience officers whom at the beginning of the war I commanded promoted to field officers, without the appearance of any extraordinary merits."

Washington recommended fairness to Congress, adding that gifted officers should not be kept from becoming generals just because there were already too many generals from their state. He said, too, that the Board of War or Congress, and not the individual states, should determine lower promotions, and that if the current system remained, it "will be injurious and become an incurable source of inquietude and disgust." The general's continual rank troubles would lead him to later insist that Congress place all promotions under the president and that the chief executive also serve as commander-in-chief.

Despite his frustrations, Washington maintained a remarkable level of self-control. It was this ability to rein in his emotions that permitted him to maintain his image as a commander completely in charge of any situation, unable to be rattled. He vented his anger to aides in private, sometimes using salty language, but was never seen raising his voice in public. He maintained his dignity in any dispute with Congress or with other generals, even in the Conway affair. He had ordered his men to give up gambling. Washington, an energetic gambler himself, gave up games of chance, too. He drank wine with dinner, but in moderation. Washington was not a womanizer; he ignored any attention by local women. He remained at his post and never went home on furlough, as everyone else did, spending a total of just eighteen hours at Mount Vernon, on his way to Yorktown, in eight years of military service. "No man ever united in his own person a more perfect alliance of the virtues of a philosopher with the talents of a general," said John Bell during the middle of the war. Even Dr. David Ramsey, a physician who usually heard nothing but complaining by sick soldiers, said, "I have never heard of one who charged him with any habitual vice or even foible."

Disorders had festered in the Commissary and Quartermaster's divisions for months. The general hoped they would end, too, with the takeover of those departments by Greene and Wadsworth.

Nathanael Greene had not joined the army to find bread and butter; he had joined it to fight the British. He was reluctant to give up his field command, even though he would keep his major general rank, to run the Quartermaster's Department. "My rank in the army and the splendor of command which I am obliged to discontinue for a time are not inconsiderable sacrifices and what I have in return [are] a troublesome office to manage and a new set of officers in the different districts to seek for."

Washington persuaded Greene to take the job. He was the best man for it and enjoyed the commander's complete trust. The commander-in-chief also assured him that when fighting resumed he would be back on the battlefield with the troops. Greene then waded into the quagmire that had become the Quartermaster's Department with the same grumbling efficiency he had shown in every other assignment the general had given him during the war, whether combat or administrative. He decided to move his office to Moore Hall, a large stone building two miles from Valley Forge, where he and his men could work untroubled by daily camp life. Once there, he named James Abeel, perhaps the only man in the army more efficient than himself, as his top assistant. He remembered the hard work of Abeel in procuring food in Morristown the previous winter.

Jeremiah Wadsworth, the new head of the Commissary, was a compassionate man who had always felt badly about the faltering supply system while he worked as a deputy in Connecticut. He had spent much of his time there arguing with locals in order to buy food and cattle at realistic prices. He was in many ways just like Greene—a hard-working officer who had to take over a badly administered department. Like Greene, he had a deep feeling for the soldiers.

He wrote one colleague upon appointment, "I fear nothing but the army's wanting food. For God's sake let that be prevented my own estate I would freely sacrifice rather than let the army want food. I wish I could rid myself of the un-Christian feelings I have toward those gentlemen who have urged me into this distressing situation but I will forgive them may heaven do so too, but their own consciences will acquit or condemn them."

The new commissary general and quartermaster took office just in time. All of the army's problems had coalesced in mid-February and again threatened its dissolution. Washington was pleased that the departments would finally be run efficiently, but angry that they had not been reorganized much sooner, as he had suggested. "Our worthy General wrote to Congress immediately upon the alteration that was made in the department [Buchanan's appointment] and exactly foretold them all the ill and dangerous consequences that would follow but they did not or would not believe him," wrote General Huntington of Connecticut.

The commander-in-chief's temper had flared again and again in the middle of the month as supplies dwindled and deaths mounted. Alexander Hamilton was ordered to begin a camp-wide investigation to discover why newly arrived food had not been distributed swiftly enough to the men. Ephraim Blaine, a quartermaster, was asked to determine how many wagons could be commandeered in southeastern Pennsylvania and had to tell the commander that altogether there would not be as many as needed to bring in enough food to keep the men alive. He ordered clerks in different departments to his office at the Potts house three and four times each day to keep him informed about any morsel of food that arrived in camp, convened extra meetings of his staff, and kept his aides working until late at night as he fired off pleas for food.

His spirits had waned, too, eliciting much sympathy from those around him. "I pity him from my heart and soul," said Thomas Jones, deputy quartermaster of issues. "There is no man more distressed...he is the most unhappy man in the world."

Life had deteriorated quickly for the soldiers, too. By mid-February the men had been put on half rations and the number of cattle in pens was far less than the amount needed. The Commissary situation had disintegrated so badly that one general called it "shocking." Men began to haphazardly cut up their field tents and wrap the shredded canvas around themselves as blankets. So many horses had died that few were left to hook up to supply carts, and the soldiers had to yoke themselves to the carts and pull them across camp. Conditions in camp had become so bleak by the end of February that one soldier, William Weeks, wrote a friend, "I should be glad if you would be careful of speaking about the bad fare of the army, as it might be a discouragement to the men to enlist...."

Wadsworth's arrival and Greene's elevation were just two of several major changes in the army, changes Washington always made to better the military. In late February, the general also welcomed the arrival of the most peculiar man in the American army, Baron Frederich William Von Steuben. The forty-eight-year-old, portly, brusque Von Steuben spoke very little English. A former Prussian "general," he had decided to join the Continental Army. His acceptance had been urged by Benjamin Franklin, in Paris, who sent him on to America and told Congress that Von Steuben was a lieutenant general in the Prussian Army and a close confidant of the legendary military leader Frederick the Great. The truth was that Von Steuben was only a deputy quartermaster in the Prussian Army, but Franklin thought he needed a far more impressive title and so he gave him one.

Upon arrival at Valley Forge, Von Steuben told George Washington that the Virginian was the commander-in-chief of a large underdisciplined fighting force that needed to be whipped into shape if the Americans were ever going to beat the British in traditional head-to-head combat and win the war. The army, he said, needed to fight more like the Europeans; he could help them reach that goal. Washington's eyes must have widened as he listened to a description of his army that matched his own assessment. The commander knew that he needed a professionally trained army that could maneuver on the battlefield as well as the British and fight them with highly sharpened military skills.

It was not enough for Washington, for the country, to stumble out of Valley Forge with a malnourished, still badly trained force and continue to lose battles or run and hide from the Redcoats. He wanted to emerge from winter camp with new resolve, with a splendid-looking, refreshed, motivated, and highly trained fighting force so that he could meet the British anywhere and defeat them. He had merged inexperienced militia with Continentals for three long years with little success beyond guerrilla warfare victories at Trenton and Princeton. That would not win what was clearly becoming one of history's great wars. He had always needed a solid, professional army and he never had one. Now, in Von Steuben, his dream might be realized.

Washington did not know what to do with Von Steuben, though, who later asked to be an inspector general and then major general. The Prussian was a foreigner in an army where many foreigners were detested. He certainly could not be made a general of any kind since he was a colonel, or perhaps even of lesser rank, according to his mysterious past in Germany. Washington had been saddled with Conway as an inspector general and was unable to employ another. Besides, it would be impossible for a hundred Prussian drill masters to whip his disorganized fighting force into shape in just a few weeks; to do so would take years.

Von Steuben met with Washington, with John Laurens speaking to Von Steuben in French and then translating. The Prussian blithely waved away all of Washington's objections and told him he would serve as a volunteer, without pay, until he could officially join the army. "I have but one aim, and that is to be useful to the United States and to participate in the glory of your armies," he told Washington.

Washington liked Von Steuben right away, as he explained to Henry Laurens in late February: "Baron Von Steuben has arrived in camp. He appears to be much of a gentleman and as far as I have had an opportunity of judging, a man of military knowledge and acquainted with the world."

The commander took him at his word and gave him free rein to train his men. Washington, and just about everyone else, was startled at what happened next. Von Steuben would not merely oversee the training at a distance, like anyone else with his experience; he decided to work with the men as a drill sergeant might, barking orders in the line and marching alongside the men as they struggled through maneuvers on the wide fields, constantly trying to understand his guttural German as he shouted commands. He had unbounded enthusiasm, and one officer said he worked "like a lieutenant anxious for promotion."

Von Steuben quickly determined what his problems were. The Americans did not march or maneuver with the same steps and commands. Each regiment had its own commands and, on long marches or in the heat of battle, this caused confusion. There were no printed instructions for maneuvers on the battlefield. There was no one who had any experience as a true drill master, and the men resented drills.

The Prussian decided that the best way to accomplish his goal was to form a model company. Its achievements would lead to the success of all the others. Washington ensured the success of the model troupe by assigning his fifty-man personal guard and one hundred other hand-picked soldiers to it. He told them that it was of great importance and they should do what the drillmaster told them without complaint. And, as a final incentive, he reminded them that the Baron was legendary Frederick the Great's right-hand man (he had already learned the truth about his real rank, which Von Steuben did not deny, but never told the men).

Washington told Von Steuben that he was dealing with unruly, shivering, hungry, angry, and cantankerous men who were in no hurry to drill. There was little time and the Baron had to simplify his procedures, streamline his tactics, and command the men as sympathetically as possible.

To create a bond between the baron and the men, Washington accompanied Von Steuben on tours through the hut city, trudging over patches of snow and mud, to introduce him to his new charges. The commander told all that he had complete confidence in the "renown" Prussian. The busy Washington also acquiesced to the Baron's demand that he and Washington meet daily to discuss the drills.

The soldiers, eager to learn from Frederick the Great's major domo, stunned Washington with their immediate enthusiasm. They were not merely happy to learn how to maneuver better, but soon came to see it as a game in which one regiment could outperform another. Progress under the shouts and epithets of the Prussian became an impressive sight. He stumbled through his new-found English while marching through the vast, grassy fields near the Schuykill with his men. They mastered simple drills and maneuvers in days, and within weeks were marching down roads, platoon after platoon, and making difficult turns. They were soon conquering complicated battlefield maneuvers and learning how to fight with two lines of men against three lines of the enemy. Attacks and retreats, which excited the men, were practiced relentlessly, as were bayonet charges. And, too, the hours of drills kept the minds of the men off their dying comrades and their own hungry stomachs.

By May, Von Steuben was able to assure Washington that he had made much progress and that the men were ready to take on the British or anybody else. The astonished general congratulated him on what seemed to him a military miracle. Von Steuben also informed Washington that he was spending his free time writing a book on military maneuvers for the Americans, *Regulations for the Order and Discipline of the Troops of the United States*, which was, in fact, ready in longhand by that summer.

Everybody was impressed at Von Steuben's exuberance. "The Baron discovers the greatest zeal and an activity which is hardly to be expected at his years. The officers in general seem to entertain a high opinion of him," said John Laurens. "Baron Steuben set us a noble example," said General Sullivan. "He shows himself to be a perfect master of [discipline]."

And the men knew it. One soldier wrote home that "the army grows stronger every day…and there is a spirit of discipline among the troops that is better than numbers.…[Y]ou would be charmed to see the regularity and exactness with which they march and perform their maneuvers. Last year…it was almost impossible to advance or retire in the presence of the enemy without disordering the line and falling into confusion. This misfortune, I believe, will seldom happen again."

Turning his enlisted men into finely trained regiments was just part of the near-miraculous overhaul of the army undertaken by the commander-in-chief in just a few months that winter. He wanted to augment his artillery, so he dispatched Henry Knox on a lengthy tour of New England to locate and purchase additional cannon. He told army officers in Maryland, Delaware, New Jersey, Connecticut and Massachusetts to procure more. This search resulted in more than two dozen cannon of different sizes.

Washington had also made up his mind to increase the size and enhance the effectiveness of his cavalry, which had fought well at Brandywine and Germantown. "We have found so many advantages from the cavalry in the course of this campaign that I am determined to augment them as much as possible against the next and enable them to take the field in a respectable manner," he told General William Heath. He sent the cavalry, under Polish Brigadier General Casimir Pulaski, to Trenton by itself for training at its own winter camp.

Washington ordered all of his generals and some colonels to write lengthy memos, which he used to supplement his own plans. These memos, some more than thirty pages in length, eventually led to the reorganization of the army into five divisions, drafts for Continental soldiers as well as militia, the replacement of many workers in the Quartermaster's and Commissary offices in camp, and reform in the army's hospitals.

The month of April in 1778 brought considerable relief to the Continental Army on all fronts. Greene and Wadsworth had streamlined the Quartermaster's and Commissary Departments. At Washington's urging, Greene hired hundreds of experienced wagon drivers from Pennsylvania and New Jersey who moved to Valley Forge and drove teams as civilians for weekly wages. The general ordered the impressment—with payment—of hundreds of wagons throughout Chester, Bucks, and Berks County in Pennsylvania and as far south as Maryland. Greene had ended most of the mismanagement in the department and speeded up deliveries. Wadsworth, although never able to completely solve the food crisis, did reorganize the department, curb most corruption, and expand the search for food and clothes. Good weather made it much easier to transport supplies and shortages eased considerably. The success of Wadsworth and Greene reaffirmed his desire, later, as president, to place all federal departments under the chief executive.

The Relentless Search for Cattle

The severest problem facing the army in the second half of that winter was food, especially after the Pennsylvania Council told the general that the state had simply run out of it. During mid-February, as supplies dwindled, Washington made a bold decision. In what seemed a nearly impossible feat of logistics, he decided to develop a network of supplies that reached all the way to Massachusetts in the North and Maryland in the South. He would obtain food in those states, where it was plentiful, and transport it hundreds of miles to Valley Forge in wagon trains in journeys that would take weeks.

While the wagon convoy was unprecedented, the bold part of the scheme was Washington's planned cattle drives to obtain needed beef. He kicked off the campaign with a strident proclamation sent to farmers throughout the Atlantic seaboard. The general implored them to sell him every head of cattle that they could:

> It is therefore recommended to the inhabitants of those states to put up and feed, immediately, as many of their stock cattle as they can spare so as that they may be driven to this army....Proprietors may assure themselves that they will render a most essential service to the illustrious cause of their country and contribute in a great degree to shorten this bloody contest.

He warned the farmers, too, that if the Americans lost the war because they hoarded their cattle, the British would steal the cows anyway, abuse their families, put the farmers in prison, and/or kill them. At the same time, the general once again pleaded with the governors he had worked so hard to bring into his confidence, telling all that he feared the collapse of the army unless the cattle drives were successful and begging them to use their considerable "means and influence" to help.

Once the farmers and officials were alerted, the commander then ordered quartermasters throughout the New England states, Delaware, and Maryland to buy up thousands of heads of cattle wherever they could find them—pleading at each and every farm they could visit—and organize them into herds. They were to use soldiers and hired farmhands to lead the herds from town to town, state to state, to Valley Forge, some from farms 250 miles away. The herds and their drivers would have to stop to rest at dozens of farms, meadows, and towns, and prior arrangements would have to be made for their stay. The cattle would have to be fed, supervised, and given medical attention if needed. The animals would be taken over snow- or ice-covered roads, and, perhaps, because of the continually changing weather, muddy highways.

Thousands of cows in different herds from New England would have to be transported across the Hudson River on ferries and later taken over the Delaware by boat. Those drives were often delayed, the herds detained on riverbanks when the Hudson became impassable. All of this had to be undertaken without drawing suspicion from British patrols or local spies. These would be the most massive cattle drives in American history until the development of the West in the 1870s. It was an historic plan and a huge gamble.

Planning for the drives had commenced back on February 7, when Washington ordered assistant commissary head Ephraim Blaine to accompany four brigades of wagons to Head of Elk, Maryland, a port town on the Chesapeake Bay that would serve as the clearing house for southern provisions. Blaine remained there for several weeks, spending most of his time looking for wagons.

The need for cattle was immediate, Washington told General Putnam in Albany, "As the resources of this country…are nearly exhausted, and the Army under my command is in consequent literally reduced in a starving condition, it becomes indispensably necessary for us to avail ourselves, as much as possible, of our more distant supplies" and urged him to forward all the cattle he could to Pennsylvania. The commander-in-chief stressed the emergency in a similar order to Henry Lee, in charge of supplies for Delaware and Maryland: "All the cattle that are fit for slaughter must be immediately consumed on account of our present necessity and therefore should be drove toward camp as far as they can be collected."

Blaine told a New Jersey officer who had promised to send him a herd, "for God's sake and my reputation, use every exertion to forward with the greatest dispatch all the stock and other cattle you possibly can [obtain] without one moment's loss of time." A New York agent was told that Washington needed more than two hundred head of cattle each week, an imposing herd, through the end of the spring, more if possible. "The quantity cannot be too great or too soon forwarded," he was told.

Washington wrote the governors of New York, Connecticut, Rhode Island, and Massachusetts of his plight and the risky, cross-country cattle drives that he proposed, gaining their support. He told them, and his agents in their states, that the army would collapse without all the cattle they could spare. "Jersey, Pennsylvania and Maryland are now entirely exhausted," he wrote. "All the beef and pork already in them or that can be collected will not by any means support the army one month longer. To the eastward only can we turn our eyes with any reasonable hope of timely and adequate succor. If every possible exertion is not made use of there to secure us immediate and ample supplies of cattle, the most fatal consequences must ensue."

As always, there were problems purchasing herds from local farmers. Washington ordered agents to either buy cattle or wagons or impress them on credit. They were to be taken, no matter how. There was no time left.

The cattle drives, which involved hundreds of soldiers and civilians, succeeded beyond anyone's expectation. New York's commissary chiefs began sending an average of 160 cattle per week and Massachusetts and Connecticut delivered 190 per week. The States of Delaware and Maryland equaled those figures, and a thousand head of cattle began to arrive at Valley Forge each week. Only one herd, out of approximately one hundred, was intercepted by the British. The Valley Forge supply warehouses and cow pens began to fill up. The good weather also brought needed supplies of salt from saltworks in New Jersey and Maryland. The precious meat seasoning—imported prior to the war—had been in short supply until Washington had ordered the militia to aid in the construction and operations of new American saltworks.

The Crisis Eases

By April, the coming of spring eradicated most of the worst conditions at Valley Forge. The hospital crisis had eased considerably as better weather, good clothing, and decent food cut down cases of pneumonia and reduced the hospital population, which in turn halted diseases being transmitted from one patient to another. The general health of the soldiers was so satisfactory that Dr. Ebenezer Crosby wrote, "The army...is tolerable healthy, better clothed and on a much more respectable footing than ever before."

Better weather enabled General Washington to go horseback riding for pleasure far more often than he had in the depths of winter and, with guards, galloped along the banks of the Schuykill and through the thick forests that surrounded the Valley Forge area. The general also encouraged sports games, and the soldiers used the large meadows for various types of ball games and croquet. Washington enjoyed watching, especially games involving the portly Henry Knox, who was surprisingly fleet-footed despite his weight. The general was thrilled when he learned that a group of soldiers had formed a theater group—he loved the stage—and attended the several plays they staged at the end of winter.

The spirits of all the soldiers improved as spring arrived. One man wrote that "the fertile ground which has long laid covered in snow seems to be renewed by the breezes of the South and the warm shining of the sun." A Rhode Island soldier wrote his wife following a walk along the Schuykill that, "the meadows on each side of that beautiful river begin to look charmingly."

And, too, on May 15, thanks to strenuous lobbying by Washington, Congress finally approved a compromise pension plan that would award all officers half-pay pensions for seven years. The men were grateful. "Congress, God bless them!" Rhode Island's Samuel Ward wrote his wife. "I am infinitely pleased with that step...me thinks I see a new ardor for the service. America is invincible." (The joy of the officers was not shared by the enlisted men, who received a paltry eighty dollar pension for their services in the war.)

The mood of the commander-in-chief had been buoyed, too, thanks to a new resolution of Congress, which reaffirmed all of the previous extraordinary powers that had been given to him in December 1776, and renewed several times. That was pleasing because it came from a Congress that had so angered him over the Conway Cabal, frustrated him over its refusal to solve the supply problem, and did little to boost enlistments. These were the delegates, too, who in private had been so critical of him. Now he once more had their support, and it gave him the political capital he needed to serve as the unquestioned head of the army.

The army's third food crisis struck in late May when the camp quartermaster told Washington that he had only a single day of meat left. Fortunately, the cattle drives now paid off. The constant arrival of beef, larger herds arriving as frantically requested, provided enough beef to prevent starvation. Purchases of fish, now available in good weather, and other items kept the men in good physical condition. They were feeling so much better that one, Samuel Ward, wrote his wife that "We have milk and sugar in plenty...our regiment begins to grow healthy as the fine season approaches." And one surgeon with a sense of humor wrote a friend that the only shortage now was of grog.

That spring, Congress ratified an agreement with France, which was impressed by the American victory at Saratoga and Washington's ability to hold the army together, in which the French recognized America as a free and independent country. The agreement also called for substantial military aid, including cannon, muskets, and ammunition. It was a foreign alliance that America needed badly. Washington was thrilled and set aside May 6 as a camp holiday to celebrate.

The day was one of the most festive of the war. Following a huge outdoor religious service attended by just about all of the troops, a parade of all fifteen thousand soldiers and officers was held, with the men performing Von Steuben's intricate maneuvers with perfection, looking as polished as any army on earth. The highlight of the day was the firing of thirteen cannons, for the thirteen states, three times each.

That salute was followed by a lengthy *Fue de Joy*, an intricate pattern of musketry discharges in which each soldier fires into the sky right after the soldiers next to him, then loads and reloads and completes the procedure three times. Directed adroitly by an officer, the *Fue de Joy* that day included three rounds by each soldier and a total of more than thirty thousand musket firings, one right after the other, followed by a lusty roar from all. Tents were set up for officers to dine and drink; enlisted men stood nearby, drinking toast after toast. It was what one soldier called an afternoon of "mirth and jollity." And, in a friendly gesture, the commander-in-chief left the officers' reception and mingled with the enlisted men.

Finally, in late afternoon, leaving the gathering, Washington mounted his white horse and reined him to one side to begin the ride back to his headquarters. At the sight, without any direction, the entire army began to cheer the general in a long, throaty roar. Washington, touched, reined his horse back to face the men, raised his hat in the air, smiled, and waved it at them in thanks. At that, thousands of men whipped off their hats and tossed them high into the air. Washington smiled, reined his horse again, turned, and galloped off.

The soldiers in the army were probably just as satisfied with themselves that sunny May afternoon as at any other time during the war, such as the surrenders of Burgoyne at Saratoga or Cornwallis at Yorktown. They had survived the valley of death that Valley Forge had become, and finally had decent clothing to wear and nutritious meals to eat. Von Steuben had transformed them into a well-trained, aggressive fighting force. They understood that they had been through much and suffered greatly, but they knew, too, that there had been dramatic changes in the army, and in them. Those who remained, and they represented the overwhelming majority of the army, had become tougher and more resilient soldiers and men of great character, capable of enduring anything. They had bonded together in that awful winter as soldiers and as Americans.

The men who left Valley Forge had been forever changed. Many had become staunch patriots, such as John Cropper Jr., a Lieutenant Colonel of the 11th Virginia regiment, who rejected numerous opportunities to go home, in order to fight on. In a tender letter, he told his wife:

> I would not have believed an angel if he'd told me that I would have stayed so long from the arms of my dear wife, my darling infant and the management of my unsettled estate at home. But, so it is, and as sure as there is a God in heaven, or that you and I exist, my motives are laudable and my intentions innocent. Let it be sufficient for the present to say that the exigency of my country's cause...have so long kept me from the enjoyment of domestic happiness. It is with the greatest reluctance I stay in camp, when I consider what you suffer in my absence. But my country's call, the greatest of all calls, demands my presence with the army for a time, to pay for the blessings I have enjoyed and expect to enjoy under the auspices of liberty.

Others were affected in a deeply spiritual way. General James Varnum was one. He wrote:

> But for the virtuous few of the army, I am persuaded that this country must long before this have been destroyed. It is saved for our sakes, and its salvation ought to cause repentance in us for all our sins, if evil and misery are the consequences of iniquity. For my own part, I believe they are and expect by this penance, to emerge into the world, after leaving this place, with all accounts fully balanced. I shall then take care how I sin again, ever having a retrospective to its consequences.

And, despite the perilous winter, they were spoiling for a fight. "Our army, though in a poor situation, seem to surmount every difficulty with uncommon patience, firmness and fortitude—subject to order and anxious for action," Captain James Gray of New Hampshire wrote his wife.

Their officers and members of Congress understood the transformation of the men, too, and were proud of them. Congressman Gouverneur

Morris, who had become very close to Washington by then, expressed the feelings of most when he said, "The poor dogs are in an enemy's country without clothes to wear, victuals to eat, wood to burn or straw to lie on. The wonder is that they stay, not that they go." And Nathanael Greene hailed their perseverance: "The soldiery discovered more patience and fortitude than was ever manifested by common soldiers under such distressing circumstances."

The men of the Continental Army had grumbled all winter about the army, but never about the commander-in-chief. He may have been conspired against by some of his fellow generals and maligned by others in Congress, but his men never lost their faith in him. That devotion was put eloquently in a letter from Major Samuel Shaw to a friend at the end of winter camp. Shaw wrote of "our illustrious Commander-in-Chief" that "he enjoys a perfect state of health, and is the same steady, amiable character he ever has been. His fortitude, patience and equanimity of soul, under the discouragements he has been obliged to encounter, ought to endear him to his country; it has done it exceedingly to the army. When I contemplate the virtues of the man, I cannot too heartily coincide with the orator for the fifth of March last, who so delicately describes him as a person that appears to be raised by heaven to show how high humanity can soar."

That feeling of affection by the men was returned by the commander-in-chief. As spring, and an end to the suffering, approached, he wrote, "To see men without clothes to cover their nakedness, without blankets to lay on, without shoes, by which their marches might be traced by the blood from their feet, and almost as often without provisions…marching through frost and snow without a house or hut to cover them…submitting without a murmur, is a mark of patience and obedience which in my opinion can scarce be paralleled."

Eager for Combat

May also brought word from Washington's spies in both Philadelphia and New York that the British might be preparing to evacuate the Pennsylvania capital and return to the shores of the Hudson. The evacuation was now being supervised by Henry Clinton. Sir Henry had arrived in

Philadelphia to succeed Howe as head of the British force; Howe was returning to London, at his request.

Would they return to New York? Would they be going back by ships? Would they march across New Jersey? Was Clinton emulating Washington and staging an elaborate hoax in order to make the Americans think the British were going back to New York when in reality they planned an all-out attack on Valley Forge? Both Henry Laurens and Henry Knox were convinced of it, Knox assuring Washington that New York was the lynchpin for "the subjugation of America" writing his brother "the enemy threaten to fight bloodily before they depart."

In mid-May, the commander put the entire army on alert, ready to move at any moment. The men were ordered to rise before dawn and conduct drills from 5 A.M. to 6 A.M. and then again in late afternoon. He ordered all of his cavalry in New Jersey to report to Valley Forge. All of the men in area hospitals healthy enough to fight were gathered up and brought to camp. General Smallwood's two brigades in Wilmington, Delaware, were called to Valley Forge.

And he was sure of the British destination, telling Congressman Richard Henry Lee that "I am convinced they are bound to New York, whether by land or water." This was no idle guess, such as the speculation engaged in by Laurens, Knox, and others. During the winter, Washington had developed a brand-new spy in New York City, an important Tory with daily access to the British high command. He was so well-known that Washington could not risk divulging his identity to anyone. The spy knew where the British in Philadelphia were headed and provided that information to the commander-in-chief.

Washington was eager for a major battle. His main army now totaled just larger than fifteen thousand men, almost as large as the British force. He had more cannon than at any time during the war. Through an exchange of prisoners, General Charles Lee was back after eighteen months as a British prisoner-of-war. The militia in several states had, as hoped, turned out to fight. His own Virginia had drafted two thousand men to serve for a year and called for five thousand volunteers to serve for six months. North Carolina had conducted a similarly strong effort to raise men.

Washington was no longer interested in a guerrilla tactics or surprise attacks. The commander wanted to engage the British head-on in open-field combat—and defeat them. The victory would convince the British that not only could they not beat the Americans in unconventional warfare, but they could not beat them in a traditional fight, either. A decisive blow against the British would rejuvenate the Continental Army and once again rally the American public to the patriot cause. A significant victory would also restore Washington to the Olympian status he had enjoyed with the people before the fall of Philadelphia and the terrible winter at Valley Forge. And, most importantly, it might end the war.

On May 28, all wagons were ordered stocked with supplies, baggage was collected, and guards at posts several miles away were told to have their equipment packed and ready to join the army if it moved.

Washington was brimming with optimism. The army had lost 2,500 men through death, expired enlistments, and desertions, and was forced to leave another 1,700 behind, still sick or recovering from smallpox inoculations. But the men he led out of Valley Forge had gained a new confidence in themselves and were a different army. Washington had crushed the cabal to depose him, convinced Congress to reorganize the Quartermaster's and Commissary departments, halted another smallpox epidemic, again gained the help and support of governors and state legislatures, held the army together, and had done a superb administrative job throughout the winter under daunting circumstances. He wrote Robert Morris:

> I rejoice most sincerely with you on the glorious change in our prospects. Calmness and serenity seem likely to succeed in some measure those dark and tempestuous clouds which at times appeared ready to overwhelm us. The game, whether well or ill-played hitherto, seems now to be verging fast to a favorable issue and cannot I think be lost, unless we throw it away by too much supineness on the one hand, or impetuosity on the other. God forbid that either of these should happen at a time when we seem to be upon the point of reaping the fruits of our toil and labor.

The battle would not be fought on the banks of the Schuykill, however. Howe was happily on his way home to the theaters and parties of London and away from the dreary war in America. He was in no mood to engage Washington. By now, in June, with three-year enlistments and militia call-ups, and a significantly improved supply chain, Howe understood through spies that the Continental Army was far stronger than when it stumbled into its winter camp the week before Christmas. Howe had nothing to gain and everything to lose in a battle with Washington. Why bother? Sir William would be roundly criticized for that decision, and for not joining forces with Burgoyne at Saratoga, as he had promised, resulting in Burgoyne's defeat there, and for being unable to crush Washington and the Americans with his overwhelming forces.

The British army crossed the Delaware on June 18 with a huge train of supply wagons and several thousand nervous Philadelphia Loyalists unwilling to remain in town (some left by ship). Clinton's army of just more than ten thousand men headed northeast, toward New York. Washington's army, prepared as always for rapid movement, crossed the Delaware and moved as quickly as possible to intercept the British, catching up with them near the Monmouth County Courthouse on June 28. By then, adding militia as he went, Washington had about twelve thousand men, giving him a slight numerical advantage, although the British had far more cannon and wagons. Since Charles Lee was officially the second in command, Washington put him in charge of the attacking army. He would have preferred handing the reins to Anthony Wayne or Lafayette. Lee bungled the attack and the Americans were confused by his jumbled orders as the British attacked. The Americans were about to be overwhelmed when a furious Washington rode into the middle of the battle, cursed out Lee in salty language his men had never heard him use before, put Wayne in charge, and in just moments devised a new battle plan. His lines held.

The British pulled back and attacked several more times. Now the Americans were configured into long defensive lines, one behind another, in order to produce rapid-fire volleys at the enemy as he advanced, one of Steuben's European tactics. Washington was determined to show the British that he could fight by their rules and win. The American successfully repulsed the British on an insufferably hot day. Clinton hurled one more charge at the Americans, sending a large force of men in one final assault at the American center. The charge almost worked. The Americans were driven back, but at the rear they were joined by the rest of the army, under Washington's personal command. As the fighting continued, with victory unsure, Washington, atop one of his signature white horses, raced up and down the American lines, an easy target for the British, urging his troops to fight harder.

They did. Clinton called off his attacks at the end of the day. He was surprised that the Americans could fight with such skill in a European-style battle. He was also surprised that an army he was assured had been decimated by the winter and on the verge of extinction was as large as his, healthy and eager for the fight.

The English, unable to defeat the superbly trained Americans, withdrew and continued toward New York. The now well-supplied American army—buoyed by Monmouth and overflowing with an energy it had never felt before—had done exactly what Washington hoped. The standoff at Monmouth gave the men confidence, renewed patriotic fervor across the country, and restored the sharply criticized Washington to the lofty position of unquestioned public trust he had held prior to the awful winter at Valley Forge.

Chapter Eleven

STARVING TO DEATH

MORRISTOWN, 1779–80

"We were absolutely, literally starved. I do solemnly declare that I did not put a single morsel of victuals into my mouth for four days and as many nights, except a little black birch bark which I gnawed off a stick of wood, if that can be called victuals. I saw several of the men roast their shoes and eat them, and I was afterward informed... that some of the officers killed and ate a favorite dog that belonged to one of them."

—Private Joseph Martin

George Washington returned to Morristown for winter camp on December 1, 1779, in the middle of a violent snow and hail storm, which made travel treacherous for hundreds of weary soldiers with their cumbersome wooden wagons and cannon. The general was in a hurry to set up headquarters and had left his personal guard behind at his summer camp in Newburgh, New York. He rode the 120 miles with the regular army, unconcerned about an enemy attack in the storm. The army moved slowly on the narrow, bumpy, snow-covered dirt highway leading from Newark to Morristown, now a much-larger village than when he left it in 1777. There was no one else on the roads, and those who lived in the small farmhouses they passed stayed indoors and kept the logs in their fireplaces burning; thin columns of gray smoke drifted out of their chimneys.

The general's eyes squinted at the driving sleet, his hat pulled down over his hair, his great blue cloak held tight around him, as riders led him off the road toward the large white mansion of Mrs. Theodosia Ford, the widow of Jacob Ford Jr., who had died during Washington's last visit to the community. The two-and-a-half story house with its high roof stood at the crest of a gentle slope overlooking the town. It was encircled by several hundred acres of rolling farmland. The house, like the rest of the area, was surrounded by a deep blanket of snow that in places measured two feet.

The winter of 1779–80 was shaping up as a stark contrast to the previous year, when the army was quartered in a series of well-appointed campsites along Bound Brook, in central New Jersey. The winter of 1778–79 featured the mildest weather of the entire war. By the time the army camped at Bound Brook, Nathanael Greene and Jeremiah Wadsworth had managed to streamline the Quartermaster's and Commissary departments and procured more than enough food and clothing to supply the troops adequately throughout the winter; the fair weather and clothing meant very little sickness. The battle of Monmouth, in June 1778, was the last major engagement of that year and the British stayed in New York all winter, deciding not to harass Washington at Bound Brook, concentrating instead on a southern expedition that resulted in the capture of Savannah, Georgia. Winter for the Continental Army in Bound Brook was so problem-free and uneventful that Washington was able to slip off to Philadelphia for two months to renew his relationships with congressional delegates.

The commander-in-chief had not decided on Morristown for his winter headquarters that year until the very end of November. He had considered remaining in Newburgh, but the soldiers had stripped the area of all its forage and there was little food left in the region. Newburgh was also too far from New York City, where the British would again spend the winter. Just as in 1777, Washington felt he needed to be close enough to monitor the British and yet far enough away to be safe from attack. The camp had to be near major highways for easy transportation and in a town whose people had proven themselves ardent supporters of the war. Most important, he needed to live in the middle of farmlands for grain, cattle, eggs, wheat, and other produce because this time he was keeping his main army, nearly thirteen thousand men, in one place, while a continent of a few hundred men remained in Newburgh and a force of 2,500 were stationed in Charleston, South Carolina.

He had lodged men in a half-dozen communities near Morristown in 1777 and was not satisfied with that arrangement. He told Nathanael Greene that this time "to encamp the whole army together is on every account desirable." Also, Congress had forbidden the quartering of men in residential homes. He also liked the idea of being close to a thriving town since so many of his problems at Valley Forge had been caused by the camp's isolation. Greene, whom he had sent ahead to survey Morristown, reminded him, too, that the area was heavily wooded; the army would have no trouble using felled trees for the construction of buildings and for firewood.

Morristown and the hamlets around it had grown since 1777, thanks to the business and notoriety the army had brought that winter. The number of residents had increased and the spacious village green and the lanes around it were more crowded. The first post office was established and two new general stores had opened; one even sold books. Business at the local taverns boomed and their number increased from two to seven. Profits had swollen for local craftsmen, such as silversmiths. Business in nearby towns had flourished, too, and by the winter of 1779–80 Morris County was home to twenty-four sawmills, thirty-six gristmills, and twenty-three taverns. Tax records showed that residents of the county owned 4,700 horses, 5,200 hogs, and 8,900 cows. The village had served as a small military base in the winter of 1778–79, while the main army stayed at Middle Brook, New Jersey, thirty miles south. The military's various supply warehouses and offices in Morristown were still there. The people in the vicinity had become used to the army, even though they were not terribly pleased about the inconvenience. It seemed a good choice.

The general was not happy as he settled into the Ford mansion and set up his office in a room on the first floor, at the rear of the building, that had served Ford as a study. It was a twelve-foot square room with a high ceiling and two large windows that let in good amounts of light, particularly in the late afternoon. There was room in it for a wooden desk, a chair, and a writing stand for one aide. The hardwood floor creaked under the force of Washington's dark brown leather boots whenever he strode into it.

There had been ominous signs that this winter would be troublesome. By mid-November, subordinates had warned Washington of a bread and flour shortage, caused by an unusually long autumn drought. The lack of food was so prevalent that Pennsylvania troops under General William Irvine had to leave the New York camp for the long trek to Morristown without any bread, and received none during their four-day march through an earlier snowstorm. Four November snowfalls in the Hudson Valley had delayed the transportation of needed cattle to be slaughtered for meat. The men were hungry and angry. The general, always worried about irritable soldiers, called the lack of bread "alarming" and told the officers to "do all in your power to keep the troops in temper."

The clothing issued the year before had been worn out, and there was, once again, a desperate need for coats, shirts, and breeches, especially with cold weather moving in. He knew there was a clothing-supply problem similar to the one he was forced to grapple with two years earlier at Valley Forge. Despite his orders, enough clothes had not arrived. The general sent an order to his officers in Newburgh to transport them immediately—but he knew that would take weeks. There was a dearth of footwear, too, just as there was at Valley Forge, which annoyed the commander. "The deficiency of shoes is so extensive that a great proportion of the army is totally incapable of duty and could not move," he wrote James Wilkinson, one of the quartermasters there, after his arrival in Morristown. And supplies that were available were hopelessly delayed or missing (one bread shipment vanished for eight days) and at one point

Washington angrily ordered an underling "to hurry the transportation of it [supplies] with all possible dispatch."

Washington had arrived in Morristown to find that he only had five of an anticipated eleven generals to help him. Some had retired. Others were sick and in bed, such as Alexander McDougall and Israel Putnam. Gates had refused a command and gone home to Virginia to sulk. Wadsworth, the commissary general, stayed in Newburgh. Lord Stirling was at his home in Basking Ridge, south of Morristown, but complaining of severe illness and not available to do very much. The reliable Greene was now wearing two hats, that of a general and quartermaster. As always, much of the work the missing generals usually did now fell on the commander-in-chief and his aides.

Washington's officer corps was even more depleted than the high command. Hundreds of officers, hopeful of spending the winter at home, had applied for and received furloughs and disappeared. This had taken place without Washington realizing it until too late. He had told his generals to grant furloughs, but only as long as they had at least half their officers in camp. Somewhere along the line the orders were ignored. Now, when he needed officers most, they were not there.

It was becoming more difficult to pay for the supplies the army needed, because by December 1779 inflation had crippled Continental currency. This had been a small problem in the winter of 1777 in Morristown, when the continental dollar had dropped to two-thirds the value of hard money, or gold pieces. The value of the American dollar was a growing dilemma at both Valley Forge and Middle Brook. Now, however, runaway inflation plagued the states and it took $30 in Continental dollars to equal $1 in hard money, ($50 to $1 in Philadelphia), and the rate was climbing. And, once again, as in 1777, the British were flooding the states with near-perfect counterfeit Continental scrip in what Washington said was an attempt to bring out "the entire ruin of our money" in order to win the war.

Most of all, Washington worried about the weather. All of the traditional omens of a bad winter, signs he knew so well from his years at Mount Vernon, were in the air. The weather began to get cold in early

November, with a light snowfall at his New York headquarters on November 2. Two small snows followed, on November 17 and 24, and a large storm lashed the area on November 26, dumping nine inches on the metropolitan New York area. Another storm on November 29 added several more inches. Roads were impassable. A sixth storm, a blizzard, hit on December 2, and a Connecticut writer jotted in his diary: "stormy snow, night rain and violent thunder." Worst of all, the temperatures remained unseasonably chilly. The storms made troop movement difficult, as evidenced in the diary of Lieutenant Robert Parker, who wrote on November 25 that "the roads are very bad and the weather cold."

All of these problems, converging, as they had at Valley Forge, were on the minds of Washington and his aides as they settled into Mrs. Ford's mansion on the night of December 1. The general took the Fords' eighteen-foot square bedroom on the second floor of the west side of the house for his own (Martha was scheduled to arrive just before Christmas) and Mrs. Ford and her four children made two downstairs rooms their apartment for the winter. Washington took two other upstairs bedrooms, all with high windows, hardwood floors, high ceilings, and fireplaces, like his own, and had them turned into crowded sleeping quarters for five of his aides. The Ford parlor was renovated into a meeting room and an office for more assistants. Dozens of soldiers flooded the foyer and hallways, and clustered about outside, to protect the commander-in-chief.

As soon as he was settled, Washington began to issue orders to his men concerning the construction of another rambling city of wooden huts, similar to those at Valley Forge, that was to be built in what locals called "Jockey Hollow," a vast, thick forest, full of glens surrounded by sharply angled slopes, three miles southwest of Morristown. The camp would house thirteen thousand men and become, in effect, the third largest city in America, smaller only than Philadelphia (twenty-eight thousand) and New York (twenty-one thousand). This time, fearful of sickness caused by damp and drafty cabins at Valley Forge, he demanded that they be built with tightly packed, thick-cut logs to prevent rain and snow from being blown in. They were all to be built into the sides of hills to afford good drainage. Stagnant water in huts had brought about many of the health problems that combined to create catastrophe at Valley Forge. Remembering the lack of ventilation at Valley Forge, the general ordered windows cut into the sides of these wooden huts. Any hut not built exactly as Washington ordered was to be torn down. Washington had learned his lesson well at Valley Forge and his army would never again live in tents or huts without heat and efficient drainage.

The city was an architectural wonder. One man who lived in nearby Basking Ridge wrote a letter to a local newspaper describing a trip he took to look at Jockey Hollow: "I rode out today on purpose to take a view of our encampments. I found it excessively cold, but was glad to see most of our poor soldiers were under good roofs. The encampments are exceedingly neat; the huts are all of a size, and placed in more exact order than Philadelphia."

Washington's problem with the construction of the city was that the men, and officers, had to live in their thin canvas tents until their buildings were completed. The erection of the huts took an undue amount of time because there were few officers on hand to supervise the cutting down of the trees, planning of the camp, and clearing of the streets.

And then, on December 6, one of the worst snowstorms in years hit Morristown, burying the village under another nine inches of snow and paralyzing towns and cities throughout the area, including New York and Philadelphia. Herbert Muhlenberg, of Philadelphia, remarked in his journal that "it began to snow hard early in the morning and continued thus throughout the whole day, that the snow lay a foot and half deep and there was no going out of doors." New York newspaper editor Hugh Gaines noted that there was "nothing stirring but snow."

The storm, which lasted two days, wreaked havoc in the camp, where few huts had been finished and the great majority of men had to take shelter in their tents to protect themselves. The hollows of the area created swirls, and the strong winds of the storm ripped up many of the tents and caused high drifts. Many of the tree stumps men had used for chairs were covered in white. Icicles hung from the roofs of the huts and sleeves of five-inch-thick snow covered large tree limbs. The hollow also created loud echoes, and as their tents collapsed, the voices of the men cursing could be heard for great distances. The earlier snows had not melted and this snowfall meant that there was again more than two feet laying on the forests and in the meadows. The snow prevented transportation of any wagons carrying food, clothing, and other provisions. The men in arriving regiments reported that they had to trudge through frigid weather and were often forced to leave their supply wagons back on the highways, buried in snow. All of Washington's worst nightmares were coming true—and at the same time.

Doctor James Thacher, an army surgeon from Massachusetts, marched into camp with his regiment the day after the storm. He described the Morristown camp with vividness in his journal:

> The snow on the ground is about two feet deep, and the weather extremely cold; the soldiers are destitute of both tents and blankets and some of them are actually barefooted and almost naked. Our only defense against the inclemency of the weather consists of brushwood thrown together. Our lodging last night was on the frozen ground. Having removed the snow, we wrapped ourselves in great coats, spread our blankets on the ground and lay down by the side of each other, five or six together, with large fires at our feet. We could procure neither shelter or forage for our horses and the poor animals were tied to trees in the woods for twenty four hours without food, except the bark which they peeled from the trees.

The weather warmed up a bit on December 8 and a few inches of snow melted away. Then, on December 14, a cold front hit the greater New York area, a front that was to keep the east coast in a deep freeze for thirteen weeks. A shivering Lieutenant Erkuries Beatty, of the Fourth Pennsylvania Regiment, one of the four men in the Beatty family in the Continental Army, wrote his brother that "if you saw my situation and way of living you would really pity me; for colder weather I never saw." The cold front gripped the entire Middle Atlantic area. Muhlenberg wrote in his diary that "we have had such a terrible and bitterly cold windstorm as we have not had in a long time. Men and beasts tremble."

By the second week of December, chaos began to grip the army's supply chain. General Greene was under siege from all sides. Wagons full of food destined for the troops at Morristown never arrived. Some were stuck in eight-foot-high snowdrifts. Others were not dispatched because spiraling inflation prevented the army from renting wagons. Orders for others disappeared in misplaced paperwork.

Local state officials had arrested Greene's foraging officers when they tried to buy food, unwilling to accept their promise that their Continental scrip would be usable. Many local farmers would not accept either scrip or loan certificates. The looming problem for General Washington was that New Jersey's farmers also refused to sell food on credit. During the Valley Forge food crisis of 1777, Pennsylvania residents complained about the economy just as loudly as New Jerseyans did in 1779, but the Pennsylvanians did reluctantly take credit notes, saving the army. Now, with scrip so badly devalued and Congress practically bankrupt, farmers refused all payment, including credit, plunging the army into a crisis far beyond any it had endured before.

Grist mills had no wheat to make bread because of the long drought, and the wheat they had could not be ground into grain due to the lack of water power. Desperately needed clothes were nowhere to be found, either unknowingly lost in warehouses in other cities or transported to the wrong towns. Regimental coats, shirts, and breeches that did arrive were usually only one third to one half the amount ordered. Belligerent officials from different states argued that they would send clothes for their own men at Morristown, but not those of other states. Water-powered sawmills under contract to cut logs and boards were closed because their nearby rivers and streams froze over. Yet, as the month wore on, thousands of additional troops arrived, clamoring for supplies and provisions that were not there. Worse, no military operations could be undertaken because soldiers did not have enough clothes. A depressed Washington had to call off sending troops to South Carolina to help the southern army defend cities against the British because five hundred of the soldiers scheduled to march there had no shoes.

Exasperated, Greene, at Washington's urging, wrote Congress a desperate letter on December 12. After explaining the army's woes, Greene told the delegates:

> Here is an expensive army to support and the difficulties hourly increasing....We are without the means either to defray the current expenses or discharge our past contracts, which are now very great, owing to the poverty of the Treasury. And so dissatisfied are the people at being kept out of their money that they have begun to sue the public agents. Nothing can be more alarming than the situation of the forage department at this time: the food magazines empty, the consumption very large, which will be greatly increased. What are we to do?

There was little assistance from Congress. Provisions dwindled. Despondent, Greene told Colonel Daniel Brodhead that he understood the anger of the public in dealing with a Congress that could not pay its bills, and he feared that "the people will pull us to pieces."

Greene had complained about Congress incessantly to George Washington, and on December 15, an irate Washington predicted the collapse of the army in a scathing note to Congress, much harsher than any he had sent before, in which he reminded members that he would run out of bread in just four days. "Our prospects are infinitely worse than they have been at any period of the war," he pleaded, "and that unless some expedient can be instantly adopted a dissolution of the army for want of subsistence is unavoidable."

The commander-in-chief was wrong about Congress, though. They did know about his plight, and they did care. They acted promptly on all of his requests in a frantic effort to rescue the army, but he did not know that because the storms prevented couriers with Congressional news from reaching Morristown. On December 6, at his urging, Congress ordered all officers on furlough back to Morristown and authorized paid advertisements in newspapers to inform them of the decision. The following day Congress began discussion of a new, three-year enlistment program, with a possible draft, and several days later authorized $61 million for the army.

Washington's friend Thomas Jefferson had already told Congress that Virginia would meet its troop quota and that the state would devote "every last schilling" to pay for them. On the 11th, Congress ordered six states to procure and forward a total of eighty-three thousand barrels of flour and twenty thousand bushels of corn to the commander. Emergency letters were sent to the governors of each state in which they were told to hurry. On the 14th, in a sharply worded formal resolution, Congress ordered all of the states to send Washington whatever he asked to save the army. Congress lamented the collapsing economy and knew what it was doing to Washington and his men and on December 6, in strong language, requested additional taxes from the states in order to pay for army supplies. "The military chest is empty, and the treasury nearly exhausted," a resolution proclaimed and urged the payment of taxes in order not "to give the most fatal blow" to the country.

All of these initial orders and requests were followed up by Congress over the next few weeks. On December 20, delegate William Houston told Governor Livingston and Caleb Camp that he had met with the army's commissary head and believed his story that there was no food left in Philadelphia and that the food that was there would never get to Morristown in time to prevent starvation. "A treasury without money and an army without bread is really alarming," he said, and advised them to hurry with their supplies. He even suggested impressing food if necessary, just as Congressmen had advised at Valley Forge. That same day Samuel Huntington, the new president of the Continental Congress, told Connecticut's Governor Trumbull that without emergency supplies the army could not make it through the winter. He told Delaware's Rodney that the cost of goods had "drained the public treasury" and that the country now had to rely on the states. One representative in Philadelphia, exasperated, said that "Congress is at its wits end" and that if the states did not pay their taxes so that Congress could feed the army, "we may be undone."

Unaware of these actions and unable to wait for a response, Washington issued an emergency circular the very next day to the governors of New York, New Jersey, Pennsylvania, Delaware, and Maryland, begging for help. "The situation of the army with respect to supplies is beyond description alarming," he told the governors, reminding them, too, that the men were out of sustenance and the war might soon be over. "Our [food] magazines are absolutely empty everywhere and our commissaries entirely destitute of money or credit to replenish them....Unless some extraordinary and immediate exertions are made by the States...there is every appearance that the army will infallibly disband in a fortnight."

He sought emergency assistance everywhere—national, state, county, and community. Washington went well beyond the limits of his military power and acted as an unelected civilian president, working for the public good in a national crisis, setting a precedent for presidents who would utilize the full resources of government in emergencies in later years.

Reaction to the plight of the army from the states was swift. His friend Livingston kept the New Jersey Legislature in session on Christmas Day. New Jersey's representatives agreed to send eight thousand barrels of flour to Morristown. They appointed one state commissary head to make the department more efficient, announced price controls on hundreds of products (set at twenty times 1774 prices), and made it a crime to hoard food if the army requested it. The legislature also ordered farmers to accept continental money and/or credit for their produce and to sell as many heads of cattle as possible (1,200 were eventually sent to Morristown). Maryland did even more, fulfilling its quotas and, at the general's suggestion, picking up five thousand barrels of flour that had just arrived on a French frigate and adding it to the state's shipment.

The governors had been glad to help and had hoped their swift action would end the crisis. All of them recognized the difficulty Congress always seemed to have in raising money, finding supplies, and getting them to the army, which caused such catastrophe at Valley Forge. The governors had, by now, understood that General Washington was relying on the states as much as on Congress and that, as he always told them, that combination of assistance was the only way he was going to win the war. He had made each of them understand that while they were responsible for the administration of their own state, they, and their people, also had a responsibility to the federal government. One could not function without the other. He, Washington, was the connection between them, serving as head of the army and the representative of the national civilian government. The general had filled what seemed to be a necessary new role in the fledgling democratic American government—a powerful and respected civilian overseer of both Congress and the states, laying the foundation for the presidency in 1789.

It had been three difficult years since the general had first begun to court the governors of the various states and their legislatures in an effort to induce them to support the army when Congress could not. Now, in 1780, he realized that not only was that important, but necessary. The country could not succeed when run only by Congress. It obviously could not function when governed only by the states. His experience in the war so far had also shown him that state governments could not achieve their goals without considerable assistance from county magistrates and local administrators. For Washington, the winters had begun to exemplify the need for a country with a strong national government that relied on help from well-run state and local governments. He also realized that the national government, weak and unstable in the war, needed some kind of single national executive as an administrator. All of these branches were necessary and none could stand alone.

The always colorful Livingston, whose new slogan, printed boldly under each of his proclamations and newspaper columns, was "God Save the People," told Washington that he and his state would always be there for assistance. In regard to supply shortages, Livingston found villains everywhere. Authorizing shipments of New Jersey supplies to the army, he wrote, "that America, after having so long been the admiration of Europe and having an army on foot that defies the power of Great Britain should at last be compelled to disband her troops by the artifices and practices of Tories and speculators and monopolizers and scoundrels of all sorts and sizes could go very near to deprive me of my senses."

At the same time, as Washington was sending couriers off with his pleas and orders, the construction on the small city rising in Jockey

Hollow resumed. But on December 18 another storm hit, depositing an additional seventeen inches of snow.

Recently arrived men had to continue to live in tents, buffeted by high winds, as the storm shut down almost all construction. Ensign Jeremiah Greenman, who arrived on Friday, December 17, the day before the storm, said that he could only work on his hut "when the weather would admit it." Ebenezer Huntington, of General John Stark's New England brigade, working on his own regiment's huts, remembered that "the severity of the weather hath been such that the men suffered much without shoes and stockings and working [on the huts] half a leg deep in snow." When they did finish their huts, they found that the snow had seeped in under the logs and boards and through the windows and froze on the floor in thick sheets. The men had to chop up the frozen snow into tiny pieces with axes and tomahawks and sweep out the ice. Worse, the officers, trapped in tents, began to steal the firewood that belonged to the enlisted men in order to keep warm.

The men who arrived late in the month, such as Private Joseph Plumb Martin, from Connecticut, had little clothing, due to the shortage and, like the men already in camp, had to get by on scraps of food. He wrote in his journal, "Our situation at this time: naked, fatigued, and starved, forced to march many a weary mile in winter through cold and snow, to seek a situation in some woods to built a habitation to starve and suffer in."

The December 18 storm, coming on the heels of the cold front, kicked off what meteorologists would later call the worst winter of the eighteenth century and one of the worst in American history. Record low temperatures would be chronicled throughout the Middle Atlantic states for months (during January the temperature would rise above freezing on only one day and on January 16 it was minus 16 degrees). The Atlantic seaboard would be pounded by twenty-six snowstorms, six of blizzard proportion, between December and April.

The foot and a half of snow that fell on December 18, combined with the cold, caused many waterways to freeze over during the next few weeks, preventing any shipping. By the last week of December, the Delaware River had frozen over, stopping all water traffic, and the

Schuykill River soon followed. Sleighs and even horse-drawn carriages rode across the river each day, to the amazement of residents. The ice would not melt until March 4, 1780. The harbor at Baltimore froze in mid-December and did not thaw until March 9. By the end of December, the Chesapeake Bay, in Maryland, froze solid so that Marylanders could walk across it. Thomas Jefferson noted in his journals that the York River, near Williamsburg, Virginia, was sheer ice, and remained impassable for months. Sections of Long Island Sound froze and the *New York Gazette* reported incidents of New Yorkers crossing the sound from Long Island to Norwalk, Connecticut, on sleds. In perhaps the most unprecedented ecological occurrence, the vast New York harbor froze over for the first and only time in recorded history during the last week of December, and the British were able to send troops on sleds back and forth over the ice on a daily basis. Sometimes British cavalry would gallop across the harbor ice, to the astonishment of all.

But the most serious consequence of the December 18 storm was that it once again made roads impassable and held up the substantial supplies ready to be transported by the states. Wagons could not move in the deep snow and even sleds found it difficult. There was no money to rent sleds or pay drivers. There were infrequent arrivals of bread, clothes, and cattle sent on by patriots, such as Timothy Shaw, who proudly took out a large ad in the *New Jersey Gazette* to announce that he would sell the army anything it needed, and for Continental money, too, to help the cause. All of this helped somewhat, but the crisis continued.

Food dwindled, and on December 22 Washington was so upset about conditions that he called his head of commissary to the Ford mansion three different times to demand food for the men—food that was just not there. There were no shoes, either, and Washington complained about their absence each day when he visited the quartermaster's warehouse to look for them. He was livid when he learned that wagon and sled drivers bringing food from other counties were seen stealing some.

Washington's Christmas Day was spent with his aides because the storms made it impossible for his wife to leave Philadelphia to join him. He was alone and angry. His desk was filled with emergency reports and desperate pleas for help as his men continued to starve. By that Christmas, flour and bread had nearly run out and Washington put the men on half rations of rice. The general had run out of money to buy more food, and daily read fervent pleas for cash from his commissary agents: "Money, money, money...for God's sake! Without it I can do little. Send me what cash you can!" pleaded Robert Hoops on Christmas Day. "Payment has been so long in coming that there is no aid," added Joseph Lewis. That same Christmas morning, Erkuries Beatty wrote his brother that the men had little to eat and were freezing. "Outside of my [hut] you will see maybe half a dozen men naked as Lazarus, begging for clothing," he said. And on that Christmas, he heard from General Greene that Wadsworth had told him with great frustration that his storehouses were empty but that "like the Israelites, I have been ordered to make bricks out of straw."

The commander had sent hundreds of horses to Pennsylvania on December 10 so that he could save the corn given to them daily. Now, on December 23, desperate for any kind of food, he began to give the soldiers the horse's corn.

Greene angrily told Washington, as he told all, that the Morristown residents, who had food, had abandoned them. "They receive us with coldness, and provide for us with reluctance." And, added to all of that, Greene's own aides were regularly petitioning him for pay raises, as were the express couriers that Washington needed to communicate with Congress and his generals.

On Christmas Day, as he sometimes did, the general rode through the camp at Jockey Hollow to check on the progress of the huts, talk to officers and survey life in the small city. This time he was appalled to see that valuable gunpowder was being used to blow up tree stumps, and that straw was left lying outside of many huts and stomped upon by dozens of men going by. "In passing through the camp, I observed with pain that there is a shameful waste of forage, the high price of this article and the difficulty of procuring it...ought to induce all possible care and economy," he told the men.

General Washington had gone through every food chain he knew and appealed to everyone he could think of in the states and in Congress.

He was frustrated. "I can only say that everything in my power has been done to keep the army supplied," he said in a letter to General Enoch Poor on the day after Christmas.

December 26 also brought other ominous news. Despite the weather, the British fleet set sail at 4 P.M. that afternoon for South Carolina, as it turned out just twenty-four hours before the harbor froze, "with a fair wind," noted one observer. More than eight thousand seasoned and well-rested, well-fed troops were on board the transports. Washington could not send men southward to foil them wherever they landed because he had few to spare. The available soldiers could not march toward South Carolina because they had no shoes. And, Washington learned, 750 of these men he planned to send south had no coats, either. General Benjamin Lincoln had twenty-five hundred troops in the Carolinas to meet the British when they arrived and those forces would not be enough; the needed reinforcements were camped outside Washington's office, shivering, immobile, and unable to walk.

Construction on the huts, so well planned in the early weeks of December, had slowed considerably and had become a nightmare. As soon as the army had arrived in Morristown, Greene had pushed the Trenton quartermaster, Moore Furman, to have boards produced by sawmills and sent, along with needed provisions, as soon as possible. "I beg you to set every wheel in motion that will give dispatch to the business," he wrote. But Furman's sawmills in Trenton were as unoccupied as Greene's in Morris County. The wide, wooden waterwheels that powered them could not move because the creeks, ponds, and rivers had frozen beneath them. The need for boards became critical after Christmas because thousands of enlisted men were still without protective huts and so were almost all of the lower-ranking officers. They battled the elements in small, thin canvas tents, which were often blown over by the high winds that swirled through the canyons formed by the oddly shaped hollows in the camp.

Morristown quartermaster Joseph Lewis had been given his job because he was the son-in-law of Rev. Johnnes. He knew all the local farmers and merchants and begged friend Will Bayard to make his sawmill

100 percent operational, and to do it at once. "Do not let your mill stand still by night or day as it will at once serve your country, which is the greatest motive which will induce any person to work," he told him.

The detailed notes and letters that Lewis kept throughout the war reflect the exasperation of those in Washington's administration. The manufacture of boards and cut logs was slow, and by January, a full month after the arrival of the army, there were nowhere near enough huts to shelter the men. Lewis wrote frantically to a subordinate that "200,000 feet of boards are still needed." He was so desperate for wood that he told his men to rip down farmers' barn walls and floors, and even the sides of latrines and "bring these at once without being [stuck] in the snowbanks." Lewis was so eager for lumber that at one point he even impressed his uncle into service: "Hurry and get 2,000 feet of board from the Allinson and Hathaway sawmill. You must not fail. Go with as many sleds as you can at once."

Those men who did finish building their huts then found that they had no straw to use for mattresses on the thin, rough boards that served as beds. The quartermaster corps had to beg the locals for straw, as they had to plead for everything. Lewis rode to the homes of several area farmers to purchase it. "I am hourly called for straw for the poor frozen soldiers that are now entering their huts," he said. He pushed locals to find it, telling one, "persuade [neighbors] to thrash out their grain and spare the straw for this purpose." The army had been on one-half and one-third rations of bread, corn, and rice for weeks and now even that was running out.

New arrivals were startled. "I was extremely shocked," General Von Steuben told Governor Clinton of New York just after he went to Morristown. "[It was] the greatest picture of misery that was ever seen, scarce a soldier among them who has sufficient [clothes] to cover his nakedness in this severe season...."

Then, on December 27, yet another storm hit New Jersey, lasting two days. The storm dumped eighteen more inches of snow on top of the foot or so still on the ground. It closed all roads and ended transportation of supply wagons. Unable to obtain food in camp, the soldiers did exactly what Washington feared—they began to plunder food, clothing, and supplies, raiding nearby homes and farms and taking what they wanted, as they had done at Valley Forge. The soldiers' theft was considerable. In addition to food, they helped themselves to tomahawks, reams of canvas, bags of rags, animals, hammers, nails, thread, hats, shoes, pitchforks, shovels, bars of iron, breeches, bridle bits, kettles, candles, canteens, chalk, forks, knives, horseshoes, ink, cups, panes of glass, writing paper, pikes, quills, shirts, stockings, stove pipes, stoves, tableclothes, and dishes. Many farmers complained that the marauding troops stole their fence poles to use for firewood, and while doing so permitted their animals to wander off—to be stolen by the troops.

One private in the Fourth New York regiment said that the men became so hungry that plunder became necessary and commonplace. The officers would not stop them, either, as one private explained: "The officers were obligated to release the soldiers and permit them to go, in great numbers together, into the country to get provisions where they could find it."

No one in the army, including those in the general's headquarters, could fault the soldiers for thievery. They had endured as much as any army in similar circumstances. They were stranded in the middle of a forest thirty-five miles from any major cities. The residents they were risking their lives to defend refused to sell them food, even on credit, to keep them alive, and their government appeared to be bankrupt. The seemingly endless storms, a snowy plague from heaven, halted whatever wagons carrying sustenance that might have reached them. And, at the same time, they assumed that the British soldiers were living in warm homes and supplied with generous meals in New York. Even Lewis, who knew the farmers they looted, did not blame the troops who stole. "We are now as distressed as want of provisions and money can make us. The soldiers have been obliged to rob the inhabitants to save their own lives," he said.

Washington wondered what had happened to the character of the army; the character of the country. It was not plausible to expect that each of the soldiers under his command would be as devoted to the service as he, but he always expected strong dedication. When the war began, men had been proud to walk about the streets of Boston and Baltimore and Philadelphia and Williamsburg in military-style coats. They had talked lovingly of independence and the virtue of their country and themselves. And what of the people? They had lusted for independence in the spring of 1775, and cheered in different villages and cities when the Declaration of Independence was read to them in July 1776. And now these same people would not sell food to the army to keep the soldiers alive. And the soldiers robbed the people.

On December 28, he issued a scalding general order outlawing any further thefts. "The General most earnestly exhorts the officers to use their utmost exertions to put an effectual stop to a practice not more oppressive to the country, than disreputable to the army, better becoming a band of robbers than disciplined troops," it read. Washington warned that "depredations of so pernicious a nature will not escape…punishment" and added that he wanted to "hear no more complaints of so disagreeable nature."

To put teeth into the order, Washington told his men that there would be several roll calls each day, nightly inspections of cabins, and daily surveillance. The punishments for plundering, he warned, would be severe.

But they were not. The general had made his bombastic public warning, let everyone know that offenders would be court-martialed and satisfied Congress, whose members abhorred such behavior, as did state and local officials. He also knew that with food running out, his men had little recourse except plunder. He privately fumed that the men who had so courageously defended America at Trenton, Princeton, Brandywine, Saratoga, and Monmouth and had survived Valley Forge were reduced to stealing turkeys to survive because the people they protected would not help them. And so George Washington simply turned his back on the plundering. He listened to daily complaints from county magistrates, farmers, and merchants about the theft of everything from jackets to horseshoes to bushels of apples. He read reports from his colonels concerning continued stealing by the men. This went on for days, and Washington simply told Congress "I have it not in my power to punish or to repress the practice." The thefts continued as the general continued to look the other way.

The final days of 1779 passed gloomily. The supply of nails ran out and the huts had to be built with handcarved wooden pegs. By the end of the month, all thirteen thousand men and officers had moved to Morristown, along with Knox and his artillery, taking up even more space and clamoring for supplies that were not available. Rations were reduced again. Some men ate the bark from trees and others ate their dogs.

Finally, just after New Year's, the army simply ran out of food. On the morning of January 1, when the temperature dropped to 28 degrees, Greene told Washington that all of the food in Morristown was gone. Two days later, Wadsworth closed his doors, too. "My opinion is that your army cannot be supplied with fresh meat of any kind," he told Washington.

January 1: Clear—cold & freezing with little wind.

Wadsworth reminded the general that without food he did not think the army would hold together. This was Washington's fear. There was already growing evidence of a slow breakup of his forces brought about by starvation. Men were starting to go home, and on the very same day he opened Wadsworth's letter eighteen men had been found guilty of desertion at a Morristown court-martial. Washington's two great concerns, always, were mass desertions and mutinies, either of which would decimate the army and end the war. He could not have either. The eighteen deserters in Morristown that morning could be a harbinger of things to come; their flight had to stop.

The commander-in-chief was angry. "It is lamentable that our magazines are so empty and that our future prospects are so alarmingly limited. The worst consequences are to be apprehended," he warned one officer. Clothes had vanished, too. The Board of War informed Congress during the first week of January that it had no money to purchase any more.

The troops were out of food and funds for clothing and the British fleet was on the ocean, probably to assault one of the southern seaports, probably Charleston, South Carolina, putting yet another major American city in their pocket. What else could possibly go wrong?

Just before noon on January 2, a Sunday, Washington stood in his small office in the Ford house and dictated a letter; he looked out the window and noticed that it had started to snow—hard. He jotted down the time in his notes because just the day before he had decided to resume his pre-war practice of charting the weather each day, a chore that had helped him as a farmer and might now help him again. He continued to watch the snow as it fell all day. Later that night he wrote in his diary: "Very cold. About noon it began to snow and continued without intermission through the day and night. The wind was high and variable, but chiefly from the west and the northwest."

The thick, wet snow continued to come down without letup. The general and his aides at the Ford home, and all the men in camp, watched as it descended for nearly three days and, accompanied by howling winds and temperatures in the low twenties, deposited more than one foot of snow in Morristown and throughout the Middle Atlantic states, leaving three feet in Albany, New York. The snow stopped falling late on the afternoon of January 4, but on January 6 a second, two-day long and equally harsh storm hit New Jersey and much of the Atlantic seaboard.

January 6: Snowing and sunshine alternately. Cold with the wind west and northwest and increasing. Night very stormy. The snow, which in general is eighteen inches deep, is much drifted. Roads almost impassable.

The storm that battered Morristown that week was a double blizzard. From Sunday through Friday, nearly four feet of snow blanketed the surrounding countryside. But the real problems were caused by severe winds, which created high drifts. In New York, a diarist said that "the wind has piled up the snow higher than a man's head" and a Connecticut man measured drifts near his house at four feet. In the Morristown area, troops reported drifts over the tops of farmer's chest-high fences.

The storm had dealt the men in the huts and tents of Jockey Hollow a savage blow when it whipped through the area. One of the most graphic descriptions of the devastation was by Dr. Thacher: "We experienced one of the most tremendous snowstorms ever remembered; no man could endure its violence many minutes without danger of his life. Several [tents] were torn asunder and blown down over the officers heads in the night and some officers and soldiers were actually covered while in their tents and buried like sheep under the snow. My comrades and myself were roused from sleep by the calls of some officers for assistance; their tents had blown down and they were almost smothered in the storm. Their blankets and baggage were nearly buried in the snow," said the doctor, who noted in his diary that in many places in camp the snow drifts were more than six feet high.

The snow completely shut down Jockey Hollow. The drifts were so high that even the plunderers could not get out. Men had to use shovels to clear out pathways and dig out pieces of wood covered with waist-high snow in order to make fires and keep warm. And hunger was everywhere. "We scarcely get anything to eat," one said.

"The sufferings of the poor soldiers can scarcely be described. While on duty they are unavoidably exposed to all the inclemency of storms and severe cold. They are badly clad and some are destitute of shoes. We are frequently for six to eight days entirely destitute of meat and then as long without bread. The soldiers are so enfeebled from hunger and cold as to be almost unable to perform their military duty or labor in constructing their huts," Thacher added.

The general felt great sympathy for his soldiers. "The troops, both officers and men, have born their distress with a patience scarcely to be conceived. Many of the latter have been four or five days without meat entirely and short of bread," he told Huntington.

His letter to Huntington reflects his division in feelings about the army and the country. He could deplore the troops for plundering or carelessness but he could also admire their patriotism for merely staying in camp. Their great strength in those snowy winters of the war was that they were simply there. This hard core of thirteen thousand and more men survived every calamity God and the British threw at them, and remained at their posts. He was angry at them, exasperated by them and puzzled by them—but he was also proud of them.

Other commanders felt compassion, too. "Poor fellows," said Lieu-tenant Colonel Huntington, "my heart bleeds for them, while I damn my country as void of gratitude." Nathanael Greene was moved by their courage. "They exhibit a picture truly distressing. More than half naked, and above two thirds starved. A country once overflowing with plenty are now suffering an army employed for the defense of everything that is dear and valuable, to perish for want of food. O foolish Galathians, who has bewitched you!" he said.

The blizzard had trapped the army and Washington knew from his farming years that the cold that followed the storm, and the winds, guar-anteed weeks of chilly weather. The snow was not going to thaw out to permit the arrival of any food. No wagon could move through these drifts, which smothered roads for hundreds of miles. Anyway, there was no food in warehouses in the New York camp, or Trenton, or Philadel-phia. There was just no food.

Washington knew that the blizzard and lack of food could only have two results. One possibility was that the men, facing death, would flee and return home, and who could blame them? Second, they could stay and die. Either way, the Revolution would end, and in only a matter of days. There would not even be a final battle, as there was supposed to be in a war of this magnitude. The British regulars would not have to march to Morristown, bayonets out and teeth clenched. The vaunted Redcoat artillery, those long trains of hundreds of huge cannons that frightened the world, would never be positioned on a field. There would no be final gallant rush, no last speeches by the generals to exhort the men to glory in the face of hopeless odds. No flags would be unfurled and waved in the cold winter air. No fife-and-drum corps would muster itself to play martial music to fire up the frigid soldiers. The American army would simply collapse.

With farmers unwilling to accept any form of payment, even credit, the only remaining avenue of action was for George Washington to declare martial law and send troops, swords drawn, to force citizens to give up their food and clothing to the military. It was a step he loathed to take. He had always been able to persuade farmers to take credit, albeit very bad credit. Despite Congressional urging, Washington had refused to do so at Valley Forge and his view had not changed. How could the commander-in-chief, so loved and respected, turn on the people, point a musket at them, and take their food?

Washington often thought about the effects of martial law on the country and on its leaders in the two years since Valley Forge. The general wrote Joseph Reed a long letter about the issue in 1780, telling him that the power was dangerous for the people because a leader could do anything he wanted under the banner of "the public safety." It was equally dangerous for the leader because factions would disagree with his unchallengeable decisions regardless of what they were. Washington warned him, too, that if martial law did not produce the desired results, the people would rise up against their leader and that he would become as much the enemy as the British. Chaos would follow. "If it is not used proportionately you will be responsible for the consequences," he said.

Martial law had been quietly discussed again between delegates in Philadelphia and the governors as an unwanted last resort, but, compared to starvation, considered "the less of the two." In a painful letter, Massachusetts delegate Sam Holton wrote his longtime friend Samuel Adams that he expected just that:

> The situation of our affairs here are truly distressing, owing to the disordered state of our money and finances. An army in want of one day's supply and demands upon the treasury daily for millions and little or no money there. Is the [Massachusetts legislature] really sensible of our distressed state? I must suppose they be, for what can Congress do more than they have done? But don't, my worthy friend, think I despair for the common cause. No, not if they army should be all disbanded, which some think will be the case....

Those in Congress and in Washington's inner circle all knew that time was running out. "We are at the very pinch of the game," said Congressional delegate William Ellery. None put it better than Nathanael

Greene, plainly scared, who said, "God have mercy upon us. We have little to hope for and everything to fear."

With all prospects for success fading fast, Washington decided to take a calculated gamble on the evening of January 8. He asked Lewis to have the county's eight magistrates, or elected leaders, meet at the small private home that served as Greene's office in Morristown. He wanted Greene to persuade the civilian leaders to help him in his desperate straits, but it was important that Lewis be there because he had known the magistrates for years. His plea, as a neighbor and friend, would be even more compelling than that of General Greene (it is unknown whether Washington himself attended the meeting).

The magistrates arrived shortly after 8 P.M. on horse-drawn sleighs and trudged through snowbanks as high as the top buttons on their winter coats to Greene's office, dimly lit by candles. It had been a cold morning, with a brisk wind from the northwest. The temperature had climbed a bit during the early afternoon, but after sundown it plunged to nineteen degrees, again with a steady northwest wind that stung the faces of the magistrates. At the meeting, perhaps the most important of the war, Greene and Lewis bluntly told the civilian administrators that the army had reached the end. The men had been out of bread and food for nearly a week because farmers would not sell the army food on credit. The soldiers were dying. The double blizzard had snowed them in; the weather insured that no emergency provisions could reach them even if some could be found. The stage set, Greene then read the men a strident, but carefully worded letter from the commander-in-chief which Washington had spent all day preparing. In it, he told them that he was calling upon them, and county leaders throughout the state, to immediately turn over assigned quotas of bushels of grain and cattle to save the army.

Washington's letter quickly outlined the needs of the hungry soldiers:

The present situation of the army with respect to provisions is the most distressing of any we have experienced since the beginning of the war. For a fortnight past, the troops, both officers and men, have been almost perishing for want. They have been alternately without bread or meat the whole time, with a very scanty allowance of either and frequently destitute of both. They have borne their sufferings with a patience that merits the approbation and ought to excite the sympathy of their countrymen. But now they are reduced to an extremity no longer to be supported.

Washington explained that the men would die in days. He did not waste any time on military or civilian legalities, simply telling them that it was "his duty to the public" to take immediate action. He ordered them to procure two hundred heads of cattle and six hundred bushels of grain (he ordered 2,200 cattle and 12,150 bushels of grain throughout the state that same night) in what he called "an emergency of so pressing and peculiar a nature."

He reminded the justices in Morristown, and others throughout New Jersey, of "the patriotism of the people of this state and of their attachment to an army making every sacrifice in defense of their country" and told them he was certain that their citizens would change their minds and turn over their cattle and grain and accept continental money or credit for it.

Then, in ominous words, he made clear that if the civilians would not comply with his emergency edict and accept credit payment he would simply take what he needed, "which will be disagreeable to me on every account."

Washington had to have an immediate answer from the magistrates. The food had to be obtained right away and brought to camp without delay, or he would order his men to seize it. To make certain of immediate possession, on the previous day he had ordered his officers to be ready to move—and to take their muskets with them. They were to offer credit payment for supplies but if that was not accepted they were to take what they needed by force. The step, of course, would place the nation under martial law.

There is no record of the discussion that followed, but before the evening was over all of the justices, fully realizing the crisis, guaranteed cooperation and told Greene that when the army sent wagons to local farms they would be able to buy whatever wheat, flour, and cattle was available, on credit.

That same busy night, Washington also turned to the logistical problem of reopening the roads. Highways would be closed indefinitely throughout the Middle Atlantic region, but the army in Morristown needed clear highways right away. Washington got word of the emergency to the leaders of the Morris and Somerset county militias, and the local civilians who were responsible for the conditions of the roads under county government.

The militia heads reached out to their members at home, also trapped by the storm, and their neighbors, with news of the highway emergency. The militiamen and locals reacted just as swiftly as the farmers and merchants did in agreeing to provide food. Several hundred men from the Morris and Somerset county militias gathered on the morning of January 9 to break open roads that most residents believed so snowbound that they would remain closed for weeks. The militiamen discovered with pleasure that the alarm had apparently spread throughout Morris and Somerset counties, and they were joined that chilly morning, when the temperature was twenty degrees, by many more men and their families, local residents with no military connections at all, who wanted to help in the crisis.

January 9: Morning clear and cold, the Wind (though not high) from the No. West. Mid-day moderate but with little wind—the evening cold, though the Wind had shifted to the Southward.

The common method of clearing roads shut down by storms in the 1770s was rather primitive. After a snowfall, by prior agreement, teams of neighbors who lived along roads that connected their farms to villages or isolated general stores would gather at a designated place. They brought large sleds pulled by horses wearing specially made steel shoes to give them traction on ice or snow or arrived with wagons with customized snow-runners attached to wheels that were locked in place, or to wheelless axles, to create "super sleds." The lead sled would be driven into the middle of the snow covering the highway, forging a narrow trail with the horses legs and the sled runners. A second sled, and then third and fourth and fifth and sixth, would follow, in reverse "V" patterns, so that the horses and runners of each sled would furrow through different sections of snow and over each other's tracks. The teams would ride over, say, three hundred yards and then turn, riding back over the same road, then turning and traversing it again. In this manner, the half-dozen wagons would pound down snow to create six or seven foot wide lanes. Finished with the stretch of three hundred yards, the men and their sleds would move on to perform the task again, and again, and again. By the end of the day they could create an open highway upon which they could all ride into the village to buy supplies. The neighbors would then clear out other roads for friends. The few hundred people living within a half mile or so of a town would have an open road in a day or two.

The problem the militia and farmers faced that morning would seem insurmountable to most, though. Their job was far more daunting than simply breaking open a half-mile of roadway as they usually did after snowstorms. They had to forge paths that could cover miles of highway to several far-away towns and to numerous farms, many quite distant, in order for the quartermaster's sleds to reach the silos and graneries and cow pens. They had to do this not on roads with a typical snowfall of one or two inches, but roads inundated by four and five feet of snow from drifts. They had to accomplish with sleds and wagons in two counties what is rarely done in contemporary times with thousands of automated snowplows and sand trucks in a single community.

The total number of sleds and wagons belonging to residents that day were never completely accounted for because the teams worked on different roadways, but nineteenth-century historians estimated their number at somewhere between three and five hundred, as many as used in any battle of the war. The teams went to work quickly and diligently and, making progress slowly, plowed through the drifts. Warmly dressed men and boys with shovels dug out the areas the wagons and sleds missed.

By the time forty-eight hours had passed, all of the major roadways connecting nearby towns and farms to Jockey Hollow—up to eight miles of them in several directions—had been plowed open in a miracle of engineering and determination. The farmers and merchants then hastily loaded up their sleds with as much food, straw, and clothing as they could, and herded their cattle out into the newly created roadways of snow and ice, taking continental scrip, loan certificates, and sometimes just a scrawled IOU in payment, and sent everything they had to the starving soldiers at Morristown. Some of the cattle arrived during a light snowfall that began just after noon on January 10.

The Herculean efforts to open the roads and promptly provide food for the troops from nearby towns was repeated in counties farther away over the next several days. So much food arrived on the now passable roads, and so quickly, that by January 11 one of the commissary officers reported with glee that his food warehouses were nearly full.

The army was saved at the eleventh hour by Americans who would not let it perish. They did it because they feared martial law—and did not want to force Washington to declare it—but they also did it out of respect for the commander-in-chief, whose persuasive, personal patriotic plea was hard to refuse. He never forgot the effort of the people during those freezing days in January, and at the end of the month issued a thankful public letter to them: "I should be wanting in justice to their zeal and attachment to that of the inhabitants of the state in general, were I not to inform Congress that they gave the earliest and most cheerful attention to my requisitions and exerted themselves for the army's relief in a manner that did them the highest honor...owing to their exertions in a great measure the army has been kept together." Later, in letters to the county justices themselves, he was equally thankful, telling them that "You will permit me to assure you gentlemen that I entertain the highest sense of the exertions which have been made [by you] and the inhabitants of this county to relieve the distresses of the army...these exertions, and those of the state of Jersey in general, the troops and in them the public have derived the most important and happy benefits."

The American Revolution would continue.

Chapter Twelve

A WAR OF ATTRITION AND UNGRATEFUL HEARTS

MORRISTOWN, 1779–80

"I despise my countrymen. I wish I could say I was not born in America. I once gloried in it, but am now ashamed of it. If you do your duty, though late, you may finish the war this campaign. You must immediately fill your regiments and pay your troops in hard monies. They cannot exist as soldiers otherwise. The insults and neglects which the army have met with from the country beggars all description. It must go no father; they can endure it no longer. I have wrote in a passion. Indeed, I scarce am ever free from it…and all this for my cowardly countrymen who flinch at the very time when their exertions are wanted and hold their purse strings as though they would damn the world rather than part with a dollar to their army."

—Lieutenant Colonel Ebenezer Huntington

The double blizzard that struck Morristown during the first week of January had caused George Washington numerous problems, but he believed that it had also presented him with a unique opportunity. Why not use the billowing snow drifts and frigid temperatures as a cover to once again launch a surprise attack, and this time on the biggest prize of all—New York City? Why not sneak down a snow-covered New Jersey highway; cross the narrow waterway that separated New Jersey from New York, the Arthur Kill, which intelligence reported as frozen; and hit the British garrison at dawn after an all-night march? The enemy would never expect an army to suddenly appear out of a snow-covered world like some magician's illusion. The same kind of attack had worked against the Hessians at Trenton and it could succeed again. The target, Staten Island, adjacent to New York City, was defended by a force of just one thousand British troops. The Americans could force them into retreat across the frozen Hudson River toward New York and confiscate much-needed grain, cattle, clothing and other supplies for the destitute troops in Morristown. A successful assault on New York would also be a public-relations coup for the Americans, a startling reminder that Washington and his men could win battles any time they chose to do so. It would also shock the British people.

But the more the general thought about the idea, the more he questioned it. Such an attack would have to be launched immediately, with little planning and no knowledge of how the British had, or had not, survived the blizzards that had lashed the Americans at Morristown.

The general sent Tench Tilghman to scout the area. He was to make certain that the ice on the narrow strip of water west of Staten Island was thick enough for thousands of soldiers and wagons loaded with cannon and supplies to cross. Washington also worried that the weather might not hold; a sudden thaw would kill the plan, trap the men on the island, and make them an easy target for a British counterattack from Manhattan. He learned that Lord Stirling, whom he picked to lead the raid, was nervous about it and had insisted on even more men, a total of three thousand, plus additional cannon. Washington did not feel that he or Stirling had enough solid information from spies, either. "We shall be able to undertake the enterprise upon more certain intelligence which at present is defective, consequently disadvantageous in forming the plan," he told him.

It was physically difficult for troops to march to Staten Island through the recent snowfall. Cannon caissons could not be moved in it with much ease and neither could wagons loaded with food, ammunition, and supplies. The only way to attack New York through the snow was on a flotilla of sleds—hundreds of them. Washington could load a half dozen or more men on to each large sleigh, drawn by strong horses. Each sleigh could handle a single cannon. Ammunition and provisions could also be loaded onto sleds. They could cut through the snow easily, and silently, and carry an entire army through the white countryside. And sleds were fast. A horse-drawn sled could travel at twelve miles per hour, compared to a horse-drawn wagon at six miles per hour and a man walking at three miles per hour. It would be a strange-looking army launching one of the most unusual attacks in military history, comparable to Hannibal and his elephants crossing the mountains to attack the Romans, but it could work.

The problem was that the Americans had neither sleds or horses. Washington had sent most of his horses to Pennsylvania in December because he had no more food to feed them. He once again turned to local Morris County officials and asked them to pressure the farmers, exhausted from opening the roads on January 9 and 10, to not only give the army their sleds, but drive them into battle themselves, risking their lives. Joseph Lewis conveyed the plea to local officials in language that was more of an order than a request. "You will please engage every man in your district. No excuses must be admitted. [No] friend to his country could be fond of making excuses at this time," he wrote. Washington was not disappointed. More than three hundred farmers agreed to provide sleighs, jammed with soldiers, cannons, ammunition, food, and blankets, and drive them to Staten Island.

One day later, the general postponed the attack because he still did not feel he had enough information; he peppered Tilghman for more facts. On the following day, he delayed the action again. Now Washington seemed uncertain about Stirling's ability to carry out the mission. The commander-in-chief had to be absolutely certain that the attack had a reasonable chance of success; he could not lose three thousand men.

He wanted to give the veteran general all the support he could, despite his reservations, for several reasons. Stirling had agreed to use his large ironworks for weapons and ammunition production at the beginning of the war. The "lord" had taken on any assignment Washington had given him without complaining and had been one of his most reliable generals during the troublesome winter at Valley Forge. He was reliable. On the political side, he was the brother-in-law of Governor Livingston. And, on the personal side, it was Stirling who had tipped off Washington to the Conway plot against him. Washington wanted him to succeed and so, from January 12 to January 14, he sent him several lengthy letters outlining the attack as he, Washington, would stage it, straining to make Stirling believe that he had great confidence in him. Finally, at precisely 2 P.M. on January 14, the first men boarded the long train of sleds that stretched for nearly a mile off the village green in Morristown and rode off in the snow toward Staten Island. At exactly 4 P.M., as skies began to darken, the cannons were loaded onto the larger sleds and sent down the highway, the sturdy farmers' horses straining to pull the heavy artillery.

January 14: Clear & Cold—Wind steadily from the West—but not hard.

This time, however, the attack was a dismal failure. British spies learned of the assault, and the Redcoats had plenty of time to position themselves behind nearly impregnable fortifications they had built or acquired. Some were made out of ten-foot-high walls of snow and ice. Other British soldiers were placed in homes and barns. Since they had ample notice from lookouts and spies that the Americans and their army on sleds was approaching, the British were able to dig in and were well armed. Since the American had lost the element of surprise, they were unable to take advantage of the cold and icy conditions. In fact, the bad weather now, for perhaps the only time in the war, played into the hands of the English. The Redcoats could not be dislodged and the military action was over soon after it commenced. Instead of cutting his losses and returning to Morristown, Stirling, for some inexplicable reason, kept his men on Staten Island for twenty-four hours. They spent a night sleeping on the icy ground in temperatures cold enough "to cut a man in two," according to one of the soldiers. "We took up our abode for the night upon a bare bleak hill in full rake of the northwest wind with no other covering or shelter than the canopy of the heavens and no fuel but some old rotten rails which we dug up through the snow, which were two or three feet deep," said Private Martin sarcastically. The next morning, covered in ice rather than glory, the lord and the Americans boarded their sleds and traveled back to Morristown.

The returning soldiers were miserable. "We arrived at camp after a tedious and cold march of many hours, some with frozen toes, some with frozen fingers and ears and half-starved into the bargain," Martin wrote in his diary. Another man estimated that five hundred soldiers suffered severe frostbite.

In his report to Washington, which was sent on to Congress, Lord Stirling covered himself well, explaining to all that "an assault was deemed unadvisable." Washington, unhappy with the failure of the three thousand-man army, even though casualties were light, was reluctant to criticize his general and the men under him. In his report to Congress, Washington outlined the difficulty of the attack and reminded the delegates that once the British knew the Americans were on their way, the element of surprise had been lost, dooming the mission. "Little hope remained of effecting the business in that manner," he told Congress on January 18. As to his own feelings, Washington carefully told the delegates that "we were disappointed in our expectations." He had managed to successfully downplay the failed raid, learning that few would dispute the view of the most powerful man in the army. This lesson would not be forgotten and he would later, as president, again minimize military losses, against American Indians, once more cutting off negative public opinion.

Even more disappointing to the general was the outrageous behavior of residents from Essex County, across the water from Staten Island, who defied pleas to remain home and took it upon themselves to follow the troops onto the island. The civilians looted homes and stores in search of needed food and clothing as they went.

For the Continental Army, the actions of the citizens were as much of a public-relations disaster as the failed raid. "From the vast multitude who greedily rushed toward plunder, our country has received such disgrace as will not be easy, I may say possibly, wiped off," an annoyed Stirling told Washington. The general, just as angry, then ordered residents to return any plunder they had run off with, under the threat of arrest and imprisonment. Few did.

Also unsettling to Washington was the fact that the army was so short on clothing that the men engaged in the Staten Island assault had to borrow their woolen caps and mittens from the supply shed in Morristown and were ordered to return them so others could use them for outdoor work the following day.

The British press pilloried Stirling, whom many thought had considerable nerve to keep his so-called English title throughout the revolution. The editor of the Tory *New York Royal Gazette* wrote that his "Lordship" was "beneath contempt" and that he "wasted his time in a state of stupid insensibility." He then asked Stirling of his decision to have copies of his official report printed in newspapers, "what could lead you openly to describe the NOTHING which you performed? Was it to convince us that you are unacquainted with your present profession?"

The members of Congress were critical, too. John Adams savaged Stirling, charging that he had little success while, at the same time, he failed to prevent the plundering that everyone in Congress denounced.

But the colonial press, which venerated Washington, turned the failure into a success, as always. *The Jersey Journal* blithely told its readers that the Americans had been quite successful and that "the enemy on all sides retired to their works." The *New Jersey Gazette* bragged about the aborted attack: "This may serve to show the British mercenaries with what zeal and alacrity the American will embrace an opportunity, even in a very inclement season, to promote the interests of their country by harassing the enemies."

British retaliation for the Staten Island attack was swift. On January 25, the Redcoats launched a nighttime assault on the New Jersey towns of Newark and Elizabeth, using troops from Staten Island and Manhattan, who crossed the frozen Hudson. In Newark, British soldiers burned down Newark Academy, one of the state's most prestigious schools. They torched the courthouse and meeting house in Elizabeth. The troops also rounded up and kidnapped several local officials, including Joseph Hedden, one of the magistrates who governed Essex County.

Their success at seizing Hedden, as well as some minor local officials, emboldened the British to attempt something their leaders had dreamed of for years—the kidnapping of General Washington. They were convinced that the capture of Washington would bring about the end of the war within weeks, months at the latest, and they were probably right. There was no other commander with the personal and military skills to hold the army together through the rest of the brutal winter. His likely successor would be Nathanael Greene, the secret choice back in 1777, when Washington nearly died. Greene was a very unhappy and worried man, though. He was mad about the lack of support he received from Congress and the locals in his ceaseless drives to obtain supplies and had recently threatened to resign as quartermaster. The tempermental Greene also had great difficulty in dealing with Congress. On top of that, Greene worried constantly about his wife, Kitty, who was going through a very difficult pregnancy. She had insisted on being with her husband and had been taken by a sled from her home in Connecticut to Morristown just days after the double blizzard. She was due to give birth any day. Greene's mind was just as much on his wife's troubles as the army and would never have the focus of Washington; he would not make a good commander-in-chief at that time.

Lord Stirling certainly could not take over the army. Despite Washington's public faith in him, he was considered old and crusty by most. Baron Von Steuben was not an American and, although a fine general, would have little support. The Americans might fight well under another popular foreigner, Lafayette, but the headstrong young marquis was home in France. General Phillip Schuyler had never been a favorite among the officers or men and now he had moved from being an unpopular general to an unpopular Congressman. The temperamental and always complaining Benedict Arnold was despised by many. The only man left who knew the workings of the army and could deal successfully with Congress was Alexander Hamilton, but he was only twenty-two years old. He would never be able to overcome his inexperience. Besides, what soldiers would fight for a mere boy?

The kidnapping of Washington would also deal a fatal blow to the American citizenry, which had accorded him a near God-like status. Ever since his stunning victories at Trenton and Princeton in 1777, he had come to individually symbolize the entire Revolution. The American people, whether public officials in Congress or in the states or simple farmers and merchants, saw him as the one man who had held the army together through all of its many trials and could lead it through more. He could, in fact, lead it through anything. Many seemed to feel that he was some sort of mythic Greek stage hero, inevitably destined for victory. The problems that confronted the army—food shortages, inflation, lack of foreign troops—did not really seem to matter to many people because they had Washington. In the army's darkest hours he had snatched victory from the jaws of defeat and could do so again, and again, and again. The British may have misjudged the pulse of the Americans on numerous occasions, but not about Washington. His capture would be a public-relations blow from which the people could never recover; it *would* end the war.

How to do it, though? Washington was guarded by two hundred armed men who slept in huts in his front yard. The Ford mansion itself was crammed with men who zealously protected the general day and night. There appeared to be only three ways to capture George Washington. One was to seize him on one of those evenings when, against the wishes of his security chiefs, he traveled to the homes of friends accompanied by only a dozen or so guards. A second was to grab him while he was riding in the countryside in the afternoon with his servant Billy Lee, protected by only a few men. Another was to send a large force of men on horseback to Morristown in the middle of the night and, in a lightning-quick strike, attack Ford Mansion, break through his protective ring, grab him, and then spirit him away to New York.

That is exactly what General John Simcoe, commander of the Queen's Rangers, and Captain John Beckwith, an aide to General Wilhelm von Knyphausen, planned to do at the end of January. They were given authorization to take five hundred dragoons on horseback into New Jersey and, using lesser-traveled roads, work their way toward Morristown and kidnap the commander of the American army.

January 31: Very cold & freezing—wind being fresh from the No. West the whole day.

But the British were spotted immediately on the morning of January 31. Washington had warning messages from spies and from Silas Condict, his friend in Morristown, that some kind of attempt to kidnap or assassinate him was underway. His aides were fearful that so large a party of dragoons, on fast horses, might succeed if they descended upon Morristown with enough surprise and speed. Intrigue and mystery still surrounds the entire affair. Washington made no effort to play the bold hero, determined to fight off abductors himself. He knew that the head of the army had to be safe in order to run the war, just as wartime presidents later discovered. It was necessary to flee. Local lore has it that the general's aides sent him off with his personal guard to the home of John Jacob Faesch, Washington's friend and an owner of the ironworks in Rockaway, seven miles distant, for protection. Washington reportedly remained in hiding for several days (he wrote Condict on February 1 that he was then "rather remote from the army"). Any British troops arriving in Morristown who did manage to reach the mansion would find it empty of its most distinguished resident.

The dragoons never got close to the Ford mansion, however. The heavy snows had closed most of the smaller roads and they were forced to travel on the main highways, where they were soon spotted and engaged by a militia unit. Some were killed, some wounded, and the rest driven off. The entire party limped back to New York, having caught, in the freezing night, nothing but colds.

Steal or Die

By the end of January, the emergency food supplies that poured in following Washington's urgent January 8 plea—and threat of martial law—began to dwindle. Ephraim Blaine, the head of commissary in camp, reported to the Board of War that the troops had just ten days of bread and twenty-four days of meat left in the Morristown warehouses, half of what was necessary to survive. "We need all the goods you can lend. Send with all possible dispatch," he wrote.

Unable to get much to eat, and fearful that their new-found supplies would run out or that storms would again trap them and prevent the transportation of food to the camp, the soldiers once more resorted to plundering. Washington was soon confronted by the magistrates of the different counties. Had not the people opened up their barns and livestock pens to the army in its time of need just two weeks before and provided food for the men? Did they not then help the militia open up the roads to save the army? And now the men that they saved were raiding their farms again. The scope and depth of the thievery was what galled the county's public officials. The soldiers did not limit their plunder to simply scarves for warmth and apples for nourishment. They had taken just about everything not nailed down, and then stole the nails.

Lengthy lists that victims later compiled for the winter of 1779–80 showed the breadth of the thievery. As an example, the soldiers looted the farm of Nicholas Kemine and absconded with four sheep, three beehives, an ox, and fifteen ducks. James Bogart filed claims for the theft of a beehive filled with honey, a saddle, two sheep, and $434 in continental money. John Eskopfon charged that Continental troops looted his residence and made off with a cloth cloak, $130 in Continental money, two shirts, six caps, six "new" handkerchiefs, one hundred pounds of flour, and one half loaf of bread. Jacob Ackerman, who appeared to be a frequent victim, told the army he had been robbed of twelve pairs of stockings, several coats and blankets, a hog, dozens of newly laid eggs, knives, a cow, two hundred bushels of apples, twelve baskets of turnips, eleven turkeys, and ten sheep, and that soldiers had, he said angrily, pulled the bolts that held his wagon together out of their sockets and taken them, too. Other residents charged that soldiers had victimized them for frying pans, muskets, jackets, spoons, pants, butter, mittens, towels, ale tankards, linen, and even women's hats.

The commander-in-chief was embarrassed. He had always maintained a careful and precarious relationship with these county leaders. He had needed their help in the past and he would need it in the future. He found it necessary to threaten them to obtain what he wanted, as he had on January 8, when the army ran out of food. Yet he had to be supportive of them and understand their own political situation. They did not represent the army or the nation at large, as the general did. They represented the people that lived in the county and their job was to seek fairness and equitable treatment for them. Here, they had begged the people in Morris County to save the army and the people had done so. The warehouses had been full of food for awhile and they did not feel the soldiers had any right to resume plundering. The general had guaranteed an end to it. Now they suggested to Washington that he had gone back on his word. He had to assure them that he had not, that the pillaging had occurred without his knowledge. He was learning quickly that in democracy, all politics is local. A national leader can only succeed when he works with state and local officials. He must meet their needs in order to gain their help to meet his.

Washington was apologetic and told the magistrates that he felt badly for the farmers who had helped him and that "no means in my power shall be wanting to put a stop to every species of such practices." He vowed to arrest and punish the looters and to make certain that the local residents were reimbursed for their losses. (This would eventually take more than three years, but the men and women would be paid.)

He was hurt, too, because he felt that his men had betrayed him, just as the magistrates had accused the army of betraying them. The next day, in a rare departure from his usually cool temperament, Washington had a scathing general order read to the troops: "The General is astonished and mortified to find that notwithstanding the order issued on the 29th of last month…that the inhabitants in the vicinity of camp are absolutely a prey to the plundering and licentious spirit of the soldiery….A night scarcely passes without gangs of soldiers going out of camp and committing every species of robbery, depredation and the grossest personal insults. This conduct is intolerable and a disgrace to the army."

The general kept his word to punish the plunderers and began imprisoning soldiers for stealing food, clothing, equipment, or money from the area residents, even hanging one man for theft on February 20.

The clothing situation remained just as bleak as the food problem. The day before the local residents and militia helped the army dig its way out of the double blizzard, one of the quartermasters wrote that only one-fifth of clothing supplies promised since mid-December had arrived. He informed the Board of War that "the situation of the troops beggars all description."

There was clothing at Newburgh, near West Point, but the string of snowstorms that buried the northeast made highways from there to Morristown impassable and the wagons, full of apparel, remained in barns. And, to make matters worse, two fires broke out in the warehouses there, destroying the provisions stored in them.

February 22: Wind at No. Et. And raining moderately all day— beginning about 7 O'clock with the hail. In the Night the Wind freshened from the same quarter.

The general had hoped that the clothing problems would be alleviated by the states, whose leaders had promised to send wagonloads of apparel to troops from their states. However, few items of clothing had arrived by early March.

Desperate for breeches, shirts, and especially winter coats, remembering vividly how the lack of proper clothing brought on disease and death at Valley Forge, Washington asked for any soldiers with experience as tailors to help. Hundreds volunteered and during the daytime dozens of huts were turned into busy makeshift tailors' shops. The shops were grim reminders of overall conditions, as Ekuries Beatty outlined in a letter to his brother at the end of January: "Outside of the tailors [huts] you will see maybe half a dozen men naked as Lazarus, begging for clothing.…[T]he hut is full of cut cloth and men run in all day to get some."

The army had no money for transportation, either. Washington had employed between five and six hundred wagons and teams of horses, and their drivers, each day for hauling and foraging, paying $20 in Continental scrip per day per wagon. By mid-February, that was cut back to $14 per day, and the farmers grumbled. Within ten days, the army could not even pay the $14, and wagon drivers refused to work.

Since their arrival in early December, a number of soldiers had also borrowed money from area residents. Now, because of inflation, they could not pay it back and a deep animosity began to set in between the residents and the troops.

By the first week of February, the army had simply run out of money. Quartermasters were forced to lie about it. Lewis pleaded with headquarters in Philadelphia to send him loan certificates, telling them "I can't let the [residents] know I have no cash." Quartermasters were afraid residents would again refuse the certificates and asked that advertisements be taken out in newspapers to inform locals that there was no money and that they had to accept them.

Worse, the farmers and merchants in New Jersey became increasingly livid that they had to adhere to the newly established state price controls, but their counterparts in nearby states did not. Despite spirited debate in the assemblies of New York, Pennsylvania, and Delaware, price-regulation bills had failed in each. So, in early February, New Jersey had to lift its price controls, which had been in effect for only six weeks. Prices soared.

Tory newspapers filled up their pages with columns denouncing Congress for plunging the people into financial ruin, and one writer even called for Congress to declare bankruptcy. "The hour is at hand," he wrote, "you see their certificates are no better than blank notes, worse than their paper dollars."

Renewed Congressional efforts to curb prices failed when a special national price-control convention adjourned in mid-February without adopting any policy. Many public officials were shaken. "I dread to mention the approaching consequences," delegate John Armstrong Sr. told Horatio Gates on February 16.

The Congressional solution to the growing national currency crisis was to simply replace old money with new. During the first week of March, it was ordered that the $200 million in Continental script circulating through the states be confiscated at a rate of $15 million a month through April 1781. The old money would be burned. New, much smaller amounts of money, issued only as the older paper bills were destroyed, would then serve as sturdier currency. This new money would be raised by taxes assessed the states. Sixty percent of the new money would be issued by the states and 40 percent by Congress. The goal of the plan was to stabilize the economy and leave the United States with a total debt of only $5 million by the end of 1781. Hopefully, the plan would end the crazy inflation that gripped the country, driving the cost of a hat to $400 and a horse to $20,000. New York congressional delegate William Floyd told friend Pierre Van Cortlandt that prices in some towns in their state had soared to one hundred times what they were at the start of the war and that "a dollar in this market is reckoned very little more than a penny."

March 3: Ground hard frozen. Morning clear & pleasant with but little wind and that from the South. Mid-Day cloudy & lowering—variable afterwards—sometimes snowing, at other times Sunshine—Wind getting westerly. The Northern lights, or aurora Borealis was seen last evening but not in a very conspicuous degree.

Continental Congress President Huntington assured everyone that the new plan would work and said it was "the happiest expedient that could be adopted to extricate these states from the embarrassment of a fluctuating [economy] and at the same time to some measure afford the necessary means for supporting the ensuing campaign."

Washington's closest confidants disagreed. They felt that in order to have a solid economy, Congress needed to back up its currency with large financial reserves. They also felt that the national debt would climb much higher than the projected $5 million because the states had started to issue loan certificates as salary to their soldiers and promised to redeem the certificates at the end of the war. They believed that these certificates, when cashed in, would bring about enormous debt. (In fact, by the time the Constitutional Convention met in 1787, national debt, due primarily to soldier payments, would reach $77 million.)

In a series of heated, highly analytical columns in the *Jersey Journal*, Washington's friend the Rev. Jacob Greene insisted on financial support for the new paper money. He suggested that between 1780 and 1783, Congress collect $15 million a year in silver and gold, so that by 1783 residents could redeem their paper bills for hard cash. The security of the silver and gold in banks would assure the people of the legitimacy of the currency and further stabilize the economy.

Hamilton, snowed in like everyone else during that frigid January, spent his time putting together an intricate plan to end inflation and assure future economic soundness, which he described in a lengthy letter to a Congressional delegate, most likely Schuyler, and surely showed to Washington. He advocated a "Bank of the United States." The bank would sell $200 million in stock to wealthy Americans who would also deposit their personal fortunes in it and make loans to it. They would convince their companies to deposit their funds in it, too. Half the stock would always be owned by the national government. The Bank would back up all of its reserves with Spanish dollars or other hard money. This money would come from the conversion of taxes raised in paper bills into specie through local or foreign banks. In addition, he urged, the U.S. had to obtain several foreign loans, supported by hard money, and suggested an initial loan of $8 million. The Bank would loan Congress money whenever necessary. Its money would be the national currency, replacing state currency and certificates.

"All our...operations are at a stand and unless a system very different...be immediately adopted through the states our affairs must soon become desperate beyond the possibility of recovery," said Hamilton of his plan, which would, with modifications, later became the basis for the American economic system.

General Greene, too, had become a believer in a strong national government. His feelings, of course, had developed in direct proportion to the lack of cooperation he received from the states and counties. He wanted Congress to have complete jurisdiction over the states. "We are a ruined people," without a strong national government, he said. "And that is not very distant."

George Washington's wartime experience had taught him by then that constant efforts to run the country with varied coalitions between Congress and state legislatures had failed. He wrote toward the end of the winter of 1780 that the proposed currency split between Congress and the states, with the states producing 60 percent of the country's money, and the power it gave the states in the new economic plan, seemed perilous. He called any plan to give the states more power than the Continental congress "a many headed monster" and warned that a national body had to supercede the various state bodies in order for America to work as a democracy. He also warned that the key to success was not a monopoly of power by either the federal, state, or local governments, but a distribution among them. His vision would later become the primary focus of the Constitutional Convention in 1787 and the cornerstone of his own presidency.

Not everyone in Congress applauded the new economic plan, either. Some were apprehensive about the reliance on local officials to carry it out. One of Congress's newest and brightest members was young James Madison, a slight, five foot, four inch, one hundred forty pound member from Virginia, who had just arrived in Philadelphia to serve his first term. Madison, who raised eyebrows in the halls of Congress by dressing in black each day (which some sneered suited his taciturn personality), was one of the most well-read men in America. He had done extensive research on the economic practices of European governments.

Upon his arrival, Madison wrote his friend Thomas Jefferson of the new scheme and its shortcomings: "If the states do not vigorously proceed in collecting the old money, and establishing funds for the credit of the new...we are undone." Madison told delegates that American currency was in free fall because Congress had no money in reserve. The people needed to have confidence that Congress could back up its money and that, more importantly, Congress would be around to do so. The war had to be won in order for people to have faith in Congress and the currency. Yet, in the winter of 1780, the Americans had no prospects of victory and the army had gone to the brink of disbanding twice in just the last two months.

French and Spanish diplomats had continually told Congress that their countries would only send troops if Washington and his men survived the winter and got through another summer against the British—and won some battles. "The critical situation of public affairs...requires the next campaign to be prosecuted with such vigor as may entirely expel the enemy from every part of the United States," North Carolina delegates John Penn, Thomas Burke, and Allen Jones said in a very carefully worded letter to Governor Richard Caswell about the foreign ultimatums.

James Lovell put it more bluntly. "We must cut throats for another year at least and we ought to do it vigorously," he told Samuel Adams.

The British Conduct Their Own "Body Counts"

There was another reason why the army had to survive the winter. Washington, with clearer vision than anyone in the army or in Congress, had always understood that the rebellion was a war of attrition. The Americans did not have to win the war; they simply had to survive long enough to convince the British to quit. And Washington knew that the decision to end it would not be made by the generals, but by the politicians in London. The politicians would continue to endorse the war until enough pressure was brought against them to abandon it by the press and the public.

Now, in the winter of 1780, that pressure continued to build. There were numerous signs that Britain's once-swaggering resolve to crush the Americans was dissipating. Both France and Spain had declared war on England and the British government had been forced to refocus its energies on their foes across the English Channel, with whom they had feuded for centuries, rather than enemies three thousand miles away. British residents' fear of attack by the two European powers, and by American privateers refitted in French ports, was so great that dozens of volunteer militias had been formed, most in seaside communities, to fight off the invaders if they landed.

These worries were not unfounded. In the summer of 1779, a fleet of sixty-six French and Spanish ships had prowled the waters around Britain, looking for vessels to sink. The American sea captain, John Paul Jones, who had already defeated two British ships, always seemed to be lurking about and had become so feared that English nannies used his name to strike fear into their toddler charges.

Opposition to the war had grown in British governing bodies. Firebrand politician John Wilkes had been ejected from Parliament in 1763 for his opposition to the king. He had fought for reinstatement for eleven years, supported by the press and public, and was finally given his seat back in 1774. Throughout the war, Wilkes, with newspaper support, championed the American cause, equating the colonists' complaint of taxation without representation with his own cry that parliament was controlled by the royals and the rich and that there was no true representation of the English common people.

By the late 1770s, groups called "Patriotic Societies" had sprung up throughout England to support the American cause. A number of county associations, or governing bodies, issued statements calling for an end to British involvement in America. In 1777, after news of British defeats at Trenton and Princeton reached England, the city of London's common council voted thirty to one against continued financial support for bounties for soldiers to fight in the States. In Parliament, Lord George Gordon, referred to it as the "mad, cruel, accursed American war." One group of wealthy young lords and businessmen not only wanted England to quit the war, but embraced Washington and his men as romantic heroes. They even renamed their yacht *The Congress*.

Disenchantment in the British army itself had been growing for three years. Troops were openly asking not to be assigned to America, and in the spring of 1779 soldiers from the 71st Highlanders had even mutinied when told they were going to New York to fight the rebels. The high command was not very comfortable battling the Continental Army, either. Lord Howe, Lord Percy, and several other generals had asked for and received permission to leave the States and return to England. Now, in the winter of 1780, the latest British commander-in-chief, Sir Henry Clinton, too, said he was tired of the endless conflict and wanted to go home. He was turned down by Lord Germain, head of the Foreign Office, who let slip in his rejection that he did not have very high prospects for victory himself, telling Clinton, stationed in New York City, that he was "the only chance we have of saving America."

There had never been much harmony among the British generals and their staffs in New York. Howe had feuded with his generals during his two years in the States. Clinton did not seem to get along with any of his subordinates, either, especially Lord Cornwallis, and by the winter of 1780 Clinton was barely on speaking terms with his own aides. No one in New York, citizens or officers, had much good to say about his aides, either, and former New Jersey Governor William Franklin, then living in New York, referred to them as "a parcel of blockheads."

By 1780, criticism had grown in the London press, too. The British media probably had more freedom than any other in Europe. Although most newspapers and magazines supported the war at first, they became critical of the conflict following the American victory at Saratoga in the fall of 1777. Their editors criticized Parliament for putting British troops' lives at risk and for spending millions on what they considered an unnecessary war. These anti-war periodicals published frequent parodies of parliamentary debate on the war and filled their pages with a substantial number of columns by English writers denouncing the war. Since the Crown censored news of the war, the papers published numerous letters from Americans providing details of the war (biased, of course). Two of the Americans published with regularity were Benjamin Franklin and John Adams. The tempo of stories in favor of American separation increased in 1779 as France and Spain declared war against Great Britain.

British publications begun to publish "body counts" as early as the winter of 1778. Their columns were filled with long lists containing the names of all the British army soldiers killed, wounded, or taken prisoner in the American war. One was *London Magazine*, read by many members of Parliament and the monarchy. The journal gave substantial prominence to its often-printed "body count." In its June 1780 issue, as an example, the magazine told its readers, many tired of the war already, that so far England had suffered 8,900 men killed, 11,000 wounded, and 9,116 captured.

Washington believed that these published reports would soon turn public opinion in Great Britain against the war. He was confident that if opposition to the war in England grew strong enough, and the British continued to have their hands full battling France and Spain, King George III would abandon the war in the colonies, which had become very costly in lives and money. There were certainly historical precedents for Washington's philosophy, and they extended back to long before the birth of Christ. A similar military/political adventure took place between 431 and 404 BC, when Athens sent an undermanned army to attack Sicily. The small Athenian force was unable to secure a speedy victory, and did not receive substantial reenforcements. The war dragged on for years and at home political chiefs squabbled amongst themselves and the people turned on the leaders, producing serious domestic discord.

The Americans could win it, Washington hoped, by merely keeping their armies on the field for another year to produce a similar result. The British people had to come to understand that although outnumbered and badly equipped, the Americans would not give up and would continue to fight on for years. The only way to end the war for Great Britain was to continue to commit large armies and accept high casualties. The Redcoats would have to move out from the comfort of the American cities where they were now headquartered and chase the rebels across the vast vistas of America, whose seaboard extended for nearly two thousand miles. They would not be able to fight the Americans on traditional British ground, open meadows, but on the Americans' turf—thick forests, mountain ridges, rock strewn valleys, and swamps. They would also have to finally defeat and capture the entire Continental Army, and its commander-in-chief, to prevent them from retreating and returning to fight another day, something they had been unable to do. Prominent English politicians such as Edmund Burke reminded their countrymen, that even a conclusive victory over the Continental Army would not end the war; the Americans would fight on as snipers and saboteurs and would never truly be defeated.

But, to accomplish all of that the Continental Army had to stay on the field for at least another year. Washington wondered, amid his numerous calamities, how could they do that?

Life in Morristown was as chaotic as it was in Congress. The temperatures had remained frigid throughout the entire month of January. Washington's weather diary entry for January 28th was typical: "very cold—the wind being fresh from the northwest—froze severe." The ice was so thick in New York harbor that one evening in late January revelers held a party in the middle of the river and for dinner consumed a huge ox they roasted there. Another New Yorker reported that many miles of Long Island Sound had frozen over.

The winter of 1779–80 was so severe that in March the American Philosophical Society, based in Philadelphia, took out ads in newspapers asking readers to send them any weather readings or notes on weather patterns they had made since the first snowfall so that their members could study the weather's effect on animals and plants. It is doubtful that anyone could match the meticulous notes of General Washington in his weather diary. Although he did not jot down daily temperatures, his notes help to tell the story of the winter and how it affected the war.

New Jersey was hit with a storm that dumped four inches of snow on the ground on January 10; the area suffered snowfalls of an inch or so on January 17 and again on the 27th. A severe snowstorm hit Morristown in early February 8 followed by more snow the next day. And then, on March 2 and on the 16th, two more big storms battered the area, each leaving nearly four inches of snow.

February 8: A fall of nine or ten Inches Snow in the Night from the No. Et. Wind continuing in the same quarter all of the forenoon with a little Snow and some rain. In the afternoon the wind got westerly & in the evening cleared.

The city of huts that had been under construction since early December was still unfinished. Almost all the enlisted men were in huts by January, but some officers didn't get into the wooden structures until mid-February and a few remained in tents, shivering, until mid-March.

It was in March that the army's money and food crisis loomed again. Greene had warned Washington for more than six weeks that the army was headed toward starvation. He told him in mid-January that he believed there was enough grain stored in local farmers' sheds, and cattle for slaughter in their pens, to keep the army going—but the army had no money to pay for them. Washington, who had come close to martial law on January 8, and felt very uneasy about military rule, had made up his mind not to declare it under any circumstances.

Greene now reminded Washington that the Congressional plan to get the states to provide provisions had failed. "The cloud thickens and the prospects are daily growing darker," he told the commander-in-chief, insisting that the army was running out of time. "There is now no hope of cash. The agents are loaded with heavy debts and perplexed with half finished contracts, and the people clamorous for their pay, refusing to proceed in the public business unless their present demands are discharged.…I see nothing, therefore, but a general check, if not an absolute stop, to the progress of every branch of business in the whole department." Greene again threatened to quit and Washington again had to remind him how grateful he was for his service to his country and persuaded him into remaining.

Greene remained morose. "There was never a darker hour in American politics than this," he said on the last day of February. "Our treasury is dry, and magazines empty. How we are to support the war is beyond my conception. Shillings cannot be had where pounds are wanting. It is in vain in my opinion to expect the people to pay taxes and grant credit at the same time. Public fraud cannot be practiced on individuals much longer." In a letter to Wadsworth, Greene sneered at a note he received from Continental Congress President Samuel Huntington assuring him that as soon as the new taxes rolled in his bills would be paid. Greene said it was the usual "folly of Congress."

Washington's friends in Philadelphia were also afraid of the future and told the commander that Congress was in chaos. On the very same day that Washington received the latest of Greene's doom-and-gloom letters, he read a note from Schuyler, who gave him his personal assessment of the new currency plan: "Our finances are completely deranged."

Baron Von Steuben, whose English was much improved, visited Congressional committees, at Washington's behest, to explain the army's needs. He then sent the commander-in-chief a harrowing report. "Every wheel of the [government] machine seemed stopped," he told the general and added that the chances of anything being accomplished were reduced by the various factions that he observed. "The civil departments of the army, at a time when their whole attention should be taken up in providing for the approaching campaign, are in such a state of dissatisfaction and confusion that I am very apprehensive they will make things still worse than they are."

Many of those in Congress agreed with him. James Madison fumed to Thomas Jefferson back in Virginia:

> Our army threatened with an immediate alternative of disbanding or living on free quarter; the public trust empty; public credit exhausted, nay the private credit of purchasing agents employed, I am told, as far as it will bear, Congress complaining of the extortion of the people, the people of the improvidence of Congress, and the army of both; our affairs requiring the most mature and systematic measures and the urgency of occasions admitting only of temporizing expedients and those expedient generating new difficulties; an old system of finance discarded as incompetent to our necessities, an untried and precarious one substituted and a total

stagnation in prospect between the end of the former and the operation of the latter....

The situation seemed so unsalvagable, friends in Congress told the
commander, that he had to send Greene to Philadelphia to explain that his
supply problems were extremely critical. Greene went to Philadelphia and
met with committees in Congress, but with little success. Greene reported
back that the "public business is in a wretched train. All things at a stand;
and I don't believe the great departments of the army will be organized for
a month to come unless the new system is adopted, which will starve and
disband the army in half the time." And, Greene added, even though he
had arrived as the personal emissary of the commander-in-chief, he was
received with little respect and, he claimed, often insulted. Greene said the
only salvation the army now had was the melodramatic arrival of Washington himself in Philadelphia, but the commander resisted the idea.

On March 20, Blaine informed Congress that the army only had
twelve days of grain left and that the troops would again be put on rice
diets. There were just four hundred cattle in pens and they would not
supply beef beyond early May. He added that just the day before he had
learned that every one of the commissary assistants in the southern
department had resigned due to poor pay.

That same week, Joseph Lewis ran out of money to pay wagon teams
and begged the local justices to talk the farmers into working without pay
until the new taxes arrived. "Surely Morris County is not so destitute of
feeling for the army that they would suffer troops to starve for want of
assistance?" he asked on March 22.

*March 22: Clear but rather cool, the wind being pretty fresh
from the No. West all day. Ground froze again.*

The next day, exasperated, Lewis warned Furman that he had just
four days of bread. "Good God!" he wailed. "Where are our resources?
We are in the most pitiful situation...distracted with calls [for food] that
are not in our power to answer."

Washington, besieged on all sides for help, poured out his skepticism of the attempted reorganization of the commissary in Philadelphia to Schuyler, telling him that the new system emananated from necessity and choice. He saw little hope in it and warned that, if adopted, "…ruin must follow."

He and the officers also fumed about civilian administrative boards they had to deal with and the bunglers who served on them. "All public bodies seem to me to act in a manner which if they were individuals they would be kicked out of their company," Pennsylvania Governor Joseph Reed said about them.

The men in the army continued to be baffled by the locals' reluctance to sell food and clothing on credit. Later, in what seemed rather spectacular disdain for the army, the Morris area families on whose land the winter camp had been built refused to let the soldiers tear down the huts and take the boards. They demanded that the hundreds of huts and their boards be left on the sides of the hills of Jockey Hollow in lieu of the money they said the army owed them.

Lieutenant Sam Shaw, who lived in one of those huts, was disgusted with his Morristown neighbors, just as he had been angry with those who held the same views at Valley Forge. He wrote in his journal, "The people of America seem to have lost sight entirely of the noble principle which animated them at the commencement of [the war]. That patriotic ardor which then inspired each breast—that glorious…enthusiasm—has given place to avarice and every rascally practice which tends to be the gratification of that sordid and most disgraceful passion." Major General Johann Kalb, another Valley Forge veteran, snapped, "And these are the people who talk about sacrificing their all in the cause of liberty!"

Morristown was different because, unlike Valley Forge, it was not an isolated plateau far from any substantial civilian population; it was a community that the army needed. In an emotional letter to quartermaster Furman in Trenton, Lewis explained that "Morristown has become the very capital to the army and will require large sums [of money] to support it. Every house is filled with troops and needs to be guarded and filled with wood for fires to cook for meal. Money is needed for boards, nails, artisans to build huts." Then he made a fervent plea for the rights of the people he knew so well, explaining that they needed to be paid "for support of their families, who were long deprived of their money. Families are helpless. Children are nearly reduced to begging. Such are the greatest sufferers. The army depends on Morristown and must pay its bills. Were I to be silent at the present distressed period I should be highly criminal in my duties."

The lack of food and clothes contributed to the growing rate of desertions and resignations in the army. Washington felt little joy in the Congressional promise to raise an army totaling thirty-two thousand troops by the end of the summer because he knew some soldiers were leaving Jockey Hollow for home each day. Within the Massachusetts line alone, twelve officers resigned during the first eleven weeks of 1780. Men stationed in Pennsylvania took advantage of their isolation on guard duty to simply leave their posts and go home. Only dramatic incentives seemed to keep men in uniform. In December, Pennsylvania again guaranteed each soldier who stayed in the army one half-pay for seven years following the end of the war, plus up to two thousand acres of free land. Washington had the notice read to his men as an incentive to keep them.

Anyone with a complaint beat a path to Washington's door. Everybody was unhappy about something. Officers in Albany reported that Tories who had fled in the spring of 1777 had returned to discover that soldiers had torn the walls off their barns to use for barracks. They were going to sue. Groups of homeowners with political influence had been able to lobby for a freeze on their taxes; others in their community, without connections, had their taxes raised. Officers said that the new taxes would ruin them. Colonel Morgan Lewis, one of Greene's aides, reported that he would now have to pay half of his army salary in taxes.

Washington was told repeatedly, through his aides, that shipments of everything from clothing to wood to meat were held up because merchants decided to hike their prices. "This is a circumstance so alarming that I request an immediate return of the quantity of meat within your district, more particularly of what is within a short distance of camp, and I must further request you to make use of every exertion to have it brought forward," Washington told one officer in the Commissary department.

Schuyler, who could look at the crisis as both a general and newly minted Congressman, was grim. He sent a blistering note to the various state legislatures on April 4: "Congress are obliged to call on the states to use every possible exertion to expedite the public supplies. The present deficiency is very great and, if continued, must be fatal."

Washington also had to once again refute rumors that swept through the country. These rumors, like most, had some truthful origin but were then exaggerated as they moved from one listener to another. Naturally, most were alarming. This time Washington had to put down the unfounded story that Spanish ships had landed thousands of troops in western Florida, and that they had captured Pensacola and were marching on St. Augustine. Another rumor was that Congress had decided to disband the quartermaster corps and rely on each state for supplies. A third was the usual gossip that tens of thousands of soldiers, from any country someone wanted to pick, were gleefully signing up to fight with the British in the spring. Yet another, perhaps the wildest of all, was that Parliament was ready to grant independence to most of the states, but that, for some unexplainable reason, insisted that Georgia, South Carolina, and the Maine territory had to remain under English control.

Stress began to bring down the general, just as it had in the winter of 1777. "It is impossible for the Commander-in-Chief to discharge the general duties of his station while he is encumbered by the many minutious details which are daily brought before him," one of his aides told the troops.

He Danced All Night

Once again, Martha came to the rescue.

Mrs. Washington had started her annual journey from Mount Vernon to winter camp in the middle of December, determined to reach Morristown by Christmas. She was trapped, like so many others, by the snowstorms that buffeted the East Coast and spent the holidays in

Philadelphia with friends. She enjoyed her stay but was eager to see her husband. Worried about travel over the winter roads, the commander-in-chief sent one of his aides to fetch her in a horse-drawn sleigh. Martha, bundled up in winter clothing and cheeks red from the ride through the snow, arrived in front of the Ford mansion in Morristown in the sled the next day, to the delight of her husband.

Martha moved into her husband's second-floor bedroom at Ford's Mansion. She took charge of the general's part of the household and Theodosia Ford ran the overall household. The home had become over-populated. Probably at Martha's urging, Washington ordered three extra buildings constructed behind the mansion, pressuring his workers to complete them in direct proportion, it appears, to his wife's pressure on him. One was a kitchen with a large stone fireplace for headquarters staff, one was an office building for his aides, and the third was a large stable for the general's horses and the horses of his staff.

Martha became friendly with the officers' wives who lived in the winter camp and probably visited the home of Kitty Greene as often as possible to help her as she labored through the final weeks of her pregnancy. She probably was present at the January 31 birth of Kitty's fourth child, Nathanael, and helped nurse her back to health as Kitty went through a difficult recovery and remained bed-ridden for several weeks. Martha also began yet another sewing organization, enlisting the wives of officers and local women, in what seemed a never-ending battle to stitch together clothes for the soldiers. She also had the chance, as did everyone else in Morristown, to follow the whirlwind romance between Betsy Schuyler and Alexander Hamilton.

Betsy, twenty-two, was the gorgeous daughter of Philip Schuyler. She arrived in late December on a visit to her aunt, Mrs. John Cochran, while her mother and father traveled on to Philadelphia (their summer home in Saratoga had been burned down by Burgoyne in the fall of 1777). Several officers, including Tench Tilghman, had already met the vivacious Betsy, a slender brunette with dark brown eyes and soft, alabaster skin. They had all been slain by her beauty. "I was prepossessed in favor of this young lady the moment I saw her," said Tilghman.

Upon her arrival she sought out General Von Steuben, on her father's orders, to deliver a formal letter of introduction. He was not near head-quarters that day and as she went from office to office and house to house seeking him, she reportedly left a train of love-struck soldiers in her wake.

It is unknown when she met Hamilton, who was consumed by her as everyone else. Their romance was the talk of the county. They were inseparable, attending all of the parties and receptions together and trav-eling by sleigh to the homes of Lord Stirling, Governor Livingston, Elias Boudinot, and others. Not a night went by when locals did not see them hand in hand somewhere, Betsy radiant and Hamilton smitten.

The young colonel wrote her numerous love letters. His heart-thumping March 17 letter, sent a week before they were engaged, was typical. He thanked her for her own letter and said of it that "I cannot tell you what ecstasy I felt in casting my eye over the sweet effusions of tenderness it contains. My Betsy's soul speaks in every line and bids me be the happiest of mortals. I am so and will be so. You give me too many proofs of your love to allow me to doubt it and in the conviction that I possess everything the world can give," he told her. The ardent suitor fin-ished, "Adieu my charmer; take care of yourself and love your Hamilton as well as he does you, God bless you."

George and Martha were eyewitnesses to the romance since the Ford Mansion was only about one-third mile from the white clapboard Cochran home, where Betsy stayed. The Washingtons approved of the relationship and the general did not seem to mind when Hamilton sneaked out of headquarters each night to woo his beloved. Hamilton wore out a trail in the snow taking a shortcut through the woods to the Cochran home. He had to check in with the commander-in-chief before he visited each evening, though, because he needed to be told the secu-rity password for entrance to the mansion, which changed daily. A story passed down by locals was that one night, deep in thought over Betsy, he trudged back to headquarters through the snow and was stopped by guards who asked for the password. Hamilton had forgotten it. He explained to the guard who he was (the guard knew), but to no avail. Orders were orders. Finally, off in the distance, he spotted Mrs. Ford's teenage son, Jacob. The amused Ford, who like everyone else in the mansion knew of his stealthy midnight returns, gave him the day's code and the guard let him through, surely with a wink.

Martha was delighted by the romance between Hamilton and Schuyler, who were married nine months later. Her biggest social triumph, though, was getting her "old man," George Washington, back on the dance floor.

She was worried about her husband's spirits, which by February had sunk lower than at any time since Valley Forge. The deep snows had prevented him from his customary afternoon riding excursions with Billy Lee. He had little recreation and, thanks to his own edicts, could not gamble. Martha did not want to see him moping at the front windows of the Ford home, staring out the panes at the snow; she wanted to see him smiling broadly, as he always did when he twirled about the floor to his beloved jigs and reels. Mrs. Washington was not alone; a number of officers and their wives thought a succession of parties would liven up the miserable winter.

There were no halls spacious enough to hold dances in the Morristown area, so the interior of one of the large warehouses was cleared to provide a makeshift dance floor (when Washington was out of earshot, men joked that there was plenty of room for dancing because there was no food). The Washingtons invited all of the officers to the first dance assembly at the end of February and asked each to purchase a subscription to the dances since somebody had to pay for the band and refreshments. Hamilton reminded the general that with inflation each subscription ticket cost four hundred dollars.

There were three officers' dances that winter, all held in the warehouse. Several dozen officers attended each. Women such as Lucy Knox accompanied their husbands. Dozens of unattached young women in the Morristown area were invited as company for the single officers. There were a number of women at two of the dances, but only a few at the first, held after a snowstorm had shut some roads.

The highlight of the evenings, of course, was watching the commander-in-chief dance. The stress of five years of war might have put some additional gray into his hair and some wrinkles under his eyes, but it had done nothing to slow down his feet. He was the central figure on the dance floor in the food warehouse just as he had been in the most luxurious mansions in Virginia. His dancing exploits were legendary. At a dance the previous winter, at Bound Brook, he had been talked into a marathon by Kitty Greene. Delighted at the challenge, the general had danced with her for three solid hours, reminding those who knew him of his dance marathons at Mount Vernon and Williamsburg, when eyewitnesses reported that he sometimes danced until dawn.

Now, in Morristown, he danced all night. Martha, who did not share his great love of dancing, shared a few jigs and reels with him, but most of the time he danced with other women as Martha rested or chatted with anyone who wanted to talk to her. All of their lives, these women on the dance floor would tell the story of the night they danced with George Washington.

The dances were popular and led to other, smaller parties for officers at the homes of local militia leaders. There was much dancing and much drinking at these parties, usually populated by lower-ranking officers and not the generals. "We kicked up a hell of a dust," wrote a rather proud Lieutenant Beatty of one.

All were cheered up by the news that on the snowy March 16 the commander-in-chief had again ordered a festival to celebrate St. Patrick's Day on the following day because the Irish, too, were rebelling against British trade restrictions. He said the lifting of their tariffs, which he termed "tyrannical oppressions," would "restore to a brave and generous people their ancient rights and freedom and by their operation to promote the cause of America." The festival was staged to give everyone a day off, reward the hard-fighting Irish soldiers in the Continental Army, and to encourage the Irish to openly rebel against the Crown, just as the Americans had.

March 16: Ground was frozen again. About Sunrise it began to Snow from the North or North a little westerly and continued without intermission the whole day—at the same time cold. Snow abt. 9 Inches deep.

The Washingtons hosted numerous dinner parties and receptions for the officers and their wives, and local couples, particularly state and county politicians, at Ford's mansion. It was considered a great honor for anyone to be invited by the general, and women often sold off livestock and grain to raise money to buy new dresses for the parties. Those not invited peppered those who did attend, and actually met the Washingtons, for all the details they could provide.

One guest was David Thompson, whose mother was thrilled that he had been asked to attend. "Mother was very much interested in my trip to Morristown," he said, "and kept asking how Mrs. Washington carried herself, and the color of the dress she wore—also, did she powder her hair—was her dress too short—did her petticoat show—what men were there...."

Martha's arrival had lifted the general's spirits, as always, especially at the dances in February and late March. He particularly needed a boost in his morale during those frigid weeks at the end of March, and whatever other sustenance he could find to brace himself, because the following week he had to tell the world about the court-martial of Benedict Arnold.

Chapter Thirteen

A HERO TURNED TRAITOR

MORRISTOWN, 1779–80

"If your Excellency thinks me criminal, for Heaven's sake let me be immediately tried and, if found guilty, executed. I want no favour; I ask only justice. If this is denied me by your excellency, I have nowhere to seek it but from the candid public, before whom I shall be under the necessity of laying the whole matter. Let me beg of you Sir, to reconsider, that a set of artful, unprincipled men in office may misrepresent the most innocent actions and, by raising the public clamour against your Excellency, place you in the same situation I am now in."

—Benedict Arnold to George Washington, May 5, 1779

The hot-tempered, sharp-tongued Benedict Arnold, the son of a shipowner who was a colonial governor of Rhode Island, had fallen in love with the military life at sixteen, when he ran away from home to join a company of colonial troops fighting with the British in the French and Indian War. The yen for the sound of musketry and the rumble of cannon never left him, and in the early 1770s he signed on with the New Haven militia and was soon elected its captain. The news of the first battles of the Revolutionary War at Lexington and Concord in nearby Massachusetts in April 1775, brought all of the military passions inside Arnold roaring to the surface. He convinced the seventy men in his militia company to leave New Haven and march to Cambridge with him to join American troops already massing there for further battles against the British.

Dozens of farmers who spotted his column advancing north on the dirt highway stopped their work, grabbed a musket, hastily kissed loved ones good-bye, and joined him. The most prominent was Israel Putnam, "Old Put," who had also fought in the French and Indian War. Putnam, at work in his fields when the regiment passed, rushed to his farmhouse, put on his old uniform, which was a bit tight, pulled his musket from a closet and joined Arnold at the head of the procession.

The American commanders in Boston were glad to have Arnold and anyone else with military experience. Arnold was a compact, muscular man, five feet, eight inches tall, with jet-black hair, blue-gray eyes, and a hooked nose. He was always well-dressed, possessed strong leadership skills, and cut a commanding figure. In short order, the ambitious Arnold fought alongside Ethan Allen and the Green Mountain Boys in their successful effort to capture Fort Ticonderoga, in New York, a victory that startled the British and garnered instant fame for both commanders. Arnold and his regiment then captured a British schooner and sailed it to St. John's, Nova Scotia, where they commandeered warehouses full of supplies. Then, in December 1775, he led an expedition on a harrowing winter journey through little-traveled backwoods areas of Maine into Canada in a failed effort to capture Quebec. In an attack against the well-fortified town, Arnold was badly wounded when a musket ball hit him just below his right knee, causing him to crumple to the ground.

Arnold was promoted to brigadier general for his courage and recovered in Montreal. He was then ordered to join General Horatio Gates's army at the northern tip of Lake Champlain, in New York. Gates told

Arnold to defend the lake the best he could against a British fleet comprised of three large schooners and two hundred gunboats and flatboats with ninety-three cannon on board. Arnold put his men to work building a small navy to do battle with the enemy. Proceeding at a mercurial pace under his supervision of Arnold, the men hastily built three schooners, three galleys, and eight gunboats, carrying a total of seventy cannons. Arnold proudly named one of the boats the *Washington.*

In early October, Arnold, acting as an unofficial admiral, engaged the makeshift American fleet in two battles against the much stronger British ships on the waters of Lake Champlain. The Americans lost, but the damage they inflicted on the British vessels forced their captains to abandon plans to sail any further south and they put into port for repairs and retired, finished for the year.

His bravery was evident again in April 1777, following the British victory at Danbury, Connecticut. Arnold led Continentals, Connecticut militia, and local farmers in a late attack that forced the British out of the area. In that fighting, Arnold had two horses shot out from under him and was shot twice himself, the bullets harmlessly ripping through his uniform collar.

Then, in October 1777, Arnold earned considerable glory at Saratoga. Atop his white horse, Arnold led his men in a succession of fearless charges into withering British fire, forcing victory. Arnold was shot again at Saratoga, this time by a wounded Hessian soldier whose musket ball shattered the American general's right thigh. The ball hit him just inches above his wound from Quebec and would make him a quasi-cripple all of his life, unable to ride a horse and at times barely able to walk.

He was named the military governor of Philadelphia in the summer of 1778. Washington, who had always been his champion, wanted to give him an important job but a post that would keep Arnold off the battlefield for his own protection. In Arnold, Philadelphians had the conqueror of Ticonderoga, the sea-faring daredevil of Lake Champlain, and the hero of Saratoga. But they also had an angry, brooding, surly man whose need for recognition and success was insatiable and whose inability to deal with others was easily discernible. The people also found themselves governed by a man with extravagant tastes and who appeared to spend far more money than he earned on his general's pay. He was also a man, they soon found out, who bent rules.

He had arrived in Philadelphia full of venom toward Congress. He had joined the army as a captain and had been promoted to brigadier general, but he had been denied promotion to major general, a rank he justifiably felt his exploits had earned him. He was turned down because of a foolish Congressional rule that limited the number of major generals from each state. Connecticut already had its allotted number and so Arnold was told he had to wait. He fumed.

He was also angry that Congress had instituted an audit of his expenditures from 1775 to 1778 following rumors from some soldiers that he had misappropriated army money. He claimed he had spent thousands of dollars of his own funds to support his men. It was a routine investigation, actually conducted because of Arnold's messy bookkeeping, but Arnold saw it as another example that Congress was not only preventing him from the success that his victories deserved, but was in fact trying to ruin his career.

Arnold had no love for the president of the Executive Council of Pennsylvania, Joseph Reed. Pennsylvania's civilian chief had written a letter to Charles Lee early in the war in which he severely criticized George Washington at a time when Reed was one of Washington's close aides. The dispute between the two men was only resolved when Reed resigned and went back to Pennsylvania, to Washington's dismay, where he became a Congressman and then head of the State Council. Arnold considered him a coward for leaving the army. After all, Arnold fought on with two bad wounds. Rather ironically, Reed's secret letter to Lee made Arnold feel that Reed was a traitor. Reed and many other civilian leaders in the state feuded often with Arnold.

The general adapted rather easily to his new role and began buying luxurious, custom-made coaches, fine horses, and expensive clothes, and hosted lavish official balls. His tastes very quickly led him into debt. He had great needs for money to pay his bills and to be a success as military governor, certain the post would garner him his long-awaited promotion.

Those needs led him to the charms of Peggy Shippen and, eventually, to the *Charming Nancy*. Shippen, eighteen, was the daughter of a prosperous Loyalist judge in Philadelphia. She had been the target of several suitors from the British Army when it occupied Philadelphia, including Major John Andre. The teenager was enamored by the officers because her dream was to leave Philadelphia, a city she loathed, and move to glamorous London where she could indulge in her fantasy to be a centerpiece of British high society. She met Arnold at a July 4 ball and they were engaged by the end of September, much to her father's chagrin. Officers in the army, and Pennsylvania officials, complained that under Peggy's influence Arnold showed too much favoritism toward local Tories, even giving some illegal passes to leave the city and travel to New York. Reed and Arnold were on a collision course.

That friction exploded over the *Charming Nancy* affair. Arnold and others had privately invested heavily in the *Nancy*, a sturdy and much-traveled cargo ship, a common practice at the time. They planned to split the profits when the merchandise was unloaded and sold. New Jersey privateers had seized the vessel at sea, however, and forced it to dock in Egg Harbor, New Jersey. Arnold, fearful that he would lose the ship, sent a dozen army wagons owned by the state of Pennsylvania to bring the cargo to Philadelphia, where it was sold, which turned out to be the beginning of all of his troubles.

Reed and the council began to keep notes on any and all complaints lodged against Arnold, and in February charged him with eight counts of corruption, starting with using public wagons for private profit concerning the *Charming Nancy*. Some of the accusations were serious: he used Pennsylvania state wagons to transport goods that he planned to sell for personal profit; he gave passes in and out of the city to Tories who sold goods to the British; he schemed with others to reap half the profits from a British ship that did not belong to them; and he wanted to leave the army and head up a fleet of privateers to make a fortune. Some were petty: he asked Congress for federal bodyguards, explaining that he would not trust Pennsylvanians to protect him; he refused to send his barber to cut the hair of an officer of the Pennsylvania council;

he behaved like some European lord; and he was not a servant of the people.

Following an investigation, a Congressional committee dismissed four of the counts but, under pressure from Pennsylvania Council, it ruled that Arnold had to be court-martialed on the others. Few in Congress paid any attention to the matter, which was considered nothing more than the latest round in the Reed-Arnold feud. Newspaper editors paid little heed, either, and those who did were in Arnold's corner, such as the editor of the *Pennsylvania Packet*, who called Arnold "the Hannibal of the American army" and said that he "has fallen into the unmerciful fangs of the Executive Council of Pennsylvania." (Reed hated Arnold with a passion, telling a friend in December 1779 of the charges against him that "a great villain is at last detected.")

Benedict Arnold limped into Norris's Tavern, in Morristown, on December 23, 1779, five days after the latest snowstorm and on the third consecutive day of brutally cold temperatures, for the opening proceedings of the court-martial, whose sessions were continually postponed due to storms and not concluded until the end of January. He reminded everyone that he had left his wife at home in Philadelphia because she was six months pregnant. He made quite an impression on the thirteen man court-martial board, whose president was General Robert Howe. Arnold looked as grand as the commander-in-chief in his elegant blue-and-buff general's uniform. As a reminder of his military honors, he wore on his shoulder the gold epaulet he was given by Washington for bravery at Saratoga; on his waist he wore the short gold sword Washington had given him for heroism.

Arnold would get a fair hearing. Robert Howe had been court-martialed himself, on trumped-up charges, and understood Arnold's feelings. The men on the board all knew about the feuds with Reed. Howe even dismissed one member of the board, General William Maxwell, when Arnold insisted that Maxwell hated him. There were no Pennsylvanians on the board.

Arnold called the charges "false, malicious and scandalous" and, working from careful notes, refuted each in a lengthy, detailed response.

What hurt most of all, he told the court-martial board in the tavern, pacing back and forth in front of them using a cane, his limp pronounced and obvious, was that anyone would question his patriotism.

"When the present necessary war against Great Britain commenced I was in easy circumstance and enjoyed a fair prospect of improving them. The liberties of my country were in danger. The voice of my country called upon all her faithful sons to join in her defense," he told them, looking into the eyes of each as he spoke. "With cheerfulness, I obeyed the call. I sacrificed domestic ease and happiness to the service of my country and in her service have I sacrificed a great part of a handsome fortune. My time, my fortune, my person have been devoted to my country in this war. I was one of the first who appeared in the field and, from that time to the present hour, have not abandoned her service."

Witnesses verified that he had, indeed, ordered Pennsylvania's army wagons used to transport goods. One, Timothy Matlack, even said he had seen Arnold's doctored books, in which wagon trips were covered up. One of his own aides testified that Arnold had told him to use soldiers to shut down stores and then buy up their contents, at a discount, for Arnold, who planned to sell them at a profit later, although there was no evidence that he had done so.

The cocky Arnold was certain that he would be acquitted. He was eager for the trial to end and blamed the entire episode on jealousy by Reed and his enemies in the army. He saw the dismissal of all charges as a public-relations coup that could catapult him to even greater fame. He made tentative plans to have the entire 179-page transcript of his trial—and acquittal—published as a book in order to earn money. He had even asked Washington to make him an admiral in charge of the entire United States Navy as soon as the court-martial was over.

Arnold was, however, found guilty of illegally permitting ships to dock in Philadelphia and of using public wagons to transport his cargo from the *Nancy*. In its findings, the court said that as military governor, the general should have shown far more "delicacy in high station in which he served." Arnold was acquitted on charges that he gave passes to Loyalists for illicit reasons and that he closed shops in order to confiscate their goods and sell them at a profit (decades later, however, much evidence was uncovered to suggest that he did so).

The court-martial board recommended merely an official reprimand from General Washington, a slap on the wrist, something to keep Reed and those who did not like the tempestuous Arnold happy. The mildest possible punishment would also be a signal to Arnold that the commander-in-chief still supported him, despite his misadventures.

Washington was satisfied with the outcome of the trial. In an effort to make the sentence less of a sting, Washington did not even mail the written reprimand to Arnold or to Congress or issue it as a separate circular. He merely had it printed in the daily General Orders for April 6, sliding it in between a request for a man to clean horses and an order to deliver firewood, pretty much dismissing it.

Washington had written several drafts of the reprimand. He wanted to be stern but he did not want Arnold to think he was unduly upset. "The Commander in Chief would have been much happier in an occasion of bestowing commendations on an officer who has rendered such distinguished service to his country as Major General Arnold," he wrote, noting Arnold's heroism at Saratoga and five years of service. "But in the present, a sense of duty and a regard to candor oblige him to declare that he considers his conduct in the instance of the permit as peculiarly reprehensible, both in a civil and military view, and in the affair of the wagons as imprudent and improper."

Later, in a personal letter, Washington reminded Arnold that high-profile generals had to be careful about their actions. "Our profession is the character of all. Even the shadow of a fault tarnishes the luster of our finest achievements. The least inadvertence may rob us of the public favor. You should have been guarded and temperate in your deportment toward your fellow citizens."

Washington was pleased with the wording of the reprimand and letter and was certain that Arnold, so lightly chastised, would now continue as one of his best generals. The commander-in-chief had completely misjudged Benedict Arnold, though. He did not understand the fury that still raged within Arnold over Congressional delay in his promotion to major general, Congress's scrutiny of his personal records, and the Morristown trial. Washington failed to see that Arnold truly did feel that he had lost his personal fortune in the war and felt that he did not have enough money to give his wife the high-society life she desired. And, perhaps most injudicious, the commander-in-chief did not understand Peggy Shippen. Not at all. He viewed her as just another woman from a Tory family who had fallen in love with an American officer and would change her politics, as had so many others, such as Lucy Knox.

And he misinterpreted his own relationship with Arnold. The suspicious, hot-headed, and sometime paranoid Arnold had come to see just about all of the important men in his life as enemies. Reed and his cronies had conspired to bring him to trial. The members of Congress had delved into his personal finances. Gates had refused to acknowledge his bravery at Saratoga. Washington, in his eyes, was the only one who had befriended him, trusted him and valued his service to his country, the only man who saw him as an untarnished patriot. It was Washington who had personally complained to Congress when it overlooked Arnold for promotion. It was the commander who made certain he *was* promoted the following year. Washington bragged to people about Arnold's bravery at Saratoga. Washington named him military governor. Washington, unlike many others, heartily approved of his engagement to Peggy. And now his mentor, benefactor, and best friend had betrayed him, too.

The court-martial, and Washington's reprimand, pushed Arnold over the edge. He had been solicited for help by the British in May 1779, but had not responded. Now, following Washington's betrayal, he felt free to talk to British Colonel John Andre about treason.

Washington had placed Arnold in charge of American defenses at West Point, on the Hudson River. Andre, a personable young officer, asked Arnold to give the British all of the plans for the defense of West Point, plus details on the size of American forces there, so that an attack could be launched. Arnold agreed to do so, but Andre was captured following a series of botched communications. He was out of uniform, with the plans on him, and charged as a spy. Suspicion fell on Arnold, and

Washington and his guard galloped to Arnold's home. A very frightened Arnold left his wife Peggy alone in their bedroom and fled, escaping on horseback just moments before Washington arrived. Peggy then threw a fit, weeping and wailing and crawling about the floor of her room, pounding her fists against the hard wooden floor as Washington entered. She screamed that soldiers were trying to kill her child and, hysterical, claimed she knew nothing about any treasonous plot or the whereabouts of her husband.

Instead of arresting her, Washington, upset by her dramatics, that others claimed were staged, let her go back to Philadelphia alone. He sent men out to find Arnold, but the traitor had too much of a head start. Arnold made it to British lines and became a British general, a rather ineffective one. His wife joined him after the war and they moved to London, where neither received the warm reception they anticipated. Despite arguments from his aides that the likable Andre was an officer and not a spy (anyone out of uniform was considered a spy and could be executed; a uniformed officer had to be jailed as a prisoner of war), a furious Washington had Andre hanged. Later, Washington authorized a raiding party to capture Arnold, threatening to hang him, too, but it failed.

But there was still another lesson to be learned from the sordid Arnold affair. Washington had complained since the beginning of the war that he was the supreme commander of all allied forces, yet it was men in Congress, few with any military background, who initially appointed and promoted the generals in the army who served beneath him. It was state legislatures who appointed middle-ranking officers, such as colonels, again with no approval from Washington. This system allowed the appointment and promotions of incompetent men, such as Thomas Conway to inspector general in 1778, to be sure, but it also prevented the promotions of highly skilled and qualified men such as Arnold. The substantial discontent that had spread through the army for years was fueled by the anger over rank by many of those disappointed officers. It was one of the major reasons why many officers resigned or deserted and even considered mutiny. None of his generals had betrayed their country, as

Arnold shortly would, but all of them were justifiably unhappy over the system.

Washington did little about it during the war beyond plead for certain promotions and urge Congress to turn down others, but after the war he would work diligently to ensure that in the future the country's most responsible civilian officer holder, the president, was also the commander-in-chief of the army. Later, the president would approve all promotions as the commander-in-chief and run the army, with the advice and assistance of his generals, not Congress. Having the national executive as the head of the army would also prevent incompetent or seditious generals from making ruinous decisions or decisions based solely on military or personal goals and not the greater public good. And, since the army was the symbol of the nation, in wartime or in peace, then the president should be its leader.

The Cupboard Is Bare

Ever since the army had moved to Morristown in December 1779, New Jersey farmers and merchants had complained to local officials that Washington had brought into their midst a virtual city of thirteen thousand men, along with hundreds of horses, that consumed millions of pounds of food. How could any small region of farmers supply that much food, especially in the middle of one of the most severe winters in memory? Pennsylvanians at Valley Forge could not. The residents had done their very best, they pleaded, and simply had no more to give.

As Governor Clinton told Washington of New York's supplies that April, "this state is so exhausted that I am persuaded there is not more grain and meal left in possession of the farmers than a bare competency for the support of the inhabitants until the new crop comes in" and that, of more food, that it was "simply not to be had."

Every five or six weeks food would run out and, in an endless litany of pleas, the commander-in-chief would again have to persuade his New Jersey neighbors to sell whatever food they had left on credit. Once again, on March 7, the army began to starve. The Board of War begged the different states to find supplies somewhere, warning that "unless the speediest relief is afforded, it is by no means improbable that the army will be obliged to disband."

By April 2, following a storm that left nine inches of snow on the ground, the provisions crisis was again at a peak and Washington wrote a quartermaster that "we have not at this day one ounce of meat fresh, or salt, in the magazine, and supposing all the supplies of this article within any reasonable distance ever collected, they would not amount to more than three or four days consumption…"

April 2: Hard frost—clear & very cold—wind fresh from the No. West & continued so all day. Toward evening it began to freeze hard. The Snow but little dissipated.

Now he recognized the plight of his neighbors, just as he had toward the end of the Valley Forge winter. "We may possibly, with the greatest difficulty, subsist for a very short time upon this almost totally exhausted country, but we ought not, nor must not depend upon it for anything more. If we do, it must be by depriving the inhabitants of what barely remains sufficient for their own support."

On April 3, Greene informed the commander that their food would run out on or about April 10. Then, to everyone's surprise, substantial food supplies somehow arrived in Trenton, sixty miles away. But the quartermaster there had no wagons to send the food to Morristown.

And so Washington again turned to the local magistrates and pleaded with them to persuade hundreds of local farmers to drive their wagons to Trenton with soldiers to pick up the food and bring it back. He was blunt. He told the local civilian leaders that he could only pay in Continental scrip, loan certificates, and credit, and that he realized how depreciated scrip had become. He told them, too, with great honesty, that he did not expect the country's finances to improve—at all. They simply had to come to his rescue. This time he did not threaten martial law, but told them carefully, "Occasions will probably more than once occur in this period which will call for exertions of virtue and patriotism from the people…I am confident that these will be never be wanting."

What he needed, the general explained to the county leaders, was a large armada of wagons, two hundred or more, to travel some sixty miles down narrow highways to Trenton, get the food and then drive back—and hope that they were not trapped in a snowstorm as they traveled. Could they help him yet again?

The following morning, April 15, Washington rode to the village green to inspect the wagons. He had no idea how many of the beleaguered farmers would be able to come to his aide in this latest crisis. He had asked for two hundred wagons, hoping for one hundred. As he reached the green, he saw a long line of sturdy wooden farm wagons, as far as he could see, more than three hundred in all, with warmly dressed local drivers, ready for the trip. The wagon train traveled to Trenton and came back the next day, returning under thick gray clouds as a snowstorm threatened. Once again, Washington's persuasive powers had saved the army from starvation. The tons of food brought to camp would keep the army going—for awhile.

April 15: Cold & raw—Wind very fresh from the Eastward. Weather lowering with appearances of Snow or Rain.

Becoming a Diplomat

Despite the food shortages, some desertions, and resignations, the troops remained at their posts, shivering and hungry, but still there. The determination of the officers and men to remain with the army, despite the hardships of the brutal winter, impressed many, but no one held these men in higher esteem than their commander. In early April, the general was confronted by a Congressman who suggested that a general should not be given a field command. Washington took the opportunity to write Congress a dramatic letter extolling the patriotism of all of his officers and men. "There is no set of men in the United States…that have made the same sacrifice of their interest in support of the common cause as the officers of the American army. That nothing but love of their country, of honor, and a desire of seeing their labors crowned with success could possibly induce them to continue one moment in service," he said. "That no officer can live upon his pay; that hundreds having spent their all in their scanty public allowance have resigned because they could no longer support themselves; that numbers are at this moment rendered unfit for duty for want of clothing, while the rest are wasting their property and some of them verging fast to the gulf of poverty and distress."

The commander-in-chief decided to stage a campaign to garner Congressional support for the army, just as he had done at Valley Forge. He again requested that a Congressional committee visit Morristown and that its members live there for several weeks in order to see firsthand the seriousness of conditions. The Congressional sojourn to Chester County had been successful in 1778 and could be again. Washington secretly lobbied some Congressmen to get his way, particularly his close friends Schuyler and Joseph Jones of Virginia. But he drafted Hamilton to perform most of the public courting.

The commander did this for two reasons. First, the loquacious aide was a far better writer than the general. He was expected to weave literary magic and he did, peppering targeted delegates such as James Duane with letters that outlined an army at wit's end: "For God's sake, my dear sir, engage Congress to adopt it [committee]. We have not a moment to lose," Hamilton wrote in his usual breathless style.

There was a second, more important reason. Washington could not ask Congress to authorize the committee to turn over even more power to him in this emergency; Hamilton could. In another use of "hidden hand" politics, Washington had Hamilton do his work for him. In persuasive language, Hamilton let Congressmen know that the general needed additional support and strength if he was to put together an alliance with the French and strike at the British. "The fate of America," said Hamilton, "is perhaps suspended on the issue; if we are found unprepared, it must disgrace us…defeating the good intentions of our allies, and losing the happiest opportunity we ever have had to save ourselves."

This tactic of using others to achieve his goals remained effective throughout the war and, as president, Washington would resort to it often, using Congressman James Madison as his secret emissary to the legislature.

Congress saw much merit in Washington's request for a committee. The three men they selected were one suggested by the General himself, Philip Schuyler, plus Nathaniel Peabody of Massachusetts and South Carolina planter John Matthews, who turned out to be the most sympathetic of the trio. The three arrived in winter camp in early May 1780, and soon produced a report that the general might have written himself. In it, they explained, yet again, that the army suffered greatly.

The winter camp was busy with visitors. The middle of April had seen the arrival of the most important visitors to any of Washington's winter camps: the new French Minister to America, Anne-Cesar; Chevalier de la Luzerne, accompanied by his secretary, Francois Barbe-Marbois; and Spanish diplomat Don Juan de Miralles. They arrived on April 19th to conduct an official inspection of the American army and to confer with General Washington and his officers in an attempt to determine if France and Spain should begin to formally supply ships, troops, and cannon to the Americans.

It was another opportunity for Washington to work as a high-level state diplomat to advance the foreign-affairs goals of the country, power given to him in 1777, as he had in talks with these ambassadors the previous winter at Bound Brook. It was another chance, too, to add foreign policy to his ever-broadening scope of responsibilities, always enhancing his own position as both military and civilian leader of the United States.

As such, the general understood that these important diplomats, whose help was needed to win the war, could not arrive in Morristown to find a disorganized band of rebels living in the woods. They had to find the army of a great nation and they had to be treated as the leaders of great empires themselves. To do so, Washington made their arrival an unprecedented event, despite a light drizzle of rain that fell most of the day and a sharp northwest wind.

The diplomats were met about ten miles from the winter camp by two hundred men dressed in their finest uniforms. They accompanied the diplomats' carriage for five miles, when they were greeted by an equally splendid-looking corps of officers led by a smiling George Washington and all of his aides. The commander-in-chief asked the diplomats to leave their carriages and ride to Morristown on two elegantly appointed horses. In the village, the parade ended in front of an ensemble of two battalions of men and hundreds of local residents who had been asked to attend. Thirteen cannons were fired in a salute as they arrived.

Five days later, following visits to Jockey Hollow and long discussions and dinners with Washington and his aides, (especially Hamilton, who spoke fluent French), the diplomats were treated to two days of military drills and parades held on the village green and on the Jockey Hollow parade ground; an elegant ball was held in honor of the visit. This time the general had some cooperation from the weather, which was crisp but fair.

April 24th: Wind in the same place but not fresh; day clear & pleasant but rather cool.

The military reviews were observed from a large, hastily constructed wooden platform upon which Washington and all of his generals sat with the diplomats. They were joined by Governor and Mrs. Livingston and several local officials and their wives. Baron Von Steuben organized the military maneuvers, all done with the timing and precision of the finest European regiments. The French were impressed. Washington's efforts to make them see the Americans as a powerful army, like any of those on the continent, had succeeded. Even more successful were his efforts to make them view him as a national leader capable of hosting reviews, parades, dinners, and balls for foreign dignitaries in the same manner they would be treated at any European court. Days later, Luzerne reaffirmed his country's full financial, political, and military support, including troops and warships, for the Americans.

Washington had succeeded, he knew, because he was able to offer all the trappings of a European court, with himself serving as head of state, stopping short of any appearance of monarchy itself. His ability to appear as a royal personage, and still be seen as a Virginia farmer, would be just as valuable to him as the nation's chief executive later as it was during the winters of the war.

Miralles did not have the opportunity to recommend anything. The suave, impeccably dressed Spanish official became violently ill during his stay in Morristown and, despite prolonged efforts by army surgeons and local doctors, died on April 29 following days of care at the Ford mansion. Again, Washington acted as a civilian head of state and insisted that the Spaniard could not simply be interred in a local cemetery. He was a Spanish diplomat and had to be given a full state funeral. It was important that America act like any great nation in burying a foreign official who died on its soil. Miralles's body was dressed elegantly in his best clothes and powdered wig, with his hands adorned with all of his diamond rings and his diamond-studded gold watch. His body was placed inside an ornately designed coffin draped in black velvet, which was carried by six uniformed army pallbearers. Hundreds of officers and soldiers, all in full dress uniform, joined by a large contingent of local residents, county magistrates, and some members of Congress summoned by the commander-in-chief, comprised the mile-long funeral procession, led by a mournful George Washington—now acting as head of state as well as commander of the army. The Spanish official was buried in the cemetery behind the Presbyterian church.

The elegant state funeral in the tiny New Jersey village, planned so carefully by the general, was another example of the lengths he went to in order to show foreign nations that America was an independent nation, whose leaders would bury foreign diplomats with the same pomp as they would be interred at home or in any other nation where they had died. A week later there was a special funeral mass for Miralles in Philadelphia, which was attended by the members of Congress. Spanish officials were very thankful for the funeral.

Despite the reassurances of help from the diplomats, Washington was still fearful that his time was running out. The Americans had been at war for nearly five years and the fighting had taken its toll on the army and the country. The army was now reeling from crisis to crisis and the men were miserable and angry. They were refusing to reenlist or were deserting; by the end of the winter, one thousand soldiers would be gone. The army had no food and no money. Washington had faced the starvation of the entire army several times during the Valley Forge winter and several more times in Morristown. Thousands of men had died and thousands more had been taken prisoner. The army could not hold out any longer if it remained bankrupt and continued to be restrained by state laws and Congressional indecision. The only solution, several influential members of Congress believed, was to make Washington the absolute dictator of America—again, they urged him to declare martial law. Others suggested that Washington head up a three- or four-member committee, the others all Congressmen, that would be given dictatorial powers to run the country. Washington's job as dictator would be to impress food, clothing, and other goods from the citizens without paying; prevent desertions or resignations from the army by force; institute a draft; give orders to state, county, and local civilian officials; overrule civilian court decisions; and oversee the spending of America's millions on the war effort.

The notion of the popular Washington as an American Caesar was the centerpiece of considerable attention. Congressional delegate Ezekial Cornell and others thought it was a sound solution to the growing problems of the country. "The necessity of appointing General Washington Dictator of America is again talked of as the only means under God by which we can be saved from destruction," he said. Washington, vehemently against martial law, much less a role as an American emperor, refused to even comment on the idea.

What Washington desired most was the promised full military commitment from the King of France, Louis XVI. His government had secretly shipped supplies to the Americans since the winter of 1777. Enthused with the American victory at Saratoga in October 1777, and lobbied with great charm by Benjamin Franklin in Paris, the French government had signed the Treaty of Amity and Commerce on February 6, 1778, which brought about springtime attacks by British warships on French frigates. In June, seeking retaliation, France formally declared war against England and entered the conflict in North America on the side of the Continental Congress. Spain also entered the war against England in the spring of 1779, but offered little military or financial help to the United States.

The Americans required ships, troops, and guns—in addition to a treaty—from France. The French had continually stalled. Then, finally, on May 10, the Marquis de Lafayette arrived in Morristown with the news that France was sending eight thousand troops under General Jean-Baptiste Rochambeau, along with a flotilla of war ships, to join forces with the Continental Army in New Jersey to defeat the British. The ships should have already departed French ports, filled with the veteran soldiers, Lafayette said, and would arrive in June or early July 1780.

Lafayette's news elated Congress and the commander-in-chief. Washington sent a letter to General Benjamin Lincoln in Charleston to tell him that the French fleet would probably anchor there sometime in mid-June to protect him from the British. But Washington's real excitement was reserved for his long-delayed attack on New York City, in the planning stages ever since the British chased him out of Manhattan in the fall of 1776, four long years ago. He could use the French fleet to bombard Manhattan and then add his own force of thirteen thousand men to the eight thousand promised French troops for an all-out assault that would, he hoped, result in the defeat of the British army there. The seizure of New York and Sir Henry Clinton's army would be a crushing military blow to England, but a far more devastating public-relations strike. Even the staunchest supporters of the American war in Parliament could not continue the costly enterprise if the Americans could take New York and imprison Sir Henry Clinton and his eight thousand soldiers.

The commander was glad just to see Lafayette again. His young friend had not been merely a romantic adventurer who, like so many other French officers, fought for a few months and then returned to the dining halls of Paris, as some Americans had predicted upon his arrival in the summer of 1777. Lafayette, wounded at Brandywine, had fought hard with the Continental Army and weathered the debilitating winter at Valley Forge with it. He had aided the cause considerably while in France and had been instrumental in obtaining an army as well as French warships. Washington needed all of the men he could muster, from France and America. The Americans were also thankful for Lafayette's family fortune. The French general had not only served without pay and shouldered all of his own expenses, but from 1777 through 1780 in public and private, contributed nearly a quarter of a million dollars to the American cause.

Mutiny

What genuinely worried the commander-in-chief, though, was a mutiny in the army. Could the Continental Army hold out for another six weeks, until the French fleet arrived? How long could his men live under the dire conditions that had plagued them since the beginning of December? How long can an army live on half rations, and sometimes no rations? How long can a soldier survive with just a thin coat, tattered shirt, and ripped breeches for protection against fierce storms and freezing temperatures? This fear of revolt had troubled him since the middle of December, when the first of the twenty-six storms battered Morristown. He learned then that one brigade of irate troops at Stony Point, New York, without bread for seven days, was "on the verge of mutiny," according to General Heath, and that two-thirds of the troops in another brigade simply went home.

On February 5, 1780, Washington received a disturbing personal letter signed by dozens of soldiers at Poughkeepsie:

> Our own wants and the sufferings of our distressed families loudly calls on us to quit a service which although of the utmost necessity promises nothing better than an increase of misery. Already scarce supportable, and we hope that our legislature have provided such gentlemen our successors, who from an equal zeal for the cause and love to the service and from being possessed of independent fortunes, may be able to render their country more eminent service. We having given that body timely notice that under present circumstances, our services could not extend beyond this day. We therefore beg your excellency to accept our resignations and grant us leave to retire from service.

And on March 24, several dozen starving soldiers from the New York camp near Fishkill deserted, complaining of food, and troops had to be sent out to look for them.

On April 3, yet another day when the ground was frozen solid and a northwest wind cut through the village of Morristown, the commander-in-chief wrote a melancholy letter to Congress's president Samuel Huntington, warning him of possible rebellion in the ranks. He said of his soldiers that "in their present state they are actually suffering every inconvenience, in fruitless expectation of a remedy that will perhaps never come" and warned that "there has never been a stage in the war in which the dissatisfaction has been so general or alarming. It has lately in particular instances worn features of a very dangerous complexion." Washington then recapped all the grievances of the men, well known to Congress, and warned: "They murmur, brood over their discontents and have lately shown a disposition to enter into seditious combination."

Nathanael Greene, too, feared some kind of uprising and told Jeremiah Wadsworth in early May that "the soldiers are neither fed or paid and are getting sour amazingly fast. Such a temper never appeared in our army before. God knows how it will end."

The mutiny that Washington feared began after dinner on May 25, following yet another week of meager food supplies. Two Connecticut regiments, comprising eight hundred men, took their muskets and left their huts. They told other soldiers in Jockey Hollow that they were starving and had not been paid in more than five months. Any money they did possess, or their families had saved, had been rendered worthless by depreciation. The men had had enough.

Private Joseph Martin was one of the mutineers and, like the rest, he was simply tired of everything. "They were truly patriots; they loved their country and they had already suffered everything short of death in its cause. And now, after such extreme hardships to give up all was too much, but to starve to death was too much also," he said in describing the surly mood of the men that night.

The mutineers warned other soldiers not to interfere. Colonel Jonathan Meigs tried to stop them, but backed off when one of the men struck him. Several other officers tried to talk them out of the uprising, but to no avail. The angry men began to leave, amid much shouting and cursing. Colonel Walter Stewart of the Pennsylvania Line, in quarters nearby, organized several hundred troops, weapons drawn, and had the Connecticut men surrounded. They surrendered without any shots fired and returned to their huts.

The mutiny frightened the high command. "We are apprehensive [they] will run through the whole line like wild fire," said Greene in a letter to the governor of Rhode Island the next day.

The commander-in-chief was angry at the men from Connecticut, but understood their motivation. "Their sufferings were too great; they wanted present relief and some present substantial recompense for their service," Washington told Congress, explaining the mutiny, and added that the uprising "has given me infinitely more concern than anything that has ever happened." He could not bring himself to order a wholesale execution of the men and only ordered one man, a leader of the revolt, executed; the rest were pardoned.

The mutiny had shaken Washington. The next day, he sent a letter to Joseph Reed, again pleading for supplies and urging Reed to pressure Congress to curb inflation. It was one of the most depressing letters Washington wrote during the war. He told Reed that he would never believe the terrible conditions that existed. Despondent, he wrote that "indeed, I have almost ceased to hope. The country in general is in such a state of insensibility and indifferent to its interests that I dare not flatter myself with any change for the better."

Worse, he complained to Reed, the mutiny came just as America finally had assurances of substantial aid from France. America's inability to supply the army and hold it together would be, he said, "proof that motives of honor, public good and even self-preservation have lost their influence upon our minds. The court of France has made glorious efforts for our deliverance, and we disappoint its intentions...we must become contemptible in the eyes of all mankind." Washington added that the French might even withdraw their aid when they found out that America's commitment was so tentative.

If Washington thought his spirits would rebound with time after the mutiny had been put down, he was mistaken. Just before Christmas, Clinton and Cornwallis had taken an army of eighty-five hundred soldiers aboard ninety transports, escorted by fourteen men of war, to Charleston, South Carolina. The journey had been constantly interrupted by bad weather and storms, which forced the fleet to anchor at different harbors on its way south, making the voyage far longer than anticipated. During the first week of May, the British blasted their way through four ships that formed all of the feeble American Naval defense of the Charleston area and staged a successful landing several miles from the wealthy southern seaport. General Benjamin Lincoln had only 3,300 men, eight hundred of them untrained militia. He had failed to formulate any workable land or sea defense of the city and was trying to formulate yet another plan to save the town when he was informed the British had landed. Lincoln could not successfully attack the British and was unable to flee. The general and his entire army were captured in a devastating defeat on May 12.

Washington, aware of the impact the loss of Charleston would cause, quickly sent out notes dismissing its importance, just as he had done following the aborted Staten Island attack. He even called it a blessing in disguise because it meant that Britain's forces were now divided and would be easier to conquer. Hamilton parroted Washington's feelings in his correspondence, but added a telling line at the end of a letter to the Marquis de Barbe-Marbois: "If it is a blessing, 'tis a blessing in a very strange disguise."

The Americans, who had boasted of their captures of British armies at Trenton and Saratoga, had now lost an entire army of their own, and a large one representing more than a quarter of all American forces. Cornwallis now controlled a key city from which to launch attacks throughout the Carolinas, and as far north as Washington's own Virginia. The British now possessed large armies in the South and Mid-Atlantic regions and seemed intent on capturing seaports up and down the coast. The fall of the world-renown city of Charleston was a considerable public-relations setback for the United States.

Washington's downplaying of Charleston's capture did not work this time. One Congressional delegate, upon hearing the news, said that "the catastrophe is indeed disastrous" and another called it "a severe blow to us." And in Pennsylvania, the executive council, fearful of a British invasion, voted to give Joseph Reed the power to declare martial law whenever he believed it was necessary.

Morale in the army was lower than at any time since Valley Forge. Martha Washington would leave camp in mid-June, and upon her arrival at Mount Vernon tell friends that her husband was despondent. Lafayette wrote on the last day of May that the army was in shambles: "An army that is reduced to nothing, that wants provisions, that has not one of the necessary means to make war, such is the situation wherein I found our troops and however prepared I could have been to this unhappy sight, by our past distresses, I confess I had no idea of such an extremity."

Washington was disconsolate, despite the news of French soldiers, ships, and supplies. He worried that the number of French troops would be less than expected and not enough to make a real difference in his plans. He wrote Congress on May 31 that he could win the war with an all-attack on New York City, but to be successful he needed a total of thirty-five thousand troops, perhaps more, including the Frenchmen. To raise that many troops, Congress would have to double its recruitment efforts and find new monies for bounties, soldier salaries, and twice as many supplies. He knew that they could not do that; they could not even pay for supplies for his current force of thirteen thousand men. His gloom deepened.

There had been some joy in the winter of 1779–80. The number of men who died in the terrible winter, when freezing temperatures and the lack of food had been continuing problems, had been less than one hundred out of an army of thirteen thousand, or less than 1 percent. It was a remarkably low fatality rate in a winter that was far more severe than that of 1777–78, which claimed more than two thousand lives at Valley Forge.

The number was so small because this time Washington, who never made the same mistake twice, made certain that the huts were built properly, the logs and the materials between them making the living quarters airtight to prevent cold and dampness. The chimneys all worked and heated the huts. The city had been designed with hundreds of fire pits to keep men warm. These conditions prevented the soldiers from being vulnerable to pneumonia or typhus, as they had been at Valley Forge. The numerous hospitals were better built and staffed and located in camp. Mindful of the spread of disease in open wards at Valley Forge, Washington ordered doctors to build hospitals with large isolation wards to keep infected men separate.

Washington, a good listener, had learned much about medical care during the disastrous winter at Valley Forge, and this time took immediately steps to prevent another medical catastrophe. He rejected Henry Knox's request to move his artillery corps back into the school southwest of Jockey Hollow that he had built the previous winter. Instead, Washington turned the large academic hall of the school and its other buildings into a huge hospital complex, run by Dr. James Tilton, and approved Tilton's request to make the main hall and several other buildings isolation wards. Now soldiers with typhus would be treated together, separate from everyone else, and those suffering from pneumonia would recover in a different building. Those with other diseases would be housed together, in some other large log building built specifically as an isolation ward. Numerous hospitals were built in camp to prevent long wagon trips to converted hospitals miles away, a real problem at Valley Forge.

Now, too, Washington persuaded dozens of doctors living in the Morristown area to assist his staff of physicians in running his hospitals and administering to soldiers in their huts. The commander made certain that the hospitals had ample food, clothing, and straw for their patients. Doctors now had more medical textbooks and supplies.

The army had not been in any major battles prior to its arrival at Morristown and the hospitals did not fill up immediately with bleeding and wounded men, or men recovering from wounds inflicted months before. The absence of any treatment for the wounded was a major factor in the low death rate at Morristown.

There was personal happiness, too. Again, as in every winter, Martha had traveled to camp and spent nearly five months with him. The dance assemblies had lifted the spirits of his officers. He, Martha, and others had shared the joy of the Livingstons on April 12, 1780, when their second oldest daughter was married at their winter camp farmhouse, and with the Greenes when their baby was born.

But there had been personal problems, too. The anger displayed by Benedict Arnold following the verdict in his trial had hurt the general. Having failed to kidnap Washington on January 31, the British had made a later attempt to kidnap Governor Livingston at his home near camp. The attempt had failed, but it reminded Washington that while he might continually escape capture, protected by his large army, some of his close friends might not (the British did manage to kidnap a Bergen County justice).

The malaise that depressed Washington was not isolated. Despondency seemed to permeate the homes and businesses of everyone in America as that horrible winter began to recede, whether they were generals, delegates to Congress, or ordinary citizens. Many in public life could not believe that the army, and the nation, had come so far in the quest for independence and yet it still seemed beyond their grasp.

In a sorrowful letter to the governor of Connecticut that winter, Congressional delegate Oliver Ellsworth recounted all of the revolution's woes—recruiting, clothing, food, depreciated currency—and informed him that the national government had once again run out of money. Then, in a plea aimed more at the Almighty than the governor, he implored, "Can it, sir, be the design of heaven that has roused us to exertions thus far, and armed mighty nations for our support, and brought us within sight of the promised [land] to leave us after all to destruction?"

A People's Army, Born to Fight

In London, Lord George Germain, rejuvenated following the fall of Charleston, now saw an opportunity to crush the states and win the war. He wrote Sir Henry Clinton that all indications seemed to be that the American public was tired of the endless conflict and that the collapse of Charleston would be such a blow to American morale that total victory would soon be in hand. The enemy, which had held up so long and so well, was finally vulnerable. "All private letters from the rebel countries are filled with representations of the general distress and sufferings of the people, the discontents of the troops and a universal wish for peace. The middle provinces are said to be so disinclined to support the Congress that no recruits are to be had and the militia will not submit to be drafted," he told Clinton on May 3.

Washington expected an attack on his northern armies from the British, brimming with confidence after the capture of Lincoln's army. They would want to add another major victory, perhaps the final extermination of the Continental Army that had eluded their clutches for five years. He knew, too, that General Wilhelm Knyphausen, commanding the remaining eight thousand British troops in New York, had learned of the May 25 mutiny and possessed extensive information concerning the American supply nightmares.

The Hessian general, left in charge by Clinton, had been studying the Americans for months. He was convinced that the Continental Army was fatigued from their grueling winter, starving, ill-clothed, and bad-tempered. The mutiny was the most telling evidence of army unhappiness. Knyphausen, relying on loyalists and spies, also believed that the New Jersey militia would not support the Continentals with much force and those men who did report would not fight well. The German general had come to believe, too, that a surprise attack on Morristown would catch Washington off guard, that he had no effective early-warning system, and that he would not be able to mobilize his men to meet a forceful attack of a large force.

But Washington was ready. The American commander just did not know whether the British would strike at Morristown or at West Point. Following the arrival of the news of the Charleston loss, he had quickly put the garrison at West Point on alert. The general then ordered all of his signal fires between Morristown and New York checked in case they had to be lit if a British invasion of New Jersey began. Lookouts were posted twenty-four hours per day and their number increased. On June 2, Washington asked Governor Livingston to call out the entire New Jersey militia. Responding with inordinate speed, the full militia was on alert by June 5. A large portion of the New Jersey brigade was sent to the Springfield and Elizabeth area as a defensive line in case of an attack.

And so, on June 6, the Hessian commander began a quiet midnight ferryboat crossing of the Arthur Kill and landed six thousand soldiers, accompanied by a few hundred loyalist troops, in just a few hours. The men marched through the still of the night to Elizabeth, confident that they could overwhelm the few troops they expected to meet there, who would be sleeping, and then press on over the Watchung Mountains to Morristown, surprising Washington by mid morning.

Elizabeth was not vulnerable, however, and the British were met head on by very wide-awake troops commanded by Colonel Elias Dayton, who had been waiting for them. They held their ground for awhile, exchanging long, rapid rounds of loud musket fire that lit up the night, then retreated westward to Connecticut Farms, (the community of Union, New Jersey today), to join forces with the New Jersey Brigade under General William Maxwell, which was positioned in front of a Presbyterian Meeting House in the village. The British attacked in full force, but were repeatedly beaten back.

The Americans at Springfield fought well and managed to hold out for more than three hours, standing up to thick hails of thousands of musket balls and hundreds of cannonballs that exploded with frightening force nearby. Overwhelmed, they were eventually forced to retreat out of the town and form a new defensive line. The British followed them. In the chaos, someone shot and killed Hannah Caldwell, the wife of the Rev. Caldwell, as she sat in her home. A villager who saw the incident claimed it was not a battlefield accident, but murder by the British.

By early morning, hundreds of militia were swarming into Springfield, men and boys, including Ashbel Green, now seventeen, the son of the Rev. Jacob Green, his musket slung over his shoulder. The militia joined Continental troops and made a stand at the edge of a thicket of trees behind a narrow wooden bridge on the Rahway River south of Springfield. At the same time, hundreds of frightened residents of Springfield and nearby communities loaded their possessions into wagons and ox carts, piling their children in with them, and began to flee westward, the carts kicking up clouds of dusts and dirt.

By 8:30 A.M. Washington had sent off a dozen or more couriers with orders to militia companies throughout the state, urging all to march to Springfield as quickly as possible. Knowing that the militia fought best on unconventional terrain, Washington told his generals to place their members in the woods for best effect. The general then sent dispatches to different brigades and regiments, ordering them into a defensive line near Springfield. He would rely on the regulars and the militia from different counties, all commanded by Nathanael Greene, to hold off Knyphausen.

The Morris County militia was led by Sylvanus Seely, who shouted profanities every few seconds as he tried to force his men to move faster as they traversed an open meadow within the range of a string of British soldiers and cannon near Springfield. The men crossed the meadow as the Redcoats opened up, sprinting for cover behind rocks, trees, and bushes. They came under terrific fire, an assault the men there that morning would remember all of their lives. "Cannon ball and grape shot…swept over us like a storm of hail, the ground trembling under us at every step. No thunder storm I have ever witnessed, either in loudness of sound or the shaking of the earth, equaled what I saw and felt in crossing that meadow," said seventeen-year-old Ashbel Green as an old man when he recalled the morning.

The Morris militia, in a long defensive line with other militia and regulars and supported by a single cannon, using trees, rock outcroppings, and bushes for cover, held off the British for hours, forcing them to retreat and abandon all hopes of crushing Washington's army.

As Knyphausen pulled back, Washington's division of the army arrived in town and aligned itself in a north/south arc across the Watchung Mountains to await another attack, as Lord Stirling and several hundred soldiers reinforced Maxwell's line. The following morning Washington ordered Colonel Edward Hand to attack the British with 1,500 men; Hand drove the Redcoats back to the eastern tip of Elizabeth, where both armies then skirmished for several days before the British returned to New York.

On June 17, eleven days after British and Hessian troops had invaded New Jersey, Sir Henry Clinton and his warships arrived back in New York from Charleston. Clinton now decided to launch a second assault. Washington had always seen West Point as the target for Clinton, who could sail his ships directly up the Hudson, loaded with thousands of troops. The American commander took two thousand men and began to march north to meet him there, but he moved cautiously, ready to turn around if the British again attacked Morristown via Springfield. He had couriers ready to bring him any news.

Morristown *was* the target of Clinton and Knyphausen, and at dawn seven thousand Redcoats again descended on Connecticut Farms. Washington's well-placed alarm guns were fired the moment the British were spotted, and warning beacon fires were lit. Within minutes, militia in the Morristown area began to mobilize. They had been waiting for another chance to engage the British, many of them aroused by a fiery June 14 newspaper story about the murder of Hannah Caldwell. By noon, five thousand militia were in the Springfield area, linking up with the twenty-five hundred Continentals under Nathanael Greene. Again, a well-prepared defensive force under Dayton held off the first furious British assault as reenforcements arrived hourly. The American line of only several hundred men under the command of Colonel Israel Angell held steady behind the bridge over the Rahway river, holding off five thousand British troops for over forty minutes "amidst the severest firing of cannon and musketry," according to one soldier. The Americans dropped back to a second line and then a third and again cut down Clinton's men with murderous cannon and musket fire, inflicting heavy casualties. In the line and just behind it were some local residents and the Rev. Jacob Green, who had ridden from Hanover to observe the fighting and to look out for his teenage son.

Knyphausen then heard that Washington and his two thousand rapidly advancing men had made astonishing progress in their return from the highway to West Point and would be at Springfield within hours. Clinton, his forces now stopped in two separate battles, decided to cut his losses and retreat back toward New York. He may have engaged Nathanael Greene, but he did not want to tangle with George Washington. "The more we advanced the more it was realized that Washington was ready to reduce further our still remaining advantage," said Major Johann Baurmeister, of the British Army, coldly explaining the retreat.

What they did not know was that a very worried Washington, frustrated by the slow movement of his troop columns, had impetuously decided to ride ahead of his men to Springfield, ignoring pleas not to leave the protection of the army. The commander-in-chief spurred on his horse and bolted ahead of his soldiers, only a single bodyguard and Billy Lee with him, and galloped as fast as his mount could take him down the highway toward the battle, an easy target for enemy snipers, arriving just after it ended.

As they withdrew, the frustrated British, fired at by militiamen posted in numerous village buildings, set fire to the entire community of Springfield as a defense. Soldiers torched and destroyed the Presbyterian Church and twenty or more residences and stores. The entire village of Springfield was engulfed in flames, and the thick, dark columns of smoke could be seen for miles.

As the British fled, Washington sent couriers on horseback to the towns within a few miles of Springfield to let residents know that they could stop loading up their wagons for flight; they were safe. The message the couriers shouted as they rode through the communities was short and sweet: "The British are flying! The British are flying!"

General Knyphausen bemoaned poor intelligence that led him into Springfield in a failed effort to capture Morristown, but he was stunned by the fierce resistance of the reportedly worn-out Continentals and militia. "I found the disposition of the inhabitants by no means such as I expected; on the contrary they were everywhere in arms," he said.

Sir Henry Clinton's report to Lord Germain about the raid was very defensive and highlighted a safe return to New York, which saved the lives of many British soldiers. The Redcoats, according to Sir Henry, had done a masterful job of not winning both battles at Springfield and had, in fact, executed a brilliant retreat and "without molestation evacuated the Jersies." In his memoirs, he defended himself further, explaining that he would have crushed Washington if he could only have gotten his hands on him: "Fortunately for the rebel affairs, that wary war chief

[Washington] acted on this occasion with his usual caution and by marching his army wide of the river [Hudson] continued to place every part of it [army] beyond our reach."

Hours after the British had left the smoldering village, residents and soldiers trudged through the burned-out buildings. It was a somber moment and captured well by the seventeen-year-old Green, who had emerged from the battle unhurt: "The whole scene was one of gloomy horror—a dead horse, a broken carriage of a field piece, a town covered in ashes, the former inhabitants standing over the ruins of their dwellings—the unburied dead covered in blood and with the flies that were devouring it. [It] filled me with melancholy."

The battles at Springfield have been overlooked by most historians, but they were two of the more important engagements of the Revolutionary War. Ever since the first day the Continental Army arrived in Morristown in early January 1777, more than three long years before, George Washington had feared a wintertime British attack of New Jersey and the annihilation of his small, undermanned force. He had chosen Morristown for specific reasons: the Watchung Mountains to the east would serve as a defensive barrier to protect the army from assault; Morris County had a well-trained, dedicated militia that could be used in case of trouble; alarms and beacon fires would serve as an early-warning system to alert him to an attack; local Presbyterian ministers would support the army; friendly state politicians would assist him; and his militia, so unreliable in the early days of the war, would fight.

All of his hopes were realized and plans validated in the Springfield battles. During the fighting, the slopes of the Watchung offered a perfect geographic landscape for the American soldiers to dig in with considerable protection in the woods, and with a height advantage from the slopes of the Watchungs, for a defensive stand. The Morris militia responded immediately, arriving on the battlefield within four hours of notification. The alarms and beacon fires, lit at once, signaled the attack as soon as the Redcoats were spotted. Rev. Caldwell's heroic work in the battles, despite the death of his wife, had fired up the American troops. New Jersey's governor, Livingston, had Washington's requested five thousand troops—spirited militia—moving toward Springfield within just two days. The militia fought hard and well and, in fact, all agreed, was responsible for the victory. Washington, who had denounced the militia with such venom in the winter of 1776–77, now told everyone how extremely proud he was of them, that they fought "with admirable spirit."

But what was demonstrated most clearly in the Springfield engagements was that the revolution, as Washington had believed for so long, despite repeated criticism, was a war fought by all the people, not just the full-time soldiers of the Continental Army and not just men in uniform. It was fought by teenagers like Ashbel Green; storeowners like militia captain Sylvanus Seely; newspaper apprentices such as Shelly Arnett and Matthias Day, who abandoned their press to join the fight; ministers like the Rev. Caldwell; ironworkers who produced cannons; farmers who drove wagons into battle; and neighborhood women in sewing circles who repaired uniforms. Springfield confirmed Washington's long-held view that he was not the commander-in-chief of just the Continental forces, but a citizens' army.

Yet, despite stopping the British twice, Washington was unhappier than ever after the enemy had been driven back across the Hudson to New York. Springfield may have seemed like a great victory to many, but to him it was yet another sign that his forces could not hold off the British forever. Although Washington never said so publicly, he was thankful that the British were afraid of his ability to defeat them regardless of the circumstances, as both Knyphausen and Clinton had demonstrated when they withdrew.

He told brother-in-law Fielding Lewis that if the British had pressed harder that day they might have won, captured Morristown, and driven the Americans back into the New Jersey forests. He then went on a rare tirade, charging that Congress could not help him because it had relinquished nearly all of its powers to the states, and that the states did not assist him either. Writing from "the bitterness of my soul," he complained to Lewis of the lack of a substantial army and a critical clothing shortage. He concluded a long and tempestuous letter by reminding Lewis of the old maxim that a country could not have peace unless it was always ready for war and complained that the United States was still not ready to win a war, even after six years of conflict.

The commander-in-chief was even more morose in a vitriolic letter he wrote that same day to his brother Jack in Virginia. "It is to be lamented, bitterly lamented, and in the anguish of soul I do lament, that our fatal and accursed policy should bring the sixth of June upon us and not a single recruit to the army," he began, and then offered his brother a litany of complaints. "We have no system" of war, he told him, and said that Americans "slumber and sleep while we should be diligent in preparation" and that the country was bringing itself "to the brink of destruction."

He went on to unload all of his unhappiness and frustration to his brother Jack, who lived in Virginia :

> To tell a person at the distance of three or four hundred miles that an army reduced almost to nothing [by the expiration of short term enlistments] should, sometimes, be five or six days together without bread, then as many without meat, and once or twice, two or three without either; that the same army should have had numbers of men in it with scarcely clothes enough to cover their nakedness and a full fourth of it without even the shadow of a blanket severe as the winter was, and that men under these circumstances were held together, is hardly within the bounds of credibility, but is nevertheless true; it is no difficult matter therefore under this view of things to form some idea of my situation.

Again, as he had so often done in the past, he begged Congress for more troops. Since that plea produced the same results as usual—none— he turned to the states and asked them for more officers and regulars. He stressed the importance of his situation and tried to get them to understand that turning back the British at Springfield signified nothing to him. "The present crisis is by far the most important and delicate that this country has ever experienced," he told state leaders, "and it pains me in the extreme that we are so backward in all our measures. Our allies would be chagrined…to find that we have but handful of men in the field and would doubt, it is more than probable, whether we had any serious intentions." He told the state leaders that if the French went home because he did not have enough men it would bring "absolute ruin."

He wrote an abrupt letter to a Congressional delegate asking him who was in charge of American foreign affairs, since he believed, but did not say, that the answer was no one. As commander-in-chief he had to frequently deal with his new French allies, but could never answer their questions about official U.S. international goals. Would not some one in charge tell him what to do about foreign policy? How could the commander of the army dealing with the soldiers of a foreign government not be permitted to participate in political discussions with leaders of those governments? It was one more reminder to Washington that the person serving as head of the civilian government had to be entrusted with foreign policy and command of the army, too. He must have muttered to himself, too, would not someone in charge tell him what to do about his bankrupt treasury, soldiers who deserted, and farmers who would not sell him food? Would not someone in charge tell him what to do about his army, often buried under snowdrifts as high as his own head, and his malnourished soldiers?

Those closest to him, especially his wife, worried about his growing despondency. "The poor General was so unhappy that it distressed me exceedingly," she wrote her brother-in-law after Springfield.

The escalating frustrations of George Washington were reflected in the growing depression of the American people. One Quaker farmer in New Jersey, who seemed to represent the opinion of many, saw the possible collapse of the army as just another disaster in a season of indescribable woe, and with great emotion wrote in his diary that America seemed not just prey to the British or victim of the elements, but caught in the grip of some Biblical plague:

The cattle and other creatures have perished this spring for want of food and the winter grain very much destroyed with the hardness of the winter, the wheat in particular. Many fields look as if there would not be more than the seed gathered. The prospect of scarcity, of cleanness of teeth and want of bread more and more appeared and the cries of the poor began to be heard in our once plentiful and peaceful land. The winter has been so hard that it has killed many trees of the woods and fruit trees and a great part of the poke and I think the summer birds are scarcer this spring.

Now there is a great deal of white oak timber and other timber, thousands of cords killed with ye hardness of the frost in this winter and many of the shade trees before our doors are killed. The birds have not been heard by us this spring. They have not come to build under the eaves of the house as usual.

These are melancholy, mourning prospects of which the signs of the times in diverse particulars have foretold this several years past. There have been many uncommon things of late in our land which seemed to threaten dissolution, the downfall of the nation or the bringing down or humbling the people, things that bespoke the displeasure of the almighty....

"These things I thought seemed to have something of a language in them like that of Jonah to Ninevah when he proclaimed yet forty days and Ninevah shall be overthrown," he wrote, citing God's threat to destroy the Assyrian city of Ninevah because its people had become depraved and corrupt.

George Washington, who referred to Providence so often, could not have agreed more.

Chapter Fourteen

THE GREAT SLAVERY DEBATE

*"Your scheme...to encourage the emancipation
of the black people of this country from that state
of bondage in which they are held is a striking
evidence of the benevolence of your heart. I shall
be happy to join you in so laudable a work."*
—George Washington to Marquis de Lafayette, April 5, 1783

*"I can only say that there is not a man living
who wishes more sincerely than I do to see a plan
adopted for the abolition of [slavery]."*
—George Washington to Robert Morris, April 12, 1786

In the winter of 1780–81, the *New Jersey Journal*, a newspaper secretly funded by the Continental Army, became the literary dueling ground for one of the most extraordinary public debates on slavery in America up to that time. The dialogues commenced just after the start of winter, on November 29, when the *Journal*, published near Morristown, printed a lengthy letter signed "Eliobo," which attacked the Rev. Jacob Green's anti-slavery sermons that had been printed in the newspaper. Green responded, beginning a series of letters between the two. A third writer, who supported slavery, joined in. The plainly written but spirited letters, overlooked by most historians, reflected the national division on the slave question. They were published in the *New Jersey Journal* throughout the winter and read with great interest by all of the soldiers in the northern wing of the army at Morristown and several thousands of residents of New Jersey, Pennsylvania, and New York, where the paper was distributed.

Eliobo, who was not a slaveholder, upheld the practice by reiterating the social and economic grounds upon which people who owned slaves defended the practice. They claimed that: 1) slaves' needs in life, such as food, clothing, and medicine, are provided by their owners; 2) blacks are lazy and can not function as free laborers; their lives as such would be worse than in slavery; 3) they are happy as slaves; 4) freed blacks will rape white women; 5) freed slaves who can use firearms will take what they want by force; 6) freed slaves will probably join forces with the American Indians to attack white villages. Seeking a psychological motive to condone the ownership of people, Eliobo even contended that slaves were actually better off than freemen: "He lives free from all anxiety...perplexing cares troubles and disappointments and these, I humbly conceive...make up the whole of our unhappiness," he said of slaves.

Green answered Eliobo in a satirical column, suggesting that slaveholders were a greater danger to liberty than their charges. The three men exchanged salvos in several more letters. Green had the final word in a January 31, 1781, letter. Summing up all of his arguments and connecting them to the timing of the revolution, he told Eliobo, and the readers of the paper, that "our avowing and endeavoring to hold a number of human creatures and their posterity from generation to generation in perpetual bondage is one of the greatest evils , tho' not the only one, that is among us. 'Tis so unnatural and cruel, so inconsistent with the principles on which the present war is founded, so inconsistent with our prayers and application to God on the occasion of the present war, that he who weighs the nations in an equal balance must be highly offended with us on this account." Then he turned to the timing of the anti-slavery movement. "To suppose this is not the proper time to do it is, in my view, much the same as for a sick man to say that the time of his sickness is not the proper time to take a disagreeable medicine, but that he will [wait] till his stomach can better bear it."

The debate was followed carefully by readers. The people of New Jersey were caught up in the slavery debates of the 1780s just as those residing in other states. There were approximately ten thousand slaves (some Native Americans were also enslaved) in New Jersey during the Revolution, or 6 percent of the total population of the state; New Jersey had the second-highest number of slaves in the northern states, behind New York. Most worked in farming, manufacturing or in the ironworks (some ironworks had as many as forty). Others worked for merchants running small stores, at the docks of the state's several seaports, or as domestics. Housewives who had slaves, such as Aaron Burr's mother, regarded them as routine household labor. There were so many household slaves that a count in the seaport of Perth Amboy showed that every house in town except one employed at least one slave as a servant. Slavery in New Jersey was authorized in 1664 by land grants from the Crown to Lord Berkeley and Sir George Carteret and blacks in chains began arriving by ship from the Caribbean shortly afterward. They were in great demand through the first half of the eighteenth century because New Jersey employers were unable to attract free, indentured white workers and did not want to pay laborers.

The growth of anti-slavery sentiment in New Jersey was rapid and greatly influenced by the Quakers, who led the movement in nearby Pennsylvania. Their first efforts were in 1693, when Quakers living in South Jersey promoted a failed plan to convince farmers to buy slaves and free them after they worked off their purchase cost. Quaker anti-slavery speakers rode from town to town on horseback denouncing the institution. They were often theatrical; one stabbed a pig bladder full of berry juice and splattered it all over his audience to convince them that slavers had blood on their hands. Others were quite eloquent, like John Woolman, a South Jersey Quaker who said that "When wickedness takes root and spreads wide amongst the inhabitants of a country, there is real cause for sorrow."

Anti-slavery advocates in Somerset County imposed a sales tax on slaves in 1713 to make their purchase costlier. Anti-slavery farmers tried to get a similar, statewide tax imposed in 1737 and 1744 and finally succeeded in 1769. Petitions to completely abolish slavery were submitted to the Assembly beginning in 1773. More petitions were submitted on the eve of the war; they came from dozens of individuals and numerous counties. None went far. The only time the legislature seriously considered eliminating slavery was in 1778 when Governor Livingston, a fierce abolitionist, sponsored an anti-slavery bill that made it as far as a committee, where it was voted down, six to four. In one of his speeches backing the bill, the governor charged that slavery was "odious and disgraceful."

While New Jersey debated slavery in committees, other states abolished it. Vermont was the first to free its slaves, in 1776. Pennsylvania followed in 1780 and Massachusetts would be next in 1783. All of the northern states would ban the practice, outright or gradually, by 1804. Several towns in New England simply freed slaves with municipal ordinances. Some states permitted individuals to free slaves if they desired.

The slavery discussions in the *Jersey Journal* that winter encompassed the arguments of all. There were few public figures as interested in the slavery question as George Washington, the man who funded the newspaper. The anti-slavery crusade expanded in Virginia as he grew into a man there, although the size of the movement was always small. The Quakers located in Virginia in the late 1750s and pressured slaveholders to sell their workers; some did. The Baptists had made the abolition of slavery part of their state-wide evangelical crusade there in the 1760s. The Quakers tried, unsuccessfully, to get the House of Burgesses to eradicate slavery by legislation in 1773 and again in 1779.

Washington's own feelings about slavery had always been mixed. He was a successful leader of the southern gentry and a longtime public official who had owned slaves all of his life (three hundred when the Revolution began, making him one of America's largest slaveholders). He bought and sold them callously and sometimes used revenue from the sale of produce to purchase slaves he needed. Washington once ordered a subordinate to sell flour in order to get money to buy workers and to look for "choice ones." On another occasion, he permitted farmers who owed him mortgage payments to use their slaves as collateral for the debt. At times he declared that blacks were dishonest. Once, when meat had been reported missing from one of his storage houses, he immediately suspected one of his slaves. "I know of no black person about the house that is to be trusted," he told his manager, William Pearce. Washington never understood why some of his slaves fled, and ran ads in the *Virginia Gazette* and other newspapers offering rewards, usually $20, for their recovery. He was, like most Virginians who owned plantations, willing to use slaves to work his land and establish his fortune.

However, everyone who knew him said the general was extremely caring for the men and women in bondage at Mount Vernon. He rarely called them slaves, usually referring to them as "his family" or "his people." He went to great lengths to provide them with good food and shelter and, when he was president, reminded his plantation manager that he had always procured extra food for his "family." "I always used to lay on a great quantity of fish for them…meat, fat and other things were given to them besides," he said. Slaves who worked especially hard were given cash or food bonuses; all the slaves received bonuses following a particularly good harvest. They were permitted to travel locally to visit family and shop in nearby villages. Many were given muskets and allowed to hunt in order to supplement their food allowances.

Washington was always anxious that the men, women, and children who worked for him at Mount Vernon were properly clothed to keep warm and prevent illness. "If you depend on me for [money] to clothe my Negroes, let me know without delay the quantity necessary that it may be sent in time," he told his manager. Washington brought in doctors at considerable cost to care for his slaves. He himself tended to them when they were sick. Managers were told to alert him to any illness in the slave quarters. He did not bark orders at them from a horse when they were at work, but toiled in the fields with them. He appointed some slaves as overseers and said that those chosen were "sober, honest and industrious."

He had nothing but the highest regard for the blacks working in his fields. None could be punished by flogging until an overseer gave Washington the reasons for the beating, in writing, and Washington approved; he often did not. Few cruel overseers were permitted at Mount Vernon and those that were employed were never permitted to administer floggings to slaves. Washington detested unfair or harshly administered punishments, and once fumed that his men had to labor under "a worthless white man," an overseer, whom he promptly fired. Washington was critical of slaveowners "who are not always as kind, and as attentive to their [slaves'] wants and usage as they ought to be."

Polish Count Julian Niemcewicz, visiting Mount Vernon, said the slaves living there seemed happy. "General Washington treats his slaves far more humanely than do his fellow citizens of Virginia. Most of these gentlemen give their blacks only bread, water and blows," he wrote.

Throughout his life, George Washington maintained mixed feelings about slavery as an institution, but he almost always remained a staunch supporter of the right of other people to own slaves. At the end of the war, he insisted that the British return slaves they had freed in areas they had occupied and taken with their army. Sometimes he angrily denounced anti-slavery groups, such as an occasion when he was president and was informed of an anti-slavery petition that Pennsylvania Quakers had introduced in Congress in 1790. He called it "very malapropos" and an "ill-judged piece of businesses [that] occasioned a great waste of time." He was adamant that slavery had to remain for the present, after the war telling Jacques de Warville, a French politician, that while slavery might end, it would not be for many years. "Time, patience and education and it will be overcome," he said.

There were times when his feelings waffled, however. Washington's unhappiness over the Stamp Act, and then the Townshend Acts, and the idea that Americans were becoming enslaved to British politicians and merchants caused him to do some hard thinking about the issue in the late 1760s, and he announced with great bravado that he was going to introduce a bill in the House of Burgesses to eliminate the importation of slaves into Virginia. His fellow Burgesses and planter friends talked him out of it. Then, again, in the summer of 1774, he authored the Fairfax Resolves, with George Mason. One of the resolves, or proposals, printed in most of the newspapers in the South, called for the elimination of the slave trade and the restriction of slavery to its present, domestic boundaries. "We take this opportunity of declaring our most earnest wishes to see an entire stop forever put to such a wicked cruel and unnatural trade," he said. It, too, went nowhere.

He tied his opposition to slavery at the time to the colonists' feeling that they were British chattel. He said that Americans had to assert their rights or be turned into as "tame and abject slaves as the blacks we rule over with such arbitrary sway." Well aware of the plight of his own slaves, he often referred to them as "the poor wretches."

Like some other planters, he did not believe that the overall cost of slave upkeep was a better economic proposition than paid labor and tenant farmers and knew that slave worker slowdowns, which could not be halted, often curbed profits. He understood, too, that over the years Virginians had embraced the idea that it was better to have tens of thousands of docile black slaves who were no threat to society than a population of angry young indentured white workers who, history had shown, were likely to cause trouble. He was always surrounded by wealthy men who argued that slaves were merely property and every man had a right to own property, that a man's liberty was gone if his property—slaves—could be taken from him.

Regardless of how he felt at different times during his life, Washington never mustered up the courage to free his slaves and run Mount Vernon with paid labor or indentured workers. He was, of course, under pressure from the gentry not to do it because that sort of action by such a prominent slaveholder might force them to do the same. His wife Martha had grown up among slaves on a large plantation and did not know any other way of life. Economically, it was always more profitable to use free labor than paying farm hands. In the end, despite eruptions of emancipation from time to time, Washington remained in the slaveholding fold until the mid 1770s, when he took charge of the army.

As commander-in-chief, Washington again turned to the slavery issue, but with a new outlook brought about by the changes in the economy and his views. In the summer of 1778, unhappy with sinking plantation profits and increased harvest troubles, he wrote his cousin Lund that he was tired of the responsibility of managing slaves at Mount Vernon and was willing to trade them all away for land and continue without them. "I every day long more and more to get rid of them," he said.

What had changed the mind of a lifetime slaveholder? All evidence points toward three reasons: 1) his years away from Mount Vernon in Massachusetts, Pennsylvania, New York and New Jersey, states where slavery was doggedly opposed by prominent political leaders and ministers of large churches and was debated publicly, and not just by the Quakers and Baptists; 2) the virulent anti-slavery attitudes of the men who were closest to him throughout the winter camps of the war: Livingston, Greene, Hamilton, Laurens, Lafayette, and Jay, among others; and 3) his growing relationship with his slave Billy Lee, with him continuously throughout the war.

The commander spent practically all of his time with aides Hamilton and Laurens and a considerable amount of time with Livingston, who had moved into his winter camp in 1777 and in 1779. He had spent countless hours at dinners with the governor and his wife and the governor's brilliant son-in-law, John Jay. Nathanael Greene was a Quaker and one of his relatives was the commander of one of the highly regarded black regiments in the Continental Army. Congressional delegate Gouverneur Morris, one of the loudest critics of bondage, spent months living in camp at Valley Forge and surely influenced Washington's thinking. They were all outspoken opponents of slavery and tried to convince Washington that the system was not only financially unsound, but immoral.

The anti-slavery activities of these men continued throughout their lives. Right after the war, Livingston signed a law to prohibit any further purchases of slaves in New Jersey, an act that paved the way for the state's emancipation bill of 1804. When the fighting ended, Jay continued his abolitionist activities and became the founder and president of the New York Manumission Society; Hamilton was its vice president. In 1799, Jay, as governor of New York, signed a bill to free the slaves in that state. He spent the last years of his life trying to convince southern leaders to abolish slavery in their states.

These men, with him nearly every day in the winters of the war, made three of the common arguments for emancipation: 1) black soldiers had fought well in the Revolution, and if blacks were free in war they should be free in peace; 2) slavery was religiously immoral; and 3) the revolution was fought to free everyone, blacks included, and that the Americans could not complain that they were "slaves" to England when they held slaves themselves.

The third argument was the strongest. Ministers had pushed for emancipation, tied to the revolution, since 1774, when New Jersey's Samuel Allinson urged Patrick Henry to make the freedom of the slaves a goal of the Continental Congress. "It is contrary to reason and inconsistent with the decrees of the Divine Legislator," he told Henry of slavery. He added that it would be to the "lasting disgrace" of Congress not to free the slaves "if they should spend so much time to secure their own liberties and leave no vestige of their regard to those of their fellow men in bondage to themselves."

It was a view shared by many. "To continue for liberty and to deny that blessing to others involves an insensitivity not to be excused," said Jay. Abigail Adams agreed. "[I question] to fight ourselves for what we are daily robbing and plundering from those who have as good a right to freedom as we do," she said. Congressional delegate James Otis warned that "those who barter away other men's liberty will soon care little for their own."

The Rev. Green, who had saved hundreds of lives during the 1777 smallpox epidemic, and who worked closely with the commander-in-chief, embraced that philosophy, too. Green hated slavery so much that in 1781 he became the first Presbyterian minister in the country to ban any slaveholders from his congregation. In a 1778 Fast Day sermon, reprinted in newspapers several times during the war, Rev. Green told his parishioners, "What foreign nation can believe that we who so loudly complain of Britain's attempts to oppress and enslave us, are at the same time, voluntarily, holding multitudes of fellow creatures in abject slavery…while…declaring that we esteem liberty the greatest of all earthy blessings." It was the same argument that Washington had made back in 1774.

Few Americans hated slavery with the passion of Lafayette. "I would never have drawn my sword in the cause of America if I could have conceived that thereby I was founding a land of slavery," he said.

Lafayette failed to convince Washington to free his slaves and to come out publicly against the institution during the revolution, but in 1783 he tried to talk him into a radical post-war experiment—never undertaken—in which the two men would run a large farm in Virginia without slave labor and make it profitable. Lafayette did make plans to proceed with a similar idea in 1786. He was going to purchase a slave plantation in French Guinea, free the residents, and hire them to work the land as freemen. Lafayette's scheme seemed to excite and yet frustrate Washington, whose response showed his true dislike for slavery. "Your late purchase of an estate in the colony of [Guinea] with a view of emancipating the slaves on it is a generous and noble proof of your humanity. Would to God a like spirit would diffuse itself generally into the minds of the people of this country, " he told him.

That same year, Washington again championed the anti-slavery cause, explaining to Robert Morris that "there is not a man living who wishes more sincerely than I do to see a plan adopted for the abolition of it" and told him he hoped that it could be abolished legislatively (again, in 1797, he urged friends, unsuccessfully, to introduce a bill to outlaw it in the Virginia state assembly). Several months later he vowed never to purchase another slave, telling a friend that it was "among my first wishes to see some plan adopted, by which slavery in this country may be abolished by slow, sure and imperceptible degrees." Two years later, Washington made up his mind not to sell slaves, either, declaring the practice morally repugnant and telling his nephew that he was "against that kind of traffic in the human species."

Washington also acknowledged the strength of the religious argument, which he had heard so often from Presbyterian ministers. He himself created the first argument in the summer of 1775 when he authorized the recruitment of black soldiers, who fought in return for their emancipation. He had urged the enlistment of all black regiments in Rhode Island but also permitted integrated units from different states, reminding officers that he did not want a "black corps." He had carefully placed Greene's relative in charge of one black unit to insure its success. More than three thousand former slaves were fighting for the army and another two thousand were working as pilots for U.S. ships in the Chesapeake area. Dozens of slaves had been recruited by Washington work as spies. He thought so much of slaves as troops that he approved a suggestion by John Laurens to travel to his home state of South Carolina to raise four battalions of them for the army, with freedom their reward (the South Carolina legislature rejected the idea). The general had been surprised and impressed with the fighting of the former slaves and happy to guarantee their freedom at war's end.

Although Washington did not free his slaves during the war, and paid little attention to the Quaker movement in 1790, he did change his mind again in 1794, following his reelection as president. Mount Vernon's profits had dropped considerably and Washington believed the best thing to do was to sell off much of the land for cash to use as a financial cushion until business improved. As part of this grand scheme, he planned to free the more than one hundred slaves who lived on those plantations and ask the purchasers to use them as free, hired help or to import English and Scottish paid laborers. He told Tobias Lear, his secretary then, that, in fact, he wanted to sell the land *in order* to free his workers, to "liberate a certain species which I possess, very repugnantly to my own feelings, but which imperious necessity compels." At the same time he told Alexander Spotswood, concerning the land sale and emancipation, that if he had his way "I would not, in twelve months from this date, be possesseed of one slave." That gesture, as president, would have stunned the nation, given considerable strength to the antislavery movement, and perhaps led to more heated legislative debates on slavery in the states and in Congress. The sale never materialized, however. The slaves remained and the first great opportunity to end slavery in America evaporated.

Washington did finally exorcise the slavery demons that had plagued him all of his adult life when he died. In his will, he freed the 123 slaves that belonged to him, stipulating that the elderly among them receive lifelong shelter and health care and that the children receive an education. In a very personal gesture, he liberated his old friend Billy Lee, "for his faithful services during the Revolutionary War." He could not free all of his workers because the remaining 130 or so legally belonged to the estate of Martha's first husband and remained in bondage to the estate and, later, Washington's grandchildren.

Washington's decision to emancipate his slaves had far greater implications than historians have acknowledged. Many have seen it as a grand deathbed gesture to rid himself of moral guilt. But Washington knew that without substantially reduced slave labor, Mount Vernon could not function very well. The plantation had, in fact, turned little profit on several occasions. In freeing his slaves, Washington ran the real risk of losing his family's lands and fortune, denying wealth and prosperity to his grandchildren and heirs. There was also the very real chance that his family, and generations of his relatives, would be socially ostracized by the landed gentry in the South. The president's bold emancipation of his slaves would have placed considerable pressure on all slaveholders to do the same, and whether or not they did so they would resent Washington for his actions. Washington was aware of all the ramifications of the emancipation of his slaves and took that gigantic step anyway.

"The unfortunate condition of the persons whose labor in part I employed has been the only unavoidable subject of regret," he said of his decision to a friend near the end of his life. "To make the adults among them as easy and as comfortable in their circumstances as their actual state of ignorance and improvidence would admit, and to lay a foundation to prepare the rising generation for a destiny different from that in which they were born afforded some satisfaction to my mind and could not I hoped be displeasing to the justice of the Creator."

Washington Gets His Own Pro-Revolutionary Newspaper

The fires of the heated slavery debate of that winter were fanned in the newspaper columns of a journal that George Washington helped to found. He had sought out a young lieutenant in the army, Shepard Kollock, to design and create a brand new newspaper that the general wanted to use as a propaganda sheet for the army, the revolution, and himself.

Like many other restless officers in the winter of 1778, Shepard Kollock wanted to resign from the Continental Army. Like them, he felt he had been unfairly overlooked for promotion. Dozens of officers petitioned the army for early resignation but military officials did not pay attention to any of them, except Kollock.

The artillery officer in Washington's army was highly regarded by Henry Knox, who did not want to lose him. Knox had learned, however, that Kollock was also an experienced editor. He had spent his teenage years as an apprentice to Isaac Collins, the editor of the *New Jersey Gazette*, the state-funded newspaper recently started by Governor Livingston at Washington's urging. Kollock also happened to be the nephew of William Goddard of Philadelphia, one of America's foremost editors. In addition, he had served as the editor of a newspaper in the West Indies, where he recuperated from an illness. And Kollock, despite his promotion dispute, was a patriot who had joined the army right after the start of the Revolution and had fought with it for three long years. The army had been so much a part of his life that he even named his first-born son Henry Knox Kollock. Knox went to Washington with the lieutenant's request for a discharge and told the general what he had discovered about his journalistic past. Washington eagerly arranged a meeting with the lieutenant.

The General had never been completely satisfied with the effectiveness of the *New Jersey Gazette*, which Livingston had so gleefully created as his own propaganda sheet. The *Gazette* was published in Burlington, in South Jersey, far from Morristown and other North Jersey communities. What the general wanted was an army-funded newspaper published close to Morristown that he could distribute to the soldiers in all of his camps. The paper would also be delivered throughout towns in northern New Jersey and New York for civilian consumption. It would be a propaganda journal filled with news of the army and opinion columns supporting the rebellion. He planned to contribute dozens of press release–style stories to it himself. The newspaper would, at the same time, boost always-waning morale within the army and generate public support for the war. He had asked Congress for funding for such a journal in 1777 and was turned down. He had made the request again in the fall of 1778, telling Congress that the people needed "a channel of intelligence that from its usual authenticity they could look up to with confidence. They might be perse-vered from that despondency which they are apt to fall into from the exag-gerated picture our enemies...commonly draw." There are no official records of a decision, but Congress apparently relented and gave Wash-ington authorization to fund the publication.

Kollock, a tall, big-boned man with a large nose, gray eyes, and shaggy eyebrows, met the commander-in-chief and Knox in Middle Brook, New Jersey. Washington's aides had done some investigating and had been told that one year before the officer had married a girl from New Providence, New Jersey, a few miles from Morristown, and that she was then pregnant, another reason that the lieutenant wanted to leave the army. Washington and Knox explained to Kollock their desire for an army newspaper that could also be circulated commercially. They told him that he would be the perfect editor. He was a military veteran him-self and understood the problems of the soldiers and the necessity for public understanding of the needs of the army. He had considerable experience as an editor. His wife had lived in New Jersey all of her life; she was a patriot and so were the members of her family. Kollock would be "safe."

Their deal was simple. The lieutenant would get his desired discharge from the army if he would serve as the editor of the newspaper, the *New Jersey Journal*. To make the offer more palatable, Washington told him that he could live at home and produce the paper in Chatham. The army would buy the printing press and other equipment he needed and supply riders, at no cost, to carry hundreds of copies of the newspaper to all of the army camps and to towns throughout the area for public sale. Wash-ington also agreed to give him—at no charge—whatever reams of paper the quartermaster could find. Later, when the army ran out of paper,

Washington approved free delivery to the *New Jersey Journal* of tons of rags and used army tents, which mills could turn into newsprint. Washington furthermore assured him that the newspaper was his as a business and that he could keep whatever profits it would produce. He also guaranteed him numerous army printing jobs, such as copies of enlistment returns, proclamations, and notices to Congress. They worked out an arrangement whereby Kollock would retain ownership of the newspaper when the war ended.

The general also promised Kollock that he would have open access to his headquarters and all the other camps. He could interview soldiers, townspeople, and public officials, such as Governor Livingston, and prisoners of war. Kollock was also allowed to witness court martials and hangings. Washington would supply him with all the army press releases he needed; the Commander would ask his minister friends to forward copies of their sermons for Kollock to publish. The general also made certain that the editor had copies of bills from the New Jersey legislature and any needed notices or legislation from the Continental Congress. (Washington did not take Livingston's advice and have aides with different handwriting using different fictitious names write letters to Kollock supporting or decrying a particular piece of legislation, as if to create a groundswell of public opinion, as the irascible governor himself did frequently with the *New Jersey Gazette*.)

In return, the general expected, and received, beginning on February 16, 1779, a highly partisan pro-army, pro-revolution newspaper, the most vocal supporter of the war in America, a public-relations dream. There are no reliable circulation figures for the *New Jersey Journal* because many copies were simply distributed free in the winter camps, but the total circulation of the paper was probably several thousand, as high as any in America.

Washington had always been aware of the power of the colonial press. He had seen it firsthand when the much-vilified Stamp Act was introduced. Newspapers had denounced it for months and the tax was repealed, a victim of relentless press pummeling. Washington realized its effect again when the Townshend Acts were issued and yet again when he and Mason introduced their non-importation proposals in 1769. Mason explained to a naïve Washington at the time that the only chance they had for public acceptance of the proposal was a lengthy story, prominently placed, in the *Virginia Gazette*, which they received.

The clever editors of the colonial newspapers, the radicals joked, had more power than ten battalions of troops. Boston newspapers had printed black borders around the front pages of their editions carrying stories of the Boston Massacre. The editor of the *Pennsylvania Journal and Weekly Advertiser* printed an illustration of a divided snake at the top of his front page banner with the unification slogan "Join or Die!"

Editors did not mince their words. "The country which our fathers purchased with their blood, we will defend with our blood," cried a writer in the *Massachusetts Spy* in 1774. A writer in the *Virginia Gazette* echoed that feeling a month later, affirming that "with the sword our forefathers obtained their constitutional rights, and by the sword it is our duty to defend them."

Newspapers had grown rapidly in America during the pre-colonial period and the Stamp Act crisis gave birth to even more. There were forty-four publications when the war started and two-thirds of them were now patriotic. Cities such as Baltimore, Boston, and Philadelphia had several newspapers and they enjoyed circulations of two thousand and more. The newspapers were not local, though. They printed articles from each other's editions so that people in South Carolina knew what was going on in Boston. The newspapers were always found in general stores, taverns, inns, and courthouses, giving them a very wide readership. Americans were quite literate in that era (75 percent of adults could read) and those that were not literate were told what was in the press by others. People living on outlying farms where newspapers were not circulated relied on the gentry to give them the news and, more importantly, to interpret it; the gentry were usually the leaders of the area's revolutionary groups.

In many cities, such as Boston, some of the leaders of the rebellion also served as editors of the newspapers (such as the men who organized the Boston Tea Party). Some of the most educated men in the country, using pseudonyms, wrote political columns that appeared in their paper and were then reprinted all over America. Many newspapers printed pamphlets in serial form, such as Thomas Paine's *The American Crisis*. Residents of Philadelphia who were unhappy with Parliament knew through newspapers that people in all the other colonies felt the same way. They all knew of each and every move the British made against any sister colony. That gave them the strength, separately and together, to strike for independence. All of this made the newspapers a powerful information network that helped radicals in different colonies unite the masses into one national tidal wave of public dissent.

Washington had come to believe, as did David Ramsay, writing just after the war, that "the pen and the press had a merit equal to that of the sword" and that, as Samuel Adams said, the press was the single most powerful weapon for independence not just in America, but in the world.

But Washington's need in the winters of the war were not merely philosophical. He wanted a strong publication in New Jersey to thwart the efforts of the well-written Tory publications in both Philadelphia and New York, especially against James Rivington's *New York Gazette*. Rivington's pro-British paper was the most widely circulated in the colonies, with a weekly subscriber list of 3,600, and was a favorite of the British high command. His well-crafted editorials had been so violently anti-American that just after the start of the war, Morris County patriots gathered up hundreds of copies of the *Gazetteer* into a huge pile and set them on fire as speakers denounced Rivington as an enemy of the American people.

As planned, the subsidized *New Jersey Journal* did serve as a morale booster for the troops and public, but it had other purposes. It was a vehicle, like other pro-rebellion papers, for the seemingly unlimited press releases from General Washington. The general had been mailing out his releases, written as letters and signed by him, since his first New Jersey winter camp in 1777. Now he sent out even more to rally support for the war. It was not unusual for the *Jersey Journal*, his own paper, to carry between three and five lengthy stories written and signed by him in each issue. These were accompanied by laudatory articles about Washington by Lafayette and other American generals and political figures. In addition, there would be notices by his staff informing soldiers about army activities. Local residents filled up the *Journal's* column with letters denouncing the British. Any letter with news of British atrocities, whether confirmed or not, was printed. The speeches of any public figure in England who disagreed with the Crown's conduct of the war were highlighted. A column of "London News" spotlighted new taxes imposed on the British to pay for the war and any in-fighting among members of Parliament. The glorification of Washington was a staple of the *New Jersey Journal,* as it was in most American newspapers. The *Journal* often ran biographical sketches of the commander-in-chief and always wove praise of him into its stories, ending sentences with "the standard of America, liberty and glorious Washington." Like the other American papers, the *New Jersey Journal* was filled with songs and poems about Washington, such as "A New Song," to the tune of "God Save the King," and "The Temple of Fame." Here and there, the *Journal,* like other papers, would repeat the new American slogan: "God Save Washington and God Damn the King!" On another occasion the general became an easy substitute for the brilliantly rising sun: "that our illustrious Washington, like the meridian sun, has dispelled those nocturnal vapors that hung around us."

At Washington's behest, Kollock devoted considerable space, often an entire page a week, printing stories connected to ongoing Irish efforts to secure independence from the Crown. Kollock wrote numerous editorials comparing it to the American war and said that the efforts of not one, but two, countries indicated that Britain was "a nation crumbling into pieces." He cheered the entry of France, and then Spain, into the war on the American side. Sometimes he simply lied to favor the revolutionary cause, such as in the winter of 1779–80, when he covered up the starvation in Morristown and wrote that the army had been "exuberantly supplied with provision and every necessity to make a soldier's life comfortable." The *Journal* was careful, too, to write stories about the punishment of any American soldiers charged with illegal plundering to let its readers know that the state and federal governments, and the army, did not condone it.

The paper printed a substantial number of sermons from local ministers and theological columns by religious figures, usually Presbyterians like himself (Kollock's uncle was a minister). There were columns on literature, education, and proper behavior for social occasions. The newspaper carried as much advertising as possible to cover expenses.

Kollock did not permit any anti-Revolution sentiment in the *New Jersey Journal*, as Washington expected of his personal press. There was no criticism of Governor Livingston or the state legislature, either. The state-subsidized *New Jersey Gazette* was different. That newspaper was sometimes critical of the legislature, Congress, and the governor himself. Its editor created quite an ethical and legal stir when he refused to divulge the name of the writer of an article overly critical of the governor, who demanded it. The governor pressured the editor as hard as he could, and so did state politicians, but the editor would not budge and won the battle. That would never happen with Kollock, who would produce a pro-army, pro-Washington sheet through the end of the war.

This adulation was gratifying to Washington, even if he was paying for it. Unfortunately for the general, he was so pleased with Kollock and his newspaper that he was never able to understand or prepare himself for the relentless attacks upon him unleashed by the press when he became president in 1789.

Mutiny Again

But it was not the slavery debate or the ownership of the *New Jersey Journal* that consumed the general's time in January 1781, when he stayed with a portion of the army quartered at New Windsor, a village on the banks of the Hudson River just north of West Point in New York, and left the majority of troops in Morristown and Pompton, New Jersey. It was yet another mutiny, an uprising at Morristown that once more threatened to destroy the army.

Mutinies had always been the great fear of the commander-in-chief. As early as October 1779, he had warned of them in a letter to Joseph Reed, telling the governor of Pennsylvania that there had been much "discontent, jealousies and uneasiness that have prevailed in the army."

He blamed some of this on arguments about rank, but warned Reed that "the temper of the general officers is at this moment a good deal soured. Their distresses proceeding from the amazing depreciation of money on the one hand and a discrimination of Congress in the allowance of subsistence on the other."

Mutinies were the result of festering unhappiness, and in the late winter of 1780 Washington had again dolefully predicted the rebellion within the ranks in May in a letter to Congress, reminding members that his men had been without food, clothing, and pay for long periods of time and, despite their patriotism, were frustrated. Many of them did not believe that they would ever obtain proper supplies from Congress and were angry that their countrymen never seemed to give them anything without a sneer and a bill attached. Washington warned Reed on May 28, the week after the mutiny of the Connecticut and New Jersey troops, that he feared more. "There is such a combination of circumstances to exhaust the patience of the soldiery that it begins at length to be worn out—and we see in every line of the army the most serious features of mutiny and sedition," he said.

Since the victories at Trenton and Princeton, Washington had been successful in keeping the army together despite numerous catastrophic events, including a smallpox epidemic, blizzards, runaway inflation, and the deaths of several thousand men at Valley Forge. His strategy was to do so until the British quit the war. The Revolution would end the moment that his army fell apart. One successful mutiny would undermine the resolve of all the other soldiers to fight on. The alliance with France would suffer irreparable damage if the government of Louis XVI found itself supporting an army riddled with mutineers. Congress would also be dealt a stunning blow.

That chain of events almost took place following the Connecticut line uprising in May of 1780. Fortunately, the battle of Springfield occurred just two weeks later. The engagement against the enemy and then the arrival of summer, along with food, defused the anger of hundreds of other troops who had not mutinied with the Connecticut men but were just as bitter. So had the swift execution of the leader of the

Connecticut mutiny. Still, there had been other disorders. In January 1780, one hundred Massachusetts men at West Point, declaring that their enlistments were up, disobeyed orders and began a march back to their state. Washington sent troops to return them to camp, where several were punished. In June 1780, after hearing of the uprising in Morristown, thirty American soldiers stationed at Fort Stanwix, on the Mohawk River in New York, starving and without pay for several months, left the fort and headed north toward a British encampment on the St. Lawrence River. A Continental Army company, among whose members were Oneida Indians, chased them and in a pitched battle killed eleven of them. The rest escaped.

Now, seven month later, another mutiny began, a very large-scale desertion that, if not checked, threatened to shatter the army. The malcontents were in the Pennsylvania Line, camped just south of Morristown and east of Jockey Hollow. The Pennsylvanians, like the other troops, had little to eat, were badly clothed, and had not been paid by their state in twelve months. They had enlisted for three-year terms or for the duration of the war and accepted mere $75 bonuses to join the revolutionary army while other states later paid their men up to $250. The Pennsylvanians had believed that if the war was still going on after three years, they could go home or reenlist and earn a new bonus of $81 plus two hundred acres of free land. In late December, they were told that was not so.

Outraged, hungry, and justly feeling that they had been misled, nearly two thousand men mutinied in the greatest army uprising in U.S. history. Just after dinner on New Year's Day, the men, whipped into a frenzy by speeches from the ringleaders, left their huts amid much shouting and cursing, fired their muskets into the air, rushed the ammunition magazines, and seized nearby cannons, which they fired off along with their guns. One officer trying to halt the mutiny was accidentally killed and two others were wounded.

The Pennsylvania general, Anthony Wayne, who had pleaded with Congress and their state council for supplies and pay, and had championed them for a year, arrived shortly before 11 P.M. in an attempt to quell the revolt. He could not contain the growing rebellion and was angered when several of the men fired their muskets over his head in an effort to chase him away. He turned and shouted at the men to kill him if they wanted, and tore open his coat to offer his chest as a target. No one fired.

The leaders of the cabal told Wayne that they were not angry at him or General Washington. Their anger was directed at Congress and the Pennsylvania legislature, which refused to pay them or permit them to reenlist and collect another bonus for it. They were going to march on Congress, in Philadelphia, and present their complaints directly to the members. The mutineers then gathered up as many muskets and as much ammunition as they could, plus whatever supplies they could find, and loaded them into wagons. Four cannons were taken and two spies that had been in a jail were brought along, too. The army of mutineers then began to assemble and left Morristown just before midnight.

Wayne had found himself in the middle of one of the most critical events of the war. There was no time to obtain direction from Washington, in New Windsor. He did send a messenger to the general that night, but had to act on his own until he received orders. A free-wheeling army of disaffected soldiers, marching through the countryside, was a severe blow to the whole country. Word about the mutiny would spread throughout the nation within days. It would weaken public support for the war and encourage British aggressiveness. Somehow, Anthony Wayne had to defuse the revolt.

He decided to capitalize on his personal popularity with the men. Taking a few aides with him, he rode alongside the dissidents, continually trying to convince them to return to camp. He finally persuaded the leaders to meet with him at Bound Brook to negotiate an end to the uprising. Talks were unsatisfactory to both sides, however, and the mutineer army left for Princeton. There, Wayne was joined by General Arthur St. Clair and the Marquis de Lafayette, sent by Washington, for peace talks. Washington himself had planned to attend, but was fearful that his own unhappy troops at New Windsor would revolt if he was not there.

The mutineers again told Wayne, and the others, that they wanted nothing more than their pay; they flatly rejected an offer from Sir Henry

Clinton to join the British army, a decision, along with the order of the mutineers, that was swiftly conveyed to the French through emissaries to keep them as allies. The Princeton talks were tense. The mutineers, fearful of an attack by other units of the army, fortified Princeton for a siege. The commander-in-chief had sent eighty officers to observe their activity, an ominous sign of a possible attack. Washington had also instructed Governor Livingston to order the New Jersey militia to surround Princeton. But Washington elected not to use force to put down the revolt. No one understood the deprivations of these men better than the general. There was little he could do to help them, as they knew, and Congress had failed them. Their state had failed them. Now, with the possible collapse in the army in the balance if the mutiny succeeded, Washington preferred talks rather than an attack.

The negotiators tried to reach an agreement with the soldiers as quickly as possible because the news of their revolt had spread quickly throughout the Congress and, naturally, the story grew as it passed from person to person. The first-day rumor, the one that reached Congress on January 21, was that many thousands had mutinied and that the entire army was at the point of disbanding. Those rumors had to be ended and the only way was with a quick settlement.

Finally, a week after the revolt, a compromise was struck. The Pennsylvania Council agreed to pay the men all of their back wages and provide new clothing. Men who elected to reenlist would be paid a bonus. Others would be permitted to resign with honor and go home (about three-quarters did so). The two British spies that the Pennsylvanians had taken from camp with them had to be turned over to the Continental Army for execution. All of the mutineers were to be pardoned. Despite a general agreement, the dissident soldiers worried that the politicians would renege on their promises and that the men would be left with nothing. Fortuitously, that same day a train of wagons arrived with the promised clothing: 1,200 shirts and pairs of shoes, 2,500 overalls, and 1,000 blankets. The deal was then struck.

The success of the Pennsylvanians encouraged another mutiny, this one in Pompton, New Jersey, just north of Morristown, on January 20.

More than two hundred New Jersey soldiers, making public the same complaints as the Pennsylvanians, staged a revolt. Washington was not so lenient this time. He had worried that the Pennsylvania mutiny would trigger others, and that is why he was glad to have it end. He could not permit another. To do so would be to entertain a long string of mutinies. If the New Jersey troops at Pompton thought that they, too, could obtain their goals through similar methods, they were badly mistaken.

The commander-in-chief ordered the Pompton rebellion to be put down with force. He sent General Robert Howe with five hundred troops and told Colonel Israel Shreve to attack the mutineers with other, reliable, New Jersey forces. This was done without a shot being fired. Washington ordered the court-martial and executions of the three leaders of the revolt. To put bite into the sentence, he ordered that the leaders were not only to be shot by their own men, but by their closest friends. The Pennsylvanians may have gambled and won, but the men at Pompton had lost. Washington's swift action to put down the Pompton revolt had succeeded. Regardless of what the spring campaign of 1781 would bring, it would not bring any more mutinies. Washington's mercy with pardons for the Pennsylvanians, and earlier forgiveness of the men from Connecticut, quite effective with the public as well as the army, would set precedent for the power of the president to pardon people later, and he would use it with dramatic effect.

Washington and Hamilton

Alexander Hamilton had yearned for a battlefield command for years. The boyish-looking Hamilton, who was twenty-four but looked younger, had served Washington faithfully as an incredibly skilled chief of staff. The general wanted him to stay right where he was, where Washington believed he could do the most good for the army. There were many men who could lead troops into battle, but no one was as smart as Hamilton and could ever replace him in the high command. Hamilton wanted out, and many in the army agreed with him. After all, he had served as the general's closest confidant for three years. It was time to put him into the field. The general had repeatedly turned down Hamilton's requests to lead attacks, particularly the January 1780 sled assault on Staten Island. He told his brilliant aide that he was always fearful that Hamilton would be captured or killed. Lafayette, Greene, and Laurens had all come to the conclusion that Washington was holding Hamilton back. Hamilton's frustration was growing, particularly now that the army had settled into winter quarters and there would be no opportunities for his field command for months. Cordial to the general all of the time, he fumed privately. Finally, an odd encounter on February 16 caused an explosion that for the time destroyed the close relationship the two men had enjoyed.

The bizarre scene was recorded in rich detail, and with much mood, in a letter Hamilton wrote to his father-in-law, Philip Schuyler. Hamilton told Schuyler that Washington and Hamilton met at the bottom of a staircase as the aide was on his way to post a letter with a courier; the general told him to meet him upstairs in ten minutes. Then, on his way back to see Washington, Hamilton met Lafayette, who engaged him in a conversation. A few moments later, Hamilton went to see the commander-in-chief, climbing up the stairs. He was totally unprepared for what happened next.

Washington snapped at him very angrily, according to Hamilton's lengthy account. "Colonel Hamilton, you have kept me waiting at the head of the stairs these ten minutes. I must tell you, sir, you treat me with disrespect," Washington said.

"I replied without petulancy, but with decision," Hamilton told his father-in-law. " 'I am not conscious of it Sir,'" he answered Washington. "But since you have thought it necessary to tell me, so we must part."

"Very well, sir," answered Washington. "If it be your choice."

Washington immediately knew that he had lost his temper and had treated his aide badly, and sent Tench Tilghman to arrange a meeting between the two. Hamilton, sulking, refused and went into a tirade about Washington to Tilghman. There would be no meeting to broker a peace between the two men.

Hamilton's letter to Schuyler describing the ugly incident included a horrible denunciation of Washington, which must have caused the father-in-law to cringe. "For more than three years, I have felt no friendship for him and have professed none. The truth is our own dispositions are the opposites of each other and the pride of my temper would not suffer me to profess what I did not feel," wrote the overheated Hamilton.

Still upset, Hamilton then send a blistering note to James McHenry, a fellow aide to Washington who now served Lafayette, recounting the incident, telling his friend that the general yelled at him "without a shadow of reason and on the slightest ground." The letter was full of sarcasm. "The Great Man and I have come to an open rupture," he said, adding that efforts by Tilghman to bring them together had failed. "I pledge my honor to you that he [Washington] will find me inflexible. He shall for once at least repent his ill-humor."

In the end, there was no resolution. Through intermediaries, Washington and Hamilton agreed to work together as before and not to discuss their falling out with anyone. Their relationship throughout the rest of the winter would be strained. Washington felt genuine sadness about the breakup, just as he had harbored much remorse about the collapse of his relationship with Joseph Reed earlier in the war. Washington understood why Hamilton felt the way he did, but did not understand why the aide refused to understand the general's position. George Washington was often incapable of understanding the emotions of the men who worked with him, even men whom he saw every day. It was ironic that Washington blithely sent Tilghman to smooth over the dispute with Hamilton because Tilghman himself was steaming inside about his own poor pay and lack of a well-deserved promotion, for which he held the general accountable. Until the Hamilton argument, Washington had never realized the ways in which he coldly treated those closest to him when it came to their own careers. The commander-in-chief had only one goal—win the war—and the personal problems of those around him did not matter.

The coldness between Hamilton and Washington would continue until the siege of Yorktown, seven months later, when Washington finally acquiesced to Hamilton's wishes and gave him the command in what would turn out to be the final major assault of the war, a charge that would result in the capture of the outer ring of Cornwallis's defenses and, within a day, bring about the fall of the city, the surrender of the British army there, and, in reality, the conclusion of the American Revolution. Washington would, in the end, with an exuberant show of public confidence, give Hamilton the glory for which he yearned. Washington did it for Hamilton and he did it for himself, to save their friendship.

And, too, he did it because the falling out with Hamilton had finally shown him the ways in which he ignored those close to him. Washington had learned from the rupture and it enabled him to grow even more. Instead of playing the role of the Great Man, too high on the mountain to be bothered with the wounded egos of underlings, Washington opted to carefully bring Hamilton back under his wing. They would remain close for years and later, as president, Washington would name Hamilton the first Secretary of the Treasury and put the country's economic future in his hands.

Thus, the winter of 1781 ended badly for Washington. The French soon confided to him that they did not have a large-enough armada to take troops to Virginia to impede British armies that moved about unchecked. His hopes that the British people would finally force their government to abandon the war were dashed when he learned in early January that the autumn elections of 1780 resulted in yet another pro-war Parliament. He had discovered, too, that a British warship had sailed up the Potomac and threatened to bombard Mount Vernon itself. Washington's tempestuous mother Mary had embarrassed him by petitioning the state legislature for a pension, falsely claiming that her illustrious son refused to support her. Then he was made aware that his stepson Jackie, elected to the Virginia legislature because of his father's fame, had acted badly, peevishly boycotting sessions when things did not go his way.

Washington's multiple problems had not simply appeared; they had festered since the first snowfalls of 1777. They were now bursting. The army had lived from hand to mouth for four years and would continue to do so. There was no permanent solution to the food or clothing crisis because there was no national government to provide these necessities. The government had so much trouble raising money in taxes from the states to pay for anything that some delegates now expressed fear that

America's "derangement" in finances, and not British bayonets, would bring down the nation. There was no resolution to the inflation woes that beset the soldiers because there was no national bank and no supply of hard money—and there would not be. The plan that was cobbled together to insure pay for the soldiers merely guaranteed it by the end of the war, which did them little good at the time. There would continue to be troubles recruiting men to serve in the military. And, too, there was deep hurt felt by Washington and everyone else in America over the defection of Benedict Arnold to the British.

The general's despondency was mirrored in letters from Congressional delegates throughout the winter. Many urged their states to collect tax money, forward food, and find clothing and other supplies for the dwindling military force, fearful, as Washington predicted, that the army would disintegrate. And, too, prominent men once again told their countrymen that the very best way to help the revolution was to join the armed forces. "When we first engaged in this contest, we declared that rather than submit to the domination of Britain we would sacrifice not only our fortunes, but our lives. This is now the time to demonstrate the sincerity of those declarations," said Pennsylvanian Charles Thomson, the Continental Congress clerk, on Christmas Day of 1780.

Most of all, the leaders of the rebellion worked hard to revive the sagging spirit of the people and convince the best of them to work for the revolution. None put it better than Samuel Adams in a letter to Richard Henry Lee that January: "It is our duty to make every proper exertion in our respective states to revive the old patriotic feelings among the people at large and to get the public departments, especially the most important of them, filled with men of understanding and inflexible virtue....Our cause is surely too interesting to mankind to be put under the direction of men, vain, avaricious or concealed under the hypocritical guise of patriotism without a spark of public or private virtue."

Time, which Washington had always used to help the rebellion because it eroded support for the British resolve at home, now began to threaten the Americans' ability to win the war. The men had been at the point of starvation for so long in the winters of the war that they no longer believed anything promised them about food. They had come to loathe many of the civilians who refused to sell them food or charged exorbitant prices, but their disgust with the civilians only mirrored the citizens' loathing of them. The distrust between the army and the people had become so great that Washington wrote in his diary at the end of winter that "we are daily and hourly oppressing the people—souring their tempers—and alienating the affections." One of the main complaints of the mutinous Pennsylvanians was that they believed their officers to be incompetent. The feuds between officers and men would only grow in the months and years ahead. The citizens were weary of sending their teenagers off to fight, having their towns burned by the British, and having their farms plundered by both sides. How long would the citizens support the war and how much longer would his soldiers continue to fight?

The people's revolution that George Washington had spurred on for so long was on the verge of collapse. His aide Tilghman, reflecting the general's feelings, explained it well in an insightful letter to Robert Morris. "The people grow tired of a war which has been of longer continuance than they were led to expect, and are alarmed and amazed to find that the enemy are at this time of day making strides which they could not effect at the beginning. The reasons are simple and would be as obvious as daylight, if there were not among us those who are determined never to see," wrote Tilghman, citing lack of cooperation between the states and the federal government, lame recruiting drives, and the depreciation of money. He told Morris, with a tinge of regret, that Americans might never grasp "the glorious prize for which we have been contenting."

Time, always his friend, was becoming his enemy. A grim George Washington knew that as the winter of 1781 faded that the war had to be ended—right now.

Chapter Fifteen

COUP D'ETAT

NEW WINDSOR, 1782–83

*"As I was among the first who embarked in the cause
of our common country. As I have never left your side
one moment, but when called from you on public duty.
As I have been the constant companion and witness of
your distresses, and not among the last to feel, and
acknowledge, your merits. As I have ever considered my
own military reputation as inseparably connected with
that of the army. As my heart has ever expanded with joy
when I have heard its praises, and my indignation has
arisen when the mouth of detraction has been opened
against it, it can scarcely be supposed, at this late stage of
the war, that I am indifferent to its interests."*
—George Washington to the officers of the Continental Army, March 15, 1783

The last battle of the war had been fought in October 1781 at York-town, Virginia, a town on a peninsula that jutted out into the Chesapeake Bay. It was an appropriate end to an eight-year-long revolution. It was accidental history. Washington appeared to want an assault on New York, and the destruction of Clinton's army there, as the *coup de grace* for the conflict. His plan was a joint land attack by combined American and French forces and a sea attack by the French Navy under Admiral Comte Francois de Grasse, now fighting the British in the West Indies. Washington had talked about an invasion of New York for years. But it was not to be. French commander Rochambeau informed Washington in mid-August that de Grasse would sail from the West Indies to America with thirty-two hundred men, but he could not make it to New York, as Washington desired. He could only make it as far as the Chesapeake Bay and could not remain past the middle of October.

Washington still publicly insisted on an attack on New York and fed disinformation concerning it to spies in that city. He then ordered part of his army to the New Jersey side of the Hudson opposite the city and began construction of what appeared to be a camp for a large-scale assault across the river, just as he had done at the Delaware at Christmas 1776. Henry Clinton was so certain that Washington was going to launch a final, heroic attack on New York that he not only refortified the city, but ordered two thousand of Cornwallis's men at Yorktown to sail back to join him. While all of this was going on, the combined armies of Rochambeau and Washington marched inland through New Jersey, unseen by the British, on their way to Yorktown. (French officers complained bitterly all the way down the Atlantic Coast that their American hosts provided weak coffee and salad dressing with too much vinegar and, worst of all, served meat and potatoes on *the same plate*.)

By the time the American army reached Yorktown, it had swelled to nearly ten thousand men as dozens of militia units and individuals, smelling the final kill, joined the ever-lengthening columns. It was outside of Yorktown that Washington again met the Marquis de Lafayette. The commander had dispatched Nathanael Greene south to Virginia to harass Cornwallis's army and prevent it from moving out of the state. He had done so, but he had ample assistance from Lafayette. The marquis had been ordered south to Virginia to assist Greene and had, in a series of skirmishes, managed to contain Cornwallis. The British general fell back to Yorktown, unworried. He did not know that now Greene's regiments and Lafayette's men were closing in on him. They were joined by Henry Knox. He had procured dozens of additional cannons on the long trek. The French had 8,800 men, giving the allied command under Washington nearly nineteen thousand men and more than two hundred cannon as they approached Cornwallis's army of just six thousand men at Yorktown. Cornwallis had the Americans and French in front of him and the French fleet anchored in the bay behind him. He was trapped.

The French and Americans dug a series of lengthy ditches for the soldiers' protection and built a series of firing areas for their long train of cannons. This was Henry Knox's winter dreams all come true. There was only one possible escape for Cornwallis. He could sneak his men out of the village and along the banks of the York River under the cover of nightfall, leaving his equipment and supplies behind, with fake campfires blazing and a show of guards. It was exactly what Washington had done before the battle of Princeton, in 1777, when Cornwallis had trapped him on the shores of the Delaware. To thwart that, Washington sent hundreds of troops to the banks of the river. Cornwallis never attempted the escape.

Instead, the British commander tried to fight it out for several days. Countless volleys of cannon battered the Yorktown defenses until Cornwallis was forced to surrender on October 18 following a final American attack on his outer protective trenches that was led by Alexander Hamilton, who at the war's final moment was given command of the army by Washington, as the young man had desired for so long.

Washington had captured Cornwallis's entire army—more than eight thousand soldiers and sailors, 244 pieces of artillery, and thousands of small arms. Cornwallis was so humiliated by the defeat that he refused to surrender the army himself, sending his second in command to hand his sword to Washington. The American commander, insulted, told Cornwallis's underling to give his sword to his own second in command, General Benjamin Lincoln.

Yorktown was the final major battle of the American Revolution. The catastrophic loss of Cornwallis's entire army and the defeat by combined French and American forces angered the British people as well as the

king. The news of the defeat caused riots in London, and in the next parliamentary elections the government of Lord North fell. The new government agreed to unconditional independence for the United States and
began peace talks with American diplomats.

The officers and men of the main American army must have sensed
that New Windsor, New York, would be the final winter camp of the Revolution when they arrived toward the end of 1781. The New Windsor
camp was large, two square miles in area, with ten thousand men housed
in eight hundred huts, similar to those constructed earlier at Valley Forge,
Bound Brook, and Morristown, with supply warehouses, offices, stables,
parade grounds, and hospitals. The army had camped there during several
summers and the veterans were familiar with the area and its small hamlets.

Washington's army, except for a few regiments sent to stay in New
Jersey, arrived in New York in January 1782, while French soldiers
camped in Virginia and the smaller southern forces of the Continental
Army under Nathanael Greene remained in South Carolina. The commander-in-chief did not join the army until the spring. Washington had
been asked to spend the winter in Philadelphia for military and administrative meetings with Congress and to monitor the now nearly defunct
British activities in Charleston and New York.

The real reason for his requested sojourn to Philadelphia was so that
he could be feted in a long procession of public and private celebrations.
The carriage carrying the general and his wife from Mount Vernon to
Pennsylvania had been greeted by cheering crowds in every village they
passed during the day; lighted candles were in the windows of every
home they drove by at night. It seemed like all of Philadelphia was illuminated for them when they finally arrived.

Washington was the guest of honor wherever he went. He was summoned to so many parties that he had to turn down many invitations.
Philadelphians then invented evening "business meetings" that he did
agree to attend, only to discover that they were really parties. He was glad
to be in the largest city in America, its social world shaking itself back to
life now that the war seemed just about over. His son Jackie had died of
fever shortly after Yorktown, where, ill, Jackie, twenty-eight, had insisted

on watching the British surrender to his father. Washington, in mourning with a disconsolate Martha, who had now lost all of her children, knew that he had to return to the armed forces for his seventh winter, and the invitation to Philadelphia was the perfect opportunity to bring Martha, who enjoyed the stay.

There, Washington had the chance to finally spend time with the men who had aided him so much in the war, such as financier Robert Morris, and to personally lobby Congress for more assistance for the army. However, after four months of meetings, lunches, receptions, and shaking hands with people who had ridden dozens of miles just to see the famous general, he was glad to return to the army in New York.

Upon arrival at the winter camp on the west bank of the Hudson, the commander-in-chief decided to make his headquarters at the two-story, Dutch-style fieldstone home of Jonathan Hasbrouck, a six-foot, four-inch farmer whom soldiers joked was probably the only man in the United States taller than Washington. The original home had been built in 1750 on a high bluff overlooking the Hudson, and extra rooms had been added to accommodate the commander and his staff. Additional buildings were erected, including large barracks for Washington's personal guard. The general would live here for sixteen months, longer than he had stayed during any other period of the war. Close by was the headquarters of General Horatio Gates, the second-ranking general in the army, restored to prominence by the commander-in-chief despite the Valley Forge controversy and his stinging defeats in the Carolinas in 1780.

Washington insisted that the army remain together until peace was absolutely certain. He had not trusted the British since the Stamp Act of 1765, and now he was apprehensive that England might trick the United States and resume the war. After all, a large British force remained in New York City. Until the ink was dry on the peace treaty, Washington wanted a full army and decided to remain on as commander-in-chief until hostilities formally ended.

However, Washington's decision to remain in charge of the army, and the seemingly endless negotiations, prompted many in both America and Europe to assume that the next logical step was for him to take over the government. It was a practice, of course, that had been followed through-out the world for thousands of years. People always expected it. Here, there was the added benefit of a leader of the army who was not merely admired by his troops, but adored by the general public, which had continued to sing his praises in newly composed songs such as "God Save the Great Washington and God Damn the King." He could assume power with lit-tle criticism and, most agreed, certainly do a better job of running the country than the bunglers in Congress. After all, even though he was a mil-itary general, everyone knew, from governors to soldiers to shopkeepers, that it was his wartime skills as an unelected political leader, a national exec-utive operating within the army, that kept the country together.

The idea of using his role of commander-in-chief to become a dicta-tor, an American Caesar, never entered Washington's thinking—not once. He became outraged when Lewis Nicola, a French printer serving in the military, suggested in 1782 that many in and out of the army wished that he would declare himself a king, George I. "Be assured, sir," he snapped at Nicola, "no occurrence in the course of the war has given me more painful sensations than your information of there being such ideas existing in the army as you have expressed and as I must view with abhorrence and rep-rimand with severity....I am much at a loss to conceive what part of my conduct could have given encouragement to an address which to me seems big with the greatest mischiefs that can befall my country. You could not have found a person to whom your schemes are more disagreeable."

The eighteen-month lag in time between the victory at Yorktown and the peace treaty itself, not signed until April 1783, caused new and dan-gerous problems for Washington. The officers and men had been engaged in little work and no fighting for more than a year when the winter of 1782–83 began. They had no sooner returned to the Hudson Valley for winter camp when they discovered that Congress had ordered a reduction in their rations, even though the area was well stocked with grain and cat-tle and, with the war over, it was not a problem to buy food. Rumors spread, too, that what little money Congress did have was not going toward feeding the army, but for raises for civilian workers in Philadel-phia. Washington shared the unhappiness of the men. "Is it policy, is it justice, to keep a sore constantly gangrened?" he wrote, worried again about the temperament of the men and fearful of another mass mutiny, similar to the uprising of January 1781.

There was so little to do in camp at New Windsor that Washington spent much time through letters running Mount Vernon from afar, as he had done each winter. He granted an inordinate amount of furloughs to his officers, which created much paperwork for him. With Billy Lee alongside, he spent most afternoons galloping up and down the western banks of the Hudson. The general once again offered prizes for the best new tent facades (in summer) and hut alterations (in winter), and designed a new hat for the enlisted men. Attendance at religious services was encouraged. He decided to institute what he called the "Badge of Military Merit" for enlisted men who had shown exceptional courage in battle, and designed a small heart of purple cloth to be worn on the left breast of the uniform. It was the first honor of its kind, and later was awarded to those wounded in combat and renamed the "purple heart."

The enlisted men, while grumbling about continued service, were eager for a peace accord so that they could return to their homes. The officers were very unhappy because the possibility of peace meant that their longstanding complaints about back pay, pensions, supplies and equipment owed them—issues that did not directly concern the enlisted soldiers—might go unresolved and they would leave the army empty-handed. They were supported by Washington, who told Congress that back pay was required; that pensions, promised since Valley Forge, were a just reward for the officers' years of service and that, in fact, Congress had already paid out numerous pensions to others who had retired earlier (they argued, however, that their total half-pay pensions would amount to five years of full wages and not the stipulated seven years). Nothing had been agreed upon for the men now in the service despite two years of debates on the subject.

He told the members of the Continental Congress that it was not right that the officers would be "turned into the world...without one farthing of money to carry them home." He argued that his officers had given up everything—their businesses, farms and family—to fight for their country, and were being treated in a shabby manner. Further, he said, he feared that an officers' revolt would trigger a general mutiny throughout the army and produce, he said, "a train of evil."

The officers' anger over these issues simmered throughout the winter and finally exploded in December 1781, when it became apparent that Congress was paying little attention to their pleas. Despite Washington's lobbying, Congress let it be known that it had no intention of paying back wages and pensions to all the officers because the national legislature was bankrupt and did not believe the states could be taxed yet again to raise money. The trio of three men, General Alexander McDougall, Colonel Matthias Ogden, and John Brooks, went to Philadelphia on December 29, 1782 to present to Congress a petition backed by all the officers in the army. It was formally turned in on January 6 and sent to a congressional committee, before which MacDougall made an impassioned plea. The committee recommended that the Congress authorize a 5 percent general tax on all citizens to raise money for the pensions. The bill was approved by delegates from seven of the thirteen states, but a parliamentary rule required authorization by at least nine. The legislation died. All Congress could raise was enough money to cover one month's back pay for each officer, hardly enough to keep the officer corps happy.

What angered the officers as much as the rejection was the cavalier attitude of the delegates, who never seemed in a hurry to do anything. That attitude of Congress was best expressed in a letter Washington received from his friend and delegate Joseph Jones about the officers at the end of February. Jones told him that the soldiers simply had to be patient, "Those acquainted with the deliberations of public bodies, and especially of so mixed a body as that of Congress, [know] allowances will be made for slow determination."

Men who had been involved in the revolution since the beginning— and who supported a more nationalistic Congress, with more federal power, and who had worked hard to get Congress to pay off state and private creditors to show its strength, were infuriated. How could the United States show the world it could pay its debts when it would not even provide pensions for its army?

Alexander Hamilton, now a Congressional delegate from New York and a leading nationalist, suggested that Washington use his stature to threaten Congress in order to help the officers. Hamilton then told several influential Congressmen that he had approached Washington on the idea of the commander siding with his troops against Congress and, he ominously told James Madison, to "exclude some other leader who might foment and misguide their councils."

Hamilton and Madison were not the only delegates to become nervous about a potential coup d'etat, perhaps led by Gates, who had been the central figure in the Conway incident five years earlier. Phillip White wrote that "both officers and soldiers are uneasy." If Washington needed any further assurances that the delegates genuinely feared an officers' coup, he received it in a letter from Joseph Jones in late February. "Reports are freely circulated here that there are dangerous combinations in the army; and within a few days past it has been said that they are about to declare they will not disband until their demands are complied with," he wrote the commander, adding that "I have lately heard there are those who are abandoned enough to use their arts to lessen your reputation in the army, in hopes ultimately the weight of your oppositions will prove no obstacle to their ambitious designs." Their pleas fell on deaf ears; Washington refused to use his power as head of the army to intimidate the nation's civilian government.

The lack of action by Congress or General Washington enraged the officers in New Windsor, who had increasingly come to believe that a huge gulf separated the army and the civilian population, whether men in Congress or regular citizens. Congressional inactivity could mean the dissolution of the army without any benefits or pensions when the peace treaty was signed. The officers, with apparent complicity by the staff of General Gates, took drastic action on March 10. They posted the "Newburgh Address," reportedly written by Major John Armstrong, an aide to Gates. In it, the officer corps threatened to ensure that the army remained together after the peace treaty was signed, regardless of Congressional orders to disband, creating the specter of a permanent, leaderless, and quite angry, military force. The officers also warned that they might not wait for the peace treaty and lead the army into the nation's interior, leaving the United States open to an attack by the British or any foreign power. Both options made it clear, too, that the army might march on Philadelphia and depose Congress in a military coup.

It was a strongly written statement and designed to inflame the emotions of the bitter officers. The Newburgh Address declared:

> If this, then, be your treatment while the swords you wear are necessary for the defense of America? What have you to expect from peace, when your voice shall sink and your strength dissipate by division? When those very swords, the instruments and companions of your glory, shall be taken from your sides, and no remaining mark of military distinction left but your wants, infirmities, and scars?…Can you consent to wade through the vile mire of despondency and owe the miserable remnant of that life to charity, which has hitherto been spent in honor? If you can—GO—and carry with you the jest of Tories and the scorn of Whigs—the ridicule and, what is worse, the pity of the world. Go starve and be forgotten.

At the same time, rumors swirled throughout Philadelphia and other cities that Washington, always the champion of his soldiers, had sided with them and would lead their march on Congress and there, after Congress had fled, would be appointed the dictator of America. The unsubstantiated rumors were so strong that the commander-in-chief had to send a letter to Congress discounting them and pledging his loyalty to the country.

But even though he pledged his continued devotion, Washington denounced Congress for reneging on promises to the army, telling Jones that if there was a mass mutiny and attack on Philadelphia, Congress and Congress alone "must be answerable for all the ineffable horrors which may be occasioned thereby."

No one appreciated the dangers of the situation more than the commander-in-chief. An officers' coup might have several effects: 1) a successful march against Philadelphia might cause the Continental

Congress to flee again, or simply disband; 2) officers might then march on various state capitals and seize power there, creating separate military states—officers from New England, the Middle Atlantic States and the southern states might turn those regions into three separate nations; 3) Congress might order the remaining army, led by Washington, to march against the officers' army, bringing about chaos and bloodshed; and 4) England might pounce on the disorder and renew the war.

And, too, as he told Hamilton later, his group of nationalist politicians, whom he quietly supported, although they did not realize it, would be smothered as a political group if the army did what they wished. Regardless of the outcome, politicians favoring strong state governments would step in to clean up the army's mess and hopes for a strong postwar national government would vanish.

Washington knew that while all of the officers publicly supported the seditious options in the address, privately many were skeptical and were looking for a negotiated settlement that would earn them their back pay and pensions and prevent trouble. The commander-in-chief decided to buy himself time to defuse the powder keg, asking for a general meeting four days later at the "Temple," a large hall constructed for recreation by the army at New Windsor. He told the officers he would not attend and that the assembly would be a chance for everyone to discuss the problem publicly; he even put Gates, who fervently supported the officers, in charge of the gathering.

The officers agreed to the public meeting, but not before they managed to publish a second address, reiterating what they insisted were nonnegotiable demands. The Temple, a large log structure that could house several hundred men comfortably, was jammed when the meeting began shortly after noon on March 15. Just as Gates had called it to order, George Washington arrived on horseback unexpectedly, without any entourage, and asked Gates for a chance to address the officers.

He walked across the stage, pulling some papers out of his coat, and turned to peer out over the group of hostile men. Hundreds were seated on rows of benches and more jammed the aisles and doorways. They were unhappy about the rejection of their grievances and unhappy that the general, whom they believed had refused to lend them enough support, had gone back on his word and insisted on addressing the group.

Washington, too, was irate. He told them that he did not want to be in the Temple that afternoon (clearly, this was orchestrated), but circumstances compelled his attendance. He read a carefully prepared speech, the best he had ever composed, and asked them to be moderate in their views and be patient in their emotions. Congress was not the villain, as they believed (even though he knew it was), but the problem was that, like any large administrative body, it moved slowly. He told them, again, that he felt that with further pressure from himself and others they would eventually obtain their goals.

After that appeal to their pocketbooks, he appealed to their patriotism and suggested that the uprising would ruin everything they had achieved in their years of bravery. The general insisted that their idea to create a marauding army might eventually result in the overthrow of the government and bring on chaos. He again promised to do everything in his power to convince leaders of Congress to develop ways to raise money and restore their back wages and provide for half-pay pensions. Washington concluded by reminding them that they were an army of patriots, and any march on Philadelphia would ruin the reputations they had developed for themselves during the revolution.

He told them, "as you value your own sacred honor, as you respected the rights of humanity, and as you regard the military and national character of America, to express your utmost horror and detestation of the man who wishes, under any specious pretenses, to overturn the liberties of our country, and who wickedly attempts to open the flood gates of civil discord and deluge our rising empire in blood," and also that "humanity revolts at the idea." He asked them not to take any action that "will lessen the dignity and sully the glory you have hitherto maintained. Let me request you to rely on the plighted faith of your country and place a full confidence in the purity of the intentions of Congress." And, then, again, he appealed to their love of country. "You will, by the dignity of your conduct, afford occasion for posterity to say when speaking of the glorious example you have exhibited to mankind, 'Had this day been wanting, the world had never seen the last stage of perfection to which human nature is capable of attaining."

He reminded them, too, that he had suffered with them for eight long years and that "I have never left your side for one moment." He talked about the distresses they had been through together, how they had shared defeats and victories as a group. He explained with great pride that he and the army were inseparable.

George Washington was an ineffective public speaker, however, and his pleas, expressed eloquently but without much passion, made little impression. He knew that he would have great difficulty swaying them with his own words and so, to underscore his remarks, he had brought along a letter from Jones in which the delegate pledged to lobby for the men in Congress. The hand-written letter was difficult to read in the badly illuminated hall, however, and, after stumbling through just a paragraph, unable to make out the words of the scrawl, Washington reluctantly removed his reading spectacles from the pockets of his coat. A murmur rose in the hall because no one except his closest aides had seen him wear the very recently purchased glasses, which his failing eyesight now required.

Lieutenant Samuel Shaw, sitting in the Temple watching the commander-in-chief, witnessed what happened next with the same feelings as everyone else in the hall. Shaw said that the general fumbled with the glasses while holding the letter; he finally managed to slide them down over his nose. "Gentlemen, you must pardon me," he said. "I have grown gray in your service and now find myself going blind as well."

The brief, unplanned sentence, a simple declaration from a soldier, touched the hearts of every man in the hall. "There was something so natural, so unaffected, in his appeal that it rendered it superior to the most studied oratory; it forced its way to the heart," wrote Shaw in his journal.

The simple sentence reminded them all, in one instant, of Washington's dedication to his country, the army, and to them. But it was more than that. It was his recognition of their own dedication, through all those battles and freezing cold winters, to a revolution to bring about the first truly democratic republic on earth. It was the public acknowledgement of their heroism and their sacrifice that they needed and wanted so badly. And, too, it served to remind them that everything the army achieved it did with the general and everything the general accomplished was done with their help. Together, he on his white horse and they with their muskets, they had defeated the greatest army and navy in the world and established independence. And now he had made them realize that to continue with their uprising would not merely ruin their honor, but the honor of the entire revolution and all of the more than 150,000 men who had fought for American freedom in it.

Some men shuddered at his words. Many became so overwhelmed that they started to weep. Some broke down and cried uncontrollably. Men hugged those next to them. Washington, on the stage, never intended that reaction and was startled at the response. A master of timing all of this life, he knew it was necessary to leave. He read Jones letter quickly, bid the men good-bye, and departed, mounting his horse and riding back to Newburgh.

There was a rather disorganized thirty-minute debate following his departure, but Gates, as moved as everyone else, refused to participate in it. Few did. The meeting ended quietly and so did the threats of the officers. They left the Temple slowly and returned to their posts. The commander-in-chief had defused the military coup that might have toppled Congress and destroyed the new nation. He did not do it with threats or force, but a simple gesture that reminded them all that they had fought for independence, to be sure, but they had fought for each other...and for George Washington.

The general kept his word to the officers after thanking them for the "affectionate sentiments expressed toward him" in the hall that afternoon. He campaigned diligently over the next few months to successfully persuade Congress to honor all of its promises concerning pensions and back pay. The decision of the officers not to revolt, he told Congress, was "the last glorious proof of patriotism which could have been given by men who aspired to the distinction of a patriot army and will not only confirm their claim to the justice but will increase their title to the gratitude of their country."

Chapter Sixteen

CINCINNATUS

CHRISTMAS, 1783

"Though I retire from the employment of public life I shall never cease to entertain the most anxious care for the welfare of my country. May the Almighty dispose the heart of every citizen of the United States to improve the great prospect of happiness before us."
—George Washington to the Common Council of Annapolis,
December 22, 1783

No one except his wife ever knew exactly when George Washington decided to resign from the army and retire to Mount Vernon to spend the rest of his years as a planter. He wrote a lengthy and passionate circular letter to the states in early June 1783, indicating that he might leave the army and telling members of Congress and the governors that "the task is now accomplished....I bid a last farewell to the cares of office and all the employments of public life." It was the first public announcement of his decision, which he apparently had contemplated for months. Later, when he moved his camp from Newburgh to Rocky

Hill, New Jersey, he explained to everyone who asked about his return to Mount Vernon that he simply looked forward to the peacefulness of retirement like anyone else, especially after what he had been through for eight years.

The general expressed that feeling to simply go home in a touching letter he later wrote to Lafayette:

> I am become a private citizen on the banks of the Potomac, and under the shadow of my own vine and my own fig tree. Free from the bustle of a camp and the busy scenes of a public life, I am solacing myself with those tranquil endowments of which the soldier who is ever in pursuit of fame, the stateman whose watchful days and sleepless nights are spent in devising schemes to promote the welfare of his own, perhaps the ruin of other countries (as if the globe was insufficient for us all); and the courtier who is always watching the countenance of his prince, in hopes of catching a gracious smile, can have very little conception. I am not only retired from all public employments, but I am retiring within myself and shall be able to view the solitary walk and tread the paths of private life with heartfelt satisfaction. Envious of none, I am determined to be pleased with all, and this, my dear friend, being the order for my march, I will move gently down the stream of life until I sleep with my fathers.

If anyone ever believed that there was any consideration by Washington of remaining on as the commander-in-chief and becoming some sort of combined commander-in-chief and civilian head of state, or even king, that consideration should have been discarded when he put down the officers' revolt at Newburgh. That was the perfect moment for him to lead the army against Congress and seize control of the United States. He could have declared that he had to take over the country and remain in charge for life because only he stood between the people and anarchy, just as Oliver Cromwell had done in England a century before. Washington's speeches, letters, and actions concerning that propsective mutiny in early March should have convinced everyone, in Europe as well as America, that he had no such plans.

Still, military leaders, public officials, newspaper editors, and monarchs throughout the world were stunned when they learned that he would resign from the army. Idolatry of Washington was so great, political observers felt, that the general did not have to do anything to be handed control of America. All he had to do was sit in his office at Newburgh and await a committee from Congress to ask him to remain as the commander-in-chief and lead the new nation.

Washington's popularity had ebbed during the terrible winter of 1777–78 at Valley Forge, when the Conway tumult began and then crumbled. He had regained the admiration of the people again with his daunting victory at Monmouth and retained it through the summer of 1781. Victory at Yorktown had given him more prestige and dramatically increased the public's admiration for him. The war had been won and Washington was now not only the commander-in-chief, but the victor. He had been transformed from beloved general to cultural phenomenon. "Old men, women and children press about him when he accidently passes along, and think themselves happy, once in their lives, to have seen him—they follow him through the towns with torches and celebrate his arrival by public illuminations. The Americans, that cool and sedate people, who in the midst of their most trying difficulties have attended only to the directions and impulses of plain method and common sense, are roused, animated and inflamed at the very mention of his name," summed up one man after Yorktown.

And so Washington's simple accession to the role of king, or Cromwellian protector, or dictatorial Caesar, seemed a natural step that had been taken by the heads of revolutionary armies for thousands of years. King George III simply could not believe what he heard of Washington's plans. He said, when told of the commander's planned resignation in June, that if the general actually did so, "he would be the greatest man in the world."

Leaders of many nations immediately drew a comparison to Cincinnatus, a Roman farmer who left his plow to rescue the empire and then ignored pleas to run the country and rode back to his fields for the harvest. This American Cincinnatus was doing the same thing, giving up the leadership of the army and perhaps the nation to ride back to the fertile fields of Mount Vernon.

Why give it all up? His pleas that he yearned to return to Mount Vernon were charming but weak; he had been away for eight long years. Washington's rustic notion that he wanted to go back to the simple life of the farmer were equally hollow; the equestrian, businessman, state legislator, militia head, fox hunter, and church elder had never been a simple farmer. The idea that he was exhausted from army life was not convincing either. Everyone else may have been tired of the army, but never him. There would probably not be much of an army to lead, either, since Washington himself acknowledged that the people did not want a large standing army and considered it "dangerous to the liberties of a country."

He had reminded people for years that he had accepted the job of commander-in-chief because he thought the war might only last six months, or a year, and that his time in service would really be equal to just a single harvest away from home. Washington had always treasured the concept of the kinsman/soldier. He told the New York legislature early in the war that all soldiers were citizens and that they would return to being citizens at the end of the conflict. Now, he would do the same. "When we assumed the soldier, we did not lay aside the citizen, and we shall most sincerely rejoice with you in that happy hour when the establishment of American Liberty upon the most firm and solid foundations, shall enable us to return to our private stations in the bosom of a free, peaceful and happy country." Later in the conflict, he addressed that idea again, writing that "as the sword was the last resort for the preservation of our liberties, so it ought to be the first to be laid aside when those liberties are firmly established."

In 1790, in an address to the people of South Carolina, Washington summed up his deeply held feelings about the men in the army:

The value of liberty was thus enhanced in our estimation by the difficulty of its attainment, and the worth of characters appreciated by the trial of adversity. The tempest of war having at length been succeeded by the sunshine of peace; our citizen-soldiers impressed a useful lesson of patriotism on mankind, by nobly returning with impaired constitution and unsatisfied claims, after such long sufferings and severe disappointments, to their former occupations. Posterity as well as the present age will doubtless regard with admiration and gratitude the patience, perseverance and valour which achieved our revolution. They will cherish the remembrance of virtues which had but few parallels in former times, and which will add new lustre to the most splendid page of history.

His entire conduct throughout the war should have led to resignation. He had never given a single thought to overthrowing Congress or even defying Congress. Washington was painstakingly careful to assure Congress that he was just a soldier doing their bidding. So when the war ended, the job completed, resignation should have been a logical next step. Yet it was not seen as such by anyone. National control was the next step all foresaw for him, and would have applauded.

The reason George Washington gave up all of his power was to remind everyone, in North America and in the world, that real power was the ability to surrender it. A strong man embraces power; a stronger man can walk away from it. By stepping down and completely severing his ties with the army and Congress, he was reminding the United States and the world that the Revolution was fought to establish a democratic republic. True power in a republic belonged to the people and leaders only obtained power from the people. Leaders in a democracy did not draw their power from wealth, political parties, or cabals, and they certainly did not draw it from the cannon of the army. The real power in America, his resignation signified, was in the Americans themselves. Democracy could not flourish with George Washington as the commanding general of the army and still the central figure of the country; he had to leave.

There was another, rather whimsical reason. Washington seems to have, in his mind, recreated himself as a character in some lengthy play about the American Revolution. The mercurial exploits of the general and his troops in the war—the escape from Brooklyn Heights, the crossing of the Delaware at Christmas, the survival of the winters at Valley Forge and Morristown, the battle of Monmouth and the address at Newburgh—were the stuff of Homerian tales. He had lived through this eight-year saga, with its twists and turns, triumphs and tragedies, as a dashing hero, irrepressibly handsome on his white horse, immaculately dressed, riding in the line of fire, waving his sword in the air.

More and more, in those closing months, Washington began to define himself in fictional and theatrical terms. He told Nathanael Greene after he resigned that, looking back, the entire war seemed like a "fiction" in which they were players because in real life "it could not be believed that such a force as Great Britain has employed for eight years in this country could be baffled in their plans of subjugating it by numbers infintely less." In general orders on April 18, 1783, the day the peace settlement with Britain was finally announced, he told his soldiers that they had been players in a drama and could now retire, hinting at his own choice. "Nothing now remains but for the actors of this mighty scene to preserve a perfect, unvarying, consistency of character through the very last act; to close the drama with applause and to retire from the military theater with the same approbation of angels and men which have crowned all their former virtuous actions," he wrote. Later, when he was the honored guest at a dinner in Wilmington, Delaware, he told that audience, in a theatrical reference, that "I shall no more appear on the great stage of action." When he finally arrived at Mount Vernon after his resignation, he wrote like a playwright to Governor George Clinton that "the scene is done." His resignation was the perfect ending to a play. The final act over, the hero could now leave the stage and permit the final curtain to ring down.

It was, perhaps, the longest resignation in America history. He had set it in motion with his June circular. The final phase began on November 23, when he rode into New York City with the army. It was an eerie ride. The fall foliage was long gone as winter began and New York was gray. There were only a few hundred New Yorkers, scattered along two miles of roadway in Manhattan leading to the city itself, to cheer him. He passed large mansions, now vacant and desolate, which had been commandeered by British officers for seven years. The army's route took them through the streets of city neighborhoods whose buildings had been destroyed or partially ruined by the great fire of 1776. Washington finally reached the gate to the center of the city, at Third and Bowery, where he was greeted by Governor George Clinton, who planned to escort him through a large crowd of well wishers that had lined the streets. Washington joined Clinton at the head of the march, ordering the New York militia to fall in behind him as a salute to the state, and proceeded on, cheered by just about every resident of the city.

The commander-in-chief was feted at several dinners and receptions, and was the guest at a fireworks in his honor, but he was in no mood to remain in the city he had longed to capture since his army was chased from its shores in 1776. The man of exquisite planning and details had a carefully arranged schedule to follow. He was to leave the city shortly and make his way to Annapolis, where the Continental Congress now met, to tender his resignation. Depending on time, along the way he would make stops at several towns and the homes of men and women who had helped him during the war. Then, after his resignation, sometime in late December, he would arrive home at Mount Vernon, where he would once again rise just before dawn to walk downstairs to his office to organize the plantation's daily activities.

There were two things he had to do first, however. He had to say farewell to his officers and he had to pay a visit to the newspaper offices of the most hated editor in America, James Rivington. The editor of the *New York Gazette*, the staunch Tory journalist who had often mocked Washington and belittled the Continental Army and the American people in his columns, had been burned in effigy in 1776 and universally despised throughout the war. Washington did not visit him to arrest him, though. He paid a courtesy call on Rivington to embrace him and thank him. It was now revealed, to the sustained shock of everyone, that from the winter of 1778 on, Rivington, the close friend of countless British officers and Sir Henry Clinton himself, had served as Washington's most trusted spy.

His final business in New York was the hardest, saying good-bye to the men who had worked with him throughout the war at Fraunces Tavern, at the foot of Wall Street. Many of his top generals and officers had returned home or were stationed too far away to join him. That final group at the small tavern numbered less than twenty. Washington would correspond with some of them, but he knew that he would never see most of them again. He lived in Virginia and the others were from different states; travel made it difficult for visits to far off towns and farms.

The general had already said farewell to the soldiers of the army in a speech read to them on April 18, the day the peace treaty was announced. In heartfelt and eloquent language, and in a letter aimed at all the men who had fought in the Revolution and not just the men in service at the end, he said:

> The glorious task for which we first flew to arms being thus accomplished, the liberties of our country being fully acknowledged and firmly secured by the smiles of Heaven on the purity of our cause, and the honest exertions of a feeble people determined to be free, against a powerful nation disposed to oppress them, and the character of those who have persevered through every extremity of hardship, suffering and danger, being imortalized by the illustrious appellation of the *Patriot Army*, nothing now remains but for the actors of this mighty scene to preserve a perfect unvarying consistency of character through the very last act, to close the drama with applause and to retire from the military theater with the same approbation of angels and men which has crowned all of their former virtuous actions.

That good-bye and soaring tribute to the soldiers had been carefully written out. This public and very personal farewell would be the most emotional moment of the war for the commander-in-chief. These men had served with him through all of the difficult times of the Revolution. They had all been away from their families for extended periods of time and suffered financially. Some had simply ended careers to join the army; others had lost businesses and farms. It was hard to say good-bye.

The afternoon was just as hard for the officers. The Continental Army had accomplished a miracle, and each of them knew that the war would not have been won without Washington as the head of the army. He had held the officers, soldiers, and the people together for eight long years against ever-mounting odds. Washington had risked everything he had for independence, including his life in several battles. The commander once said that "in winter we dream of independence and peace" and now they were here this final winter—thanks to him.

The men arrived in the low-ceilinged second-floor dining room of Fraunces' tavern at 4 P.M. as the winter light began to fade. Washington, even when seated much taller than everyone else, barely touched the platters of cheese, bread, and beef placed by waiters on the hardwood tables. Those present said they had never seen him so overwrought. He rose to propose a toast, trembling, eyes watery. His voice was thick and barely audible in the tiny room. "With a heart full of love and gratitude, I now take leave of you. I most devoutly wish that your latter days may be as prosperous and happy as your former ones have been glorious and honorable," he said, looking out at the men he trusted most in the world. He drank silently, and then they all did. There was no applause, no cheering, just an eerie quiet.

No one seemed to know what to do. "I cannot come to each of you, but shall feel obliged if each of you will come and take me by the hand," he finally said.

Henry Knox, the bookseller who had dragged fifty-five cannon across New England for him in the winter of 1776, was closest. Knox could not bring himself to speak; neither could Washington. They grasped each other's hand and hugged. The stoic Washington, so often accused of being without emotion other than anger, suddenly began to cry. Benjamin Talmadge, who had run his incredibly successful spy ring for eight years, was next. He took a step toward the commander, shook his hand, kissed him on the cheek, embraced him, and stepped back, unable to say anything. Many of the others did the same. Few could mutter more than a word or two and all wept. "The simple thought...that we should see his face no more in this world seemed to me utterly insupportable," said Talmadge later.

When he had finished embracing each man, the general simply walked out of the room, leaving his trusted officers to regain their composure. He left with a single aide, wiping tears from his cheeks, and then met with Governor Clinton and other public officials for a short farewell. Then he climbed into a carriage that took him to the wharf. There, the waters of New York harbor lapping up against the wooden docks, Washington walked, ramrod straight, through a long line of soldiers to a barge and began the long journey home.

Washington took a carriage from New Jersey to Annapolis. He was accompanied by two servants and three aides, plus an army honor guard from West Point. Two wooden wagons carried his possessions. Among them were Washington's field bed, a thirty-foot-long tent, and a box of utensils, which he purchased himself. On the way he finalized his carefully itemized expense bill, which included meals for his entire staff and spy salaries. The total bill came to $100,000, or just over $1,000 a month, in modern currency, which was the greatest bargain in American history. There was no charge for his services. He ruminated, too, about his acute financial losses in the war. He had served without pay. A corporate head serving without pay for eight years today would have lost $40 million or more while in the service. Currency depreciation and losses at Mount Vernon for eight years, due to his absence and the war, meant that his net worth had declined by almost half. Independence had cost George Washington dearly.

What followed next had no parallel in the nation's young history, or would for generations. The eighteen-month-long, frustrating peace negotiations following the American victory at Yorktown had not only angered many Americans, but prohibited any universal celebration of independence. Unable to enjoy a national holiday, Americans who lived in the towns the Washingtons would pass through on their way to Annapolis arranged hasty, but lusty, celebrations for him as a grand substitute. People lined the streets of the towns through which his small procession passed and cheered him. Farmers drove from miles away, their families in the backs of their wagons, just to get a glimpse of him. He stopped at the homes of several individuals to thank them for their service during the war, including his trusted Trenton spy John Honeyman.

There was jubilation in Philadelphia when Washington arrived on December 8, 1783. The First City Troop of Light Horse rode out to meet him, along with dozens of revolutionary leaders and city dignitaries. They led his carriage and entourage in a nightime parade through the city, accompanied by the pealing of the bells of every church in the city and booming cannon salutes from ships anchored in the Delaware and artillery on shore. Hundreds of homes and stores were illuminated by thousands of candles as a tribute. Nearly every resident of the city where Washington had been elected commander-in-chief, and had defended twice, turned out to line the streets and cheer loudly as his carriage passed by. The next day he was greeted with loud applause by members of the Pennsylvania Assembly packed into Independence Hall. Never a man for long speeches, Washington told them that "I consider the approbations of a free and generous people as the most enviable reward that can ever be conferred on a public character."

The general departed the following day, after some shopping, eager to end the celebrations and get back to Mount Vernon and his wife. Washington thanked the West Point guard and then sent them home; they were no longer needed. He continued toward Annapolis with just his aides and servants. They stopped off at Wilmington, Delaware, for a reception and lavish dinner at a hall surrounded by dozens of large bonfires that lit up the night sky. In what was to become a standard phrase in his numerous retirement speeches and letters, he told the well wishers that "I shall no more appear on the great theater of action." Then it was off to Baltimore for yet another large dinner followed by a ball that lasted until the early hours of the morning. And then the very thankful, but very tired, Washington began the next-to-last leg of their journey, to Annapolis.

There were those in Congress, what there was left of that governing body, who did not believe that Washington would actually resign from the army, and that he would refuse any seat in Congress, the House of Burgesses, or any other political body. Thomas Jefferson, who had met with Washington at Princeton, in October, was told of the plan and asked to keep it a secret. Washington also told him that despite his tattered relations with Congress throughout the war, he fervently believed it was the heart of democratic government.

Washington left it to Jefferson to arrange the details of his formal resignation at Annapolis and to put together whatever receptions or tributes Congress might approve. Washington also told Jefferson he was delighted that his young friend from Virginia had joined the Congress. The Congress, rarely with full attendance after 1777, was a skeleton by the end of the war and it was unusual when more than twenty of its twenty-six members were ever assembled at once. As Washington headed toward Annapolis, in fact, only seven of the thirteen states had representatives there. Congress had become the butt of numerous jokes, too, when, threatened by groups of soldiers over the back-pay issue, they left Philadelphia and fled to Annapolis. The national governing body was castigated in the press and snubbed by the state legislatures. Congress badly needed Thomas Jefferson.

Following his pre-arranged plan with Jefferson, Washington arrived in Annapolis on December 19, and the following day handed the president of Congress, Thomas Mifflin, a note informing him of his retirement. Mifflin was shocked, as were many others in Congress. The general really meant it. He was actually going to return to his farm and leave his role as the most powerful man in America. Mifflin was then quickly informed of Washington's desires and Jefferson's own plans for the retirement celebrations, which the Congressional leader approved. That evening Mifflin hosted a formal dinner for the general. On Sunday, Washington made personal visits to public and military leaders in town, including a friendly sojourn to the home of Horatio Gates. The following night, Monday, the Common Council of Annapolis and General Assembly of Maryland met and listened to notes of retirement and thanks from the general.

That evening, Congress hosted an extravagant dinner to honor the commander-in-chief (which Jefferson missed, complaining of yet another migraine). The dinner was at Mann's Tavern, the largest in Annapolis. More than two hundred guests were invited for a sumptuous meal. When Washington was asked to give his own toast, following thirteen others, he chose his words carefully in order to let everyone know where he stood in the formation of the government of the United States: "Competent powers to Congress for general purposes," he said, and downed his drink to the cheers of the crowd.

The dinner was merely the start of the evening, which was crowned by a lavish ball in the newly completed, elegant red-brick Maryland State House and was attended by more than six hundred people. There were cheers, toasts, thirteen-gun salutes, food, and wine. And there was dancing. The commander-in-chief once again strode on to the dance floor and spent much of the night dancing jigs, reels, and minuets. He danced with different women in the hall, many of whom could not dance at all, but merely wanted to touch him and remember the moment vividly in order to retell it again and again to their grandchildren.

All who wished him well during those few, last winter days of the war assumed, like the general, that the final curtain on his career had, indeed, come down As Elbridge Gerry remarked to a friend, "thus he will retire to life a finished character."

Early on Tuesday morning, December 23, the commander-in-chief sent a letter of thanks to the governor and Council of Maryland in which he told them that "the flattering sentiments you entertain of my exertions in defense of our country, and the favorable point of light in which you place my character, too strongly demonstrate your friendship." At noon, George Washington arrived by carriage at the State House, cheered again by men, women, and children in the huge crowd, which had gathered hours earlier.

Charles Thomson, the secretary of the Congress since the beginning of the war, led Washington and several of his aides to the front of the assembly, to join the Congressmen, all with their tri-corned hats on and in their best clothes. The balcony was packed with spectators. Every seat on the first floor was filled and more than two hundred soldiers, who had donned their old uniforms for the occasion, were squeezed together along the walls or sat in the window seats to see the general for the last time.

Mifflin pounded his gavel to bring the house to order and asked Washington to speak. The general could have walked up to the podium to talk, but he chose to remain at his chair, his figure silhouetted against the high, wide windows of the hall. He stood and nodded as the delegates lifted their hats upward, then put them back on their heads in acknowledgement. The general had difficulty talking. He was overcome with emotion again, as he had been at Fraunces Tavern. He pulled a speech from the pocket of his coat. James McHenry, one of his former aides who was in the audience, noted that the commander was uneasy. "The General's hand which held the address shook as he read it. When he spoke of the officers who had composed his family, and recommended those who had continued in it to the present moment to the favorable notice of Congress he was obliged to support the paper with both hands." He spoke for three and a half minutes, and when he finished everyone in the hall, Congressmen, soldiers, and spectators, was weeping, according to David Howell, also in attendance.

Washington's voice completely broke only once, when he asked God to watch over the United States, and then he ended, telling the hushed chamber that "having now finished the work asigned me, I retire from the great theater of action; and bidding an affectionate farewell to this august body under whose orders I have so long acted, I here offer my commission, and take my leave of all the employment of public life."

McHenry was as overwrought with feeling as everyone else in the chamber. He wrote:

> So many circumstances crowded into view and gave rise to so many affecting emotions. The events of the Revolution just accomplished, the new situation into which it had thrown the affairs of the world, the great man who had borne so conspicious a figure in it, in the act of relinquishing all public employments to return to private life, the past, the present, the future, the manner, the occasion, all conspired to render it a spectacle inexpressibly solemn and affecting.

The commander-in-chief took a few steps forward and handed Mifflin his resignation letter. Mifflin, who had been his close friend and sometimes foe, then read a citation from Congress to the throng. In it,

Congress thanked Washington for conducting the war "with wisdom and fortitude" and for always remaining subservient to civilian authority. The president of the Congress told him that his glory would not end that afternoon, but would "animate remotest ages." He paused when he reached the final lines. "For you," he read to the crowd, looking down at the commander, "we address to Him our earnest prayers that a life so beloved may be fostered with all his care, that your days may be happy as they have been illustrious, and that he will finally give you that reward which this world cannot." As Mifflin finished, the crowd let out a roar that lasted several minutes and reverberated through the State House for Washington, "our illustrious hero," said a spectator.

Washington had no desire to remain in Annapolis for what promised to be a long round of parties and receptions. He was eager to get home to Mount Vernon and his wife, whom he missed dearly. After one final bow to Congress and the crowd, Washington left the hall and mounted a horse. He reined him in, waved slowly to the crowd gathered outside the building, and turned his mount southward. Accompanied only by Billy Lee and two aides, Washington then began the trip to his plantation on the Potomac. They arrived there on Christmas Eve, where Martha and the house staff greeted them with applause. George Washington spent his first full day at Mount Vernon on Christmas Day, 1783, when he rose at dawn, as always, quietly pulled his six-foot, three-inch frame out of the canopy bed so as not to disturb Martha, dressed, and walked downstairs to look at the business books of Mount Vernon for the first time in years. He shaved near the east window, dried his hands, and sat down at his large wooden desk to begin reading the most recent letters that had arrived. It was December 25, 1783, exactly seven years, to the day, since he crossed the Delaware and changed the history of the world.

Epilogue

"I DO SOLEMNLY SWEAR..."

"You must be the President.
No other man can fill that office."
—Gouverneur Morris to George Washington, December 6, 1788

"I little thought, when the war was finished, that any
circumstances could possibly have happened which
would call the general into public life again...I will
not, however, contemplate with too much regret
disappointments that were inevitable. Though the
General's feelings and my own were perfectly in
unison with respect to our predilection for public life,
yet I cannot blame him for having acted according to
his duties in obeying the voice of his country."
—Martha Washington

The country had never seen anything like it. The monarchs of
Europe and the pashas of the Far East may have been coronated
with more elaborate ceremonies and fanfare, but the ascension to power
of all of those storied potentates together could not match the fervor of

the people that greeted George Washington, fifty-seven, on his triumphal ride from Mount Vernon to New York City for his inauguration as the first president of the United States in April of 1789.

The president-elect was apprehensive about his future as he left his plantation at precisely 10 A.M. on April 16. "I bade adieu to Mount Vernon, to private life and to domestic felicity; and with a mind oppressed with more anxious and painful sensations than I have words to express, set out for New York," he wrote in his diary that evening.

The newspapers had published numerous stories describing the unanimously elected first president's route to New York. He was greeted by immense crowds of cheering citizens wherever he went. Ferry stops teemed with people eager to talk to him or, in most cases, to simply brush his coat with their hands. Every large city and tiny village through which he rode staged elaborate parades and celebrations in his honor. Thirteen cannon bursts, one for each state, announced his arrival at numerous receptions. Girls spread flowers on the highway in front of him as he rode through Trenton, the town he captured at Christmas 1776, and turned the tide of the war. Choirs gathered to sing newly written songs to commemorate his life. He met with Congressmen and Senators in Elizabeth. He offered a fond thanks to the Presbyterians at the College of New Jersey in Princeton and spent the night at the home of its president, Rev. John Witherspoon, who had sent seventy-seven graduates of his seminary into the Continental Army to serve as chaplains.

A few days later, Washington crossed the Hudson River to New York to prepare for his inauguration. The river was jammed with vessels, large and small, American and foreign, their decks overcrowded with passengers who cheered lustily as Washington's barge left the Elizabeth docks. Traveling alongside him were two other barges. One carried an honor guard of smartly dressed Continental Army soldiers and a smiling Henry Knox. On the other rode members of an orchestra and a choir of men and women who sang as their boat moved through the water. A Spanish man-of-war anchored in the harbor fired a fifteen-cannon salute.

On the New York side of the harbor, soldiers had to hold back thousands of citizens eager to get a glimpse of Washington. The president-elect, stunned at the reception, smiled softly, stepped into an elegant horse-drawn carriage, and rode away, the coach moving slowly down the streets lined with people surging toward it, screaming out his name.

Creating the Presidency

According to the sparse language of the Constitution, the president of the United States was authorized to execute laws passed by Congress, periodically inform Congress of the state of the union, and offer bills. He could veto legislation. He would serve as the head of state and be in charge of foreign policy with the advice and consent of the Senate, communicate with the state governors, and serve as commander-in-chief of the armed forces. The description was vague but delegates, certain that George Washington would be the choice for the first chief executive, trusted him to develop the office properly because he had performed so admirably during the war.

Washington's work in the Revolution with the thousands of people he came in contact with in some capacity became the foundation for the office of the president as it was created at the convention to write a new Constitution for the United States in 1787. The men who were most responsible for the formation of the presidency, and the ratification of the Constitution by the states, were the men closest to Washington throughout the war. Alexander Hamilton, John Jay, and James Madison were the authors of *The Federalist Papers*, the series of eighty-five newspaper columns published in just about every journal in America to advocate the ratification of the Constitution and the presidency. During the convention itself, held over several months in summer of 1787 in the same town where some of these same men had signed the Declaration of Independence, they had been joined by other wartime associates to form a cadre of delegates who lobbied hard for a presidency. James Wilson, for example, had been a wartime delegate in Congress for several years, where he became friendly with the commander-in-chief. Another delegate, Gouverneur Morris, was one of the members of the Congressional Committee-at-Camp who lived at Valley Forge for several weeks with Washington and came to admire him greatly.

466 George Washington's War

These men saw the perfect president as their friend the general. That opinion was formed by their friendship with him during the winters of the Revolution. They observed how he operated both politically and militarily—often under intense pressure—and how he was able to forge bonds between Congress, states, counties, municipalities, the press, the army, and the people. His experience in the war had given him many of the skills they believed were necessary for a national leader.

They had considerable help in constructing the presidency from Washington himself. Publicly, he made it known to everyone that he would simply preside over the Constitutional Convention as a figure-head, but he was just as active behind the scenes in Philadelphia as he had been in Williamsburg a generation before, offering his opinions on each and every subject the delegates had discussed on the floor. He dined with just about all of the delegates during the weeks of deliberations and, through persuasion, convinced many to accept his own views on what the United States—and its president—should be like. These views reflected all of his experiences during the Revolution. He voted with Virginia for a strong national government with extended powers that far exceeded those of the states. He favored a national legislature and a single, active president who could serve an unlimited number of four-year terms, remembering the ineffectiveness of the one-year terms of the presidents of the Continental Congress. He favored small Congressional districts to give more people a voice in representative government, and hard money as opposed to paper money (his nightmare in the war). The latter measure, however, to his amazement, did not pass. He enthusiastically favored the presidential veto and insisted that a three-quarters majority vote of the Senate, and not a proposed two-thirds, be required to override it, confident that it was better for a country to abide by the wishes of a single leader who knew what was best, just as the army had followed a single commander. He favored national taxes to support the government, including a tax on exports (which would hurt him as a planter) remembering all too well the bankruptcy of the Congress during the war that nearly wrecked the army. He supported and, off the floor, convinced others to support, Congressional authority over all interstate commerce, giving the new national government the power to develop the great American west that had been important to Washington.

Federal jurisdiction would also end the squabbling between the states over taxes, prices, and transportation that had caused such friction during the war. He voted for national supremacy over states in any dispute concerning laws, with a judiciary to make the final determination (vividly recalling the loud battles between Congress and the state of Pennsylvania during the Valley Forge winter). He was emphatic that the president should also be the commander-in-chief of the army, and this seemed natural. Since the delegates all assumed that Washington would be the first president, who could be better suited to serve as commander-in-chief than the former commander-in-chief? And so, despite their fear of giving too much civilian power to one man, the delegates were quite happy to give him the army and navy, too.

They did not fear the emergence of a military dictator, though, because Washington had shown them that he had no lust for power when he resigned from the army in 1783, four years before the constitutional convention convened. They did not put the president in charge of the army because they thought every chief executive would exercise that power wisely, but because they knew George Washington.

Washington, then, through backroom lobbying and through his votes in the Convention, helped to create a potentially strong presidency, specifically designed for him—if he wanted it. He was not giving himself new powers he thought would be useful as a prospective president, but merely utilizing old ones he had used so well for success during the Revolution.

Washington made his views emphatically clear while publicly convincing most observers that he had participated in the deliberations only minimally. But those at the Convention knew the truth, as James Monroe wrote Thomas Jefferson at the end of the deliberations: "be assured that [George Washington's] influence carried this government." Washington did reveal his backroom politicking for a strong presidency in an initial draft of his first inaugural address, but quickly discarded it: "Although the agency *I* had in forming this system, and the high opinion

I entertained of my colleagues for their ability and integrity may have tended to warp my judgment in its favor...."

⸎

Although he had worked hard to create the presidency, George Washington insisted that he did not want the office. He wrote Lafayette that he enjoyed his new-found peace and quiet at Mount Vernon, where he planned to spend his remaining years: "I called to mind the days of my youth and found they had long since fled to return no more; that I was now descending the hill I had been 52 years climbing, and that tho' I was blessed with a good constitution, I was of a short lived family and might soon expect to be entombed in the dreary mansions of my fathers...I have had my day." And he told aide David Humphreys that his lone wish "is to live and die on my own plantation." He even seemed annoyed at the prospect of serving as the first chief executive, writing Henry Knox that "my movement to the chain of government will be accompanied by feelings not unlike those of a culprit who is going to his place of execution."

The men and women who knew him best understood his desire for a well-deserved retirement, but all shared the feelings of Jay, who wrote Washington in 1786 that he, of all people, could not sit idly by as the nation was being rocked by troubling post-war events. "I am persuaded," he said, "that you cannot view them with the eye of an unconcerned spectator."

Washington slowly came to believe, too, as his wife told him, that serving as the first president was something he had to do. Congress, with a president elected by its members, had continued to govern the nation under the Articles of Confederation for more than a year because the supporters of the new Constitution had great difficulty getting the states to ratify it. There was still resistance of many smaller states to the idea of a powerful national government, just as there had been during the war. These states would not cooperate with the new government, Washington was convinced, unless they had great respect for the president in the new government. He had to leave his plantations. History had called him again.

He did not want to leave his beloved Mount Vernon, "but when the exigence of my country seemed to require me once more to engage in public affairs, an honest conviction of duty superseded my former resolutions and became my apology for deviating from the happy plan which I had adopted," he wrote a church group of his decision to plunge back into public life, and added in a note to Lafayette that he only took the job with "unfeigned reluctance."

Once committed, though, Washington was determined to succeed in his new post, just as he had been driven to excel at everything he ever attempted in his life. Independence gave America the opportunity to forge a free and democratic government, run by the people, and he felt competent to lead the new nation. He was proud of the United States, telling a friend "that the government, though not absolutely perfect, is one of the best in the world, I have little doubt…an unequivocally free and equal representation of the people in the legislature, together with an efficient and responsible executive were the great pillars on which the preservation of American freedom must depend…."

George Washington had been one of the very first proponents of a strong federal government. The army had nearly disbanded on several occasions during the winters of the war because of the weakness of the Continental Congress. The national legislative body had the authority to write and pass legislation, but no real power to force anyone to comply with those laws. It had not been able to stabilize continental currency, and the devalued American script had become practically worthless. The delegates could not draft soldiers and had to send requests for regular troops and militia to the states. Congress had the right to order the production and purchase of provisions for the soldiers, but could not force anyone to actually supply them, and the army nearly starved in several winters of the war. Congress could levy taxes, but had no authority to collect them and had to rely on the states to do so.

While the government consisted of just Congress, Washington kept in close touch with political leaders in America from 1783 until 1787 with voluminous correspondence. He entertained dozens of public figures at Mount Vernon and maintained subscriptions to numerous newspapers. Even though he was once again happily engaged in raising crops on his Virginia plantations, the general kept himself updated on national and international politics and, when asked, offered advice to others on events. These events brought him nothing but anxiety.

Foreign countries, such as Morocco, knowing that Congress could do little under the Articles of Confederation, had seized American merchant ships, sometimes selling the sailors into slavery. The financial institutions of other nations, fearful of America's still uncertain economy, charged the U.S. exorbitant interest on loans. Britain refused to evacuate the Northwest Territories, despite a treaty obligation to do so. Spain had closed the Mississippi River to traffic for a time in a border dispute.

At home, states bickered with each other. Legislatures ran amuck, with members of unwieldy, oversized assemblies all pushing special interests, turning meetings into chaos. Crowds marched on the homes of legislators with petitions. Counties and towns created their own assemblies, which passed bills that contradicted state law. Mobs closed courthouses. Citizens refused to pay taxes. Cities saw the emergence of political "associations," which ignored the law and often engaged in rioting.

The most jarring episode was the Shays Rebellion. The insurrection was named after Daniel Shays, a Continental Army veteran and farmer who, with an "army" of more than one thousand local men, refused to pay high Massachusetts taxes, ignored Congressional orders to do so, fought off local sheriffs, closed a courthouse, and captured a federal arsenal. Finally, unable to quell the tax rebellion on its own, which threatened to spread to other parts of the state, Massachusetts called in native son Henry Knox, with a Continental Army force, to put down the rebellion. Knox surrounded the arsenal with a group of artillery batteries, forcing those inside to surrender. It was a blatant example of the Confederation's inability to govern well.

The tumult changed Washington's thinking about a life of easy retirement on the banks of the Potomac. Back in 1783, his final year in the army, Washington had become convinced that without a strong national government America was destined for chaos and would again be a target of foreign powers. "This may be the ill fated moment for relaxing the powers of the Union, annihilating the cement of the Confederation and exposing us to become the sport of European politics, which may play one state against another to prevent their growing importance, and to serve their own interested purposes," he wrote then. "Without an entire community to the spirit of the Union, we cannot exist as an independent power." And, too, he told a friend that summer, that under the Confederation the United States was quickly becoming, as he had foretold in the middle of the war, a nation "directed by thirteen heads" and feared that the country might "sink into...anarchy and confusion" and "moulder into dust."

He told friends that the hopes of the new nation were being crippled by the jealousy of the states and wrote Virginia governor Benjamin Harrison that the states had "run riot until we have brought our reputation to the brink of ruin." His dismay grew in 1784, when he griped to Jay that "our affairs are drawing rapidly to a crisis" and reminded him that "to be fearful of investing in Congress, constituted as that body is, with ample authorities for national purposes, appears to me the very climax of popular absurdity and madness." He snapped to Humphreys about the people, "What, gracious God, is man that there should be such inconsistency and perfidiousness in his conduct?"

Political chaos spread at such an alarming pace that by 1787 Washington was writing friends that the nation was in a "critical period." Clearly, some new Constitution was not only desirable, but necessary. And now, Washington told friends with great pride, that Constitution was admirable and the first national legislature was a good one. "I cannot help flattering myself [that] the new Congress, on account of the self-created respectability and various talents of its members, will not be inferior to any assembly in the world."

While he was going to be a strong president, he felt confident that neither branch of government could ever overwhelm the others, proudly explaining to Lafayette "these powers...are so distributed among the Legislative, Executive and Judicial branches into which the general government is arranged, that it can never be in danger of degenerating into a monarchy, an Oligarchy, an aristocracy or any other despotic or oppressive form, so long as there shall remain any virtue in the body of the people."

Under the terms of the Constitution, an electoral college, with representatives elected by state legislatures, selected the first president and vice president (the practice continues today, but the people of each state vote for the electors that are pledged to particular candidates). The electoral-college voters chose Washington unanimously and selected John Adams as vice president. The popular Washington's triumphal arrival in New York for his inauguration on April 30, 1789, much like his wartime triumphs at Trenton and Princeton, had given him enormous political capital with which to mold the presidency. He could make the office whatever he wanted and so, he knew, great care had to be taken with the task. The president, he believed, had to be a very strong national leader, but not a tyrant. He had to be respected and popular with the people, but not appear as a monarch. He had to work with Congress, but never be considered an equal partner with Congress. And, in this new democratic system, the chief executive at all times had to represent the people.

Looking for reliable solutions to his new and daunting problems, and trying to fill a brand-new office, Washington did not consult political theorists; he simply recreated his role as commander-in-chief as the president. It had worked before and it could work again. The president, he determined, needed to be a successful administrator who could persuade men and women of different political views, in or out of the government, to work with him to construct this new democratic institution. What he needed to do now in his four-year term as president in civilian clothes was exactly what he had done in his eight years as commander-in-chief in uniform.

President Washington understood that the people wanted the national executive to look and live like a king without being one (one of his first official decisions was to refuse flowery titles and to insist on being addressed as simply Mr. President). The people had dreamed wistfully of Bolingbroke's Patriot King for years and now they had one. Washington understood the people's need for an esteemed national leader; he had become just that during the war. Now, as the first chief executive, he simply continued that role. He insisted on living in a large home in New York and, later, in Philadelphia. He and his wife rode about in fine carriages. The president was the best-dressed man in town, just as he had been in the army. The Washingtons shopped in the most expensive stores and cordially greeted everyone they met while walking the streets. The president's home was staffed with neatly dressed servants, and aides were always seen busily tending to the nation's business.

This political home had the same ornate trappings that Washington had found so helpful at his meticulously run winter camps to facilitate his need to impress people during the Revolution. Washington had used his daily wartime dinners to build relationships with his staff and national, state, and local public figures. Now, as president, he hosted twice-weekly gatherings for government workers and their families, twice-weekly receptions at which any member of the public could visit his mansion and meet him, and a Friday evening tea party for friends and close federal aides. He attended hundreds of public ceremonies, too, so that the citizens could see the president.

He understood the need of the president to not only be the people's representative but to speak publicly on the peoples' behalf in outlining his plans to Congress. Discarding advice to simply have his speeches to Congress read by another, Washington read his inaugural and his annual State of the Union addresses, plus other speeches, each year. He perused several newspapers each day in order to find out what the press thought of his administration. The president read all of his own mail. He corresponded with trusted friends to ask that they write him frequently, informing him about the public's reaction to him, positive as well as negative, in their states. He sent his aides into the streets to mingle with the people and make every possible effort to overhear what they were saying about the new federal government—and him.

And, finally, in a move that future presidents would repeat again and again with equal success, he made lengthy tours throughout the country to make public appearances in all of the states so that the people could see and meet their president. These tours did much for his legislative agenda, garnering local support for his policies and the Federalist Party, and were a public-relations coup. They provided Washington with an opportunity to realize, again, how incredibly popular he was, as evidenced by a large banner in Cambridge, Massachusetts, that welcomed him on his New England Tour, "TO THE MAN WHO UNITES ALL HEARTS."

A newspaper described his arrival at a Virginia town in the spring of 1791 on his southern tour:

> On Monday the second at 2 o'clock p.m., the beloved and excellent GEORGE WASHINGTON, Esq., President of the United States of America, arrived in this city, with his suite, to the inexpressible satisfaction as well of the citizens as of strangers. Never, it may be truly said, was joy, love, affection and esteem more universal upon any one occasion—and never did these amiable passions of the human heart animate or more brilliantly display themselves than upon this occasion.

In the army, he had treated everyone in the same direct and respectable manner, whether a governor or a courier. Now, as president, that same modest demeanor once again impressed those who met him, such as Louis, Count of Fontanes, a French diplomat: "In all of his negotiations, the heroic simplicity of the President of the United States, without elevation or debasement, was brought into communication with the majesty of Kings. He sought not in his administration those conceptions which the age calls great, but which he regarded as vain. His ideas were more sage than bold; he sought not admiration, but he always enjoyed esteem."

Through all of this he was deliberately creating a careful image of the president of the United States. He held a unique office in the dying days of the eighteenth century in a world ruled by kings and queens. His job, he believed, was not simply to fill the office and hope for the best. Washington always had a vision of the future and now he tried to look far ahead in order to create an executive office whose occupant would never be merely an elected official, but an extraordinary leader of a remarkable people.

Other men had multiple aims in the new government—political, economic, social, cultural; Washington did not. Others were political theorists steeped in the analysis of governments going back to ancient Greece; Washington was not. Others saw in the new government the chance to propose and pass hundreds of bills that each addressed one of the myriad problems of the new Republic; Washington did not.

As a general, Washington had just one goal, to win the war. As president, he also had but a single goal, one united country, run by a very strong central government, that was sound enough to move on into history after he was, finally, entombed with his fathers. He was never sidetracked from that simple overriding dream. Political scientists and historians have criticized him for his lack of intellectual brilliance, limited education, and simplistic political views. He did not need the mental wizardry of Hamilton, the brilliance of Jefferson, or the wisdom of Madison to maintain his simple desire to hold the United States together in its infancy.

"This object has uniformally been to overlook all personal, local and partial considerations to contemplate the United States as one great whole," he wrote of the administration, and understood that none of the hundreds of dreams of his countrymen would be realized if the nation were not united.

He fully understood the magnitude of the position of the first president of the United States. John Adams had correctly predicted that Washington's service as commander-in-chief of the army would make him a great character in the world; the presidency could make him an even greater one. He had to be extremely circumspect about how he filled an office that could, in his hands or the hands of future leaders, become either beneficial or dangerous to the democratic cause. He had to move carefully, he told James Madison, because everything he did would be important and set precedent. "Many things which appear of little importance in themselves at the beginning may have great and durable consequences." The first president was walking, he concluded in a note to an

Englishman, "on untrodden ground."

And he trod slowly, disinclined to make a critical mistake in the name of expediency, just as he had moved cautiously during the war. "Perhaps the strongest feature in his characters was prudence, never acting until every circumstance, every consideration, was maturely weighted; refraining, if he saw a doubt; but, when once decided, going through with his purpose whatever obstinacies opposed," said Jefferson.

Washington never saw the president as an independent character who acted on his own without any responsibility to Congress. His vision of the president was that of an elected leader who could work with Congress on legislation he proposed or they submitted and act as a liaison between Congress and the states to ensure that the federal and state governments acted in conjunction with each other in the national interest. And, tied directly to that at all times, he saw the president as the one man elected to represent all of the people who always had to have the people's interest at heart.

Forming the Cabinet

As he honed his concept of the presidency, Washington returned again and again to formulas that had worked during the war and the people who assisted him in the Revolution. Every single member of his cabinet was a close associate during the war. Henry Knox beame the first Secretary of War. Hamilton was named the first Secretary of the Treasury. Thomas Jefferson, the Secretary of State, was not only his fellow House of Burgesses member and friend, but one of the war governors of Virginia (at cabinet meetings, Washington, Knox and Hamilton called each other by their army titles, such as "General Knox" and "Colonel Hamilton," which always annoyed the civilian Jefferson).

Others named to lead departments that later became cabinet posts, or powerful ambassadors, were friends from the Revolution, too. Fellow Virginian Edmund Randolph was selected as Attorney General. The President tapped Gouvuernor Morris, a wartime Continental Congress delegate, as minister to England, succeeded by Thomas Pinckney, another army veteran. The French diplomatic post at first went to

Charles Pinckney, who fought as a soldier in the Continental Army, and later to James Monroe, wounded badly at Trenton. Elias Boudinot, his wartime spymaster, was named Director of the Mint. The president's propensity to fill the nearly one thousand jobs with former generals, aides, and soldiers extended to every level of the federal government, including nominees to innocuous posts such as seaport customs agents. The president even took great care to appoint the members of his wartime spy rings, such as Joshua Mercereau, to federal posts. He was relying on wartime colleagues he trusted without reservation and at the same time rewarding them. It was a patronage practice that future presidents would warmly embrace.

The president's cabinet, which has been an integral part of the executive branch of American government since 1789, was Washington's invention. The Constitution never mentioned a cabinet. Its authors only suggested that department heads send written opinions to the president when required, nothing more. Washington, though, saw an opportunity to create a powerful and productive advisory council by uniting his department heads into a "cabinet" that met as a group and worked closely with him. It was a unique consortium created by the president to prevent the problems the government had faced daily during the Revolution.

President Washington controlled each department of the national government directly. He did not do this merely through meetings or personal conversations, but via endless notes and queries and attention to the business of each, following his wartime mania for detail. The cabinet did not meet together during Washington's first term, but by the start of his second administration, and the worry over the French Revolution, he began to call meetings of his secretaries on a regular basis. The discussions of his cabinet in that and other crises were invaluable to the president.

The peacetime cabinet was a carbon copy of his military councils. During the war, Washington required all of his generals and some of his aides to write lengthy memos in response to his questions about the army. The generals would meet with Washington, with aides present or conferred with later. At these frequent councils of war, the generals informed the commander-in-chief about the operations of their divisions of the army or administrative responsibilities and offered opinions on the war. The generals would discuss the war with each other, in meetings that lasted several hours, all carefully managed by Washington. He took that model and used it for his cabinet, with his cabinet secretaries assuming the roles of the generals and aides. The cabinet was not created out of political theory, but out of his wartime experience.

And, too, Washington was shrewd enough to realize that he would have difficulty managing any cabinet made up of men who had not served in the military with him and did not understand his style of leadership or share the grim memories of the war. Any mix of former officers and men with no connection to the war would create a room full of individuals who did understand each other's motivations and experience. In creating a cabinet and government of people who would still deal with him as the beloved commander-in-chief, Washington had constructed a federal government that worked as smoothly as his army councils.

The president's cabinet became a fixture in American government, as did his staff. Washington's vision of the cabinet/staff as a close advisory consortium expanded and grew in the nineteenth and twentieth centuries and is today, itself, a powerful arm of the federal government.

When he exercised his Constitutional power to select justices to the new Supreme Court, Washington once again chose men who were close to him during the Revolution. His choice for chief justice was John Jay, the chief justice of the New York Supreme Court and former president of the Continental Congress. Jay certainly had the proper judicial and administrative credentials to serve as the head of the court, but it was his friendship with Washington, formed during dozens of dinners in winter camp at Morristown, that earned him the job.

Jay was not his only wartime judicial choice. Washington named the first five justices and then, during his two terms, nominated another six. Out of the eleven jurists, six were members of the Continental Congress who worked closely with him in the winters of the war. Three of the eleven were signers of the Declaration of Independence. Three served in the army. Others were connected to the war in different ways, such as William Paterson, New Jersey's wartime attorney general. Several of the eleven, such as John Rutledge and James Wilson, had also been Washington's colleagues at the Constitutional Convention. Two additional war-related Supreme Court nominees did not serve. Robert Harrison, one of his military aides, withdrew in order to become the chancellor of the University of Maryland. Patrick Henry declined in order to remain governor of Virginia.

The presidency of the United States, and the democratic framework of its government, it seems clear, was not created at the Constitutional Convention, but during the winters of the American Revolution. George Washington selected the men around him to lead the new nation because they had been trusted comrades during the Revolution. They had stood by him during the series of crises presented by the war and he knew that he could count on them to stand by him now, in a new set of crises to confront the infant republic.

American heritage is not a Fourth of July parade down Main Street on a warm day or flags flying in the summer sunshine. It is a heritage of snow and cold and ice and an extraordinarily gifted leader who grew from a farmer into a general into a president.

George Washington was a strong supporter of the separation of church and state, but wanted the national government to recognize the freedoms of all religions—even the Quakers, who gave him so much trouble during the Revolution. He wanted America to expand westward. A man of little formal schooling himself, he had learned the value of education from wartime colleagues such as Hamilton and John Laurens and was determined to have the federal government establish a national university. He championed a sound economy. Washington wanted a standing army to be used to put down insurrections such as the Shays Rebellion, curb Indian raids in the western parts of the states, and to be on the alert for any attacks by a foreign power. He had pushed for a permanent national army during every winter of the war as his Continental troop numbers dwindled and his militia men, terms expired, went home.

He wanted an America free from overly complicated ties to foreign powers. He supported Patrick Henry's call for a "bill of rights," added to the Constitution in 1791.

Also on his agenda were plans to support efforts to increase manufacturing in the United States. A lifelong planter in a nation that was basically an agrarian society in the 1790s, Washington had always been convinced that farming was the backbone of life and said that it was "the proper source of American wealth and happiness." However, the war had taught him that the U.S. needed more manufacturing. There were no factories to produce the uniforms, cannon, and shoes he had needed.

And there was one final role—an irresistible role—remaining from his days in the war that Washington sought to play as president, that of spymaster. The world of shadow and intrigue had always fascinated him, and during the winters of the Revolution he ran a successful spy ring. That urge to know what was going on in the enemy camp never left him, and as president he secretly employed several spies to work in Florida to uncover the plans of the Spanish government there. His small spy ring was the forerunner of the Central Intelligence Agency.

Washington had arrived in New York as not only the most popular man in the country, but a genuine national hero. His prestige engendered a desire in Senators and Congressmen to work with him to pass legislation because they not only respected him, but knew that the public venerated him; they needed to associate with him to ensure their own electoral futures. They knew, too, that he was in private a persuasive man and a man with extensive experience as a state legislator and, most of all, he had become a good politician and skilled administrator during the winters of the war. Although he may have been a reluctant president, he arrived in office as a man well-suited for the job.

Creating a Currency

The wildly depreciating Continental paper currency throughout the war had posed as strong a threat to the security of the United States as British troops. The dollar began to depreciate in the winter of 1777, within two months of Washington's arrival in Morristown with his exhausted men.

It slipped further in value during the Valley Forge winter the following year and went into a spiraling freefall in the winter of 1779–80.

One of the first efforts of the new administration toward financial security was the establishment of a national bank, the brainchild of Hamilton. The bank, the headstrong secretary of the treasury assured the president, would not only attract corporate investment from American companies, but substantial foreign interest because its monies would be guaranteed by the national government. The bank was controversial. Jefferson saw it as a threat to all local financial institutions. He argued that a national bank was not provided for in the Constitution. Hamilton asserted that it was, under Article I, Section 8 of the Constitution that gave Congress what he and Madison claimed were "implied powers" that were as important as expressed powers and that "the former are as effectually delegated as the latter."

Washington's decision was rather simple, though. Hamilton's proposal was nothing new. He had drafted the exact same bank proposal during the winter of 1779–80 in snow-bound Morristown to show Washington what was needed to shore up the collapsing Continental paper dollar, a proposal supported by Washington's friend, the Rev. Jacob Greene, in the general's newspaper, the *New Jersey Journal.* At that time, one of Washington's major concerns, expressed again and again in letters to colleagues in Congress and friends, was the strength of the American dollar. In a rather prophetic letter to Gouverneur Morris in 1779, Washington wrote "it is well worthy the ambition of a patriot statesman at this juncture to endeavour to pacify party differences to give fresh vigor to the springs of government, to inspire the people with confidence, and above all to restore the credit of the currency." Now, a decade later, that same "statesman" had a chance to implement the same plan, which he believed in. Washington signed the bill without hesitation, giving the United States the economic framework it has used ever since.

Part of that financial stability was an agreement by Washington, following rancorous debates in his cabinet and in Congress, to have the federal government assume the individual states' war debts of $23 million. Washington had seen the settling of the government's accounts as critical during the war, writing in 1783 "let us as a nation be just, let us fulfill the public contracts , which Congress had undoubtedly a right to make for the purpose of carrying on the War, with the same good faith we suppose ourselves bound to perform our private engagements." As president, he was just as stern in his desire to pay the nation's bills, and the money owed all the citizens who gave him needed supplies on credit during the winters of the war. "No pecuniary consideration is more urgent than the regular redemption and discharge of the public debt; on none can delay be more injurious, or an economy of time more valuable," he reiterated in 1793.

The opposition in Congress to the federal assumption of state debts, which some saw as giving the national government too much power over the states, was overcome with an agreement to build the nation's capitol on the banks of the Potomac (eventually Washington, D.C.).

Presidential Powers and Civilian Rebellion

The president's conviction that the chief executive should be the commander-in-chief of the army was tested in two critical instances. In the first, residents of western Pennsylvania balked at paying a new federal excise tax on home-brewed whiskey they sold. Washington at first sent warrant officers to collect the tax; they were turned back by angry mobs. A regional federal tax collector's home was attacked and burned, and a man was killed in the melee. Washington asked Pennsylvania to send its state militia to the region to collect the tax; state officials refused. The president then turned to the courts, but Supreme Court justice James Wilson, a Pennsylvanian, told Washington there was no legal grounds for his appeal. Angered and concerned that this refusal to pay taxes would spread throughout the country, Washington assumed his powers as commander-in-chief of the army, called out twelve thousand militia from four states, and ordered them to gather at Bedford, Pennsylvania, where he rode to meet them, wearing his old Continental Army uniform, now a bit tight around the waist.

The president had made an historic decision to use the army and militia to put down a civilian rebellion. Throughout the Revolution, he had worried constantly that a single successful mutiny among the troops would bring about the collapse of the army. Now, he worried that one rebellion would bring about the downfall of the country. And he realized, too, as he had so many times in the Revolution, that at these times the leader had to take emergency action to end a crisis.

Washington was uncertain how the battle would be fought, but he was clearly willing to put his life in danger, as he had during the war. The president was spared any fighting when the rebellion collapsed following news of his decision to lead the attack. A magnanimous Washington then did what he had done so often during the war—he pardoned the convicted leaders of the uprising and sent them home to pay their taxes.

The president was extremely pleased with the dramatic results of his actions and the establishment of civilian rule, backed by the army. He told Congress of the people's favorable reaction to the incident that "it has demonstrated that our prosperity rests on solid foundations; by furnishing an additional proof, that my fellow citizens understand the true principles of government and liberty, that they feel their inseparable union; that notwithstanding all the devices which have been used to sway them from their interest and duty, they are now as ready to maintain the authority of the law against licentious invasions, as they were to defend their rights against usurpation [in the Revolution]. It has been a spectacle, displaying to the highest advantage, the value of Republican Government."

His second action as commander-in-chief came when he decided to oversee a five-year campaign to drive Indians out of the Northwest Territories (what is now Ohio) and to stop Native American raids on villages there. He had been tough on Indians throughout the war, ordering General John Sullivan's summer 1779 expedition through New York in which he burned dozens of Indian villages in retaliation for tribes' attacks on settlers. Washington would not let the tribes, particularly the Six Nations and Miami in the northwest and the Creek and Cherokee in the southwest, intimidate him as president. Part of Washington's vision was the westward expansion of America, and he was not going to be thwarted.

The president maintained very mixed feelings about American Indians. He had fought against them during the French and Indian War and in the Revolution. As president, he tried to create a policy under which Indians could be assimilated into the white population as long as they remained peaceful. At first, they did not. The Indians felt very threatened as Americans moved west, taking their land by force and treaty, and fought back. President Washington, angered, did not want a wholesale war on the Indians, but needed to stop them.

The president urged Congress to let him raise a five thousand–man army to attack the Indians. Some Congressmen balked, charging that Washington was waging a one-man war, but went along with his request. In October 1790, Washington sent troops under Brigadier General Josiah Harmar to stop Indian raids, but his troops were routed. The president then replaced Harmar with General Arthur St. Clair, but that army was defeated in 1791 and eight hundred Americans were killed in a military disaster. Despite sharp criticism from Congress for doggedly continuing the war, Washington replaced St. Clair with General Anthony Wayne, his trusted Continental Army general, who finally crushed the Indians in the summer of 1794.

The president was pleased that the threat had ended, but he felt compassion for Native Americans, especially when he later learned that dozens had been killed by unruly white settlers in Georgia. In his State of the Union address on December 6, 1795, he told Congress that Indian rights had to be protected in order to preserve peace on the frontier. "Unless the murdering of Indians can be restrained, by bringing the murderers to…punishment, all the exertions of the government to prevent destructive retaliations by the Indians will prove fruitless," he said in his 1795 State of the Union address, adding that the killings "shock humanity."

The President and Foreign Affairs

Another first president might have turned over the foreign affairs of the United States to Thomas Jefferson with a feeling of comfort because the former Virginia Governor was not only versed in world history and politics but had served as the U.S. Ambassador to France for several years.

Washington, however, was convinced from his experience in the war that it was necessary for the president, and not a Cabinet officer, to frame the foreign policy of the nation.

Washington had substantial experience with foreign diplomats, political philosophers, and generals, such as Von Steuben, Pulaski, and De Kalb. One of his closest friends was Lafayette. He had countless discussions about foreign government and politics with Hamilton and had issued a lengthy analysis of world politics one winter, crafted by Hamilton, which showed a shrewd understanding of European palace intrigue. He had learned much about Dutch politics from his friend Livingston and received considerable background on the British-Irish struggle from the Irish officers in his army.

He had learned from the failed invasion of Canada in 1776 that it was foolhardy to force the British off the North American continent entirely. Two years later, during the Valley Forge winter, Congress authorized another Canadian foray, placing Lafayette in charge of an American army to push the British out and claim the country for France. Washington did not want the French, or any other foreign power, to gain a foothold in North America and refused to sanction the invasion, which was abandoned because of his lack of cooperation and mounting logistical problems.

He was, as the president, well prepared for foreign affairs. He had a problem, though, and that was the language in the Constitution, which required the president to mold foreign policy with the "advice and consent" of the Senate. The Senate wanted to form a permanent three-member committee to consult with the president on all foreign-policy decisions. Washington must have cringed at the notion, remembering the incompetence exhibited by Congressional committees during his supply crises during the winters of the war. In August of 1789, preparing for negotiations on a new treaty with Indian nations, Washington went to a session of the Senate with Knox and told the members that he needed their "advice and consent" on it. John Adams read the treaty, which had to be read a second time because of noise from carriages on the street outside. Senators began talking to each other and paid little attention to Adams.

It was then read a third time. Senators then barraged Washington with inane questions. An exasperated Washington, either out of impulse or design, used the squabbling of the Senate as an excuse to stand up and, losing his temper, scowled that "this defeats every purpose of my coming here." He and Knox then stormed out of the chamber. Washington never returned to the Senate for foreign-policy advice. The three-member–committee idea was dropped and the Senate left relations with foreign powers up to the president.

His desire to direct foreign policy was tested severely twice and gave Washington a chance to show what the president could do in foreign crisis, setting a course for U.S. foreign relations that lasted more than a century.

The first crisis arose when the United States came under intense pressure to enter the ongoing war between France and several European powers on the French side, as part of the alliance formed in 1778. Washington held firm against the crusade by Congressmen and the press, and kept America out of the conflict with his Neutrality Proclamation. He did not want the U.S. involved in the conflict for several reasons: the country was still recovering from the Revolution; the nation did not have the financial resources to send an army and navy to Europe for the fight; and this conflict might eventually lead to war with England, which Washington knew would be catastrophic for trade. The president was also firm in his belief that the new nation needed time to grow on its own and become a free and independent country by staying out of the seemingly endless wars in Europe. He issued the controversial proclamation as part of his role as head of state, without Congressional approval, a step which further expanded the scope of the office.

Dismissing the complexities of the diplomatic problem, the president simply told anyone who would listen that, frankly, he just did not want to stick his nose into Europe's business. "I have no inclination to touch, much less to dilate, on politics. For in politics, as in religion, my tenets are few and simple; the leading one of which, and indeed that which embraces most others, is to be honest and just ourselves, and to exact it from others; meddling as little as possible in their affairs where our own are not involved. If this maxim was generally adopted, wars would cease and our swords would soon be converted into reap-hooks and our harvests be more abundant, peaceful and happy," he wrote Dr. James Anderson on Christmas Eve, 1795.

Again, that year, he had increased the powers of the presidency when he sent John Jay to London to establish an arbitration commission to settle a dispute involving the British seizure of dozens of American merchant ships in the West Indies. Washington was severely criticized by the Senate for extending his powers, but the treaty, which averted bloodshed, was approved. It gave Washington yet another chance to broaden the powers of the president when he refused to submit certain documents concerning the negotiations to Congress, just as he had never submitted all of his intelligence reports to Congress during the Revolution, claiming, for the first time, executive privilege. A heated debate followed in the House of Representatives but, in the end, Washington's decision was final and a presidential prerogative, controversial to this day, was established.

Washington had held firm on neutrality and the Jay treaty to define the presidency, but also to test the American system and its three branches of government. Would his decision stand or would Congress, the states, and the press (fearful of French vessels raiding American harbors and more British seizures) clamor for war? He had his answer soon enough when, despite some bickering, he obtained universal support for his bold foreign-policy moves.

A stronger reason for neutrality was that he remembered his experiences with European politicians during the war. The Americans loved their French allies dearly, but the troops and ships needed from France did not arrive for three long years. And the talks with the French to earn that treaty had been laden with deception and treachery by Parisian diplomats. Washington had buried Don Juan Miralles during the winter of 1779–80 in Morristown and the Spanish had thanked him for honoring their diplomat with a state funeral, yet despite numerous promises the Spanish did not aid the American cause for a long time. Washington's trusted young friend Jay had been sent to Spain at the end of the war in an effort to work out a peace treaty and obtain aid, and had been received in a very shabby fashion by the Spanish court. All of Washington's letters with British Generals Howe and Clinton seeking prisoner exchanges and better treatment for American prisoners-of-war during the winters of the Revolution had been met with double talk and inaction. The English peace offer during the winter of 1778 was almost laughable, full of half-promises.

Washington had learned lessons in foreign relations well during the winters of the war, and as president was not going to become entangled with foreign powers again. He stated that forcefully on numerous occasions, delivering his views emphatically in his farewell address. He warned that America would become indebted to any European power with whom it sided in a war, "a slave in its animosity or to its affection." The president did not want any ties with anybody anywhere, asking Congress "to steer clear of permanent alliances with any portion of the foreign world."

He cautioned, too, that the corruption and ambition connected to alliances he feared on foreign shores could just as easily poison America: "How many opportunities do they afford to tamper with domestic factions, to practice the arts of seduction, to mislead public opinion, to influence or awe the public councils! Such an attachment of a small or weak, toward a great and powerful nation, dooms the former to be the satellite of the latter."

A former general, he was eager to avoid any possibility of being drawn into a European military dispute. His disgust for war never left him, and he repeated his hatred for fighting often. Washington called war "a plague to mankind" and told friends he wanted it "banished from off the Earth, and the sons and daughters of this world employed in more pleasing and innocent amusements than in preparing implements and exercising them for the destruction of mankind."

Washington took full advantage of the vagueness of the Constitution's description of the presidency, just as he was quite liberal in his interpretation of his role as commander-in-chief. The first president simply assumed authority he wanted. He garnered power first, then let Congress decide whether or not it was proper. Washington did this because he knew that he had the public popularity to overcome Congressional objections. And, of course, he had the votes. It did not hurt that the most influential Congessman, James Madison, the author of the Constitution, often went along with Washington's interpretations, telling fellow Congressmen that the president had to have inherent powers in order to run the country.

Washington pushed as far as he could. The president assumed extensive powers in the field of foreign policy, establishing direct ties between himself as head of state and foreign leaders and visiting diplomats, bypassing Congress. He knew that only the head of the American government had the prestige to deal effectively with foreign leaders. The war had taught him that he was able to accomplish more to influence foreigners than any of the various committees of Congress that dealt with diplomats from abroad.

Washington, with Hamilton's encouragement, established the presidency, and not Congress, as the office of response to threats from other countries. He acknowledged that only Congress had the power to declare war, but argued that in incidents involving warlike circumstances it was the president who had to act in America's best interests. Under this interpretation, he retained for himself the power to deal with the seizure of American cargo ships on the high seas, to threaten foreigners with military action, and to retaliate swiftly against any attacks. It was under this interpretation that he issued the Neutrality Proclamation.

But Washington did defer to Congress on many matters, sharing power he might have appropriated and often simply giving some up. He established the long practice of senatorial courtesy concerning presidential appointments when he withdrew a nomination that was opposed by a state's senator. He established the precedent of the presidential veto, giving the chief executive enormous power over Congress, yet during his eight years in office he only vetoed two bills, unwilling to bully Congress with that power. And, too, he welcomed a Congressional investigatory committee to review his actions against the American Indians, remembering how valuable those kind of committees that visited him at Valley Forge in 1778 and Morristown in 1780 had been.

The first president was also careful not to thwart the law-making function of Congress. Although he outlined goals in his Inaugural Address, he proposed no legislation during the term of the first Congress in 1789 and, over the next eight years, offered few bills. He was content to let Congress grow as a legislature while he served different functions as the chief executive.

One of his first moves was to assert his right to fire any employee in the executive branch, overriding Congressional objections that these departments were created by Congress. Washington remembered vividly the disastrous operations of Congressional departments during the winters of the war and his inability to fire incompetent and corrupt employees of the Quartermaster's and Commissary Departments. He would end that practice now. Congress grudgingly approved.

As the head of the national government, he shared power with the states. He never agreed with fellow Virginians that all authority not specifically given to the federal government belonged to the states, as demonstrated by his own expansion of power, but he did believe in the separation of the federal government and the states. Except for the collection of taxes and the Indian Wars, Washington did not intrude upon the operation of state governments. He did not do so because he knew that the men running those states had shown their skills as leaders during the Revolution, when he had befriended them. They had convinced him then that the states had to be part of a national government, but also needed autonomy. As president, Washington continued to maintain good relations with the governors and other states leaders, communicating with them through letters and emissaries, meeting with them on his various tours, and greeting them upon their arrivals in New York and Philadelphia. He told them as the president, as he had during the war as a general, that he was always glad to see them.

He also simply surrendered on some policy matters he believed were essential. One was the establishment of a large standing army. Congress, as fearful as the public of standing armies of any kind, despite their respect for the Continental Army, refused to sanction one. Later, without a trained army in place, the U.S. would be unprepared for several world conflicts.

But most of the legislation Washington pushed did pass, thanks to his "hidden hand" politicking, usually accomplished through James Madison. The two men had struck up a close friendship in the winter of 1781, when Washington spent several months in Philadelphia following the victory at Yorktown. He found Madison, a fellow Virginian, a kindred spirit, and the young Congressman found in Washington the real-life heroic figure he had read about so often in Greek and Roman classics, referring to him again and again in his correspondence and public speeches as "our great General."

Madison became the forerunner of the modern party "whip" for Washington in the House of Representatives, where he wielded considerable influence. Washington would meet with Madison and have him introduce in his name bills sent over by the president or pressure Congressmen to approve previously introduced bills. Madison would also keep Washington informed about the activities of each and every Congressman, Federalist or Anti-Federalist.

The president trusted Madison completely. He permitted Madison to read his mail and write responses to correspondents for him. Madison helped Washington write his first Inaugural and some of his State of the Union addresses. Because of his literary skills, Madison was asked to write the formal messages from Congress to the president. Then, after a secret meeting with the president, Madison wrote Washington's response to Congress, essentially writing back and forth to himself. Madison was constantly asked for advice by the president and had considerable influence in all appointments. More than anyone except Hamilton, he helped George Washington mold the first presidency.

Washington turned the office into a powerful one in small ways, too. During the war, he had urged the governors to issue proclamations of Thanksgiving at the end of each November. Congress had decided that it was the right of the state, not the national government, to do so. Now, as president, seeing Thanksgiving Day as a very visible symbol of American freedom, Washington superceded the states and issued the proclamation himself, adding a blessing for the nation and the Constitution. During the Revolution, his frequent calls to Providence to watch over the United

States had served to stimulate the belief in the people that God was watching over the Revolution; he now achieved the same goal with the new nation, once again connecting it to the Almighty.

Washington's belief in democratic government and his own ability to lead it was shaken badly toward the end of his first term, though, when a severe breach developed between Jefferson and Hamilton. Jefferson favored a national government with limited powers and state governments with substantial authority while Hamilton, like Washington, championed a very strong national government. Washington pleaded with the duo to get along so that he could run the country. He told them it would be difficult for him "to manage the reins of government" without "mutual forbearances and temporising yieldings on all sides." That appeal had always worked in the Revolution, but it did not work in national politics, particularly with two headstrong men like Hamilton and Jefferson, and the strong political parties they had created.

George Washington was politically savvy enough to create a strong and efficient federal union out of thirteen squabbling states, negotiate treaties with foreign countries, keep America out of a European war, put down the troublesome Whiskey Rebellion, and develop a sound, capitalist, economic system. Yet, despite all of his acumen, he was genuinely surprised by the rise of political parties and worried that their development would destroy what he had built during his eight years in office. He expected that some legislators would oppose his nationalistic views, but was stunned and angered that they would create a formal political party to advance their own policies, and work to have men who believed in those views to be elected to office as Anti-Federalists, later Republicans.

He fretted to friends and political colleagues that these "factions," as he called them with considerable disdain, would wreck the Republic. At the height of the Jay Treaty debates, frustrated, he blurted out about protest crowds gathered by the Anti-Federalists that they were "at all times improper and dangerous." The president complained to Henry Knox in 1795 of political organizations: "Such (for wise purposes, it is to be presumed) is the turbulence of human passions in party disputes; when victory, more than truth, is the palm contended for..."

He wanted everyone to be just like him, without private interest and only concerned, as he had said repeatedly during the war, with the "public good." He told Timothy Pickering, who had replaced Knox as Secretary of War, that he was a man "of no party...whose sole wish is to pursue with undeviating steps a path which would lead this country to respectability, wealth and happiness" and could not understand why everyone in political life did not think the same.

Washington summed up his feelings in his Farewell Address when he charged that "[parties] may now and then answer popular ends, [but] they are likely in the course of time and things, to become potent engines by which cunning, ambitious and unprincipled men will be enabled to subvert the power of the people and to usurp for themselves the reins of government; destroying afterwards the very engines which have lifted them to unjust dominion" and called parties the "worst enemy" of popular government.

It was Washington, in the early days of the war, who was one of the first prominent leaders of the Revolution to complain about factions, lamenting that "...nothing but disunion can hurt our cause, [faction] will ruin it, if great prudence, temper and moderations is not mixed in our counsels." Later, in the middle of the conflict, Washington again groaned about feuding interest groups, telling Joseph Reed, "It is also most devoutly to be wished that faction was at an end and that those to whom everything dear and valuable is entrusted would lay aside party views and return to first principles...."

The president had dealt with small factions since his days in the Virginia legislature, but he was bewildered by the emergence of large, formal parties. Organized political associations had existed in some form since the 1720s in Pennsylvania. Upstate and downstate political groups had formed in New York in the early 1780s. Political organizations had formed in numerous states to oppose the ratification of the Constitution in 1787. Washington had supported Hamilton and the "nationalist" faction in the Continental Congress when they united as a lobbying group in 1782. Washington himself had been one of the leaders of a faction in the House of Burgesses that rallied against the Stamp Act and later urged independence. Washington also knew that opposing candidates had clashed in seeking Congressional seats in the very same 1788 election in which he had been chosen president. Still, he was astonished at the rapid growth of parties, writing Rhode Island Arthur Fenner during his first year in office that "…if we mean to support the liberty and independence which it has costs us so much blood and treasure to establish, we must drive far away the demon of party spirit…"

Washington's failure to understand the rise of political parties, and the public turmoil they created, was accompanied by his shock at the shift in newspaper coverage from unequivocal support for him during the war to a far more critical, and at times hostile, media in peace time. The sea change in press coverage of the government was tied to the development of political parties. It was the parties, and their leaders, who began to provide financial subsidies to numerous newspapers. It would seem obvious that newspaper editors of political parties would slant their news coverage toward the views of the party leaders who paid their salaries, yet Washington never seemed to understand that.

His friends did not wait until his inauguration to begin publishing their own newspaper, the *Gazette of the United States*, with John Fenno as its editor. The paper, with a circulation of about 1,500, paid its bills through advertising and circulation, plus a subsidy from the Federalists. The journal was a staunch supporter of Washington. The Anti-Federalists wasted little time to do the same thing. Shortly after the president's inauguration, the *National Gazette*, with Philip Freneau as editor, and the *Aurora*, edited by Benjamin Franklin Bache, Benjamin Franklin's grandson, appeared to criticize the president and champion the policies of their beneficiaries, states'-rights champions such as the Secretary of State. Jefferson, in a brazen move, even put Freneau, the *National Gazette* editor, on the payroll as a State Department translator, a no-show job, which infuriated Washington, who had, of course, done the very same thing when he hired Shepard Kollock as the editor of his private wartime newspaper, the *Jersey Journal*.

The president was pilloried for just about anything he said or did by the anti-Federalist press. Its editors flogged him in their columns for his support of Hamilton's national bank, the catastrophic battles of General Arthur St. Clair against American Indians, the Whiskey Rebellion, and just about all of his foreign-policy decrees.

One writer said that the president maintained the "seclusion of a monk and the supercilious distance of a tyrant." Another said that he harbored "dark schemes of ambition" and suffered from "political degeneracy." Several charged that victory in the Revolution under his leadership was nothing more than dumb luck. When out of political ammunition, his critics in the press dredged up his gambling days in Williamsburg, his consumption of wine during the war, and, just for good measure, for being "a swearer and blasphemer." The president's cabinet officers, aides, and government workers were accused, among other things, of being rascals, atheists, liars, jackals, and drunks.

An editor in the *National Gazette* took Washington to task for allowing others to celebrate his birthday as if it were a national holiday, a practice started in the middle of the Revolution. Another accused him of becoming another Cromwell. Others charged him with attempting to become an American king. Even Tom Paine, whose works Washington had read to his troops during the winters of the war for inspiration, turned on him, using press columns to called the president "a hypocrite," an "apostate," and an "imposter."

The Republican editors would not even let Washington resign and return to Mount Vernon in peace. Bache suggested that the nation declare a day of jubilee to celebrate the exit of Washington from the political arena:

> If ever a nation was debauched by a man, the American nation was debauched by Washington. If ever a nation has suffered from the improper influence of a man, the American nation has suffered from the influence of Washington. If ever a nation was deceived by a man, the American nation was deceived by Washington. Let his conduct be an example to future ages. Let it serve to be a warning that no man may be an idol and that a people may confide in themselves rather than in an individual. Let the

history of the federal government instruct mankind, that the masque of patriotism may be worn to conceal the foulest designs against the liberties of a people.

Publicly, Washington claimed not to be hurt by them, writing the governor of Virginia, "I care not; for I have consolation within that no earthly ambitions nor interested motives have influenced my conduct. The arrows of malevolence, therefore, however barbed and well pointed, never can reach the most vulnerable part of me...."

Privately, though, the president engaged in venomous denunciations of his critics, whom he frequently referred to in scalding language as "the infamous scribblers." The president was just as thin-skinned about criticism from the press as he was about attacks by party leaders. He wrote Attorney General Edmund Randolph near the end of his first term that neither he or the government could function under the press assault, which he referred to as a "malignancy." "If the government and the officers of it are to be the constant theme for newspaper abuse, and this too without condescending to investigate the motives or the facts, it will be impossible, I conceive, for any man living to manage the helm or to keep the machine together."

He told Jefferson during discussions of the Jay Treaty that the press made him out to be the enemy of America and that he could not believe that "every act of my administration would be tortured and the grossest and the most insidious misrepresentations of them made" and that the papers referred to him "in such exaggerated and indecent terms as could scarcely be applied to a Nero, to a notorious defaulted, or even to a common pickpocket."

And in his cabinet meetings he sometimes exploded over press criticism, particularly that of Freneau. Jefferson remembered his most savage blast, triggered by an attack on him in the *National Gazette* during the delicate negotiations to stay out of the France-England conflict in the summer of 1793. "The President was much inflamed; got into one of those passions when he cannot command himself," Jefferson wrote of one cabinet session. "[He] ran on much on the personal abuse which had been bestowed on him; defied any man on earth to produce one single act of his since he had been in the government which was not done on the purest motives; that he had never repented but once having slipped the moment of resigning his office; and that was every moment since; that *by God* he had rather be in his grave than in his present situation; that he had rather be on his farm than to be made *Emperor of the World*, and yet that they were charging him with wanting to be a King. That *rascal Freneau* sent him three of his papers every day, as if he thought he would become the distributor of his papers; that he could see in this nothing but an impudent design to insult him."

Still, Washington supported press freedom. The president refused suggestions to shut down critical publications and lobbied to kill a bill to raise postal rates to cut into newspaper profits.

According to Jefferson, the president's crucifixion in the opposition-party press was the primary reason he decided to step down as the nation's first president at the end of his second term. Hamilton said it was the virulent animosity between the two political parties. Friends said it was a yearning to spend his last years at his Mount Vernon. There was his sense of theater, too, stepping off the stage to loud applause, just as he had done at the end of the war when he resigned from the army.

But there was a final, far more important reason for his departure from an office he could have held until death—his sense of history. Just as he knew that democracy could not be put in place in America unless he resigned from the army in 1783, Washington was cognizant in 1796 that the United States could not survive if its presidents remained in office for life. Perhaps he had been a good choice, but others might not be wise selections. By seizing control of the political party machines that had developed, and would surely expand, they might retain brutish power for a lifetime. Young leaders might serve for decades. Washington was convinced that America could not grow without fresh leadership, renewed often, regardless of party, and that the only way to permit that was for the most popular man in the nation's history to step down.

George Washington had served sixteen years in the Virginia State Legislature, eight years as commander-in-chief of the Continental Army, and eight years as president of the United States. One could not blame him for being tired of public life. And he *did* look forward to mounting his white horse and riding away from the politicians, the critics in the press, and the celebrity he had nurtured so well, and reach his beloved Mount Vernon. He was so glad to leave that when it was time, at John Adams inauguration in 1797, Washington told his successor, "I am fairly out and you fairly in. See which of us will be happiest!"

He left office hopeful that competent men, and particularly those who had been with him during the Revolution and its winters, would follow him as president. He was correct. The man who had nominated him as commander-in-chief, aided him throughout the war, and served as his practically hand-picked vice president, John Adams, was elected the second president of the United States. He served one term. Adams was replaced by Thomas Jefferson, Washington's lifelong friend. They had served together in the Virginia House of Burgesses, and as the war governor of Virginia Jefferson had helped Washington considerably throughout the Revolution with men and troops, particularly at critical junctures of the conflict. Jefferson served two terms and was succeeded as president by James Madison, one of Washington's key friends in the Continental Congress during the war, instrumental in Congressional assistance during the cruel winters. Madison was also the primary author of the Constitution and the "whip" of his administration. Madison was succeeded as president by James Monroe, who fought with Washington in the war and was shot at the battle of Trenton. Monroe was succeeded in office by John Quincy Adams, the son of John Adams. The first president to hold office not directly connected to Washington and the Revolution in some way was Andrew Jackson, who took office in 1828. Washington and his closest confidants in the war served as presidents of the United States for thirty-nine years. In addition to the presidents, there were numerous others who were close to him during the war who went on to be elected Senators, Congressmen, and governors. Washington and those he trusted during the war, especially his close friends in the winters, not only created the American government, but ran it for nearly four decades.

Washington had created the presidency, just as he had invented his unique role as head of the Continental Army. He gave the United States a national bank and a stable economy, asserted his powers as commander-in-chief of the army to put down the Whiskey Rebellion and quell several Indian uprisings, oversaw passage of the Bill of Rights, restrained from imposing any restrictions on a free press, established the chief executive's right to determine all foreign policy, and kept the nation out of a European war. Washington had made good use of the powers outlined for the chief executive in the Constitution, but he had also seized what he claimed were inherent powers to greatly expand the scope of the office; future presidents would use his inherent-powers doctrine often. He had made the president a very powerful man, but a man who was a full and equal partner in the three branches of government, never a bully attempting to dominate the other two.

But, more importantly, George Washington made the president of the United States a leader who functioned as the true representative of the people, a man who used his considerable personal skills to mobilize the national Congress, state legislators, county and local officials, and the people, together, for the public good—in war and peace. He had left an office of great power and prestige because he had constructed it, an office respected at home and abroad because he had filled it, an office which in time, regardless of its tenant, would become the most powerful in the world—because he had been its first occupant.

As his successor, John Adams, said of Washington and the presidency, "His example is...complete and it will teach wisdom and virtue to magistrates, citizens and men, not only in the present age, but in future generations, as long as our history shall be read...."

Farewell

Just after breakfast on December 12, 1799, George Washington emerged from the first floor office on the southern wing of Mount Vernon, walked fifty yards downhill to the stables, mounted one of his horses, and went for the morning inspection of his farms. It was cold and windy on the banks of the Potomac; snow had been falling gently since dawn. The general rode for several hours as three inches of snow began to accumulate on the ground. He returned to the stables with a thin covering of sleet on his hat and jacket and, despite pleas from aide Tobias Lear, insisted on dining in his wet clothes. The next evening the ex-president complained of a severe sore throat. It was the beginning of another bout with quinsy, his nemesis, which had almost killed him during the war. His doctors were summoned immediately. The physicians gave him some medicines, which were ineffective. Then they continuously bled him, which worsened his condition. The room was quiet; Martha held his hand as he weakened.

George Washington, sixty-seven, died the following night, December 14, in the middle of winter, as frost formed on the panes of his second-floor bedroom windows and a sharp wind swept across his fields and the sprawling Virginia countryside. All of the land around him was covered with snow, as it had been twenty-three years earlier, when he and his small army crossed the ice-filled Delaware River in New Jersey and turned the world upside down.

ACKNOWLEDGMENTS

M y research on *George Washington's War* carried me to the sites of the winter camps of the Revolution and other historical places. Historians there opened up their vast depositories of books, magazines, diaries, journals, and collections of letters for me and spent a considerable amount of time helping me to find information in order to tell the story of George Washington during the war.

Lee Boyle, recently retired, the author and longtime historian at Valley Forge, spent nearly a week pulling down journals and books for me from the dark wooden shelves in the old stone building that serves as the library there. Eric Olson, the historian at the Morristown National Historical Park, who also speaks around the country about the Revolution, assisted me in finding sources and in shaping the overall story of the army's cruel winters in the small New Jersey village. His colleague, David Vecchioli, the head librarian at the Morristown park, was also of great assistance. They all helped me to understand the war, the people who lived near the army camps, and Washington, as did David Fowler, the former historian at Washington's Crossing State Park, in Pennsylvania. Each also read through chapters of the book and made helpful suggestions.

Special thanks go to Dr. Edward Lengel, the author, historian, and senior editor at the George Washington Papers project at the University of Virginia. Lengel read through the entire book for me, helped in the editing, answered my historical questions, and aided me in interpreting the events of the colonial era and the war. Veteran editor Jere Herzenberg went over the manuscript and suggested constructive changes. Dr. Fran Moran, of New Jersey City University, a specialist in political theory, aided in my interpretation of Washington as president. Thanks, too, to Dr. Fred Greenstein of Princeton University, for his comments on the manuscript.

My thanks also go to the staff of the Rockefeller Library, at Williamsburg, Virginia, who worked with me on a long visit as I tried to put together the early life of Washington. Many thanks, too, to the researchers at the David Library of the American Revolution, at Washington's Crossing; the librarians at the Washington Cantonment Historical Park, in Newburgh, New York, who did the same; and to the librarians at Rutgers, Princeton, and New Jersey City Universities. Especially valuable in my work, too, was Marie Heagney at the Morris County Free Library, in Whippany, New Jersey.

Dawn Bonner, the head of photo services at Mount Vernon, helped me select illustrations from among hundreds of images of the first president's estate on the banks of the Potomac. Scott Houting, of the museum services division at the Valley Forge National Historical Park, worked with me in picking pictures to accompany the chapters on the awful winter of 1777–78 there. Johnni Rowe, at the Morristown, New Jersey, National Historical Park, did the same. Andrea Ashby-Leraris provided photos from the vast collection at the Independence National Historical Park collection in Philadelphia. I also received photo assistance from Christine Jochem and Suzanne Gulick at the Morristown-Morris Township library.

I would like to thank Hillel Black, the gifted editor of *George Washington's War* at Sourcebooks, with whom I have worked before. Hillel possesses an unusual sense of history, drama, and good writing that makes his relationships with writers a joy for them.

My literary agents, Carolyn Krupp and Lisa Queen, were kind enough to read the book, chapter by chapter, and were instrumental in getting it into print. Thanks, too, to my wife Marjorie, who assisted me in my research.

BIBLIOGRAPHY

ARCHIVAL SOURCES

Abeel, James. Papers. Morristown National Historical Park.
Bauman, Sebastian. Papers. New York Historical Society.
Blaine, Ephraim. Morristown National Historical Park
Bogart, John. Letters. Rutgers University Library, Special Collections.
Boudinot, Elias. Stimon-Boudinot Papers. Princeton University Library.
Chaloner, John. Papers. Connecticut Historical Society.
Eccleston, John. Papers. Rutgers University Library, Special Collections.
Gates, Horatio. Papers. New York Historical Society.
Greene, Nathanael. Papers. New York Historical Society.
Hoff, Joseph. Letter book. Morristown National Historical Park.
Huntington, Jedediah. Letters. Connecticut Historical Society.
Knox, Henry. Papers, on microfilm, Morristown National Historical Park and the Massachusetts
    Historical Society.
McDougall, Alexander. Papers. New York Historical Society.
Neilson, John. Papers. Rutgers University Library, Special Collections.
Palfrey, William. Papers, Massachusetts Historical Society.
Pearse, John. Hopewell Furnace day book. Rutgers University Library, Special Collections.
Pierson, Abraham. Pierson and Sargent Papers. New York Historical Society.
Records of Chester County, Pennsylvania. Valley Forge National Historical Park.
Smith, John. Papers. Valley Forge National Historical Park.
Stewart, Charles. Papers. New York Historical Society.
Sullivan, John. Papers. University of New Hampshire Library.
Turner, Peter. Papers. Library of Congress.
Varnum, James. Papers. Harvard University Library.
Wadsworth, Jeremiah. Papers. Connecticut Historical Society.
Ward, Samuel. Papers. Rhode Island Historical Society.
Washington, Martha. Mount Vernon Library Collection.
Wayne, Anthony. Papers. Pennsylvania Historical Society.
Wild, Ebenezer. Papers. Massachusetts Historical Society.

NEWSPAPER SOURCES

Connecticut Journal. 1777.
Freeman's Journal. 1777.
Maryland Journal. 1777-82.
New Jersey Gazette. 1778-80.
New Jersey Journal. 1777-83.
New York Gazette and Weekly Mercury. 1776-82.
Pennsylvania Evening Post. 1777.
Pennsylvania Gazette. 1777.
Pennsylvania Packet. 1777.
Philadelphia Journal. 1777.
Virginia Gazette. 1768-89.

JOURNAL ARTICLES AND BOOK CHAPTERS

"Extracts from the Memoirs of Jonas Ingram, late Captain of the Bucks County, Pennsylvania, Militia." *Pennsylvania Magazine of History and Biography* 26, No. 3, 1902.

"Letters of George Washington to Lord Dunmore." *William and Mary Quarterly* April 1940.

"Lieutenant Andreas Wiederholt's Diary," *Pennsylvania Magazine of History and Biography* 22, 1898.

"Quartermaster's Receipt Book in the Revolution." *New Jersey Historical Society Proceedings*, July, 1920.

"The Marriage of George and Martha Washington," *The Daughters of the American Revolution Magazine*, February, 1977.

Alexander, William. "The Letters of William Alexander, Lord Stirling." *New Jersey Historical Society Proceedings*, July, 1942.

Allen, William. "George Washington and the Standing Oak." Gregg, Gary, and Matthew Spalding, eds. *Patriot Sage: George Washington and the American Political Tradition.* Wilmington: ISI Books, 1999.

Beatty, Erkuries. "Letters of Erkuries Beatty." *Pennsylvania Magazine of History and Biography*, vol. 14, 1890.

Bodle, Wayne. "Generals and 'Gentlemen': Pennsylvania Politics and the Decision for Valley Forge." *Pennsylvania Magazine of History and Biography*, Winter, 1995.

Boorstin, Daniel. "American Revolution: Revolutionary or Non-Revolutionary? Part Two." Grob, Gerry, and George Billias, eds. *Interpretations of American Historical Patterns.* 2 vols. New York: Free Press, 1967.

Bradford, S. Sydney. "Hunger Menaces the Revolution." *Maryland Historical Magazine*, March 1966.

Bradley, Harold. "The Political Thinking of George Washington." *Journal of Southern History*, November, 1945.

Breen, T.H. "Horse and Gentlemen: The Cultural Significance of Gambling Among the Gentry of Virginia." *William and Mary Quarterly*, April, 1977.

Danforth, George. "Lord Stirling's Hibernia Furnace," *New Jersey Historical Society Proceedings*, April, 1953.

Duncan, Louis. Medical Men in the Revolution. *Army Medical Bulletin* No. 25.

Falkner, Leonard. "A Spy for Washington." *American Heritage*, August, 1957.

Gerlach, Larry. "Smallpox Inoculations in Colonial New Jersey," *Journal of the Rutgers University Library*, 1967.

Gould, E.R.I. "Local Self Government in Pennsylvania." *Pennsylvania Magazine of History and Biography*, vol. 7, 1882.

Jameson, Franklin. "The American Revolution: Revolutionary or Non-Revolutionary? Part One." In Grob, Gerry, and George Billias, eds. *Interpretations of American Historical Patterns.* 2 vols., New York: Free Press, 1967.

Jensen, Merrell. "Historians and the Nature of the American Revolution." *The Re-Interpretations of Early American History.* Ray Billington, ed. San Marino, California: Huntington Library Association, 1966.

Kibler, J. Luther. "Washington in Williamsburg." Monograph, February, 1933. Rockefeller Library, Williamsburg.

Kohn, Richard. "The Inside History of the Newburgh Conspiracy: the Army and the Coup d'Etat." *William and Mary Quarterly*, 27, 3: 1970.

Longworth, Polly. "Portrait of Martha Washington." *Journal of the Colonial Williamsburg Foundation*, Summer 1988.

Ludlum, David. "The Weather of Independence: Trenton and Princeton." *Weatherwise*, August, 1975.

McLaughlin, William. "The Role of Religion in the Revolution: Liberty of Conscience and Cultural Cohesion in the New Nation," Stephen Katz, and James Hutson, eds. *Essays on the American Revolution.* Williamsburg: Institute of Early American History and Culture, 1973.

McMichael, James. "The Diary of James McMichael." *Pennsylvania Magazine of History and Biography* 16, 1892.

Meader, Lewis. "The Council of Censors." *Pennsylvania Magazine of History and Biography*, vol. 22, 1898.

Middleton, William. "Medicine at Valley Forge." *Picket Post*, July, 1962.

Mitros, David. "Shepard Kollock and the New Jersey Journal." *The County Circular*, Winter, 2001.

Newcomb, Benjamin. "Washington's Generals and the Decision to Quarter at Valley Forge." *Pennsylvania Magazine of History and Biography*, October, 1993.

Paltsits, N.H. "John Holt: Printer and Postmaster." *New York Public Library Bulletin*, vol. 24, 1920.

Parker, Robert. "Robert Parker's Diary." *Pennsylvania Magazine of History and Biography*, vol. 28, 1904.

Peale, Charles Wilson. "Journal of Charles Wilson Peale." *Pennsylvania Magazine of History and Biography* 38, 1914.

Phelps, Glenn. "George Washington: Precedent Setter." Thomas Cronin, ed. *Inventing the American Presidency*. Lawrence: University of Kansas Press, 1989.

Ramsey, David. "The View From Inside." Jack Greene, Ed., *The Ambiguity of the American Revolution*. New York: Harper and Row, 1968.

Robson, Eric. "The American Revolution in its Political and Military Aspects." Edmund Morgan, Ed., *The American Revolution: Two Centuries of Interpretation*. Englewood Cliffs: Prentice Hall, 1965.

Rozell, Mark. "Washington and the Origins of Presidential Power." Gregg, Gary, and Matthew Spalding, eds. *Patriot Sage: George Washington and American Political Tradition*. Wilmington: ISI Books, 1999.

Smelser, Marshall. "George Washington and the Alien and Sedition Acts." *American History Review*, January, 1954.

Spieler, Gerhard. "Peter Hasenclever: Industrialist." *New Jersey Historical Society Proceedings*, October, 1941.

Thatcher, Harold. "The Social and Economic Ideas of New Jersey's First Governor," *New Jersey Historical Society Proceedings*, October, 1942.

Torres-Reyes, R. "A Study of Medical Services in the 1779-1780 Encampment." Monograph. Morristown National Historical Park, 1971.

Vernon-Jackson, H.O.H. "A Loyalist's Wife: Letters of Mrs. Philip Van Cortlandt," *History Today*, 1917.

White, Joseph. "The Good Soldier White." *American Heritage*, June, 1956.

Wordham, George. "A Physical Description of George Washington." *Daughters of the American Revolution Magazine*, February, 1974.

Wright, William. "The Colonial Plantation Settlement in New Jersey: Iron and Agriculture Examples." Wright, William, ed. *Economic and Social History of New Jersey*. Newark: New Jersey Historical Association, 1973.

BOOKS

200 Years Ago Today at Valley Forge. Valley Forge: Valley Forge Historical Park, 1979.

Adams, Charles. *The Letters of Mrs. Adams*. 2 vols. Boston, 1841.

Addington, Larry. *Patterns of War Since the Nineteenth Century*. Bloomington: University of Indiana Press, 1984.

Ambrose, Stephen. *Supreme Commander: The War Years of General Dwight D. Eisenhower*. Garden City: Doubleday Co., 1970.

Annals of Medical History, Third Series, III. Madison, Wisconsin, 1841.

Anderson, John R. *Shepard Kollock: Editor for Freedom*. Chatham: Chatham Historical Society, 1973.

Anderson, Troyer. *The Command of the Howe Brothers During the American Revolution*. New York: Octagon Books, 1872.

Arita, I., F. Fenner, D.A. Henderson, Z. Jelek, and I.D. Ladnyi. *Smallpox and Its Eradication*. Geneva: World Health Organization, 1988.

Arnold, James. *Presidents Under Fire: Commanders-in-Chief in Victory and Defeat*. New York: Orion Books, 1994.

Atwood, Rodney. *The Hessians: Mercenaries From Hessan-Kassel in the American Revolution*. Cambridge: Cambridge University Press, 1980.

Bailyn, Bernard, and John Hench, eds. *The Press and the American Revolution*. Worcester: American Antiquarian Society, 1980.

Baxin, Herve. *The Eradication of Smallpox*. New York: Academic Press, 1984.

Bergh, Albert, ed. *The Writings of Thomas Jefferson*. 28 vols. Washington, D.C.: Thomas Jefferson Memorial Association, 1907.

Berlin, Ira, and Phillip Morgan. eds. *Cultivation and Culture: Labor and the Shaping of Slave Life in the Americas*. Charlottesville: University of Virginia Press, 1993.

Bezanson, Anne, Robert Gray, and Miriam Hussey. *Price and Inflation During the American Revolution, Pennsylvania*. Philadelphia: University of Pennsylvania Press, 1935.

Bill, Alfred. *New Jersey and the Revolutionary War*. New Brunswick: Rutgers University Press, 1964.

Billias, George, ed. *George Washington's Generals*. New York: W. W. Norton Co., 1964.

Binger, Carl. *Revolutionary Doctor: Benjamin Rush, 1746-1813*. New York: W. W. Norton, 1966.

Bingham, Hiram Jr. *Five Straws Gathered From Revolutionary Fields*. Cambridge, 1901.

Black, Jeremy. *War for America: The Fight for Independence, 1775-1783*. New York: St. Martin's Press, 1991.

Bodle, Wayne and Jacqueline Thibault. *Valley Forge Historical Society Research Report*. 2 vols. Washington, D.C.: U.S. Department of the Interior, 1980.

Boller, Paul Jr. *George Washington and Religion*. Dallas: Southern Methodist University Press, 1963.

Bolton, Charles, ed. *Letters of Hugh Early Percy From Boston and New York, 1774-1776*. Boston: Gregg Press, 1972.

Bonwick, Colin. *The American Revolution*. London: MacMillan Co., 1991.

Boudinot, Elias. *Journal of Events in the Revolution*. New York: New York Times/Arno Press, 1968, reprinted from Frederick Bourquin, 1894.

Bourdin, H.L., and R. H. Gabriel. *Sketches of Eighteenth Century America*. New Haven: Yale University Press, 1925.

Bourne, Miriam. *First Family: George Washington and His Intimate Relations*. New York: W.W. Norton, 1982.

Bowman, Allen. *The Morale of the American Revolutionary Army*. Port Washington: Kennikat Press, 1943.

Boyer, Charles. *Early Forges and Furnaces in New Jersey*. Philadelphia, 1931.

Boyle, Lee. *Writings from the Valley Forge Encampment of the Continental Army, December, 1777—June 19, 1778*. Bowie, Md.: Heritage Books, 2001.

Bray, Robert and Paul Bushnell, eds. *Diary of a Common Soldier in the American Revolution, 1775-1783; An Annotated Edition of the Military Journal of Jeremiah Greenman*. DeKalb, Ill.: Northern Ilinois University Press, 1978.

Brown, Gerald. *The American Secretary: The Colonial Policies of Lord George Germain, 1775-1778*. Ann Arbor: University of Michigan Press, 1963.

Brunhouse, Robert. *The Counter-Revolution in Pennsylvania, 1776-1790*. Harrisburg: Pennsylvania Historical Commission, 1942.

Bryant, Arthur. *The American Ideal*. Freeport: Books for Libraries Press, 1969.

Burke, Edmund. *Speeches on the American War and Letter to the Sheriffs of Bristol*. Boston: Gregg Press, 1972.

Budka, Metchie, trans. Niemcewicz, Julian. *Under the Vine and Fig Tree: Travels through American, 1797-1799, 1805, With Some Further Account of Life in New Jersey*. Elizabeth, N.J. : Grassman Publishing, 1965.

Butterfield, L.H., ed. *The Letters of Benjamin Rush*. Princeton: Princeton University Press, 1951.

Callahan, North. *Daniel Morgan: Ranger of the Revolution*. New York: Holt, Rinehart, Winston, 1961.

Callahan, North. *Henry Knox: George Washington's General*. New York: Rinehart Co., 1958.

Carp, Wayne. *To Starve the Army at Pleasure: Continental Army Administration and American Political Culture, 1774-1783*. Chapel Hill: University of North Carolina Press, 1984.

Chase, Philander. *Baron Von Steuben in the War of Independence*. Diss. Duke University, 1975.

Chestnut, David, ed. *The Papers of Henry Laurens*. 15 vols. Columbia: University of South Carolina Press, 1988.

Christiano, Terri, ed. *History of Rockaway, New Jersey*. Morristown, 1973.

Clark, Dora. *British Opinion and the American Revolution*. New Haven: Yale University Press, 1930.

Clark, Walter. Ed. *The State Records of North Carolina*. Winston: M, I & J.C. Stewart Co., 1895.

Cody, Edward. *The Religious Issue in Revolutionary New Jersey*. Trenton: New Jersey Historical Commission, 1975.

Collines, Varnum. *A Brief Narrative of the Ravages of the British and Hessians at Princeton in 1776-1777*. New York: New York Times/Arno Press, 1968 reprint of original published by Princeton University Press, 1906.

Cooley, Henry. *A Study of Slavery in New Jersey: Johns Hopkins University Studies in Historical and Political Science*. New York: Johnson Reprints, 1973.

Correspondence and Public Papers of John Jay. 4 vols. New York: G.P. Putnam's Sons, 1893. Reprint, New York: DeCapo Press, 1971.

Cowen, David. *Medicine and Health in New Jersey*. Princeton: Van Nostrand Books, 1961.

Cresswell, Nicholas. *The Journal of Nicholas Cresswell*. New York: Dial Press, 1924.

Damient, Lincoln. *Chaining the Hudson: The Fight for the River in the American Revolution*. New York: Carol Publishing, 1989.

Davidson, Philip. *Propaganda and the American Revolution 1763-1783*. Chapel Hill: University of North Carolina Press, 1941.

Davis, David Brion. *The Problem of Slavery in the Age of Revolution*. Ithaca: Cornell University Press, 1965.

Davis, K.G., ed. *Documents of the American Revolution, 1770-1783* (Colonial Office Series). 14 vols. Dublin: Irish University Press, 1976.

DeConde, Alexander. *Presidential Machismo: Executive Authority, Military Intervention and Foreign Relations*. Boston: Northeastern University Press, 2000.

Doyle, Joseph. *The Life of Frederick William Von Steuben, a Major General in the Revolutionary Army*. Steubenville, Ohio: Stanton Monument Association, 1913.

Duane, William, ed. *Christopher Marshall: Extracts from the Diary…Kept in Philadelphia and Lancaster during the American Revolution, 1774-1781*. Albany, 1877.

Duer, William. *The Life of Lord Stirling*. New York: Wiley and Putnam, 1847.

Duffy, John. *Epidemics in Colonial America*. Baton Rouge: Louisiana State University Press, 1953.

Dupuy, Ernest and Trevor. *The Compact History of the Revolutionary War*. New York: Hawthorn, 1963.

Dwyer, William. *The Day is Ours*. New York: Viking, 1983.

Einstein, Lewis. *Divided Loyalties: Americans in England During the War for Independence*. Freeport, N.Y.: Books for Libraries Press, 1933.

Esposito, Frank. *The Madison Heritage Trail*. Madison Bicentennial Commission, 1985.

Ewald, Johann. *Diary of the American War*. New Haven: Yale University Press, 1979.

Field, Edward, ed. *The Diary of Colonel Israel Angell, Commanded the Second Rhode Island Continental regiment During the Revolution*. New York: New York Times/Arno Press, 1971. Reprinted from Providence: Proctor and Rounds Co., 1899.

Fields, Joseph, ed. *Worthy Partner: The Papers of Martha Washington*. Westport: Greenwood Press, 1994.

Fitzpatrick, John. *The Writings of George Washington*. 38 vols. Washington, D.C.: United States Government Printing Office, 1932.

George Washington Diaries, 1748-1799. 4 vols. Mount Vernon Ladies Association of the Union. Boston: Houghton-Mifflin, 1925.

Fleming, Thomas. *First in Their Hearts: A Biography of George Washington*. New York: W.W. Norton Co., 1984.

Fleming, Thomas. *The Secret War in Morristown*. Morristown: Morris County Historical Society, 1980.

Flexner, James. *George Washington and the American Revolution*. Boston: Little, Brown Co. 1968.

Ford, Worthington, ed. *Defense of Philadelphia in 1777*. New York: DeCapo Press, 1971.

The Correspondence and Journals of Samuel Blachley Webb. 3 vols. New York: New York Times / Arno Press, 1969.

Freeman, Douglas Southall. *George Washington: A Biography*. 6 vols. New York: Charles Scribner's Sons, 1951.

Freeman, Joanne. *Affairs of Honor*. New Haven: Yale University Press, 2000.

Gerlach, Larry. *New Jersey in the Coming of the American Revolution*. Trenton: New Jersey Historical Commission, 1970.

Gilbert, Albert, trans. Machiavelli, Nicolo. *Chief Works and Others*. 3 vols. Chapel Hill: University of North Carolina Press, 1965.

Gillett, Mary. *The Army Medical Department, 1775-1818*. Washington, D.C.: Center of Military History, U.S. Army, 1901.

Gregg, Gary, and Matthew Spalding, eds. *Patriot Sage: George Washington and the American Political Tradition*. Athens, Ga.: University of Georgia Press, 1999.

Hammond, Otto. *The Letters and Papers of John Sullivan, Continental Army*. Concord, N.H.: New Hampshire Historical Society, 1931.

Hansen, Richard. *The Glorious Hour of Lieutenant Monroe*. New York: Athenaeum, 1976.

Harris, Mary. *Trade of the Delaware District Before the Revolution*. Smith College Studies in History. Northampton: Northampton Press, 1917.

Harwell, Richard. Ed. Douglas Southall Freeman. *George Washington*. Abridged ed. New York: Collier, 1968.

Hendrickson, Robert. *Hamilton II: 1789-1804*. New York: Mason/Charter, 1976.

Hester, Alan. *South Jersey, A History*. New York, 1924.

Heusser, Albert. *George Washington's Map Maker*. New Brunswick: Rutgers University Press, 1966.

Hibbert, Christopher. *Rebels and Redcoats: The American Revolution Through British Eyes*. New York: W.W. Norton, 1990.

Hirschfield, Fritz. *George Washington and Slavery: A Documentary Portrayal*. Columbia: University of Missouri Press, 1997.

Historical Sketches of the Town of Leicester, Massachusetts. Boston, 1860.

History of Morris County, New Jersey, with Illustrations and Biographical Sketches of Prominent Citizens and Pioneers. New York: W.W. Munsell, 1882.

History of Picatinny Arsenal. Picatinny: War Planning Division, 1931.

Hoskins, Barbara. *Washington Valley: An Informal History*. Ann Arbor, 1960.

Howard, Michael, and Peter Paret, eds. Carl Von Clausewitz. *On War*. Princeton: Princeton University Press, 1976.

Howell, Hazell. *Research Report on the John Faesch House*. Rockaway Township, 1973.

Iron Mines of New Jersey. New Jersey Documents. Trenton: New Jersey Historical Commission, 1973.

Jackson, Donald, ed. *Diaries of George Washington*. 6 vols. Charlottesville: University of Virginia Press, 1976.

Jackson, John. *Valley Forge: Pinnacle of Courage*. Gettysburg: Thomas Publications, 1999.

Johnston, Henry, ed. *Records of Connecticut Men in the War of the Revolution, 1775-1793*. Hartford, 1889.

Jones, Alfred. *The Loyalists of New Jersey*. Newark: New Jersey Historical Society, 1927.

Jones, Joseph. *The Life of Ashbel Green*. New York: Robert Carter and Brothers, 1849.

Journals of the Continental Congress. 34 vols. Washington, D.C.: U.S. Government Printing Office, 1824.

Kapp, Friedrich. *The Life of Johann Kalb, Major General in the Revolutionary Army*. New York, 1884.

Karlsen, Carol, and Laurie Crumpacker, eds. *Journal of Esther Edwards Burr*. New Haven: Yale University Press, 1984.

Ketchum, Richard. *The Winter Soldiers*. Garden City, N.Y.: Doubleday and Company, 1973.

Klein, Philip and Ari Hoogenboom. *A History of Pennsylvania*. University Park: The Pennsylvania State University Press, 1980.

Kobre, Sidney. *The Development of the Colonial Newspaper*. Gloucester: Peter Smith, 1960.

Koch, Adrienne, *Power, Morals and the Founding Fathers: Essays in the Interpretation of the American Enlightenment*. Ithaca: Cornell University Press, 1961.

Kollenberg, Bernard. *George Washington: The Virginia Period, 1732-1775*. Durham: Duke University Press, 1967.

Land Use Study of Valley Forge Historical Park. Philadelphia: University of Pennsylvania Press, 1989.

Lands, Edward. *The Hessian and the Other German Auxiliaries of Great Britain in the Revolutionary War*. New York: Harper and Brothers, 1884.

Lauber, Almon. Ed. *Orderly Books of the Fourth New York Regiment, with the Diaries of Samuel Tallmadge, 1780-1782*. Albany, 1932.

Leckie, Robert. *George Washington's War*. New York: HarperCollins, 1992.

Leibiger, Stuart. *Founding Friendship: George Washington, James Madison and the Creation of the American Republic*. Charlottesville: University Press of Virginia, 1999.

Letters Written by Ebenezer Huntington during the American Revolution. New York: C.F. Heartman, 1915.

Longmore, Paul. *The Invention of George Washington*. Los Angeles: University of California Press, 1988.

Lucas, Stephen. *The Quotable George Washington: The Wisdom of an American Patriot*. Madison: Madison House Press, 1999.

Ludlum, David. *Early American Winters, 1604-1828*. Boston: American Meteorological Society, 1966.

Lundin, Leonard. *Cockpit of the Revolution: The War for Independence in New Jersey*. Princeton: Princeton University Press, 1940.

Macmillan, Margaret. *The War Governors in the American Revolution*. New York: Columbia University Press, 1943.

Main, Jackson Turner. *The Sovereign States, 1775-1783*. New York: Franklin Walls, 1973.

Malberg, Edward. *Slavery as an Institution: New Jersey and the South*. Diss. Rutgers University, 1966.

Manuscripts of the Earl of Dartmouth. 2 vols. Boston: Gregg Press, 1972.

Martin, Joseph. *Private Yankee Doodle: Being A Narrative of Some of the Adventures, Dangers and Sufferings of a Revolutionary Soldier*. Boston: Little, Brown Co., 1962.

Mattern, David. *Benjamin Lincoln and the American Revolution*. New York: Columbia University Press, 1995.

Mattia, Mark. *New Jersey and the Loyalists During the First British Invasion and Occupation of the State in 1776-1777*. Master's Thesis. Rutgers University, 1975.

Mays, David. *The Letters and Papers of Edmund Pendleton, 1774-1803*. Charlottesville: University Press of Virginia, 1967.

McCants, David. *Patrick Henry: Orator*. Westport: Greenwood Press, 1990.

McDonald, Forrest. *The American Presidency: An Intellectual History*. Lawrence: University of Kansas Press, 1994.

Meir, Louis, *The Healing of an Army, 1777-1778*. Norristown: History Society of Montgomery County, Pennsylvania, 1991.

Memoirs of Long Island: George Washington and Mount Vernon. 4 vols. Brooklyn, 1899.

Meyers, Frank, ed. *The Papers of Josiah Bartlett*. Hanover: University Press of New England, 1979.

Michaelsen, William. *Creating the American Presidency, 1775-1789*. Boston: University Press of America, 1987.

Milton, George. *Use of Presidential Power, 1789-1943*. Boston: Little, Brown Co., 1944.

Minutes of the Committee and of the First Commission For Detecting and Defeating Conspiracies in the State of New York. 3 vols. Albany: State of New York, 1909.

Mitchell, Broadus. *Alexander Hamilton: The Revolutionary Years*. New York: Thomas Crowell, 1980.

Mitchell, Broadus. *Alexander Hamilton: Youth to Maturity*. 2 vols. New York: MacMillan Co., 1957.

Mitros, David, ed. *Jacob Green: Observations on the Reconciliation of Great Britain and the Colonies*. Mendham, N.J.: Morris County Heritage Association, 1975.

Mitros, David. *Jacob Green and the Slavery Debate*. Mendham: Morris County Heritage Commission, 1975.

Montross, Lynn. *The Reluctant Rebels: The Story of the Continental Congress, 1774-1789*. New York: Harper and Brothers, 1930.

Morris, Margaret. *Private Journal Kept During the Revolutionary War*. New York: New York Times/Arno Press, 1969.

Nell, William. *The Colored Patriots of the American Revolution*. Boston: Robert Walcott, 1855. Reprint, Salem, N.H.: Ayer Co., 1986.

Nelson, Paul. *William Alexander: Lord Stirling*. Birmingham: University of Alabama Press, 1987.

Nelson, William. *The American Tory*. Boston: Beacon Press, 1961.

Niebuhr, Reinhold and Alan Heimert. *A Nation Conceived: Reflections on the History of America From Its Early Visions to Its Present Power*. New York: Charles Scribner's Sons, 1963.

Niles, Hezekiah. *Principles and Act of the Revolution in America*. New York: A.S. Barnes, 1876.

Noss, Theodore. *The Awakening of the Quaker Movement Against Negro Slavery in Colonial Pennsylvania and Western New Jersey*. Diss. University of Chicago, 1934.

Oberholtzer, Ellis. *Robert Morris: Patriot and Financier*. New York: MacMillan Co, 1903.

Ogden, Horace. *CDC and the Smallpox Crusade*. Washington, D.C.: U.S. Department of Health, Center for Disease Control, 1972.

Otis, James. *The Rights of British Colonists Asserted and Proved*. Boston, 1766.

Paine, Lauren. *Benedict Arnold: Hero and Traitor*. London: Robert Hale, 1963.

Palmer, David. *The Way of the Fox: American Strategy in the War for America, 1775-1783*. Westport: Greenwood Press, 1975.

Palmer, John. *General Frederick Von Steuben*. New Haven: Yale University Press, 1937.

Pancake, John. *1777: Year of the Hangman*. Birmingham: University of Alabama Press, 1972.

Paul, Ed, ed. *Journals of Hugh Gaines, Printer*. 2 vols. New York: Dodd, Mead and Co., 1902.

Pearse, John. *A Concise History of the Iron Manufacture in the American Colonies*. 1876.

Pederson, William, Mark Rozell and Frank Williams, eds. *George Washington and the Origins of the American Presidency*. Westport: Praeger Publishing, 2000.

Peterson, Harold. *The Guns of the Continental Soldier*. Harrisburg: Stackpole Books, 1968.

Phelps, Glenn. *George Washington and American Constitutionalism*. Lawrence: University Press of Kansas, 1993.

Pierce, Arthur. *Iron in the Pines*. New Brunswick: Rutgers University Press, 1957.

Preston, John. *A Gentleman Rebel: Mad Anthony Wayne*. Garden City: Garden City Books, 1930.

Prince, Carl. *William Livingston: New Jersey's First Governor*. Trenton: New Jersey Historical Commission, 1975.

Quincy, Josiah. *The Journals of Major Samuel Shaw: The First American Consul at Canton*. Boston: William Brosby and H.P. Nichols, 1847.

Randall, Willard. *Benedict Arnold: Patriot and Traitor*. New York: William Morrow, 1990.

Randall, Willard. *George Washington: A Life*. New York: Henry Holt, 1997.

Rasmussen, William, and Robert Tilton. *George Washington: The Man Behind the Myths*. Charlottesville: University Press of Virginia, 1999.

Razwell, Peter. *The Conquest of Smallpox*. Sussex, England: Caliban Books, 1977.

Read, D.B. *The Life and Times of General John Graves Simcoe*. Toronto: Virtue Publishing, 1890.

Reed, John. *Valley Forge: Crucible of Victory*. Monmouth Beach, N.J.: Philip Freneau Press, 1969.

Reed, Wilfred. Ed. *A Reprint of the Original Letters from Washington to Joseph Reed During the American Revolution*. Philadelphia: Carey & Chart, 1852.

Reiss, Oscar. *Medicine in the American Revolution*. Jefferson, North Carolina: McFarland and Company, 1998.

Rhys, Isaac. *The Transformation of Virginia, 1740-1790*. New York: W. W. Norton, 1982.

Risch, Erna. *Supplying Washington's Army*. Washington, D.C.: Center of Military History, 1981.

Roberts, Lemuel. *The Memoirs of Lemuel Roberts*. New York: New York Times/Arno Press, 1969. Reprinted from Bennington: Anthony Haswell, 1809.

Rodney, Thomas, *The Diary of Thomas Rodney, 1776-1777*. Wilmington: Historical Society of Delaware. 1888.

Rossman, Kenneth. *Thomas Mifflin and the Politics of the American Revolution*. Chapel Hill: University of North Carolina Press, 1963.

Royster, Charles. *A Revolutionary People at War*. Chapel Hill: University of North Carolina Press, 1979.

Ryan, Dennis. *New Jersey's Loyalists*. Trenton: New Jersey Historical Commission, 1975.

Sabine, Lorenzo. *A Historical Essay on the Loyalists of the American Revolution*. Springfield, Mass.: Walden Press, 1957.

Saffron, Morris. *Surgeon General to Washington: Dr. John Cochran, 1730-1817*. New York: Columbia University Press, 1977.

Scheer, George, and Hugh Ranken, eds. *Rebels and Redcoats*. New York: World Publishing Company, 1957.

Schlesinger, Arthur. *Prelude to Independence.* New York: Alfred Knopf, 1958.

Schmidt, Hubert. *Slavery and Attitudes on Slavery in Hunterdon County, N.J.* Flemington: Hunterdon County Historical Society, 1941.

Schroeder, John, ed. *Maxims of George Washington: Political, Military, Social and Religious.* Mount Vernon: Mount Vernon Ladies Association, 1989.

Selby, John. *The Revolution in Virginia, 1775-1793.* Williamsburg: Colonial Williamsburg Foundation, 1988.

Sherman, Andrew. *The History of Morristown, New Jersey: the Story of Its First Century.* Morristown, N.J.: Howard Publishing, 1905.

Showman, Richard. *The Papers of Nathanael Greene.* 6 vols. Chapel Hill: University of North Carolina Press, 1989.

Shreve, I.G. *Tench Tilghman: The Life and Times of Washington's Aide-de-Camp.* Centreville, Md.: Tidewater Publications, 1982.

Sipe, C. Hale. *Mount Vernon and the Washington family: a concise handbook on the ancestry, youth and family of George Washington, and history of his home.* Butler, Pa.: Ziegler Printing, 1927.

Smallpox in Colonial America. New York: New York Times and Arno Press, 1977.

Smith, James. Ed. *The Republic of Letters: The Correspondence between Thomas Jefferson and James Madison, 1776-1826.* 3 vols. New York: W.W. Norton Co., 1995.

Smith, Paul, ed. *Letters of Delegates to Congress, 1774-1789.* 26 vols. Washington, D.C.: Library of Congress, 1976.

Smith, Paul. *Loyalists and Redcoats.* Williamsburg: Institute of Early American History and Culture, 1964.

Soceano, Mara, and Duran Echevarria, trans.Warville, Jacques Pierre Brissot de. *Travels in the United States of America, 1788.*Cambridge: Harvard University Press, 1964.

Soderlund, Jean. *Quakers and Slavery: A Divided Spirit.* Princeton: Princeton University Press, 1985.

Sparks, Jared, ed. *Correspondence of the American Revolution Being Letters of Eminent Men to George Washington from the Time of His Taking Command of the Army to The End of His Presidency.* 4 vols. Freeport, N.Y.: Books for Libraries Press, 1979.

Stewart, Bruce. *Morristown: A Crucible of the American Revolution.* Trenton: New Jersey Historical Society, 1975.

Stryker, William, ed. *Archives of the State of New Jersey Newspaper Extracts.* 2d Series. 2 vols. Trenton: John Murphy Co., 1901.

Stryker, William. *The Battles of Trenton and Princeton.* Boston: Houghton and Mifflin Co., 1898.

Syrett, Harold. *The Papers of Alexander Hamilton.* 27 vols. New York: Columbia University Press, 1961.

Tappert, Theodore and John Doberstein. *The Journal of Henry Muhlenberg.* Philadelphia: Muhlenberg Press, 1942.

Tatum, Edward. *The American Journal of Ambrose Serle.* New York: New York Times/Arno Press, 1969.

Tebbel, John. *Turning the World Upside Down: Inside the American Revolution.* New York: Orion Books, 1993.

Thacher, James. *Military Journal of the American Revolution from the Commencement to the Disbanding of the American Army, Comprising a Detailed Account of the Principal Events and Battles of the Revolution With Their Exact Dates and a Biographical Sketch of the Most Prominent Generals.* Hartford: Hurlbut, Williams and Co., 1862.

Thane, Elswyth. *The Fighting Quaker: Nathanael Greene.* New York: Hawthorn, 1972.

Thane, Elswyth. *Washington's Lady.* New York: Dodd, Mead and Co., 1960.

Thayer, Theodore. *Nathanael Greene: Strategist of the American Revolution.* New York: Twayne Publishers, 1960.

The History of the George Washington Bicentennial Association. 3 vols. Washington, D.C. United States Government Printing Office, 1932.

The Proceedings of a General Court Martial for the Trial of Benedict Arnold, With an Introduction, Notes and Index. New York, 1865.

Thomson, Charles. *Revolutionary War Papers of Charles Thomson, Secretary to the Continental Congress, 1774-1789.* New York: New York Historical Society, 1879.

Thompson, Ray. *Benedict Arnold in Philadelphia*. Fort Washington, Pa.: The Bicentennial Press, 1975.

Thompson, William. *Israel Shreve: Revolutionary War Officer*. Ruston, La: McGinty Trust Fund Publications, 1979.

Tilghman, Tench. *The Memoirs of Tench Tilghman*. Albany: S. Munsell, 1876.

Tomlinson, Richard, Jr. *A Community Under Stress: Morristown, 1740-1800*. Diss., Princeton University, 1972.

Trussel, John Jr. *Birthplace of an Army: A Study of the Valley Forge Encampment*. Harrisburg: Pennsylvania Historical and Museum Collection, 1998.

Tuttle, Joseph. *Index to Annals of Morris County*, Morristown, 1876. Reprint, Morristown: American Civilization Institute of Morristown, 1968.

Tuttle, Joseph. *Centennial Collection of Morris County*. Morristown, 1877.

Tuttle, Joseph. *Reverend Jacob Green of Hanover, N.J. as Author, Statesman and Patriot*. Newark: Advertising Printing, 1894.

Uhlendorf, Bernard. Trans. *Revolution in America: Confidential Letters and Journals, 1776-1784 of Adjutant General Major Baurmeister of the Hessian Forces*. New Brunswick: Rutgers University Press, 1957.

Upton, Leslie, ed. *Revolutionary Versus Loyalist*. Waltham, Mass.: Blaisdell Publishing, 1968.

Van Doren, Carl. *Mutiny in January*. New York: Viking Press, 1943.

Volm, M.H. *The Hessian Prisoners in the American War of Independence and their Life in Captivity*. Charlottesville: University of Virginia, 1977.

Wallace, Willard. *Traitor and Hero: The Life and Fortunes of Benedict Arnold*. New York: Harper Bros., 1954.

Ward, Christopher. *The War of the Revolution*. 2 vols. New York: MacMillan Co., 1952.

Warner, Michael. *The Letters of the Republic: Publication and the Public Sphere in Eighteenth Century America*. Cambridge: Harvard University Press, 1990

Washington, George. *General Orders of George Washington Issued at Newburgh-on-the-Hudson, 1782-1783*. Harrison, N.Y.: Harbor Hills Books, 1973.

Weeks, Stephen. *Southern Quakers and Slavery: A Study in Institutional History*. Baltimore: Johns Hopkins University Press, 1896.

Wharton, Anne Hollingworth. *Martha Washington*. New York: Charles Scribner's Sons, 1897.

White, Donald. *A Village at War: Chatham, New Jersey and the American Revolution*. London: Associated University Presses, 1979.

Wickwire, Franklin and Mary. *Cornwallis: The American Adventure*. Boston: Houghton and Mifflin Co., 1970.

Wilcox, William, ed. *Sir Henry Clinton, the American Rebellion: Sir Henry Clinton's Narrative of His Campaign, 1775-1782, With an Appendix of Original Documents*. New Haven: Yale University Press, 1954.

Wilkinson, James. *Memoirs of My Time*. 3 vols. Philadelphia: Abraham Small, 1816.

Williams, Catherine. *Biographies of Revolutionary Heroes, Containing the Life of Brigadier General William Barton and Also of Captain Stephen Olney*. Providence: Catherine Williams, 1839.

Williams, William. *America Confronts a Revolutionary World*. New York: William Morrow, 1976.

Wills, Garry. *Cincinnatus: George Washington and the Enlightenment*. Garden City: Doubleday, 1984.

Wingo, Barbara. *Politics, Society and Religion: The Presbyterian Clergy in Pennsylvania, New Jersey and New York and the Formation of the New Nation, 1775-1808*. Diss. Tulane University, 1976.

Wood, Gordon. *The Creation of the American Republic, 1776-1787*. New York: W. W. Norton Co., 1969.

Woolman, John. *Some Considerations on the Keeping of Negroes*. Philadelphia: James Chattin, 1754, Viking Reprint, 1976.

Zagarri, Rosemary, ed. David Humphreys. *The Life of George Washington, with General Washington's "Remarks."* Athens, Georgia: University of Georgia Press, 1991.

NOTES

GW = George Washington
CONG = Library of Congress
GWW = The Writings of George Washington
JCC = *Journals of the Continental Congress*
HK = Papers of Henry Knox, Morristown National Historic Park
DGW = *The Diaries of George Washington*
PGW = *The Papers of George Washington*
NJHS = New Jersey Historical Society
GB = *Documents of the American Revolution*
LAURENS = *The Papers of Henry Laurens*
ABEEL = James Abeel Papers
GREENE = Nathaniel Greene to William Livingston
VFR = *Valley Forge Historical Society Research Report*
Reed = John F. Reed, Valley Forge: Crucible of Victory
VFHP = Valley Forge Historical Park Collections
NJJ = *New Jersey Journal*

Chapter One: Christmas, 1776

4   *"a little paltry colonel"*: Edward Tatum, Jr., ed., *The American Journal of Ambrose Serle*, New York: New York Times/Arno Press, 1969, p. 35.

5   *"I feel for Washington"*: William Hooper to Joseph Hewes, November 30, 1776, in Paul Smith, ed., *Letters of Delegates to Congress, 1774–1789* (CONG), 26 vols., Washington, D.C.: Library of Congress, 1976, vol. 5, pp. 557–58.

5   *"I think our affairs"*: George Washington (GW) to Jack Washington, December 18, 1776, in John Fitzpatrick, *The Writings of George Washington* (GWW), 38 vols., Washington, D.C.: United States Government Printing Office, 1932, vol. 6, p. 397.

5   *"they fall dead on the roads"*: George Ross to James Wilson, November 26, 1777, in CONG V: 547.

6   *"rushed like a torrent"*: Richard Henry Lee to Patrick Henry, December 3, 1776, in CONG V: 564.

6   *"The enemy move rapidly"*: William Hooper to Joseph Hewes, December 3, 1776, in CONG V: 564–65.

7   *"leave no room for joy"*: Robert Morris to Silas Deane, December 20, 1776, in CONG V: 620.

7   *"that until they should otherwise"*: The resolution was passed on December 12, 1776, and later sent to the general. *Journals of the Continental Congress* (JCC).

7   the British planned to recruit: Samuel Adams to James Warren, December 25, 1776, in CONG V: 660–61.

7   they could easily attack his army: GW to Major General Joseph Spencer, December 22, 1776, in GWW VI: 426–28.

7   *"You may as well attempt"*: GW to Robert Morris, December 22, 1776, in GWW VI: 420–21.

8   *"The enemy are daily gathering strength"*: GW to the president of the Continental Congress, John Hancock, December 20, 1776, in GWW VI: 400–409.

8   *"I am almost led to despair"*: GW to Jonathan Trumbull, December 21, 1776, in GWW VI: 411.

8   *"the prospects are gloomy"*: GW to Nicholas Cooke, December 21, 1776, in GWW VI: 412–13.

8   *"my situation"*: GW to Major General William Heath, December 21, 1776, in GWW VI: 417–19.

8   *"I tremble for Philadelphia"*: GW to Lund Washington, December 10, 1776, GWW VI: 345–47.

9   *"devise some other rule"*: GW to John Hancock, December 24, 1776, GWW VI: 433.

9   *"Washington ordered the leaders"*: GW to the Passamaquoddy chief and chiefs of the St. John's Indians, December 24, 1776, in GWW VI: 434–36.

9   *There seemed to be no respite*: William Dwyer, *The Day Is Ours*, New York: Viking, 1983, pp. 152, 213.

11   *"He was a very sociable man"*: Lieutenant Andreas Wiederhholt's Diary, *Pennsylvania Magazine of History and Biography* 22 (1898): 462–67.

12   *"Victory or death"*: Dwyer, *The Day Is Ours*, p. 213.

13   *"Very stormy"*: Margaret Morris, *Private Journal Kept During the Revolutionary War*, New York: New York Times/Arno Press, 1969, p. 20.

14   *the crossing of the Delaware began*: Theodore Thayer, *Nathaniel Greene: Strategist of the American Revolution*, New York: Twayne Publishers, 1960, pp. 140–43.

15   *"The army crossed the river"*: Henry Knox to Lucy Knox, December 26, 1776, Papers of Henry Knox, Morristown National Historic Park (HK); originals at the Massachusetts Historical Society.

15   *"It was as severe"*: William Stryker, *The Battles of Trenton and Princeton*, Boston, Mass.: Houghton and Mifflin Co., 1898, p. 133.

16   *"the worst day of sleet"*: David Ludlum, "The Weather of Independence: Trenton and Princeton," in *Weatherwise* (August 1975): 75–83.

16   *"There was no making a retreat"*: GW to Congress, December 27, 1776, in GWW VI: 441–44.

16   *"Press on boys"*: Christopher Ward, *The War of the Revolution*, 2 vols., New York: MacMillan, 1952, vol. 1, p. 295.

17   *"every devil one of them"*: Dwyer, *The Day Is Ours*, p. 249.

18   *"Grant writes me"*: Stryker, *The Battles of Princeton and Trenton*, p. 70.

18   *Trenton scouts reported*: Leonard Falkner, "A Spy for Washington," *American Heritage* (August 1957), pp. 58–64.

18   *"the rebels could not do so"*: Dwyer, *The Day Is Ours*, p. 219.

19   *"My brave soldiers, advance!"*: William Stryker, *The Battles of Trenton and Princeton*, pp. 165–93.

19   *Several Hessians scrambled*: Narrative of Joseph White, "The Good Soldier White," *American Heritage* (June 1956): 74–79.

19   *The Hessians fled*: Richard Hansen, *The Glorious Hour of Lieutenant Monroe*, New York: Athenaeum, 1976, p. 153.

19   *The battle was over*: Henry Knox to Lucy Knox, December 30, 1776, HK.

19   *Just two Americans*: James Flexner, *George Washington in the American Revolution*, Boston, Mass.: Little Brown Co., pp. 176–79.

19   *"This is a glorious day"*: James Wilkinson, *Memoirs of My Time*, 3 vols., Philadelphia, Pa.: Abraham Small, 1816, vol. 1, p. 131.

20   *"Providence seemed to have smiled"*: Henry Knox to Lucy Knox, December 28, 1776, HK.

20   *"Their behavior upon this occasion"*: GW to John Hancock, December 27, 1776, in GWW VI: 444.

20   *"The officers and the men"*: GW to General John Cadwalader, December 27, 1776, in GWW VI: 446.

21   *Washington had other reasons to attack*: GW to John Hancock, January 5, 1777, in GWW VI: 468.

21   *a second engagement*: GWW VI: 467.

23   *one veteran slowly stepped forward*: Charles Wilson Peale, "Journal of Charles Wilson Peale," *Pennsylvania Magazine of History and Biography* 38: 278.

23   *"We have no money"*: GW to Robert Morris, December 31, 1776, GWW VI: 45–458.

24   *Morris wrote back*: Ellis Oberholtzer, *Robert Morris: Patriot and Financier*, New York: MacMillan, 1903, pp. 1–12.

25   *"over our shoetops"*: Peale, "Journal of Charles Wilson Peale," p. 278.

25   *"We've got the old fox"*: Geoffrey Ward to GW, 310.

25   *"Even the most sanguine"*: Josiah Quincy, *The Journals of Major Samuel Shaw: The First American Consul at Canton*, Boston, Mass.: William Brosby and H. P. Nichols, 1847, pp. 30–33.

26   *meticulous weather diaries*: Donald Jackson, ed., *The Diaries of George Washington* (DGW) 6 vols., Charlottesville: University Press of Virginia, 1976, vol. 2, p. 49. The weather that night was exactly the same as on the night of March 24, 1768.

26   *"Mar. 22—Calm, clear"*: DGW I. Weather diary for March, 1768.

26   *He was certain*: DGW I: 283–88. Washington had tracked snows, rains, and frosts that he followed carefully in short notations in his weather diary, separate from his general diary.

26   *These conditions would not last*: Ludlum, "The Weather of Independence," p. 82.

27   *Shortly after midnight*: Peale, "Journal of Charles Wilson Peale," pp. 279–80.

27   *"The morning was bright"*: James Wilkinson, *Memoirs of My Time*, vol. 1, p. 66.

27   *"The road which the day before"*: Catherine Williams, *Biographies of Revolutionary Heroes, Containing the Life of Brigadier General William Barton and Also of Captain Stephen Olney*, Providence, R.I.: Catherine Williams, 1839, p. 196.

27   *Washington and the rebels had simply vanished*: Henry Knox to Lucy Knox, January 7, 1777, HK; Franklin and Mary Wickwire, *Cornwallis: The American Adventure*, Boston, Mass.: Houghton-Mifflin Company, 1970, pp. 95–100.

28   *"About 150 of my men"*: Stryker, *The Battles of Trenton and Princeton*, pp. 438–42.

28   *The British were too strong*: Varnum Collins, ed., *A Brief Narrative of the Ravages of the British and Hessians at Princeton in 1776–1777*, New York: New York Times/Arno Press, 1968 reprint of the Princeton University Press edition, 1906, pp. 40–50.

29   *"Fire!"*: Thomas Rodney in Stryker, *The Battles of Trenton and Princeton*, p. 440.

29   *The General never moved*: *Pennsylvania Evening Post*, January 6, 1777.

29   *The British troops were unnerved*: Thomas Rodney, *The Diary of Thomas Rodney, 1776–1777*, Wilmington: Historical Society of Delaware, 1888, pp. 34–36.

29   *"It is impossible"*: Shaw, p. 29.

30   *"I thank the God"*: Henry Knox to Lucy Knox, January 7, 1777, HK.

30   *Just after the fighting*: Richard Ketchum, *The Winter Soldiers*, Garden City, N.Y.: Doubleday and Co., pp. 370–73.

30   *would soon arrive in the area*: Dr. Benjamin Rush in a letter published in the *Maryland Journal*, January 7, 1777.

30   *Washington's calculations*: GW to John Hancock, January 5, 1777, in GWW VI: 467–71.

31   *"They were drubbed"*: Jonathan Potts to Owen Biddle, January 5, 177, in Stryker, *The Battles of Trenton and Princeton*, p. 445.

31   *"The enterprises"*: Harold Syrett, ed., *The Papers of Alexander Hamilton*, New York: Columbia University Press, 1961, vol. 5, p. 349.

31   *"The news from General Washington"*: James Smith to Eleanor Smith, December 31, 1776, in CONG V: 714–15.

31   *"A few days ago"*: Dwyer, *The Day Is Ours*, p. 279.

32   *"The late success"*: *Pennsylvania Evening Post*, January 21, 1777.

32   *"The men behaved"*: *Freeman's Journal*, January 21, 1777.

32   *"in utmost confusion"*: *Connecticut Journal*, January 22, 1777.

35   *"a painful shock"*: Stryker, *The Battles of Trenton and Princeton*, p. 401.

35   *The Prince's subordinates*: Rodney Atwood, *The Hessian Mercenaries from Hessen-Kassel in the American Revolution*, Cambridge: Cambridge University Press, 1980, p. 100.

35   *"the most brilliant"*: Flexner, *George Washington in the American Revolution*, p. 189n.

35   *"George Washington's coup"*: Johann Ewald, *Diary of the American War*, New Haven, Conn.: Yale University Press, 1979, p. 50.

35   *"all of our hopes"*: Dwyer, *The Day Is Ours*, p. 279.

35   *"the most consumate ignorance"*: Franklin and Mary Wickwire, *Cornwallis*, p. 98.

35   *"It may be doubted"*: Ernest and Trevor Dupuy, *The Compact History of the Revolution*, New York, 1963, p. 174.

Chapter Two: The Squire of Mount Vernon

37   *"for the wisdom of his counsel"*: H. R. McIlwaine and J. P. Kennedy, eds., *Journals of the House of Burgesses*, 13 vols., Richmond, Va.: Colonial Press, E. Waddy Co., 1905–1915, vol. 13, p. 191.

38   *The delegates were looking*: Douglas Freeman, *George Washington: A Biography*, 6 vols., New York: Charles Scribner's Sons, 1951, vol. 3, pp. 444–45.

39   *"His features strong"*: *History of the George Washington Bicentennial Celebration*, 3 vols., Washington, D.C.: U.S. Government Bicentennial Commission, 1932, vol. 1, pp. 31–35.

39   *"The resources of Britain"*: Flexner, *Washington: The Indispensable Man*, Newtown, Fla. : American Political Biography Press, 2003, p. 60.

39   *"He seems discreet and virtuous"*: Eliphalet Dyer to Joseph Trumbull, June 17, 1775, CONG I: 499.

40   *"He is a complete gentleman"*: Thomas Cushing to James Bowdoin, Sr., June 21, 1775, CONG I: 530.

40   *"There is something charming"*: John Adams to Elbridge Gerry, June 18, 1775, CONG I: 503.

40   *"the generalissimo of American forces"*: *Virginia Gazette,* July 6, 1775, p. 3.

40   *"one of the most important characters"*: John Adams to Abigail Adams, June 17, 1775, CONG I: 497.

42   *By the time he was eighteen*: George Wordham, "A Physical Description of George Washington," *The Daughters of the American Revolution Magazine*, February, 1974, pp. 85–88.

42   *"a commanding countenance"*: Freeman, *George Washington: A Biography*, vol. 3, p. 141.

43   *"He is a very excellent and bold horseman"*: Howard Rice, ed. and trans., Marquis de Chastellux, *Travels in North America*, 2 vols., Chapel Hill: University of North Carolina Press, 1963, vol. 1, p. 111.

46   *Washington became quite ill*: Robert Leckie, *George Washington's War*, New York: HarperCollins, 1992, pp. 138–42.

47   *Martha Custis was different*: Polly Longsworth, "Portrait of Martha Washington," *Journal of the Colonial Williamsburg Foundation* (Summer 1988): 6.

47   *Martha Custis and George Washington*: Anne Hollingsworth Wharton, *Martha Washington*, New York: Charles Scribner's Sons, 1897, pp. 34–35.

47   *Washington was riding*: Willard Randall, *George Washington: A Life*, New York: Henry Holt, 1997, pp. 173–75.

48   *He saw in Martha*: "The Marriage of George and Martha Washington," *The Daughters of the American Revolution Magazine*, February 1977, pp. 109–11.

48   *"prepare in the best manner"*: GW to John Alton, April 5, 1759, W. W. Abbott, ed. *The Papers of George Washington* (PGW), Charlottesville, University of Virginia Press, 1983, PGW VII, Colonial Series: 200.

48   *"I am now, I believe"*: GW to Richard Washington, September 20, 1759, GWW II: 336–37.

49   *bad harvests on the continent*: John Fitzgerald, ed., *Diaries of George Washington, 1748–1799*, 4 vols., Mount Vernon Ladies Association of the Union, Boston, Mass.: Houghton-Mifflin, 1925, vol. 1, p. 303.

49   *twice as much wheat to Europe*: John Selby, *The Revolution in Virginia, 1775–1783*, Williamsburg, Va.: Colonial Williamsburg Foundation, 1988, p. 32.

49   *He raised sheep*: DGW I: 216 (Fitzgerald version).

49   *breeding of buffalo*: GW to James Cleveland, January 10, 1775, GWW III: 260–61.

49   *His holdings were vast*: DGW II: 81 (Fitzgerald version).

49   *Washington did not delegate*: DGW I: 107.

50   *"goes on better"*: GW to Bryan Fairfax, July 4, 1774, GWW III: 227.

50   *"Mrs. Washington was blooded"*: DGW I: 151–52 (Fitzgerald version).

50   *Washington, a good judge of land*: Thomas Fleming, *First in Their Hearts: A Biography of George Washington*, New York: W.W. Norton Company, 1984, pp. 33–36.

51   *Washington was apparently sterile*: GW to Robert Cary and Co., September 20, 1759, GWW II: 498–99.

51   *"I carried little Patsy"*: Martha Washington to Nancy Burwell, Anne Wharton, *Martha Washington: A Portrait*, New York: Charles Scribner's Sons, 1897, p. 56.

52   *everything he could for the girl*: Miriam Bourne, *First Family: George Washington and His Intimate Relations*, New York: Norton, 1982, p. 36.

52   *"my dear little girl is much better"*: Martha Washington to Margaret Green, September 29, 1760, Joseph Fields, ed., *Worthy Partner: The Papers of Martha Washington*, Westport, Conn.: Greenwood Press, 1994, p. 131.

52   *"[She] expired in less than two minutes"*: GW to Burwell Bassett, July 20, 1773, GWW III: 138–39.

53   *"I must confess to you"*: Jonathan Boucher, quoted in Fields, *Worthy Partner*, p. xxii.

53   *cut off Jack's charge accounts*: GW to Cary and Co., July 10, 1773, PGW IX, Colonial Series: 271.

53   *"He lacks that attention"*: GW to Jonathan Boucher, June 5, 1771, GWW III: 42–44.

53   *"lost time"*: GW to Jonathan Boucher, April 20, 1771, PGW VIII, Colonial Series: 448–49.

53   *"has ever bestowed"*: GW to Burwell Bassett, April 20, 1773, PGW IX, Colonial Series: 219.

54   *"affections and regard"*: Jack Custis to GW, February 20, 1774, PGW IX, Colonial Series: 491.

54   *begging for assurances*: Jack Custis to Martha Washington, August 21, 1776, *Worthy Partner*, pp. 170–71; Custis to Martha Washington April 3, 1778, *Worthy Partner*, pp. 178–79.

54   *Throughout those years*: JOHB IX: 66.

54   *"Your modesty is equal to your valor"*: Fleming, *First in Their Hearts*, pp. 35–36.

54   *He became an elder*: Bernard Knollenberg, *George Washington: The Virginia Period, 1732–1775*, Durham, N.C.: Duke University Press, 1967, p. 106.

55   *His civic responsibilities*: Paul Longmore, *The Invention of George Washington*, Los Angeles: University of California Press, 1988, pp. 106–07.

55   *Washington's great vice*: T. H. Breen, "Horses and Gentlemen: The Cultural Significance of Gambling among the Gentry of Virginia," *William and Mary Quarterly* (April 1977): 339–57.

55   *fanatic for the lotteries*: *Virginia Gazette*, April 4, 1768, p. 3.

55   *His diaries showed*: DGW II: 57. As an example, between March 9 and 17, 1772, Washington played cards for money at Campbell's "gaming club" seven out of nine nights.

55   *parlors jammed with card tables*: DGW I: 238.

55   *Washington put up purses*: "Washington in Williamsburg" monograph, February 22, 1956, pp. 23–25, PARK.

55   *Washington loved to see plays*: J. Luther Kibler, "Washington in Williamsburg" monograph, February 10, 1933, Rockefeller Library, Williamsburg, Va.

55   *viewing matinees*: DGW II: 57–62.

56   *Washington recorded the exact time*: DGW I: 299.

56   *was a very fashionable dresser*: "Washington in Williamsburg," p. 26.

56   *"a handsome suit of clothes"*: Note added to letter from GW to Richard Washington, PGW Colonial Series, VII: 81.

56   *"fine clothes make fine men"*: GW to Bushrod Washington, January 15, 1783, Stephen Lucas, ed., *The Quotable George Washington: The Wisdom of an American Patriot*, Madison, Wis.: Madison House Press, 1999, p. 15.

56   *bought silverware with great care*: Washington's diary notes on expensive purchases are frequent, such as one for a large marble chimney piece he personally uncrated in on April 6, 1775. DGW II: 357.

56   *was kept in museum condition*: GW to Lund Washington, August 20, 1775, GWW III: 435.

56   *"No estate in United America"*: C. Hale Sipe, *Mount Vernon and the Washington Family: A Concise Handbook on the Ancestry, Youth, and Family of George Washington, and History of his Home*, 4th ed., Butler, Pa.: Ziegler Printing, 1927, p. 61.

57   *Washington's six brothers and sisters*: Most of Washington's siblings died before 1760, but a few enjoyed lengthy lives. His oldest brother Sam, who borrowed substantial amounts of money from George and rarely paid him back, lived out his years in the western part of Virginia and died in 1781. Older brother Charles also moved to the western part of the state and died on 1790. John Augustine ("Jack"), his closest brother, died in 1787. His sister Betty, with whom he was also close, lived in nearby Fredericksburg on a large plantation, Kenmore, and died in 1797.

57   *"He keeps an excellent table"*: Nicholas Cresswell, *The Journal of Nicholas Cresswell*, New York: Dial Press, 1924, pp. 254–56.

57   *"elegant hospitality"*: Elizabeth Powel to Martha Washington, Fields, *Worthy Partner*, p. 198.

57   *Washington enjoyed helping people*: Fleming, *First in Their Hearts*, pp. 35–36.

58   *"The general seems"*: Cresswell, *The Journal of Nicholas Cresswell*, p. 256.

58   *would soon change everything*: William Rasmussen and Robert Tilton, *George Washington: The Man Behind the Myths*, Charlottesville: University of Press of Virginia, 1999, pp. 92–94.

58   *"great satisfaction"*: JOHB IX: xiii.

58   *ban hogs from running wild*: JOHB IX: 248.

59   *"destroy American freedom"*: David McCants, *Patrick Henry: Orator*, Westport, Conn.: Greenwood Press, 1990, p. 121.

59   *"torrents of eloquence"*: JOHB X: xv–xvii.

59   *His diary records dozens*: His diaries include long calendar lists on which are noted dining and social engagements with the leaders of British and American political factions in Williamsburg.

59   *"Colonel Fairfax and myself"*: GW to Lord Dunmore, May 30, 1772, "Letters of George Washington to Lord Dunmore," *William and Mary Quarterly* (April 1940): 162.

59   *George Washington had come to believe*: J. Franklin Jameson, "The American Revolution: Revolutionary or Non-Revolutionary? I," in Gerry Grob and George Billias, eds., *Interpretations of American Historical Patterns*, vol. 1, New York: Free Press, 1967, pp. 199–200.

59   *By 1775*: William Appleman Williams, *America Confronts A Revolutionary World*, New York: William Morrow Company, 1976, pp. 28–31.

60   *The Crown thought nothing*: Randell, *George Washington*, pp. 260–61.

60   *The colonists also feared*: David Ramsay, "The View From Inside," Jack Greene, ed., *The Ambiguity of the American Revolution*, New York: Harper and Row, 1968, pp. 33–34.

62   *"We had borne much"*: GW to Joseph Reed, February 10, 1776, GWW IV: 321.

62   *"Psychologically, the residents"*: Daniel Boorstin, "American Revolution: Revolutionary or Non-Revolutionary? II," in Grob and Billias, *Interpretations of American Historical Patterns*, pp. 221–28.

62   *They felt compelled*: Adrienne Koch, *Power, Morals and the Founding Fathers: Essays in the Interpretation of the American Enlightenment*, Ithaca, N.Y.: Cornell University Press, 1961, pp. 122–26.

62   *It was an ideal that could not*: Arthur Bryant, *The American Ideal*, Freeport, N.Y.: Books for Libraries Press, 1969, pp. 8–10.

62   *Americans were convinced*: Gordon Wood, *The Creation of the American Republic*, New York: W.W. Norton Company, 1969, pp. 108–14.

63   *purity of their character*: Reinhold Niebuhr and Alan Heimert, *A Nation So Conceived: Reflections on the History of American From Its Early Visions to Its Present Power*, New York: Charles Scribner's Sons, 1963, pp. 126–29.

63   *This view made it possible*: Merrell Jensen, "Historians and the Nature of the American Revolution," in *The Re-Interpretation of Early American History*, Ray Billington, ed., San Marino, Calif.: Huntington Library Association, 1966, pp. 106–107.

63   *Virginians protested the various acts*: JOHB XI: Special section about the Committee of
      Correspondence.
63   *The turning point*: *Virginia Gazette*, October 25, 1765, p. 1.
63   *there was such protest*: *Virginia Gazette*, April 4, 1766. The *Gazette* devoted several pages of
      coverage to the controversy in all of its April issues.
63   *The debates continued*: *Virginia Gazette*, March 21, 1766, p. 3.
64   *"dreadful attack upon their liberties"*: GW to Francis Dandridge, September 20, 1765, GWW
      II: 426.
64   *generated much hatred towards the crown*: *Virginia Gazette*, May 24, 1767, p. 2.
64   *"No man should scruple"*: GW to George Mason, April 28, 1769, PGW VIII, Colonial Series:
      182.
64   *"violated the rights of Americans"*: JOHB XIII: 214.
64   *"hearts filled with anguish"*: JOHB XIII: 216.
64   *Washington and Mason then retaliated*: *Virginia Gazette*, May 25, 1769, p. 1.
64   *so irritated over the issue*: Fleming, *George Washington: The Indispensable Man*, pp. 49–53.
64   *"intolerable acts"*: Leckie, *George Washington's War*, p. 143.
65   *The Intolerable Acts caused an uproar*: *Virginia Gazette*, January 6, 1774. The *Gazette* ran full
      front page stories about the closing of the port, with inside stories and letters, for several
      weeks and discussions in Virginia were dominated by the event.
65   *"an unexampled testimony"*: Quoted in Flexner, *Washington: The Indispensable Man*, p.
      58.
65   *"Shall we"*: Leckie, *George Washington's War*, p. 143.
65   *"conquered country"*: *Virginia Gazette*, August 4, 1774, p. 2.
65   *Both men were also insulted*: Eric Robson, "The American Revolution in its Political and
      Military Aspects," in Edmund Morgan, ed., *The American Revolution: Two Centuries of
      Interpretation*, Englewood Cliffs, N.J.: Prentice-Hall, 1965, pp. 143–46.
65   *"dangerous attempt"*: JOHB XIII: 73–76.
65   *The resolution was published*: *Virginia Gazette*, May 26, 1774.
66   *"Have we not addressed the Lords"*: GW to Bryan Fairfax, July 4, 1774, PGW X, Colonial
      Series: 212.
66   *"I was much pleased"*: Edmund Pendleton to anonymous correspondent, September of 1774,
      David Mays, ed., *The Letters and Papers of Edmund Pendleton, 1774–1803*, 2 vols.,
      Charlottesville: University Press of Virginia, 1967, vol. 1, p. 98.
67   *In Philadelphia in the fall*: Fleming, *First in Their Hearts*, p. 52.
69   *"I this day declare"*: Leckie, *George Washington's War*, p. 125.
69   *"I have launched"*: GW to the captains of several independent companies in Virginia, CONG
      I: 527.
69   *"I am now embarked"*: GW to Burwell Bassett, CONG I: 515.
69   *"a trust too great"*: GW to Martha Washington, June 18, June 23, 1775, CONG I: 509–11;
      GWW III: 301.
69   *"I shall relay therefore"*: GW to Martha Washington, CONG I: 509–11.
70   *"This Congress doth"*: Flexner, *Washington: The Indispensable Man*, p. 61.

Chapter Three: The Army Will Die
71   *"Many of our poor soldiers"*: GW to John Hancock, January 5, 1777, in GWW VI:
      467–72.
72   *"Greene was a thirty-four-year-old Quaker"*: Elswyth Thane, *The Fighting Quaker: Nathaniel
      Greene*, New York: Hawthorn, 1972, pp. 3–16.
73   *Lord Stirling had been*: Alan Valentine, *Lord Stirling*, New York: Oxford University Press,
      1969, pp. 94–95.
73   *Morristown would serve*: Flexner, *Washington: The Indispensable Man*, p. 181.
73   *Morristown was also about midway*: Flexner, *Washington: The Indispensable Man*, p. 545.
74   *"A storm will burst soon"*: GW to Robert Morris, GWW VII: 32.
74   *"We are now in one of the most critical periods"*: GW to Joseph Reed, February 23, 1777,
      GWW VII: 190–92.

74   *The general was not just looking*: Josiah Bartlett to William Whipple, March 15, 1777, in Frank Meyers, ed., *The Papers of Josiah Bartlett*, Hanover, N.H.: University Press of New England, 1979, pp. 151–53.

75   *Washington felt comfortable*: Larry Gerlach, *New Jersey in the Coming of the American Revolution*, Trenton: New Jersey Historical Commission, 1970, pp. 8–20.

75   *"the asylum for the sons"*: David Mitros, ed., *Jacob Green: Observations on the Reconciliation of Great Britain and the Colonies*, Mendham: Morris County Heritage Association, 1975, p. 24.

75   *The head of the regular militia*: Andrew Sherman, *History of Morristown, New Jersey: The Story of Its First Century*, Morristown, N.J.: Howard Publishing Co., 1905, p. 145.

75   *It was Winds' militia*: Richard Tomlinson Jr., *A Community Under Stress: Morristown, 1740–1800*, PhD diss., Princeton University, 1972, pp. 86–88.

76   *"You cannot travel"*: Elswyth Thane, *Washington's Lady*, New York: Dodd, Mead and Co., 1960, p. 159.

76   *No "luxuriant" small village*: Bruce Stewart, *Morristown: A Crucible of the American Revolution*, Trenton: New Jersey Historical Commission, 1975, pp. 1–10.

76   *Most of the buildings in Morristown*: Sherman, pp. 212–13.

77   *"floorboards were rather cold"*: Peale, "The Journal of Charles Wilson Peale," p. 285.

77   *"are very fond of the soldiers"*: James McMichael, "The Diary of James McMichael," *Pennsylvania Magazine of History and Biography* 16 (1892): 129.

77   *troops began to convert local buildings*: Alfred Hoyt Bill, *New Jersey and the Revolutionary War*, New Brunswick, N.J.: Rutgers University Press, 1964, pp. 48–52.

78   *"He is the honestest"*: Tilghman, p. 40.

78   *"I cannot discuss politics"*: Tench Tilghman to his father, April 21, 1777, Tench Tilghman, *The Memoir of Tench Tilghman*, Albany, N.Y.: S. Munsell, 1876, appendix.

79   *They were never to relate*: L. G. Shreve, *Tench Tilghman: The Life and Times of Washington's Aide-de-Camp*, Centreville, Md.: Tidewater Publications, 1982, pp. 116–30.

79   *"Great number of them"*: GW to John Hancock, September 2, 1776, GWW VI: 4–5.

79   *He fired off an angry letter*: GW to Nicolas Cooke, January 20, 1777, GWW VII: 42–44.

79   *"Your troops are in comfortable barracks"*: GW to William Duer, January 14, 1777, in GWW 7: 13–14.

79   *"There certainly must be roguery"*: GW to General William Heath, April 18, 1777, GWW VII: 429–30.

79   *"Surely you meant this"*: GW to General Samuel Weedon, March 17, 1777, Worthington Ford, ed., *The Correspondence and Journals of Samuel Blachley Webb*, 3 vols., New York Times/Arno Press, 1969, vol. 2, p. 197.

80   *"cannot be carried into execution"*: GW Washington to Robert Morris, March 2, 1777, GWW VII: pp. 224–25.

80   *He could complain about petty things*: GW to Caleb Gibbs, May 6, 1777, PARK.

80   *After the war*: Robert Norton Smith, *Patriarch: George Washington and the New American Nation*, Boston, Mass.: Houghton-Mifflin Company, 1993, p. 123.

80   *Security in Morristown was tight*: John Sullivan to GW, February 13, 1777, PGW VIII: 330.

81   *Washington had also received*: Anonymous letter to GW, February 7, 1777, PGW VIII: 266–67.

81   *twenty-six soldiers guarded the tavern*: *History of Morris County, New Jersey, with Illustrations and Biographical Sketches of Prominent Citizens and Pioneers*, New York: W.W. Munsell, 1882, p. 19.

82   *"Two waistcoats, and two pair of breeches"*: GW to Caleb Gibbs, May, 1777, PARK.

83   *"His Excellency, George Washington"*: James Flexner, *Young Hamilton*, Boston, Mass.: Little, Brown Co., 1978, p. 138.

83   *"I have been much gratified"*: James Thacher, *Military Journal of the American Revolution, from the commencement to the disbanding of the army, Comprising a detailed account of the Principal events and battles of the revolution with their exact dates and a biographical sketch of the most Prominent Generals*, Hartford: Hurlbut, William and Co., 1862, p. 30.

83   *"Never shall I forget the impression"*: Barry Schwartz, *George Washington: The Making of an American Symbol*, New York: MacMillan, 1987, pp. 18–19.

84   *The final flourish was his personal guard*: GW to Colonel Caleb Gibbs, April 22, 1777, in GWW VII: 452–52; to Colonel Alexander Spotswood, April 30, 1777, GWW VII: 494–95.

85   *colonial newspapers he had delivered*: It took days for newspapers to learn of battles, so most of those brought to Washington were ten to fourteen days old. Local papers from Philadelphia and New York reached him sooner, however.

85   *"Show yourselves worthy"*: *Philadelphia Freeman's Journal*, April 15, 1777.

85   *"had he lived in the days of idolatry"*: *Pennsylvania Journal*, February 19, 1777.

85   *Many saw him as an eighteenth century Moses*: Robert Hay, George Washington: American Moses, *American Quarterly* (Winter 1969): 780–91.

86   *"our brave general...fearless of any danger"*: Shaw Journal, p. 29.

86   *Washington's position in America had transcended*: Longmore, *The Invention of George Washington*, pp. 200–201.

87   *"heaven, no doubt for the noblest purposes"*: *The History of the George Washington Bicentennial Celebration*, p. 31–35.

87   *"military genius"*: Carl Von Clausewitz, *On War*, Michael Howard and Peter Paret, eds., Princeton, N.J.: Princeton University Press edition, 1976.

88   *these same qualities had to be*: Royster, *A Revolutionary People at War: The Continental Army and American Character, 1775–1783*, New York : Norton, 1981, p. 256.

88   *The Congressmen, like the soldiers*: Longmore, *The Invention of George Washington*, pp. 66–67, 179.

88   *"To merit the approbation"*: Lucas, *Quotable George Washington*, p. 84.

89   *"Washington was born for"*: David Richard Palmer, *The Way of the Fox: American Strategy in the War for America, 1775–1783*, Westport, Conn.: Greenwood Press, p. 38.

90   *The disease claimed the lives*: Horace Ogden, *CDC and the Smallpox Crusade*, Washington, D.C.: U.S. Department of Health, Center for Disease Control, 1972, pp. 3–4.

90   *It had hit America, too*: John Duffy, *Epidemics in Colonial America*, Baton Rouge: Louisiana State University Press, 1953, pp. 69–109.

90   *Smallpox struck quickly*: Herve Bazin, *The Eradication of Smallpox*, New York: Academic Press, 1984, p. 6.

90   *The disease might have been carried*: DGW I: 138–39.

91   *Washington's fear of smallpox*: F. Fenner, D. A. Henderson, I. Arita, Z. Jelek, and I. D. Ladnyi, *Smallpox and Its Eradication*, Geneva, Switzerland: World Health Organization, 1988, pp. 238–40.

91   *When he was summoned to Philadelphia*: Flexner, *George Washington in the American Revolution*, p. 81.

91   *The General was in charge*: GW to Horatio Gates, January 28, 1777, GWW VII: 72–73.

91   *"The smallpox is so thick"*: John Adams to Abigail Adams, February 20, 1777, in CONG VI: 326–27.

91   *had stopped dispatching couriers*: John Hancock to the Executive Committee, January 29, 1777, CONG VI: 159.

91   *"We beg leave to remind"*: Medical Committee to GW, February 13, 1777, CONG VI: 271.

92   *Doctors studied ways*: Smallpox in Colonial America, New York: New York Times/Arno Press, (reprints of colonial pamphlets), 1977, section four.

92   *American doctors*: Larry Gerlach, "Smallpox Inoculations in Colonial New Jersey," in *the Journal of the Rutgers University Library*, December, 1967, pp. 21–28.

92   *American doctors, like their European counterparts*: David Cowen, *Medicine and Health in New Jersey*, Princeton, N.J.: Van Nostrand Books, 1961, pp. 2–3.

92   *Washington did not have time*: Peter Razwell, *The Conquest of Smallpox*, Sussex, England: Caliban Books, 1977, pp. 15–17.

92   *"I know it is more destructive"*: GW to Patrick Henry, April 13, 1777, GWW VII: 408–409.

93   *"Finding the smallpox"*: GW to Dr. William Shippen, January 6, 1777, GWW VI: 473.

93   *All of the three thousand troops*: Dr. Carl Binger, *Revolutionary Doctor: Benjamin Rush, 1746–1813*, New York: W.W. Norton Co., 1966, p. 122.

93   *Soldiers were forbidden*: GW to Dr. William Shippen, January 28, 1777, in GWW VII: 75–76; letter from Washington to the New York Convention, February 10, 1777, in PGW, Series 3C, microfilm.

93   *It was a decision Washington made*: Medical Committee to GW, February 13, 1777, in CONG: VI: 271–72.

93   *There was some dissent*: Donald White, *A Village at War: Chatham, New Jersey, and the American Revolution*, London: Associated University Presses, 1979, p. 92.

94   *"I shudder at the consequences"*: GW to Robert Harrison, January 20, 1777, GWW VII: 37–38.

94   *It was a ground-breaking*: Robert Morris and George Clymer to John Hancock, February 22, 1777, in CONG: VI: 342–43.

94   *It was one of Washington's first opportunities*: Leonard Lundin, *Cockpit of the Revolution: The War for Independence in New Jersey*, Princeton: Princeton University Press, 1940, p. 233.

95   *Fear of the dreaded smallpox*: *Harper's Monthly*, February, 1859, p. 294.

95   *Use every means possible*: GW to Dr. John Cochran, January 20, 1777, GWW VII: 44–45.

95   *"Vigorous methods must be adopted"*: GW to Robert Harrison, January 20, 1777, GWW VII: 38.

96   *"many, many sick"*: Joseph Tuttle, *Reverend Jacob Green of Hanover, N.J. as an Author, Statesman, and Patriot*, Newark, N.J.: Advertiser Printing, 1894, p. 33.

96   *Green's small church*: Peter Livingston to Gerard Barcke, March 3, 1777, in Proceedings of the New Jersey Historical Society (NJHS) 13: 3 (1928), p. 381.

96   *There were so many patients:* Larry Wilgers, *Ashbel Green: Advocate of Practical Christianity*, PhD diss., Vanderbilt University, 1973, p. 13.

96   *"be ugly for the rest of her life"*: Joseph Tuttle, *Annals of Morris County*, 1876, pp. 51–54.

96   *"You will want to know"*: Lucy Knox to Henry Knox, April 13, 1777, in HK.

96   *"I had many pocks on my face"*: "The Revolutionary War in Morristown," NJHS, 51: 3, p. 253.

97   *The experimental procedure*: R. Torres-Reyes, "A Study of Medical Services in the 1779–1780 Encampment," paper, National Park Service, Washington Association, 1971, p. 52.

97   *The same success was reported*: Richard Henry Lee to Patrick Henry, April 22, 1777, in CONG VI: 633.

97   *humor in the recuperation of the troops*: Dr. Isaac Knight note, April 4, 1777, PARK.

97   *Recuperating privates with a sweet tooth*: Dr. John Cochran to Edward Duff, April 1, 1777, PARK.

97   *many Morristown and Morris County area residents*: Joseph Tuttle, *Centennial Collection of Morris County*, Morristown, 1877, p. 104.

97   *That winter also saw*: Vogt monograph, p. 22.

97   *local heroism and tragedy*: Frank Esposito, *The Madison Heritage Trail*, Madison, Wis.: Bicentennial Commission, 1985, p. 38.

98   *He came down with smallpox*: White, *A Village at War: Chatham, New Jersey, and the American Revolution*, pp. 98–110.

98   *Abiel Tompkins, volunteered as a nurse*: Tuttle, *Centennial Collection of Morris County*, p. 106.

98   *His orders for the treatment*: GW to John Washington, June 1, 1777, PGW, Revised Series VIII: 586–87.

99   *"Inoculation at Philadelphia"*: GW to Joseph Trumbull, March 3, 1777, in PGW Series 3C, microfilm.

99   *The British apparently did not learn*: Henry Thursfield, "Smallpox in the American War of Independence," *Annals of Medical History*, 3rd series, vol. 2, pp. 312–16.

Chapter Four: The Patriot King

102 *"When the civil and military powers"*: GW to New York Committee of Safety, April 20, 1776, GWW IV: 497.

102 *He knew many of the governors*: Margaret Macmillan, *The War Governors in the American Revolution*, New York: Columbia University Press, 1943, pp. 149–51.

103 *He attempted to include*: Macmillan, *The War Governors in the American Revolution*, pp. 152–55.

103 *During their visits or in letters*: Flexner, *Young Hamilton*, p. 153.

103 *Washington assured them*: GW to Joseph Trumbull, January 24, 1777, in PGW, Series 3C, microfilm; to Nicholas Cooke, April 21, 1777, GWW VII: 451.

103 *He promised to investigate*: GW to the Massachusetts Bay legislature, February 28, 1777, in PGW, Series 3C, microfilm.

103 *they have given the highest*: GW to the Massachusetts Bay legislature, February 2, 1777, in PGW, Series 3C, microfilm.

103 *The general changed*: GW to Joseph Trumbull of Connecticut, December 14, 1776, in PGW, Series 3C, microfilm.

103 *He sometimes replaced*: GW to William Livingston, February 1, 1777, in PGW, Series 3C, microfilm.

104 *"my reasons for making"*: MacMillan, *War Governors of the American Revolution*, p. 146.

104 *"reflect the highest honor"*: GW to Caesar Rodney, February 18, 1777, GWW VII: 160.

104 *"hidden hand" politics*: Fred Greenstein, *The Hidden Hand Presidency: Eisenhower as Leader*, New York: Basic Books, 1982, pp. 58–84.

104 *He kept a watchful eye*: MacMillan, *War Governors of the American Revolution*, pp. 154–55.

104 *"which I can see you performed"*: GW to Joseph Trumbull, February 6, 1777, in PGW, Series 3C, microfilm.

105 *"I flatter myself"*: GW to the Pennsylvania Council of Safety, March 29, 1777, to Massachusetts Legislature, February 4, 1777, in PGW, Series 3C, microfilm.

105 *He also told them*: GW William Livingston, February 15, 1777, in PGW, Series 3C, microfilm.

105 *"cheerful concurrence with me"*: Macmillan, *War Governors*, p. 163.

105 *"I took the liberty"*: GW to the Massachusetts Bay Assembly, April 25, 1777, PGW, Series 3C, microfilm.

106 *"Let us do our part"*: Livingston speech to state assembly on February 26, 1777, *Pennsylvania Packet*, March 4, 1777.

106 *Livingston had published*: Livingston wrote as "an American whig" for several Philadelphia newspapers; *Pennsylvania Packet*, March 4, 1777.

106 *Both were devoted family men*: GW to William Livingston, February 15, 1777, in PGW, Series 3C, microfilm.

107 *Alexander Hamilton later said*: Carl Prince, *William Livingston, New Jersey's First Governor*, Trenton: New Jersey Historical Commission, 1975, p. 22.

107 *Apprehensive about his welfare*: General Orders, January 15, 1777, GWW VII: 16–17.

107 *"As for the personal friendship"*: Lundin, *Cockpit of the Revolution*, p. 275n.

109 *The Awakening also changed*: Rhyss Isaac, *The Transformation of Virginia*, 1740–1790, New York: W.W. Norton Co., 1982, pp. 192–93.

109 *The ministers of the Awakening preached*: Alan Heimnert and Perry Miller, *The Great Awakening*, New York: Bobbs-Merrill Co., 1967, pp. xvii–xxviii.

109 *"the necessaries of life"*: GW to Francis Dandridge, September 20, 1765, GWW II: 425.

109 *He wrote George Mason*: Isaac, *The Transformation of Virginia*, p. 251.

109 *The Great Awakening energized*: William McLaughlin, "The Role of Religion in the Revolution: Liberty of Conscience and Cultural Cohesion in the New Nation," in Stephen Kurtz and James Hutson, eds., *Essays on the American Revolution*, Williamsburg, Va.: Institute of Early American History and Culture, 1973, pp. 198–200.

110 *The revolution was an end to one era*: Stephen Marini, *Radical Sects of Revolutionary New England*, Cambridge, Mass.: Harvard University Press, 1982, pp. 172–73.

110   *"eternal happiness"*: Edward Cody, *The Religious Issue in Revolutionary New Jersey*, Trenton: New Jersey Historical Commission, 1975, p. 21.

110   *"When God, in his providence"*: Stearns quoted in Philip Davidson, *Propaganda and the American Revolution, 1763—1783*, Chapel Hill: University of North Carolina Press, 1941, p. 206.

110   *"We may for a considerable time"*: Simeon Vanartsdalen to John Bogart, March 23, 1777, Bogart Letters, Rutgers University.

110   *"The liberty enjoyed by the people"*: Lucas, *Quotable George Washington*, p. 80–81.

111   *"the preachers look upon the war"*: Manuscripts of the Earl of Dartmouth, 3 vols., Boston, Mass.: Gregg Press, 1972, vol. 2, p. 427.

111   *"the Presbyterians are the chief"*: Barbara Wingo, *Politics, Society, and Religion: The Presbyterian Clergy in Pennsylvania, New Jersey, and New York and the Formation of the New Nation, 1775–1808*, PhD diss., Tulane University, 1976, p. 241.

111   *The commander*: Paul Boller Jr., *George Washington and Religion*, Dallas, Tex.: Southern Methodist University Press, 1963, p. 237.

111   *He became friendly*: *History of Morris County*, pp. 116–117.

111   *He ordered all of the soldiers*: General Orders, April 19, 1777, GWW VII: 442–43.

111   *He hired as many chaplains*: GW to General William Heath, GWW VII: pp. 429–30.

111   *He also made sure*: Wingo, *Politics, Society, and Religion*, p. 271.

111   *Several chaplains in winter camp*: Allen Bowman, *The Morale of the American Revolutionary Army*, Port Washington, N.Y.: Kennikat Press, 1943, pp. 96–97.

112   *Washington also referred*: Boller, *George Washington and Religion*, pp. 95–97.

112   *"with wonder and affection"*: David Mitros, *Jacob Green and the Slavery Debate*, Morristown: Morris County Heritage Commission, 1975, pp. 8–9; Larry Gerlach, ed., *Jacob Green: Observations on the Reconciliation of Great Britain and the Colonies*, pp. 15–31.

112   *Johnnes' Morristown Presbyterian Church*: History of Morristown, p. 135.

112   *They offered material*: Tomlinson, *A Community Under Stress, 1749–1800*, p. 26.

113   *The press particularly enjoyed*: William Stryker, ed., *Archives of the State of New Jersey Newspaper Extracts*, Second Series, vol. 2, Trenton: John Murphy Co., 1901.

114   *highly partisan New Jersey Gazette*: John Pancake, *The Year of the Hangman*, Birmingham, Ala.: University of Alabama Press, 1977, p. 95.

114   *Washington's officer councils*: Niccolo Machiavelli, trans. Allan Gilbert, *Chief Works and Others*, 3 vols., Chapel Hill: University of North Carolina Press, 1965, vol. 1, p. 223.

114   *the idea of the "Patriot King"*: Longmore, *The Invention of George Washington*, pp. 200–201.

114   *Washington's great fear*: Horatio Gates Papers, Box 6, NYHS.

114   *"I believe the enemy"*: GW to John Hancock, March 14, 1777, GWW VII: 287.

115   *in one skirmish*: *Pennsylvania Evening Post*, March 3, 1777.

115   *"they serve to harass"*: Freeman, *George Washington*, vol. 5, p. 383.

115   *"Scarce a day passed"*: Anonymous letter to the *Pennsylvania Gazette*, April 9, 1777.

115   *The success of the foragers*: Troyer Steele Anderson, *The Command of the Howe Brothers During the American Revolution*, New York: Octagon Books, 1972, p. 256.

115   *Washington wanted as many skirmishes*: *Philadelphia Evening Post*, March 13, 1777; *Pennsylvania Journal*, March 5, 1777.

115   *The foragers seemed to be everywhere*: Howe to Lord Germain, January 20, 1777, K. G. Davis, ed., *Documents of the American Revolution, 1770–1783* (GB), Colonial Office Series, vol. 14, Dublin: Irish University Press, 1976.

116   *Washington told townspeople*: Joseph Jones, *The Life of Ashbel Green*, Robert Carter and Brothers, 1849, pp. 100–101.

116   *He also issued strict orders*: *Pennsylvania Packet*, February 11, 1777.

116   *By the winter of 1777*: Palmer, *The Way of the Fox*, p. 42.

117   *If they adopted that strategy*: Palmer, *The Way of the Fox*, p. 138.

117   *This was, in fact*: Gerald Saxon Brown, *The American Secretary: The Colonial Policy of Lord George Germain, 1775–1778*, Ann Arbor: University of Michigan Press, 1963, pp. 81–117.

117   *The Americans*: Brown, *The American Secretary*, pp. 84–85.

117 *"We should on all occasions"*: GW to John Hancock, September 8, 1776, GWW VI: 28.

117 *He would fight*: Palmer, *The Way of the Fox*, pp. 136–40.

117 *Although he complained endlessly*: Larry Addington, *The Patterns of War Since the Nineteenth Century*, Bloomington: University of Indiana Press, 1984, pp. 14–16.

117 *He now knew where*: Colin Bonwick, *The American Revolution*, London: MacMillan Company, 1991, p. 113.

117 *"It is really a strange thing"*: Lucas, *Quotable George Washington*, p. 100.

119 *Washington's recruitment drive*: Theodore Thayer, *Colonial and Revolutionary Morris County*, Morristown, N.J.: Morris County Heritage Commission, 1975, pp. 167–69.

119 *It was estimated*: Bonwick, *The American Revolution*, p. 113–15.

119 *Most of these men and women*: Leslie Upton, ed., *Revolutionary Versus Loyalist*, Waltham, Mass.: Blaisdell Publishing, 1968, p. 75.

119 *They agreed with Joseph Galloway*: William Nelson, *The American Tory*, Boston, Mass.: Beacon Press, 1961, pp. 66–67.

119 *Several thousand Loyalists*: Lorenzo Sabine, *A Historical Essay on the Loyalists of the American Revolution*, Springfield, Mass: Walden Press, 1957, pp. 14–15.

119 *"the inhabitants are afraid"*: Israel Shreve to GW, March 29, 1777, in William Thompson, *Israel Shreve: Revolutionary War Officer*, Ruston, La.: McGinty Trust Fund Publications, 1979, pp. 27–28.

119 *There were small loyalist armies*: Nelson, *The American Tory*, pp. 110–11.

119 *whose troops had been promised*: Dennis Ryan, *New Jersey's Loyalists*, Trenton, N.J.: New Jersey Historical Society, 1975, pp. 12–13.

119 *"undesirables of the lowest order"*: Quoted in David Mitros, "Shepard Kollock and the New Jersey Journal," *The County Circular*, Winter 2001, p. 7.

120 *apparently on a personal front*: Royster, *Revolutionary People*, p. 130.

120 *Some were driven*: Lewis Einstein, *Divided Loyalties: American in England During the War of Independence*, Freeport, N.Y.: Books for Libraries Press, 1933, p. 189–94.

120 *"They have been lost"*: Proclamation, January 25, 1777, GWW VII: 61–62.

120 *There was another reason*: Paul Smith, *Loyalists and Redcoats*, Williamsburg, Va.: Institute of Early American History and Culture, 1964, pp. 42–44.

120 *"The more united the inhabitants"*: GW to John Hancock, February 5, 1777, GWW VII: 102–106.

121 *"the destruction of the opposition"*: GW to an unknown Congressional delegate, February 14, 1777, GWW VII: 144.

121 *"They have warred upon"*: William Livingston's speech to the New Jersey Legislature, Hezekiah Niles, *Principles and Act of the Revolution in America*, New York: A.S. Barnes, 1876, p. 91.

121 *"Washington remembered that Livingston"*: William Livingston to Jonathan Deare, July 9, 1776, in LIV I: 87–88.

121 *As soon as he became Governor*: Carl Prince, *William Livingston: New Jersey's First Governor*, pp. 8–10.

121 *"He [Washington] hath assumed"*: Abraham Clark to John Hart, February 8, 1777, CONG VI: 240–41.

121 *violated the civil rights*: Abraham Clark to Elias Dayton, March 7, 1777, CONG: VI: 413–14.

122 *"An execution or two"*: Alexander Hamilton to the New York Committee of Correspondence, April 21, 1777, HAM I: 237–38.

122 *"It is the ardent wish"*: Alexander Hamilton to William Livingston, April 29, 1777, HAM I: 242–44.

122 *"No form of an oath"*: GW to Samuel Parsons, February 8, 1777, GWW VII: 119.

123 *"It is not in my power"*: GW to Thomas Mifflin, February 14, 1777, GWW VII: 151.

123 *"pests to society"*: William Whipple to Joseph Whipple, February 19, 1777, CONG VI: 326.

123 *"most dangerous"*: Roger Sherman to Jonathan Trumbull, April 9, 1777, CONG VI: 561.

123 *"banish all the wretches"*: William Whipple to John Langdon, January 15, 1777, CONG VI: 111.

123   *"cowardly, selfish"*: Royster, *Revolutionary People*, p. 106.

123   *Some states and counties*: Pancake, *The Year of the Hangman*, p. 110.

123   *New York created*: John Pancake, *1777: The Year of the Hangman*, pp. 140–41.

123   *The New Jersey Committee of Safety*: Mark Mattia, *New Jersey and the Loyalists During the First British Invasion and Occupation of the State in 1776–1777*, Rutgers University Master's thesis, 1975, pp. 49–54.

123   *The Council heard*: William Livingston to John Witherspoon, May 7, 1777, in LIV I: 322–24.

123   *One group of suspected Loyalists*: Thomas Wharton Jr., to William Livingston, March 26, 1777, in LIV I: 285–86.

123   *Washington was a key figure*: Sherman, p. 223.

123   *Council did not have enough evidence*: *Minutes from the New Jersey Council of Safety*, August 21, 1777, pp. 14–15, PARK.

123   *John Duyckman was held*: *Minutes from the New Jersey Council*, pp. 22–23.

123   *Many were kept*: *Minutes from the New Jersey Council*, p. 15.

124   *John Johnson*: Minutes of May 3, 1778, *Minutes of the Committee and of the First Commission for Detecting and Defeating Conspiracies in the State of New York*, 3 vols., Albany: State of New York, 1909, vol. 3, p. 45.

124   *One of most zealous boards*: *Minutes of the Committee*, 5/15/78.

124   *That commission imprisoned*: *Minutes of the Committee*, 5/27/78.

124   *The Dutchess County board*: *Minutes of the Committee*, 10/1/78.

125   *he also ignored property*: GW to William Livingston, April 1, 1777, LIV I: 289–91.

125   *The attacks on the Loyalists*: Joseph Hedden Jr., to William Livingston, June 21, 1777, and an Order of the Council of Safety, signed by Livingston, LIV I: 358–59.

125   *The crusade even reached*: Sherman, p. 231–32.

125   *During the campaign*: Alfred Jones, *The Loyalists of New Jersey*, Newark: New Jersey Historical Society, 1927, p. 101.

126   *"I will not give a drop of milk"*: H.O.H. Vernon-Jackson, "A Loyalist's Wife: Letters of Mrs. Philip Van Cortlandt," in *History Today*, August, 1964, pp. 574–80.

126   *The New Jersey Council on Safety*: MacMillan, p. 87.

127   *The New Jersey Council*: Thayer, *Colonial and Revolutionary Morris County*, p. 190.

127   *The governor*: Ruth Keesey, "New Jersey Legislation Concerning Loyalists," NJHS: 79, April, 1961, pp. 74–94.

127   *Brother has been fighting*: Henry Laurens to Henry Laurens Jr., March 24, 1777, David Chestnut, ed., *The Papers of Henry Laurens* (LAURENS), 15 vols., Columbia: University of South Carolina Press, 1988, vol. 11, p. 317.

127   *By late April*: Alexander Hamilton to William Livingston, April 21, 1777, PGW, reel 23.

127   *"Private pique and resentment"*: Alexander Hamilton to William Livingston, April 29, 1777, in HAM I: 242–44.

128   *"It has been represented to me"*: GW to the Sussex County Magistrates, April 15, 1777, PGW, reel 23. Despite his orders and pleas, local committees in some states continued to pursue loyalists through the spring of 1778.

129   *The government had flooded*: *Pennsylvania Gazette*, March 16, 1777.

129   *Shaken by the rising cost*: *Journals of the Continental Congress*, Washington, D.C.: U.S. Government Printing Office, 1907, vol. 1, pp. 27–28, JCC.

129   *The New England states met*: Jackson Turner Main, *The Sovereign States, 1775–1783*, New York: Franklin Watts, 1973, pp. 235–40.

129   "The people paid little attention": Bonwick, *The American Revolution*, pp. 113–20.

129   *"the whole power"*: From Benjamin Rush's notes of the price control debates, CONG VI: 274–77.

129   *Washington called the British counterfeiters "villains"*: GW to John Hancock, April 18, 177, GWW VII: 434–36.

129   *"a diabolical scheme"*: Josiah Bartlett to William Whipple, April 21, 1777, Bartlett, pp. 157–58.

129   *Prices soared*: Theodore Tappert and John Doberstein, trans., *The Journals of Henry Melchior Muhlenberg*, 3 vols., Camden, Pa.: Muhlenberg Press, 1942, vol.1, 166–67.

130   *sugar costs were up*: William McLoughlin, ed., *The Diary of Isaac Backus*, Providence, R.I.: Brown University, 1979, vol. 2, p. 991.

130   *"Everything here bears a high price"*: Oliver Wolcott to Laura Wolcott, March 11, 1777, CONG VI: 435.

130   *would set two prices:* Henry DuFouer to James Abeel, March 27, 1777, in James Abeel Papers (ABEEL), National Historic Park, Morristown.

130   *Very few farmers*: Edward Duff to James Abeel, March 26, 177, in ABEEL.

130   *Civilians argued*: Robert Hoops to James Abeel, May 10, 1777, in ABEEL.

130   *If asked to lease wagons*: Edward Dunlop to James Abeel, May 6, 177, in ABEEL.

130   *"I will blow out your brains"*: Edward Duff to James Abeel, March 26, 1777, in ABEEL.

130   *By the end of the winter*: Joseph Thornburgh to James Abeel, July 5, 1777, ABEEL.

130   *Some farmers would not*: Azariah Dunham to Jonathan Stiles, January 10, 1777, PARK.

130   *The refusal even extended*: Jonathan Horton to Henry Knox, January 13, 1777, in HK.

130   *"It will be an example"*: William Whipple to Jonathan Trumbull, February 12, 1777, CONG VI: 265.

130   *"to remedy the evils"*: John Hancock to the States, February 20, 1777, CONG VI: 332.

131   *"The cry of want"*: Baker, *Itinerary of George Washington*, p. 69.

131   *"No army was ever worse"*: GW to Eldridge Gerry, July 19, 1777, in GWW VIII: 448.

131   *"The treasury has been"*: GW to Hancock, January 22, 1777, GWW VII: 51.

131   *he complained in a letter*: GW to John Augustine Washington, February 24, 1777, GWW VII: 197–98.

131   *all dead within the last month*: Theodore Thayer, *Nathaniel Greene: Strategist of the American Revolution*, New York: Twayne, 1960, pp. 113–16.

131   *"the bright side of our affairs"*: Robert Morris to GW, February 27, 1777, PGW VIII: 456–58.

131   *"I give into no kind"*: Broadus Mitchell, *Alexander Hamilton: Youth to Maturity*, New York: MacMillan Co., 1957, vol. 1, p. 110.

131   *"The weight of the whole war"*: Tilghman, p. 147.

132   *The endless work*: Lundin, *Cockpit of the Revolution*, p. 245.

132   *aides had been dramatically reduced*: Tench Tilghman to his father, February 22, 1777, Tilghman, Memoirs, appendix.

132   *Yet another*: Freeman, *George Washington*, vol. 4, p. 391.

132   *George Johnston*: Shreve, *Tench Tilghman*, p. 220–21.

132   *Washington could not replace*: Thayer, *Nathaniel Greene*, p. 117.

132   *"an extraordinary storm"*: Tappert and Doberstein, *Journals of Henry Melchior Muhlenberg*, vol. 1, pp. 3, 16.

133   *Snow fell for twenty-four hours*: Phineas Pemberton, Ms. notes for Metropolitan Observatory, Philadelphia, February, 1777.

133   *streets were impassable*: Hugh Gaine, *The Journal of Hugh Gaine*, New York; Dodd, Mead & Co., 1902, p. 19.

133   *over fifteen inches fell*: David Ludlum, *Early American Winters, 1604–1820*, Boston, Mass.: American Meteorological Society, 1966, p. 100.

133   *Washington surely led the storm clean up*: Flexner, *George Washington in the American Revolution*, p. 202.

133   *Dr. Cochran rushed to his side*: Morris Saffron, *Surgeon General to Washington: Dr. John Cochran, 1730–1817*, New York: Columbia University Press, 1977, pp. 33–38.

134   *Hamilton had arrived in Morristown*: Sherman, *A History of Morris County*, p. 118.

134   *"His Excellency General Washington"*: Nathaniel Greene to William Livingston, March 8, 1777, 6 vols., in Richard Showman, ed., *The Papers of Nathaniel Greene*, Chapel Hill: University of North Carolina Press, 1989, vol. 2, p. 36.

134   *"very much indisposed"*: Alexander Hamilton to Alexander McDougall, March 10, 177, HAM I: 201–202.

134   *"The only answer"*: Alexander Hamilton to Alexander McDougall, March 10, 177, HAM I: 201–202.

134   *"perfectly recovered"*: *The Continental Journal*, March 27, 1777.

134   *His hometown paper*: *Virginia Gazette*, April 4, 1777, p. 3.

135   *Martha Washington had left*: Elswyth Thane, *Washington's Lady*, pp. 150–52.

135   *"universal joy"*: Baker, p. 71.

Chapter Five: Rebuilding the Army

138   *Young Hamilton had been easily assimilated*: Flexner, *Young Hamilton*, pp. 134–38.

138   *"There are few men"*: Washington quoted in Flexner, *George Washington in the American Revolution*, p. 412.

140   *The two were constantly together*: Mitchell, pp. 105–12.

140   *The Commander often rode*: Sherman, *A History of Morris County*, p. 219.

140   *a strong bond with his troops*: This sense of trustworthiness as a bond between troops and their leaders was similar to that felt between soldiers and General Dwight Eisenhower in World War II. A good description of that 1940s relationship, which helps explain the revolutionary soldiers' confidence in Washington, is given by Stephen Ambrose in *The Supreme Commander: The War Years of General Dwight D. Eisenhower*, Garden City, N.Y.: Doubleday Co., 1970, pp. 323–26.

142   *"Washington is brave without temerity"*: Howard Rice, ed., Marquis de Chastellux, trans., *Travels in North America in the Years 1780, 1781, and 1782*, Chapel Hill: University of North Carolina Press, 1963, p. 114.

142   *"the serenity of his countenance"*: Thacher, *Military Journal*, p. 48.

142   *"His face is much more agreeable"*: Flexner, *George Washington in the American Revolution*, p. 541.

142   *"in conversation"*: Humphreys quoted in Smith, *Patriarch*, pp. 6, 15.

142   *"He commands both sexes"*: "Washington in Williamsburg" monograph, p. 27.

142   *"he is polite with dignity"*: Abigail Adams to March Cranch, January 5, 1790, Adams Papers, Massachusetts Historical Society.

143   *"he looks the hero"*: Flexner, *George Washington in the American Revolution*, pp. 368–71.

143   *"he speaks of the war"*: *The History of the George Washington Bicentennial*, pp. 31–35.

143   *"modest and worthy"*: Shreve, *Tench Tilghman*, pp. 88–89.

145   *Mrs. Washington invited*: Thane, *Washington's Lady*, pp. 158–61.

145   *"Her graceful and cheerful manners"*: Wharton, *Martha Washington*, p. 117.

145   *"As militia must be our dependence"*: GW to John Hancock, January 19, 1777, in GWW VII: 29–30.

146   *Washington continued his frantic pleas*: JCC I: 41–42.

146   *"We have a full army"*: Circular to the New England States, January 24, 1777, GWW VII: 59.

146   *"in the most pressing terms"*: GW to Nicholas Cooke, January 20, 1777, GWW VII: 42–44.

146   *"Reinforcements come up"*: GW to John Hancock, January 26, 1777, GWW VII: 66.

146   *He enlisted Elias Boudinot*: Elias Boudinot, *Journal of Events in the Revolution*, New York: New York Times/Arno Press, 1968, reprinted from Philadelphia: Frederick Bourquin, 1894, pp. 44.

147   *Boudinot's 40,000 figure*: Boudinot, *Journal of Events*, pp. 54–55.

147   *"Nothing but ignorance"*: GW to Samuel Parsons, March 6, 1777, in GWW VII: 259–60.

148   *"You might suppose"*: Robert Morris to American Commissioners in Paris, March 28, 1777, in CONG VI: 503–504.

148   *"single men in the night"*: GW to Anthony Wayne, July 10, 1779, GWW XXV: 397.

148   *"he paid all of his spies"*: GW to Nathaniel Sacket, February 4, 1777, in GWW VII: 101.

148   *"You will keep as many spies"*: GW to Israel Putnam, January 5, 1777, in GWW VI: 471–72.

148   *"a man of intrigue"*: William Duer to GW, January 24, 1777, Jared Sparks, ed., *Correspondence of the American Revolution Being Letters of Eminent Men to George Washington from the Time of His Taking Command of the Army to the End of His Presidency*, 4 vols., reprinted, Freeport, N.Y.: Books for Libraries Press, 1970, pp. 329–30.

148   *Sackett recruited others*: Sparks, *Correspondence of the American Revolution*, vol. 1, pp. 337–40.

149   *The chain of command*: Thomas Fleming, "GW: Spymaster," *American Heritage* (February/March 2000): 45–51.

149   *Some operatives were women*: Fleming, "GW: Spymaster," p. 48, and Boudinot, *Journal of Events*, pp. 50–51.

150   *One very attractive woman*: Thomas Fleming, *The Secret War in Morristown*, Morristown: Morris County Historical Society, 1980, pp. 8–14.

150   *Entire families worked as spies*: William Livingston to Hugh Mercer, July 26, 1776, LIV I: 106–107.

150   *The head of the operation*: Bakeless, p. 128.

150   *The Mercereaus were so trusted*: John Mercereau to Elias Boudinot, September 19, 177, in Boudinot, *Journal of Events*, p. 182.

151   *"I wish you to use diligence"*: The newly found letters are from the Neilson family papers, Special Collections, Rutgers University.

151   *The Washington-Neilson letters*: Washington fully explained the liquid's use in a May 3, 1779, letter to Boudinot. Boudinot, *Journal of Events*, pp. 180–81. By then, Boudinot had become one of his most trusted spymasters.

152   *Washington employed double agents*: Boudinot, *Journal of Events*, pp. 66–67.

152   *Three of them were captured*: Fleming, "GW: Spymaster," p. 49.

152   *One of the first*: John Adams to Abigail Adams, March 31, 1777, in CONG VI: 511–12.

152   *"infernal foes"*: John Hancock to Horatio Gates, April 18, 1777, in CONG VI: 610.

152   *Washington ordered subordinates*: John Eccleston to a friend, winter 1778, in Eccleston Papers, Special Collections, Rutgers University.

153   *"The unfortunate policy"*: GW to John Augustine Washington, April 12, 1777, GWW VII: 395.

153   *Recruitment efforts to enroll men*: Royster, *Revolutionary People*, p. 133; GW to Robert Harrison, January 29, 177, GWW VII: 37–38; Washington to John Cadwalader, March 3, 1777, GWW VII: pp. 238–39.

153   *"Let us have a respectable army"*: GW to John Hancock, December 16, 1776, in GWW VI: 379–81.

154   *"The enclosed return"*: GW to John Hancock, March 14, 1777, GWW VI: 286–87.

154   *"To place any dependence"*: GW to John Hancock, September 24, 1776, GWW VI: 110–11.

154   *"Their officers are generally"*: GW to William Livingston, January 24, 1777, in GWW VII: 56–57.

154   *"the total loss of our liberties"*: Circular to the New England States, January 24, 1777, in GWW VII: 58–60.

155   *compete for bonus soldiers with state militias*: Henry Knox to GW, February 1, 1777, PGW VIII: 213–16.

155   *"a dearth of public spirit"*: Flexner, *George Washington in the American Revolution*, p. 55.

155   *"if...(sending) only one hundred men"*: GW to Samuel Holden Parsons, March 6, 1777, in GWW VII: 258–60.

155   *allow entire regiments of men*: GW to General Philip Schuyler about a New Jersey regiment, January 18, 1777, in GWW VII: 26–27.

156   *"a motley crew"*: GW to Jack Custis, January 22, 1777, in GWW VII: 52–54.

156   *Washington could not get money*: *Pennsylvania Evening Post*, January 11, 1777.

156   *"The treasury has been"*: GW to Hancock, January 22, 1777, GWW VII: 48–53.

156   *"I have to deal with"*: Freeman, *George Washington*, vol. 5, p. 386.

157   *In one troubling incident*: GW to Lord Stirling, January 19, 1777, in GWW VII: 33.

157   *Washington told Stirling*: GW to Lord Stirling, January 19, 1777, GWW VII: 33.

157   *Six weeks later*: David Mattern, *Benjamin Lincoln and the American Revolution*, Columbia: University of South Carolina Press, 1995, pp. 36–37.

157   *A number of officers quit*: Lundin, *Cockpit of the Revolution*, p. 237.

157   *"Any man that has friends here"*: John Eccleston to a friend, April 5, 1777, Papers of John Eccleston, Rutgers University Library.

158   *"Explicit and frequent promises"*: Freeman, *George Washington*, vol. 4, p. 414.

158 *"This practice in the militia"*: GW to Major General Philemon Dickinson, January 21, 177, in GWW VII: 45–46.

158 *"They often walk off"*: GW to Joseph Trumbull, March 3, 1777, in PGW, Series 3C.

158 *One of Washington's aides*: Robert Harrison to friend, May 20, 1777, in PARK.

158 *"to His Excellency"*: Note from Richard Meade for George Washington, April 25, 1777, PARK.

159 *"our army…will waste away"*: George Washington Proclamation to the Governors, January 31, 1777, PARK.

159 *He persuaded newspaper editors*: Pennsylvania Journal, February 18, 1777; *Pennsylvania Evening Post*, February 22, 1777.

159 *He pressured Congress*: JCC I: 115–18.

159 *He asked Livingston*: Thayer, *Colonial and Revolutionary Morris County*, p. 175.

159 *"we shall be obliged"*: GW to John Hancock, January 31, 1777, in GWW VII: 80–81.

159 *In Philadelphia*: Thomas Burke's notes on desertion debates, February 25, 1777, CONG VI: 356–63.

159 *"I really believe"*: Richard Henry Lee to Thomas Jefferson, April 29, 1777, in CONG VI: 675–76.

160 *"They are determined"*: Peale, "Journal of Charles Wilson Peale," p. 280.

160 *"I tried all in my power"*: Rodney, *The Diary of Thomas Rodney*, p. 42.

160 *Late on the morning*: Rodney, *The Diary of Thomas Rodney*, p. 45.

160 *"Slept poorly on account"*: Kenneth Rossman, *Thomas Mifflin and the Politics of the American Revolution*, Chapel Hill: University of North Carolina Press, 1952, p. 79.

160 *Washington had always relied*: Pancake, *1777: The Year of the Hangman*, p. 77.

160 *"With respect to the prisoner's"*: GW to General Israel Putnam, May 12, 1777, GWW VIII: 50.

161 *"run the gauntlet"*: Sherman, *A History of Morris County*, p. 216.

161 *"Reprieve! Reprieve!"*: George Scheer, ed., Joseph Plumb Martin, *Private Yankee Doodle, being a narrative of some of the adventures, dangers and sufferings of a revolutionary soldier*, Boston: Little Brown Co., 1962, pp. 45–46.

162 *"The trembling criminals"*: Thacher, *Military Journal*, pp. 195–196.

162 *"to strike terror"*: John Fitzgerald to General Benjamin Lincoln, May 10, 1777, PARK.

162 *Washington was so angry*: GW to Samuel Webb, April 7, 1777, in *The Diary of Samuel Blachley Webb*, vol. 2, p. 203.

163 *"no human prudence"*: GW to John Hancock, February 23, 1777, in GWW VII: 193–95.

163 *The soldiers who did not depart*: General Orders, February 11, 1777, PGW Revised Series VIII, p. 305.

163 *One group of officers*: Jones, *Ashbel Green*, pp. 100–112.

163 *Soldiers subscribed to private lotteries*: Ryden, p. 154.

163 *Women went to headquarters*: Sherman, *Historic Morristown*, p. 241.

163 *"few vices with more pernicious consequences"*: JCC I: 192, *Pennsylvania Evening Post*, May 13, 1777.

164 *Faced with unhappy men*: Thayer, *Colonial and Revolutionary Morris County*, p. 178.

164 *"greatly embarrassed"*: Alexander Hamilton to William Duer, May 6, 1777, HAMIL I: 246–47.

164 *"to hear their pretensions"*: GW to Horatio Gates, February 20, 1777, GWW VII: 177–78.

164 *This evil*": GW to John Hancock, February 20, 1777, GWW VII: 170.

164 *"He bristled when several generals*: GW to John Hancock, February 11, 1777, in PGW VIII, Revised Series: 305.

165 *"I cannot get a man"*: GW to John Hancock, January 26, 1777, GWW VII: 66.

165 *"I think I am excusable"*: GW to Nicolas Cooke, April 3, 1777, GWW VII: 351.

166 *"What then remains"*: GW to Patrick Henry, May 17, 1777, PGW, Series 3C.

166 *Local officials commiserated*: Samuel Chase to the Maryland Council on Safety, February 20, 1777, CONG VI: 329.

166   *"We have not a thousand men"*: John Adams to Abigail Adams, April 28, 1777, CONG VI: 366–67.

167   *"truly distressing"*: GW to Alexander MacDougall, April 28, 1777, GWW VII: 487.

167   *"While Washington survives"*: Cesar Rodney to aide William Killen, January 27, 1777, George Ryden, ed., Thomas Rodney to Cesar Rodney, January 14, 1777, in *Letters to and from Cesar Rodney, 1756–1784*, Philadelphia: University of Pennsylvania Press, 1933, p. 172.

167   *A private from Massachusetts*: Robert Bray and Paul Bushnell, eds., *Diary of a Common Soldier in the American Revolution, 1775–1783: An Annotated Edition of the Military Journal of Jeremiah Greenman*, Dekalb, Ill.: Northern Illinois University Press, 1978, p. 73.

167   *It is the earnest desire*: John Hancock to GW, February 25, 1777, in Spark, *Correspondence of the American Revolution*, vol. I, pp. 347–48.

168   *"the safety of our country"*: North Callahan, *Daniel Morgan: Ranger of the Revolution*, New York: Holt, Rinehart, Winston, 1961, pp. 118–19.

168   *"The enemy armies are moving"*: Josiah Bartlett to the Committee of Safety, May 1, 1777; to the leaders of the New Hampshire Militia, May 3, 1777, BART, pp. 160–61.

168   *In late April came*: GW to John Armstrong, March 5, 1777, in GWW VII: 249–50.

168   *The state of Maryland*: Aide John McKinley to Rodney, April 29, 1777, Ryden, *Letters to and from Cesar Rodney*, p. 185.

168   *fifteen hundred troops*: Alexander Martin to GW, May 16, 1777, PGW VIII, Revised Series: 444–45.

168   *Several hundred men*: *The Memoirs of Lemuel Roberts*, New York: New York Times/Arno Press, 1969, reprint from Bennington: Anthony Haswell, 1809, p. 52.

169   *By the time Washington's wing*: Pancake, *1777: The Year of the Hangman*, p. 79.

Chapter Six: The Army's War Machine

171   *Washington probably learned*: DGW II: 112.

172   *It is not known whether*: Paul David Nelson, *William Alexander, Lord Stirling*, Birmingham: University of Alabama Press, 1987, pp. 50–51.

172   *Lord Stirling wasn't Washington's only contact*: Jacob Ford Sr. to William Livingston, September 2, 1776, in LIV I: 134–35.

172   *Later that season*: Sherman, p. 8.

172   *Stirling's critics charged*: George Danforth, "Lord Stirling's Hibernia Furnace," NJHS 71: 178–88.

173   *The first iron forge*: William Wright, ed., "The Colonial Plantation Settlement in New Jersey: Iron and Agriculture Examples," in *Economic and Social History of New Jersey*, Newark: New Jersey Historical Association, 1973, p. 9.

173   *who ran it with seventy slaves*: Wright, "The Colonial Plantation Settlement in New Jersey," p. 9.

173   *Their success spurred others*: *Iron Mines of New Jersey*, New Jersey Documents, 1973, Trenton, p. 5.

173   *The larger ones required*: Munsell, *The History of Morris County, New Jersey, 1739–1882*, p. 40.

173   *The Rockaway River*: Charles Boyer, *Early Forges and Furnaces in New Jersey*, Philadelphia, 1931, p. 9.

173   *By 1775*: Arthur Pierce, *Iron in the Pines*, New Brunswick, N.J.: Rutgers University Press, 1957, p. 17.

174   *The mining town contained*: Pierce, *Iron in the Pines*, p. 18.

175   *The owners of the ironworks*: Dr. Hazel Howell, ed., *Research Report on the John Faesch House*, Rockaway, 1973, pp. 8–20.

175   *It was a two and one half story high*: Thayer, *Colonial and Revolutionary Morris County*, p. 57.

175   *Paid labor was costly*: Munsell, p. 43.

175   *They were turned down*: Nelson, *William Alexander, Lord Stirling*, p. 55.

175   *The blast furnaces*: Mary Alice Harris, "Trade of the Delaware District Before the Revolution," *Smith College Studies in History*, vol. 2, Northampton: Northampton Press, 1917, p. 286.

175   *"the furnace is making"*: Joe Hoff to Lord Stirling, May 20, 1775, in Hoff Letterbook, PARK.

175   *The financial troubles*: Munsell, p. 42.

177   *A week later*: Hoff Letterbook.

177   *"All the powder"*: Hoff Letterbook.

177   *"Lord Stirling told me"*: Hoff Letterbook.

178   *"Will you carry on works"*: Hoff Letterbook.

178   *"I am afraid the miners"*: Hoff Letterbook.

178   *The Continental Army*: Flexner, *George Washington in the American Revolution*, p. 151.

178   *"And [the cannon fire]"*: North Callahan, *Henry Knox: George Washington's General*, New York: Rinehart Co., 1958, p. 37.

178   *At Fort Ticonderoga*: George Athan Billias, ed., *George Washington's Generals*, New York: W. W. Norton Co., 1964, p. 241.

178   *Knox, though, was despondent*: Henry Knox to Richard Gridley, October 8, 1775, HK.

179   *He needed money*: Hoff Letterbook, August 31, 1776, PARK.

179   *Knox, fed up with his supplies*: Henry Knox to the president of the Continental Congress, September 1, 1776, HK.

179   *One reason Knox wanted to utilize*: Harold Peterson, *The Guns of the Continental Soldier*, Harrisburg, Pa.: Stackpole Books, 1968, p. 110; Calahan, *Henry Knox*, p. 242.

179   *Washington pressed Knox*: Francis Lewis to Robert Morris, January 15, 1777, CONG VI: 109–110.

179   *Congress reached an agreement*: Freeman, *George Washington*, vol. 3, p. 308.

180   *"Have weapons"*: Gabriel Ogden to Henry Knox, February 12, 1777, HK

180   *"Willing to cast"*: Hoff letterbook.

181   *for use by the Continentals*: Hoff Letterbook.

181   *"I have given Directions"*: GW to Philip Schuyler, March 12, 1777, GWW VII: 272–76.

181   *"an air furnace"*: GW to Benjamin Flowers, January 16, 1777, GWW VII: 18–19.

182   *"The furnace is now"*: Hoff Letterbook.

182   *"We'll give you 50 tons"*: Hoff Letterbook.

182   *The ironworks of Morristown*: GW John Hancock, February 14, 1777, GWW VII: 145–49.

183   *Many of the ironworks*: Wright, "The Colonial Plantation Settlement in New Jersey," p. 4.

184   *the slaves toiled alongside hundreds of indentured servants*: Boyer, *Early Forges and Furnaces in New Jersey*, p. 55.

184   *Those people agreed*: Richard Hofstadter, *America in 1750*, New York: Random House, 1973, p. 33.

184   *New Jersey still contained several hundred Indians*: John Pearse, *A Concise History of the Iron Manufacture in the American Colonies*, 1876, p. 34.

184   *In 1777*: Thayer, *Colonial and Revolutionary Morris County*, p. 210.

184   *Washington captured hundreds of Hessians*: *History of Picatinny Arsenal*, Picatinny: War Planning Division, 1931, p. 5.

184   *"I am informed"*: Hoff Letterbook.

185   *By the spring of 1778*: Christiano, *History of Rockaway*, p. 9.

185   *Washington approved of three classifications*: GW to Robert Morris, January 1, 1777, GWW VII: 108.

185   *Some were prisoners-of-war*: Rodney Atwood, *The Hessians: Mercenaries From Hessan-Kassel in the American Revolution*, Cambridge: Cambridge University Press, 1980, pp. 198–201; Edward Lands, *The Hessian and the Other German Auxilliaries of Great Britain in the Revolutionary War*, New York: Harper and Brothers, 1884, pp. 285–91; M. H. Volm, *The Hessian Prisoners in the American War of Independence and Their Life in Captivity*, pamphlet, University of Virginia, 1977, p. 6.

186   *The ironworks managers*: Hoff Letterbook.

186   *This was a major problem*: Hoff Letterbook.

186   *People here begin to think*: Hoff Letterbook.

186   *We have lost some fine fellows*: Hoff Letterbook.

187   *They had won a temporary*: Christiano, *History of Rockaway*, p. 9.
187   *"Every preparation should be made"*: Hoff Letterbook.
187   *"happy in the service of my country"*: Hoff Letterbook.
187   *"Why should the ironmasters'"*: GW to Richard Henry Lee, April 24, 1777, GWW VII: 462–65.
187   *Washington agreed to the exemption*: GW to Richard Henry Lee, April 24, 1777, GWW VII: 462–65.
188   *"It is highly expedient"*: JCC, October 7, 1777.
188   *"Wanted at Batsto"*: *Pennsylvania Gazette*, June 27, 1777.
188   *Even the exemptions*: GW to General Nathaniel Heard, April 23, 1777, PGW IX: 244.
189   *"I have desired"*: Lord Stirling to the Springfield Militia, "The Letters of William Alexander, Lord Stirling," NJHS, vol. 60, no. 3, July, 1942.
189   *The ironworks owners*: Gerhard Spieler, Peter Hasenclever: Industrialist, NJHS, vol. 59, 1941, p. 253.
189   *Washington listened to any ideas*: Lincoln Damient, *Chaining the Hudson: The Fight for the River in the American Revolution*, New York: Carol Publishing, 1989, pp. 110–12.
190   *A second chain*: Albert Heusser, *George Washington's Map Maker*, New Brunswick, N.J.: Rutgers University Press, 1966, p. 176–81.
190   *Toward the end of the winter*: Erna Risch, *Supplying Washington's Army*, Washington, D.C.: Center of Military History, 1981, pp. 361–62.
190   *The commander-in-chief*: *Pennsylvania Evening Post*, May 27, 1777.
190   *A large munitions factory*: GW to General Nathaniel Heard, April 23, 1777, GWW VII: 461–62.
191   *Despite Washington's unhappiness*: John Pearse, *A Concise History*, pp. 34–50. Hopewell Furnace day book, Rutgers University, special collections, p. 34.
191   *in mid-April*: John Hancock to GW, March 26, 1777, in Sparks, *Correspondence of the American Revolution*, vol. 1, pp. 358–59.
191   *"I have as many as tolerable"*: GW to Philip Schuyler, January 27, 1777, PGW, VIII: 165–66.
192   *Lord Howe and the British*: Earl Hugh Percy to Lord George Germain, September 2, 1776, ed. Charles Bolton, *Letters of Hugh Earl Percy from Boston and New York*, Boston, Mass.: Gregg Press, 1972, reprinted from Boston, Mass.: Charles Goodspeed, 1902, p. 71.
192   *"The rebels will not"*: Lord Howe to George Germain, April 2, 1777, GB XIV: 64–65.
192   *"We shall be able"*: Shaw, p. 33.
192   *"it would be madness"*: Alexander Hamilton to Gouverneur Morris, May 12, 1777, HAM I: 251–52.

Chapter Seven: Valley Forge

195   *"open to the ravages"*: Wayne Bodle and Jacqueline Thibaut, *Valley Forge Historical Society Research Report* (VFR), 3 vols., Washington, D.C., U.S. Department of the Interior, 1980, vol. 1, pp. 70–71, 113–15.
195   *Members of the council*: Wayne Bodle, Generals and "Gentlemen": Pennsylvania Politics and the Decision for Valley Forge, *Pennsylvania Magazine of History* 62, 1 (Winter 1995).
195   *They also demanded*: John F. Reed, *Valley Forge: Crucible of Victory* (Reed), Monmouth Beach, N.J.: Philip Freneau Press, 1969, pp. 4–7, GW to John Augustine Washington, November 26, 1777, GWW X: 113.
196   *"the military chest is bare"*: GW to Henry Laurens, November 8, 1777, GWW X: 22–23.
196   *The general was naturally worried*: Wayne Bodle and Jacqueline Thibaut, VFR I: 56–58.
197   *Valley Forge was advocated*: Abraham Clark to Lord Stirling, December 20, 1777, CONG IX: 444.
197   *Many disagreed*: Worthington Ford, ed., *Defense of Philadelphia in 1777*, New York: DeCapo Press, 1971, pp. 236–37.
197   *Several others told Washington*: Benjamin Newcomb, "Washington's Generals and the Decision to Quarter at Valley Forge," *Pennsylvania Magazine of History and Biography* 67, 4 (October 1993), p. 319.

197 *our men, our horses*: Jedediah Huntington to Joshua Huntington, December 20, 1777, Huntington Letters, Connecticut Historical Society.

197 *"Good advice was not taken"*: Baron DeKalb Comte de Broglie, December 25, 1777, Friedrich Kapp, *The Life of Johan Kalb, Major General in the Revolutionary Army*, New York: 1884.

198 *"We should [not] leave"*: General Orders, December 17, 1777, GWW X: 167–68.

198 *"impossible to comply"*: GW to William Livingston, October 1, 1777, GWW IX: 487.

198 *"On October 13"*: GW to Congress, October 13, 1777, PGW War II: 497–501.

198 *"On November 6"*: GW to Thomas Jefferson, November 6, 1777, GWW X: 15.

198 *Two days later*: GW to Henry Laurens, November 8, 1777, GWW X: 23.

198 *On November 10*: GW to Thomas Nelson, November 11, 1777, GWW X: 27.

198 *The absence of shoes*: General Orders, November 22, 1777, GWW X: 94.

198 *"The stock of goods"*: GW to Patrick Henry, November 13, 1777, GWW X: 55.

199 *Three weeks later*: VFR II: 285.

199 *A Pennsylvania officer:*: VFR II: 286.

199 *"My people"*: Anthony Wayne letter, Dec. 30, 1777, Wayne Papers IV: 61, PHS.

199 *"they are destitute of shoes"*: Spy Peter DuBois to Sir Henry Clinton, December 18, 1777, Clinton Papers.

199 *General Washington had monitored*: GW to James Mease, November 12, 1777, GWW X: 45–46.

199 *That same day*: General Orders, November 12, 1777, GWW X: 47–48.

199 *"provide each man"*: GW to Lt. Colonel James Innes, January 2, 1778, GWW X: 254–55.

199 *There was no one that the army*: VFR II: 246–47.

199 *In late November*: Powers to Officers to Collect Clothing, Etc., November, 1777, GWW X: 124.

200 *After he watched*: General Orders, November 26, 1777, GWW X: 105.

200 *"The officers and soldiers"*: General Orders, December 17, 1777, GWW X: 158.

200 *"pleasant for the season"*: John Smith Diary, January 1, 1778, Valley Forge Historical Park Collections (VFHP).

200 *"very fare and pleasant"*: Diary of Ebeneezer Wild, January 1–14, 1778, Massachusetts Historical Society.

202 *Food was so scarce*: Return of Joseph Trumbull, August 8, 1777, VFHP; VFR I: 22.

202 *"further proof of the inability"*: GW to Henry Laurens, December 23, 1777, GWW X: 192–98.

202 *the army's beef needs*: GW to Henry Laurens, December 23, 1777, GWW X: 192–98; January figure the returns of the army for that month, VFHP.

203 *farmers had reduced their wheat harvest*: Anne Bezanson, with Robert Gray and Miriam Hussey, *Price and Inflation During the American Revolution*, Philadelphia: University of Pennsylvania Press, 1935, p. 49.

203 *plundered by the British*: Records of Chester County residents seeking reimbursement from the British or American government after the war, submitted in 1782, VFHP. *Land Use Study of Valley Forge Historical Park*, Philadelphia: University of Pennsylvania Press, 1989, pp. 70–80.

203 *"this starved country"*: Jedediah Huntington letter, December 25, 1777, VFHP.

203 *The resignations*: VFR II: 12.

204 *"the whole race [of them]"*: Hughes to Horatio Gates, August 24, 1777, Gates Papers.

204 *"no person knows"*: Peter Colt to John Hancock, October 4, 1777, VFHP.

204 *The problems with Trumbull's successor*: Captain Thomas Cartwright to GW, February 14, 1778, VFHP.

204 *"There is not a Cross Road"*: Tench Tilghman to GW, February 19, 1778, Library of Congress, George Washington Papers.

204 *The Commissary was run so badly*: William Buchanan to Charles Stewart, November 13, 1777, Charles Stewart Papers, NYHS.

204 *Buchanan blamed all of his troubles*: William Buchanan to the Board of War, March 4, 1778, PGW, reel 47.

204 *"We have lived upon lean beef"*: Jedediah Huntington to Andrew Huntington, December 20, 1777, Stewart Papers.

205 *who blamed the commissary*: Joseph Chambers to Charles Stewart, November 21, 1777, Stewart Papers.

205 *"I was almost a stranger"*: Henry Laurens to Jonathan Trumbull, January 5, 1778, CONG VIII: 533.

205 *In a private letter*: Henry Laurens to John Laurens, CONG VIII: 549.

207 *"like a family of beavers"*: Quoted in Freeman, *George Washington*, vol. 4, p. 571.

207 *offered a monetary reward*: General Orders of December 20. Freeman, *George Washington*, vol. 4, p. 571.

207 *The city of huts*: GW General Orders, December 20, 1777, GWW X: 180–91.

208 *"To see our poor"*: John Brooks to anonymous correspondent, January 5, 1778, VFHP.

208 *Men drank dirty water*: Reed, p. 14.

208 *The rotting carcasses*: Miscellaneous notes of Nathanael Greene, February 26, 1777, Greene Papers, NYHS, VFR II: 199.

208 *The horses that remained*: John Laurens to Henry Laurens, February 17, 1778, *Correspondence of John Laurens*, p. 127.

208 *These hardships*: William Middleton, "Medicine at Valley Forge," *Picket Post Magazine*, July 1962, p. 22.

208 *Washington's ability to deal*: Flexner, *The Young Hamilton*, pp. 202–20.

209 *Officers complained*: Reed, p. 12.

209 *Hungry soldiers sneaked*: GW, General Orders of December 25, 1777, GWW X: 207.

209 *"had a body of the enemy"*: GW to Henry Laurens, December 22, 1777, GWW X: 184.

210 *"No man, in my opinion"*: GW to Henry Laurens, December 23, 1777, GWW X: 192–198.

210 *"you ought to know"*: GW to Henry Lutterloh, December 27, 1777, GWW X: 214.

211 *"in whose bosoms the sparks"*: Henry Laurens Circular to the States, December 23, 1777, CONG VIII: 465.

211 *Laurens, a short, heavy-set man*: Henry Laurens to James McLene, December 23, 1777, CONG VIII: 463.

212 *"Within a few days"*: Henry Laurens to William Livingston, December 30, 1777, Laurens, XII: 227.

212 *Laurens worked at an enormous disadvantage*: John Laurens to Henry Laurens, March 9, 1778, *Correspondence of John Laurens*, p. 137.

212 *He re-organized the Board of War*: Report of the Committee on Conference to Congress, February 6, 1778, GWW XI:

213 *"not only the Commissarial"*: Henry Laurens to Jonathan Trumbull, January 5, 1778, LAURENS XII: 251.

213 *"I am sorry to hear"*: Ichabod Ward to Abraham Pierson, January 19, 1778, Pierson and Sargeant Family Papers, Connecticut State Library.

214 *"The people of the country"*: Lord Stirling to GW, December 27, 1777, PGW, reel 46.

214 *"the most infamous"*: Francis Lightfoot to Samuel Adams, December 22, 1777, CONG VIII: 459.

214 *"My fear is that of dying"*: James Varnum to Colonel Nathan Miller, March 7, 1778, Varnum Papers, Harvard University Library.

214 *"The cursed Quakers"*: Quoted in VFR I: 156, Isaac Gibbs to his brother, March 5, 1778, VFHP.

217 *Stalemated by Congress*: Thomas Jones to John Magee, November 25, 1777, frame 142, reel 13, PA, PHMC.

217 *"knowing how exceedingly"*: GW to Patrick Henry, December 27, 1777, GWW, X: 209.

217 *Here in Pennsylvania*: VFR II: 12–14.

218 *Unlike Morris County*: E. R. I. Gould, "Local Self-Government in Pennsylvania, *The Pennsylvania Magazine of History and Biography* 7 (1882): 164.

218   *The state's new constitution*: Philip Klein and Ari Hoogenboom, *A History of Pennsylvania*, University Park: The Pennsylvania State University Press, 1980, p. 91.

218   *County public officials*: Robert Brunhouse, *The Counter-Revolution in Pennsylvania, 1776–1790*, Harrisburg: Pennsylvania Historical Commission, 1942, p. 13.

218   *The state officials*: Lewis Meader, "The Council of Censors," *The Pennsylvania Magazine of History and Biography* 22 (1898): 284.

219   *Congress then passed a bill*: JCC, January 15, 1778.

219   *"This measure must go"*: Nathanael Greene to GW, December 3, 1777, GREENE II: 234.

219   *"I can assure those gentlemen"*: GW to Congress, December 23, X: 192–98.

220   *"the work has indeed"*: Henry Laurens to GW, January 5, 1778, National Archives, Papers of the Continental Congress.

220   *Washington's pleas*: Pennsylvania Council to the Pennsylvania delegation to Congress, December 20, 1777, Pennsylvania Archives.

220   *the varying prices*: Robert Hooper to Frederick Leinback, December 2, 1777, Charles Stewart Papers.

220   *there were supply miscues*: John Fitzgerald to GW, February 16, 1778, PGW, reel 47.

220   *A shipment of clothes from Virginia*: VFR II: 287.

220   *Shipments of food upstream*: William Duer to Francis Lightfoot, February 19, 1778, VFHP.

220   *An investigation by John Ladd Howell*: Jackson, *Pinnacle of Courage*, Gettysburg, Pa.: Thomas Publications, 1992, p. 101.

220   *Fifteen tons of much-needed hay*: Jackson, *Pinnacle of Courage*, p. 103.

221   *Tench Tilghman discovered*: Jackson, *Pinnacle of Courage*, p. 103.

221   *"dogs were never more naked"*: Lt. Col. Nathanael Ramsey to General John Sullivan, January 11, 1778, Sullivan Papers, vol. 1, p. 4.

221   *Reports came in from Boston*: VFR II: 330.

221   *Washington had lost so many shipments*: GW to John Sullivan, mid-January, 1778, Sullivan Papers, vol. 2, p. 7.

221   *"today was the most beautiful"*: Burgoyne, *Diaries of Two Ansbach Jaegers*, p. 34.

221   *"bad weather and broken roads"*: GW to William Buchanan, December 28, 1777, GWW X: 217.

221   *"The badness of roads"*: Ephraim Blaine to Thomas Wharton, February 12, 1778, Pennsylvania Archives, Series 1, vol. 1, p. 252.

221   *"intolerably bad"*: John Jackson, *Pinnacle of Courage*, p. 34.

221   *The rainfall that winter*: John Smith Diary, January 2, 1778, VFHP.

222   *"the troops are worn out"*: Nathanael Greene to Christopher Greene, January 5, 1778, GREENE II: 248.

222   *"dying of the 'Meases'"*: Anthony Wayne to Richard Peters, May 4, 1778, Pennsylvania Archives.

222   *"Complaining is the fashion"*: James Mease to Francis Dana, January 28, 1778, Papers of Continental Congress, National Archives.

223   *Needing someone*: VFR II: 434–35.

223   *referring to those who did*: General Orders, December 26, 1777, GWW X: 206–207.

224   *bring two hundred cows back to camp*: John Armstrong to GW, December 26, 1777, VFHP.

224   *Washington ordered American patrols*: VFR I: 145.

224   *Learning that a large British force*: GW to Nathanael Greene, February 12, 1778, GWW X: 454.

224   *The general also refused*: GW to Board of War, November 11, 1777, GWW X: 39–40.

224   *His 219 tailors*: David Forman to GW, December, 1778, Library of Congress, George Washington Papers.

224   *He contacted newspaper editors*: *Virginia Gazette*, December 5, 1777.

224   *In a rather simple move*: VFR, pp. 340–41.

224   *Unable to procure enough supplies*: GW to William Livingston, February 16, 1778, GWW X: 465; Tench Tilghman to GW, February 19, 1778, GWW X: 471.

225 *"I address myself to you"*: GW to Patrick Henry, February 19, 1778, GWW X: 483–85.

225 *The food supply*: Randell, *George Washington*, p. 157.

225 *"No meat"*: Flexner, *George Washington in the American Revolution*, p. 262

225 *"No meat! No soldier!"*: William Duane, ed., *Christopher Marshall, Extracts from the Diary…Kept in Philadelphia and Lancaster during the American Revolution, 1774–1781*, Albany, N.Y., 1877, pp. 152–53.

225 *"the poor soldiers had hardships"*: Martin, *Private Yankee Doodle*, p. 288.

225 *"the present managers"*: John Laurens to Henry Laurens, February 17, 1778, *Correspondence*, p. 126–27.

226 *"the army under my command"*: GW to Israel Putnam, February 5, 1777, GWW X: 423.

226 *"we cannot but disband"*: GW to Jonathan Trumbull, February 6, 1777, GWW X: 424.

226 *"we are supplied from hand to mouth"*: GW to William Livingston, February 14, 1776, PGW.

226 *"total want and dissolution"*: GW to William Buchanan, February 7, 1778, GWW X: 427.

226 *"we shall have not a horse left"*: GW to Robert Hooper Jr., Nathaniel Falconer and Jonathan Mifflin, February 15, 1778, VFHP.

226 *The crisis moved the Pennsylvania Assembly*: Resolution of the Pennsylvania General Assembly, December 6, 1777, Pennsylvania Archives.

226 *Americans had complained*: E. Wayne Carp, *To Starve the Army at Pleasure: Continental Army Administration and American Political Culture, 1775–1783*, Chapel Hill: University of North Carolina Press, 1984, p. 76.

226 *War in the late 1750s*: Carp, *To Starve the Army at Pleasure*, p. 78.

227 *Impressment laws*: Reed, p. 16.

227 *They gave the commander-in-chief*: Henry Lee to John Howell, February 19, 1778, Reed Collection, VFHP.

227 *Some states*: Carp, *To Starve the Army at Pleasure*, pp. 79–81.

227 *"Some recommendations"*: William Ellery to William Whipple, December 21, 1777, CONG VIII: 466.

227 *"may, on critical exigencies"*: Quoted in Burnett, *Letters of the Continental Congress*, p. 270.

227 *"Nothing can be expected"*: George Gibson to GW, February 22, 1778, PGW, reel 47.

228 *He was further appalled*: GW to the Board of War, November 11, 1777, GWW X: 39–40.

228 *"such a procedure"*: GW to Board of War, November 11, 1777, GWW X: 39.

228 *"an evil much to be apprehended"*: GW to Henry Laurens, December 14, 1777, X: 155–59.

228 *"The people at large"*: GW to Henry Laurens, in December 15 fragment addition, p. 160.

228 *"I am not without power"*: GW to William Livingston, December 31, 1777, GWW X: 231–234.

229 *"Nothing in nature"*: GW to William Livingston, June 15, 1781, GWW XXII: 223.

229 *He feared authorization*: Anthony Wayne to GW, December 26, 1777, PGW, reel 46.

229 *Commissary agents*: John Chaloner to John Howell, January 12, 1778, Lee Boyle, *Writings from the Valley Forge Encampment of the Continental Army, December 19, 1777—June 19, 1778*, 3 vols., Bowie, Md.: Heritage Books, 2001, vol. 2, pp. 22–23

229 *"never failed"*: GW to Henry Laurens, January 5, 1778, GWW X: 267.

229 *"these requisitions are not the result"*: GW to Governor Thomas Johnson, November 6, 1777, GWW X: 15.

229 *He told his agents*: GW to Henry Lee, February 16, 1778, GWW X: 468.

229 *"as the inhabitants can spare"*: Powers to Officers To Collect Clothing Etc., November, 1777, GWW X: 124–125.

230 *"We are well disposed"*: Mercer County Magistrates to GW, January 2, 1778, Library of Congress, George Washington Papers.

230 *"the country in the vicinity"*: General James Varnum to Nathanael Greene, February 12, 1778, PGW, reel 47.

230 *"the country has been"*: Nathaniel Greene to GW, February 16, 1778, Library of Congress, George Washington Papers.

230   *"this council must acknowledge"*: Supreme Executive Council to GW, March 10, 1778, Pennsylvania Archives.

230   *"All the magazines provided"*: GW to George Clinton, GWW X: 469–70.

Chapter Eight: The Angel of Death
232   *"the weather frequently changes"*: General James Varnum to Mrs. William Greene, March 7, 1778, Boyle, *Writings From the Valley Forge Encampment of the Continental Army*, p. 76.

232   *"noting that in January"*: Blagden to Banks, January 21, 1778, Blagden Letters, pp. 416–17.

232   *A thaw on January 5*: Baurmeister, *American Revolution*, p. 151.

232   *"this day was the worst"*: Israel Angell Diary, VFHP.

232   *Soldiers sometimes went to sleep*: Wild Diary, January 3, 1778.

232   *Snowfalls of March 9 and 10*: John Trussell Jr., *Birthplace of an Army: A Study of the Valley Forge Encampment*, Harrisburg: Pennsylvania Historical and Museum Collection, 1998, pp. 37–38.

233   *"I need not explain"*: GW to Rev. John Ettwein, March 28, 1778, GWW XI: 170–71.

235   *"remarkably kind"*: Leven Powell to Sarah Powell, January 21, 1778, Boyle, *Writings from the Valley Forge Encampment*, p. 34.

235   *The only hospital*: Oscar Reiss, M.D., *Medicine in the American Revolution*, Jefferson, N.C.: McFarland and Company, 1998, p. 196–97; Gibson, *Dr. Bodo Otto and the Medical Background of the American Revolution*, Springfield, Ill.: Charles Thomas Co., 1937, p. 154–55.

235   *Doctors and officers*: Minutes of the Uwchlain Monthly Meeting, January 8, 1778, quoted in William Middleton, "Medicine at Valley Forge," Madison, 1841, *Annals of Medical History*, 3rd series, vol. 3, p. 473.

235   *The church and parsonage*: Ibid.

235   *All of these medical centers*: William Middleton, "Medicine at Valley Forge," *Picket Post Magazine*, pp. 22–25.

236   *"flying hospitals"*: Middleton, "Medicine at Valley Forge," p. 25.

236   *There was no truly effective cure*: Middleton, "Medicine at Valley Forge," p. 200–204.

236   *There was a constant shortage*: General Orders, April 14, 1778, GWW XI: 261.

237   *"You are authorized"*: GW to Brigadier General Lachlan MacIntosh, April 4, 1778, GWW XI: 206–208.

237   *All of the hospitals:* Governor Livingston and others complained often to both Washington and Congress, Livingston to Henry Laurens, December 25, 1777, LAURENS XII: 200–202.

238   *"I gits better but a number died"*: Fisher Journal, p. 7.

238   *An example was a horrific outbreak*: Louis Meier, M.D., *The Healing of an Army, 1777–1778*, Norristown: History Society of Montgomery County, Pennsylvania, 1991, p. 18.

238   *"the misery…cannot be"*: Dr. Benjamin Rush to GW, February 25, 1778, Library of Congress, George Washington Papers.

238   *Hundreds of men without shoes*: Walter Clark, ed., *The State Records of North Carolina*, Winston: M. I. & J.C. Stewart, 1895.

238   *Some medical centers*: Meier, *The Healing of An Army*, p. 11.

238   *One man arrived*: Elijah Fisher Journal, VFHP, p. 7.

238   *Men who lived within seventy miles*: "Extracts from the Memoirs of Jonas Ingram, late Captain of the Bucks County, Pennsylvania, Militia," *Pennsylvania Magazine of History and Biography* 26, 3 (1902) p. 409.

239   *"There are medicines"*: Potts quoted in James Gibson, *Dr. Bodo Otto and the Medical Background of the American Revolution*, p. 155.

239   *The death rates*: Potts quoted in James Gibson, *Dr. Bodo Otto and the Medical Background of the American Revolution*, pp. 22–24, Mary Gillett, *The Army Medical Department 1775–1818*, Washington: Center of Military History, U.S. Army, 1901, p. 82.

239   *As an example*: Reed, p. 44.

239   *"sickness and mortality"*: Committee in Camp report, quoted in Trussell, *Birthplace of an Army*, p. 40.

239   *"Young men under twenty"*: Louis Duncan, *Medical Men in the Revolution*, Carlisle, Pa: Army Medical Bulletin, no. 25, p. 240–42.

240   *"Who, sir, can bear"*: Dr. Benjamin Rush to GW, January 1, 1778, Washington correspondence, VFHP.

240   *"stink of human life"*: Ibid., p. 243.

240   *"There cannot be a greater calamity"*: Benjamin Rush to GW, December 26, 1778, Library of Congress, George Washington Papers.

240   *In another acidic remark*: Benjamin Rush to Nathaniel Greene, February 1, 1778, GREENE II: 267.

240   *General Jedediah Huntington*: General Jedediah Huntington to GW, January 1, 1778, Library of Congress, George Washington Papers.

241   *"quackery substituted"*: General James Varnum to GW, January 3, 1778, Library of Congress, George Washington Papers.

241   *The general at first*: GW to William Heath, December 17, 1777, GWW X: 165.

241   *What appeared to be a cautious plan*: GW to General William Heath, December 17, 1777, GWW X: 165–66.

241   *Washington then ordered a canvass*: Enoch Poor to Meshech Weare, March 4, 1778, VFHP.

241   *He told doctors*: GW to William Smallwood, February 25, 1778, GWW X: 511.Enoch Poor to Meshech Weare, March 4, 1778, VFHP.

242   *in areas where isolated*: General William Smallwood to GW, February 15, 1778, Library of Congress, George Washington Papers.

242   *Doctors ran the inoculation program*: GW to General William Heath, January 22, 1778, GWW X: 335; Middleton, "Medicine at Valley Forge," p. 22.

242   *More than four thousand troops*: Reiss, *Medicine and the American Revolution*, p. 196.

242   *before the last group*: Alexander Scammell to John Sullivan, April 8, 1778, Boyle, *Writings from the Valley Forge Encampment*, vol. 2, p. 104.

243   *This second mass inoculation*: Trussell, *Birthplace of an Army*, p. 45.

243   *"It would be shocking to humanity"*: Duncan, *Medical Men in the Revolution*, p. 223.

243   *"I am not fond of danger"*: Middleton, *Medicine at Valley Forge*, Annals of Medical History, vol. 3, p. 467.

243   *He received a letter from Dr. Rush*: L. H. Butterfield, ed., *The Letters of Benjamin Rush*, Princeton: Princeton University Press, 1951, pp. 140–50.

243   *"I sincerely feel for the unhappy"*: GW to William Livingston, December 31, 1777, GWW X: 233.

244   *"My disorder increases"*: Joseph Holt to GW, April 1, 1778, Boyle, *Writings from the Valley Forge Encampment*, vol. 2, pp. 101–102.

244   *"If I turn from beholding"*: Thacher, *Military Journal*, p. 113.

244   *Stress and fatigue caused*: Reed, p. 31.

245   *The Shippen-Rush feud*: Saffron, *Surgeon to Washington*, pp. 44–48.

245   *"the accommodation of the sick"*: GW's report to the Committee of Congress With the Army, January 29, 1778, GWW X: 495.

245   *"as nothing adds more"*: General Orders, December, 1777, GWW X: 241.

245   *Washington had ashes and tallow*: Meier, *The Healing of an Army*, 1777–1776, pp. 18–19.

245   *The general ordered doctors*: Gillett, *The Army Medical Department*, p. 83.

246   *"peculiarly distressing"*: GW to the Board of War, January 3, 1778, GWW X: 251.

246   *in early January*: GW to the Board of War, January 3, 1778, GWW X: 251.

246   *No matter how low*: General Orders, February 22, 1778, GWW X: 499.

246   *In mid-January, Washington*: General Orders, January 2, 17778 and January 21, 1777, GWW X: 333.

246   *The commander ordered wagons*: Brigadier General Jedediah Huntington to GW, January 1, 1778.

246   *he issued a lengthy memorandum*: General Orders, January 30, 1778, GWW X: 405–407.

246 *"It is to be regretted"*: GW to Benjamin Rush, January 12, 1777, GWW X: 297.
246 *"the carcasses of dead horses"*: General Orders, quoted in, Middleton, "Medicine at Valley Forge," *Picket Post*, p. 21.
247 *Washington ordered officers*: General Orders, quoted in, Middleton, "Medicine at Valley Forge," *Picket Post*, p. 21.
247 *"the smell of some place"*: General Orders, quoted in Trussell, *Birthplace of an Army*, p. 44.
247 *On the advice of Baron Von Steuben*: Middleton, "Medicine at Valley Forge," *Annals of Medical History*, p. 480.
247 *doctors turn in regular reports*: GW to General Lachlan McIntosh, April 4, 1778, *200 Years Ago Today at Valley Forge*, Valley Forge: Valley Forge Historical Park, 1979.
247 *The Commissary Department was ordered*: Ephraim Blaine to Dr. Potts, May 2, 1778, Blaine Letterbook.
247 *"I am obliged to you for"*: GW to Francis Hopkinson, March 28, 1778, GWW XI: 166.
247 *Later in the winter*: General Orders, April 10, 1778, *200 Years Ago Today at Valley Forge*.
247 *One thing that infuriated*: Middleton, "Medicine at Valley Forge," *Picket Post*, p. 21.
248 *"Such a scene of mortality"*: Middleton, "Medicine at Valley Forge," *Picket Post*, p. 22.
248 *"Our brethren who are unfortunately"*: Waldo Diary, p. 309.
249 *"Our soldiers in the hands"*: William Ellery to William Whipple, December 21, 1777, CONG VIII: 454.
249 *"cruelty unheard of"*: Daniel Roberdeau to John Adams, January 21, 1778, CONG VIII: 625.
249 *"cruel and unjustifiable treatment"*: GW to the Board of War, January 2–3, 1778, GWW X: 250–54.
249 *"I can only assure you"*: William Howe to GW, February 21, 1778, Library of Congress, George Washington Papers.
249 *Washington warned Howe*: GW to William Howe, January 20, 1778, GWW X: 323.
250 *"That some have been dragged"*: William Howe to GW, February 21, 1778, Washington correspondence, VFHP.
251 *"Poor food"*: Waldo Diary, pp. 306–309.
251 *Conditions continued to deteriorate*: Orders, February 28, 1777, GWW X: 537.

Chapter Nine: The Fall from Grace
254 *The American public*: Royster, *Revolutionary People*, pp. 184–85.
254 *"success sanctifies everything"*: Greene to GW, November 24, 1777, GREENE II: 208–209.
254 *Members of Congress*: Burnett, *Letters of the Continental Congress*, p. 268–69.
254 *"such blunders as might"*: Burnett, *Letters of the Continental Congress*, pp. 270–71.
255 *"I found myself infinitely"*: Hamilton, quoted in Flexner, *Young Alexander Hamilton*, p. 199.
256 *"You know the importance"*: GW to Charles Lee, December 11, 1776, GWW VI: 348.
256 *"But what could he do?"*: Nathanael Greene to GW, December 4, 1777, GREENE II: 231.
256 *"one cause of (the Thanksgiving)"*: John Adams to Abigail Adams, October 26, 1777, *Adams' Family Letters*, pp. 322–23.
256 *"the army was not inclined"*: James Lovell to Samuel Adams, December 20, 1777, CONG VIII: 450–51.
256 *Washington himself was partially*: Scheer and Rankin, *Rebels and Redcoats: The American Revolution through the Eyes of Those Who Fought and Lived It*, Cambridge, Mass.: Da Capo Press, 1988, p. 293.
256 *Washington had no champions*: Sidney Kobre, *Development of Colonial Newspapers*, Gloucester: Peter Smith, 1960, pp. 148–57.
258 *"I have been a slave to the service"*: GW to Richard Henry Lee, October 17, 1777, GWW IX: 387–88.
258 *"was not the man people imagined"*: Ephraim Blaine's recollection of conversation with innkeeper Jones to GW aide Robert Harrison, January 18, 1778, Washington correspondence, VFHP.
258 *"Heaven has been determined"*: Freeman, *George Washington*, vol. 4, p. 550.

258   *A suspicious Stirling*: Scheer and Rankin, *Rebels and Redcoats*, p. 295.
258   *A rumor spread that Congress*: Nathanael Greene to Alexander McDougall, Feb. 5, 1778, McDougall papers, NYHS.
258   *His generals and aides*: Flexner, *George Washington in the American Revolution*, p. 248.
258   *"wicked duplicity of conduct"*: Freeman, *George Washington*, vol. 4, p. 550.
258   *Hamilton said it was*: Alexander Hamilton to George Clinton, February 13, 1778, Syrett, *The Papers of Alexander Hamilton*, vol. 1, p. 428.
259   *The commander's other generals*: Flexner, *George Washington in the American Revolution*, pp. 271–73.
259   *"the sole defender"*: Quoted in Leckie, *George Washington's War*, p. 450.
259   *"dangerous incendiary"*: GW to Horatio Gates, Jan 4, 1778, GWW X: 263–65.
259   *"doing all in my power"*: GW to Henry Laurens, January 31, 1778, GWW X: 410–11.
260   *"a military genius"*: Horatio Gates recommendation to Congress for Wilkinson's promotion, Washington correspondence, VFHP.
260   *"whether any members of Congress"*: GW to Landon Carter, July 30, 1778, GWW XI: 493.
260   *"I am told a scheme"*: GW to Rev. William Gordon, January 23, 1778, GWW X: 338.
261   *"intrigues of a faction"*: GW to Patrick Henry, March 28, 1778, GWW XI: 163.
261   *"Washington seethed about Gates"*: GW to Lafayette, December 31, 1777, GWW X: 236–37.
261   *"The attempt was made"*: GW to Archibald Blair, June 24, 1799, GWW XXXVII: 245.
261   *"my inveterate enemy"*: Lafayette to GW, December 31, 1778, Lafayette College Library.
261   *It would be best leave*: GW to Lafayette, December 31, 1777, GWW X: 237.
261   *"You shall see very plainly"*: Lafayette to GW, December 30, 1777, Lafayette College Library.
261   *His generals and aides*: Otto Hammond, *The Letters and Papers of John Sullivan, Continental Army*, 3 vols., Concord: New Hampshire Historical Society, 1931, vol. 1, p. 1.
262   *"reflects disgrace and dishonor"*: Hamond, *The Letters and Papers of John Sullivan*, vol. 1, p. 1.
262   *"universal disgust"*: John Laurens to Henry Laurens, January 1, 1778, LAURENS XII: 231.
263   *"but (they) do not bear"*: Lafayette to Laurens, January 5, 1778, LAURENS XII: 255–57.
263   *"feelings and opinion"*: GW to Henry Laurens, January 2, 1778, GWW X: 249.
263   *"is capable of all the malignity"*: GW to Horatio Gates, January, 4, 1778, February 9, 1778, GWW X: 437–41.
264   *"I solemnly declare"*: Horatio Gates to GW, February 19, 1778, Gates Papers, Library of Congress, George Washington Papers.
264   *"to give the least cause"*: Hammond, *The Letters and Paper of John Sullivan*, vol. 1, pp. 2–3.
264   *"Conway wrote the General"*: Thomas Conway to GW, December 31, 1778, Library of Congress, George Washington Papers, Tench Tilghman to General John Cadwalader, January 18, 1778, Historical Society of Pennsylvania, Cadwalader Papers.
264   *"He is a great incendiary"*: Nathanael Greene to GW, January 3, 1778, GREENE II: 243.
264   *"like moles who work"*: Tilghman, quoted in *Pennsylvania Magazine of History and Biography* 32, 2 (1908): 167–70.
265   *"My feelings will not permit"*: GW to Henry Laurens, January 2, 1778, GWW X: 249–50.
265   *"guilty of the blackest"*: Laurens quoted in Freeman, *George Washington*, vol. 4, p. 591, Laurens note upon receipt of letter, Laurens Papers, XII: 273.
265   *The purported effort*: Lund Washington to GW, February 18, 1778, Library of Congress, George Washington Papers.
266   *"A long connection"*: Joseph Reed to Jonathan Smith, February 8, 1778, CONG VIII: 60–61.
266   *"Be not alarmed"*: Henry Laurens to Lafayette, January 12, 1778, CONG VIII: 572.
266   *"I thank you sincerely"*: GW to John Fitzgerald, February 28, 1778, GWW X: 128–29.
268   *"sending for Mrs. Washington"*: Major General John Armstrong to GW, December 30, 1778, Library of Congress, George Washington Papers.
268   *"But Mrs. Washington"*: GREENE II: 276; PGW note, February 5, 1778, Washington correspondence, VFHP.
268   *"I must go"*: Martha Washington to Burwell Basset, December 22, 1777, Mount Vernon Library Collection.
268   *"a dreary kind of place"*: GW to Jack Custis, February 1, 1777, GWW X: 414.

268   *"The General's apartment"*: Martha Washington to Mercy Otis Warren, March 7, 1778, Fields, *Worthy Partner*, pp. 177–78.

269   *"indecently and most shamefully"*: Pickering, I: 199.

269   *She quickly resumed her role*: Flexner, *George Washington in the American Revolution*, p. 283.

269   *Martha also organized a party*: John Trussell, Jr., *Birthplace of an Army: A Study of the Valley Forge Encampment*, Harrisburg: Pennsylvania Historical and Museum Commission, 1998, p. 98.

270   *She also worked with Charles Wilson Peale*: Miller, Peale Papers I: pp. 230, 236–37; John Laurens to Henry Laurens, March 9, 1778, LAURENS XII: 533.

270   *Martha took on unpleasant responsibilities*: Elizabeth Drinker's Diary, quoted in *200 Years Ago Today at Valley Forge.*

271   *"She is small and fat"*: Chastellux, *Travels in North America*, vol. 1, p. 298.

271   *"a social, pretty kind of woman"*: Drinker diary.

271   *Martha had always been*: Flexner, *George Washington in the American Revolution*, p. 283.

271   *General Washington had to constantly quell*: Richard Caswell to GW, February 15, 1778, Library of Congress, George Washington Papers.

271   *In December, a rumor flew*: Waldo diary, December 22, 1777, p. 313.

271   *And then, on March 27*: Elias Boudinot to Hannah Boudinot, March 27, 1778, Stimon-Boudinot Collection, Princeton University Library.

272   *the French had already landed*: *Pennsylvania Gazette*, December 20, 1777.

272   *Just before Christmas*: William Palfrey to GW, January 5, 1778, Palfrey Family Papers, Massachusetts Historical Society.

272   *It was during the Valley Forge*: William Gordon to GW, January 8, 1778, Library of Congress, George Washington Papers.

272   *Another that floated*: Lafayette to GW, January 5, 1778, Lafayette College Library.

272   *"The cry against Congress"*: Clark, NJHS VII, p. 104.

273   *"[Peace talks] will require"*: GW to John Augustine Washington, May, 1778, GWW XI: 501.

274   *"injustice, delusion and fraud"*: GW to Henry Laurens, April 18, 1778, GWW XI: 276–277.

274   *"the object of the war"*: British Admiralty Board to Richard Lord Howe, March 22, 17778, quoted in Mackesy, *War for America*, p. 186.

274   *He stopped talking*: GW to Congress, January 29, 1778, GWW X: 362–403.

274   *The four man investigative*: Freeman, *George Washington*, vol. 4, pp. 584–65.

275   *They were shaken*: JCC IX: 505.

276   *"Good God!"*: Francis Dana to Elbridge Gerry, February 16, 1778, CONG 9: 108–109.

276   *"the number of little piddlin"*: Committee of Congress at Camp to resident of Congress, February 25, 1778, PCC.

276   *The acerbic letters to Congress*: Carp, *To Starve the Army at Pleasure*, pp. 49–50.

277   *"In short, everything seems"*: Thomas Jones to Charles Stewart, February 18, 1778, Stewart Papers, NYHS.

Chapter Ten: The New American Army

280   *"a great and growing disgust"*: Thomas Wharton to GW, February 17, 1778, Pennsylvania Historical Society and Museum.

280   *Washington constantly pressed*: Thomas Wharton to GW, January 14, 1778, VFHP.

280   *"I have no expectation"*: General William Smallwood to GW, December 30, 1778, Library of Congress, George Washington Papers.

280   *"There were one thousand"*: VFR I: 56.

280   *Washington was unhappy*: The Subalterns of Virginia to GW, April 1778, Library of Congress, George Washington Papers.

280   *To keep them in the army*: GW to Henry Laurens, Nov. 13, 1777, VFHP.

280   *"It is very surprising"*: General Alexander McDougall to GW, February 17, 1778, Library of Congress, George Washington Papers.

281   *"We may be assured"*: Circular to the States, December 20, 1778, GWW X: 222.

281   *This direct plea*: The liquor was Lord Stirling's idea, Stirling to GW, January 1, 1778; GW to Captains William Scull, Alexander Patterson and William Wilson, February 23, 1778.

281   *"I am sorry to find you have"*: GW to Samuel Holden Parsons, January 16, 1778, GWW X: 309.

282   *Washington was so fearful*: GW to General James Varnum, April 9, 1778, quoted in *200 Years Ago at Valley Forge*.

282   *"the situation of the army"*: GW to John Glover, January 8, 1778, GWW X: 280.

282   *"as expeditiously as circumstances"*: GW to Henry Knox, February 21, 1778, GWW X: 489–90.

282   *"Resign…you will meet"*: GW to Colonel William Malcolm, January 6, 1778, quoted in *200 Years Ago Today at Valley Forge*.

282   *"possess more virtue"*: GW to Charles Lewis, March 21, 1778, GWW X: 121–22.

282   *"I am astonished"*: GW to James Bowdoin, March 31, 1778, quoted in *200 Years Ago at Valley Forge*.

282   *"an epidemical disease"*: GW to Major Isaac Beall, quoted in *200 Years Ago Today at Valley Forge*.

282   *"our wives, our children"*: Archelaus Lewis to Jesse Partridge, February 1, 1778, VFHP.

282   *"When an officer"*: Waldo Diary, pp. 314; the surgeon was referring to one of his patients.

283   *"If they were confined"*: GW to Henry Laurens, April 30, 1778, XI: 327.

283   *"Nothing else will preserve"*: Doctor Sam Tenney to Dr. Peter Turner, March 22, 1778, Turner Papers, Library of Congress.

283   *Washington argued*: GW to the Committee of Congress, January 29, 1778, GWW X: 365.

283   *"hold the army together"*: GW to Henry Laurens, December 23, GWW X: 192–196.

283   *Several thousand soldiers*: Reed, p. 26.

284   *Washington acknowledged them*: Committee in Camp to Henry Laurens, February 5, 1778, CONG VIII: 30.

284   *Washington also asked*: GW to Committee of Congress With the Army, January 29, 1778, GWW X: 362–403.

284   *"the fatal policy of host"*: GW to William Livingston, March 25, 1778, quoted in *200 Years Ago at Valley Forge*.

284   *"If the states do not exert"*: Henry Laurens to Isaac Motte, January 26, 1778, CONG 8: 653.

284   *Rank among officers*: VFR I: 148–49.

285   *a source of great honor*: Joanne Freeman, *Affairs of Honor*, New Haven, Conn.: Yale University Press, 2000, pp. xiii–xv.

285   *"near daggers points"*: George Fleming to Sebastian Bauman, March 26, 1778, Bauman Papers, NYHS.

285   *"my reasons for leaving"*: James Eldredge to GW, January 1, 1778, VFNHP.

285   *"will be injurious"*: GW to the Committee of Congress With the Army, January 29, 1778, GWW X: 380–381.

286   *"No man ever united"*: Quoted in the *History of the George Washington Bicentennial*, vol. 1, p. 37.

286   *"I have never heard"*: Schroeder, *Maxims*, p. 197.

286   *"My rank in the army"*: Nathanael Greene to Colonel Hugh Hughes, April 16, 1778, GREENE II: 342–43.

287   *"I fear nothing but the army's"*: Jeremiah Wadsworth to Henry Champion, June 8, 1778, Wadsworth Papers, Connecticut Historical Society.

287   *"Our worthy general"*: Jedediah Huntington to Andrew Huntington, March 6, 1778, Huntington Papers, Connecticut Historical Society.

287   *The commander-in-chief's temper*: Charles Jones note, February 16, 1778, VFHP.

287   *Ephraim Blaine, a quartermaster*: Ephraim Blaine, "An Estimate of Provisions in the Middle District," February 14, 1778, VFHP.

287   *"I pity him"*: Thomas Jones to Charles Stewart, February 18, 1778, Stewart Papers, NYHS.

288   *Life had deteriorated quickly*: Ephraim Blaine to Thomas Wharton Jr., February 12, 1778, VFHP.

288   *"shocking"*: Jedediah Huntington to Jeremiah Wadsworth, March 5, 1778, Wadsworth
Papers, Connecticut Historical Society.

288   *Men began to haphazardly*: Joseph Reed to Henry Laurens, February 23, 2778, William Reed,
Life and Correspondence of Joseph Reed, 2 vols., Philadelphia, Pa.: Lindsay and Blakiston,
1847, vol. 1, p. 361.

288   *"I should be glad"*: William Weeks to anonymous, February 16, 1778, in Hiram Bingham Jr.,
Five Straws Gathered from Revolutionary Fields, Cambridge, 1901, p. 25.

288   *The truth was that Von Steuben*: John Jackson, *Pinnacle of Courage*, p. 124.

289   *"I have but one aim"*: Fredrick Von Steuben to Henry Laurens, March 12, 1778,
VFHP.

289   *"Baron Von Steuben"*: GW to Henry Laurens, February 27, 1778, GWW X: 518–19.

290   *"like a lieutenant"*: John Laurens to Henry Laurens, April 18, 1778, Laurens Correspondence,
p. 160.

290   *The Prussian decided*: Philander Chase, PhD diss., *Baron Von Steuben in the War of
Independence*, Durham, N.C.: Duke University, 1975, p. 59.

290   *He told them that*: General Orders, March 19, 1778, GWW XL: 163.

290   *the "renown" Prussian*: John Palmer, *General Frederick Von Steuben*, New Haven, Conn.: Yale
University Press, 1937, p. 137.

291   *The soldiers, eager to learn*: Joseph Doyle, *General William Von Steuben and the American
Revolution*, Steubenville, Ohio: Stanton Monument Association, 1913, p. 90.

291   *By May, Von Steuben*: Doyle, *General William Von Steuben*, pp. 95–100.

291   *Von Steuben also informed*: Friedrich Kapp, *The Life of Frederick William Von Steuben, a
Major General in the Revolutionary Army*, New York: Mason Brothers, 1859, p. 199.

291   *"The Baron discovers"*: John Laurens to Henry Laurens, March 25, 1778, quoted in *200 Years
Ago Today at Valley Forge*.

291   *"Baron Steuben set us a noble"*: General Alex Scammel to John Sullivan, April 8, 1778,
Sullivan, p. 322.

291   *"the army grows stronger"*: Anonymous, quoted in *200 Years Ago Today at Valley Forge*.

292   *Turning his enlisted men*: GW to Horatio Gates, February 21, 1778, GWW X:
486–87.

292   *"We have found so many advantages"*: GW to General William Heath, January 2, 1778,
GWW X: 257–58.

292   *Washington ordered*: Colonel Daniel Brodhead was one of many who submitted
reorganization memos. Brodhead to Tench Tilghman, December 30, 1778, Library of
Congress, George Washington Papers.

293   *The severest problem*: Ephraim Blaine to Robert Huggins, February 15, 1778, Blaine
Letterbook, PARK.

293   *He warned the farmers*: GW Proclamation, February 18, 1778, VFHP.

293   *"means and influence"*: GW to Maryland Governor Thomas Johnson, February 16, 1778,
Maryland Hall of Records.

294   *the commander then ordered*: Henry Lee to GW, February 21, 1778, GWW X: 471–473.

294   *They were to use soldiers*: GW to General William Smallwood, February 16, 1778, GWW X:
467.

294   *Thousands of cows*: Henry Champion to GW, February 28, 1778, Library of Congress,
George Washington Papers.

294   *All of this had to be*: GW to Henry Hollingsworth, February 16, 1778, GWW X:
468.

294   *Planning for the drives*: Ephraim Blaine to Colonel Ludwick, February 7, 1778, Blaine
Papers, MNHP.

294   *Blaine remained there*: Ephraim Blaine to Henry Lutterloh, February 18, 1778, Blaine
Letterbook, MNHP.

294   *"As the resources of this country"*: GW to Israel Putnam, February 6, 1778, GWW X:
423.

294   *"All the cattle that are fit"*: GW to Henry Lee, February 25, 1778, GWW X: 513–14.

295 *"for God's sake and my reputation"*: Ephraim Blaine to Azariah Dunham, February 9, 1778, VFHP.

295 *"The quantity cannot be"*: John Chaloner to Henry Champion, March 17, 1778, Chaloner Papers, Connecticut Historical Society.

295 *"Jersey, Pennsylvania and Maryland"*: GW to Henry Champion, February 17, 1778, GWW X: 474.

295 *there were problems purchasing herds*: Henry Hollingsworth to Washington, February 18,1778, Library of Congress, Papers of George Washington.

295 *The cattle drives*: Henry Champion to Washington, February 18, 1778, Jeremiah Wadsworth to Washington, February 20, 1778, VFHP, GW to Anthony Wayne, February 28, 1778, GWW X: 524.

296 *"The army...is tolerable"*: Dr. Ebeneezer Crosby to Norton Quincy, April 14, 1778, HUL.

296 *"the fertile ground"*: Lieutenant B. Howe to Major Sebastian Bauman, April 23, 1778, Bauman Papers, NYHS.

296 *"the meadows on each side"*: Samuel Ward to Phoebe Ward, April 1778, Ward Papers, RIHS.

296 *Congress finally approved*: JCC XI: 502.

296 *"Congress, God bless them!"*: Sam Ward to Phoebe Ward, May 15, 1778, Ward Papers, RIHS.

297 *The mood of the commander-in-chief"*: GW to Henry Laurens, April 27, 1778, GWW XI: 313

297 *The army's third food crisis*: John Chaloner to Charles Stewart, May 23, 1778, Stewart Papers.

297 *Fortunately, the cattle drives*: Samuel Ward to Phoebe Ward, May 5, 1778, Ward Papers.

297 *"We have milk and sugar"*: Dr. S. Tenny to Dr. Peter Turner, April 10, 1778, Peter Turner Papers, Library of Congress.

297 *one of the most festive*: Elisha Stevens: Fragments of Memorandum, the War of Revolution, family published, 1924, p. 3.

298 *Directed adroitly by an officer*: John Laurens to Henry Laurens, May 7, 1778, *Correspondence of John Laurens*, pp. 168–71.

298 *Finally, in late afternoon*: Diary of George Ewing, quoted in *200 Years Ago Today at Valley Forge*.

299 *"I would not have believed"*: John Cropper Jr. to Peggy Cropper, May 29, 1778, Boyle, *Writings from the Valley Forge Encampment*, pp. 139–41.

299 *"but for the virtuous"*: James Varnum to Mrs. William Greene, March 7, 1778, VFHP.

299 *"Our army, though in"*: James Gray to his wife, Gray Papers, Huntington Library.

300 *"The poor dogs are"*: Gouverneur Morris to George Clinton, February 17, 1778, CONG IX: 117.

300 *"The soldiery discovered"*: Nathanael Greene to George Weedon, March 7, 1778, VFHP.

300 *"our illustrious Commander-in-Chief"*: Shaw, p. 45.

300 *"To see men without clothes"*: GW to John Bannister, April 21, 1778, GWW XI: 292.

300 *May also brought word*: Israel Shreve to GW, May 18, 1778, GWP.

301 *"the subjugation of America"*: Henry Knox to GW, January 3, 1778, Library of Congress, George Washington Papers.

301 *"the enemy threaten"*: Henry Laurens to John Laurens, May 31, 1778, Laurens XII; Anthony Wayne to Sharp Delaney, May 21, 1778, Boyle, *Writings from the Valley Forge Encampment*, p. 134; Henry Knox to William Knox, May 28, 1778, HK.

301 *In mid-May*: GW to Colonel Stephen Moylan, May 24, 1778, GWW XI: 446.

301 *All of the men*: GW to Major Richard Campbell, May 24, 1778, GWW XI: 446.

301 *General Smallwood's two brigades*: GW to William Smallwood, May 25, 1778, GWW XI: 449.

301 *"I am convinced"*: GW to Richard Henry Lee, May 25, 1778, GWW XI: 451.

301 *Washington was eager*: Quoted in a letter from a soldier at Valley Forge, March 9, 1778, *New Jersey Gazette*, March 18, 1778.

302 *On May 28*: General Orders, May 28, 1778, GWW XI: 463–64.

302 *Washington was brimming*: Annals of Medical History, p. 482.

302 *"I rejoice most sincerely"*: GW to Robert Morris, May 25, 1778, GWW XI: 453.

302 *The battle would not be fought*: Christopher Hibbert, *Redcoats and Rebels: The American Revolution through British Eyes*, New York: W.W. Norton Co., 1990, p. 222.

302 *The British army crossed*: Hibbert, *Redcoats and Rebels*, p. 223

Chapter Eleven: Starving to Death

305 *George Washington returned*: Scheer and Rankin, *Rebels and Redcoats*, p. 367; Robert Parker Diary, *Pennsylvania Magazine of History and Biography* 28 (1904): 23.

306 *The general's eyes squinted*: Miers, *Crossroads of Freedom: The American Revolution and the Rise of a New Nation*, New Brunswick, N.J., Rutgers University Press, 1971, p. 191.

306 *The commander-in-chief had not decided*: GW to General Alexander McDougall, November 13, 1779, GWW XVII: 100–102.

307 *"to encamp the whole army"*: GW to Nathanael Greene, November 23, 1779, GWW XVII: 167–68; GW to Congress, December 4, 1779, GWW VII: 216–17.

307 *He also liked the idea*: Greene to GW, November 27, 1779, GREENE V: 118–20.

307 *Morristown and the hamlets*: Thayer, *Colonial and Revolutionary Morris County*, pp. 210–13.

308 *There had been ominous signs*: William Irvine to Joseph Reed, December 12, 1779, in Irvine Papers, NYHS.

308 *Four November snowfalls*: GW to Jeremiah Wadsworth, November 27, 1779, GWW XVII: 201.

308 *"alarming"*: GW to General William Heath, November 18, 1779, GWW XVII: 123.

308 *"do all in your power"*: GW to Alexander McDougall, November 22, 1779, GWW XVII: 161–62.

308 *The general sent an order*: GW to James Wilkinson, December 6, 1779, GWW XVII: 221.

308 *"The deficiency of shoes"*: GW to James Wilkinson, December 22, 1779, GWW XVII: 300.

309 *"to hurry the transportation"*: GW to James Wilkinson, December 22, 1779, GWW XVII: 300.

309 *He had arrived in Morristown*: Miers, *Crossroads of Freedom*, p. 195.

309 *Somewhere along the line*: GW to General William Heath, November 16, 1779, GWW XVII: 113.

309 *difficult to pay for the supplies*: John Cox to Greene, December 6, 1779, GREENE V: 151.

309 *British were flooding the states*: GW to Congress, December 7, 1779, GWW XVII: 231

309 *Washington worried about the weather*: Almon Lauber, ed., *Orderly Books of the Fourth New York Regiment, With the Diaries of Samuel Tallmadge, 1780–1782, and John Barr, 1779–1782*, Albany, N.Y.: 1932, p. 717.

310 *"stormy snow"*: Ludlum, *History of Early American Winters*, pp. 120–21.

310 *made troop movement difficult*: Parker, *Pennsylvania Magazine of History* 28, p. 23.

310 *As soon as he was settled*: GW to General Nathanael Greene, November 17, 1779, GWW XVII: 118–19; General Orders, November 19, 1777, GWW XVII: 137.

311 *"I rode out today"*: *New Jersey Gazette*, December 18, 1779, p. 3.

311 *"it began to snow"*: Ludlum, *History of Early American Winters*, pp. 120–21.

311 *The storm, which lasted*: Edward Field, ed., *The Diary of Colonel Israel Angell, Commanded the Second Rhode Island Continental Regiment During the Revolution*, New York: New York Times/Arno Press, 1971, reprinted from Providence: Proctor and Rounds Co., 1899, p. 100.

312 *"The snow on the ground"*: Thacher, *Military Journal*, pp. 180–81.

312 *"if you saw my situation"*: Erkuries Beatty to Reading Beatty, December 29, 1779, "Letters of Erkuries Beatty," *Pennsylvania Magazine of History and Biography* 14, 1890, p. 205.

312 *"we have had such a terrible"*: Ludlum, *Early American Winters*, pp. 120–23.

313 *Grist mills had no wheat*: GW to General William Heath, December 20, 1779, PGW IV, Revised Series, microfilm.

313 *A depressed Washington*: GW to Samuel Huntington, December 10, 1779, Anthony Wayne to GW, December 9, 1779, PGW IV, Revised Series, microfilm.

314 *"Here is an expensive army"*: Nathanael Greene to Samuel Huntington, December 12, 1779, GREENE V: 166.

314   *"the people will pull"*: Nathanael Greene to Daniel Brodhead, December 18, 1779, GREENE V: 182.

314   *"Our prospects are infinitely worse"*: GW to Huntington, December 15, 1779, GWW XVII: 272–73.

314   *The commander-in-chief was wrong*: JCC XV: 135–36.

314   *The following day Congress*: JCC XV: 1358–59, XVI: 44–45.

315   *"every last schilling"*: Thomas Jefferson to Congress, December 10, 1779, PGW IV, Revised Series.

315   *Congress ordered six states*: JCC XV: 1368–72.

315   *Emergency letters*: Samuel Huntington to Maryland Governor Thomas Johnson, CONG XIV: 267–68.

315   *On the 14th*: PGW IV, Revised Series, December 14, 1779.

315   *"The military chest"*: JCC XV: 1354.

315   *"A treasury without money"*: William Houston to William Livingston and Caleb Camp, December 20, 1779, CONG XIV: 282–83.

315   *That same day*: Samuel Huntington to Jonathan Trumbull, December 20, 1779, CONG XIV: 284.

315   *"drained the public treasury"*: Samuel Huntington to Caesar Rodney, December 20, 1779, CONG XIV: 290.

315   *"Congress is at its wits end"*: William Ellery to William Greene, December 21, 1779, CONG XIV: 288.

316   *"Our [food] magazines"*: Circular, GWW XVII: 273–74.

316   *New Jersey's representatives*: *New Jersey Gazette*, December 29, 1779, p. 1.

316   *The legislature also ordered*: A cavalry leader, Henry Champion, had complained to Washington on December 14 that he could not feed his men because local residents refused credit to buy cattle, PGW IV, Revised Series.

316   *Maryland did even more*: S. Sydney Bradford, "Hunger Menaces the Revolution," *Maryland Historical Magazine* 61, March 1966, pp. 1–23.

317   *"that America, after having so long"*: William Livingston to GW, December 21, 1779, LIV III: 277.

318   *"But on December 18"*: Ludlum, *Early American Winters*, pp. 120–21.

318   *"when the weather would admit"*: Bray and Bushnell, *Diary of a Common Soldier*, p. 145.

318   *"the severity of the weather"*: Henry Johnston, ed., *Records of Connecticut Men in the War of the Revolution, 1775–1783*, Hartford, Conn.: 1889.

318   *When they did finish*: Lauber, *Orderly Books of the Fourth New York Regiment*, pp. 264, 205.

318   *"Our situation at this time"*: Joseph Plumb Martin, *Private Yankee Doodle*, p. 166.

318   *The December 18 storm*: The number of storms and their intensity were recorded by a professor Atwater at Yale College, Ludlum, pp. 114–15.

318   *The foot and a half of snow*: *New Jersey Gazette*, February 9, 1780, p. 3.

319   *The ice would not melt until*: *New York Gazette*, February 16, 1780.

319   *In perhaps the most unprecedented*: Ludlum, *Early American Winters*, pp. 115–16.

319   *Sometimes British cavalry*: *New York Gazette and Weekly Mercury*, February 22, 1780.

319   *But the most serious consequence*: *New Jersey Gazette*, March 13, 1780.

319   *Food dwindled*: GW to Anthony Wayne, December 19, 1779, GWW XVII: 288.

319   *He was livid*: Bradford, "Hunger Menaces the Revolution," p. 10; Risch, *Supplying Washington's Army*, p. 424.

320   *"Money, money, money"*: Ibid., p. 9.

320   *"Payment has been so long"*: Joseph Lewis to GW, December 25, 1779, Joseph Lewis letterbook, PARK.

320   *"Outside of my [hut]"*: Ekuries Beatty to Reading Beatty, December 26, 1779, Beatty letters, PARK.

320   *"like the Israelites"*: Jeremiah Wadsworth to Greene, December 23, 1779, GREENE V: 199–200.

320   *The commander had sent*: Bradford, "Hunger Menaces the Revolution," p. 11.

320   *"They receive us with coldness"*: Nathanael Greene to General George Weedon, December 25, 1779, GREENE V: 209.

320   *Greene's own aides*: Petition of Col. Udny Hay, December 9, 1779, petition of express riders, December 26, 1779, GREENE V: 220.

320   *"In passing through the camp"*: General Orders, December 25, 1780, GWW XVII: 320.

321   *"I can only say"*: GW to General Enoch Poor, December 26, 1779, GWW XVII: 325.

321   *"with a fair wind"*: Ed Paul, ed., *Journals of Hugh Gaines, Printer*, 2 vols., New York: Dodd, Mead and Co., 1902, vol. 1, pp. 74–75.

321   *More than eight thousand seasoned*: New Jersey Gazette, January 5, 1780, p. 3.

321   *"I beg you to set"*: Nathanael Greene to Moore Furman, December 1, 1779, GREENE V: 135.

322   *"Do not let your mill"*: Joseph Lewis to Will Bayard, January 3, 1780, JL.

322   *"200,000 feet of boards"*: Joseph Lewis to Major Peter Gordon, January 26, 1780, JL.

322   *He was so desperate for wood*: Joseph Lewis to Major Peter Gordon, to Constant Cooper, February 2, 1780, JL.

322   *"bring these at once"*: Joseph Lewis notation, January 8, 1780, JL.

322   *"Hurry and get 2,000"*: Joseph Lewis note to uncle, January 1, 1780, JL.

322   *"I am hourly called"*: Joseph Lewis to Sam Haines, January 1, 1780, JL.

322   *"persuade [neighbors] to thrash"*: Joseph Lewis to John Carle, January 1, 1780, JL.

322   *"[It was] the greatest picture of misery"*: Thayer, *Colonial and Revolutionary Morris County*, p. 224.

323   *The soldiers' theft*: Quartermaster General's Receipt Book in the Revolution, NJHS (July 1920) 11: 364–68; *Claims to Damages Done by Americans, Morris County*, New Jersey State Library, Archives and History.

323   *The officers were obligated*: New Jersey Journal, January 26, 1780, p. 3.

323   *"We are now as distressed"*: Joseph Lewis to Moore Furman, January 8, 1780, JL.

324   *"The General most earnestly"*: General Orders, Dec. 28, 1779, GWW XVII: 331–332.

324   *"I have it not in my power"*: GW to Huntington, January 5, 1780, GWW XVII: 357–358.

325   *simply ran out of food*: Nathanael Greene to Moore Furman, January 4, 1780, GREENE V: 230.

325   *Two days later Wadsworth*: Jeremiah Wadsworth to GW, January 3, 1780, PGW IV, Revised Series.

325   *Wadsworth reminded the general*: General Orders, January 3, 1780, GWW XVII: 343.

325   *It is lamentable*: GW to Royal Flint, January 4, 1780, GWW XVII: 351.

325   *The Board of War informed Congress*: JCC XVI: 35–36.

326   *The thick, wet snow*: George Clinton to GW, January 6, 1780, Papers of George Clinton V: 446.

326   *"the wind has piled up"*: Ludlum, *Early American Winters*, pp. 122–26.

326   *"We experienced one of the most"*: Thayer, *Colonial History of Morris County*, p. 185.

327   *"We scarcely get anything to eat"*: Martin, *Private Yankee Doodle*, p. 178.

327   *"The sufferings of the poor soldiers"*: Thayer, *Colonial History of Morris County*, p. 185.

327   *"The troops, both officers and men"*: GW to Samuel Huntington, January 5, 1780, GWW XVII: 358.

328   *"Poor fellows"*: Thayer, *Colonial and Revolutionary Morris County*, p. 256.

328   *"They exhibit a picture"*: Nathanael Greene to Moore Furman, January 4, 1780, GREENE V: 230.

328   *The blizzard had trapped*: Hoyt, *New Jersey and the Revolutionary War*, p. 92; Lundin, *Cockpit of the Revolution*, p. 420.

329   *"If it is not used"*: GW to Joseph Reed, July 4, 1780, William Reed, ed., *A Reprint of the Original Letters from Washington to Joseph Reed during the American Revolution*, Philadelphia, Pa.: Carey & Chart, 1852, p. 146.

329   *"the less of the two"*: William Houston to Caleb Camp and William Livingston, December 20, 1779, CONG XIV: 283.

329   *"The situation of our affairs"*: Samuel Holton to Sam Adams, January 4, 1780, CONG XIV: 318.

329 *"We are at the very pinch of the game"*: William Ellery to William Greene, December 21, 1779, CONG XIV: 288.

330 *"God have mercy upon us"*: Greene to Wadsworth, January 5, 1779, GREENE V: 230

331 *"which will be disagreeable"*: GW to the Justices of Morris County (and New Jersey), January 8, 1780, GWW XVII: 362–65.

333 *The total number of sleds*: The best description of how snow-covered roads were opened for traffic is by St. John de Crevecoeur in H. L. Bourdin, R. H. Gabriel, and S.T. Williams, *Sketches of Eighteenth Century America*, New Haven, Conn.: Yale University Press, 1925, pp. 39–50.

334 *"I should be wanting in justice"*: GW to Samuel Huntington, January 27, 1780, GWW XVII: 449–50.

334 *"You will permit me"*: GW to the Justices of Morris County, January 27, 1780, GWW XVII: 452.

Chapter Twelve: A War of Attrition and Ungrateful Hearts

335 *"I despise my countrymen"*: Ebenezer Huntington to Andrew Huntington, July 7, 1780, Ebenezer Huntington, *Letters Written By Ebeneezer Huntington during the American Revolution,* New York: C.F. Heartman, 1915, pp. 87–88.

336 *He learned that Lord Stirling*: GW to Henry Knox, January 13, 1780, GWW XVII: 399.

336 *"We shall be able to undertake"*: GW to Tench Tilghman, January 10, 1780, GWW XVII: 372.

337 *"You will please engage"*: Joseph Lewis to Morris County Justices, January 12, 1780, JL.

338 *Washington wanted him to succeed*: GW to Stirling, January 12, 1780, GWW XVII: 379.

338 *Finally, at precisely*: GW To Lord Stirling, January 14, 1780, GWW XVII: 391.

338 *attack was a dismal failure*: British Brigadier General Thomas Sterling to General Wilhelm Knyphausen, January 15, 1780, in GB XVIII: 39.

339 *"We took up our abode"*: Thayer, *Colonial and Revolutionary Morris County*, p. 229.

339 *"We arrived at camp"*: Martin, *Private Yankee Doodle*, p. 171–72.

339 *Another man estimated*: Thacher, *Military Journal*, p. 188.

339 *"Little hope remained"*: GW to Samuel Huntington, January 18, 1780, GWW XVII: 406.

339 *"we were disappointed"*: *New Jersey Gazette*, January 26, 1780.

340 *Even more disappointing*: William Duer, *The Life of Lord Stirling,* New York: Wiley and Putnam, 1847, pp. 205–207.

340 *"From the vast multitude"*: Lord Stirling to Washington, January 16, 1780 PGW, Series 3C.

340 *Also unsettling to Washington*: General Orders, January 22, 1780, GWW XVII: 424.

340 *"Lordship" was "beneath contempt"*: *New York Royal Gazette and Weekly Mercury*, February 9, 1780.

340 *The members of Congress*: Miers, *Crossroads of Freedom*, p. 199.

340 *"the enemy on all sides"*: *New Jersey Journal*, January 18, 1780.

340 *"This may serve to show"*: *New Jersey Gazette*, January 19, 1780.

341 *On January 25*: Lundin, *Cockpit of the Revolution*, p. 425, *Jersey Journal*, February 2, 1780.

343 *"rather remote from the army"*: GW to Silas Condict, February 1, 1780, GWW XVII, p. 474.

343 *The dragoons never got close*: D. B. Read, *The Life and Times of General John Graves Simcoe,* Toronto: Virtue Publishing, 1890, pp. 67–68.

344 *We need all the goods*: Ephraim Blaine to Board of War, February 6, 1780, Ephraim Blaine letterbook, PARK.

344 *Lengthy lists*: These were some of hundreds of claims filed in 1783 when the government agreed to compensate civilians who had been plundered. Local Magistrates investigated each claim to make certain that none were fraudulent.

345 *"no means in my power"*: GW to the Justices of Morris County and New Jersey, January 27, 1780, GWW XVII: 452.

346 *"The General is astonished"*: General Orders, January 28, 1780, GWW XVII: 459–460.

346   *The general kept his word*: Thacher, *Military Journal*, p. 190.

346   *"the situation of the troops"*: James Wilkinson to the Board of War, January 7, 1780, PGW Revised Series, reel 3C, microfilm.

346   *There was clothing at Newburgh*: Tench Tilghman told Greene this in a February 18, 1780, letter, GWW XVIII: 23.

346   *two fires broke out*: GW to Huntington, February 14, 1780, GWW XVIII: 8.

346   *The general had hoped*: GW to Col. Josiah Starr, Lt. Col, Isaac Sherman of the First Connecticut, GWW XVIII: 117.

347   *"Outside of the tailors"*: Ekuries Beatty to Reading Beatty, January 25, 1780, Beatty letters, PARK.

347   *no money for transportation*: Joseph Lewis to Azariah Dunham., February 16, 1780, JL.

347   *Within ten days*: Joseph Lewis to Nathanael Greene, February 26, 1780; to Moore Furman, March 3, 1780, JL.

347   *"I can't let the [residents]"*: Joseph Lewis to Benjamin Freeman, January 20, 1780; to Constant Cooper, February 5, 1780, JL.

347   *Quartermasters were afraid*: Joseph Lewis to Constant Cooper, February 7, 1780. JL.

347   *"The hour is at hand"*: *New York Gazette and Weekly Mercury*, March 6, 1780.

348   *"I dread to mention"*: John Armstrong Sr. to Horatio Gates, February 16, 1780, CONG XIV: 423.

348   *The Congressional solution*: *Jersey Journal*, March 29, 1780.

348   *The goal of the plan*: William Floyd to Pierre Van Cortlandt, January 11, 1780, CONG XIV: 232.

348   *"the happiest expedient"*: Samuel Huntington's Letter to the States, March 20, 1790, CONG XIV: 521.

349   *Jacob Greene insisted on financial support*: Jacob Greene, writing as "Eumenes," *Jersey Journal*, December 13, 1779.

349   *"All our...operations"*: Anonymous letter by Alexander Hamilton, January, 1780, HAM II: 234–51.

350   *"We are a ruined people"*: Thayer, *Colonial and Revolutionary Morris County*, p. 246.

350   *He called any plan to give the states*: GW to Fielding Lewis, May 5, 1780, GWW XIX: 132.

351   *French and Spanish diplomats*: Notes of the French Minister recorded in the Secret Journal, Foreign Affairs, January, 1780, JCC XVI: 109.

351   *"The critical situation"*: Penn, Burke, and Jones to Caswell, February 9, 1780, CONG XIV: 404.

351   *"We must cut throats"*: James Lovell to Sam Adams, February 8, 1780, CONG XIV: 396.

352   *In the summer of 1779*: Hibbert, *Redcoats and Rebels*, pp. 258–59.

352   *groups called "Patriotic Societies"*: For the best summary of the British public's opposition to the war, see Dora Clark, *British Opinion and the American Revolution*, New Haven, Conn.: Yale University Press, 1930.

352   *Disenchantment in the British army*: Hibbert, *Redcoats and Rebels*, p. 261.

353   *"the only chance we have"*: Hibbert, *Redcoats and Rebels*, p. 249.

353   *"a parcel of blockheads"*: Hibbert, *Redcoats and Rebels*, p. 253.

354   *Washington believed that these published reports*: *London Magazine*, May 1780, reprinted in the *New Jersey Journal*, June 14, 1780.

354   *There were certainly historical precedents*: Victor Davis Hanson, "The Meaning of Tet," *American Heritage*, May 2001, p. 46.

355   *Edmund Burke reminded their countrymen*: Edmund Burke to John Farmer and John Harris, Sheriffs of Bristol, in Burke, *Speeches on the American War and Letter to the Sheriffs of Bristol*, Boston, Mass.: Gregg Press, 1972, pp. 172–73.

355   *"very cold—the wind being fresh"*: William Floyd to George Clinton, January 28, 1780, CONG XIV: 379.

355   *Another New Yorker reported*: Robert Livingston to John Jay, February 10, 1780, CONG XIV: 407.

355   *New Jersey was hit with a storm*: Lauber, *Orderly Books of the Fourth New York Regiment*, p. 717.

356   *"The cloud thickens"*: Charles Pettit to Greene, February 3, 1780, GREENE V: 339, GW to Greene, March 8, 1780, GWW XVIII: 89.

356   *"Our treasury is dry"*: Nathanael Greene to Alexander McDougall, March 1, 1780, GREENE V: 428.

357   *"folly of Congress"*: Nathanael Greene to Jeremiah Wadsworth, March 17, 1780, GREENE V: 459–60.

357   *"Our finances are completely deranged"*: Philip Schuyler to GW, March 7, 1780, Sparks, *Correspondence of the American Revolution*, vol. 2, p. 412.

357   *"Every wheel of the (government)"*: Baron Von Steuben to GW, March 26, 1780, Sparks, *Correspondence of the American Revolution*, vol. II, p. 420.

357   *"Our army threatened"*: James Madison to Thomas Jefferson, March 27, 1780, quoted in James Smith, ed., *The Republic of Letters: The Correspondence between Thomas Jefferson and James Madison, 1776–1826*, 3 vols., New York: W.W. Norton & Company, 1995, vol. 1, p. 126.

358   *"public business is in a wretched train"*: Nathanael Greene to GW, March 31, 1780, Sparks, *Correspondence of the American Revolution*, vol. 2, p. 424.

358   *"Blaine informed Congress"*: George Morton to Samuel Huntington, March 20, 1780, Blaine letters.

358   *"Surely Morris County is not so destitute"*: Joseph Lewis to Justice Brookfield, March 22, 1780, JL.

358   *"Good God!"*: Joseph Lewis to Moore Furman, March 23, 1780, JL.

359   *"ruin must follow"*: GW to Philip Schuyler, March 22, 1780, GWW XVIII: 137–138.

359   *"All public bodies"*: Joseph Reed to Nathanael Greene, February 14, 1780, GREENE V: 383.

359   *The men in the army*: Joseph Lewis to Nathanael Greene, August 6, 1780, JL.

359   *"The people of America"*: Shaw, p. 58.

359   *"And these are the people"*: John Kalb quoted in Miers, *Crossroads of Freedom*, p. 209.

360   *"for support of their families"*: Joseph Lewis to Moore Furman, January 31, 1780, JL.

360   *Washington felt little joy*: GW to General Robert Howe, March 30, 1780, GWW XVIII: 181.

360   *Men stationed in Pennsylvania*: General William Irvine to GW, George Clinton Papers V: 458.

360   *Colonel Morgan Lewis*: Col. Morgan Lewis to Nathanael Greene, February 4, 1780, GREENE V: 345.

360   *Washington was told repeatedly*: Col. Sidney Berry to Nathanael Greene, February 7, 1780, GREENE V: 351.

360   *"This is a circumstance so alarming"*: GW to Azariah Dunham, April 5, 1780, GWW XVIII: 220.

361   *"Congress are obliged"*: Philip Schuyler note, read in Congress, April 4, 1780, JCC XVI: 326.

361   *"It is impossible"*: General Orders, February 12, 1780, GWW XVIII: 5–6.

362   *birth of Kitty's fourth child*: Thane, *The Fighting Quaker*, p. 269.

363   *It is unknown when she met Hamilton*: Mitchell, *Alexander Hamilton: Youth to Maturity, 1755–1788*, pp. 196–98.

363   *"Adieu my charmer"*: Alexander Hamilton to Betsy Schuyler, March 17, 1780, HAM II: 186–87.

365   *"We kicked up a hell of a dust"*: Ekuries Beatty to Reading Beatty, March 13, 1780, Beatty letters, PARK.

365   *"tyrannical oppressions"*: General Orders, March 16, 1780, GWW XVIII: 120.

366   *"Mother was very much interested"*: Barbara Hoskins, Caroline Foster, Dorothea Roberts, and Gladys Foster, *Washington Valley: An Informal History*, Ann Arbor, Mich., 1960, pp. 57–58.

Chapter Thirteen: A Hero Turned Traitor

371   *That friction exploded*: Lauren Paine, *Benedict Arnold: Hero and Traitor*, London: Robert Hale, 1963, pp. 137–39.

371   *he asked Congress for federal bodyguards*: Samuel Huntington to Benedict Arnold, October 6, 1779, CONG XIV: 35.

372   *Following an investigation*: Samuel Huntington to GW, March 11, 1780, CONG XIV: 487. Congress confirmed the sentence of the court martial, as required, but there was little discussion of it and the matter was promptly forgotten. Congressmen who informed legislators or friends in their home states of the verdict did so in a line or two, without opinion, William Houston to the N.J. Assembly, March 18, 1790, CONG XIV: 516.

372   *the Hannibal of the American army*: Reed, quoted in *The Proceedings of a General Court Martial for the Trial of Benedict Arnold, With an Introduction, Notes, and Index*, New York: 1865, p. 26.

372   *Benedict Arnold limped into Norris's Tavern*: Willard Randall, *Benedict Arnold: Patriot and Traitor*, New York: William Morrow, 1990, p. 186.

372   *"false, malicious and scandalous"*: Ray Thompson, *Benedict Arnold in Philadelphia*, Fort Washington, Pa.: The Bicentennial Press, 1975, pp. 117–21.

373   *"When the present necessary war"*: Arnold's testimony from *The Proceedings of a General Court Martial for the Trial of Benedict Arnold*, p. 102.

373   *One, Timothy Matlack, even said*: Matlack testimony from original transcript of court martial, first published in 1790, reprinted within *The Proceedings of a General Court Martial for the Trial of Benedict Arnold*, p. 41.

373   *The cocky Arnold*: Willard Wallace, *Traitor and Hero: The Life and Fortunes of Benedict Arnold*, New York: Harper Bros., 1954, p. 191.

373   *"delicacy in high station"*: Wallace, *Traitor and Hero: The Life and Fortunes of Benedict Arnold*, pp. 191–93.

374   *Washington did not even mail*: General Orders, April 6, 1780, GWW XVIII: 222–25.

374   *"Our profession is the character"*: Quoted in Paine, *Benedict Arnold: Hero and Traitor*, p. 139.

377   *farmers and merchants had complained*: E. Wayne Carp, *To Starve the Army at Pleasure*, p. 55.

377   *"this state is so exhausted"*: George Clinton to GW, April 24, 1780, Sparks, *Correspondence of the American Revolution*, vol. 2, pp. 440–41.

377   *"unless the speediest relief"*: Board of War to the Maryland legislature, March 7, 1780, quoted in Freeman, *George Washington*, vol. 5, p. 152.

378   *"We may possibly"*: GW to Henry Champion, April 12, 1780, GWW XVII: 252.

378   *On April 3 Greene informed*: Freeman, *George Washington*, vol. 5, pp. 155–56.

379   *He had asked for two hundred wagons*: GW to the Magistrates of New Jersey, April 15, 1780, GWW XVIII: 266–67.

379   *"There is no set of men"*: GW quoted in George Greene, *The Life of Nathanael Greene*, 3 vols., Cambridge, Mass.: Riverside Press, 1891, vol. 2, p. 329.

380   *"The fate of America"*: Mitchell, *Alexander Hamilton: Youth to Maturity, 1755—1788*, pp. 184–85.

381   *The diplomats were met about ten miles*: Miers, *Crossroads of Freedom*, pp. 207–208.

383   *Miralles did not have the opportunity*: Thacher, *Military Journal*, pp. 181–93.

384   *"The necessity of appointing"*: Ezekial Cornell to William Greene, August 1, 1780, CONG XV: 527–28.

385   *Lafayette's news elated Congress*: JCC May 21, 1780, XVII: 441, 447.

385   *Washington sent a letter*: GW to General Benjamin Lincoln, May 15, 1780, GWW XVIII: 362–363.

385   *Washington's real excitement*: GW to the Marquis de Lafayette, May 16, 1780, GWW XVIII: 369–73.

386   *"on the verge of mutiny"*: General William Heath to Governor George Clinton, December 16, 1780, Clinton Papers V: 109.

386   *"Our own wants and the sufferings"*: Letter from the troops at Poughkeepsie, February 5, 1780, Clinton Papers V: 479.

386   *And on March 24*: GW to Colonel Francis Johnston, March 24, 1780, GWW XVIII: 147.

387   *"in their present state they are actually suffering"*: GW to Samuel Huntington, April 3, 1780, GWW XVII: 207–211.

387   *"the soldiers are neither fed or paid"*: Nathanael Greene to Jeremiah Wadswroth, May 8, 1780, GREENE V: 550.

387   *"They were truly patriots"*: Martin, *Private Yankee Doodle*, p. 182.

387   *The mutineers warned other soldiers*: Thacher, *Military Journal*, pp. 197–98; Martin, *Private Yankee Doodle*, pp. 181–83.

388   *"We are apprehensive [they] will run"*: Greene to William Greene, May 27, 1780, GREENE V: 582–83.

388   *"Their sufferings were too great"*: GW to Samuel Huntington, May 27, 1780, GWW XVIII: 429–31.

388   *"indeed, I have almost ceased to hope"*: GW to Joseph Reed, May 28, 1780, GWW XVIII: 434–40.

388   *"proof that motives of honor"*: GW to Joseph Reed, May 28, 1780, GWW XVIII: 434–40.

388   *Just before Christmas*: Miers, *Crossroads of Freedom*, p. 210.

389   *"If it is a blessing"*: Alexander Hamilton to the Marquis de Barbe-Marbois, May 31, 1780, HAM II: 331–32.

389   *"the catastrophe is indeed disastrous"*: William Houston to William Livingston, June 5, 1780; Daniel of St. Thomas Jenifer to Thomas Sim Lee, June 5, 1780, CONG XV: 250, 255.

390   *And in Pennsylvania*: William Houston to William Livingston, June 4, 1780, CONG XV: 246.

390   *"An army that is reduced"*: Lafayette to Joseph Reed, May 31, 1780, quoted in Freeman, *George Washington*, vol. 5, p. 166.

390   *Washington was disconsolate*: GW to Joseph Jones, May 31, 1780, GWW XVIII: 454.

392   *"Can it, sir, be the design of heaven"*: Oliver Ellsworth to Jonathan Trumbull, March 28, 1780, CONG XIV: 549.

392   *"All private letters from the rebel countries"*: Lord George Germain to Sir Henry Clinton, May 3, 1780, GB XVIII: 82–64.

393   *But Washington was ready*: Diary of Sylvanus Seely, June 5, 1780.

393   *A large portion of the New Jersey brigade*: Thayer, *Colonial and Revolutionary Morris County*, p. 246.

394   *Elizabeth was not vulnerable*: White, *A Village at War*, p. 173.

395   *By 8:30 a.m. Washington*: GW to Major Jeremiah Talbot, June 7, 1780, GWW XVIII: 487.

395   *Knowing that the militia fought best*: GW to Lord Stirling, June 7, 1780, GWW XVIII: 490.

395   *"Cannon ball and grape shot"*: Green, *The Life of Ashbel Green*, pp. 112–14.

395   *On June 17*: Martin, *Private Yankee Doodle*, p. 188.

396   *Morristown was the target*: *New Jersey Journal*, June 14, 1780.

396   *"amidst the severest firing"*: Thacher, *Military Journal*, p. 201.

396   *Knyphausen then heard*: Thayer, *Colonial and Revolutionary Morris County*, p. 253.

396   *"The more we advanced"*: Bernard Uhlendorf, trans., *Revolution in America: Confidential Letters and Journals, 1776–1784 of Adjutant General Major Baurmeister of the Hessian Forces*, New Brunswick, N.J.: Rutgers University Press, 1957, p. 354.

397   *What they did not know*: Green, *The Life of Ashbel Green*, V.D.M., p. 121.[

397   *As they withdrew*: Scheer and Rankin, *Rebels and Redcoats*, p. 374.

397   *Soldiers torched and destroyed*: White, *A Village at War*, p. 173.

397   *"The British are flying!"*: White, *A Village at War*, p. 174.

397   *"I found the disposition of the inhabitants"*: Wilhelm Knuyphausen to Lord Germain, July 3, 1780, GB XVIII: 110.

397   *"without molestation evacuated the Jersies"*: Sir Henry Clinton to Lord Germain, July 4, 1780, GB XVIII: 112–13.

397   *"Fortunately for the rebel affairs"*: William Willcox, Ed., *Sir Henry Clinton, The American Rebellion: Sir Henry Clinton's Narrative of His Campaign, 1775–1782, With an Appendix of Original Documents*, New Haven, Conn.: Yale University Press, 1954, p. 194.

397   *"The whole scene was one of gloomy horror"*: Green, *The Life of Ashbel Green*, p. 121.

399   *"with admirable spirit"*: GW to General Robert Howe, June 10, 1780, GWW XVIII: 494–96.

399   *He told brother-in-law Fielding Lewis*: GW to Fielding Lewis, July 6, 1780, GWW XVIV: 129–34.

400   *"To tell a person at the distance"*: GW to John Augustine Washington, July 6, 1780, GWW XVIV: 135–37.

400   *"The present crisis is by far the most important"*: GW's Circular Letter to the States, June 30, 1780, GWW XVIV: 104–105.

401   *He wrote an abrupt letter to a Congressional delegate*: GW to James Bowdoin, June 14, 1780, GWW XVIV: 10.

401   *"The poor General was so unhappy"*: Martha Washington to Burwell Bassett, July 18, 1780, *Worthy Partner*, p. 183.

402   *"These things I thought seemed"*: John Hunt's Diary, May 30 and 31, 1780, NJHS, pp. 237–39.

Chapter Fourteen: The Great Slavery Debate
403   *"Your scheme...to encourage the emancipation"*: GW to Lafayette, April 5, 1783, GWW XXVI: 297–301.

404   *"To suppose this is not the proper time"*: Mitros, "Shepard Kollock and the New Jersey Journal," pp. 48–69.

405   *The debate was followed carefully*: Allen Hester, *South Jersey, A History*, New York, 1924, p. 49.

405   *New Jersey had the second highest*: Henry Cooley, *A Study of Slavery in New Jersey: Johns Hopkins University Studies in Historical and Political Science, 14th Series*, New York: Johnson Reprint, 1973, p. 31.

405   *Most worked in farming*: Hubert Schmidt, *Slavery and Attitudes on Slavery in Hunterdon County, N.J.*, Flemington: Hunterdon County Historical Society, 1941, p. 10.

405   *Others worked for merchants*: See Carol Karlsen and Laurie Crumpacker, eds., *Journal of Esther Edwards Burr*, New Haven, Conn.: Yale University Press, 1984.

405   *There were so many household slaves*: Jean Soderlund, *Quakers and Slavery: A Divided Spirit*, Princeton, N.J.: Princeton University Press, 1985, p. 75.

405   *Their first efforts were in 1693*: *Pennsylvania Magazine of History and Biography* 13, p. 268.

405   *Quaker anti-slavery speakers rode*: Theodore Noss, *The Awakening of the Quaker Movement Against Negro Slavery in Colonial Pennsylvania and Western New Jersey*, PhD diss., Chicago: University of Chicago Press, 1934, p. 56.

405   *When wickedness takes root*: John Woolman, *Some Considerations on the Keeping of Negroes*, Philadelphia, Pa.: James Chattin, 1754, Viking reprint, 1776.

406   *Anti-slavery advocates in Somerset County*: Edward Malberg, *Slavery as an Institution: New Jersey and the South*, PhD diss., New Brunswick, N.J.: Rutgers University, 1966, pp. 13–16.

406   *"odious and disgraceful"*: Cooley, *A Study of Slavery in New Jersey*, p. 23.

406   *While New Jersey debated*: *Historical Sketches of the Town of Leicester, Massachusetts*, Boston, Mass: 1860, p. 442–43.

406   *The slavery discussions*: Stephen Weeks, *Southern Quakers and Slavery: A Study in Institutional History*, Baltimore, Md.: Johns Hopkins University Press, 1896, pp. 201–15.

407   *"choice ones"*: PGW IX, Colonial Series: 70.

407   *On another occasion*: GW to James Mercer, July 19, 1773, PGW IX, Colonial Series: 282.

407   *I know of no black person*: GW to William Pearce, March 22, 1795, *Memoirs of Long Island: George Washington and Mount Vernon*, Brooklyn: 1899, vol. 4, p. 206.

407   *Washington never understood why*: Virginia Gazette, May 4, 1775.

407   *"I always used to lay"*: GW to William Pearce, December, 1793, *Memoirs of Long Island*, IV, pp. 17–28.

407   *"If you depend on me"*: GW to William Pearce, February 15, 1795, *Memoirs of Long Island*, p. 159.

407   *"Washington brought in doctors"*: Frtiz Hirschfield, *George Washington and Slavery: A Documentary Portrayal*, Columbia: University of Missouri Press, 1997, pp. 40–41.

407 *"sober, honest and industrious"*: GW to William Pearce, March 22, 1795, *Memoirs of Long Island,* IV, p. 178.

408 *"a worthless white man"*: GW to William Pearce, August 26, 1793, *Memoirs of Long Island,* IV, p. 5.

408 *"who are not always as kind"*: GW to Arthur Young, June 18, 1792, GWW XXXII: 65.

408 *"General Washington treats his slaves"*: Methie Budka, trans. Juliam Niemcewicz, *Under the Vine and Fig Tree: Travels through America, 1797–1799, 1805, With Some Further Account of Life in New Jersey,* Elizabeth, N.J.: Grassman, 1965, pp. 101–102.

408 *Throughout his life*: "Letters of George Washington Bearing on the Negro," *Journal of Negro History,* October 1917, pp. 411–22.

408 *"very mal-apropos"*: GW to David Stuart, March 28 and June 15, 1790, GWW XXXI: 30, 52.

408 *"Time, patience and education"*: Jacques Pierre Brissot de Warville, *New Travels in the United States of America, 1788,* trans. Mara Soceano Vamos and Durand Echevarria, ed. Durant Echevarria, Cambridge, Mass.: Harvard University Press, 1964, pp. 329–30.

408 *There were times when his feelings*: July 18, 1774, PGW X, Colonial Series: 154–56; *Virginia Gazette,* July 24, 1774.

409 *"We take this opportunity"*: Ibid.

409 *"tame and abject slaves"*: GW to Bryan Fairfax, August 24, 1774, PGW X, Colonial Series: 154–56.

409 *"the poor wretches"*: GW to Lund Washington, GWW XIV: 147–49.

409 *Like some other planters*: Alfred Cornwell and John Meyer, *The Economics of Slavery and Other Studies in Econometric History,* Chicago: Aldine Co., 1964, pp. 45–84.

409 *slave worker slowdowns*: Ira Berlin and Phillip Morgan, eds., *Cultivation and Culture: Labor and the Shaping of Slave Life in the Americas,* Charlottesville: University of Virginia Press, 1993, pp. 2–3.

409 *Virginians had embraced*: David Brion Davis, *The Problem of Slavery in the Age of Revolution,* Ithaca, N.Y.: Cornell University Press, 1965, p. 261.

409 *He was always surrounded by wealthy men*: Davis, *The Problem of Slavery in the Age of Revolution,* p. 267.

410 *"I every day long more and more*: GW to Lund Washington, August 15, 1778, GWW XII: 326–28.

410 *The anti-slavery activities of these men*: John Jay to Elias Boudinot, 1819, *Correspondence and Public Papers of John Jay,* 4 vols., New York: G.P. Putnam's Sons, 1893, vol. 4., pp. 430–43, reprint, Henry Johnston, ed., New York: DeCapo Press, 1971.

411 *lasting disgrace*: Samuel Allinson to Patrick Henry, October 12, 1774, Allinson Papers, Rutgers University Special Collections.

411 *"To continue for liberty"*: Charles Adams, ed., *The Letters of Mrs. Adams,* 2 vols., Boston, Mass.: 1841, vol. 1, p. 24.

411 *"those who barter away"*: James Otis, *The Rights of British Colonists Asserted and Proved,* 3rd ed., Boston, Mass.: 1766, pp. 43–44.

411 *"What foreign nation can believe"*: Mitros, "Shepard Kollock and the New Jersey Journal," p. 19.

412 *"I would never have drawn"*: William Nell, *The Colored Patriots of the American Revolution,* Boston, Mass.: Robert Eallot, 1855, p. 388

412 *"Your late purchase of an estate"*: GW to Marquis de Lafayette, May 10, 1786, PGW III, Confederation Series: 43.

412 *"there is not a man living"*: Lucas, *Quotable George Washington,* p. 89; GW to Laurence Lewis, August 4, 1797, GWW XXXVI: 2.

412 *"among my first wishes"*: GW to John Mercer, September 9, 1786, GWW XXIX: 5.

412 *"against that kind of traffic"*: "Letter of George Washington Bearing on the Negro," *Journal of Negro History,* pp. 419–20.

413 *"black corps"*: GW to William Heath, June 29, 1780, GWW XIX: 93.

413 *More than three thousand former slaves*: Major Henry Lee to GW, July 26, 1779, GWW XV: 488.

413 *He thought so much of slave"*: Alexander Hamilton to John Jay, March 14, 1779, HAM II: 17–18.

413 *"liberate a certain species"*: GW to Tobias Lear, May 6, 1794, GWW XXXIII: 358.

413 *"I would not, in twelve months"*: GW to Alexander Spotswood, November 23, 1794, GWW XXXIV: 47.

414 *"for his faithful service"*: GW will, July 9, 1799, GWW XXXVII: 277.

414 *"To make the adults among them"*: Quoted in Rosemary Zagarri, *David Humphreys, The Life of George Washington with General Washington's "Remarks,"* Athens: University of Georgia Press, 1991, p. 332.

415 *The army had been so much*: John Anderson, *Shepard Kollock: Editor for Freedom*, Chatham: Chatham Historical Society, 1975, pp. 6–7.

416 *"a channel of intelligence"*: GW to Philip Livingston, Elbridge Gerry and George Clymer, July 19, 1777, GWW V: 498–99.

416 *The lieutenant would get*: Kollock's obituary, *Newark Daily Advertiser*, July 30, 1839.

416 *To make the offer more palatable*: There were numerous deliveries of paper reams, as indicated in army records starting with a December 6, 1778, shipment. Kollock or his apprentice routinely picked up paper at Bound Brook or Morristown, ABEEL, December 6, 1778.

416 *when the army ran out of paper*: John Cox to Abeel, July 19, 1779, ABEEL.

417 *Washington furthermore assured him*: Richard Claiborne to Abeel, April 9, 1779, ABEEL.

417 *Washington did not take Livingston's advice*: Harold Thatcher, "The Social and Economic Ideas of New Jersey's First Governor," NJHS, vol. 60, no. 4, 1942, p. 236.

418 *Mason explained to a naïve Washington*: George Mason to GW, April 5, 1769, GWW II: 504.

418 *"Join or Die!"*: Sidney Kobre, *The Development of the Colonial Newspaper*, Pittsburgh, Pa.: Colonial Press, 1944, p. 153.

418 *"The country which our fathers"*: Arthur Schlesinger, *Prelude to Independence*, New York: Alfred Knopf, 1958, p. 201.

418 *Newspapers had grown rapidly*: Bernard Bailyn and John Hench, eds., *The Press and the American Revolution*, Worcester, Mass.: American Antiquarian Society, 1980, pp. 132–36.

418 *served as editors of the newspapers*: John Holt to Samuel Adams, January 29, 1776, N.H. Paltsits, "John Holt: Printer and Postmaster," *New York Public Library Bulletin* 24, 1920, p. 494.

419 *the newspapers a powerful information network*: Michael Warner, *The Letters of the Republic: Publication and the Public Sphere in Eighteenth-Century America*, Cambridge, Mass.: Harvard University Press, 1990, pp. 68–69.

419 *"the pen and the press"*: Schlesinger, *Prelude to Independence*, p. vii.

419 *the press was the single most powerful*: Warner, *The Letters of the Republic*, p. 32.

419 *Rivington's pro-British paper*: Warner, *The Letters of the Republic*, p. 222.

419 *the subsidized New Jersey Journal*: New Jersey Journal (NJJ), May 10, 1780.

420 *The Journal often ran*: Anderson, *Shepard Kollock: Editor for Freedom*, p. 35.

420 *the standard of America*: NJJ, May 31, 1780.

420 *that our illustrious Washington*: NJJ, October 31, 1781.

420 *a nation crumbling to pieces*: NJJ, March 8, 1780.

420 *"exuberantly supplied with provision"*: NJJ, quoted in David Mitros, "Shepard Kollock and the New Jersey Journal," *The County Circular*, Morris County Heritage Commission (Winter 2001), p. 7.

420 *The* Journal *was careful*: NJJ, February 9, 1780.

421 *"discontent, jealousies and uneasiness"*: GW to Joseph Reed, October 22, 1779, Reed, *A Reprint of the Original Letters*, p. 145.

422 *Mutinies were the result*: Jeremy Black, *War for America: The Fight for Independence, 1775–1783*, New York: St. Martin's Press, 1991, p. 53.

422 *"There is such a combination"*: GW to Joseph Reed, May 28, 1780, Reed, *A Reprint of Original Letters from Washington to Joseph Reed During the American Revolution*, p. 136.

423 *Outraged, hungry and justly feeling*: Lundin, *Cockpit of the Revolution*, pp. 439–40.

423 *The Pennsylvania General, Anthony Wayne*: John Hyde Preston, *A Gentleman Rebel: Mad Anthony Wayne*, Garden City, N.Y.: Garden City Books, 1930, pp. 210–14.

424   *Wayne had found himself:* Carl Van Doren, *Mutiny in January*, New York: Viking Press, 1943, pp. 41–50.

424   *He decided to capitalize:* Flexner, *George Washington in the American Revolution*, pp. 406–407.

424   *The mutineers again told Wayne:* Leckie, *George Washington's War*, pp. 592–94; John Sullivan to the Chevalier de la Lucerne, January 13, 1781, CONG XVI: 597.

425   *The negotiators tried to reach:* Lynn Montross, *The Reluctant Rebels, The Story of the Continental Congress, 1774–1789*, New York: Harper and Brothers, 1930, pp. 304–305.

425   *a compromise was struck:* Committee on the Pennsylvania Mutiny Draft Proclamation, January 10, 1781, CONG XVI: 585.

425   *Despite a general agreement:* John Tebbel, *Turning the World Upside Down: Inside the American Revolution*, New York: Orion Books, 1993, pp. 367–70.

427   *"For more than three years":* Alexander Hamilton to Philip Schuyler, February 18, 1781, HAM II: 561–68.

428   *"without a shadow of reason":* Alexander Hamilton to James McHenry, February 18, 1791, HAM II: 569.

428   *In the end, there was no resolution:* Broadus Mitchell, *Alexander Hamilton: The Revolutionary Years*, New York: Thomas Crowell Company, 1970, pp. 272–75.

429   *the winter of 1781:* Oliver Wolcott to Oliver Ellsworth, January 2, 1781, CONG XVI: 542.

429   *The government had so much trouble:* Charles Thomson to John Dickinson, December 25, 1780, CONG XVI: 486.

430   *The general's despondency was mirrored:* Oliver Wolcott and Jesse Root to Jonathan Trumbull, January 16, 1781, CONG XVI: 605.

430   *"When we first engaged in this contest":* Charles Thomson to John Dickinson, December 25, 1780, CONG XVI: 493.

430   *"It is our duty to make every proper exertion":* Samuel Adams to Richard Henry Lee, January 15, 1781, CONG XVI: 599.

431   *"we are daily and hourly oppressing":* DGW II: 207–208.

431   *"One of the main complaints":* Royster, *Revolutionary People*, 304–305.

431   *"the glorious prize":* Tench Tilghman to Robert Morris, December 22, 1780, Charles Thomson Papers, vol. 1: 455–58.

Chapter Fifteen: Coup d'Etat

435   *Washington had captured:* Flexner, *Washington: The Indispensable Man*, pp. 154–64.

438   *"Be assured, sir":* GWW XXIV: 272.

438   *The eighteen-month lag:* GWW XXIV: 295–96.

438   *"Is it policy, is it justice":* GWW XXIV: 289–90.

439   *They were supported by Washington:* JCC, October 21, 1780, XVIII: 257.

440   *"a train of evil":* GWW XXV: 227–28.

440   *The officers' anger:* Burnett, *Letters of the Continental Congress*, VII: xiv–xiv.

440   *Despite Washington's lobbying:* GWW XXV: 430.

440   *"Those acquainted with the deliberations":* Joseph Jones to GW, February 27, 1778, CONG XVIX: 745–46.

441   *Alexander Hamilton:* Alexander Hamilton to GW, February 13, 1783, Syrett, *The Papers of Alexander Hamilton*, vol. 2, pp. 253–55.

441   *"exclude some other leader":* Madison's "Note on Debates," William Hutchinson and William Rachal, *The Papers of James Madison*, 17 vols. Chicago: University of Chicago Press, vol. 6, p. 266.

441   *Hamilton and Madison:* Richard Kohn, "The Inside History of the Newburgh Conspiracy: the Army and the Coup D'Etat *William and Mary Quarterly*, 3rd series 27 (1970): 187–220.

441   *"both officers and soldiers":* Bartlett, p. 303.

441   *"Reports are freely circulated":* Joseph Jones to GW, February 27, 1783, PGW, reel 90.

442   *"If this, then, be your treatment":* JCC XXIV: 295–96.

442   *rumors swirled throughout Philadelphia:* GW to Congress, March 12, 1783, GWW XXVI: 211–12.

442 *"must be answerable"*: GW to Joseph Jones, March 12, 1783, GWW XXVI: 213–16.

443 *And, too, as he told Hamilton later*: GW to Hamilton, April 16, 1783, Syrett, *The Papers of Alexander Hamilton*, vol. 3, pp. 329–30.

443 *The commander-in-chief decided to buy himself time*: General Orders, March 12, 1783, *General Orders of George Washington Issued at Newburgh-on-the-Hudson, 1782–1783*, Harrison, N.Y.: Harbor Hill Books, 1973, p. 70.

443 *He walked across the stage*: Flexner, *George Washington in the America Revolution*, pp. 506–508.

444 *"as you value your own sacred honor"*: Newburgh Speech, written March 12, 1783, delivered March 15, GWW XXVI: 222–27.

445 *"I have never left your side"*: Newburgh Speech, written March 12, 1783, delivered March 15, GWW XXVI: 222–27.

445 *"There was something so natural"*: Shaw, p. 104.

446 *Some men shuddered at his words*: Randell, *George Washington*, p. 396.

446 *"affectionate sentiments expressed"*: General Orders, March 18, 1783, *General Orders Issued at Newburgh*, p. 72.

446 *"the last glorious proof of patriotism"*: GW to Congress, March 18, 1783, GWW XXVI: 229–230.

Chapter Sixteen: Cincinnatus

447 *"the task is now accomplished"*: Circular Letter to the States, June 8, 1783, GWW XXVI: 483–96.

448 *"I am become a private citizen"*: GW to Lafayette, February 1, 1784, GWW XXVII: 317.

449 *"he would be the greatest man"*: George II quoted in Garry Wills, *Cincinnatus: George Washington and the Enlightenment*, Garden City, N.Y.: Doubleday, 1984, p. 13.

450 *"dangerous to the liberties"*: GW, Sentiments of a Peace Establishment to Congress, May 2, 1783, GWW XXVI: 375.

450 *"When we assumed the soldier"*: GW to the New York Legislature, June 26, 1775, GWW III: 305.

450 *"as the sword was the last resort"*: GW to Robert Morris, George Clymer and George Walton, January 1, 1777, GWW VI: 464.

452 *"it could not be believed"*: GW to Nathanael Greene, February 6, 1785, GWW XXVI: 104.

452 *"Nothing now remains"*: General orders, April 18, 2001, GWW XXVI: 336.

452 *"I shall no more appear*: GW to George Clinton, December 28, 1783, GWW XXVII: 288

454 *"The glorious task"*: General Orders, April 18, 1783, GWW XXVI: 334–37.

455 *"The simple thought"*: Freeman *George Washington*, vol. 5, p. 466; *Memoir of Benjamin Talmadge*, quoted in Meltzer, pp. 182–84.

456 *When he had finished embracing*: Flexner, *George Washington in the American Revolution*, p. 524.

457 *There was jubilation in Philadelphia*: Freeman, *George Washington*, vol. 5, pp. 469–72.

457 *"I consider the approbations"*: GW to Lafayette, February 1, 1784, GWW XXVII: 318.

457 *"I shall no more appear"*: Randall, *George Washington*, pp. 404–406.

458 *Washington arrived in Annapolis*: GW letters to the Common Council and General Assembly, December 22, 1783, GWW XXVII: 281–83.

459 *"Competent powers to Congress"*: GW to Lafayette, February 1, 1784, GWW XXVII: 318.

459 *The dinner was merely the start*: James Tilton to Gunning Bedford Jr., December 25, 1783, CONG XXI: 232.

459 *"thus he will retire"*: Elbridge Gerry to Samuel Holten, December 20, 1783, CONG XXI: 215.

459 *"the flattering sentiment"*: GW to the Governor of Maryland, December 23, 1783, GWW XXVII: 182–83.

460 *"having now finished the work assigned me"*: GW to Congress, December 23, 1783, GWW XXVII: 284–85.

460 *"So many circumstances"*: James McHenry to Margaret Caldwell, December 23, 1783, CONG XXI: 221.

461 *"our illustrious hero"*: David Howell to William Greene, December 24, 1783, CONG XXI: 224–29; Burnett, *Letters of the Continental Congress*, p. 591; Thacher, *Military Journal*, p. 349.

461 *Washington had no desire to remain in Annapolis*: David Howell to William Greene, December 24, 1783, CONG XXI: 224–29.

Epilogue: "I Do Solemnly Swear..."

464 *"I bade adieu to Mount Vernon"*: DGW V: 445.

464 *"Washington crossed the Hudson river"*: DGW V: 477.

464 *On the New York side of the harbor*: DGW V: 478 note.

467 *Washington made his views*: William Michaelsen, *Creating the American Presidency, 1775–1789*, Boston, Mass: University Press of America, 1987, pp. 70–76.

467 *"be assured that [George Washington's] influence"*: Richard Harwell, ed., Douglas Southall Freeman, *George Washington*, abridged ed., New York: Collier Books, 1968, p. 554.

467 *"Although the agency"*: Discarded address quoted in William B. Allen, "George Washington and the Standing Oak," Gary Gregg and Matthew Spalding, eds., *Patriot Sage: George Washington and the American Political Tradition*, Wilmington, Del.: ISI Books, 1999, p. 119.

468 *"I called to mind the days"*: GW to Marquis de Lafayette, December 8, 1784, GWW XXVIII: 7.

468 *"is to live and die"*: Rosemary Zagari, ed., David Humphreys, *The Life of George Washington, with General Washington's "Remarks,"* Athens: University of Georgia Press, 1991, pp. 43–47.

468 *"my movement to the chain of government"*: GW to Henry Knox, PGW II.

468 *"I am persuaded"*: John Jay to Washington, cited in John Schroeder, ed., *Maxims of George Washington: Political, Military, Social, Moral and Religious*, Mount Vernon, N.Y.: Mount Vernon Ladies Association, 1989, p. 193.

469 *"but when the exigence"*: Gary Gregg II, "The Symbolic Dimensions of the First Presidency," Gregg and Spalding, *Patriot Sage*, p. 185.

469 *"unfeigned reluctance"*: GW to Marquis de Lafayette, January 29, 1789, PGW I, Pres. Series: 263.

469 *"that the government"*: GW to Catherine Macauley Graham, January 9, 1790, GWW XXX: 496.

470 *The most jarring episode was Shays Rebellion*: Gordon Wood, *The Creation of the American Republic, 1776–1787*, New York: W.W. Norton Co., 1969, pp. 277–465.

470 *The tumult changed Washington's thinking*: Harold Bradley, "The Political Thinking of George Washington," *Journal of Southern History* (November 1945), pp. 472–74.

470 *Back in 1783, his final year in the army*: Glenn Phelps, *George Washington and American Constitutionalism*, Lawrence: University Press of Kansas, 1993, pp. 67–69.

471 *"Without an entire community"*: GW's Circular to the States, June 8, 1783, GWW XXVI: 484–86.

471 *"directed by thirteen heads"*: GW to the Rev. William Gordon, July 8, 1783, GWW XXVII: 49.

471 *"He told friends that the hopes"*: GW to Bushrod Washington, January 10, 1784, GWW XXVII: 417.

471 *"run riot until we have brought our reputation"*: GW to Benjamin Harrison, January 18, 1784, GWW XXVII: 305–306.

471 *"our affairs are drawing rapidly"*: GW to John Jay, August 1, 1786, GWW XXVIII: 502.

471 *What, gracious God*: GW to David Humphreys, December 26, 1786, GWW XXIX: 125.

471 *"critical period"*: GW to Charles Carter, December 14, 1787, GWW XXIX: 339.

471 *"I cannot help flattering"*: GW to Marquis de Lafayette, January 29, 1789, PGW I, Pres. Series: 262.

471 *"these powers...are so distributed"*: GW to Marquis de Lafayette, February 7, 1788, GWW XXVIII: 410.

473 *This political home*: GW to David Stuart, July 26, 1789, PGW I, Pres. Series: 321.

473 *He corresponded with trusted friends*: GW to David Stuart, July 26, 1789, PGW I, Pres. Series: 321.

473 *he made lengthy tours*: Mark Rozell, "Washington and the Origins of Presidential Power," Gregg and Spalding, *Patriot Sage*, p. 125.

474 *"TO THE MAN WHO UNITES ALL HEARTS"*: DGW V: 457.

474 *"On Monday the second"*: *Virginia Herald*, May 26, 1791.

474 *"In all of his negotiations"*: Contannes quoted in *History of the George Washington Bicentennial Celebration*, vol. 1, p. 37.

475 *He had to move carefully*: GW to James Madison, May 5, 1769, GWW XXX: 311.

475 *"Many things which appear"*: "Queries on a line of conduct," GW's notes, May 10, 1789, GWW XXX: 321.

476 *"on untrodden ground"*: Smith, *Patriarch*, p. 24.

476 *"Perhaps the strongest feature"*: Jefferson quoted in George Milton, *Use of Presidential Power, 1789–1943*, Boston, Mass.: Little, Brown and Company, 1944, pp. 25–26.

477 *The president even took great care*: Joshua Mercereau to GW, July 13, 1789, PGW I, Pres. Series: 189.

477 *President Washington controlled*: McDonald, *The American Presidency*, pp. 226–28.

477 *The cabinet did not meet*: Milton, *The Use of Presidential Power, 1789–1943*, pp. 29–33.

478 *Washington was shrewd enough*: Neustadt, *Presidential Power and the Modern Presidents*, pp. 138–39.

478 *The president's cabinet*: Glenn Phelps, "George Washington: Precedent Setter," Thomas Cronin, ed., *Inventing the American Presidency*, Lawrence: University of Kansas Press, 1989, pp. 271–73.

480 *"the proper source of American wealth"*: GW to Theodorick Bland, August 15, 1786, GWW XXXVIII: 517.

480 *war had taught him that*: Smith, *Patriarch*, p. 80.

480 *Washington had arrived in New York*: Neustadt, *Presidential Power and the Modern Presidents*, pp. 150–51.

481 *"implied powers"*: Hamilton quoted in Robert Hendrickson, *Hamilton II: 1789–1804*, New York: Mason/Charter, 1976, pp. 80–81.

482 *"let us as a nation"*: Circular to the States, June 8, 1783, GWW XXVI: 489.

482 *"No pecuniary consideration"*: GW to the House of Representatives, December 3, 1793, GWW XXXIII: 168.

483 *Washington was uncertain*: Randall, *George Washington*, pp. 488–89.

483 *"has demonstrated that our prosperity"*: Address to Congress, November 19, 1794, GWW XXXIV: 34.

484 *President Washington, angered*: GW to General Arthur St. Clair, October 6, 1789, PGW IV, Pres. Series: 141.

484 *The president urged Congress*: James Arnold, *President Under Fire: Commanders-in-Chief in Victory and Defeat*, New York, Orion Books, 1994, p. 72.

484 *The president then replaced Harmar*: Alexander DeConde, *Presidential Machismo: Executive Authority, Military Intervention, and Foreign Relations*, Boston, Mass.: Northeastern University Press, 2000, pp. 214–17.

484 *"shock humanity"*: State of the Union address, December 6, 1795, GWW XXXIV: 387–92.

486 *"this defeats every purpose"*: McDonald, *The American Presidency*, p. 222.

486 *Washington held firm*: Ryan Barilleaux, "Foreign Policy and the First Commander-in-Chief," Gregg and Spalding, *Patriot Sage*, pp. 250–52.

486 *He issued the controversial proclamation*: McDonald, The *American Presidency*, pp. 237–38.

487 *"I have no inclination to touch"*: GW to Dr. James Anderson, December 24, 1795, GWW XXXIV: 407.

487 *he had increased the powers of the presidency*: McDonald, *The American Presidency*, pp. 241–42.

486 *Washington had held firm on neutrality*: Washington's speech to a group of men in Alexandria, Virginia, is from Smith, *Patriarch*, p. 169.

488   *"How many opportunities"*: Farewell Address, September 19, 1796, GWW XXXV: 233.

488   *"a plague to mankind"*: GW to David Humphreys, July 25, 1785, GWW XXVIII: 202.

489   *Washington, with Hamilton's encouragement*: Ryan Barilleaux, "Foreign Policy and the First Commander in Chief," Gregg and Spalding, *Patriot Sage*, p. 152–54.

490   *He also simply surrendered*: Gregg and Spalding, *Patriot Sage*, p. 157.

491   *"our great General"*: Stuart Leibiger, *Founding Friendship: George Washington, James Madison, and the Creation of the American Republic*, Charlottesville: University of Virginia Press, 1999, p. 21.

491   *The president trusted Madison*: Leibiger, *Founding Friendship*, pp. 21–30, 105–121.

491   *Washington turned the office*: Phelps, "George Washington, Precedent Setter," Thomas Cronin, *Inventing the American Presidency*, p. 276.

492   *Washington's belief in democratic government*: Hendrickson, *Hamilton II*, p. 252.

492   *"to manage the reins of government"*: GW to Jefferson, August 23, 1792, GWW XXXII: 130–31.

492   *"at all times improper and dangerous"*: GW to John Adams, August 20, 1795, GWW XXXIV: 280.

492   *"such (for wise purposes, it is to be presumed)"*: GW to Henry Knox, July 27, 1795, GWW XXXIV: 251.

493   *"of no party...whose sole wish"*: GW to Timothy Pickering, July 27, 1795, GWW XXXIV: 251.

493   *"worst enemy"*: Farewell Address, September 19, 1796, GWW XXXV: 226.

493   *"nothing but disunion can hurt"*: GW to Joseph Reed, April 15, 1776, GWW IV: 483.

493   *"It is also most devoutly"*: GW to Joseph Reed, November 27, 1778, GWW XXXIII: 347.

493   *The president had dealt with small factions*: Forrest McDonald, *The Presidency of George Washington*, Lawrence: The University of Kansas Press, 1974, pp. 4–6, 100–104.

494   *Washington also knew*: McDonald, *The Presidency of George Washington*, pp. 7–8.

494   *"if we mean to support the liberty"*: GW to Arthur Fenner, June 4, 1790, XXX: 48.

495   *"seclusion of a monk"*: *The Aurora*, August 22, 1795.

495   *"dark schemes of ambition"*: *The Aurora*, September 27, 1795

495   *"a swearer and blasphemer"*: *The Aurora*, October 21, 1795.

495   *The president's cabinet officers*: Forrest McDonald, *The American Presidency: An Intellectual History*, Lawrence: University of Kansas Press, 1994, p. 243.

495   *An editor in the National Gazette*: *National Gazette*, December 12, 1792.

495   *Another accused him of becoming*: *National Gazette*, March 2, 1793,

495   *Others charged him with attempting*: Carol Sue Humphrey, "George Washington and the Press," Mark Rozell, William Pederson, Frank Williams, eds., *George Washington and the Origins of the American Presidency*, Westport, Conn.: Praeger Publishing, 2000, pp. 157–69.

495   *Even Tom Paine*: Marshall Smelser, "George Washington and the Alien and Sedition Acts," *American History Review*, January 1954, pp. 323–28.

495   *"If ever a nation was debauched by a man"*: *The Aurora*, December 23, 1796.

496   *"I care not; for I have consolation"*: Ward, *George Washington*, p. 26.

496   *"the infamous scribblers"*: Smelser, "George Washington and the Alien and Sedition Acts," p. 327.

496   *"If the government and the officers"*: GW to Edmund Randolph, August 20, 1792, GWW XXXII: 136–37.

496   *"in such exaggerated and indecent terms"*: GW to Thomas Jefferson, July 6, 1796, GWW XXXV: 120.

496   *"[He] ran on much on the personal abuse"*: Thomas Jefferson, "Anas," August 1–3, Albert Bergh, ed., *The Writings of Thomas Jefferson*, 28 vols., Washington, D.C.: Thomas Jefferson Memorial Association, 1907, vol. 1, pp. 253–354.

498   *"I am fairly out and you fairly in"*: John Adams to Abigail Adams, March 3, 1797, *Adams Letters to His Wife*, p. 244.

499   *"His example is...complete"*: Adams quoted in *History of the George Washington Bicentennial Celebration*, vol. 1, p. 37.

INDEX

Ackerman, Jacob, 344

Adams, Abigail, 411

Adams, John, 68, 81, 91, 129, 159, 166, 253, 256–57, 340, 353, 472, 475, 485–86, 498, 499

Adams, Samuel, 255, 256, 329, 351, 419, 430

Allen, Ethan, 368

Alton, John, 48

Amboy, Perth, 405

American Crisis, The, 14, 194, 419

Anderson, James, 487

Armstrong, John, 224, 441

Arnold, Benedict, 67, 117, 194, 257, 259, 342, 366–77, 392, 430

Articles of Confederation, 468, 470

Aurora, 494

Ball, Martha, 89

Bartlett, Josiah, 129, 168

Basset, Fanny, 268

Bassett, Burwell, 69

Beatty, Erkuries, 312, 320, 347, 365

Beckwith, John, 343

Bell, John, 286

Blaine, Ephraim, 287, 294–95, 344, 358

Board of War, 219, 223, 228, 260, 263–64, 285, 325, 344, 346, 377

Bogart, James, 344

Boston Harbor, 64–65

Boucher, Jonathon, 53

Bowdoin, James, 282

Braddock, Edward, 45

Bradford, William, 256

Brandywine Creek, 194, 235, 254, 262, 268, 292, 324, 385

Brethren House, 238

Brodhead, Daniel, 314

Brooklyn Heights, 27, 33, 248, 452

Brooks, John, 440

Bunker Hill, Battle of, 67

Burgoyne, John, 117, 194, 255, 298, 303, 362

Burke, Edmund, 355

Burkeley, Norborne, 60

Cadwalader, John, 12, 13, 20, 265

Caldwell, Hannah, 394

Camp, Caleb, 315

Carpenter's Hall, 38

Carteret, George, 405

Chamberlayne, William, 47

Charming Nancy, 371, 373

Chastellux, Chevalier, 271

Clark, Abraham, 255

Clinton, George, 102–5, 187, 230, 322, 377, 452–53, 456

Clinton, Henry, 35, 150, 300, 353, 385, 392, 395, 397, 424–25, 434, 453

Collins, Isaac, 415

Commissary Department, 201–06, 286–88

Committee of Correspondence, 63

Common Sense, 14

Concord, Battle of, 2, 67, 117, 176, 368

Condict, Silas, 343

Connecticut Journal, 32

Continental Army: desertions, 157–63; enlistments, 7, 153–69, 279–84; hospitals, 6, 232–40; munitions, 171–73, 176–92; mutiny, 386–92; public and, 213–16; soldiers, condition of, 5, 71–73, 89–99, 198–200, 201–6, 221–30; thievery among, 323–25, 344–46; training of, 290–93

Continental Congress: enlistments and, 167–69; Morristown food crises and, 314–17, 379–86; munitions and, 190; Valley Forge and, 216–30, 274–77; Washington and, 6–9, 37–40, 67–70, 80, 88, 216–21, 253–67, 379–86

Custis, Martha. *See* Washington, Martha

Conway, Thomas, 257, 258–69, 272, 285, 289, 297, 338, 376, 441, 449

Cooke, Nicholas, 8, 79, 105, 146

Cornwallis, Charles Earl, 4, 10, 18, 19, 21, 24–25, 27, 30–31, 33, 35, 118, 298, 353, 388–89, 428, 434, 435

Council of Safety, 218

Cresswell, Nicholas, 31, 57

Crosby, Ebenezer, 296

Cushing, Thomas, 40

Custis, Jack, 51, 53–54, 156, 171, 271

Custis, Patsy, 51–53

Dana, Francis, 274, 276

Dartmouth, 64

Dayton, Elias, 394

de Miralles, Don Juan, 381, 383

de Villiers, Jujmonville, 44

Deane, Silas, 262

Declaration of Independence, 61, 182, 194, 218, 324, 465, 478

DeKalb, Baron Johann, 197, 254

Delaware River, 1, 4–8, 12–17, 20–21, 25, 31–32, 86, 102, 194, 224, 294, 303, 318, 434, 452, 457, 500

Drinker, Elizabeth, 270

Duane, James, 380

Duche, Jacob, 254

Dunmore, Lord, 65

Dyer, Eliphalet, 39

Eldredge, James, 285

Eliobo, 404

Ellery, William, 227, 249, 329

Ellsworth, Oliver, 392

Ewing, James, 12, 13

Faesch, John Jacob, 141, 172, 175, 181, 183, 189, 343

Fairfax Resolves, 65, 409

Fairfax, Bryan, 50, 66

Fairfax, George, 47

Fairfax, Sally Cary, 47–48

Fauquier, Francis, 64

Federalist Papers, The, 144, 465

Fenner, Arthur, 494

Ferry Farm, 41

Fisher, Elijah, 237

Fitzgerald, John, 78, 132, 143, 266

Flower, Benjamin, 222–23

Folsom, Nathaniel, 274

Ford, Theodosia, 306, 310, 362, 364

Fort Duquesne, 44, 45

Fort Necessity, 44

Fort Ticonderoga, 13, 67, 166, 168, 178–80, 257, 368–69

Fort Washington, 4, 33, 156, 178

Franklin, Benjamin, 75, 256, 288, 353, 384, 494

Franklin, William, 75, 353

Frederick the Great, 35, 264, 288, 290, 291

Freeman's Journal, 32

French and Indian War, 37–38, 44, 46, 54, 57, 61, 68, 75, 86, 148, 226, 267, 367–68, 484

Fulling Mill, 234

Furman, Moore, 321

Gates, Horatio, 5, 9, 91, 194, 208, 215, 255–61, 263–67, 271, 309, 348, 368, 375, 437, 441, 443, 446, 458

Gazette of the United States, 494

George I, 29

George III, 35, 62, 65, 114, 354, 449

Germain, George, 392

Germantown, 194, 235, 248, 254–55, 292

Gibbs, Caleb, 268

Gist, Christopher, 44

Glover, John, 3, 4, 13, 282

Gordon, George, 352

Gordon, William, 260

Grant, James, 18

Gray, James, 299

Great Awakening, The, 108–13

Greene, Kitty, 269, 362, 365

Greene, Nathanael, 72, 132–34, 138, 191, 219, 221, 224, 230, 242, 254, 263–64, 275–76, 286–88, 292–93, 300, 306–9, 313, 314, 320–21, 325, 328, 330–31, 341, 350, 356–58, 378, 387–88, 392, 395–96, 410, 427, 434–36, 452
Greene, Rev. Jacob, 75, 349, 481

Hamilton, Alexander, 10, 17–18, 29, 31, 89, 107, 115, 122, 127, 132–40, 143–44, 147, 164, 192, 208–9, 255, 258, 263–64, 287, 342, 349–50, 362–64, 380, 382, 389, 410, 426–29, 435, 441, 443, 465, 475–76, 479, 481, 485, 489, 491–95, 497
Hancock, John, 8, 20, 30, 38, 79, 115, 130, 145–46, 153, 156, 159, 163, 167
Harlem Heights, 4
Harrison, Benjamin, 88
Harrison, Robert, 78, 132, 134, 137, 479
Harvie, John, 274
Hasbrouck, Jonathan, 437
Heath, William, 292
Hedden, Joseph, 341
Henry, Patrick, 58–59, 63, 67, 92, 102, 106, 166, 168, 198, 217, 225, 260, 411, 479, 480
Hessians, 3, 11, 33, 35, 132, 184–85, 221, 369, 393–95
Holt, Joseph, 244
Holton, Sam, 329
Honeyman, John, 10, 11, 456
Hooper, William, 5, 7
Hoops, Robert, 320
House of Burgesses, 37, 58, 63–64, 68, 102, 144, 166, 267, 406, 408, 457, 476, 493, 498
Howe, Richard, 3
Howe, William, 2–10, 24, 27, 33, 35, 71, 74, 111, 115–18, 120–21, 129, 131, 146–47, 151, 165, 192, 195–96, 249–50, 255–56, 274, 301, 303, 353, 372, 488
Howell, David, 460
Howell, John Ladd, 220
Hudson River, 3, 116, 124, 180, 189, 294, 336, 375, 421, 464
Humphreys, David, 468

Huntington, Ebenezer, 318, 335
Huntington, Jedediah, 204, 240, 287
Huntington, Samuel, 315, 357, 387
Hutchinson, John, 125

Iron Act, 61, 175
ironworks, 171–192
Irvine, William, 308
Jay Treaty, 496
Jay, John, 144–45, 151, 410–11, 465, 468, 471, 478, 487
Jefferson, Thomas, 62, 88, 102, 106, 198, 315, 319, 350, 357, 457–58, 467, 475–76, 481, 484, 492–96, 498
Jersey Journal, 340, 406
Jockey Hollow, 310, 311, 317–318, 320, 326–27, 333, 359–60, 382, 387, 391, 423
Johnson, Thomas, 229
Jones, John Paul, 352
Jones, Joseph, 380, 440

Kalb, Johann, 359
Keith, William, 1, 2
Knox, Henry, 10, 13–20, 30, 72, 96, 130, 138, 155, 164, 178–82, 187, 190, 208–9, 284, 292, 296, 301, 391, 415–16, 435, 455, 464, 468, 470, 476, 485–86, 492–93
Knox, Lucy, 13, 15, 20, 96, 364, 375
Kollock, Shepard, 415–17, 420–21, 494

Lafayette, Marquis de, 118, 261–66, 276, 303, 342, 385, 390, 403, 410, 412, 420, 424, 427–28, 434–35, 448, 468–71, 485
Laurens, Henry, 205, 209, 211–12, 220, 225, 262–63, 276, 284, 301, 410
Laurens, John, 209, 259, 262–63, 289, 291, 413, 479
Lear, Tobias, 413
Lee, Billy, 78, 140, 342, 364, 397, 410, 414, 439, 461
Lee, Charles, 5, 8–9, 38, 73, 131, 256, 258, 272, 301, 303, 370
Lee, Richard Henry, 6, 159, 187, 258, 301, 430
Lewis, Charles, 282
Lewis, Fielding, 43, 399

Lewis, Joseph, 321–23, 330, 358
Lewis, Morgan, 360
Lexington, Battle of, 2, 67, 117, 176, 177, 368
Lincoln, Benjamin, 385, 389
Livingston, William, 75, 78, 102, 106–7, 113–14, 121–22, 125, 134, 139, 141, 144, 152, 159, 187, 198, 217, 224–29, 243, 284, 315, 317, 338, 363, 382, 391–93, 398, 406, 410, 415, 417, 421, 425, 485
London Magazine, 354
Louis XVI, 384
Loyalists, 119–128

Madison, James, 350–51, 357, 380, 441, 465, 475, 481, 489, 491, 498
Malcolm, William, 282
Martin, Joseph, 225, 387
Mason, George, 42, 64, 109, 409, 418
Massachusetts Spy, 418
Matlack, Timothy, 373
Mawhood, Charles, 27
Maxwell, William, 372, 394
McCarty, Thomas, 16
McDougall, Alexander, 280, 282, 309, 440
McHenry, James, 460
McIntosh, Lachlan, 237
McKonkey's Ferry, 20
Mease, James, 222
Meigs, Jonathan, 387
Mercer, George, 57
Mercer, Hugh, 28, 29, 42, 131
Mercereau, Joshua, 477
Mifflin, Thomas, 201–4, 257–64, 267, 458–61
Monroe, James, 10, 19, 477, 498
Morris, Gouverneur, 299, 465, 476
Morris, James, 248
Morris, Robert, 7, 74, 80
Morristown encampment, 1777: desertions, 157–63; economic inflation, 128–31; enlistments, 153–56; headquarters at, 76; ironworks at, 171–73, 176–92; security at, 80–81, 115; selection of, 73–74; setup of,

74–75; smallpox epidemic, 89–99; spy network, 145–52; Washington's illness at, 132–35
Morristown encampment, 1779–80: attempted Washington kidnapping, 341–44; Benedict Arnold affair, 367–77; community and, 344–46; finances and, 346–51; food crises, 314–34; mutiny during, 386–92; political support during, 379–86; selection of, 305–7; setup of, 307–11; supply problems, 355–61, 377–79; weather at, 311–12, 318–20, 327–32
Morse, Jedediah, 39
Mount Vernon, 8, 81–82, 98, 135, 138, 206, 268, 271, 286, 309, 361, 365, 390, 407–10, 413–14, 429, 436, 439, 447–48, 450, 452–53, 456–57, 461, 464, 468–70, 495, 497–99, 502
Muhlenberg, Peter, 196, 282, 312

National Gazette, 494–96
Neilson, John, 150, 151
Neutrality Proclamation, 486
New Jersey Committee of Safety, 123
New Jersey Gazette, 114, 319, 340, 415, 417, 421
New Jersey Journal, 403–4, 416–17, 419–21, 481
New York Gazette, 319, 419, 453
New York Royal Gazette, 340
Newburgh Address, 442
Nicola, Lewis, 438
Niemcewicz, Julian, 408
Norris's Tavern, 372

Ogden, Gabriel, 180, 181, 188
Ogden, Matthias, 440
Olney, Stephen, 27

Paine, Thomas, 14, 120, 194, 207, 419, 495
Parker, Charles, 204
Parliament, 35, 60–64, 66–67, 73, 119, 176, 273, 352–54, 361, 385, 419–20, 429

Parsons, Samuel Holden, 281
Peabody, Nathaniel, 381
Peale, Charles Wilson, 25, 270
Pearce, William, 407
Pendleton, Edmund, 66
Pennsylvania Assembly, 218, 226, 228, 280, 457
Pennsylvania Council, 256, 284, 293, 371–72, 425
Pennsylvania Evening Post, 32
Pennsylvania Gazette, 256, 272
Pennsylvania Journal and Weekly Advertiser, 85, 256, 418
Pennsylvania Packet, 256, 372
Philadelphia Freeman's Press, 85
Pickering, Timothy, 493
Pinckney, Thomas, 476
Pope's Creek Plantation, 41
Potts, Isaac, 207
Potts, Jonathon, 31, 238, 244, 245
Powel, Elizabeth, 57
press, 414–21, 496–99
Princeton, Battle of, 25–29
prisoners of war, 185–87, 248–49
Pulaski, Casimir, 292, 485
Putnam, Israel, 225, 368

Quaker Bridge Road, 27
Quakers, 214, 218, 233–35, 250, 405–6, 410, 479

Rall, Johann, 7, 10–11, 16–19
Ramsey, David, 286
Randolph, Edmund, 476, 496
Randolph, Peyton, 59
Reading Hospital, 235
Reed, Joseph, 61, 74, 102, 103, 224, 266, 274, 329, 359, 370–75, 388, 390, 421–22, 428, 493
Regulations for the Order and Discipline of the Troops of the United States, 291
religion, 108–13
Revolutionary War: beginning of, 2–5, 58–66; Benedict Arnold affair, 367–77; British homefront troubles, 351–55;

Concord, Battle of, 2; Delaware crossing (Dec. 25, 1776), 11–16; Delaware crossing (Dec. 29, 1776), 21; enlistments and, 153–56; Europe and, 34–35; finances and, 128–31, 346–51; Lexington, Battle of, 2; Monmouth, battle at, 302–4; munitions and, 171–73, 176–92; officer revolt, 436–46; politics and, 101–8, 253–67; press and, 31–32, 113–14; Princeton, Battle of, 25–29; Princeton, battles at, 392–99; public support of, 5; religion and, 108–13; Staten Island attack, 1780, 336–40; Trenton, battles at, 16–20; Yorktown, Battle of, 433–36. *See also* Morristown encampment, 1777; Morristown encampment, 1779-80; Valley Forge encampment
Roberdeau, Daniel, 249
Rodney, Caesar, 104, 167–68, 280, 315
Rodney, Thomas, 15, 17, 28, 160
Ross, George, 5
Royal Gazette and Weekly Mercury, 99
Royal Navy, 41
Rush, Benjamin, 30, 91, 129, 231, 239–40, 243–46, 248, 255, 275
Rutledge, Edward, 67
Rutledge, John, 479

Saratoga, 257, 259, 263, 297–98, 303, 324, 353, 362, 369, 372, 374–75, 384, 389
Schuylkill River, 189, 196, 207, 220, 223, 284, 319
Schuyler, Phillip, 181, 191, 257, 342, 349, 357, 359, 361–64, 380, 427
Seely, Sylvanus, 395
Sergeant, Jonathon, 254
Serle, Ambrose, 4
Shaw, Samuel, 25, 300, 359, 445
Shays Rebellion, 470
Shippen, Peggy, 371, 375
Shippen, William, 244–45
Shreve, Israel, 426
Simcoe, John, 343
slavery, 403–414
smallpox, 89–99, 128, 240, 241–42

Smallwood, William, 280
Smith, Jonathon, 266
Sons of Liberty, 64, 67
Spotswood, Alexander, 413
St. Clair, Arthur, 484
Stamp Act, 24, 59, 63, 75, 109, 175, 408, 417–18, 437, 493
starvation, 221–230, 314–334
State Constitutional Convention, 218
Staten Island, 338, 339, 340, 341, 389, 427
Stewart, Walter, 387
Stirling, Lord, 9, 55, 72–73, 107, 132, 141, 157, 171–72, 175, 177, 188–90, 196, 214, 223, 258, 269, 309, 336, 338–40, 363, 395
Sugar Act, 61
Sullivan, John, 5, 9, 17–19, 29, 72, 80–81, 92–93, 198, 223, 261, 280, 282, 291, 483

Talmadge, Benjamin, 455
Thacher, James, 244, 312, 326
Thompson, David, 366
Thomson, Charles, 430, 459
Tilghman, Tench, 78, 131–34, 137, 143, 221, 225, 264, 336–37, 362, 427–28, 431
Tilton, James, 243, 391
Tories. *See* Loyalists
Townshend Acts, 61, 64, 408, 417
Troup, Robert, 264
Trumbull, Jonathon, 8, 201, 212, 226, 315
Trumbull, Joseph, 99, 104, 201–4

Valley Forge encampment: Commissary Department troubles, 201–6, 286–88; community relations, 213–16; Congress and, 216–21; construction of, 206–13; end of, 296–300; enlistments and, 279–84; hospitals, 232–47; medical emergencies, 231–51; political battles during, 253–67; rumors at, 271–74; selection of, 194–98; smallpox at, 242–43; starvation at, 221–30, 293–96; training during, 290–93; weather at, 200–1
Van Cortlandt, Catherine, 125–26

Van Cortlandt, Philip, 125–26
Varnum, James, 214, 230, 232, 240, 282, 299
Virginia Association, 64
Virginia Gazette, 40, 63, 134, 407, 418
Von Clausewitz, Carl, 87
von Knyphausen, Wilhelm, 343, 393, 395–97, 399
Von Steuben, Frederich William, 247, 288–91, 298, 322, 341, 357, 363, 382, 485

Wadsworth, Jeremiah, 286, 288, 292–93, 306, 309, 320, 325, 357, 387
Ward, Samuel, 296, 297
Washington, Augustine, 40
Washington, Jack, 52, 57, 272, 400
Washington, George: aides and, 76–79, 80, 137–40; appointed commander-in-chief, 37–40, 69–70; attempted kidnapping of, 341–44; Billy Lee and, 140; Constitutional Convention and, 465–68; Continental Congress and, 6–9, 67–70, 80, 88, 216–21, 253–67, 379–86; death of, 499–500; early life of, 41–43; farming and, 48–51; in French and Indian War, 44–46; gambling and, 55; Gates and, 253–67; Hamilton and, 139–40, 426–31; health of, 132–35; Livingston and, 143–44; Loyalists and, 119–28; military strategy of, 33, 114–19, 300–2; Mount Vernon and, 42, 48–51, 56–57; politics and, 58–66, 101–8, 216–21, 253–67, 379–86; Shays Rebellion, 470–71; press and, 31–32, 113–14, 414–21, 496–99; public image of, 81–82, 85–86, 253–67, 451–53; religion and, 108–13; retirement as commander-in-chief, 447–61; slavery and, 403–14; smallpox epidemics and, 89–99, 242–43; social life of, 54–56, 141–45; soldiers and, 83–86, 163–69, 300, 323–25; spying and, 145–52; stepchildren of, 51–54; Von Steuben and, 288–93; winter and, 9–10, 26, 30, 33–34, 311–12, 318–20, 327–32

Washington, George *(continued)*
    Martha Washington and: at
        Morristown, 1780, 361–66; at Valley
        Forge, 267–71; marriage to, 46–48
    as president: Cabinet, 476–79; civil
        rebellions, 482–84; currency,
        480–82; foreign affairs, 484–89;
        inauguration of, 463–65; policies,
        468–70, 479–80; political parties,
        492–96; presidential image, 472–76
    Revolutionary War: Benedict Arnold
        affair and, 367–77; British discord
        and, 353–55; camp administration,
        206–13, 271–74; Commissary
        Department, 201–6, 286–88;
        desertions, 157–63; enlistments and,
        8–9, 21–23, 153–56, 163–69,
        279–84; finances and, 21–23,
        128–31, 279–84, 346–51; food
        crises, 221–30, 293–96, 314–34;
        hospitals, 232–40, 242–47;
        munitions, 171–73, 176–92; mutiny
        and, 386–92, 421–26; officer revolt
        and, 436–46; prisoners of war,
        185–87, 248–49; public and, 5,
        213–16, 344–46; selection of
        Morristown (1777), 73–74; selection
        of Morristown (1779–80), 305–7;
        selection of Valley Forge
        encampment, 194–98; supply
        problems, 355–61, 377–79

Revolutionary War battles: Delaware
    crossing, 11–16; Monmouth, 302–4;
    preceding Delaware crossing, 2–5;
    Princeton (1780), 392–99; Princeton,
    Battle of, 25–29; Staten Island attack,
    1780, 336–40; Trenton, 16–20;
    Yorktown, 433–36
Washington, Lawrence, 41–42, 46, 48
Washington, Martha: at Morristown 1777,
    135, 141–45; at Morristown 1780,
    361–66; at Valley Forge, 267–71; children
    of, 51–54; health of George Washington
    and, 135; marriage to George Washington,
    46–48
Washington, Mary, 40, 41
Wayne, Anthony, 243, 423–24, 484
Wharton, 280
Whiskey Rebellion, 281, 492
White Plains, 4, 150
Wiederholt, Andreas, 11
Wilkes, John, 352
Wilkinson, James, 19, 27, 308
Wilson, James, 129, 465, 479, 482
Winds, William, 75, 124
winter, 9–10, 26, 30, 34
Witherspoon, John, 111, 129, 464

Yellow Springs, 234–35, 239, 242

ABOUT THE AUTHOR

Bruce Chadwick, Ph.D., lectures in American History at Rutgers University while also teaching writing at New Jersey City University. He is a former journalist and the author of four other historical books: *Brother Against Brother: The Lost Civil War Diaries of Lt. Edmund Halsey*, *Two American Presidents: Abraham Lincoln and Jefferson Davis 1861-1865*, *Traveling the Underground Railroad* and *The Reel Civil War: Mythmaking in American Film.*